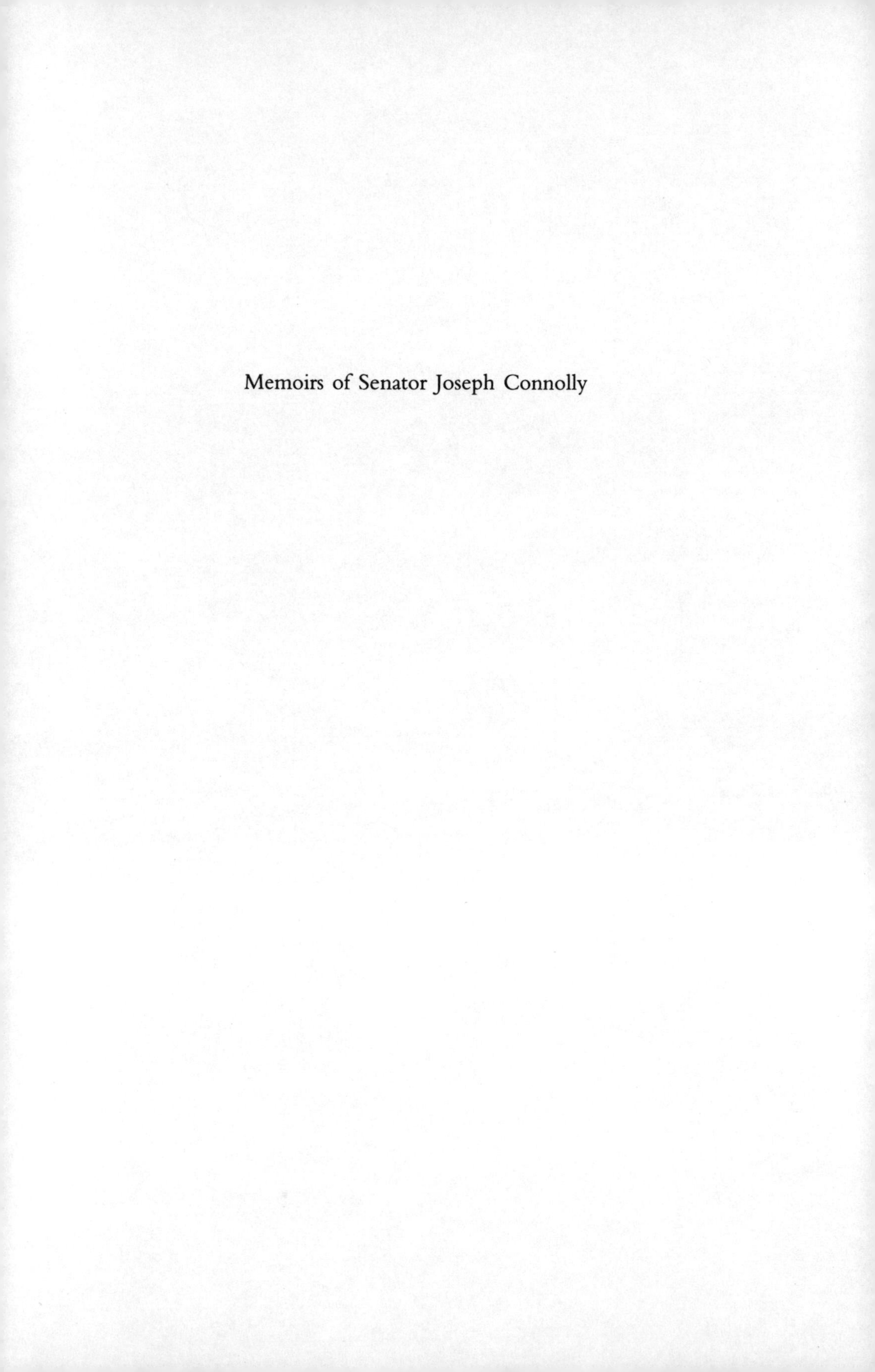

Memoirs of Senator Joseph Connolly

Memoirs of Senator Joseph Connolly (1885-1961)

A founder of modern Ireland

Edited by
J. ANTHONY GAUGHAN

IRISH ACADEMIC PRESS

First published in 1996 by
IRISH ACADEMIC PRESS
Northumberland House,
44, Northumberland Road,
Ballsbridge, Dublin 4

and in North America by
IRISH ACADEMIC PRESS
c/o ISBS, 5804 NE Hassalo Street,
Portland, OR 97213

Reprinted 1998

British Library Cataloguing in Publication Data

Connolly, Joseph, b.1885
The memoirs of Senator Joseph Connolly
1. Connolly, Joseph, b.1885 2. Legislators – Ireland – Biography 3. Ireland – Politics and government – 1922–1949
4. Ireland – History – 20th century
I. Title II. Gaughan, J. Anthony (John Anthony), 1932–
941.5'082'092

ISBN 0 7165 2611 5

Library of Congress Cataloguing-in-Publication Data
A catalog record for this book is available from the Library of Congress

Printed in Great Britain by
Bookcraft (Bath) Ltd, Midsomer Norton, Avon

To
Reverend F. X. Martin, O.S.A.,
who encouraged Joseph Connolly to write his memoirs

Contents

List of Illustrations

Foreword

There have been frequent complaints about the dearth of Irish political memoirs. Fr J. Anthony Gaughan has already made an inestimable contribution to Irish history by reviving the memory of people who were important public figures in their time, such as Tom Johnson, first leader of the Irish Labour Party, Austin Stack, Thomas O'Donnell and Professor Alfred O'Rahilly. Fr Gaughan is now performing an important service in publishing the memoirs of Joseph Connolly. Thanks to Fr Gaughan, the existence of these important memoirs has been known for some time and they have been made available to historians. But putting them into print will make them accessible to every student of history. They make a substantial contribution to a deeper understanding of the history of twentieth-century Ireland. Written in the 1950s, they have a great breadth, covering the North prior to partition, the Irish State in the first decades of independence, with interesting insights into Irish-America in the 1920s.

The memoirs are important from a number of aspects. The early chapters describing life in Belfast in the first twenty years of this century from the point of view of a nationalist businessman are in themselves a fascinating social document. They describe what life was like for Northern nationalists before partition and before conditions became even more difficult. They provide a valuable complement to Eamon Phoenix's study of Northern nationalism. Connolly describes the difficult dilemmas confronting Northern nationalists and illuminates some of the labour history of the period. He also provides a fine pen-portrait of the Presbyterian minister, Dr James Alexander Hamilton Irwin, who supported the republican cause on a speaking tour in 1920 in North America.

Joseph Connolly, who helped organise the Volunteers in the North, was directly involved in the struggle for independence and was interned in 1916. He describes in his memoirs most of the leaders, whom he knew, such as Collins, MacSwiney, Griffith and de Valera. He was one of the organisers of the Belfast boycott. He also went as one of the country's early diplomatic emissaries to the United States.

He was a close associate of Eamon de Valera and was one of the very few people ever appointed to the cabinet from the senate. His memoirs provide an inside account and reflections on his work in the 1930s and 1940s, first as a minister, later as a senior public servant, in relation to issues such as land division, forestry and industrial policy. His account is of comparable value, in the administrative history of the State and its agencies, to the memoirs of Todd Andrews. Connolly was also involved in the launch of the *Irish Press*.

He attended the League of Nations assembly in 1932 with de Valera and presided over the assembly in de Valera's absence. His memoirs contain interesting accounts of international figures and events in the early 1930s. He met President Franklin D. Roosevelt in 1933 and was his warm admirer, except in relation to Yalta. On his return from the United States he represented the Irish Free State at the World Economic Conference in London in 1933.

Like some other members of the founding generation, he gradually became somewhat disillusioned and became less close to de Valera.

As someone who has for some time encouraged Fr Gaughan to publish these memoirs, I am very glad he has now done so. We tend today very often to have a naïve, negative and simplistic view of the hard task of State-building that faced a pioneering generation in exceptionally difficult conditions. These memoirs, the first that have been published by someone who was a Fianna Fáil cabinet minister, but I am sure not the last, will help to deepen our understanding and empathy with a period that is very much out of fashion today, but which, along with its shortcomings, was also one of real achievement.

MARTIN MANSERGH
Leinster House
Kildare Street
Dublin 2
7 March 1996

Introduction

Joseph Connolly was born at 41 Alexander Street West, Belfast, on 19 January 1885. He attended the national school at Milford Street from 1889 to 1897 and St Malachy's College from 1897 to 1900. On leaving St Malachy's he spent a year and a half assisting his father in the family bakery. Owing to clashes between himself and his father, the family decided that he should re-start his working life as an apprentice in the engineering firm of Coombe, Barbour & Coombe in January 1902. Finding this as uncongenial as his former employment, he joined the firm of Maguire & Edwards in January 1903. Connolly remained with this firm of wholesale and retail house furnishers until April 1915, when he set up his own house-furnishing business. He married Róisín MacGavock (1892-1983) in January 1916 and continued his business in Belfast until the autumn of 1921.[1]

In recalling his early life in Belfast Connolly provides a fascinating insight into the lives of linen-mill workers, those working in the engineering industries, skilled workmen and unskilled labourers. He describes the occasional Orange *versus* Green riots, the more colourful 'No popery' evangelists and the 1907 strike led by Jim Larkin. He traces the evolution of the Home Rule movement and the reaction it provoked, culminating in Ulster's 'Covenant Day'. Most importantly, he indicates how the celebration of the 1798 rebellion, the Boer war, the journals edited by Arthur Griffith and D. P. Moran and especially the Gaelic League and the Gaelic Athletic Association contributed to a new nationalist awakening among the Catholics of Belfast.

Connolly's involvement in the independence movement began in 1911 when, with a few others, he founded a 'Freedom Club' to spread the separatist gospel of Sinn Féin. This was to become the archetype of a number of others throughout the country. In 1914, on his initiative, a conference was held, as a result of which a company of the Irish Volunteers was established in Belfast, with Connolly as deputy chairman of the organising committee. At the outset the company attracted some five hundred members, but when the Irish Party supported the movement its strength rose to almost five thousand. When the leadership of the Irish Party attempted to take control and persuade members to become involved in the Great War, the movement split into the Irish National Volunteers and the Irish Volunteers. In Belfast the former followed the lead of Joseph Devlin, M.P., the latter, numbering a mere two hundred, remained loyal to the movement's original leadership.

1. For an account by Connolly of his family background, see Appendix 1.

In an increasingly hostile environment Connolly and his comrades continued drilling and resisted the vigorous recruitment campaign for the British army. He had not much confidence in the leadership qualities of those in charge of the Belfast company of the Volunteers and on Easter Saturday 1916, on learning of the imminence of a Rising by Irish Volunteers, travelled to Dublin to take part in it. After meeting Eoin MacNeill, chief of staff of the Volunteers, he became aware of the confusion among the leadership and on his way back to Belfast delivered a message to the Volunteers at Drogheda. This was one of the messages sent by MacNéill to Volunteers throughout the country cancelling the nationwide parades which had been organised in preparation for the Rising. On the Friday after he returned home Connolly was arrested and taken to Crumlin Road jail. Subsequently he was held in Richmond Barracks in Dublin and in Knutsford and Reading jails in England. In these institutions he met Belfast comrades such as Alf Cotton, Denis McCullough, Seán Neeson and Herbert Moore Pim. He also fraternised with members of the Volunteer movement from other parts of the country, who were to contribute significantly to the subsequent struggle for independence. Among the best known of these were Ernest Blythe, Harry Boland, Con Collins, Darrell Figgis, Arthur Griffith, Alderman Tom Kelly, Pierce McCan, Tomás MacCurtain, Terence MacSwiney, Seán Milroy, Paudeen O'Keeffe, Seán T. O'Kelly, George Count Plunkett and Austin Stack. With other untried political prisoners Connolly was released from Reading jail on 22 and 23 December 1916.

On his return to Belfast, Connolly applied himself to his business which prospered. His home was a 'safe house' where visiting Sinn Féin/Volunteer leaders stayed, if it was necessary for them to remain overnight in the city. On business trips to Dublin Connolly occasionally conferred with Arthur Griffith who had become a close friend. He unsuccessfully contested the mid-Antrim constituency on behalf of Sinn Féin in the general election of 1918.

After the Sinn Féin M.Ps had established Dáil Éireann in January 1919 he offered his services to it and was appointed to its Commission of Inquiry into the Resources and Industries of Ireland in September of that year. Notwithstanding the dangers involved and the difficulties placed in the functioning of the Commission, Connolly was one of its most effective members. The attitude of the British authorities to the Commission can be gathered from his description of one of its sessions: 'I was in Cork in early 1920 to attend special sessions of the Commission which had been arranged to take evidence from people in the area. The meetings were to be held in the city hall and we had just assembled when the military arrived and ordered us out. The members of the Commission were staying at the Imperial Hotel and after a brief consultation we decided to return to the hotel . . . and proceed with our work there. We had started but a short time when the room was invaded by another detachment of military and again we were driven out'. However, it seems Professor Alfred O'Rahilly, a member of the Commission, made his residence available and the Commission was thus able to complete its work in Cork.

Connolly witnessed the pogroms launched against the Catholics in certain parts of Belfast especially those in 1921-2 which had been prompted by I.R.A. activities elsewhere in the country. Some Belfast employers insisted on their Catholic employees making declarations of loyalty to the British government. Many simply dismissed their Catholic workers. In reaction to this members of Sinn Féin in Belfast organised the 'Belfast boycott'. The aim of the boycott was to force Belfast employers to desist from their discrimination against Catholic employees. Although the organising committee of the boycott failed to persuade Dáil Éireann to sanction their actions, the boycott, with the help of I.R.A. members, was successful. Connolly was one of the most active and influential members of the organising committee and, with his considerable experience of business, contributed significantly to its success.

At Arthur Griffith's request Connolly went to the U.S.A. as consul-general of the Irish Republic in September 1921. Before departing he sold his business. In his new post he was engaged in developing trade between Ireland and the U.S.A., in countering British propaganda, addressing meetings and attending social functions. He was deeply disappointed with the Anglo-Irish treaty, but did not publicly campaign against it. At that time Jim Larkin was serving a prison sentence in New York for provoking public disorder. On Connolly's initiative a case was brought which resulted in Larkin being released. In May 1922 Connolly went on a lecture tour in Canada, during which he had an opportunity to brief the Canadian prime minister, William Lyon Mackenzie King, on the situation in Ireland.

Connolly returned to Ireland in July 1922 to find that the civil war in the infant Irish Free State had begun. During the following month Arthur Griffith died and Michael Collins and Harry Boland were killed. Connolly was back at his desk in the consul-general's office in New York in September. However, dismayed by newspaper reports of the continuing fratricidal conflict at home, he resigned his post and arrived back in Ireland on 26 November 1922.

On 17 December Connolly wrote to de Valera. He deplored the civil war and the failure of both sides to find 'constitutional ways of settling their differences'. He pointed out that the Irish Free State was a *fait accompli*, that a prolongation of the civil war was a futile and tragic waste of life and energy and that the only sane course for him and his Party was to end it and adopt a policy of political opposition. In a reply, dated 26 December 1922, de Valera told Connolly that Republicans would not regard the Free State government as an established government either *de jure* or *de facto*. He blamed his adversaries for the fratricidal conflict, but stopped short of expressing his own attitude to the civil war. He suggested that Connolly should discuss the matter further with Austin Stack. This Connolly did some time later but with no greater success. At the end of their discussion Connolly informed Stack that he would be steering clear of both sides in the conflict.

In February 1923 Connolly joined the National Land Bank, of which his friend, Lionel Smith-Gordon, was managing director. Three months later he received an invitation from de Valera to meet him. At this meeting they discussed Connolly's letter of December 1922. De Valera requested Connolly to act as chairman of a committee which would act along the lines suggested in the letter. Connolly consented to do so and, apart from him and Eoin O'Keeffe who was secretary, the committee included: Michael Comyn, S.C., George Daly, Michael Foley, Dr Kathleen Lynn, Dr Conn Murphy, Philip Ryan, Mrs Hannah Sheehy Skeffington and Robert E. Whelan.

The committee launched 'Sinn Féin Re-organised' at a well-attended public meeting in the Mansion House. There followed other meetings throughout the country, the one in Cork being presided over by Daniel Corkery. As a result of these political activities, Connolly was forced to resign his post in the National Land Bank in June. Thereafter he spent all his time in the service of 'Sinn Féin Re-organised' and preparing for a general election which had been fixed for 27 August.

Connolly was involved in the most dramatic incident of that election campaign. De Valera who was still 'on the run' from the authorities in the Irish Free State decided to address his constituents in Ennis on 15 August. T. V. Honan, the chairman, opened the meeting. Connolly followed outlining the Party's policy and emphasising the importance of the impending election. As de Valera came forward to address the gathering, Free State soldiers fired over the heads of those on the platform, arrested de Valera and led him away.

Considering the circumstances Connolly was well pleased with the results of the election. The government Party secured a first-preference vote of 415,000 and returned 66 members to the new Dáil, while 'Sinn Féin Re-organised' or Republican first preferences totalled 286,000 and elected 44 members. After the election Connolly resigned from the organising committee, as he did not wish to become a professional politician. In that September of 1923 he returned to the U.S.A. and, with Dan McGrath, a former colleague in the consul-general's office in New York, he became until 1929 a distributor of suitings, serges, tweeds and hand-knit sports wear which were imported from Ireland. In 1926, at the request of Senator James Douglas, he took over the management of Alesbury's, a firm of coach builders and furniture manufacturers, with factories at Edenderry and Navan. In 1931, because of the general trade depression, he had to close down the factory at Edenderry to ensure the viability of the one at Navan. He severed his connection with this firm in 1932 on becoming a member of the Fianna Fáil cabinet.

Towards the end of 1928 Connolly, Mrs Kathleen Clarke, Michael Comyn, S.C., / Seán McEllin, Joseph O'Doherty and Séamus Robinson were elected to the Seanad in the Fianna Fáil interest. After they had taken their seats Connolly was appointed chairman or leader of the group. Of his colleagues in the upper house, who were from both the old and the new Ireland, he was most impressed by James Douglas and Thomas Johnson. He and his Fianna Fáil colleagues were kept busy continuing their Party's opposition to legislative measures passed on to the Seanad for ratification. He was outraged by the manner in which the majority in the upper house rushed through the Public Safety Act of 1931. In his memoirs he quotes Thomas Johnson's comment on this episode: 'Personally I think that any claim for respect as a legislative chamber that the Seanad has made hitherto has been forfeited by its conduct on this bill'.

At de Valera's invitation Connolly became a member of the board of directors of the proposed *Irish Press* in 1930. He saluted the appearance of the first issue of this newspaper on 5 September 1931 as significant not only for Republicans but for all who welcomed a new outlook and direction from the daily press. The influence of the new daily soon became apparent. After the general election of 1932 Fianna Fáil was able to form a government with the support of seven Labour T.Ds. When selecting his cabinet de Valera offered the ministry of education to Connolly, who declined to accept it on the grounds that he was not a fluent Irish speaker or a university graduate. However, he agreed to become minister for posts and telegraphs.

As minister for posts and telegraphs and leader of the government party in the Seanad, Connolly was second only to de Valera in promoting legislation to abolish the oath of allegiance which arose from the Anglo-Irish treaty and as an apologist for the government's policy with regard to the payment of the land annuities. He intervened directly to provide the equipment which made it possible for the pope to broadcast to the Eucharistic Congress in Dublin in June 1932. Although he acknowledged the importance of forging relations with Australia, Canada and South Africa, he opposed the attendance of Free State representatives at the imperial economic conference at Ottawa in July. He was one of de Valera's staunchest supporters in the economic war with Great Britain which began in the same month.

Connolly accompanied de Valera to the inaugural meeting of the League of Nations assembly at Geneva in September 1932 on the occasion of the Irish Free State's presidency of the council. He subsequently represented his leader at the working sessions of the assembly. At Geneva he observed the unsuccessful attempts to deal with the seeds of World War II, notably the Manchurian conflict between China and Japan and difficulties arising out of the treaty of Versailles. He met many of the world's leading political leaders and statesmen. Those who impressed him most were: Beneš of Czechoslovakia, Colijn of the Netherlands, Hambro of Norway, Herriot of France, Hymens of Belgium, Litvinov of the Soviet Union, Matsuoka of Japan and Wellington Koo of China. Apart from being critical of the activities of the British delegation, he was given little reason to have much regard for the hapless Ramsay MacDonald and his minister at the foreign office, Sir John Simon.

After Fianna Fáil's victory in the general election of January 1933 Connolly was appointed minister for lands. Before he took up his post he was requested by de Valera to visit the U.S.A. His brief was to pay off the Republican Bonds, which had been bought in 1919-21 by American supporters. These he was to dispose of with a bonus of twenty-five per cent in lieu of deferred interest. He was also directed to meet influential American politicians to ensure that they were friendly or at least sympathetic to the cause and interests of the Irish Free State and specifically to counter British propaganda on the various issues at the root of the economic war. In the event, he was remarkably successful in this exercise. Apart from Irish-Americans he conferred with a number of important politicians in Washington and had two long and useful interviews with Franklin D. Roosevelt. In addition, he became a friend of Raymond Moley, one of the president-elect's most influential advisers. On his return voyage to Ireland in mid-May 1933 he met and had as his constant companion a German Jewish professor of art and history who was returning to Hamburg after a lecture tour in the U.S.A. From him he learned at first hand about the anti-Jewish pogroms in Germany.

Within three weeks of his return from New York Connolly was in London representing the Irish Free State at the World Economic Conference which opened on 12 June 1933. He was disappointed at the manner in which delegates from the various countries attempted to turn to their advantage the course of the conference's deliberations. In this regard he was particularly critical of the U.S.A., Great Britain and France. However, he was not forgetful of Ireland's interests. At a meeting of the economic sub-committee on commercial policy he intervened to bring to the attention of the conference the punitive tariffs imposed by Great Britain on the Irish Free State because of its refusal to pay over monies which it regarded as neither legally or morally due. Subsequently he engineered a publicity *coup* by having himself ruled out of order at a debate by the conference's economic sub-commission on a resolution proposing a pact of 'economic non-aggression'. This enabled him to ensure that a statement prepared by him on the economic war between the Irish Free State and Great Britain received world-wide coverage in the press.

Connolly agreed with most observers that the policy of the U.S.A. to refuse to agree to the stabilisation of currency and an intervention by Franklin D. Roosevelt were mainly responsible for the abject and disappointing failure of the world economic conference. He considered U.S. policy intelligible in the light of the country's efforts at that time to climb out of its worst economic depression. However, he also ascribed the chaos and confusion in the U.S. delegation and ultimately in the world economic conference to weaknesses in the American president's character. The first of these he described as Roosevelt's '. . . tendency to think and believe that if he insisted vehemently enough that a thing was to be done it was already accomplished'. The second was the president's '. . . tendency to put a new man "on the job" without withdrawing the one originally appointed and in many cases without advising either of them of the true position'.

During the conference Connolly declined invitations to nearly all the social events arranged in connection with it. He was particularly cautious when invited by General Jan Smuts to a private meeting with George V. Suspicious of the motivation of the South African prime minister and anxious not to compromise his own government in any way, he graciously declined the opportunity to meet his majesty.

On his return from the World Economic Conference Connolly took charge of the department of lands. It was not an easy assignment. The new government regarded the department to be in dire need of reform and

Connolly was expected to make a substantial improvement in its operations. The land commission was one of the department's responsibilities. It had been established to facilitate the acquisition and division of estates. Thereby it was hoped that land would be made available for the landless men who had worked on the estates and that it would be possible to enlarge contiguous, small, uneconomic holdings.

In his memoirs Connolly is generous in his praise of the members of the land commission. In his first year at the department he had, with their assistance, 118,510 acres of land divided. He regarded his years in the department as among the most satisfying of his life. In the nation-building in which he and his colleagues were then engaged, he considered that there were few things as important as ensuring the welfare and comfort of thousands of his own people by establishing them in homes and farms where they could live and work and rear their families in reasonable comfort and security. The urgency in the acquisition and re-distribution of land seems to have diminished with Connolly's departure from the department, a fact of which he was severely critical subsequently.

The department of lands included a section on fisheries and the department of agriculture a section on forestry. While settling in to his new department, Connolly was persuaded by Dr Jim Ryan, minister for agriculture, to exchange 'fisheries' for 'forestry'. He set about his new brief on 'forestry' with his customary enthusiasm. By 1934 he had increased the number of acres planted each year from 4,000 to 8,500 and had introduced measures which were to greatly improve the department's section on forestry.

Another section of the department of lands dealt with the Gaeltacht. Much of the department's work for the Gaeltacht consisted of making available to the poorer residents of those areas grants and loans for the rebuilding of their homes or their replacement by new houses. In 1934 Connolly carried out the first experiment in a policy of migration. He established twenty families from the poorer districts of Connemara on twenty-two acre farms at Athboy in County Meath. In a second scheme sixty families from Donegal, Mayo and West Kerry were transferred to more lands which had become available in County Meath.

The Gaeltacht section also managed industries which had been established to ensure the social viability of the Irish-speaking parts of the country. There was much dissatisfaction at the inefficient manner in which they were run. Connolly, with his business background, was considered by his cabinet colleagues as an ideal person to reorganise them. Notwithstanding the opposition and unpopularity which it attracted, this he did with a fair measure of success.

In June 1936 the Seanad ceased to exist and thereby Connolly's career as a minister. He subsequently served on a commission to advise the government on the creation of a new Seanad or Second Chamber of the Oireachtas. He contributed to the majority report of the commission, but this was not accepted by the government which set up the Seanad in accordance with the recommendations of a minority report.

In June 1936 Connolly became chairman of the Commissioners of Public Works. The Office of Public Works or Board of Works was responsible for essential services required by State departments, including accommodation, furnishing, heating, lighting and maintenance. In addition, it had under its care national schools, training colleges and all other State institutions except military barracks. It was responsible for public parks, such as the Phoenix Park, St Stephen's Green and the Muckross Estate in Killarney, as well as the harbours at Dún Laoghaire, Howth and Dunmore East. Authority for arterial drainage was also vested in the Board.

The first serious challenge faced by Connolly in his new post was to procure and store supplies in anticipation of the war which even by 1938 appeared to be inevitable. In this he was remarkably successful, particularly with regard to fuel. As a result of his bulk purchase of coal in 1938 and use of turf supplies, the Board of Works was able to provide reasonable heating for government departments throughout the war and at the end of which it had still 3,000 tons of the coal purchased in 1938.

In September 1938 the government set up a commission to deal with arterial drainage on a national scale. By July 1940 the commission had reported to the government which, as Connolly, a member of the commission, proudly noted, passed the necessary legislation to initiate a programme of extensive drainage work.

At the outbreak of the world war Connolly was appointed the controller of censorship. Under his supervision, the press censorship was successfully conducted by Michael Knightly, editor in chief of the reporting staff of the Oireachtas. Connolly recalled having difficulty in persuading R. M. Smyllie of the pro-British *Irish Times* that at that time the freedom of the press would have to give way to the priority of preserving the country's neutrality.

The control of the post was a more difficult undertaking. Initially between ten and fifteen per cent of foreign-addressed letters were checked but eventually, it seems, all such mail was intercepted. Here most of the problems were caused by pro-British correspondents falsely alleging that German U-boats were taking on supplies at places on the south-west coast and that German agents were active in their districts.

The censorship of the use of the telegraph services by journalists was particularly difficult, as most representatives of British and American newspapers deeply resented Irish neutrality and not a few attempted to create incidents that could endanger it. During this time as controller of censorship, Connolly was exposed to the ire of David Gray, the U.S. ambassador, of whom he was to write: 'I have met many members of the diplomatic service representing various countries when in Geneva, London and Washington and here at home, and the only one that seemed to me to be dangerously incompetent was the one who represented the U.S. government here during the war and misrepresented Ireland to the U.S. at that critical time.'

In 1941 Connolly successfully requested to be relieved of the post of controller of censorship so as to give his entire attention to his responsibilities at the Board of Works which had increased considerably. Accommodation had to be found for emergency staffs for new services such as rationing, passports and emigration. Also as the war continued it became more urgent to ever more carefully supervise the supply reserves.

In January 1950 Connolly retired from the Board of Works where he had been an outstanding public servant. He was acutely conscious of his responsibility to spend public monies wisely and the commitment and integrity he brought to his duties was clear for all to see. A person of courage as well as conviction, he successfully challenged political superiors on the issue of political interference with regard to the employment of staff. In looking back with pride on his time in the Board of Works he expressed satisfaction at being able to facilitate the renewed use of the Chapel Royal in Dublin Castle for daily Mass. He also had some regrets. Among these were: his inability to initiate a programme of refurbishing the buildings in the Dublin Castle area, his failure to realise his ambition to set up a short-wave radio station at Donnybrook and the lack of enthusiasm and support, save from the Tuairim lobbying and study group, for his plan to re-site the new University College, Dublin, in Iveagh Gardens and its frontage on St Stephen's Green and Harcourt Street. In a retrospective look at his time in politics and service in the Board of Works he called for more attention to ethics by people in public life, was critical of retired ministers being appointed to government boards and deprecated lavish spending on legations and embassies disproportionate to the size and importance of the country.

Five years before Connolly retired from the Board of Works a close relationship between him and de Valera had ended. From 1923 onwards de Valera frequently consulted Connolly on most aspects of government activity and policy. Connolly had acted as de Valera's roving ambassador in the U.S.A. in the spring of 1933 and was practically his *alter ego* at meetings of the League of Nations in Geneva in September of 1932 and at the World Economic Conference in London in June 1933. The two were of one mind on most important issues faced by the government. The break between the two came when de Valera asked Connolly's advice on how the malaise which had engulfed the work of the land commission could be dispelled. Connolly, who was never other than forthright in expressing his opinion, reminded de Valera that he and the other land commissioners had on several occasions indicated the solution to the problem but, since nothing had been done, he had concluded that de Valera had a change of mind with regard to the government's original policy in the matter. The two parted after Connolly curtly rejected de Valera's angry denial that this was so.

Connolly subsequently expressed his bewilderment at the manner in which de Valera had changed his mind on this and other policies which prior to 1932 had been 'articles of faith'. He further complained that de Valera had never attempted to explain to his supporters or the electorate his change of mind on these issues. He also recalled that in his later talks with de Valera he found that the Fianna Fáil leader no longer welcomed discussion much less criticism and that he seemed to wish to have beside him only a group of 'yesmen'.

After his retirement Connolly, who earlier had his hobbies listed in *Who's Who* as work, walking and the theatre, enjoyed hill-walking and frequently attended the theatre. He was less in contact with political life than when he had been chairman of the Board of Works. However, he continued to be an interested observer of political events. He was gravely disappointed with political developments in the mid-1940s and early 1950s. The rise and fall of Clann na Poblachta he considered to be particularly damaging to public life because of the sense of general disillusionment which it left in its wake. In 1953, at his own expense, he published a pamphlet *How does she stand? An appeal to Young Ireland* which was intensely critical of the Irish political establishment. Connolly claimed that the country was being rapidly 'put in pawn' to foreign combines, that unacceptably high emigration continued, that people were not being settled in farms or homes of their own by the land commission and that a 'mountain of debt bearing heavy interest rates had been built up to lay on the shoulders of future generations'. He was particularly critical of the purchase of farms by foreigners.

Early in 1913 Connolly wrote *The mine land* which before the end of that year he managed to have performed by the Abbey Theatre in Dublin and the Ulster Group Theatre in Belfast. Subsequently, on 29 April 1915, it was presented by the Holy Rosary Dramatic Society in their hall on the Ravenhill Road. After his retirement in 1950 Connolly resumed playwriting and by 1952 had completed *Master of the house*, a satirical study of a modern tycoon and his domineering attitude to his workers, business associates and members of his family. Under the title of 'Children of the light' this was presented by the Dublin Group Theatre at Archbishop Byrne Hall, Harrington Street, Dublin, on 7 and 8 May 1953. After failing to interest the Abbey Theatre in this play, he succeeded in having it presented by the Belfast Theatre Group from 12 April to 1 May 1958. On Good Friday 1959 he survived a serious heart attack. Subsequently, with some difficulty, he completed his memoirs, which he concluded with the following *L'envoi*: 'Old contemporaries will disagree with some or many of my views and that will not distress me. Young Ireland may learn at least a little of what, to many of them, is a somewhat confusing period of our history. If they can glean some few grains of inspiration from the best of those that I have mentioned and learn some few lessons of what to avoid, then my reward will be more than adequate'.

Connolly complemented the memoirs of his public life with a postscript concerning his happy married and family life. This he described as 'the simple, ordinary story of the family, quietly going their separate ways without fuss or excitement but a great comfort and consolation to an old man in his seventy-sixth year who can almost see the stage manager ready to give the signal to ring down the curtain on the last act. I pray that it may be a good "curtain" and that I may have a favourable and merciful reception when it falls'. The curtain came down for Joseph Connolly on 18 January 1961.

In connection with the preparation of these memoirs for publication I wish to thank the library staff of the Jesuit House of Studies, Milltown Park; the National Library of Ireland; the Royal Irish Academy; Trinity College, Dublin; and University College, Dublin; for their courtesy and help; Darach Connolly and Fr Colm Gallagher for allowing me to consult and use the items listed on p. 450; and all who gave me information, especially those whose names appear on pp. 452-3.

I am indebted to Darach Connolly, Helen Murray, Pádraig Ó Snodaigh, C. J. Woods and especially Maurice O'Connell for their continuing and practical interest in the progress of this work.

I am grateful to Mrs Eileen Francis for preparing the material for Stan Hickey who, as usual, has done a splendid job in preparing the book for printing; and to Michael Kane for seeing it through the printing stage.

My thanks are due to Jarlath Hayes for the design and layout of the book.

I feel honoured in having the book published by Irish Academic Press and the foreword provided by Martin Mansergh.

J. ANTHONY GAUGHAN
56 Newtownpark Avenue
Blackrock
County Dublin
1 March 1996

1

Early days in Belfast – The Catholic Association 'Split' – The '98 centenary – The riots of 1898 and 1899 – The Gaelic League and Gaelic Athletic Association – Arthur Griffith and D. P. Moran

Just as one has to declare his name and credentials, whether as a prisoner being brought to jail or as a guest at a guildhall banquet and I have experienced both, I may explain that I was born in Belfast on 19 January 1885, that I was baptised in St Peter's church, Belfast, and given the name of Joseph. The street in which I was born was known as Alexander Street West, which ran parallel to the Falls Road, and our home was a modest 'parlour house'. I attach no significance to the fact that the late Joseph Devlin[1] lived in the same house some years after our family had moved, and I am sure he would have been equally indifferent to the fact. If I say that my mother was the gentlest and most saintly mother that any son could wish for, that my father covered an entirely kind and generous nature by a brusque manner and a highly-strung sensitive temperament, I am summing up briefly all that I think I am justified in asking my readers to know. I grew up as thousands of comparatively poor but comfortably-living, decent, Catholic children grew up in the city of Belfast.

It is not my intention to record the details of my personal or family life save such as may have a bearing or reflected value on the course of my experiences and on the national and sociological evolution of my period.

And yet it is tempting to recall my early and first conscious impressions. There was the national school which my brothers and I attended. There was a kindly but wildly irascible headmaster, who not infrequently exploded in an exhilarating frenzy of bad temper and frustration, banged the desk, and yelled to his assistant teachers: 'Gentlemen, they are taking the shop from us', or again 'Gentlemen, this place is a perfect pandemonium'. It was small wonder, for the poor man with his eight assistants was trying to control some three hundred pupils of all ages from four to fourteen years of age, all crowded into two big but very depressing school rooms.

1. Joseph Devlin (1871-1934): born Belfast, journalist, secretary of United Irish League 1902, Irish Parliamentary Party M.P. for North Kilkenny 1902-6, re-established Ancient Order of Hibernians and its president 1905-34, M.P. for West Belfast 1906-18, member of Irish Volunteers 1913, M.P. for the Falls 1918, M.P. for West Belfast in the Northern Irish Parliament, 1922, M.P. for Fermanagh and Tyrone at Westminster 1929-34.

I have nothing but gratitude and deep respect for some of the masters whom I was privileged to have had over me there and for the sound ground work they gave us, particularly in grammar, mathematics and English. When one recalls that these masters were paid the miserable salaries of from £50 to £70 a year, and that their pittance was paid to them at the end of every three months, the mystery is how the Board of Education ever secured so many splendid men of real quality and ability. Teaching with most of them was really, as it should be, a vocation not a job for a wage.

We had some interesting types among my classmates, some of whom stood out almost as museum pieces amongst us ordinary pupils. 'Thirsty' was one of them. 'Thirsty' was a complete delight to us. He could sketch, draw or paint anything that was in line with his squint and 'Thirsty' had a squint that gave an added look of impishness to his humorous face. My first introduction to horse racing was when 'Thirsty' produced for our admiration a vivid picture of *Ladas*[2] winning the Derby with a life-like representation of the extended horses in full gallop passing the winning post. No doubt it had been copied from some racing paper which 'Thirsty's' dad, who was a racing punter, had left on the kitchen sofa, but even now I can recall the perfection of the drawing. 'Thirsty' was eventually expelled for an exquisite drawing of 'old Jack', our headmaster, administering a caning to the exposed bottom of an unfortunate pupil. There was less tolerance for advanced art in those days so the picture was deemed obscene or indecent. 'Thirsty' and I were good friends and kept contact after he had left our school.

He reaped a golden harvest during the 1898 centenary celebrations. In that year all Ireland was celebrating the centenary of the 1798 Rising[3] and the nationalists of Belfast played their part. A special demonstration and procession took place to commemorate the battle of Antrim and every road, street and entry in the Falls Road district was bedecked with flags, bunting and arches. 'Thirsty', who was then barely thirteen years of age, was working day and night painting the bannerettes that were hung. Pictures of Henry Joy McCracken, Jimmy Hope, William Orr, Samuel Neilson[4] as well as some of the contemporary Irish leaders were turned out

2. *Ladas* won the Derby in 1894.

3. On 7 June 1798 United Irishmen, led by Henry Joy McCracken (1767-98), attacked Antrim town and were repulsed with heavy loss. On the previous day McCracken had issued a proclamation calling United Irishmen in Ulster to arms. He was executed in Belfast on 17 July.

4. Prominent figures in the pantheon of the United Irishmen of Ulster.

by the dozen and, although it was by no means a one-man show, 'Thirsty', I think, made the biggest single contribution to the Falls Road gallery. For some years I lost track of him and then one day he called to see me. I was shocked. He looked a dissipated ruin and was practically down and out. He still had his irrepressible humour. He had been at all sorts of activities, but could not settle to a fixed job or residence. He had travelled with shows and circuses as a lightning cartoonist. This he explained was the easiest and pleasantest job he knew. He came before his audience with a block of large, white sheets on the easel and the audience was invited to call out for their favourites to be drawn. 'Thirsty' evidently gave them the picture ordered, sketching rapidly in charcoal. Chamberlain, Gladstone, De Wet and Kruger[5] came as easily to 'Thirsty' as the popular jockeys and footballers of the period. Poor 'Thirsty', he could not have been more than seventeen or eighteen when he called to me and a few months later he was dead. A precocious genius, a motherless childhood, bad care and dissipation, yet withal a good humoured kindly soul, he was the joy and the tragedy of my early schooldays.

Then we had 'Cocky' who chewed tobacco when he was about ten. Later he was involved in some burglary, did a spell in Philipstown reformatory, and later still acquired wealth and respectability as a second-hand dealer in Scotland. 'Cocky' knew all the mysteries of life at an early age!

There was Hughie who became a national teacher and playwright and Tim who was later one of the shrewdest and wisest of our colleagues in the national struggle for independence and a man of the highest character and courage. Most of them have gone to their rewards and I pray peace and eternal rest to them. A few are left and the most interesting of the latter I met recently. Little Jerry in our national schooldays resembled one of Raphael's chubby angels but had a temper that was cyclonic. We left Milford Street school at the same time to go to St Malachy's College and here Jerry eventually headed into trouble. I can see him as he stood on the seat of the desk, a tiny figure with his angelic face and curly head, a

5. British and South African political figures then much in the news. The involvement of Christian De Wet and Paul Kruger in the Boer war was followed with great interest in nationalist Ireland. Joseph Chamberlain (1836-1914): born London, began work in his father's business at age of sixteen, mayor of Birmingham 1873-5, M.P. for Birmingham from 1876, leader of Liberal-Unionists and life-long opponent of Home Rule. William Ewart Gladstone (1809-98): born Liverpool, prime minister 1868-74, 1880-85, 1892-94, life-long champion of Home Rule. Christian De Wet (1854-1922): born Leeuwkop, Orange Free State, South Africa, Boer general and politician. Oom Paul Kruger (1825-1904): born Cape Colony, South Africa, Boer military and political leader, president of the Transvaal 1883-1903.

wood-framed slate in his hand and daring the master, a man of about fifteen stone, to lay a hand on him. The master retreated and the next morning there was no Jerry. He transferred to Blackrock College where he was contemporary with de Valera,[6] did brilliantly there and eventually graduated to the British consular service in China.[7]

It was in 1897 that I transferred to St Malachy's College[8] which was and is the diocesan college as well as the principal Catholic college in the city and served, with the three large schools run by the Irish Christian Brothers, as the secondary or intermediate schools for the young Catholic boys of the city. My recollection of St Malachy's is not impressive. The professors and masters were kind and considerate, but for the junior boys those who were

6. Eamon de Valera (1882-1976): born New York, president of Dáil Éireann 1919-21, president of the executive council of the Free State 1932-37, Taoiseach 1937-48, 1951-54 and 1957-59 and president of the Republic of Ireland 1959-73.

7. Two subsequent notices on Jerry threw light on Milford Street school and on his remarkable subsequent career. The *Blackrock College Annual 1908* included the following excerpt from *The Catholic Home Journal*: 'Mr Gerald Byrne is a native of Belfast, where he was born in April 1884, his mother being principal of the Milford Street school, in which he received his early education at the hands of Mr McManus, one of the most eminent mathematicians in Ireland. Mr Byrne subsequently passed to St Malachy's College, Belfast, and Blackrock College, Dublin . . .'. The *Blackrock College Annual* 1967 provided the following further account: 'Dr Gerald P. Byrne, son of John Byrne, Crumlin Road, Belfast, had his early education at Milford St school. He went to St Malachy's College and C.B.S., Belfast, passing junior grade, 1898, at the latter school. He won exhibitions in junior and middle grades at Blackrock. Taking high places in the examinations for excise and revenue services, he elected to remain in the inland revenue, and meantime continued to study for the student interpreterships of the foreign office, and took 2nd place in the British empire, 1st place in Ireland, and was appointed to the British legation in Peking, setting off, some sixty years ago, on the fortnight-long journey by Trans-Siberian railway. He was present in Peking for the funeral of the empress, the last of the Manchu rulers, 1912, and he remained in the Far East until about 1923, when the communist revolution was building up after a series of conflicting regimes that followed the fall of the Manchus. He became a barrister of the Irish bar in 1914, and held the post of magistrate of the mixed court in Shanghai for a time, and was also British pro-consul in Shanghai. Having a good knowledge of Russian, Chinese, French, Italian and Arabic, and having a sympathetic interest in the Chinese, he fitted well into the international life of Shanghai, and made many friends, including the foreign minister in Hankow, Eugene Chen, one of China's more remarkable figures.

On returning on pension to Ireland he decided to take up medicine, and qualified L.A.H., Dublin, 1931, D.P.H., Queen's University, 1942, and practised in Belfast and as medical officer at a mental hospital near Manchester'. Jerry died on 22 July 1967.

8. *St Malachy's College, Sesquicentennial* (Belfast 1983) includes 'St Malachy's College, Belfast 1833-1933' by Patrick Rogers. While in his overview Rogers does not refer to the period when Connolly attended the college, of the years just before he wrote: 'The decade 1880-1890 will always occupy a place of honour in the annals of St Malachy's. It was a period which produced many students, whose future success in life not alone brought credit

responsible for our education were, with one or two exceptions, quite uninspiring. No doubt the star teachers, both lay and clerical, were reserved for the higher classes, but I can safely say that it was the grinding that I got from Dan Donnelly and Barney Brannigan in the national school that enabled me to do slightly more than hold my own with those who had graduated from St Malachy's own primary division. Some of our masters, all of whom were designated by the title of 'Professor', were interesting. The one who intrigued me most was Professor O'Gorman who, for some reason that I never learned, was known to us as 'Biddy'. A more inappropriate nickname I cannot imagine for 'Biddy' was a real man in every sense, dignified, courtly and scrupulously just. He despised cant, snivelling and priggishness and was devastating when he came up against any of them. I cherish the memory of the day when one of the 'very nice' boys of the class gave as his excuse, for failure to have a Latin exercise done, the fact that he had to go as an altar boy to serve at evening devotions in his parish church. 'Biddy' did not look at him, he glowered at him and I can even yet recall the contemptuous attack: 'You sanctimonious scoundrel. You are the worst sort of fraud, a pious fraud.' As a class we were loyal to one another, but I knew everyone of us agreed with 'Biddy's' verdict. 'Biddy' was our Latin master and he was a good classical scholar and a fine teacher. Many years later we renewed our association and often during the early days of Sinn Féin he would come into my office and regale me with his recollections of Irish political events and the conflicts, lay and clerical, of the Parnellite split. To me he was the outstanding personality of St Malachy's amongst our teacher-professors.

My contemporaries in class were the usual assortment to be found in an intermediate school with one or two outstanding characters. 'Paddy Mac'[9] who later became a classical scholar at Maynooth was the outstanding wit and joker of the crowd. Jimmy Stuart who led all his classes as a medical student and the turbulent Jerry already mentioned. Some of the others

---

to the college but contributed greatly to the spread of the Catholic culture. Earliest of these was Danial O'Loan, later dean and professor of church history in Maynooth. The names of Vincent McNabb, O.P., of John McErlean, S.J., and of Eoin MacNeill are honoured elsewhere . . . From 1879 onwards the story of the college is one of steady progress . . . Year by year, there passed from the halls boys who embraced the priesthood or the religious state, or who entered the professions or the commercial world and in their various ways ventured further afield, many going as missionaries beyond Europe'.

9. Patrick MacLaverty (1885-1960): student in St Patrick's College, Maynooth, for the diocese of Down and Connor 1903-9, left the College during his fourth divine year and just before ordination, emigrated to U.S.A., where he had a successful career in the clothing business.

went to Maynooth and became priests of the diocese, while others, like myself, had to set their course to prepare to earn their living in trade, profession or business.

My own immediate future was determined by family business needs. It had been decided to open a branch shop and I became a necessary pillar in the enterprise. By all the laws of equity it was a mistake. I had done well at my examinations but I was not particularly happy in St Malachy's and, like most schoolboys of my age and period, welcomed the suggestion that I should turn to take a hand in the small, family business. It should never have happened and yet looking back over the years I think it had its values.

My father and I never really hit it off harmoniously working together. We were too much alike in temperament. We were both hot-tempered and somewhat unyielding and it was not long until the occasional clashes led to a crisis and I decided to break and seek a new field for my activities.

It was while I was at St Malachy's college that I got my first glimpse of the political activities that would later develop into acute conflict between two groups of the Catholic Nationalist population. About the year 1897, when the grand old dame Victoria was celebrating her diamond jubilee as queen and empress, the bishop of Down and Connor, the Most Reverend Dr Henry, had succeeded in his efforts to get some share of the representation in the Belfast City Council and other local boards for the Catholic minority in the city. He had formed a Catholic Association[10] and had succeeded in having, under a new Franchise Act, the local wards rearranged so that in two of the city wards the Catholic population was assured of a majority vote. This would enable them to have two aldermen and six councillors in the city council and similar representation on the boards of guardians, water commissioners, and other boards.

As one looks back to those days all this may seem trivial and to savour of parish-pump politics, but at the time the advance marked a very real achievement. Until then the Catholic minority which constituted about one third of the population had neither voice nor vote on any of the local councils or boards.[11] It may be well to make it clear that the movement

10. The Belfast Catholic Association was founded by Dr Henry Henry, bishop of Down and Connor (1895-1908), as the local political organisation in 1896. Subsequently Dr Henry opposed the United Irish League which became the constituency organisation of the Irish Parliamentary Party under John Redmond in 1900. Henry's attitude towards the United Irish League lost him support among his clergy and he consented to the disestablishment of the Belfast Catholic Association in 1905.

11. This was effected mainly by the Orange Order. A dominant force in Ulster politics, this Protestant organisation was founded after a clash on 21 September 1795 between the Catholic Defenders and the Protestant Peep O'-Day Boys at the Diamond, County

was on purely religious lines. The Catholic Association was not and did not claim to be in any sense either a national or a nationalistic movement. It was local and protective. It recognised that the Catholic population, although a minority, was a substantial minority in the community, contributing its share to the work and prosperity of the city and its proportionate share of the rates. Its representation would not displace the ascendancy control by the Conservative and Orange majority, but its voice would be heard in the council chamber, and publicity and the fear of exposure might help to redress some of the grievances under which the minority suffered. I do not think Dr Henry envisaged anything beyond this policy in the formation of his Catholic Association.

At the outset his Association met with opposition from a body which claimed to be the local national political organisation. This was the Belfast National Federation, an anti-Parnellite group headed by a young, budding politician, Mr Joseph Devlin. When the first big public meeting was held in St Mary's Hall and the bishop had outlined his programme, Mr Devlin spoke and asserted what he claimed was the right of his organisation to take charge and control the representation of the Catholic-Nationalist interests. This was immediately contested by the big majority present and the issue was knit. Devlin announced his determination and that of his party to contest every seat in the impending elections against the Catholic Association candidates who from that time forward were known as 'the bishop's men'. All this, let it be remembered, took place before there was any unity in the ranks of the elected Irish Parliamentary members. At that time, 1897, the members elected to Westminster were still divided after the Parnell[12] debâcle. There were Healyites and Dillonites and various other groups and it was not until some years later that the United Irish League[13] with John

---

Armagh. It has consistently opposed any movement including that of Home Rule threatening Protestant hegemony. The Orange Order played a prominent role in the Northern Ireland State, established in 1921. Most Ulster Unionists were members of Orange lodges, as were Northern Ireland's prime ministers. The protests of the Civil Rights Association in the 1960s and I.R.A. campaign 1970-94 forced the British government to deal seriously with the legislation and discrimination against the Catholic population by the Orange ascendancy. The Orange lodges hold processions on 12 July to commemorate William of Orange's victory at the Boyne in 1690.

12. Charles Stewart Parnell (1846-91): born Avondale, County Wicklow, M.P. for Meath 1875-91, leader of Irish Parliamentary Party 1879-91.

13. United Irish League, was founded by William O'Brien, M.P., on 23 January 1898 at Westport, County Mayo. With Michael Davitt as president, the League under its slogan 'The land for the people' called for the redistribution of large estates among the small farmers and attacked land-grabbers. Fearing that the political initiative would fall

Redmond[14] as chairman was formed. It was also some four or five years before Mr Devlin was elected as member for North Kilkenny in the British parliament and eight or nine years before he would win the West Belfast seat for the United Irish League and his Ancient Order of Hibernians.[15] Naturally I knew but little of the finer shades of political differences of the time, but when the election campaign was launched I was frequently on the fringe of the crowds eagerly listening to all the speeches.

One night stands out vividly in my memory. It was a miserably wet one at the end of October or beginning of November. A meeting was in progress almost opposite the Christian Brothers School in Barrack Street. A man stood up to speak. He was a tall man with a long thin face and a somewhat wispy beard. He looked tired and old and, even to my twelve-year old eyes, looked sad. He wore what was known as the 'Ulster', a top coat with a cape, and it looked old and shabby. I saw the empty sleeve and I listened to his speech though I cannot recall any of his statements, but I knew that I was seeing for the first time Michael Davitt[16] about whom I had heard so much at home. So this was that great man, the man who had fought the land war, the man who had lost his arm in a mill, the man who had suffered for so many years in an English prison. I remembered all that I heard my father and Henry O'Gorman and all his other old friends

---

to O'Brien, John Dillon, leader of the anti-Parnellites, and John Redmond, leader of the Parnellites, re-united the Irish Party in 1900 and invited O'Brien to join them. Redmond then assumed the presidency of the League which became the Party's new constituency organisation. The League was decimated outside Ulster when Sinn Féin overwhelmed the Irish Party in the 1918 general election. However, although wound up elsewhere, it continued to operate in Ulster, where it was the organ of Joseph Devlin and his nationalist supporters until 1928.

14. John Redmond (1856-1918): born Ballytrent, County Wexford, M.P. for New Ross 1881-85, North Wexford 1885-91, Waterford 1891-1918, leader of Irish Parliamentary Party 1900-18.

15. Ancient Order of Hibernians was founded in 1641 but took its modern form as a Catholic reaction to the Orange order. It supported the Irish Parliamentary Party under John Redmond. In 1904 Joseph Devlin became national president of the Board of Erin which represented the majority of the organisation's membership. It became an important part of the political machine and during the 1920s was the principal guardian of Catholic rights in Northern Ireland. It is no longer politically active and has become a friendly society and social club.

16. Michael Davitt (1846-1906): born Strade, County Mayo, a member of the Irish Republican Brotherhood, he was involved in the raid on Chester Castle 1867, he was instrumental in establishing the Land League 1879, M.P. for Meath 1882, North Meath and North East Cork 1892 and East Kerry and South Mayo 1895-99, with William O'Brien he co-founded the United Irish League, he visited South Africa to lend support to the Boer cause, in his later years he championed undenominational education, socialism and land nationalisation.

telling about Davitt and all he had done and suffered for our people. I was thrilled to see him and hear him and yet on that night of early winter I felt instinctively that he was tired, sad and lonely. No doubt the weather and the circumstances were responsible and yet I think not entirely so.

The elections followed in due course with an overwhelming success for all the bishop's candidates and a complete rout for the Devlinite party. These successes were repeated at all the subsequent elections during Dr Henry's lifetime. After his death the control of the local Catholic paper passed into the hands of his opponents and the Catholic Association gradually melted out of existence. The subsequent growth of the United Irish League and the purely Catholic organisation of the Ancient Order of Hibernians served for what passed as national and Catholic political bodies in support of the Home Rule movement.

The 'split', as it was called, had many unfortunate repercussions both immediate and ultimate for the nationalist cause in Belfast and indeed throughout the North-East corner of Ireland. Immediately, it caused dissension and friction amongst our people and even the clergy were very much divided in their loyalties. Minorities such as ours in a definitely hostile and bigoted area cannot afford disunion and it was not disunion, but bitter antagonism that prevailed for many years following the 'break'.

But what was far more serious from the national point of view was the fact that both forces were running on purely Catholic sectarian lines. It was in this that, to my view, Devlin was guilty of a major blunder in his handling of the nationalist situation in the North. The North had always a formidable leavening of intelligent nationalist and even republican opinion amongst the non-Catholics. Belfast, Antrim and Down had led in the Republican movement of the United Irishmen and its main strength lay in the sterling independence of the Presbyterian republican. Those who had sacrificed all, like McCracken, Orr and Munro, and who had fought at Antrim and Ballynahinch and had given up everything in the cause of independence had left a deeply ingrained tradition.[17] It is true that many of their successors had fallen away from this tradition and had accepted the loaves and fishes, and in their fiery oratory preached bigotry from platform and pulpit. Nevertheless there was still a considerable volume of support for independence descending from the '98 period and the tenant-right

17. United Irishmen, led by Henry Munro, were defeated at Ballynahinch, County Down, on 16 June 1798. This brought the rebellion in the north to an end and Munro was executed at Lisburn two days later.

movement[18] down to the strong Liberal party that existed in the early years of the century. Many of these were alienated by the sectarian bias that was given to the Home Rule movement by the development of the Ancient Order of Hibernians and its synonymity with the purely political Home Rule movement known as the United Irish League.

I can recall most of the stirring activities that marked the years of the late nineties and the turn of the century. We had the '98 celebrations commemorating the Rising of 1798 and its centenary. Every nationalist district had its commemoration club. These were named after one or other of the leaders of the 1798 Rising. We had clubs called after William Orr, Henry Joy McCracken, Samuel Neilson, Jimmy Hope and all the others. It was the age of colour patriotism and green flaggery. Every club had its banner and bannerettes and the various clubs and branches were mainly concerned with this visible demonstration of their faith and loyalty in the same way as the Orange lodges concentrated on their banners and fife-and-drum bands. This is not a cynical criticism though, if the truth must be told, I formed the notion early in my life that bands and banners and perfervid oratory were among the greatest obstacles to intelligent political thought.

Our big celebration in 1898 was fixed for 6 June which was the anniversary of the battle of Antrim. Bands, banners and people assembled in Smithfield Square which was ideally situated for marshalling of all the thousands who were taking part in the parade. The procession was led by a sturdy man well known to everyone on the Falls Road, one Johnnie Yaugh whose leadership of the parade was shared by a lady as 'Maid of Erin'. Johnnie was dressed in an all-green velvet coat and white buckskin pants, top boots and white cockade, while his companion was a picture in white linen with a gorgeous, green velvet cloak.

Led by these picturesque figures, Johnnie on a bay charger and his fair companion on a white one, the cavalcade tramped the four or five miles to Hannahstown where the big meeting was held. I watched the procession from the window of a friend's house and was thrilled by the music of the bands and the blaze of colour.

The sixth of June 1898 was stamped on my memory for that afternoon the riots started. They continued for five or six weeks and were, I think, typical of the Belfast riots which I had often heard discussed by my elders.

18. There was a number of organisations associated with 'tenant right'. It is possible that the one referred to here was the Ulster Tenant Right Association, founded in 1847 by William Sharman Crawford and others, following the defeat of Crawford's tenant right bill which had sought to legalise the 'Ulster Custom', which involved the recognition of the tenant's saleable interest in his or her holdings.

My father's recollections included what he called the 'sixty-four riots', the 'seventy-two riots' and the 'eighty-six riots' and we occasionally heard him and his contemporaries referring to them. I always felt that 'riots' was almost a misnomer for these outbreaks for, both in period of duration and lists of casualties, they would make a South American revolution seem like a picnic. The ''86' outbreak lasted almost three months and there was much shooting of both sides, while the casualties caused by the batons and the paving stones were considerable. In those days the streets were paved with heavy 'kidney' stones and the sidewalks with smaller ones so that a ready supply of effective ammunition was literally on hand once rioting started. The streets connecting the Falls and Shankill Roads were the chief battlegrounds for within these streets was the line of demarcation between the Catholic and Protestant areas of residence. Despite the Arms Acts there was a fair amount of gun-fire, but the engagements were mostly attacks and counterattacks by groups armed with sticks and covered by a rear battalion of expert stone-throwers. The 'Peelers', as the Royal Irish Constabulary-men were called, had the miserable job of lining up between the opposing forces to keep them apart and alternated their attacks against both sides to try and clear a 'no-man's land' between them. Invariably it proved necessary to call out the military to end the hostilities.

That was 1898 as I remember it and there was a recurrence of similar 'trouble' in 1899. The riots of 1899 had, however, an unusual aftermath. In all the previous rioting it had been the practice of the magistrates to deal leniently with the many prisoners that had been caught and charged by the police and military, but 1899 was to see a startling change in regard to them.

At the winter assizes of that year the presiding judge was Chief Baron Palles[19] and to the consternation of those involved he proceeded to hand out penal servitude sentences to the worst offenders. It was, perhaps, a somewhat trivial thing to do a month or two in the Crumlin Road jail for defending the glorious, pious and immortal memory of William of Orange but when the Chief Baron continued to say 'Three years penal servitude' that was a new sort of medicine altogether. My own guess, made long afterwards, was that the Castle authorities, urged on by all the city

19. Christopher Palles (1831-1920): born Dublin, barrister 1853, solicitor-general for Ireland, attorney-general 1872, chief baron of Irish court of exchequer 1874-1916, commissioner of Irish national education 1890-1913, chairman of Board of Intermediate Education for Ireland 1896-1910, chairman of the commissioners of Irish university education and chief draftsman of the Constitution of the National University 1908, privy councillor of Ireland (1872) and of England (1892) and a devout Catholic.

industrialists and magnates, decided to put an end to those recurring outbreaks and make an example of those who had the misfortune to be caught.

However that may be, it is noteworthy that the riots of 1899 were the last of the serious outbreaks until 1907, and in these latter the cause of the conflict was entirely different. The riots of 1907 were not the traditional upheaval between orange and green, but a fierce conflict between the employers and their underpaid workers which will be referred to in a later chapter.

At the beginning of the century we experienced the early stirrings of a new national awakening. Most of this sprang from the Gaelic League[20] and from the spread of the Gaelic Athletic Association[21] in the North. There was a new consciousness of what it meant to be Irish and of the duties and responsibilities that rested on our people and particularly on the young people of the period.

The 1898 centenary celebrations had reawakened the memories of old and young to the long struggle that had continued against the old enemy and the fact that we were still a subject race. The Boer war which had shaken the British empire to its roots had a double repercussion in Ireland. The whole of Nationalist Ireland sympathised with the Boers in their struggle for freedom from British imperialism and an Irish brigade led by John MacBride,[22] who was to pay the deferred penalty before a firing squad in 1916, symbolised the sympathy with the Boers and the antagonism to empire that was universally felt by nationalist Ireland. There was another factor which, to my mind, had an even deeper effect on our people. As I remember it, the Boer war saw the peak point of vulgar expression of the arrogant spirit of British imperialism. Jingoism it came to be called and we in Ireland got our full share of it. Our theatre, our music-halls, which at that time were the favourite haunts of those seeking amusement, our newspapers and all the media of public expression were soaked in the propaganda that proclaimed the glory of *Britannia* and contempt for the lesser breeds. We had Kipling[23] with his 'Absent-minded beggar'. We had

20. The Gaelic League was founded in 1893 by Douglas Hyde, Eoin MacNeill and Fr Eugene O'Growney. Its aim was to de-Anglicise Ireland through the revival and preservation of Irish as a spoken language.

21. The Gaelic Athletic Association was founded in 1893 by Michael Cusack and Maurice Davin to preserve and promote traditional Irish games such as football, hurling and handball.

22. Major John MacBride (1865-1916): born Westport, County Mayo, with Arthur Lynch he organised the pro-Boer Irish brigade, member of the Irish Republican Brotherhood, he took part in the 1916 Rising for which he was executed.

23. Rudyard Kipling (1865-1936): prolific author, British imperialist, apologist for conscription and 'the rights of Ulster' and opponent of democracy and women's suffrage.

'*Britannia* rules the waves', 'We don't want to fight, but by jingo if we do', 'The British navy' and so on *ad nauseam*. As our theatres and music halls at the time were all visited, week by week, by London companies and British touring entertainers and these merely repeated their performance that had won applause in Leeds, Sheffield, Edinburgh and elsewhere in Britain, our Irish audiences got the same medicine. There was a revulsion of feeling against all this. Not only was it due to the fact that the mighty British empire had to fight for nearly three years to suppress the 'handful of Boer farmers', but its vulgar stupidity and boastfulness aroused the antipathy of anyone with any vestige of national feeling.

The Gaelic League was rapidly spreading all over Ireland. Apart from its chief aim of the restoration of the Irish language, the Gaelic League taught the gospel of self-development in every phase of Irish life. It was our duty to support our own industries, to study our own history and the problems that faced our people and to develop all branches of our own culture. It was, of course, non-sectarian and it was non-political. It was definitely non-sectarian and in its branches were to be found many members of different religious denominations. It was non-political in the local or internal national sense, and there was no barrier to anyone whether he was Redmondite, Unionist, Sinn Féin or Labour in his politics, but, in the wider sense, it was by its very nature and purposes separatist.

The Gaelic League had an extraordinary influence on the young men and women who came into its ranks in those early days. It definitely gave them a mould of character and idealism that was reflected in their everyday life. It is difficult to appraise it accurately at this late date, but it seemed to impose a sense of personal responsibility for the honour of Ireland on the individual member. They were not puritanical, but they were sober and aimed at the clean healthy life of a decent Irish citizen. They lived in Ireland and meant to live in Ireland and work for Ireland. They had their sport and their fun and I do not think it is an exaggeration to claim that there was more life and clean, wholesome fun and entertainment to be found in the Gaelic League and the Gaelic Athletic Association in the first decade of the century than has ever been experienced by young Ireland since that time.

There were other forces operating at the same time. Arthur Griffith[24]

24. Arthur Griffith (1871-1922): born Dublin, supported the Boers, with William Rooney, he founded Cumann na nGaedheal, began editing the *United Irishman* 1900, published *The resurrection of Hungary: a parallel for Ireland* 1904, his paper *Sinn Féin* replaced *United Irishman* 1906 and continued to appear until suppressed 1914, led the Irish delegation to the treaty negotiations 1921, president of Dáil Éireann 1921-22.

was preaching the doctrine of Sinn Féin[25] which was in harmony with the Gaelic League psychology from the political point of view, while D. P. Moran[26] was spreading the gospel of Irish Ireland in his weekly journal *The Leader*. Griffith was probably the most brilliant journalist that Ireland had produced in a century. His searching analyses of the evils that had eaten into and were still festering in the national being and the remedies he prescribed did more than any other single thing to awaken the conscience of the more thoughtful and intelligent youth of our period. In his weekly journals, *The United Irishman* and later *Sinn Féin*, he laid the foundation on which the independence movement grew, and created the receptive mind that later formed the Volunteers and destroyed the servile parliamentary movement. He did more than that. His paper was outstanding in the quality of its literary contributions. A brilliant writer himself, he attracted to his columns some of the ablest and best of our young writers of the period. Here writers like Padraic Colum,[27] James Stephens,[28] Séamus O'Sullivan,[29] Seumas O'Kelly,[30] Daniel Corkery[31] and a number of others were first brought to the notice of Irish readers. During those years in which Arthur Griffith carried on with his paper he was anathema to all who exercised power and influence. To the Irish Parliamentary Party he was public enemy No. 1. To the authorities in the Castle he was the danger signal that must have revived their memories of Mitchell[32] and Davis[33] and

25. Sinn Féin was a movement which developed between 1905 and 1908 under the direction of Arthur Griffith and Bulmer Hobson, absorbing the Dungannon Clubs and Cumann na nGaedhael. The movement's newspaper was *Sinn Féin*, edited by Griffith from 1906 until its suppression in 1914. After the Easter Rising 1916 the Sinn Féin and independence movements were indistinguishable.

26. Denis Patrick Moran (1872-1936): born Waterford, edited *New Ireland Review* 1898-1900, in 1900 founded *The Leader* which became an influential force in the Irish-Ireland movement.

27. Padraic Colum (1881-1972): born Longford, poet, playwright and biographer of Arthur Griffith.

28. James Stephens (1882-1950): born Dublin, poet, novelist.

29. Séamus O'Sullivan – real name, James Sullivan Starkey (1879-1958): born Dublin, poet, founder of *The Dublin Magazine*.

30. Seumas O'Kelly (1880-1918): born Loughrea, County Galway, assisted Arthur Griffith in editing *Nationality* and was found dead at its editorial desk following a raid by the crown forces.

31. Daniel Corkery (1878-1968): born Cork, national teacher, T.D. for County Cork 1921-23, professor of English, U.C.C., 1931-47, senator 1951-54.

32. John Mitchel (1815-75): born Dungiven, County Derry, contributed to *The Nation*, founded the *United Irishman* 1948, transported to Tasmania 1848, M.P. for North Tipperary 1875, his *Jail journal* first appeared in 1854 in his New York newspaper *The citizen*.

33. Thomas Osborne Davis (1818-45): born Mallow, County Cork, poet, joint editor with John Blake Dillon of the *Dublin Morning Register* with Dillon and Charles Gavan Duffy was co-founder of *The Nation*.

the 'felons' of '48.[34] To the merchants and magnates his was a journal that must be denied advertisements. To continue the paper week by week was a constant struggle, but Griffith struggled on and the paper appeared though it is safe to say that during all that time he existed on a precarious income that would have been scorned by a third-rate invoice clerk. Tempting offers were made to him of important journalistic posts abroad, but he was not interested. Arthur Griffith was more than an outstanding journalist. He was an Irishman with a vision and a mission and however hopeless the future of his policy might seem to be and despite the comparative poverty to which his work condemned him he had the grim tenacity to hold on and fight on against all opposition.

D. P. Moran founded *The Leader*, a weekly newspaper that had an immense influence on the mind of Young Ireland in the early years of the century. *The Leader* concentrated on the language and industrial revival movements and it probably did more than any other single element to awaken our people to the responsibility they owed to the country by buying Irish-made products in preference to the imported goods which in the main came from Britain.

The Leader also set out to kill the slave spirit of Shoneenism and cheap snobbery in all its phases and was remarkably successful in doing so. Moran preached a gospel of material and cultural nationalism; of pride in Ireland and being Irish; of contempt for the cheap and shoddy in people, in goods, and particularly in our cultural and entertainment activities.

There was the utmost contrast between the respective journalism of Griffith and Moran, but both were, in their different ways, all out in their efforts for the same objectives. Moran was a vehement and cyclonic force with a flair for the devastating phrase and withering criticism. Most of those who did not respect him really feared him. I do not imply that he was either scurrilous or unjust, but he saw the evils that had been and were undermining the self-respect and independence of our people and he went out to kill them. His special facility in coining phrases such as the 'Castle Cawtholic' did more to end the slave spirit of the respectable social 'climbers' than most of the preaching directed to the same end. His journal was bright and pungent and, apart from these qualities, carried many well written and constructive contributions on finance, taxation and the whole issue of national reconstruction.

34. William Smith O'Brien, Terence Bellew McManus, James Stephens and a hundred of their associates who engaged about forty police at Boulogh Commons, near Ballingarry, County Tipperary on 29 July 1848.

The Leader policy on the industrial revival meant a great deal to many of our home industries and it also meant much to the success of the paper itself. Inevitably these manufacturers appreciated the value of such a medium for their advertisements and they did not want to come into the category that Moran had shrewdly designated as the 'Dark Brotherhood' meaning those who were manufacturing, but were not adequately advertising their products.

Griffith's papers, *The United Irishman* and later *Sinn Féin* followed a more cultured and intellectual course than *The Leader*. It did not seek to be a 'highbrow' production, but it just so happened that its editor and those who associated themselves with him were people of fine intellect and the gift of fine expression without unnecessary flamboyancy. Griffith's own articles – and he contributed many under different pen-names in nearly every issue of the paper – were probably the most brilliant contributions to national thought since the time of Davis, Mitchel and Fintan Lalor.[35] While he had no predilection for the flamboyant and tended to write with an austere, hard logic, he could be satirical, humorous or devastating at will, and his turn of phrase and grace of expression were a joy to those of us who, week by week, sought our stimulus from his paper. They are both gone now and there has been nothing of equal value to replace them. How much we need intelligent direction by a new Griffith and a new Moran is evident from the growth of the modern decadence that has crept insidiously into the national being and which in their own time they had so nearly exterminated.

35. James Fintan Lalor (1807-49): born Tenakill, County Laois, his view that only those who work on the land could own it, expressed in *The Nation* during 1847, attracted the attention of the more militant Young Irelanders, co-edited John Mitchel's paper *The Irish felon* with John Martin, his brother Peter (1823-89), led insurgent miners in Australia at Eureka stockade in 1854 and rose to the rank of postmaster-general and later that of speaker in the Australian parliament.

2

I start 'engineering' – Social conditions in Belfast in 1902 – The 'half-timers' – Belfast's Sunday gloom – The evangelists of the Custom House steps

As mentioned earlier, I had the clash with my father and we decided that for both our sakes it would be wise for me to part company and seek a career in outside employment. That was at the latter end of 1901 and, for some reason or another, I decided on the engineering trade. I emphasise the word 'trade' because there was no possibility of aspiring to the professional side of the business. For one thing, the family resources were too slender to provide for a university course and my scholastic career at St Malachy's was ended before I reached matriculation standard.

After various family conferences it was finally arranged that I should enter the firm of Coombe, Barbour & Coombe as an apprentice and I did so in January 1902. It was an experience, a very tough experience, which ended happily for me some eight months after I had joined the firm. It is difficult to write dispassionately of that period and of that concern and its methods. No doubt it was not unique in those days, but when I recall the system, the exploitation of the young apprentices, the petty tyrannies of 'gaffers' and foremen, I can appreciate the spirit of revolt that created strikes and labour unrest. I was not long in the firm when I realised that it was a semi-'black shop', that is to say, that many of the employees were non-union men and that many, if not most of them, were simply 'one job' men. The technique adopted to achieve this end was interesting. A youth, whether he was an apprentice or a mere learner, was put at a machine and kept at it, or he might be tried at several machines if the need arose. Inevitably he became proficient at a particular operation and, after he proved himself, he was awarded a few extra shillings per week and so progressed until he was earning about 25 shillings per week. Beyond that he seldom went. It is true that those of us who entered specifically as apprentices were supposed to pass out after a year to the fitting shops, the machine shop or what was known as the 'tool shop' but it did not always happen. It was the general understanding that the only two really worthwhile shops where apprentices could become competent engineers was the tool shop and machine shop, but unless one had very special influence with the top level bosses, the chances of getting into one or other of those branches were pretty remote. Of course all the realities of the position only became known to us after we had entered on our employment and it was a gradual process of awareness at that.

The system was interesting from another point of view. The foremen were hard-driven for cheap production. It was as 'drivers' they had been selected and they tried to fulfil their obligations. Our particular boss was a prize specimen of the type. Hawklike and with a lean, cadaverous and nervous look, he cast an aura of strain and antagonism all around him from six o'clock in the morning until the final siren sounded at a quarter past five in the evening. Yes, work started at 6 a.m. in those days and fines were imposed if you failed to have your brass check into the box before it closed at 6 a.m. sharp. At eight o'clock there was a three-quarters-of-an-hour stoppage for breakfast, and a similar period was allowed for dinner at one o'clock. On Saturday the week's grind ended at noon. It was a fifty-four hour week and there was little or no respite during those fifty-four hours.

Checking-in at 6 a.m. meant for me rising at 5.15 a.m., and that I should be abed by 10.30 p.m. if I was going to last out the strenuous labour of the day. It was somewhat restrictive on one's social life, but it was the system, and it is worth remembering that the system continued until 1917 when, during World War I, the factory psychiatrists apparently came to the conclusion that, from the point of view of economic production, the six o'clock start with the breakfast and dinner breaks was unsound.

It is unpleasant to have to refer to anything in the nature of bigotry, but in Belfast of those days it was difficult to escape it. I am sure that our hawk-like boss, whom we knew as 'Sam', was a religious, God-fearing man. He had that appearance and the Sabbatarian look was not uncommon in the Belfast of my youth. Sam had the solemnity of a chief warden at an execution. I always expected him to wheel around suddenly on me and ask me: 'Young man, where do you expect to spend eternity?' The ice-cold blue eye was unrelenting. We all knew he taught Sunday-school and that a black suit and a bowler hat completed the gloom that he brought to his young pupils.

I was reasonably aware from my earliest days under his control that Sam had no particular love for 'papists' and as time went on my suspicions gave way to certainty and finally touched crisis. The incident was in its way trivial. I was engaged on a relatively simple operation of preparing spinning 'fliers' for their first grind and polish.

I had to cut them to a gauge and bore them at one end. It so happened that Sam himself was engaged on the next operation. In other words, I was working to him and had to keep him supplied. All foremen in the concern were 'working' foremen. I was working away steadily when Sam swept around to my machine bench, threw down a bundle of the 'fliers' and said I had spoiled them and then, just as quickly, went off again. I examined them and saw at once that my job had been done correctly, but that Sam himself had ground them at the wrong end. Without a moment's delay, I took the bundle over to the under-foreman, put them on his bench and asked him: 'Jack, what's wrong with these fliers?', without asking why I wanted to know. Jack examined them and told me they were ground on the wrong end. I took the bundle and dumped them down beside Sam. 'Jack says that these have been ground at the wrong end' I told him. Perhaps I should draw a veil over what followed. Sam became livid and I was in no sweet temper myself. I do not think his language was quite up to Sunday-school standards and I know mine was not, but I did succeed in conveying to him my appreciation of his qualities and character. That, thank God, finished me with Sam and the firm of Coombe, Barbour & Coombe.

I have recorded this, my personal experience, to give an indication of what was, more or less, the general system of petty tyranny that operated in many of our Belfast workshops and factories. I have mentioned the fact that work commenced at 6 a.m. and that this meant for me rising at about 5.15 a.m. My home was about fifteen or twenty minutes walk from the works and I always had a hot jug of coffee or cocoa to prepare and devour before I left. I had commenced working in Coombe, Barbour & Coombe Ltd. in January. It was typically cold, wet and stormy and we had often spells of heavy snow. It was neither pleasant nor comfortable, but I was well equipped with heavy overcoat and muffler and had a warm, if hurried, meal before setting out. On my way to the works I had to pass quite a few of the large mills which were the basic enterprise of the linen trade and were engaged in the spinning, weaving and finishing of the 'piece goods'.

I shudder even now when I recall those cold winter mornings, not for my personal experiences, but for the sight that met me each morning of droves of women, young girls and children making their way into the steaming spinning-rooms of the huge factories. I say 'children' for that is what many of them were!

In those days the mill owners employed 'half-timers'. Half-timers worked alternate days and attended school on the others. Their working life began at eleven years of age and those who survived until they reached the mature age of fourteen might hope to be continued as 'full-timers' or whole time workers in the mill. 'Half-timers' worked the same long hours as the others. That is to say from 6 a.m. until 6 p.m. with a three-quarters of an hour interval at 8 a.m. for breakfast and an equal break at 1 p.m. for dinner. The 'half-timers' were mostly engaged at the wet spinning, which meant that they lived and worked their day in an atmosphere of heat and moisture. Many of them went barefooted to their work, their scanty clothing covered by a poor, thin shawl. I am not describing what was occasional or unusual. I am merely recording what was the universal system of the linen industry.

The 'whole-timers' earned, on an average, eight to nine shillings per week of fifty-eight and three-quarter hours and the 'half-timers' averaged three shillings and nine pence to four shillings. They were subject to fines for being late and there were exactly six recognised holidays, apart from Sundays, out of the 365 days. These were Christmas Day and St Stephen's Day; Easter Monday and Easter Tuesday; and of course the 12th and 13th of July to celebrate the liberty that had been won for Belfast by the glorious, pious and immortal William of Orange at the battle of the Boyne. Needless to add, holidays were not paid for by the employers. To those of my fellow townsmen who, at times, become almost lyrical about the great industry of our native city, I would recommend an occasional meditation on how that success was achieved, and the very big percentage of young children who were a spent labour force before they could attain the status of 'full-timers' at the age of fourteen years. There are no statistics recording specifically the percentage of the 'half-timers' who were laid to rest in the local cemeteries. I think it must have been high!

Belfast was prospering in the first decade of the century and, if wages were relatively low, there was little unemployment. The city was growing and new areas were being developed on the traditional lines of long streets of monotonously-similar kitchen-and-parlour houses. William J., later Lord, Pirrie[1] was in control at Harland and Wolff ship-building yards and was also at the head of the White Star Line. As a result, the Queen's Island, as the yards were known locally, was fully occupied and working day and night to build the giant liners that earned the firm and the city a world-wide reputation. Here the *Celtic*, the *Adriatic* and others were built. These were vessels up from twenty to twenty-five thousand tons and set a new

1. Viscount William James Pirrie (1847-1924): born Quebec of Irish parents, raised near Belfast, entered the shipbuilding firm of Harland and Wolff 1862, became a partner 1874 and after the firm was converted into a limited company became chairman of the board, Harland and Wolff were the sole shipbuilders for the White Star Line and the Bibby line and supplied important ships for the Peninsular and Oriental Company, the Royal Mail Steam Packet Company and other leading lines, Pirrie built up Harland and Wolff until the works at Belfast covered 230 acres, he established other yards on the Clyde and ship repairing works at Liverpool and other ports, the enterprises under his control employed about 50,000 men, Pirrie's philanthropic activities were considerable especially in the field of education, his prominent place in the life of Belfast was recognised by his election in 1898 as the city's first honorary freeman, served as lord mayor 1896-7 and appointed lieutenant for the city 1911, he became Baron Pirrie of Belfast 1906 and received a viscounty 1921.

standard for trans-oceanic transport in speed, efficiency and luxury to be outclassed year after year by bigger and better liners until perhaps the peak achievement was reached by the ill-fated and reputedly unsinkable *Titanic*, which was sunk by an iceberg on its maiden voyage to New York.

Pirrie, at this time, was something of an idol to the Belfast people. He was lord mayor of the city for a number of years and Mrs Pirrie was a popular favourite with the people. She was a woman of charm and character and was sincerely interested in all the charitable activities of the period. Her consistent drive for the building and equipment of the Royal Victoria Hospital gave Belfast one of the finest hospitals in these islands and it must be recorded to her credit that she was equally active in her help to complete the other great Belfast hospital, 'the Mater', which was being enlarged and modernised by the Catholic bishop and his flock.

A few years later the Pirries came under the cloud of political bigotry and antagonism. Billy Pirrie, as he was affectionately known to the men on the 'Island', was a Liberal in politics and a Home-Ruler and when the Liberal party came into office in 1906 and Home Rule became a major issue, indeed the only issue, for the Belfast citizen, the Pirrie popularity waned to vanishing point. He made no secret of his views and presided at many Liberal and Home Rule meetings. He was now Lord Pirrie and a member of the privy council, but he was a Home-Ruler and, although he still continued as the dominant head of both Harland and Wolff and the White Star Line, his local social activities would seem to have ended. The Carsonite movement which spread its tentacles into every activity, commercial, religious and social, tolerated no opposition and the Pirries were outside the Pale.

It may be of interest to review briefly the conditions of labour and the economic position of the workers during the years prior to 1914.

The average wage for skilled workmen, that is, tradesmen such as carpenters, painters, bricklayers, cabinet-makers, fitters and mechanics had crept up to thirty-eight shillings per week for a week of fifty-four hours. Exceptional jobs in these trades might carry an extra few shillings per week and there were a number of highly-specialised jobs in the shipyards such as platers and riveters where the workers could earn more than double this rate. Labourers, apart from shipyard workers, seldom earned more than twenty shillings per week and many had to be content with a few shillings a week less. It was something of a mystery to most of us how families were reared on such wages, but living was cheap and there was then less temptation to spend on non-essentials. The kitchen house was rented at three shillings and sixpence to four shillings per week; the two-pound loaf was two pence-farthing to two pence-halfpenny; butter was nine pence or ten pence per pound and margarine was as low as four pence or five pence per pound. Tea could be bought at one shilling and four pence per pound and sugar was two pence per pound. A pint of Guinness was two pence and Woodbine cigarettes were five-a-penny.

Even with these prices, it was obvious that a real struggle was always being waged to make ends meet. An emergency, caused by sickness or unemployment, created a real crisis for in those early days of the century there was no unemployment doles or sick benefits. Bearing these factors in mind, one can understand how the children came to be rushed into the mills at eleven years of age. Their miserable slave wage of three and nine pence or four shillings a week meant a real contribution to the economy of the pound-a-week labourer and his struggling family. Looking back on it all, one realised how depressing the social conditions of the vast majority of the labouring masses were. Mean streets of small kitchen houses with a 'pub' at every corner and a group of 'corner boys' at most pubs; the usual sprinkling of pawn offices and small traders and shoals of poorly-clad youngsters trying to make play on the sidewalks; these constituted the conditions under which most of the working population lived. The conditions described were, for the most part, what prevailed for the unskilled and casual labourer and for the tradesman, whose love for the bottle outweighed his concern for his family.

For the sober tradesman who aspired to 'respectability' conditions were decent and tolerable. At a rent of five shillings a week he could enjoy a small comfortable parlour house in a decent street. He could afford a 'Sunday suit' and decent clothing for his wife and children. His daughters need not go into the mills as 'half-timers', but could continue their education and daily attendance at school until they reached the age of fourteen. At that age they generally found employment in one of the 'warerooms'. In my time, a 'wareroom girl' was one who might be employed at any branch of the 'making-up' trade. She might be a hem-stitcher or a folder or a machine sewer in a clothing factory, but by far the greatest number of the Belfast girls were engaged in the innumerable branches of the linen trade. They were quite a social 'cut' above the mill worker. Their work did not start until 8 a.m. and with an interval of an hour for lunch or dinner they continued until 6 p.m. The 'wareroom girl' never wore a shawl. She was neatly dressed in a costume or blouse and skirt, and was always conscious of her need to keep up appearances.

These girls seemed to me to be the backbone of the family life in the city. They were often the social and economic bridge which linked the early years of the family struggle to the comparative security and progress that followed their graduation to the ranks of wage earners. They were in those days more dependable than the boys of the family. They were home and house conscious and when the family had reached the stage when one, two or more of the girls had started work in the warerooms, a new sense of security was achieved. Many of them earned 'good money', as they called it. A girl of fourteen would go into the works as a learner at a wage of a few shillings a week. After a short period she would 'get a machine' and, as they were often paid on a 'piece-work' basis, she would soon be earning from ten to fifteen shillings a week or more. The additional income to the family budget usually meant the difference between comparative struggle and real comfort. They were, in the main, a gay, jolly and carefree group of workers. Going into the big rooms, where a hundred or more machines were being operated, one was usually met by a whole chorus of voices chanting the latest music hall or pantomime song. They had to work hard and constantly to make a decent wage and they did, but the conditions were, in most cases, reasonably comfortable and pleasant.

There was one branch of employment linked with the linen trade that was widely developed in those days and that was the 'outwork'. This included embroidery, 'sprigging' and hemstitching. Widows with children, wives with husbands who were delicate or what was far more common who spent much of their earnings in the pub, and delicate women who could not do a full day's work at the factory, were glad to get their share of this work. It was often fine delicate work requiring great care and expert needle-craft and it was wretchedly paid, but the few shillings that were earned were a welcome addition to the family income.

Such were the conditions as I remember them in Belfast in the first few years of the century. The skilled tradesmen had their trade unions and were reasonably protected by them, but the big mass of unskilled labour and this included dock-workers, van-drivers, navvies, shop-workers and the like were unorganised and were at the mercy of their employers. Women workers, including the mill hands, were in a similar defenceless state. The organisation of the underprivileged in industry could come later and be productive of far-reaching results. We will hope to deal with that phase in due course.

One of the most memorable developments of the period was the organising of the hurling and football clubs under the auspices of the Gaelic Athletic Association. A playing pitch was secured on the Whiterock Road and later an open space at Willowbank. In a short time there was at least a dozen or more teams of senior rank competing for the championship, while the schoolboys and the teenagers all had innumerable teams out hurling. One of my early recollections of G.A.A. activities was to be introduced to Michael Cusack,[2] one of the founders of the Gaelic Athletic Association. He was a venerable-looking old man, sturdy and squarely-built with a long flowing beard, that, strange as it may seem, I always associated with two directly-opposite types: the old Fenian and the diehard grandmaster of the Orangemen. Old man Cusack had travelled up from Dublin to 'Throw in the ball' at the big match and, at the céilidhe that rounded off the big day, he spoke a few words of advice and encouragement to those of us who were there to welcome him. The revival of the Gaelic games had an extraordinary effect on the whole life of our Catholic and nationalist people in Belfast, or perhaps it would be more correct to say in West Belfast and particularly in the area of West Belfast that is known as the Falls Road.

Belfast was and maybe still is a Sabbatarian city. The Belfast Sunday of my youth was a day of gloomy depression. The brightest Sunday in summer was made melancholy by the almost sullen silence of the streets and the black-garbed stream of solemn church-goers. A favourite walk, when we were young boys of ten or twelve years, was to one of Belfast's beauty-spots at Shaw's Bridge. Here the river Lagan wound its easy way through the quiet country-side and one could follow its course on the tow-path. It was wonderfully beautiful and pleasant, but the journey to it through Great Victoria Street, Botanic Avenue and the Stranmillis on a Sunday afternoon filled me with gloom. As a young boy I could not and did not attempt to analyse it but, even now, I feel an involuntary shudder when I recall the effect of it. I can only describe it as a sense of loneliness or homesickness, a depression that was atmospheric, and it can only have been caused by the solemnity and the appearance of severity which the church-goers presented.

On the Falls Road it was entirely different. After early Mass we had walks up and around Falls Road and the Black Mountain and there was unorganised and scrappy football here and there in what were known as the convent fields, but games in the public parks were not permitted. With the growth of the G.A.A. came a real sporting renaissance and it was an entirely salutary and healthy development. Crowds of young boys and men could be seen making their way to the playing pitches with their hurleys.

2. Michael Cusack (1847-1907): born An Carn, Ennis, County Clare, teacher at Blackrock College and Clongowes Wood, he founded a school to assist young people entering the civil service or the university, soon afterwards he founded the civil service academy hurling club and this experience germinated the idea of a Gaelic Athletic Association, of which he was co-founder in 1884.

They had been to Mass and were now out to have their few hours of recreation; surely a saner and more healthy way to occupy their one day of freedom than to sit brooding behind drawn curtains or sneaking off surreptitiously to the nearby pub.

It was symptomatic of Belfast that we should have our open-air preachers and evangelists. The great forum for these was the Custom House steps. 'The steps' surrounded a fine stone building at the dock-side at the foot of High Street, and here from about three o'clock on Sunday afternoons various hot-gospellers bellowed their dogmas. It was difficult for any reasonably intelligent listener to form any notion of what their dogmas were. For the most part the preachers were illiterate or semi-illiterate and seemed determined to harrow the feelings of their audience with recitals of their horrible pasts and the glory of their salvation which was apparently now secure beyond question. There was Billy Hutton, a swarthy, thick-set, powerful man who never minced his words when he recited all the horrible sins and crimes he had committed until, as he explained, he 'met God coming out of a public house on the Shankill Road'. His tales of his drunken bouts, his poverty caused by drink, his fights and his escapades generally were hair-raising, but were relieved by his reports on his present-day comfort and success.

Then there was a Mr Ballantine, an entirely different type to Billy. Ballantine was somewhat more refined, quoted much from the Bible, but had a viciously mean constancy in his attacks on convents and all that he alleged went on therein. They were frank to the point of embarrassment in publishing their private home life. I remember Ballantine describing how on the previous Sunday he went home to find consternation and alarm in the household because 'Wee Maggie', his daughter, was lost. They had searched everywhere for her, had sought her in the houses of the neighbours and around the nearby streets, but no trace could be found of Maggie. 'Then later on', said Ballantine, 'I had occasion to go out to the back yard and there in the W.C. I found Wee Maggie reading her Bible. I said to her: "what do you mean Maggie sitting out here and us all out looking for you?" Maggie looked up at me and says she: "But da I read in the Bible to go into my closet and pray".' Ballantine seemed happy that his influence in the home was effective.

The pivotal point at the Custom House was the rostrum held by one Arthur Trew and here literally thousands gathered each Sunday to listen to the super bigot and firebrand of militant Protestantism. Trew's performances were really a source of shame and humiliation to the respectable Church of Ireland Episcopalians, but there was no public condemnation.

He spoke for the Belfast Protestant Association[3] which had close ties with similar organisations in Liverpool and Glasgow. He was a small man, somewhat deformed, with the fiery look of a fanatic. He had a hard, strident voice that carried well and had a ready flow of fierce invective which was entirely devoted to abuse of the pope and popery, and anything that remotely tended in that direction. Ironically enough it was his conflict with the 'trimmings of popery' that led to his undoing. The history of Trew and its repercussions on things in Belfast is, I think, interesting and worthy of record.

Next to the Catholic Church and Catholics generally, Trew preached an insensate hate against all forms of what he called ritualistic practices. Now there were in Belfast at that time at least two ministers of the Protestant religion who were conducting what we understood were 'High Church Services' and had religious emblems in their churches. These included sacred pictures, crucifixes, confessional boxes and such furnishings as are usually associated with the Catholic faith. There may have been quite a number of such churches in Belfast, but I know that Trew concentrated his attacks on two of them. One was in the care of the Reverend Mr Peoples. Trew, week by week, waged his war of words from the 'steps' and, having worked up his audience to the necessary pitch of excitement and anger, eventually led mobs to the churches to demonstrate against the popish practices therein. The result was inevitable; clashes took place between Trew's followers and the police authorities, who were called out for the protection of the congregations, and minor riots followed. Ultimately, Trew was arrested and charged with incitement to riot and sentenced to twelve months imprisonment. It seemed to most people that he had achieved his purpose. He was now a martyr for his faith and a hero to his fanatical supporters. Trew differed from the other evangelists in one respect. However influenced the others were, they preached without reward or collections whereas Trew's Sunday collections for his organisation averaged £12 to £15 per meeting.

After his arrest it was announced that the meetings would continue and that his place would be taken by a Mr Thomas Sloan[4] who would give his

3. Belfast Protestant Association: Working-class, anti-Catholic organisation founded in 1900 from Belfast lodges of the Orange Order. It was led by Arthur Trew and Thomas H. Sloan. When Trew was imprisoned for twelve months in 1901 for inciting riots the Belfast Protestant Association was taken over by Sloan. Subsequently Sloan used it to establish the Independent Orange Order.

4. Thomas Henry Sloan (1870-1941): born Belfast, worked at Harland and Wolff's and was a prominent member of the Orange Order, from which he was expelled for criticising Colonel Edward T. Saunderson, leader of the Ulster Unionists, founded the Independent Orange Order 1902, M.P. for South Belfast 1902-10.

services voluntarily until their hero returned from prison. Sloan fulfilled his engagement and became the star-turn 'preacher' at all the meetings. He was somewhat of a contrast to Trew. He was more polished, but no less forcible and in a short time seemed to have gained the approval and full support of Trew's adherents.

Just about this time a parliamentary vacancy occurred in South Belfast which was always a safe seat for the local Unionist party. The Belfast Protestant Association felt that they had not the approval of the highly respected leaders of the Unionist party and no doubt the fact that it was possible in Orange and Protestant Belfast for a defender of the faith like Trew to be put away for a year in prison for resisting popery added to their wrath. However that may have been, it was decided that Trew's association would fight the official candidate.

Trew was in prison and could not be nominated and there was the one obvious choice and that was his deputy, Tom Sloan. Accordingly Sloan was nominated against Lord Arthur Hill and, to the consternation of the whole Unionist camp, defeated him at the polls and was the new member of parliament for the division. What Trew's feelings must have been when he emerged from his cell and found his deputy installed as a fully blown member of the mother of parliaments while he, Arthur, had suffered his dreary spell in jail can only be imagined. Trew, a real demagogue, had doubtless envisaged parliament, but the fates had been unkind. He had missed the tide; the wave that sent him to prison had floated his successor to the House of Commons. The rift between Trew and Sloan was soon evident and recriminations were many and fierce, but from that time Trew's influence diminished to vanishing point, while Sloan led a major split with the Orange Order and was, nominally at least, the leader of a new organisation of Independent Orangemen.

This new organisation showed evidence for a time of being a much more enlightened body than the parent one from which it stemmed. Encouraged, no doubt, by more intelligent and less bigoted elements that saw an opportunity of counter-acting the evil influences of the diehard and ascendancy control, the Independents seemed to veer to a more Irish point of view and almost 'liberal' attitude to the various political and social problems of the period. Sloan was not a leader, however, and even as a parliamentary representative he did not measure up to the minimum requirements and his reign was short and not very glorious. My old friend, John McBurney, the artist and a fellow member of the Ulster Theatre, introduced me to Sloan some years later, and I could not help feeling that it was a personal tragedy for Sloan that he had ever been translated from his highly-paid trade on the Queen's Island to the floor of the House and ultimate oblivion. The short period of passing glory had unfitted him for the Island and he had not the 'know-how' to make a nest in politics.

It may seem strange why young Catholic boys should be at the 'Steps' to listen to any and all of these preachers on a Sunday afternoon. The answer is, I think, that none of us took them seriously as religious meetings and that they were the only 'live' shows that Calvinistic Belfast provided. There was always the possibility of a row or a scene and speakers like Hutton and Ballantine usually provided more humour, however unconscious it may have been, than many of the professional comedians who appeared in the local music-halls. It was about the time that Trew was reaching the crisis of his career that the Church specifically warned all Catholics that they must refrain from attending the Custom House meetings. It was not that they feared for any injury to their faith, but they wisely decided that they were not only a source of scandal but were likely to provoke civil disturbance, and so our lessons in public speaking and the theology of Belfast bigotry ended.

3

I join the furnishing trade – Contact with variety halls – The Ulster Theatre – The Liberals come into power – Home Rule on the horizon – An era of patronage

It was in January 1903 that I made what was, for me, an important and decisive change in my career. Having abandoned any idea of the engineering trade, I entered the furniture trade. I was fortunate in securing a position with one of the best-established concerns in the business where I was to spend a reasonably happy and contented twelve years. I was fortunate, too, in having as my proprietor-boss a kindly decent man with whom I worked in real harmony and friendship. Alfred Edwards was a Welshman who had spent most of his business life in Belfast, and at the time I joined the firm he was the surviving partner and sole proprietor of Maguire & Edwards, Ltd. There were two main sections of the business; the first was engaged in manufacturing for the wholesale trade and the other was devoted to the better-class retail furnishing business. The factory was mainly engaged in bedding and wire-mattress making, but cabinet and upholstering shops and chair-making were also part of it. In the shop and retail end we did good business in every grade of carpets, curtains and all the essentials for good-class furnishings. From the beginning I liked the business and was keenly interested in acquiring an intimate knowledge of every branch of the trade. Old man Edwards was a first class mentor and under his guidance I quickly assimilated all he taught me and it was but a short time until we became more like collaborators in our work than master and man. I am not going to write a thesis on furniture or the furnishing trade, nor attempt to compile a history of another 'Quinncys', but I still have the 'feeling' for beautiful things like the satin finish of good mahogany and the soft glow of a Donegal or oriental carpet.

Edwards had an additional commercial activity and it was inevitable that, due to our close association and intimate trust, I should become involved in it. He was chairman of the directors in the Belfast 'Empire'[1] and a director of the Dublin 'Empire', the two principal music halls of the period in their respective cities. Adam Findlater[2] of Dublin was the dominating

1. In fact, Edwards was never chairman. He was a very active director from 1906 to 1911 and a supplier prior to that.

2. Adam Seton Findlater (1855-1917): born Dublin, managing director of Alex Findlater & Co. Ltd., wine merchants, director of a number of other companies, chairman of Kingstown Township Commissioners 1895-6, chairman of Belfast Empire Theatre of Varieties Ltd. and Star Theatre of Varieties Ltd., Dublin, 1895-1911.

co-partner in both and I think was by far the biggest shareholder. My connection with the concerns was external and confined to my co-operation with Edwards. It was a gradual, but speedy enough growth. It commenced with him asking me to help him draft reports and letters and eventually reached the stage of constant consultation when I might well have claimed to be an unofficial director without fees.

I can remember the old man at his desk in those days. I do not know for certain, but I think he was more or less typical of the late Victorians in the care and precision that he took in his correspondence. A rough draft would be prepared and then carefully scanned and passed to ensure that no grammatical or punctuation error had crept in and that no ambiguity or misconception could be conveyed to the recipient of the letter. At times I found it irksome and would protest that such and such a letter could be dealt with by a simple direct dictation to the typist but no, Alfred would have none of that for such letters as were to bear his own signature.

The engagement of artists for the 'Empire' afforded an informative sidelight of the music-hall world. In those years the music hall was the major centre of entertainment for the masses. The cinema was just beginning to creep in, and it is interesting to recall that in the 'Empire' only one short film billed as the 'Bioscope' was shown each evening. It was thrown on the screen as the last item on the programme and afforded an equal opportunity to those who wanted to get 'one for the road' and to those others who did not want to be present when 'God save the king' was being rushed through by the orchestra.

The two 'Empires', Dublin and Belfast, were linked up in what was known as the Moss-Thornton tour which covered a circuit of cities and towns in Britain and Ireland. Artistes invariably came to Belfast from Glasgow or Liverpool, played a week with us, proceeded to Dublin for another week and then resumed their tour of the English and Scottish cities and towns. Usually I spent one night a week seeing the show and enjoyed my visit. Apart from that, it was almost essential, as the old man was always anxious to have my opinion on this or that 'turn'. We disagreed frequently, but that made no difference between us for he had that splendid quality in a boss that demanded that you should speak your mind and had no use for a 'yesman'.

In the early nineteen hundreds the music halls were at the peak of their popularity, but were still frowned on as being not quite respectable by a great many people who were by no means ultra-Puritanical or Calvinistic. There was considerable justification for their hostility for there was much on the stage and around the bars that was objectionable. Old Alfred and

I often discussed this, and it is to his credit that he set his face against anything that would be unseemly. I remember him summing it up to me briefly when he said: 'A lady doing her show at the "Empire" can come in, go to her room, go on and do her stuff, go back to her room, dress, turn the key in the door and go to her hotel or lodgings just as your typist in the office does'. Maybe it did not all work out so smoothly as that, but that was how Alfred wanted it and how the manager was directed to run the house. Similarly on the stage it was his policy to have anything objectionable cut out. I seldom go to anything in the way of variety entertainment now, but I have seen and heard within the last five or six years on the stage in Catholic Dublin and by artistes, from which one would expect better, passages of alleged humour of the deepest indigo that old man Edwards would not have tolerated in his Belfast 'Empire'.

Most of the leading stars touched Belfast for their week as they followed the course of their circuit. Harry Lauder, R. G. Knowles, Chirgwin, Tom Costelloe, Marie Loftus, Will Fyffe, Mark Sheridan, Minnie Cunningham, Cinquivalli, and a host of others all came and drew packed houses. I sometimes think that their work was harder than that of their successors of today and for one main reason above all others. Most of these entertainers came on alone. The stage was bare, and the backcloth was their only support behind them and the orchestra their sole help in front. They depended on themselves and their ability to 'put themselves across' and to do it fairly quickly. The average period allowed for each artiste was about fifteen minutes. The audiences were reasonably quick in their reactions and not slow to express their views. Old favourites were generously welcomed, but I have heard unfortunate newcomers who missed fire being advised to 'go away and work', an ironical commentary on how some members of the audience regarded life on the stage generally.

There were frequently big shows like the Fred Karno troupes, the Boisetts, the big illusionists like Goldin and the pseudo-Chinaman, Chung Ling Loo. I had occasion to get hold of the boss one Monday morning, while he was down at the 'Empire'. Rehearsals were in action and the 'Chinaman' was supervising the planning and staging of his very elaborate equipment. He was working like a Trojan, moving this and that and swearing and ordering his staff about in tough English. I was amazed to watch him on the stage that night and find that a young 'Chinese' girl was acting as his interpreter and to hear her explain that 'my father he will now walk up the ladder of naked swords'. Chung was actually a Mr Robinson of New York, but his show was one of the cleverest and most elaborate then on the circuit. He concluded his performance by an extremely smart piece of sleight-of-hand work. He stood in the centre of the stage with a plate in his hands, while his attendants came into the stalls and got four bullets marked by members of the audience. These were then loaded into four rifles and his four gunmen aimed at his heart over which he held the plate. After the guns were fired we heard the rattle of the bullets and they were right on his plate. We knew it did not happen that way, but it was expert showmanship. Years afterwards I read of poor Chung-Robinson. This time something happened for it was no illusion and one of the bullets did not go on to the plate but into his body and that was Chung Ling Loo's last show. I do not think that mystery was ever solved. Like most of his many extremely clever mysteries, his last turn left his audience guessing.

I remember on another occasion being present for an opening night of a new show by one of the Karno companies. These Karno shows were invariably 'dumb' shows and mostly acrobatic comedy, but this was different. It was the 'Miming Birds' and represented a theatre show with a stage within the stage. The whole company gave an extremely amusing performance of acting and miming, but the outstanding act was that of an intoxicated 'toff' in a side box who had seemingly drifted in to the show. It was miming at its best. I still think it was the most ludicrously funny performance that I ever saw not excluding the clown Grock. There were no names of the individual performers on the programme, but some few years later, when films became popular, I had no difficulty in recognising the clever 'drunk' of the Karno show. It was Charlie Chaplin.

Although I have given so much attention to this side of my activities with Alfred Edwards and his music hall enterprises, I must make it clear that this formed a very minor sideline in our normal work which was concerned with the furnishing trade and factory. 'Empire stuff' as we called it was something that Alfred and I squeezed in during a quiet half-hour or more frequently by doing an extra hour or so after tea.

While I had a more or less enforced interest in the variety stage, I had a very real interest in the 'legitimate' theatre. It was an interesting period in the theatre proper. In Belfast we had, week, by week, the usual London companies with musical comedies and the smash hits such as 'The merry widow', 'The waltz dream' and the like, as well annual visits of the Carl Rosa Opera Company, and the D'Oyley Carte company with Gilbert and Sullivan productions. The operas, both light and 'grand', were, to some of us, the high spots of the theatre year and it was our practice to save enough to enable us to get gallery seats for all or most of the grand operas, and the lighter shows of Gilbert and Sullivan.

A new element was gradually creeping into the Belfast theatre and this was an occasional visit of a company which would stage a short repertoire of modern plays by Shaw,[3] Stanley Haughton[4] and an occasional play by Ibsen.[5] In those days Belfast received them coldly indeed and had little appetite for plays of ideas or drama that dealt with 'subjects'. I think preference was for the matinee idol and musical comedy. I am not criticising them for that. I am merely recalling the position as I remember it.

Many of us were interested in the theatre and some of us were especially interested in the Irish theatre. The Abbey Theatre[6] in Dublin had begun to set its individual stamp on the theatre world in general and in the Irish theatre in particular. In Belfast an equally worthy effort was being made by the Ulster Literary Theatre.[7] I had the good fortune to be associated with the latter from its early days and, though my contributions to its work were slender indeed, my interest and enthusiasm for it was unbounded.

Thc Ulster Theatre, the 'Literary' was soon dropped as being too pretentious, as I remember it began its career with a couple of performances in the Clarence Place hall. Bulmer Hobson,[8] who was one of the prime movers in the venture, wrote a play, *Brian of Banba*, and this, with a play on St Patrick by Joseph Campbell,[9] constituted their first bill. Soon

3. George Bernard Shaw (1856-1950): born Dublin, playwright, Nobel Prize for Literature 1925.

4. Stanley Haughton: born Belfast, playwright.

5. Henrik Johan Ibsen (1828-1906): born Skien, Norway, poet and playwright.

6. Abbey Theatre (1904-): founded from a merger of the National Dramatic Company, owned by Frank and William Fay, and the Irish Literary Theatre Society. It was gutted by fire in 1951 and the company was housed at thc Queen's Theatre until 1966, when it moved to the present site in Lower Abbey Street, Dublin.

7. Ulster Literary Theatre, founded in 1902, aimed at providing a native peasant drama to accomplish for Belfast and Ulster what the Abbey Theatre was doing for Dublin. It never had the repertory of actors and writers upon which the Abbey could rely and disappeared in the 1930s.

8. Bulmer Hobson (1883-1969): born Belfast, founded Na Fianna Éireann 1903, member of I.R.B. 1904, and later became a member of its supreme council, founded Dungannon Clubs 1905, vice-president of Sinn Féin 1907, founded and edited *The Republic* 1906-7, helped to establish the Irish Volunteers 1913, lost the confidence of colleagues in the Republican leadership when in June 1914 he supported a demand by John Redmond for half of the seats on the controlling body of the Volunteers, after he discovered plans for the Easter Rising he informed Eoin MacNeill and helped him in his efforts to prevent it, he withdrew from public life after the 1916 Rising and later held a minor civil service post in Dublin until his retirement to Connemara in 1946.

9. Joseph Campbell (1879-1944): born Belfast, poet, spent much of his time collecting Ulster traditional songs and setting them to music, opposed the treaty and interned during the civil war, on his release he went to New York and taught at Fordham University from 1924 until 1935 when he retired to Ireland and settled at Glencree, County Wicklow.

after, David Parkhill, whose pen name was Lewis Purcell,[10] wrote *The enthusiast*, and Rutherford Mayne[11] gave us *The turn of the road*. It is worth recalling that all these efforts were, in the wider sense, serious plays and reflected the growing feeling for national cultural development. *The enthusiast* dealt with the work of the co-operative movement in Ireland and the forces that confronted the idealist in the shape of local and historical prejudices and bigotry. *The turn of the road* similarly showed the struggle of the individual to pursue a musical career despite all the hard-headed practical wisdom and opposition of his Puritanical family. Other plays followed. Purcell's *The pagan*; Rutherford Mayne's *Red turf*; Lynn Doyle's[12] *Lilac Ribbon* and George Shiels'[13] *Away from the Mass* were some of the earliest efforts of the theatre.

A collaboration of Lewis Purcell and Gerald MacNamara,[14] the latter being the pen name of Harry Morrow, gave us an historical extravaganza called *Suzanne and the sovereign*. This was a fantastic and extremely funny re-enactment of the invasion of Ireland by William of Orange and his military exploits against James II in Derry and at the Boyne. It was a very ambitious effort requiring a huge cast and elaborate costuming and it ran for a week in the Exhibition Hall. We played to packed houses, but at the end of the week our treasurer, Artie Gilmer, announced that we were just four shillings short of the cost. It was but a short time later when Rutherford Mayne completed *The drone* as it was when first produced in the Abbey Theatre, Dublin. It was originally a two-act play and was a big success from the beginning. Very soon afterwards the author added a third act and I remember the considerable controversy as to whether this was wise or not. My own view was and is that artistically it was a mistake but, from the point of view of the manager and the box office, the three act *Drone* justified itself.

10. Lewis Purcell – real name David Parkhill: born Belfast, playwright, associated with Ulster Literary Theatre, of which he was a co-founder.

11. Rutherford Mayne – real name Samuel Waddell (1878-1967): born Japan, educated Belfast, he was a distinguished Latin scholar, acted in, and wrote plays for the Ulster Literary Theatre, chief inspector in the Land Commission.

12. Lynn Doyle – real name: Leslie Alexander Montgomery (1873-1961): born Downpatrick, County Down, bank official 1889, short-story writer, playwright, associated with Ulster Literary Theatre, member of Censorship Board 1936-37.

13. George Shiels (1886-1949): born Ballymoney, County Antrim, emigrant in Canada, short-story writer, prolific playwright, associated with Ulster Literary Theatre.

14. Gerald MacNamara – real name Henry C. Morrow (1866-1938): born Belfast, associated with Ulster Literary Theatre as actor and writer 1902-34, his *Thompson in Tír na n-Óg* was constantly revived, he wrote about a dozen quirky comedies for the Ulster Literary Theatre.

Harry Morrow gave us *Thompson in Tír-na-n-Óg*, which was the most popular and successful play that the theatre produced. It was Morrow's usual broad satire and in his cleverest vein and, as in *Suzanne and the sovereign*, it had many historical and local reflections on the religious and political issues of the North. Success was now smiling on the theatre and soon Fred Warden who controlled the two principal theatres, the Opera House and the Theatre Royal, booked the company for the Opera House. They were highly successful from the beginning, and packed houses were the rule at every performance.

Ironically enough, the success of *The drone* and *Thompson*, and particularly the association of their success with Warden's Opera House was the beginning of the end for the Ulster Theatre as originally conceived and, for many years, conducted.

The departure of Davey Parkhill/Lewis Purcell, for Australia for health reasons was a serious loss to the theatre, not alone for what he contributed by his plays and his flair for production, but even more so for the basic ideas that guided his work in the theatre. I remember that shortly before he left for Australia we met and had a meal together. He told me that he feared for the future of the theatre and urged me to work closely with two or three others that he named to keep the original plans for the development of theatre in the foreground. The theatre, he emphasised, was not to be a mere group of actors, but a school for playwriting and production which was to concern itself in creating a real Ulster school in the Irish theatre movement.

It was only later that I fully grasped the force of Davey's fears. The popularity of the company attracted many whose sole interest was to be connected with it and if possible to secure parts in the shows. Warden's interest was purely commercial and, as *The drone* and *Thompson* could always be relied on to fill the house, these became almost the only productions that the company staged. It was a fairly rapid disintegration. Various elements crept more and more into the scheme of things and, with the gradual disappearance of the old members, the original purpose of the theatre was forgotten and the theatre as we know it just faded out.

While life for me had many interests and activities and its share of problems and strains, it seems, in retrospect, to have been comparatively uneventful. I was busy at my work every day and quite happy in it and building up a very real business connection. My social connections were interesting and pleasant, and included all sorts from sporting athletes to those who were interested in books, the theatre, politics and the social problems of the day.

Our life was simple by comparison with present-day standards. It was our usual practice to enjoy the week-ends by having a few long walks. Saturday afternoons and Sundays were often spent in this way. The seven or eight miles to Lisburn going out by the Upper Falls and Suffolk village was one of our favourite tramps. A group of four or five would set out and having reached Lisburn would have a simple tea in a cafe and return leisurely either by the same route or by the Lagan valley. Another day we would make for the Black Mountain and either go on to the further Divis or wheel around and return by Ligoniel. Belfast was admittedly an uninspiring city, with the big majority of its citizens living in monstrous streets of drab houses, but few cities had more pleasant surrounding country on all sides. Divis Mountain, the Cavehill, the Castlereagh hills and the Lagan valley provided welcome escapes and we availed of them as frequently as we could.

It is, I think, of economic interest to recall some of the opportunities for recreation and their cost in those days. One excursion which we favoured was a Lough cruise on the *S.S. Bernach*. Embarking at the Queen's Quay on this pleasant paddle-steamer we sailed into Bangor where we discharged passengers and took on others for the cruise. We then sailed across the Lough towards Carrickfergus, skirted the Antrim coast, passed the Gobbins cliffs and anchored in Larne harbour. Here we were free to make the most of the little that the town of Larne had to offer in the way of excitement, but we could have an excellent meal in one of 'Knockem down' MacNeill's hotels at a very reasonable rate. After a couple of hours we re-embarked and cruised over to Bangor where we had the alternative of continuing our journey back to Belfast by the steamer or of spending the rest of the evening in Bangor and returning by train up to 11 p.m. We had five hours actual cruising time on the Lough, the 'break' at Larne and Bangor and the return journey by rail and for how much? Saloon on boat and first-class railway journey cost two shillings and sixpence, while if one was really economical, a shilling and sixpence paid for the same services but with steerage on the boat and third-class rail from Bangor. I recall this merely as an example of pre-World War I values and the relative simplicity of our self-entertainment of the period.

There was, however, a mental if not intellectual 'stirring' about this period which was weaving its thread into the pattern of the comparatively placid life of myself and my associates. Maybe it always seems so as one leaves the adolescent stage and passes into that of young manhood. However that may be, those early years of the century seem in retrospect to have had many vital, if not revolutionary, effects on our generation. There were a number of writers, Irish, English, Scottish and foreign, whose books afforded us a stimulus to thought and discussion and added a generous spice to our everyday life. Perhaps we were unduly impressed by the art and literary craft of the authors, or it may have been that we took ourselves too seriously in the pursuit of the ideas that they spread.

While making all allowances for these factors, the period that gave us Chesterton, Yeats, Belloc, Shaw,[15] William Archer[16] and opened the doors to the plays of Ibsen, Maeterlinck,[17] Bjornson[18] and others was, I think, noteworthy. Equally or more important to us was the output of our own Irish writers not only in the dramatic field, but in all branches of literature. The political situation for us who shared the views of Griffith and Sinn Féin was not encouraging. There was but little political support for Sinn Féin throughout the country and the people had not yet shed their susceptibility to the spell-binding oratory of the Irish party politicians. There seemed to me something paradoxical in the situation of the time. There was much healthy growth in the 'Irish Ireland' sense of national outlook. The Gaelic League and Gaelic Athletic Association were growing and flourishing, and yet the country resisted the idea of breaking with the House of Commons and still clung to the Home Rule policy.

In 1906 the situation hardened still more. In that year the great English Liberal party had swept into power. Led by Campbell-Bannerman[19] and supported by the Irish Parliamentary party, we in Ireland were assured that Home Rule was just 'around the corner' and would be definitely passed by the British government which had made Home Rule for Ireland one of the chief planks in its political platform. Redmond had appealed to the whole Irish race to be given a free hand to secure legislative freedom and, while many were sceptical, he certainly had no political opposition. Sinn Féin and Griffith's paper carried on, but they were practically voices crying in the wilderness. The mildest condemnation was that we were all 'rainbow-chasers' and 'hair-brained dreamers', but there were not lacking those who

15. Hilaire Belloc (1870-1950), G, K. Chesterton (1874-1936), George Bernard Shaw (1856-1950), and W. B. Yeats (1865-1939) were among the outstanding men of letters of their time. Belloc and Chesterton were English and Catholic, Shaw and Yeats were Irish and in the Protestant tradition.

16. William Archer (1856-1924): born Perth, Scotland, theatre critic, translator of the works of Ibsen, playwright.

17. Maurice Maeterlinck (1862-1949): born Ghent, poet and playwright, Nobel prize for literature.

18. Björnstjerne Björnson (1832-1910): born Österdal, Norway, poet, playwright, Nobel prize for literature 1903.

19. Sir Henry Campbell-Bannerman (1836-1908): born Glasgow, Liberal M.P. for Stirling Burghs 1868-1908, prime minister 1905-8.

attributed sinister and less worthy motives to those who distrusted all British promises and pledges. The Campbell-Bannerman ministry was regarded as a team of all the talents, and from the point of view of those who thought in terms of politicians, and House of Commons politicians at that time, they were outstanding. Asquith, Lloyd George, Churchill, Simon, Reginald McKenna, Augustine Birrell[20] and company made a favourable vanguard which impressed everybody, but the talent and political ingenuity would eventually crack when faced with the intrigues of the real power in Britain, the court, the army and navy groups, and the inner circles who chose a square-jawed Irish lawyer named Edward Carson[21] to be their spokesman. That would come later and meantime the little Welsh lawyer would give Britain and Ireland its first Unemployment Insurance Act and old age pensions for those over 70; Winston Churchill would be 'Leader of the King's Navee' and Augustine Birrell would, as chief secretary for Ireland, get some understanding of the hidden Ireland, but do little or nothing about it.

Although they could hardly have been so planned, the Insurance Act and the Old Age Pension Act constituted, to my mind, a serious menace to the nationalist movement. My reason for that view is that both opened wide the doors of political preferences and recommendations. With the Liberals in power and their close association with the Irish Party it soon became evident that many of the 'plums' of office were being made available to the henchmen and supporters of the Party. It is true that for the most part it was the smaller 'fruit' that fell to the lot of the Party, and, though the jobs were many, the seekers were even more numerous. Even the miserable and unpaid offices of justice of the peace were eagerly sought and many a heart-burning was caused in the soul of the unsuccessful applicant. Professional men, lawyers, doctors and the like, got occasional preferences on the recommendation of the Irish Party leaders and now and again we would

20. Herbert Henry Asquith, Winston Spencer Churchill and David Lloyd George were British prime ministers in 1908-16; 1940-45, 1951-55; and 1916-22 respectively, Augustine Birrell was chief secretary for Ireland 1907-16, Reginald McKenna was president of the board of education 1907-8 and lord of the admiralty 1908-11, home affairs secretary 1911-15, chancellor of the exchequer 1915-16. Sir John Simon was home affairs secretary, 1915-16, foreign affairs secretary 1931-5, home affairs secretary 1935-7, chancellor of exchequer 1937-40, lord chancellor 1940-5.

21. Baron Carson of Duncairn, Edward Carson (1854-1935): born Dublin, Unionist M.P. for Dublin University 1892-1918, English solicitor general 1900-6, leader of the Irish Unionist Party 1910, led signing of the Anti-Home Rule Ulster Covenant 1912, M.P. for Duncairn (Belfast) 1918-21, resigned leadership of Unionist Party to become lord of appeal at Westminster 1921-9.

have a prominent nationalist 'be-knighted' by Edward VII or his deputy in the viceregal lodge. Parnell's doctrine of accepting no favours was forgotten and the history of Sadleir[22] and Keogh, which belonged to the bad old days of Irish politics, was being revived.

22. John Sadleir (1815-56) and William Nicholas Keogh (1817-78) were members of the Independent Irish Party founded in September 1852. Members were pledged to be independent of and in opposition to all British governments which did not (1) concede the demands of the Tenant League for Land Reform and (2) repeal the Ecclesiastical Titles Act. The party also sought the disestablishment of the Church of Ireland. The election of 1852 resulted in a Tory administration led by Lord Derby who refused to consider the League's land reform bill. The party helped to unseat the government which was succeeded by a Liberal administration under Lord Aberdeen. Sadleir and Keogh accepted office from the government, breaking their pledges and dealing the party a severe blow when their example was followed by other members. Both men eventually committed suicide.

4

The strike of 1907 – Jim Larkin – Belfast newspapers – Parliament Act of 1911 – Carson and the Ulster Volunteers – The Ulster Liberals – The Covenant – Francis Joseph Bigger in 'Ardri'

While all seemed to flow favourably for Ireland, it was on the whole superficial, and, although the 'Haves' in Belfast were enjoying a period of peaceful prosperity, there were undercurrents running. As I have already indicated, the standard of wages for the unorganised labourers and unskilled workmen was low and the conditions of employment were framed without much consideration for the wage earner. The position of the dockers, quayside workers, van and lorry drivers was extremely grim. Stevedores stood by and were engaged as and when required by the bosses. Their employment and 'stand-by' idle periods were dictated by the arrival and departure of the steamers. This might seem a natural and reasonable course of policy, but it meant long periods of 'standing-by', uncertainty as to the amount of employment if any, and poor remuneration for the heavy manual labour involved. Moreover, at least some of the employing stevedore bosses had saloons in the vicinity of the docks, and it was not unusual, to say the least of it, to pay the dockers over the pub counter. The objections to such a practice will be obvious. Loading and unloading cargoes must be thirsty work particularly if the cargo happens to be coal or grain, and to pay men after each 'shift' or spell of the day's work is not the way to ensure that he will have a pay packet to bring home to his wife and family.

The carters and lorry drivers were poorly paid. Their work was heavy and their day was long. It was of course the period of horse traffic. The main carriers had long, four-wheel floats, drawn by splendid big Clydesdale horses capable of pulling a load of upwards of two tons. The drivers started at about 8 a.m., yoked their horses and kept on the job until they returned to the stables at about 7 or 7.30 p.m. Their dinner hour was 'fitted in' to the day's assignment and was a simple arrangement. The driver brought horse and van opposite his own residence, put a nose bag with a ration on the horse's head and went in to have his own meal. The wage paid to the driver was about a pound a week. A vanman driving a lighter outfit might be paid sixteen to eighteen shillings. Porters and male messengers who had grown old in the service of some of our prosperous business houses earned as little as fourteen shillings a week. There were occasional mild rumblings, but these workers were unorganised and, if there was discontent and grumbling, it was an individual protest here and there and nothing much happened.

It was into this setting that a new power appeared in the person of Jim Larkin,[1] the most dynamic personality that ever swept over the Irish labour stage in modern history. Jim Larkin came over from Liverpool, he was one of the Liverpool Irish who had already smarted under the conditions of employment on the Mersey docksides. It was in 1907 he came to Belfast and in a very short time by his personality and his eloquence he had fired the minds and imagination of his followers. Having quickly established himself as their spokesman and leader he organised the under-privileged of the Belfast workers into a union and demanded new conditions and terms. The result was inevitable as things were in those days. The Belfast employers were adamant and were not used to the dictation of a mob orator and demagogue. That was how they viewed and expressed it, but Larkin was equally adamant and called the men out on strike. It was a bitter fight while it lasted and had one unique development.

There was a period of rioting following various minor and major clashes when the employers and their staffs, helped out by such 'blacklegs' as could be recruited, vainly tried to carry on their work. The rioting assumed serious proportions. The police were called on to protect the property and the horses and vans, and eventually the military had to take over. The unique feature of the 1907 riots was that for the first time in modern Belfast history the contending parties were not orange and green, nor Catholics against Protestants, but the combined forces of Catholics, Protestants and non-conformists, all united together as labour, against the hard-boiled and unyielding Belfast employers. It was an incredible position to witness in our city and some of us wondered what the outcome would be.

The big industrialists, the shipping magnates, the linen lords and the big bosses generally were definitely alarmed at this hitherto unknown menace, a union of workers, orange and green, which was simply concentrating on fighting for an increase in wages and more tolerable conditions in their working lives and forgetting all about William of Orange, the battle of the Boyne and the supposed special interest that the pope took in their city. It was a situation that could not be endured. Something must be done about it! It was.

1. James Larkin (1876-1947): born Liverpool, organiser of National Union of Dock Labourers 1907, leader of 1907 strike in Belfast, founder of Irish Transport and General Workers Union 1908, leader of workers in 1913 strike and lock-out in Dublin, 'visit' to and active trade unionist in U.S.A. 1914-23, with his brother, Peter, he formed Workers Union of Ireland 1924, stormy petrel of trade union and labour politics 1923-47, Independent Labour T.D. 1926-32, 1937-8, Labour T.D. 1943-4.

The press got busy. The rumour mongers got busy. Soon Protestant workers learned that the strike was a Fenian plot; that Larkin was a papist and that Catholic agitators like Larkin must be chased from amongst them. The propaganda and the inside work of the lodges had their effect and in a short time the strike 'petered out' and the men drifted back to their jobs.

The strike failed or seemed to have failed, but actually it did not. Larkin did leave his workers' unions behind him and he did make the Belfast employer realise that his workers were something more than mere cogs in his business machine. Conditions changed for the better, slowly at first but, as the unions became organised, the old exploitations gave way to a more tolerable system for the workers. Larkin was a highly controversial figure in Irish Labour and indeed in Irish life generally. Many of his colleagues would protest that, while as an orator who could inspire the masses he had no equal, he was extremely difficult if not altogether impossible to work with as a member of a team.

This, I think, is probably a reasonable enough estimate. I met him many years later and will have occasion to refer to him further, but let me say now that, if he was impatient of routine and discipline and tended to dominate in leadership, surely these were the defects of his great qualities. To me he had the burning urge to improve the lot of the under-privileged and faced opposition of every type to get them to assert their manhood and their rights. He hammered home his arguments for sobriety and self-respect and he killed the iniquitous practice of the docker being paid his daily wage at the public-house bar. Later we may be able to review his activities in Dublin and elsewhere, but let it not be argued that Larkin failed in either Dublin or Belfast. The strikes may have 'petered out' but they were not failures. From 1907 onwards conditions for the unskilled worker and the labourer improved beyond recognition, and many of these who deserted him and helped to chase him from the Orange capital as an undesirable papist soon after benefited materially from his efforts. Incidentally, it was ironical that Jim Larkin's career in Belfast was practically ended by the cry that he was a papist, while later in 1913 he was denounced in Dublin for the very opposite reason.

Some time afterwards there was a small but noticeable spirit creeping into what I might call the 'upper ten' of the trades unions. I mean the highly organised unions of the skilled trades. Branches of the Independent Labour Party[2] were emerging, not in any great numbers nor in any great

2. Independent Labour Party: This was founded by Keir Hardie at Bradford, Yorkshire, in 1893. It prompted the establishment in 1900 of the British Labour Party which was initially known as the Labour Representation Committee, a federation of socialist societies, trade unions, trade councils and local labour electoral bodies, to promote independent labour representation in the House of Commons and in local government

strength, but nevertheless sufficient to beget the hope that the more thoughtful of the rank and file of the unions were beginning to think for themselves and might eventually escape from the leading strings of the Orange lodges. Simultaneously the North of Ireland liberals were becoming more closely welded together and were active and articulate in favour of Home Rule and the policies of their party, which was the government in power in Britain. These Belfast and Ulster liberals were only a small minority of the non-Catholic population, but they included many leading industrialists like Lord Pirrie and some of his associates in Harland and Wolff's great shipbuilding concern, quite a few of the linen magnates, and a number of the leading professional and business men of the city. The Presbyterian Church, which had given Antrim and Down many heroic figures in the struggle for independence, was, in the main, anti-Home Rule and Unionist but not entirely so. Ireland had still some fearless defenders of her rights and liberties amongst the men of the Manse. The Reverend Mr Armour[3] of Ballymoney and the Reverend Doctor Irwin[4] of Killead were only two of the more outspoken of the Presbyterian ministers who would in due course pay dearly for their honesty and courage. The Liberals at this time ran a weekly journal, the *Ulster Guardian*, which had a wide circulation among the farmers of Ulster and the liberal minority in Belfast. It was a well-edited and creditable newspaper, but its influence was slight in trying to counteract the consistent barrage of Unionism served up by the three principal dailies: the *Evening Telegraph*, the *Belfast News-Letter* and the *Northern Whig*.

The only Catholic newspaper was the *Irish News* which appeared daily and was the organ representing not only the Catholic viewpoint but, more emphatically, the views of Joseph Devlin and the Irish Parliamentary Party. It was, on the whole, a poor production lacking any distinctive quality in its literary or journalistic efforts.

The *Evening Telegraph* was almost universally bought by all sections of the community, Protestant, Catholic, and non-conformist alike. In the

3. Rev. James Brown Armour (1841-1928): born Lisboy, Ballymoney, County Antrim, Presbyterian minister in Ballymoney 1869-1928, founder of Intermediate school, Ballymoney, and lecturer in Magee College, Derry, he campaigned for Tenant Right, Home Rule and a Catholic university, condemned the Ulster Unionism which developed in 1886 as a device to maintain the Ascendancy in its privileges, he opposed the Ulster Unionist Party and the establishment of Northern Ireland.

4. Rev. James Alexander Hamilton Irwin (1876-1954): born Feeny, County Derry, served in the Presbyterian church at Killead, County Antrim, 1903-26, Edinburgh 1926-28, Leith 1928-35, Lucan, County Dublin, 1935-54, member of Commission on Vocational Organisation 1939-43, member of national executive of Fianna Fáil 1945-54.

majority of the Belfast homes, the *Evening Telegraph* was as essential as the milk for their evening tea, and in a great many it was the only paper taken in. There were several reasons for this. It was an evening paper and the average worker had no time nor opportunity to read a morning one. Apart from its politics and its consistently anti-Catholic and imperialist outlook, it was a good newspaper. The *Telegraph* was a prosperous concern and spared no expense in getting the news. It might distort it or colour it to its own shade, but it got it. It was, however, mainly to the skilful organisation of its sporting and racing news that it owed its enormous circulation and success. At the time of which I write it had no less than five city editions. Two midday editions were concerned with racing. An afternoon edition with early racing results appeared at 5 p.m. One at 7 p.m. had the final results and an edition issued between 8 p.m. and 9 p.m. gave the following day's racing programme. The editorials, commentaries and articles dealing with politics and the affairs of the day were invariably in the best tradition of British imperialism and hostility to any movement to advance the cause of Ireland or the Catholic community in the North.

Backed by the two morning dailies, it was the spearhead of the Carsonite and Ulster Volunteer Force.[5] It was the political bible and gospel of the big majority of the non-Catholic workers of Belfast as well as being the *Ruff's Guide* to the sporting punter. In many cases it was the only bible or gospel which he read and, if his primary and main interest was the results from Newmarket or Kempton Park, he could assimilate later the 'glorious pious and immortal' dope for which he had an insatiable appetite.

I do not know how the 'Tally', as it was familiarly called, has evolved since those days, but I think it is entitled to the major credit, or blame, for creating the unique bigotry and antagonism that have left their mark on the Northern capital.

There was, superficially, a comparatively calm period of life in Belfast around 1910. Trade was good and there was little or no unemployment. The Liberals were still in power and Home Rule was, according to the Irish Party spokesmen, well on the way to the statute book. Two general elections had been fought and won by the Liberals, aided by the staunch support of the Irish Party. In 1911 the House of Lords had accepted the Parliament Act rather than face the threat of having a sufficient number of peers created to pass the legislative measures passed and sent on to them

5. Ulster Volunteer Force: was founded in January 1913 by the Ulster Unionist Council from local corps in Ulster, its purpose was to resist Home Rule, due to become effective in 1914.

by the House of Commons. This seemed to remove the ultimate obstacle to the passing of the Home Rule Act for Ireland.

The Parliament Act provided that:

> If any Public Bill was passed in three successive sessions and was sent to the House of Lords at least one month before the end of the session and was rejected by the House of Lords in each of these sessions, it should, on its rejection for the third time, become an Act of Parliament on receiving the royal assent.

As was to be expected there was much jubilation in both Liberal and Irish Party circles. The power of the Lords had been crippled and the stone wall obstruction that had defeated Gladstone had been breached and the way was now clear for giving the Irish people 'statutory freedom'.

Despite the fuss and enthusiasm for the progress that seemed to have been made, little or none of it was felt by those of us who were disciples of Arthur Griffith and Sinn Féin. However we were, at the time, a negligible quantity and particularly so in Belfast and the North generally. Redmond had asked for a free hand and he had got it, and now it did seem as if a Home Rule Bill would at least become an Act and that a parliament of our own would be functioning in the near future or as the parliamentarians expressed it 'at no far distant date'.

Some of us were not so sure. We did not quite accept the order to 'trust Asquith', or 'trust Lloyd George' and in any event we knew that there was little hope of any Home Rule Act giving the Irish people any measure of real independence as a nation. A leading article with a banner headline proclaiming 'England. Damn your concessions. We want our Freedom', which appeared in the separatist *Irish Freedom* really expressed our sentiments.

The passing of the Parliament Act of 1911 may have seemed to clear the way for Home Rule and an Irish parliament, but instead it created a revolutionary spirit not only amongst the Ulster Unionists but amongst all the privileged elements of British Conservatives. It was these latter that ultimately counted. They provided all the essentials for effective opposition. No one can dispute the sincerity and fanaticism of the Ulster Unionist or Orangeman however misguided or stupid they may appear to a national thinker, but it was not the Belfast and Ulster fifer or drummer that really made the trouble. No: it was the Londonderrys,[6] the

6. 6th Marquess of Londonderry: Charles Steward Vane-Tempest Stewart (1852-1915): born London, M.P. for County Down 1878-84, opposed Home Rule, helped to organise the Solemn League and Covenant against it and the Larne gun-running.

Henry Wilsons,[7] the F. E. Smiths[8] and the inner court circles of the aristocracy that gave Edward Carson the real power to become the dictator of Ulster.

Henry Herbert Asquith may have believed in democracy, but he wilted before the powers opposed to him, and the Welsh wizard would play his three-card tricks on Asquith, his friends and colleagues and eventually on Ireland itself.

The history of the period has been written and it is outside my province to cover it anew. There were, however, several illuminating factors which registered at the time and which merit repetition in the records. Early in the Ulster campaign we had one of the leaders, Captain Craig, M.P., who would later become Lord Craigavon[9] and prime minister of the six-county parliament, proclaiming:

> There is a spirit spreading abroad, which I can testify to from my personal knowledge, that Germany and the German emperor would be preferred to John Redmond, Patrick Ford[10] and the Molly Maguires.[11]

Loyalty to the king and empire would seem to have been merely bargaining counters to the future premier.

7. General Sir Henry Wilson (1864-1922): born Currygrane, County Longford, served in Boer war, supported Curragh-based, British officers who refused to protect military storage centres in Ulster 1914, M.P. for County Down 1921, adviser to Sir James Craig, implacable foe of Sinn Féin, assassinated by the I.R.A.

8. 1st Earl of Birkenhead: Frederick Edwin Smith (1872-1930): born Birkenhead, A.D.C. to Edward Carson in Ulster Volunteer Force, 1913, solicitor-general 1915, attorney general, led the prosecution at trial of Sir Roger Casement, 1916, lord chancellor 1919-22, secretary for India 1924-28, member of British team at treaty negotiations 1921.

9. 1st Viscount Craigavon: Captain James Craig (1871-1940): born Belfast, served in Boer war and in World War I, prominent member of Ulster Unionist Council, Orange Order and Ulster Volunteer Force, M.P. for East County Down 1906-18, Mid-Down 1918-21, leader of Unionist Party and prime minister of Northern Ireland 1921-40.

10. Patrick Ford (1837-1913): born Galway, arrived in Boston 1841, editor and publisher of *The Boston Sunday Times* 1855-60, editor *The Charleston Gazette* 1864-66, founder, editor and publisher, *Irish World* 1870-1913, supported the Fenians, Land League and John Redmond, accepted Home Rule bill of 1912 as the answer to Ireland's demand for self-government.

11. Molly Maguires: This was an anti-landlord, secret, agrarian society which flourished in Ireland between 1835 and 1855. It spread to the U.S.A. where, as an off-shoot of the Ancient Order of Hibernians, it was active in the Pennsylvania coalfields. Members dressed as women when they engaged in violence, arson and sabotage against those whom they considered their oppressors. In 1875 they organised a strike in the coalfields of Pennsylvania which was broken through the efforts of a Pinkertons' agent. The society was disbanded in the U.S.A. in 1877.

Another of the leaders, Mr Thompson,[12] M.P., who was chairman of the Belfast Harbour Board, was reported to have said on 8 April 1912:

> It is passing strange that, as I learned a few months ago, Germany has been looking after Ulster developments. She had the drawings all complete of every dock we have in the harbour, including the new large dock opened for the *Olympic* and *Titanic*. She has also drawings of the approaches to these docks and, still more, she has an officer named to carry out the necessary campaign.

This could only mean that an officer of the German high command was ready to lead the revolt against King George and his British ministers, and that the plans for the 'necessary campaign' which he was to lead were in an advanced stage of preparation. The 'ghost of Roger Casement'[13] must smile. What the shadow of F. E. Smith must do does not interest me! In view of the fact that the situation between Britain and Germany was at the time very much strained and that World War I was to begin two years later, an ordinary rational person must have been bewildered in trying to assess the so-called loyalty of Ulster.

From the time that the Parliament Act of 1911 became law, the organisation of opposition to Home Rule was intensified. Ulster loyalty became loyalty to Ulster, Unionism, and the Orange Order, and threats to 'kick the crown into the Boyne' became a common feature of the Unionist meetings. Edward Carson 'adopted' Ulster, or so it seemed from the press reports, but it was more reasonable to assume that the inner circles of the Conservative party, urged on by the die-hard ascendancy landlords and anti-Irish forces, adopted Carson and booked him as producer, stage manager and principal actor in the drama that was to be staged. Carson, a Dublin man and a graduate of Trinity College, Dublin, became the idol and hero of the hard-headed Belfast merchant, shopkeeper, tradesman and farm labourer, to say nothing of the landlords and ship-owners. Despite the support and adulation that all these accorded him, it is reasonable to doubt if he would have accepted his 'brief' if it had not been endorsed by

12. Robert Thompson (1838-1918): born Belfast, Unionist M.P. for North Belfast 1910-18, proprietor of Lindsay Thompson & Co., Linen Mills, Belfast.

13. Sir Roger Casement (1864-1916): born Sandycove, County Dublin, entered British foreign service 1892, acquired international reputation for reports on atrocities in Belgian Congo and South America, member of provisional committee of Irish Volunteers 1913, organised shipment of arms from Germany to Irish Volunteers, attempted to raise an Irish brigade of Irish prisoners-of-war in Germany to fight alongside the Irish Volunteers 1914-16, captured at Banna Strand on 20 April and executed in London on 3 August 1916.

practically every member of the landed aristocracy and plutocracy of England itself. Carson was a good lawyer and a skilled tactician, and he handled his 'brief' with cunning, but he knew where his power lay. It lay in the hands of those who dominated the army and navy, in the big houses of Britain and the councils of the Conservative Party. To preach rebellion and sedition under these conditions was a perfectly safe course for Carson, as it was for 'Galloper Smith', the mutinous Gough,[14] the Henry Wilsons and their like. Their 'heroic' adventures, their gun-running and their armed parades were assured of the necessary protection before they were launched.

One day stands out uniquely in my memory of this period. This was 'Covenant Day', the day when the disciples of Carson signed their solemn covenant pledging their resistance 'to the death' to any attempt to make them subject to an Irish government. To me it was a day of depressing atmosphere. That is the only way I can describe it. The city seemed quiet as if we were attending a wake or a funeral. The city hall where the Belfast 'rebels' lined up to sign their names was the house of mourning where the corpse was being 'waked' and the corpse was a suicide. That may seem an exaggeration, but I walked around Donegal Square entirely alone on that evening of the twenty-eight of September 1912 and that was precisely how I felt. The Belfast of 1798, of William Orr, of Jimmy Hope, of Henry Joy McCracken, of Neilson, Steel Dickson and Henry Munro and all the other patriots was gone. There was no recollection of patriotic Presbyterian ministers and laymen who believed in freedom and who went to their deaths in their efforts to achieve it. Instead we had this unending stream of misled men who proclaimed to the world that they were unfit to govern themselves in their own country and preferred to have their lives ruled and directed by an alien brood. The sturdy farmers who had been the mainstay of the Tenant-Right movement as well as the insurgents of 1782 and 1798 were repudiated and disowned by their descendants. The latter, with the tradesmen and the artisans of the city, were following the lead of their titled landlords and a clever politician-lawyer from Dublin. These and similar thoughts passed through my mind on that day.

Sometime in 1911 a small group of us decided to start an organisation for the spread of Sinn Féin and Irish Republican ideas. We could only muster a small following, but we decided to persevere and we held weekly

14. General Sir Hubert De La Poer Gough (1870-1963): born London, served in India and South Africa and in World War I, when the war office ordered General Sir Arthur Paget, O.C. Ireland, to prepare to protect arms depots in Ulster Gough led the mutiny of the officers in the Curragh in March 1914 and travelled to London, where, after a meeting with General Sir Henry Wilson, he succeeded in having the original order revoked.

meetings devoted to lectures, debates, and the reading of papers on various aspects of Irish affairs. This was the first of the 'Freedom clubs', and it was followed up by the formation of similar clubs throughout the country. At times our efforts seemed depressingly futile, for the overwhelming majority of the Nationalists of Belfast were, at least nominally, followers of the Irish Parliamentary Party and, in a particular way, devoted supporters of Mr Devlin, the local Parliamentary leader. Despite our limited and slow progress, we felt that it was essential that some voice, however weak it might be, must be raised to protest against the slavish loyalty to British liberalism and to assert the national right to complete independence.

Attached to the Freedom club were the young boys of the Fianna[15] and it was with them we did our most effective work. Many of these boys were to prove their worth in the later struggle for independence.[16]

It would be entirely misleading to convey the impression that those of us who were connected with Sinn Féin at the time were living as a

15. Na Fianna Éireann: Republican youth movement founded in Dublin in August 1909 by Countess Markievicz and Bulmer Hobson, modelled on an earlier movement of the same name founded by Hobson in Belfast in 1902. The organisation continues to be active in the pursuit of its object, namely, to re-establish the independence of Ireland.

16. *The Irish News* of 26 June 1913 included an account of another initiative taken at this time by Connolly and the Freedom Club to which he belonged. It reported that: 'For the first time within the memory of the present generation, a pilgrimage to McArt's Fort, Cavehill, was held last Sunday in commemoration of the birth of Theobold Wolfe Tone.

At 11.30 a.m. six sluaighte of Na Fianna Éireann (Neilsons, McCrackens, Betsy Grays, O'Neills, Orrs, Tones) left Willowbank (Falls Road) and marched to Cavehill via Antrim Road. The bright uniforms of the boys attracted much attention on the march. More interest still was centred on the sluagh of caílíní, upwards of 30-strong, marching at a swinging pace, with all the innate grace of young Irish womanhood.

On McArt's Fort, sanctified for all time by the oath-bond of Tone and his companions, the Fianna were joined by some members of Cumann na Saoirse (Freedom Club) and others who went to pay tribute to the memory of the great dead. Shortly after one o'clock, Seosamh Ó Conghaile (Joseph Connolly) delivered an eloquent and impressive commemorative address on Wolfe Tone and the causes for which he made the supreme sacrifice.

Dealing with the salient features of the great patriot's career in feeling tones, he dwelt on the noble character, lofty aims and high endeavour of the founder of the United Irishmen. 'Twas a meet oration and a good thought to hold the commemoration on McArt's Fort a hundred and fifty years after Tone's birth. And it was a grand, inspiring spectacle to see so many young and hopeful people gathered round the lecturer as he retold the old, old tale of effort and battle for Ireland's sake.

After the oration, there was a selection of songs and recitations appropriate to the occasion. At the end, Nora Ní Chonghaile sang "The Memory of the Dead", the whole body saluting at the last stanza. The commemoration wound up with Three Shouts On A Hill for Tone, for Ireland and for the cause for which Tone died.

In the evening, the Fianna held a short but thoroughly enjoyable aeridheacht, enjoyed alike by those who took part and a large crowd of onlookers.'

depressed and despised minority beating our heads and hands against a 'wailing wall' of Belfast obduracy. We were young and had all the buoyancy and resilience of youth. We had an instinctive faith that time would prove us right, and that the tricks and deceits of the politicians would ultimately be exposed. We had our work to do and our livings to earn, but we had also the appetite for fun and enjoyment that is the most priceless asset of the young. We went to theatres and dances and céilidhes. We had our long tramps over the hills and we had as happy and congenial associations as anyone could wish for.

During those years, some of us had an open door and hearty welcome to the hospitable home of Francis Joseph Bigger[17] at 'Ardri' on the Antrim Road. Frank Bigger was a bachelor and 'Ardri' was a perfect bachelor's home. It was delightfully situated under the shadow of Cavehill and overlooking Belfast Lough and the County Down coast on the opposite shore. It was a fine house, surrounded by a garden that was a pleasant blend of order and natural wildness. Here Frank prided himself on the production of most of the fruit and vegetable supplies that were necessary for his hospitable board, and here too he was happy to gather around him on an occasional Saturday afternoon a host of kindred spirits to meet a notable or promising Irish poet, patriot, writer or musician. There would be tea and nourishment, strawberries and cream or whatever else might be in season. Here I remember meeting many birds of passage like Shane Leslie[18] who gave us readings from his latest book; Erskine Childers,[19] quiet and retiring; Lord Ashbourne[20] who was less so, and many others. Mrs Alice Stopford Green[21] and Roger Casement was there for long periods as Frank's guests.

It was customary for the 'intimates' to gather inside the house after the garden party was over and the passing guests had dispersed, and in the big library and on the landing adjoining it have a real céilidhe until midnight

17. Francis Joseph Bigger (1863-1926): born Belfast, solicitor 1888, member of Royal Irish Academy, fellow of Royal Society of Antiquaries of Ireland, editor of *Ulster Journal of Archaeology* 1894-1914, an enthusiast for all aspects of Irish culture, from his own resources he restored ruined castles and churches and re-erected ancient grave-stones and crosses.

18. Sir Shane Leslie (1885-1971): born Glaslough, County Monaghan, poet, prolific author, convert to Catholicism.

19. Captain Robert Erskine Childers (1870-1922): born England, reared Glendalough, County Wicklow, served in Boer war and World War I, a principal in Howth gun-running 1914, member of secretariat of Irish Convention 1917-18, T.D. for Kildare-Wicklow 1919-22, Sinn Féin director of publicity 1919-21, secretary to the Sinn Féin representatives who negotiated the treaty 1921, prominent anti-treatyite 1921-22.

20. 2nd Baron Ashbourne: William Gibson (1868-1942): born Dublin, scholar, member of Gaelic League, of which he became president.

21. Mrs Alice Stopford Greene (1847-1929): born Kells, County Meath, historian, supporter of Home Rule, raised funds to buy arms for Irish Volunteers 1914, senator 1922-29.

or later. The library was what a friend of mine aptly described as a 'noble room'. It ran the full length of one side of the first floor. It was lined from floor to ceiling with books with occasional 'breaks' for pictures, sketches, and memorials and mementoes of historical interest. There was a big wide fireplace and hearth and on this blazed the heaped up fire of turf and logs. With the rugs rolled back and the polished floor cleared there was ample space for forty or fifty people to dance comfortably and still have plenty of room for the less active to sit around and talk and argue and joke to their hearts' content. We enjoyed many big evenings and nights in 'Ardri', and almost equally the innumerable quiet evenings with the wonderful library at our command or the quiet talks with some of those whose shadows must still hover around the corners of that grand room.

'Ardri' was the high spot of our meeting places, made so not only because of its hospitality and social life, but more particularly by the interesting contacts and associations it gave us. I will have more to say about these later and in their proper sequence.

It was of course only one of our happy haunts. We were in our early twenties, the period when one's interests and energy are almost inexhaustible and our hours of leisure were fully occupied. Looking back on it all at half a century's distance, the evenings would seem to have been spent on much calling and visiting, reading voraciously, occasional walks and many visits to theatres, lectures and discussions. There was nothing much of outstanding notice in all this, and it was doubtless very different from the ordinary humdrum routine of thousands of others like me who concentrated solidly on their day's work from 9 a.m. to 6 p.m., and afterwards sought their relaxation or the pursuit of their interests until bedtime.

I was happy and content in my business life. After I completed my apprenticeship I discussed terms with Old Man Edwards. He put up a proposal which I rejected, and I in turn outlined my terms. These created a difficulty for the old man, for my proposal meant that my salary would be in excess of that of his eldest son who was a director. I had realised this, but I had also the comparative figures of turnover, and when he examined and checked these he capitulated, with the result that I remained with him for a period of seven more years and only severed the connection in 1915 to set up my own concern in that year. We parted amicably. It was quite a wrench for me and I venture to think it was no less for him. We had worked together for over twelve years and, save for two minor but critical disagreements, it was a period of harmonious and pleasant association. He knew I was an uncompromising Catholic, that my views were national and anti-British, but Edwards respected them, was singularly devoid of bigotry or prejudice, and treated them as entirely outside the scope of our business and friendly relationship.

It would again be tempting to mention some of the characters one encountered during that period, but it has its dangers. What provided interest and humour to me would not necessarily be of equal or indeed of any interest to others. A few exceptions may be made and the outstanding one was our bookkeeper Bob Hillock. Bob was reared in Belfast, but was of Armagh stock. An Episcopalian, he was a man of outstanding character and integrity and gifted with the most delightful flow of spontaneous wit and good humour that I have ever known. He joined the firm a few days after me, and we spent all the years together in the concern. Later I was fortunate enough to have him in the same capacity in my own concern, and during the years of trouble Bob was always willing to help out and keep the financial and accountancy end in order for several of my colleagues who had been locked up for their political and national activities.

We had the inevitable pan-handlers who paid us their weekly visits, amongst them was Harry Pickles who had in his time been chief clown in Ginnett's circus and who invariably swept in with a whoop as if he were entering the ring. 'Poor old Pickles!, the old firm again!, a tanner for poor old Pickles, I'm leaving Europe, I'm going to Glasgow on to-night's cattle boat' were a few of his favourite sallies. Then we had the silent man who did not beg but looked at you with his big sombre brown eyes and when you handed him a copper or two merely raised his hand a few inches in what was almost an ecclesiastical salute and passed on. He had a mass of brown curly hair and a brown beard. He was prematurely stooped, very dirty and unkempt. He invariably slept out in one of our delivery vans which was tilted up at the entry at the back of the factory. As Hillock said: 'He pulled the sheets of corrugated iron around him and slept peacefully there'. His was a queer history. His father had been a successful doctor and his brother had succeeded to the practice, but the family could do nothing with him. Several times he had been brought home, washed and cleaned and rehabilitated, but to no purpose. He just would not wash or change his clothes and on being pressed or urged to do so walked out and resumed his circuit. I often wanted to talk to him and hear his story, but he had a quiet gentle aloofness that made me feel it would be an impertinence.

At that time there was an old glazier who wandered about the streets with a big frame of window pane glass harnessed on his back. He was an occasional visitor. He would saunter in and tell you that there was a pane of glass cracked or broken in some of the back premises. As Hillock said: 'He could see a pain in the back of your head'.

One day he arrived as usual. There was a cracked window in the back office and he was commissioned to replace it. It was a large window much bigger than any of his stock sheets and he asked Hillock to advance enough to purchase the glass. This was done and he proceeded with the job. In the course of the work of removing the old pane he got a tiny chip which lodged just at the corner of the eyelid. I was nearby and immediately took my handkerchief and was lucky to get it removed without harm. Now our glazier was anything but clean, in fact he was a very dirty old man. His protestations of gratitude were both absurd and embarrassing the chief cry being that I would do this 'for a dirty old Jew'! I shut him up about that by saying I would do it for any old dog that I knew was in pain. When he had finished the job and collected his few shillings I had a chat with him and asked him why he continued this poor unprofitable glazing when he could, like so many of his co-religionists, get into trade and selling and make money as they did. I suggested that Sir Otto Jaffe[22] or some of his wealthy co-religionists would finance him until he got 'on his feet'. He smiled at that in a sad tired sort of way and shook his head. 'Sir Otto Jaffe offered to start me in business but I refused', he told me. 'I do not want to be rich. I read the Talmud and I think I save my soul if I am poor and work'. He told me other things before we shook hands and parted. I always felt like raising my hat as I passed him with his frame of glass harnessed on his back and he making his rounds.

'Johnny look up at the moon' was a picturesque figure who swept through the streets as if he was competing in a marathon race. He had a very bad squint poor fellow and with his head thrown back he seemed to be scanning the clouds. He was very tall and dressed in 'shorty long' grey pants and old frock coat and, as he literally swept up to you, barked out his plea which was invariably: 'You wouldn't have a happenny yourself, Sir?' You had to be quick with your responsive help or Johnny would have been off on his marathon. Watching and enjoying the famous old-time music hall star the American R. G. Knowles, I was almost convinced that he had copied his effective stage costumes from our old friend 'Johnny look up at the moon'.

Up the Falls we had our own special characters like 'Taghragh' who was a harmless poor soul but, as he was constantly waving a big stick and talking loudly to himself, was a terror to the youngsters. 'Jimmy Scallion' was a particular intimate of ours, as from the earliest days that I can remember

22. Sir Otto Jaffe (1846-1916): born Belfast, chairman of Jaffe Bros. Ltd. and of Jaffe Spinning Co. Ltd., lord mayor 1899-1901, high sheriff 1901, lord mayor 1904-05, alderman and justice of the peace 1910-1912.

until his last illness and death, dinner and supper were always provided for Jimmy in our home. He was a saintly old man with a mania for collecting medals and religious objects. He had a fine voice which could be heard in St Peter's church at evening devotions, but his interpretation of the Latin in the 'O Salutaris' and 'Tantum ergo' was fantastic.

There was 'Larry Cory' who swore that he would never work until Ireland got Home Rule and kept his oath. Cory somehow managed a few drinks and on many occasions was well under the weather. On one such occasion he ran full tilt into the famous Father Pat Convery[23] who was an ardent temperance man. Father Pat gave him the 'once over' as he passed and said in his abruptest manner: 'Drunk again, Cory'. 'So am I, Father' was the immediate comeback, as Cory stumbled on.

I wonder if notable characters of these types have disappeared in our cities and towns or is it that the present generation has neither the time nor the tolerance for them. Maybe the welfare state has provided for them, or that the art of seeking help has become more subtle in its technique. Maybe it is all to the good, but somehow they seemed to add a spice of colour and character to everyday life.

From about 1911 and 1912 and with the development of the Carsonite volunteer movement the 'atmosphere' in Belfast perceptibly changed. While there was little or no evidence in ordinary business circles of open hostility, there was a sense of strain and tension and a more careful and discreet attention to the expression of views and opinions. In the big industrial concerns, in the shipyards and foundries and at the Saturday evening football matches there were occasional incidents, but on the whole there was comparatively little disturbance. It was generally believed that this was due, in the main, to the attitude of Lord Pirrie. The Queen's Island, which he controlled, had often been the storm centre and starting place of most of the Belfast rioting. The attacks on Catholic workmen and the 'chasing' of these from the yards were the usual preliminaries to the troubles. It was understood that Pirrie had issued a warning that, if any such outbreaks occurred, Harland and Wolff would close their Belfast yards and transfer all their activities to their other branches. As they had extensive establishments on the Clyde and at Southampton and elsewhere, the threat was not an empty one. There was therefore peace on the 'Island' and when the 'Island' was at peace Belfast was generally at peace.

The Carsonite volunteers grew rapidly in numbers and soon not only the city, but every town, village and hamlet in Ulster was drilling, parading

23. Fr Patrick Convery (1850-1931): administrator, St. Peter's, Belfast 1881-95, parish priest, Cushendall, 1896-1905, parish priest, St. Paul's, Belfast 1905-31.

and getting ready to meet and exterminate the British army or any other army that would attempt to force them into an Irish parliament. It has all been recorded in great detail and I leave it at that.

There was one group of our Northern people who suffered very severely for their convictions at this time and who merit more sympathy than they ever received. I refer to those liberals who, despite all pressure and opposition against them, held firmly to their principles and refused to be cajoled or bullied into the Carsonite camp. Many liberals took the line of least resistance and conformed for the simple reason that their businesses and their livelihood depended on their doing so. Of those who did not and who continued to profess their faith openly, some were reasonably independent and could afford to do so, but there were many who paid the penalties of commercial and social ostracism. They were condemned as 'rotten Protestants' and 'traitors' and earned a special brand of contempt and hatred as such. Your Belfast Unionist and anti-Home Ruler would express it vigorously: 'Damn it all, you expect the papishes to be agin' us and to be all Home Rulers: that's only natural and it would be quare if they weren't, but these fellas ought to know better than to be putting us under the pope'. In those days your Belfast Orangeman seemed to believe that the Holy Father devoted the major portion of his day to watching what went on in Belfast. These honest liberals, as I say, suffered and they represented many sections of the community: clergymen, lawyers and teachers as well as businessmen and tradesmen. Many weathered the storm, but there were many who were forced to seek a more tolerant field for their activities abroad. Once Carsonism had reached its peak, the Liberal party and avowed liberalism in the old political sense practically ceased to exist.

5

The Irish Volunteers – The Irish Party splits the Volunteers – The World War – I commence my own business – Marriage – War prosperity in Belfast – Mr Devlin and Belfast 'Nationalism'

It is a matter of history that following the formation of the Ulster Volunteers, an all Ireland organisation known as the Irish Volunteers[1] was formed. Its avowed object was to ensure that such freedom as would be legislatively enacted and granted to Ireland would not be thwarted by organised and armed opposition. All that is, as I say, a matter of history, and in this part of the record I wish to confine myself to my experiences in Belfast and the North and to such repercussions as we felt there.

It was obvious that the Irish Parliamentary Party did not look with favour on the Irish Volunteer movement. They still proclaimed the doctrine of 'Trust Asquith' and believed that it was the duty of the British government to see that its laws were carried out, if necessary by the armed forces of the crown. Moreover, it was quite obvious that the driving force behind the Irish Volunteers was not made up of the Party supporters, but on the contrary did contain most of the best and most advanced members of the Sinn Féin and Republican movements.

In Belfast our small group watched the position with great interest and some anxiety. I think it would be fair to say that, generally speaking, the attitude of the Dublin headquarters was that it would be unwise to launch the movement in the North-East corner. The fear of doing so was no doubt due to the risk of precipitating local rows and rioting, and the fact that the big majority of the Catholics and Nationalists were staunch supporters of the Irish Party and of the local leader, Mr Devlin. Some of us did not agree with this 'go safe' policy, and at a meeting of the Freedom Club I read a paper, 'The Need in the North', in which I endeavoured to examine the position from various angles.

The gist of my summing up was that we needed the organisation in the North and that, even from the point of view of our own defence, it was essential. Now for quite a long time I had been contributing occasional

1. Irish Volunteers: founded on 25 November 1913 as a result of an article by Eoin MacNeill in *An Claidheamh Soluis* of 1 November. In the article, entitled 'The North Began', MacNeill suggested that southern nationalists should form a Volunteer movement on the lines of the Ulster Volunteer Force. By May 1914 membership was around 80,000. On 21 January 1919 the First Dáil Éireann met and proclaimed the Irish Republic. In 1920 the Irish Volunteers took an oath to the Republic and became the Irish Republican Army.

articles to Griffith's paper sometimes over my own name and sometimes over a *nom-de-plume*. I was on intimate terms with Griffith and invariably had a meal and a chat with him, when I visited Dublin.

Soon after I had read my paper, I wrote him a note and gave him such news as I had of the North and enclosed the script of my paper. Now I did not send the paper for publication, but intended it merely as an indication to him of what some of us thought. Much to my surprise the whole paper was published in the following issue of *Sinn Féin*.[2] It attracted a good deal of attention and provoked a good many inquiries and discussions, and eventually resulted in a decision to call together representatives of all the Nationalist organisations in the city for a conference. It should be noted that the conference was not called to form a Belfast company of Irish Volunteers, but to decide whether or not such a company should be organised.

The Freedom Club took the initiative and the responsibility for calling the conference and each of the following organisations was invited to send two delegates: The United Irish League, that is, the Parliamentary Party; the Ancient Order of Hibernians, also a Party organisation; the Gaelic League; the Gaelic Athletic Association; and the Irish National Foresters.[3] These, with two representatives of the Freedom Club, constituted the conference.

The representatives of the United Irish League and the Hibernians opposed the motion to form a company of Volunteers and indicated that their leader, Mr Joseph Devlin, was not in favour of any such move. This, so far as I can recall, was their only argument against the proposal. As, however, the others present were all in favour of going on, a committee and officers were elected to launch the Belfast company.

2. In *Sinn Féin* of 7 March 1914 an article by Seasomh Ó Conghaile, headed 'The need in the north' and described as 'a lecture delivered at the Belfast Freedom Club' concluded: 'To the members, then, I would plead for a quiet, determined analysis of themselves, to see in what way they can spread the principles of Irish nationality, and to remember that in their work they must keep themselves and the movement above suspicion or taint of unworthiness. If the [Home Rule] Bill fails, we must join up in the already big army of Volunteers, which are yet, please God, going to sound the death-knell of our slavery and proclaim our liberty. All these are necessary, and that we may not be taken unawares, let us, at least, begin the Volunteers at once'.

3. Irish National Foresters was founded in Dublin in 1877 as a benefit society to provide relief for members and their families. The leaders included members of the Irish Republican Brotherhood. To qualify for membership one had to be Irish by birth or descent. The organisation was regarded with great suspicion by Dublin Castle. It continues as a benefit society, whose main purpose is to assist members in search of employment.

Denis McCullough[4] was elected chairman of the organising committee, I was deputy chairman, Michael Carolan[5] was secretary and Seán Neeson[6] was treasurer. With an energetic committee to aid us, we got under way at once and arranged for opening meetings and drill at 'The Huts' at Willowbank, where the Fianna boys had their headquarters. 'The Huts' were an interesting link with the near past. They were in fact the residual buildings of what had been a British military barracks and where, some twenty or thirty years earlier, General Baden-Powell[7] was commanding officer. I can recall as a very young boy seeing the mixture of redcoats and the busbies of the 'Black Watch' parading there. The atmosphere of the Falls Road, which was almost an entirely Nationalist and Catholic area, cannot have been very congenial or sympathetic to the British tommies and this may have been the cause of their transfer to other barracks and the abandonment of the Willowbank encampment.

We had over a hundred at our first signing-on. The following week our numbers doubled, and inside a month we had upwards of five hundred. It became apparent that, despite the ukase of the Parliamentary Party and Mr Devlin, recruitment was going on steadily and we were hard pressed to deal with all the recruits who joined us. Halls were rented and we were granted the use of the G.A.A. sports ground.

We secured the services of some volunteers to train the men. These were, for the most part, former British soldiers who had been non-commissioned officers and an excellent group they were. It was rigidly laid down that all party politics were prohibited and that the only consideration was the intending member's willingness to defend Ireland's rights. Everyone joining signed the enrolment form and was on an equal footing with everyone else, irrespective of his social or political status outside the

4. Denis McCullough (1883-1968): born Belfast, a piano tuner, he established his own business in Belfast 1909, moved it to Dublin 1919, member of I.R.B. 1901, co-founder Dungannon Clubs 1905, president of Supreme Council, I.R.B. 1916, led Belfast Irish Volunteers to Coalisland, Easter week 1916, returned them to Belfast, Easter Sunday evening, owing to general confusion surrounding the Rising, supporter of treaty 1921 and Fine Gael Party.

5. Michael Carolan (1875-1930): born Belfast, member of Irish Volunteers 1914, interned Frongoch 1916, member of Belfast Corporation, I.R.A. 1919-24, opposed the treaty, director of intelligence in anti-treatyite forces 1922-23 and I.R.A. 1923-30.

6. Seán Neeson (1890-1964): born Belfast, member of Irish Volunteers 1914, interned at Frongoch and Reading jail after Easter Rising 1916, teacher in Cork 1920, director Cork Radio Station 1927-33, lecturer in Irish music, U.C.C. 1933-64.

7. Baron Baden-Powell: Robert Stephenson Smyth (1857-1941): born London, British army 1876-1910, served in India and in South Africa, where he was the hero of Mafeking, served in Ireland 1892-95, founded the Boy Scout movement in 1907.

movement. Such meetings as had to be held were concerned only with the military organisation and the training of the men.

As the numbers continued to increase the Redmondite Party finding that their prohibition against joining was being ignored decided on a complete reversal of policy. The prohibition was not only withdrawn, but the Party supporters were urged to join up and get control of the whole movement. That is part of our national history of the period. In Belfast we were swamped out and our figures leapt ahead until there were upwards of five thousand men in the regiment.

Then came the party 'squeeze', led by Mr Devlin in Belfast, and it followed the same pattern with us as elsewhere throughout the country, but with a significant difference. In Belfast Mr Devlin occupied a somewhat unique position. He was not only the Nationalist member of Parliament for West Belfast, but he was the idol of his followers. His word was law and he tolerated neither question nor opposition. The war came in August 1914 and the issue was knit. The Irish Party went out on a recruiting campaign for the British army. The cry of 'Catholic Belgium' was more potent than the one proclaiming that 'Your King and Country need you', but to us, who were more concerned with 'Catholic Ireland', the position was menacing in the extreme.

We saw the danger of our ranks being swept into the British army, and the force that had been recruited for the defence of Ireland being transferred to the defence of the only enemy that we knew, namely, the British government and forces that continued to keep us in subjection.

We decided to have a 'showdown' and each company of the volunteers was ordered to hold a company meeting at which the simple issue of allegiance to the Irish Volunteers and a refusal to be stampeded into the British forces would be put to the members. It should be stressed that this course of action was decided by the Belfast organisation and was so decided because of the particular circumstances operating there and the grip of Mr Devlin exercised over the majority of our members.

The meetings of the companies were indecisive. I represented headquarters at a number of them and found it difficult to preserve order and get a vote recorded. However Mr Devlin took the position into his own hands and called a mass meeting in St Mary's Hall. It would be merciful to draw a veil over that experience, but it must be mentioned. Recording the event simply and dispassionately, I have only to say that the meeting was 'packed', not only by the normal decent party supporters, but by a well distributed gang of 'toughs', whose duty was to silence by force any dissenting voice to the vague and nebulous arguments put forward by Devlin.

There were scuffles and rows and ejectments, covered over by a screen of yelling and cheering and general chaos and eventually a relatively small group of us, who had held out for loyalty to the original pledges and purposes of the Irish Volunteers, were forcibly driven out. Some of our friends had suffered slightly in the melee, but we shook ourselves, pulled ourselves together and arranged that we would meet a few nights later. When we did we found that, of the whole Belfast regiment, less than two hundred had remained loyal to the original body and to the constitution of the Irish Volunteers.

Later, those supporting the Parliamentary Party adopted the title of the Irish National Volunteers. The change by the introduction of the word 'National' into the name struck me as somewhat ironical. If there was any honesty whatever in their leader's policy surely 'International' would have been more appropriate.

The succession of events all over Ireland has been recorded in the history of the period, and I repeat that I am merely recording my experience of what happened in Belfast. The 'National' volunteers proceeded with their activities which were entirely of the political parade type. The funds which we had collected for the purchase of arms were taken over by the usurping body. This was achieved by applying pressure and threats on our honorary treasurer who happened to be a civil servant.

The aftermath was depressing and I felt bitter beyond expression. Apart from the fact that all our work and efforts for the past few months were shattered overnight, there was the consciousness of the tactics employed and the realisation that what could have been a really effective local defence force was dispersed.

The new 'brass hats' of the Irish National Volunteers became the chief recruiting agents for the British army. A number of them, to their credit be it said, joined up and left their bones in Flanders, but there were many others who were content to line up their misguided followers for the British forces, while they remained at home.

And here I must intervene briefly with some personal history. In the year 1913 I was twenty-eight years of age, and a reasonably contented bachelor living comfortably at home with my parents. Needless to say I had the usual fleeting passages of romance, but with one exception and that was when I was 'too young to know any better' they were fleeting indeed. It was not that I avoided the company or society of young women; on the contrary I think nobody enjoyed mixed company more. I had lots of friends of both sexes and we went to dances and parties and theatres regularly, but I had no desire and no intention of changing my way of life. I had a comfortable job which I liked and at which I worked hard and earned a decent income adequate for my needs. I had a comfortable home, my walks and books and friends and I had started to try and do some serious writing. I had had a three-act play, which I had submitted, produced by the Abbey Theatre,[8] and Yeats[9] had written me favourably about another and made various encouraging suggestions. I had my contacts with the Ulster Literary Theatre and the Arts Club and I was doing occasional articles for Griffith. Although politics absorbed a good deal of time and energy, I did preserve that other life that was definitely my own and which formed an inner sanctuary of my mind and thoughts.

About this time I remember my mother speaking to me about getting married. We were sitting together, the family Rosary had been said and the others had gone off to bed. I was reading at the fireside when without any preliminaries she asked me if I had a notion about getting married. I was surprised by her query, but quickly assured her that nothing was further from my mind. She then said that, while she realised that it would be a big break and a somewhat serious matter for her domestic economics, still she thought that it was really time for me to consider the matter. 'You are twenty-eight now and a man should not leave it too late' was how she expressed it. I told her that I was perfectly content as I was and that I really meant to go on in my bachelor way. Then it happened! We had often met before, but beyond that detached admiration and appreciation that any attractive and intelligent young woman merits, my interest did not go. Then, one way or another, in the autumn of 1913 we met more frequently and then it began to dawn on me that this was the one person for whom I had been waiting all down the years. I am not writing a romance and there are things that are too personal and too sacred for print and so let me content myself by saying what surprised me most was my own deep and instinctive conviction that our union was inevitable, that it was the only possible one for me, that it would be good and that, failing it, there would be none other.

I am writing this forty-four years afterwards, forty-two years after our marriage and after a very varied life of 'ups and downs' and I can only confirm that my conviction was fully justified.

8. Connolly's, *The mine land,* was presented by the Abbey Theatre, Dublin, and the Ulster Literary Theatre, Belfast, in 1913. Later, on 28 and 29 April 1915, the Holy Rosary Dramatic Society produced it in their hall on Ravenhill Road, Belfast.

9. William Butler Yeats (1865-1939): born Dublin, poet, journalist, stimulated a national literature, helped to establish Abbey Theatre 1904, senator 1922-28, first Irish person to receive the Nobel Prize for Literature 1923, resided mainly in France 1924-39.

Róisín was at that time in her final year studies for her arts degree in Queen's University, Belfast, and was resident in the Dominican Convent, which provided hostel accommodation for a limited number of university students. It must have been a difficult final year for her for there were many things we wanted to do together, so many temptations in the way of plays and pictures and all the rest which were serious distractions to the grind and study for a final exam. However, June 1914 came and with it the examination. She got her honours degree and, while we made no specific announcement of the fact, we became engaged.

We could not fix a definite date for our wedding for the simple reason that, although very comfortable circumstanced as a bachelor, it was entirely a different matter to prepare for the responsibilities of marriage and a home of our own.

I had often contemplated launching out on a business of my own, but only in the vaguest passing way, and I am afraid that my bachelor life and my varied interests did not tend to make me give it very definite consideration. Now the whole situation was changed and I realised the urgent need to get down to the problem of planning my future. For the first time in my life I started to save and to take stock of my business prospects. I knew I had very valuable connections with whom I had been doing good business for many years and that I would have little difficulty in getting all the reasonable credit from manufacturers and suppliers of factory materials. My capital would be small and, although I knew I could raise substantial capital from various friends, I had a complete aversion to doing so. It was not any false pride that deterred, but a convinced business philosophy that has, rightly or wrongly, guided me all my life. This was and is that, while a manufacturer or trader is justified in seeking and taking credit from those who are suppliers in his particular line, or getting overdraft facilities from his bankers, he is not entitled to risk the capital of his friends to achieve his commercial ambitions. Traders and bankers are in business for profit and can be relied on to assess the risks and make their decisions, but a friend's loan is a strain on lender and borrower and a menace to the friendship.

The position was further complicated by the outbreak of World War I. I remember setting off with Michael Carolan for a couple of weeks holiday. It was the first Saturday in August 1914 and our destination was Carnlough. The Volunteer situation was working up to the crisis that I had already described. We left the train at Larne to join the 'long car' for the coast road and heard the news of the British ultimatum. The war was on, and the days of peace were over for our generation. However, we did not realise all this at once. We were young and full of energy and optimism and we made the most of our holiday. We came back to struggle through all the local conflict of the Volunteer situation and to adjust ourselves to the war that involved us all irrespective of our views or work. Belfast settled down to a feverish existence. Thousands of young men joined up, and, whatever else might be charged against them, the cream of the young business and professional men who were Carsonite and anti-Home Rule in their outlook were soon in their officers' uniforms and many of them never returned from France. Old man Edwards lost his youngest son Billy during the first six months of the war. A grand lad he was, the ablest and best of the family. He had but a year before got his final examination as an accountant and he had had his first international cap on the Irish rugby team. He was typical of so many others that we knew and liked, notwithstanding our differences in religion and political outlook.

Despite the confusion and conflicting forces which surrounded us all, I determined to go ahead and make all possible preparations to start my own business. I consulted the various representatives of the many firms with whom I had been doing business over the years and, being satisfied that I would have no difficulties regarding supplies or credit, sought suitable premises and was fortunate enough to get just what I required in Upper Arthur Street, almost opposite those where I was employed.

It is unnecessary to recount in detail all that transpired during the succeeding months, but in April 1915 I opened the door and the firm of 'J. Connolly & Company' was launched. The '& Company' was purely titular. I had no partners. I had seen enough firms break up through unhappy partnerships that I had resolved that, however small my concern would be, it would be my own. I had, however, a sensitive objection to the first person singular being used in all correspondence and transactions and this, and this only, explained the '& Company'.

I was fortunate in getting off to a good start. I had but a small amount of capital and moderate overdraft facilities at the bank. My supplying firms were generous in their credit terms, but my instinctive urge, apart from my business sense, was to meet my liabilities promptly and establish my credit with my traders. At the end of the year, following stock-taking and the accountant's report, the business position seemed to be satisfactory.

Róisín and I were more than content with the prospects and on 31 January 1916 our good friend Father Bob Fullerton[10] united us for life and said the Nuptial Mass in St Paul's church, Belfast.

10. Fr Robert Fullerton (1879-1938): born Maghera, County Derry, St Malachy's College, Belfast 1904-7, parish of St Matthew, Belfast 1907-11, parish of St Paul 1911-34, parish of St John 1934-38, a life-long supporter of and a senior officer in the Gaelic League, a life-long supporter of Sinn Féin, temporarily assigned to the parish of Portaferry,

We had a modest but pleasant home, a semi-detached villa, 38 Divis Drive, where our windows overlooked the upper reaches of the Falls Park which in turn stretched out to the foothills of the Black Mountain. Here we were happy together and here four of our eight children were born between the years 1917 and 1922 and here we remained until circumstances forced us to transfer to Dublin in September 1922 and purchase the home, 'Melford', 5 Westfield Road, Harold's Cross, in which we still live.

They have a saying in the North of Ireland and it may be elsewhere that: 'You can't get married and do well in one year'. There was an element of truth in it in so far as we were concerned, for I have often reflected on the fact that I started business on my own account, got married and got into jail in the one year, or so near to one year that made no difference. I had, however, the one great consoling comfort that transcended all else and that was that I had as my life partner a girl of great courage and good humour, unselfish to the last degree and who was cheerful and optimistic, however dark the horizon might appear to be.

I have no wish to publish our personal or domestic life record, but I have said I think the minimum necessary to reflect the lights and shades of those days.

Early in 1916 there were various ominous rumblings. The line of cleavage between the Volunteers had been complete since the split. Large numbers of the Redmondites had been drawn into the British army and many had already made the supreme sacrifice, while at the same time the parent Volunteer organisation had been growing in numbers and efficiency in most parts of Ireland except the North. In Belfast and the North generally we were weak in numbers and organisation. This might be attributed to a number of factors. We were living in an overwhelmingly hostile atmosphere surrounded by a jingoistic war-spirit and a population that had gone 'off the rails' with war-time prosperity. Apart from the day and night activities of the shipyards, the foundries and engineering shops were swamped with orders for munitions, the clothing manufacturers with contracts for the army and navy, while the linen mills were hard pressed to supply all the aeroplane canvas that was demanded. It was an orgy of big wages and big spending, of fur coats and jewellery and heavy drinking. Perhaps the biggest single factor against us was the political control of the so-called nationalist population by the local leader, Joseph Devlin. It would be hard to conceive any political leader that could command an equal

---

County Down, Aug.-Dec. 1916 after General Maxwell threatened to have him arrested, a prolific writer on religious and social questions.

personal loyalty to that which Mr Devlin enjoyed at the time. The Home Rule bill was on the Statute Book suspended of course by an accompanying Act for the duration of the war and obviously seriously menaced by the emergency movements and changes that were taking place in the British government itself. Still, Mr Devlin would reassure his adherents that all would be well. 'You are statutory freemen' he proclaimed at a meeting in Toomebridge to which I somewhat reluctantly escorted Mrs Stopford Greene at her request. The phrase and statement outraged her, but it served its purpose. To have any views contrary to those of Mr Devlin and his political supporters ranked as near heresy, which was barely tolerated. I mention these factors not to excuse, but to explain our weakness as a unit in the Irish Volunteers and in the scheme of things then being planned.

6

Holy Week 1916 – Dublin on Holy Saturday – MacNeill's conference – Thomas MacDonagh calls – MacNeill cancels all activities – The Rising – Executions – Arrests and deportations – Various prisons – Releases – My bank manager says 'No'

It was Holy Week in 1916. There had been many rumours for some weeks, including the persistent one that the government intended to make a swoop of all the Volunteer leaders, seize all the arms they could lay their hands on and then enforce conscription on the young men of the country.

Early in that week Colm Ó Lochlainn[1] arrived from Dublin. He was one of the original members of the Provisional Committee of the Volunteers. He had messages from MacNeill[2] including a copy of the document which purported to be the secret instructions from Dublin Castle directing the operations of arrests and arms seizures which Alderman Tom Kelly[3] was to make public at a meeting of the Dublin corporation. Ó Lochlainn stayed overnight with us and I learned from him that the Rising was definitely planned to take place on the following Sunday which was Easter Sunday. The news was not unexpected, but it was definite and specific in contrast to the various rumours that had been current.

After discussing various points and possibilities, I arranged with him to

1. Colm Ó Lochlainn (1892-1972): born Dublin, member of I.R.B. 1913, member of Provisional Committee of Irish Volunteers 1913, teacher, St Enda's school 1914, student of Old Irish under Eoin MacNeill, on being asked to print the 'Castle Document' realised it was not authentic and informed MacNeill who thereupon called off the Rising, in *Irish Times* 9 March 1964 Ó Lochlainn wrote: 'After 1916 I was rather disillusioned by discovering a certain amount of deceit and duplicity in those who engineered the Rising and, although helpful in elections and in various subversive activities, I did not give my whole enthusiasm to the cause. I kept on with Gaelic studies, taught and lectured but refused to stand for the Dáil', he founded the Three Candle Press 1926, lecturer in U.C.D. 1933-43, publisher, editor, best-known for his collections of Irish street ballads, founder member of An Óige, piper, actor and Irish language enthusiast.

2. Eoin MacNeill (1867-1945): born Glenarm, County Antrim, co-founder, in effect, of Gaelic League, Feis Ceoil, Irish Volunteers, appointed professor of early and medieval Irish history, U.C.D. 1908, as chief of staff, Irish Volunteers, he attempted to cancel the 1916 Rising, T.D. for Derry 1918-21, held ministerial appointments in Dáil Éireann, provisional government and Free State government, Free State representative in Boundary Commission.

3. Thomas Kelly: born Dublin, member of Irish Volunteers, vice-president, Sinn Féin 1913, lord mayor of Dublin.

travel to Dublin on Holy Saturday, bringing with me such 'material' as I had and join up with his company on the Sunday.

The decision to go to Dublin was not a hurried, spontaneous or impulsive one, but had been formed in my own mind after some thought and consideration, and after some rather blunt discussions with some of our local leaders.

I do not propose to go into all these matters now nor to cast the slightest reflection on any particular member of our group. It will suffice to say that I had no confidence whatever in the military capacity of some of those on whom military control and responsibility would fall. Perhaps I can best explain my outlook by recording an incident that occurred in the early days of our volunteer activities.

In those days we depended largely on ex-British soldiers to provide the military training for the men. We had gathered together quite a competent team, including some ex-sergeants and drill instructors. These men carried out their duties very efficiently, while those of us who lacked their experience and training were almost wholly occupied by the work of organisation and administration. It was, of course, laid down as a general rule that all must 'fall in' and do our training and drill. A military sub-committee of those who trained and drilled us was formed and joint meetings of the military and the general committee were frequent. At one of these I was somewhat shocked to hear from the reading of the military sub-committee's report that I had been promoted to the rank of captain and that one of my colleagues had been given a still higher rank. I immediately protested that I had no qualifications whatever for the rank of captain; that I could not possibly accept any position or rank of a military nature and that, while I was doing my best to train and drill, I was content to be a private and could not be anything other than a private. This was the simple truth and a definite conviction with me. Temperamentally, I hated the necessity for military activity of any sort. I disliked regimentation and the strict discipline and, while I was at the time physically fit and often enjoyed a ten to fifteen mile tramp over the Black Mountain and Divis, I got no pleasure out of five or six mile route-marching.

Having made my position clear to the committee and got my proposed commission and promotion withdrawn, I proposed to the committee and particularly to the military sub-committee that no promotion to officer rank should ever be made except on the results of strict examination tests laid down by the military committee. This was eventually agreed.

Following this particular meeting, which, I must confess, shocked me considerably, I spoke pretty bluntly to one or two of my colleagues and pointed out the serious moral and practical responsibility that would rest on any of us who found himself in charge of a company or even a small squad, and who had not the necessary training or competence to lead or direct them. As I put it to one of these colleagues: 'The movement is almost certainly going to lead to conflict. If and when it does you, with your present rank, will have certain responsibilities; you will be expected to lead your men, to give orders and see that they are carried out. You know that you have done no serious preparation for such an occasion. Unless you are prepared to work seriously and get down to military studies, then I suggest that you should give up your military rank and be content to become an ordinary private'.

It should be noted that all that I have described took place early in 1914 and before the split in the Volunteers. Shortly afterwards, and following the disruption of the Volunteers by the Irish Party politicians, the Belfast regiment which remained loyal to the original body was reduced to about two hundred. Most of the force, which at the time of the split numbered nearly five thousand men, followed the Irish Party leaders or drifted out of the movement.

Having learned definitely that the Rising was planned for Easter Sunday, I set about making my preparations. As already mentioned, I had commenced business on my own account in April 1915 and my wife and I were settled in our comfortable home. The prospect of breaking up our home and business life cast more than a shadow over us, but there it was and, however things might work out, it had to be faced. If the Rising was taking place, then there was only one thing to do and that was to join in with the others. Away back in 1914, following a lecture which he had delivered to the Belfast Volunteers, Pádraig Pearse[4] had, with a few of our colleagues, come home with me for supper. We sat late and naturally our talk was almost entirely concerned with the movement and the possible developments in the future. The night stands out clear-cut in my memory for it was the first time that I heard Pearse propounding clearly his doctrine of the need for the blood sacrifice and the necessity for the re-baptism of the country for the salvation of the national soul. What struck me at the time was the quiet, calm, deliberate way in which he gave us his views.

It was with something of this outlook that I spent Holy Week. The Rising, to my mind, could have little hope of success, unless of course the reports and rumours which we were hearing were adequately fulfilled and

4. Patrick Pearse (1879-1916): born Dublin, founder of St Enda's school, founder member of Irish Volunteers 1913, member of I.R.B., chairman of the military council which planned the Easter Rising 1916 and as chairman of the Provisional government of the Irish Republic read the Proclamation of Independence on 29 April, was executed on 3 May after the surrender.

justified. These were mainly to the effect that ample supplies of arms and ammunition would be landed at various points around the coast by the Germans and would be quickly distributed to the Volunteers, and that simultaneously the ports would be guarded by submarines to prevent the British landing troops. It must be stressed that these reports and rumours were quite indefinite, and naturally so, for one could sense even from published reports that there were two opposing schools of thought amongst the leaders in Dublin.

It was clear to anyone who knew a little of what was moving that, reading between the lines of what Bulmer Hobson had said at a meeting a couple of weeks before Easter Sunday, he and others with him were opposed to any precipitate action by the Volunteers at that stage. The history of that has already been covered to some extent and I am not in a position to add anything authoritative or from personal knowledge to it. I am merely recounting my personal recollections of the period, the sum total of which was that the Rising was to take place on Easter Sunday and that the Belfast group was to proceed to Coalisland, County Tyrone, on the Saturday. It is hardly necessary to add that all activities of the Volunteers were to take place on the pretext that 'manoeuvres' were to be held by Volunteers all over the country on Easter Sunday. I met several of my colleagues and told them that I had already arranged to 'fall in' with some associates in Dublin and gave my reasons. I believed that to send our handful of men, about one hundred to one hundred and fifty was the most we could expect to turn out, to an outside pocket in Tyrone seemed stupid and futile and, apart from that, I had no confidence whatever in the ability of those who would be leading them. I summed it up to the one with whom I was most intimate by telling him: 'I believe that we will all be wiped out. If it has to be, it has to be, but at least I prefer to be under the command of someone who is reasonably competent to lead me and give me a fighting chance'. It was this latter view that really swayed me and I was quite frankly sick at heart at the decision and the prospect of any of our lads going out to Tyrone under what passed for military leadership of the group. However, I had no rank and no authority and so all that remained for me was to try and put my affairs in order and get ready to leave for Dublin on Holy Saturday.

My brother, Alec,[5] was a civil servant, but he had had four years' training

5. Alexander J. Connolly (1892-1982): born Belfast, civil service 1909-57, member of Sinn Féin and Irish Volunteers 1914, interned at Frangoch following Easter Rising 1916, department of industry and commerce 1932-53, private secretary to Seán F. Lemass 1932-39, 1941-48.

in our business before entering the service and I discussed the position with him. I told him I proposed to leave the business to my wife, Róisín, and himself as joint partners and that he would throw up his job and go in and run the business with her, and that all the evidence showed that it would be satisfactory for both of them. I told him I thought we would be wiped out, and that in the circumstances one of us was all the family could afford to give, if any provision was to be made for Róisín and the other members of the family; that as I was the elder of the two and, moreover, had been more prominently active in the movement, it was my job to turn out. I urged that, however he might feel about it, it was clear to me that it was his job to stay out of the Rising and take over the business and responsibilities. I must have been particularly persuasive for he left me with the feeling that he agreed and would co-operate as suggested.

I went along to see Frank Bigger my friend and solicitor and, without being very specific as to days or dates, explained what I wanted to be drafted in a will. Frank shied away from the whole business, told me to have sense and not to be worrying about a will or anything else. His attitude stunned me, but I could not persuade him to do anything for me. I did not see him again until some weeks after we were released from prison and I realised that the whole period must have been a nightmare of shock and apprehension to him.

However the need or usefulness of drawing up a will, my plan was extinguished the next day when Alec informed me that he was not prepared to agree with my plans; that he also was a private in the Volunteers and that if things were going to happen it was his duty to be there. There was no answering that and so it was arranged that we should both go up to Dublin on the Saturday afternoon, contact Colm Ó Lochlainn and fall in with his company.

Each of us had a German mauser automatic and several hundred rounds of ammunition, as well as a rifle with ammunition. The problem of taking these with us presented difficulties. I was well known to the 'G men' in Dublin and was always shadowed from the time I stepped off the train at Amiens Street until I boarded it on my return journey. As we did not know what might eventuate in the way of search or arrests, and we certainly did not relish the idea of losing our valuable 'supplies' we were perplexed to know just how we could ensure their safety. A colleague of Alec's and a good friend of us both, Seán O'Sullivan, solved our difficulty. We decided that we could not manage the rifles, but O'Sullivan volunteered to take the automatics and the ammunition with him. He was travelling by the same train and was in no way suspect to the 'G Division'. He added to the security of the 'goods' by bringing them in a heavy leather government dispatch case engraved with the royal crest of 'G.R.'.

Good Friday was a day to remember. Róisín and I attended the religious ceremonies, went to Confession and got through the day somehow. In so far as it was possible, I put things in order in the business and left such directions as I could, but it was, I am afraid, with the feeling that it was all rather futile, and that I was really closing a chapter and possibly the final chapter. I drew a veil over the rest; the quiet partings when little or nothing is said because all are thinking the same thoughts and there is nothing that needs to be said.

We arrived in Dublin in due course on Saturday afternoon and, true to our expectation, the ubiquitous 'G man', who was the most constant of the 'G men' on the Amiens street platform 'beat', was there, if not to greet us at least to spot and shadow us.

On arrival Alec and I went to Mrs Wyse-Power's[6] restaurant for tea and more particularly to hear what might be available in the way of news or developments. Whilst we were seated, Mrs Wyse-Power herself came along. She told us in a semi-whisper that she was afraid that there was bad news from Kerry. She did not know if the news was correct, but she understood that an attempt to land arms there had failed and that a car with a party from Dublin had been lost. Beyond these rumours she had no information for us, but she was obviously worried and anxious.

After tea Alec and I parted having made our arrangements to meet the next morning. He went to stay with our eldest brother who lived out at Clontarf, while I went to spend the night with my old friend, Hugh MacCartan.[7] I had advised Ó Lochlainn of my address so that he could contact me at any time and advise me of the arrangements for Sunday's 'manoeuvres'. Arriving at MacCartan's home in Gilford Avenue, Sandymount, I found that Hugh was out seeing a friend of his off to join his regiment of the British army on its way to the 'front' in France.

He came in later and was very much excited as he told me of seeing a very handsome distinguished-looking man being escorted on to the mail

6. Mrs Jennie Wyse-Power—née O'Toole (1862-1941): born Baltinglass, County Wicklow, from 1880 onwards she joined every Nationalist organisation, of which a woman could be a member, a member of Sinn Féin from its establishment, she held many of its highest offices, a founder member of Cumann na mBan, member of Dublin Corporation, married John Wyse-Power (a versatile journalist), member of Gaelic League, proprietor of restaurants run by the Irish Produce Company, senator 1922-36, member of Fianna Fáil 1936.

7. Hugh A. MacCartan: born Belfast, member of Irish Volunteers 1914, contributed poems to *Sinn Féin* of 18 February 1911 and 28 September 1912.

boat by a squad of soldiers. MacCartan described the scene graphically, how the man looked weary and worn and yet carried himself with dignity and aloofness. He was manacle and closely guarded. His conclusion was that the British had caught a very important person, probably a master spy or somebody of equal concern to them, judging by the strength and closeness of the guard that surrounded the prisoner.

It never occurred to either of us who the prisoner might be. I, of course, never thought of Roger Casement as I was satisfied that he was in Germany, but I often wondered afterwards that MacCartan did not recognise Roger, for I had brought him up specially to Frank Bigger's to meet Casement in 1913 or 1914. However, it was only much later that we realised that Hugh had witnessed the final departure from his beloved Ireland of one of our most gallant patriots who was to find a hangman's rope and prison grave in Pentonville. The incident made a deep impression on MacCartan who could scarcely talk of anything save the dishevelled but dignified figure and the sad despairing look in his eyes.

At my suggestion we retired early, which meant about 11 p.m. and that was early for us. Usually when MacCartan and I visited one another's home our first night's talk lasted well into the small hours, but tomorrow would be a different sort of day. I must be up and about early. Early Mass and early breakfast and then contact Ó Lochlainn! I was ready to step into my pyjamas when we heard a knock under our bedroom. I stopped in my tracks and listened while Hugh went down to admit a visitor. It was Colm Ó Lochlainn who had come from Eoin MacNeill with the request that I would accompany him back as MacNeill wanted to see me without delay. I dressed at once and set off with Ó Lochlainn. It was a good stretch from Sandymount to our destination which was the house of Dr Séamus O'Kelly[8] on Rathgar Road and it was close to midnight when we arrived there. On our way over Ó Lochlainn had told me that things were 'at sixes and sevens', that he understood that the news from down south was bad, but he did not give me definite details beyond the fact that MacNeill as chief of staff was not in the counsel of those who were out for action and that those who made up the immediate-action group had carried on with their plans without consultation with MacNeill or his friends in the Volunteer committee. This did not altogether surprise me, and for two reasons. The first was that, as I have already said, one could sense the conflict of views implicit in the lines of Hobson's statement, which was a plea

8. Dr Séamus O'Kelly (1879-1953): born Belfast, gynaecologist in Dublin, not involved in the national movement but made his residence available as a 'safe house' for Irish Volunteer, Sinn Féin and I.R.A. leaders.

for patient waiting and a warning against being stampeded into precipitate action before they, the Volunteers were ready for it. The other reason was that several months before Easter I had a talk with James Connolly[9] in Belfast when he introduced tentatively the possibility of having a group that would press forward more intensively the work of the Volunteers. Whether or not it was due to my comment that I always hated any suggestion of having a 'movement within a movement' and that such 'always produced rows and disagreements', he did not pursue the subject, but the talk and the reference registered.

When Ó Lochlainn and I arrived at Séamus O'Kelly's we were shown into the sitting-room and MacNeill greeted me, asked about my wife Róisín, who is his niece, and then asked me what I had come to Dublin for. My reply was short and to the point: 'To do anything I am told'. He took me slightly aside and we stood and talked at a little table near the door. He explained to me that he, as chief of staff, was calling off all parades and manoeuvres that had been arranged for the following day, Easter Sunday. Actually it must have been already Easter Sunday as we talked. He told me that, although he had already reluctantly consented to the general uprising, the reports that he had received from different parts of the country indicated that such action would be disastrous and that he was convinced would only result in useless sacrifice and the wiping out of the whole movement. He said that there was evidence that adequate planning of activities had not been made, that the arrangements about the arrival and reception of arms had completely miscarried and that in the circumstances he felt under a definite moral obligation to countermand all the orders that had been issued for Easter Sunday.

While we were talking or rather when MacNeill was telling me all this, for I was merely listening, the door opened and Thomas MacDonagh[10] was shown in. As I say, we were practically at the door of the room and MacDonagh just came in and no more. He looked tense, but was calm and cool. He asked MacNeill about his countermanding order and MacNeill

9. James Connolly (1868-1916): born Edinburgh, organiser for the Dublin Socialist Society 1896, founder of Irish Socialist Republican Party and *The Worker's Republic* 1898, propagator of socialism in U.S.A. 1903-10, Belfast organiser for Irish Transport and General Workers' Union 1911, co-founder of Labour Party 1912, led Irish Citizen Army alongside Irish Volunteers, Easter 1916.

10. Thomas MacDonagh (1878-1916): born Cloughjordan, County Tipperary, teacher at St Kieran's College, St Colman's College, St Enda's 1901-12, lecturer, U.C.D. 1912-16, co-founder of Irish Theatre 1915, founder member of Irish Volunteers 1913, member of Irish Republican Brotherhood 1915, member of military council which planned Easter Rising.

showed him a small typed note that he was sending to Volunteer units all over the country. MacDonagh read it and having done so said to MacNeill: 'Of course you realise that your order may not be obeyed'. MacNeill's reply was equally terse: 'The responsibility for disobedience will fall on those who disobey'. MacDonagh paused for a moment as if in thought and then said: 'Well I must consult my friends about this'. Folding the paper, he then left. He spoke to none but MacNeill and the whole incident was over in a few minutes. I can recall the sinking feeling that the brief conversation gave me. I was not 'in' on the talk and it was purely accidental that I happened to be standing beside them. In the room there were perhaps upwards of a dozen men some of whom I knew, others I was to know later. Amongst these whom I knew were James MacNeill,[11] Dr O'Kelly, Arthur Griffith, Seán Fitzgibbon[12] and Colm Ó Lochlainn, whilst among the others I remembered Paudeen O'Keeffe,[13] whom I was to meet later as a fellow prisoner in Richmond Barracks. Of all those gathered together, I was, I think, the only one who heard the brief discussion between MacDonagh and MacNeill and that purely by the chance circumstances that I have mentioned.

MacDonagh having gone, MacNeill asked me if I would be prepared to leave by early morning train and bring the countermanding order to our boys in the North. I agreed, but later it was arranged that I would cover the Drogheda area and that Ó Lochlainn would proceed to Tyrone. We were given copies of the countermanding order signed by MacNeill with instructions to show the orders to the person concerned and, having done so, to destroy the copy. Similar orders were given to most, if not all, of those present and some of these who were going to more distant parts of the country were setting off by car. There was nothing more to be said or done. Our instructions included the direction that, having delivered our messages, we were to proceed to our homes and dispel as far as possible any suggestion of unusual activity.

Ó Lochlainn and I left to spend the remainder of the night in his home which was but a short distance from Dr O'Kelly's. We did not talk much. The whole situation depressed me. I thought bitterly that it was the old

11. James MacNeill (1869-1938): born Glenarm, County Antrim, brother of Eoin, Indian civil service 1890, chairman, Dublin County Council 1922, high-commissioner of Free State 1922-28, governor-general 1928-32.

12. Seán Fitzgibbon: born Dublin, member of Irish Volunteers 1913, O.C., Kilcoole gun-running, August 1914.

13. Paudeen O'Keeffe: general secretary of Sinn Féin 1915-22, member of Irish Volunteers 1913, I.R.A. 1919-21, Free State army 1922, governor of Mountjoy jail 1923.

story repeated. 'Differences at the top!', 'More splits', 'Bad planning' and so on. The one phrase that stuck in my memory and remained there for long afterwards was MacDonagh's: 'Well I must consult my friends about this' and the emphasis to me was on the word 'my'. Let me be quite frank about the position as I saw it then. I did not see what other course MacNeill could have adopted. He knew that the arms ship was lost and that the four men who had motored down to complete the arrangements were lost or missing and that in many if not most parts of the country the plans for operation were anything but complete or perfect. However, it is not my purpose to attempt to judge the merits or defects of all those concerned, but merely to put on record my own personal experience in what was to me a historic moment. I never saw MacDonagh again and I think I can assume that he and MacNeill never met afterwards.

Easter Sunday morning came and Ó Lochlainn and I went to early Mass and after breakfast made our way to Amiens Street station. I got off the train at Drogheda leaving Ó Lochlainn to continue his journey to Portadown and from there to Coalisland. There were very few people about as I came out of the station and the town had all the charm that one associates with a quiet peaceful Sunday morning.

The Sunday papers carried MacNeill's countermanding order cancelling all Volunteer activities that had been arranged for the day. I made discreet inquiries and was soon directed to the address which MacNeill had given me and having explained my mission to the gentleman I showed him the order. I impressed upon him the urgency of getting in touch with the local leaders and delivering the message. He assured me that this would be done.

There was no train to Belfast until late in the afternoon and I was invited to stay for lunch. Sometime later on my host suggested a short run in the car along the Boyne valley to put in the time before my train was due to leave. I gladly agreed and we set off on our run. We had only gone a short distance outside the town when I saw a group of young men who were obviously Volunteers and who were more than ordinarily equipped, for not only did they carry knapsacks but they had various packages strapped in with their 'kits'. There were, I should say, over twenty young men in the group and, immediately sensing that not only were they Volunteers but that they made a very business-like group of lads indeed, I asked my host to pull up so that we could find their leader and speak to him. When we stopped and hailed them, a young man came forward and we explained the direction which I had brought from MacNeill and which had been published in the morning papers. The young man was obviously perplexed and unwilling to accept any such direction. I had destroyed the actual signed order after I had conveyed its message, but my host confirmed my statement and anyhow I pointed out that the direction was published in that morning's papers. The young man, I think, mentioned something about orders from others than MacNeill but, whether I am right or wrong on this recollection, it was clear that he was very reluctant to call off his activities and send his boys back to their homes. I did not argue or reason with him, contenting myself by telling him that such was the order that MacNeill had asked me to deliver.

Some weeks later I met the same young man as a fellow-prisoner in Richmond Barracks. He was Phil Monahan,[14] a teacher in Drogheda and later city manager of Cork. Phil told me that when I met him and his group they were on their way to destroy one of the main-line bridges on the permanent way. I have often wondered what would have happened if, following the failure of MacNeill's friend in Drogheda to convey his message to the local leaders, Phil and his companions had carried on and destroyed the bridge. But for my chance encounter with the Drogheda contingent the bridge operation would, I am satisfied, have been carried out.

I left Drogheda in the late afternoon and, as instructed, returned home. I was mentally exhausted and confused trying to figure out all that I had experienced during my brief absence. It was hard to realise that it was only the afternoon before that I had left for Dublin and since then had learned enough of divided and conflicting opinions and divergent policies to make one despair. As I saw it, the movement was heading towards chaos unless by the grace of God the differences and difficulties could be ironed out. It has to be remembered that at this time I, like practically everyone else in the country, knew nothing about Casement's arrest and, while I had heard rumours and suggestions about a failure to land arms in Kerry, I had learned nothing definite about the real position. MacNeill had of course told me and the others of the general lack of organisation and bad planning, but we had no details.

I was not long at home when one of my best friends and one of the most competent and reliable men of our Belfast group arrived at the house. He was Tadhg Smyth.[15] Tadhg had gone with the boys to County Tyrone and I was surprised when he came in. I learned from him that those in command had decided to 'dismiss' and order the men to return home. At first I assumed that this was the result of Ó Lochlainn's arrival with MacNeill's

14. Philip Monahan (1893-1962): born Dublin, member of Irish Volunteers and Sinn Féin 1913, interned at Frongoch after Easter Rising 1916, Cork City manager 1929-58.

15. Tadhg Smith: born Belfast, member of Irish Volunteers 1914, interned following Easter Rising 1916.

message and I was perplexed to learn from Tadhg that at the time of their dismissal there was no sign of Ó Lochlainn nor had they any word of MacNeill's order. Tadhg did not know or if he knew he did not say how the decision was made. He held no military rank and was, like myself, content to be in the ranks. He told me that after Mass they marched some miles to the station where they were able to get a connection to Belfast. I have, deliberately, never tried to probe into the circumstances of the decision to disband in Tyrone, nor in what way the decision was reached but I have always believed that, in the circumstances, it seemed the only sane decision to take. The fundamental mistake was in sending a small group to lose themselves in an isolated position in County Tyrone and in the Belfast military leaders agreeing to such a course of action.

It may have been that headquarters in Dublin knew or thought they knew of some connecting links in the area which would effect some military purpose. They may have been misled by the local reports, but from the little I knew, or learned later, there was never the slightest justification for sending the one-hundred and twenty or so Belfast boys to County Tyrone.

Before bedtime Ó Lochlainn arrived. I had invited him to come on to Belfast and spend a few days with us on the assumption that everything was off and he agreed. He told us of his arrival at Coalisland and his inquiries about the boys and finding that they had left early that morning to join the train for Belfast.

While somewhat bewildered at the time, I felt that there was nothing that could be done about it. If MacNeill's order had not been received, it had at least been acted on and even anticipated. The men were back in their homes, the manoeuvres had been called off and the authorities would assume things were no more abnormal than they were a week ago. But would they? I kept on thinking about the rumours I had heard about the failure to land arms and I could not forget Thomas MacDonagh's final word to MacNeill that he would have to consult 'his' friends. Well, that was Easter Sunday 1916, and we were a somewhat perplexed and depressed group when we retired for the night.

Easter Monday was a general holiday in Belfast and all business was closed down for the day. We idled somewhat aimlessly after breakfast. I was still feeling the tension of the week-end or perhaps it would be more correct to say that I was turning over one question after another in my mind without finding any satisfactory answer. In the afternoon we went out for a walk, Róisín, Colm Ó Lochlainn and a couple of visitors who had arrived. I cannot remember now how or from whom we heard the first rumours of 'trouble having broken out in Dublin', for it was thus the first news was conveyed to us, but it was on our way back from our walk that the rumours reached us.

For the next day or two there were all sorts of stories and rumours floating around. At first the papers were reticent and it was later in the week before we began to get any real information. For ourselves we were cut off from any hope of making contact. To travel or to attempt to travel by train was out of the question. All roads were guarded and patrolled and we were isolated and detached with no knowledge of what was going on save the very brief and uninformative official items of news permitted by the censor. The week was a nightmare, a nightmare not only of frustration but of complete sterility. Then came the news of the burning of Dublin, the shelling of the General Post Office and the final surrender of the Volunteer and Citizen Army forces. One went down to business, but one did not go to do business but to move about restlessly with a sense of futility and hopelessness. After the surrender the papers carried the news or so much of it as the British authorities and their censors considered good for us. At that particular time condemnation of the 'rebels' was almost unanimous and it was pretty grim to sense the hostility not only from the loyal Unionists of Belfast, but from others who would lay claim to the title of 'Nationalists'.

Then came the news of the first executions. We were not surprised, but infinitely saddened. And yet I could not help thinking that Tom Clarke[16] would go gaily to his death, smilingly defying the powers of the empire which he hated as an unclean evil. I knew Tom not so intimately as some of my friends did but well enough to consider myself a friend and to feel that the firing party would be for him a more welcome climax to a glorious week of defiance than a resumption of the cruel torture that they inflicted on him as Convict Henry Wilson.

Pearse too had fulfilled his destiny. There had certainly been the baptism of blood and fire, but that was over as he stands dignified before the firing squad. Some years earlier he had given us his beautiful play *The singer* in which MacDara who had 'quickened the dead years and all the quiet dust' declaimed to his friends: 'One man can free a people as one man redeemed the world. I will take no pike. I will go into the battle with bare hands. I will stand up before the Gall as Christ hung naked before men on the

16. Thomas J. Clarke (1858-1916): born Isle of Wight, member of Clan na Gael in U.S.A. 1880, prison in England for Fenian activities 1883-98, tobacconist in Dublin 1906-16, member of Supreme Council, I.R.B., first signatory to the Proclamation of Independence of 1916.

tree'. Would his dream of an Ireland renewed in spirit, in courage, and in determination be realised? Frankly there seemed little chance of it in the days that immediately followed his execution. To those of us of lesser faith everything seemed doomed. We were beaten and crushed. The rising had been a wretched failure, badly planned and badly organised with conflicting opinions and directions at the top, and the result that only Dublin and a few isolated spots had been able to rise.

We did not get much time to brood over the situation. On Friday morning, 5 May, we had been out at early Mass for the 'First Fridays' and I proceeded after breakfast to business. As I went in I was immediately seized by a couple of plain clothes men of the G Division and saw several more of them at the back of the showrooms. They permitted me to hand over my keys to Miss Rogan, who was chief assistant, and kept a controlling grip on me, while I did so. They immediately marched me off to the police courts and, after a short delay there, transferred me by taxi to the Crumlin Road jail. There I found a group of my colleagues who had been similarly 'rounded up' that morning. There were, I think, twenty-seven of us in all but they included my brother Alec, Tadhg Smyth, Pim,[17] Denny McCullough, Mickey Carden,[18] Jerry Barnes.[19] We were stripped, fingerprinted, checked in the usual way and afterwards brought to our cells.

There is no need to describe in detail either the cell or the conditions. These have become so well known both by experience and description that they are intimately known to our generation. When the fuss of installation was over, I had leisure to try and review the position. The prospect did not look very bright, but naturally my chief worry was about my young wife Róisín and how things would work out for her, our home and our future.

Here I was, I thought grimly. I had started business on my own account, got married and settled happily into our new home and now was a prisoner, all inside one year. The business I felt would be smashed, not because of insolvency, for I was satisfied that my assets would much more than out-balance my liabilities, but because all my creditors would most likely pounce immediately for their 'pound of flesh'. That, however, was a secondary worry and the chief one was the loneliness I felt for my dear girl at home. There was too the bitter sense of humiliating defeat and the

17. Herbert Moore Pim (1883-1934): born Belfast, poet, novelist, his non-fiction work includes *Unconquerable Ulster* (with foreword by Sir Edward Carson, M.P.) 1919.

18. Michael Carden: born Belfast, member of Irish Volunteers 1914, interned following Easter Rising 1916.

19. Jeremiah Barnes, born Belfast, member of Irish Volunteers 1914, interned at Frongoch following Easter Rising, 1916.

circumstances surrounding it. The conflicting elements at headquarters, the lack of proper planning and the confusion of orders as a result of which the Insurrection was practically confined to Dublin; these and many other thoughts pounded away in my head.

That First Friday was a long day. I suppose everyone's first day in jail is inevitably so. The night was nearly as bad. I found it difficult to adjust myself to the plank-bed and the mustard-coloured cover outraged all my sense of decency. On Saturday morning we were marched out to the exercise yard. It was a morning of fine drizzling rain, the sort that seeps into you. I was fortunate in the possession of a light raincoat, but I noticed that most of the men had been arrested without one. Alec was one of them, and there was a very delicate looking youth who was also without one. I did not know him at the time, but I learned later that he was a student of Queen's University and a very brilliant student at that. Barney McMackin died within a short period after release, and I have always been convinced that poor Barney got his death warrant on that Saturday morning when, for an hour, we were paraded around the circle in the Crumlin Road jail in the soaking rain.

The Crumlin Road jail abuts on to the grounds of St Malachy's College. In our young days at St Malachy's it was not unusual for some of the bigger boys to sling over small pieces of chewing tobacco in the hope that some of the unfortunate prisoners would get them. The Catholic chaplain to the prison is invariably a member of the College staff and apparently it is customary for him to attend on Saturday forenoons to hear Confessions.

I knew nothing of these arrangements and so was somewhat surprised when my cell door swung open and I saw Father John MacAuley[20] standing there and heard him say in his pronounced north-Antrim accent: 'Joe, this is a terrible business'. Father John was at that time dean of the College. He had been at Malachy's with me and was classmate with my elder brother Séamus. He was kind and consoling, but there was nothing that I could ask him to do for me beyond telling him to let Róisín know I was quite all right and feeling well. After he had visited all the men he went to the prison chapel to hear Confessions. As it was the day after the First Friday, I do not think he had many penitents, but we all filed into the chapel and were thus able to note all those who had been rounded up.

We were brought back to our cells and locked in and after about an hour we were each served with a rather forbidding-looking tin which contained a mess of some sort of stew. I tried it but revolted and left it. How foolish

20. Fr John McAuley: dean of St Malachy's College 1907-23, parish priest, Sacred Heart parish, Belfast 1923-4.

I was, for I did not know that it would be twenty-six hours before I would be offered any further ration.

We were not long settled down to our thoughts after 'dinner' when the cell door opened and we were all told to pack up and get ready to go. We were then marshalled together in the main hall, checked and cross checked and then ordered to climb into two large Pantechnicon vans such as are used for furniture removals. We were accompanied by a strong contingent of young soldiers and brought to the Great Northern Railway station and put on board the train for Dublin. In our carriage we had four soldiers to the three of us who were prisoners. The soldiers were fully armed and carried full kits. They were very young and all had very pronounced English accents. They were kindly, decent boys. They could not give us food and as we had been relieved of all property on arrival at the jail we had no money to purchase anything. They had cigarettes and were generous in sharing them with us on the journey.

We arrived in Amiens Street and the only noteworthy incident on arrival was that a man met us there and, seeking out Herbert Moore Pim, got permission from the officer in charge to hand over to Pim a heavy coat and a parcel containing a magnificent and beautifully 'frogged' dressing gown. That dressing gown was to prove a mark of distinction for Herbert during the ensuing months. With his beautifully-cultivated, Parnell-like beard, he was already someone to note and observe: with the addition of the dressing gown he was raised to the level of a mystery man in the eyes of the unsophisticated 'Tommies'. I have a distinct recollection of one of these tugging my sleeve and, pointing at Pim, saying: 'Say, matey, 'Os's the bloke with the beaver and the swell gown. Is he your bloody king, eh?'

We were formed into rank on the platform and started the long trek to Richmond barracks. Around Amiens Street and indeed through most of the city centre, many lined the footpaths to look us over. Most of them were quiet and sullen, but not a few of them were openly hostile and were not slow to express their views. We arrived in the barrack square and were 'stood at ease' by our military guards and left at 'ease' for several hours. The square was dotted all over with similar groups to our own, some of them smaller, but most of them much bigger than ours. It was late in the evening when, after much going to and fro by the officers, we were eventually marched into one of the big rooms of the barracks. There was neither food nor water and latrine service was limited to a couple of buckets on the landing which served our room and the room opposite. There was neither blanket nor mattress nor any other furnishing in the room so, as night fell, we just huddled together to try and keep warm. We got through the night somehow, shook ourselves and stood up to greet our first Sunday morning as guests of George V.

We were not long up when the door opened to admit several of our old acquaintances of the G Division who started a close scrutiny of all the men. They picked out one here and there and told him to stand aside. My old attendant H- [Detective Officer Daniel Hoey, Dublin Metropolitan Police, who was shot by the I.R.A. in 1920] I observed talking to Alec and then I saw him nodding in my direction. He came across to me, looked me over and asked me where I had gone after my arrival on the Saturday. I told him I hardly thought he needed to be told that. He did not pursue the matter, but merely told me to stand aside with the others. There were, I think, seven or eight of us and we were then transferred to another room, L.5, which was to be our bedroom, sitting-room and dining-room for most of the next month, while we were detained in Richmond barracks.

When we had got installed in L.5 we found quite an interesting collection of colleagues and quite a few of our Belfast colleagues. Cathal O'Shannon,[21] Alf Cotton[22] and Seán Neeson were there, and I was not long there when I spotted a little man whom I immediately recognised as one of those whom I had noticed at the gathering in Dr Seámus O'Kelly's on Holy Saturday night. Shortly afterwards he came across to me and asked me if he was right in thinking that he had seen me there and I confirmed that he was. This was my introduction to Paudeen O'Keeffe whom I was to know intimately for years afterwards and whom I am still glad to meet and whose vehement and picturesque analyses of things past, present and to come are always stimulating. Harry Boland,[23] with whom I was afterwards to be associated in America, was also there as were Luke Kennedy[24] and the ubiquitous Thomas Shine Cuffe[25] who alternated his singing of Dublin

21. Cathal O'Shannon (1889-1969): born Randalstown, County Antrim, member of I.R.B., founder-member of Irish Volunteers 1913, prominent member of Labour Party and Irish Trade Union Congress, founder-member of Socialist Party of Ireland, T.D. for Louth-Meath 1922-3, editor of *The Voice of Labour* and *The Watchword* 1930-32, member of Labour Court 1946-69.

22. Alf Cotton: born Belfast, civil servant in Tralee, member of Irish Volunteers 1913, interned in Frongoch following Easter Rising 1916, after the treaty resumed his civil service employment in Dublin and became a prominent member of the Gaelic League.

23. Harry Boland (1887-1922): born Dublin, member of Irish Republican Brotherhood 1904-21, secretary of Sinn Féin 1917, T.D. for Roscommon 1918-22, prominent anti-treatyite.

24. Luke Kennedy, born Dublin, member of Irish Volunteers 1913, interned in Frongoch following Easter Rising 1916.

25. Thomas Shine Cuffe, born Dublin, member of Irish Volunteers 1913, interned in Frongoch following Easter Rising 1916.

ballads with fierce arguments with his friend Paudeen O'Keeffe. Seán Milroy,[26] who was to be a close associate in other prisons, was also with us. Of course, all these acquaintanceships were to come later. On the Sunday morning we were somewhat exhausted. We were dirty and unwashed and we were, if not hungry, at least empty. It was ten or eleven o'clock in the morning and I realised that it was some twenty-six hours since I had tried without success to take the 'skilly' that had been served as breakfast to us in the Crumlin Road jail, and that we had not even had a drink of water since we left that institution. Very soon we were making demands to our young sentries and later to one of the officers who came in to look us over. After another hour or two we were each given a couple of ship's biscuits, and a small tin of bullybeef was allotted to every two of us. The fare was scanty enough, but it served for the time. I realise that in these days, when we have become aware of all the horrors, including near starvation, which have been inflicted on unfortunate prisoners in Belsen, Dachau and in the horror camps of Russia and Korea, the treatment we received will read like luxury entertainment.

However, in 1916 we had yet to learn of the modern methods of treatment of prisoners, and anyhow the experience was new to us and therein, no doubt, lay its punishment. The bullybeef and hardtack rations continued until the British premier, Henry Herbert Asquith, visited the barracks, when the ration was improved by bread and margarine and a stew that was edible.

When we got together in L.5 we decided that a certain measure of order and discipline would be desirable and, accordingly, we elected a commandant who would have authority to direct our very limited activities and serve as our spokesman to the military authorities. We selected Harry Boland and no better selection could have been made. Harry was gay and happy and full of life and vitality. He was good-humoured and kindly and at the same time was a rock of sense and shrewdness. We did not get many days to enjoy Harry's company for during the following week he was taken off for his court-martial and was given five years penal servitude.

During our first days in Richmond Barracks the courts-martial and the executions continued. There were all sorts of rumours and not infrequently we got information from some of the young soldiers who provided the day and night guard over us. It was thus we learned of Harry's sentence, but what completely depressed us was the news of the execution of Seán

26. Seán Milroy (1877-1946): born Maryport, Cumberland, journalist, close friend and associate of Arthur Griffith, helped to establish Irish Self-Determination League of Great Britain, M.P. for Fermanagh-Tyrone 1921, T.D. for Cavan 1921-24, senator 1928-36.

MacDermott[27] and James Connolly. Poor Seán, I thought, but then corrected myself for I immediately thought how Seán would resent the idea of commiseration. He too had fulfilled his destiny, but not perhaps with that calm philosophical intensity that marked Pearse but with the gay, joyous spirit of a cavalier that covered the intense burning hatred of all the evil he saw in the British occupation of his beloved country. The gay spirit, with the infectious laughter and wit that where his, had been extinguished but Seán, I felt sure, went to his death with the serene conviction that the work of his life was crowned by his sacrifice. It was later that we learned how Connolly had died. Wounded and suffering much pain, he had been propped up in position to receive the death-dealing volley. He had promised to pray 'for all brave men' when he was asked by one of the firing squad to pray for him. Quiet and reserved, so that those who did not know him might have well thought him taciturn or even grim, Connolly's spirit and heart were ever in unison with the under-privileged and had no room for the time-server or opportunist.

Recently I was talking to an old friend, a saintly priest who had been a much-loved classmate of mine when we were young boys at St Malachy's College. The talk came round about 1916 and some of the men of that time. He told me that he had had the privilege of giving their first Holy Communion to both Mrs James Connolly and to Mrs Joseph Plunkett. He told me that when Mrs Connolly visited James for the last time before his execution she told him that she intended to become a Catholic, and that at this James smiled and told her that that made him supremely happy, that in fact it was the one thing needed to make him so. I think it is desirable to put this on record, if only to dispel some of the ill-informed gossip that one has occasionally heard about him.

The execution of Connolly and MacDermott were the last of the sixteen that Maxwell[28] had carried out, but day by day men were being sentenced to long terms of penal servitude ranging from three years to life-imprisonment.

27. Seán MacDermott (1884-1916): born County Leitrim, member of I.R.B. 1906, its full-time organiser 1908, co-founder and editor of *Irish Feedom* 1910, member of Military Council of Irish Volunteers 1916, and member of Provisional government of Irish Republic declared on Easter Monday 1916.

28. General Sir John Grenfell Maxwell (1859-1929): born Liverpool, was appointed commander-in-chief of British forces in Ireland in April 1916 to deal with the Easter Rising, after its collapse he governed Ireland through the British army and Royal Irish Constabulary for a few months under a proclamation of martial law.

After Harry Boland had been taken from us and sentenced to five years, my room mates in L.5 elected me as commandant. My duties were indeed light and save for a couple of incidents were purely nominal. The men were good-humoured and our programme was easily defined. One of the chief difficulties was to keep ourselves clean and free from vermin. It was not easy and it was not always successful. We were spending twenty-four hours of the day within the four walls of the room save for relief parties to the latrines which were always under military escort. Three blankets were allocated to each pair of prisoners, one as a ground sheet and two as our blankets. We were getting no vegetables, no open-air exercise and, although we were after the first ten days or so allowed reading matter and cigarettes from our friends outside, it was at least a couple of weeks before we were taken out in small groups to get a bath. We slept head to the wall, feet facing the centre with our shoes wrapped in our coats serving as pillows.

A few nights after I had taken over we were aroused by a commotion on the landing. I got up to find out the cause and just then two or three soldiers arrived with a new prisoner. They almost literally hurled him into the room, banged the door and left him to us. He was a big, tall man and a place was found along the wall for him. He was violently offensive and damned and condemned the whole lot of us. It was late at night and, despite his vehement and lurid language, we took no notice and eventually he subsided into silence. The next morning he opened up more or less in similar terms and clearly expressed his condemnation of the Rising and everybody connected with it. The situation was unpleasant. Until his arrival we were a reasonable collection of comrades. We were not comfortable nor by any means happy, but we were cheerful and friendly as circumstances permitted, and the banter, and the gag, the story and the song and good humour carried us through. Seeing that his attitude to his roommates showed no sign of amendment, I proposed to the boys that as our new inmate had no disposition to have anything to do with us and in fact entirely disapproved of us that his wishes were to be respected and no one was to have any communication with him. This was unanimously approved.

I think he was very sorry for himself in a day or two and, although some of the boys would answer a direct question if he asked one, the big man was left severely alone. A couple of weeks later he was called out for court-martial and acquitted.

We had another interesting gentleman with us who caused us a good deal of concern not indeed due to his hostility nor his unfriendliness, but to his continuous recording. He had got some visiting friends to bring him a supply of writing pads and pen and ink and he wrote continuously. I should perhaps explain that, at the time I speak of, we were being allowed to get in parcels from visitors who were allowed to meet us and talk to us through a high wire fence. Our friend's constant writing began to worry some of us particularly when it transpired that he was putting on the record all his activities before and during Easter Week. Now at this time men were still being taken out for courts-martial and penal servitude sentences were being given daily. We knew that at any time we were liable to search and that every prisoner's parcel was subject to examination. It certainly seemed a most inopportune time and the least appropriate place in which to record one's experiences, but what concerned most of us was that the scrivener might easily implicate or involve some of his former associates. A few of us discussed the problem quietly with the result that I had to put an entire ban on further writing about the Rising or his activities and arrange for the immediate disposal of his already considerable sheaf of records. It was with considerable reluctance that he eventually agreed. We met later on in Reading where again he was something of a problem and we met occasionally for years afterwards. On all such occasions I had the feeling that he never forgave me for arresting his literary and historical contributions to the military records of the period.

Right from the beginning large batches of men were being deported daily from Richmond barracks, but none were taken from our room for the first couple of weeks.

In a small ante-room on our landing Count Plunkett[29] was accommodated. Except that he had privacy and perhaps a stretcher to sleep on he had no concessions other than the rest of us. I managed to have a couple of talks with him, thanks to the indulgence of the soldier on guard. It was sad to see the dignified old gentleman there, but there was no complaint. He accepted his lot quite cheerfully and philosophically and with complete resignation. He was released early, his place and room to be occupied by Alderman Tom Kelly. Poor Tom, whom everybody loved and respected, suffered untold agonies not indeed at the hands of the enemy, but due to

29. George Noble Count Plunkett (1851-1948): born Dublin, founder and editor of *Hibernia* director of the National Museum 1907-16, vice-president of Royal Irish Academy 1908-9, 1911-14, president of Royal Society of Antiquaries of Ireland, became a political figure after 1916 Rising in which his son was executed, independent abstentionist M.P. for North Roscommon 1917-22, minister of foreign affairs 1919-21, minister of fine arts 1921-2, opposed the treaty, Sinn Féin absentionist T.D. for County Roscommon 1922-7.

internal digestive trouble. This left him quiet and morose, but always infinitely patient.

Two weeks after my arrival at Richmond barracks my wife managed to get permission for a visit. Arrangements for it had of course to be negotiated from Belfast and this meant delay. However, eventually she was able to get the necessary permission and arrived with all sorts of comforts in the way of clothing, books and delicacies. It was wonderful to see her again and to hear all the news of the folk at home. Needless to say her reports were all cheerful, everything was going fine, including the business, and all our friends were in good form and only too anxious to be helpful. I accepted all her assurances or pretended to do so for I knew then, as I have known all my life since, that, however dark the horizon, Róisín would always pick out the silver lining for you and assure you that 'the Lord will take care of us whatever happens'.

She did bring one message which thrilled me. She told me that the day after my arrest our dear old friend Simeon O'Leary[30] had called at the shop and, taking her into the office, had written out a cheque made payable to her and left the amount to be filled in. 'Now Róisín', he said, 'you can fill that in for any amount up to two thousand'. Róisín was dumbfounded and told him that she could not possibly take any money on loan and certainly not such an amount. She assured him that we were all right at the bank and promised that, if she really did need any cash, she would go to him immediately. 'Well listen daughter', he said in his kindly fatherly way, 'this business has got to be kept going until Joe is back home and I mean to see that it is, so the money is there for you'. She did not borrow from Simeon and we and the business survived successfully, but to both of us it was just the same as if we had taken it. Simeon was not a particularly wealthy man in the accepted sense. He had a prosperous business which was going well, but he had a large young family and many commitments and a 'bite' of two thousand at the time would definitely have been felt. Simeon had a heart of gold and an open hand for anyone in trouble. He died at the age of ninety loved by all who knew him and I feel sure welcomed home by many whom he had helped by his kindly counsel and his open-handed generosity.

It was lonely after Róisín's departure, but I was cheered by all her news and particularly by the report of Simeon's offer and goodness. I did not get long to brood, however, for soon after I returned to the room I saw little

30. Simeon O'Leary (1863-1953): born Belfast, acted as election agent for Charles Stewart Parnell, journalist and agent for Reuter's in Belfast, founder-member of Ulster Arts Club 1907, proprietor of John McGuinness & Co., hide and skin merchants.

Paudeen stamping up and down fiercely from one end of the room to the other and muttering incomprehensible 'gibberish' to himself. It sounded like 'God o' God these stupid weemin!' I ventured to ask him what was getting in his hair and he turned briskly on me and fixed me with that implacable stare that is still characteristic of him. 'Weemin', said Paudeen, 'are the devil. My missus has just been up at the fence. She told me that they were at the house and asking her about my movements at Easter. Do you know what she said to them? "Why, God bless you, I did not see him since Holy Thursday night", God o' God'. And he resumed his stamping up and down the room. I could hardly refrain from laughing at the quaint recital, though I realised that Paudeen was, like the rest of us, expecting the call out for court-martial at any time and his wife's contribution to the evidence might be serious. However, a short time afterwards Paudeen was deported to be interned in some jail in England.

The days dragged on, deportations were taking place every day and gradually our numbers dwindled. Then came a day when L.5 was cleared altogether. Seán Milroy, my brother Alec and myself and the prisoner whom we had 'put in Coventry' were transferred to the room across the landing and all the others were dispatched for internment and were marched off the barrack square to the steamer.

In the room to which we had been transferred there were only four prisoners and here I met for the first time Con Collins[31] and Austin Stack.[32] Collins and Stack were awaiting court-martial in connection with the attempted landing of arms near Tralee and the arrival of Casement. It seemed ominous to have been left over with them particularly as Richmond barracks was now entirely cleared of all prisoners save our little group and our friend Alderman Tom Kelly, who still occupied the single room on the landing. It did look like being reserved for trial, but somehow we had become attuned to the acceptance of whatever came next without fretting too much about it. To me it was really a pleasant variant from the previous weeks. I found Con Collins a pleasant companion, but I have often thanked God for the opportunity I had of meeting, knowing and becoming a close friend of Austin Stack. I am anything but a sentimentalist and my reputation is, I fear, that of a rather acidulous and cynical realist,

31. Cornelius Collins: born Limerick, post-office official, member of Irish Volunteers 1913, arrested at Tralee, Easter 1916, opposed the treaty, T.D. for West Limerick.

32. Austin Stack (1880-1929): born Tralee, founder-member of Irish Volunteers in County Kerry, leader of a number of prison hunger-strikes, secretary of Sinn Féin, returned as M.P. for West Kerry 1918, minister for home affairs 1921-2, opposed the treaty, returned as Sinn Féin T.D. for Kerry and West Limerick in 1923.

but I have met very few men in a somewhat long life who struck the same chord of appeal as did Austin. It was not that he was either exceptionally clever or brilliant or had any special accomplishments in the way of learning or culture. Granted that he was highly intelligent, but that was in no way exceptional among our contemporaries. No, there was something about Stack which I can only attempt to define by saying that he had an aura of sheer goodness which he seemed to share generously with those in his company. We became fast friends then and, despite many differences of opinion in later years, remained so until his untimely death, hastened by all he had endured in various hunger-strikes, took one of Ireland's best and most loveable souls to the peace and reward which he had so well earned.

We were, perhaps, less than a week in our new location when most of us were told to pack up and get ready to leave. Leaving behind us Collins and Stack, the rest of us formed a small party and were marched off to the North Wall and taken aboard the steamer for Holyhead. We were brought down to the lower regions of the ship where, with our military guards, we sat or lay on the floor. We entrained at Holyhead, changed trains at Chester and arrived at Knutsford. In the prison in Knutsford we found ourselves in the midst of hundreds of our fellow deportees. The regime had been well established long before we had arrived. There were two 'breaks' of almost two hours each, one in the forenoon from about ten to twelve o'clock and one in the afternoon from about two o'clock to four. For these periods we were turned out of our cells to enjoy the fresh air and exercise in the prison yard. In the forenoon we had a period of strenuous physical drill, at which a sergeant-major with an amazingly loud voice bellowed his orders so that all in the compound could hear. Apart from these two intermissions for exercise, the remaining hours were spent in the cells. The prison was entirely under military control, the warders all being soldiers, who had returned from the European war front, or reservists and pensioners who had been called up, but were beyond the active service age. My particular custodian was the typical old soldier, good-natured enough in a rough and ready way and eager to exchange talk and ideas when opportunity offered. I 'weighed him up' at the first opportunity and found that he was not averse to earn a honest shilling or two from posting a letter or ordering in a few parcels from the village. Róisín had brought me some cash on her visit which I had managed to retain and it proved useful. It was only for a day or two, however, for on our second or third day in Knutsford I was surprised when two or three soldiers came into my cell and ordered me to gather up my gear and accompany them. I asked them what was the next move and where I was going, but they gave me no information. I was marched along various halls and across to another wing, shown into a cell, locked in and left there to try and figure out what the change portended. It was after breakfast the following morning when, on being brought out to exercise, I saw that there were only eight of us in the wing to which I had been transferred. There was no opportunity to learn the reasons for our transfer to the new location for we were marched round and round the ring so many paces apart and we were 'covered' by four armed guards who twirled their automatics menacingly as we marched round the circle. It was an unpleasant change to have to preserve silence all the time and to do the circle as a forced, exercise march. Moreover, our exercise time was curtailed. We were not released from our cells until all the other prisoners were out in the big compound and we had to be brought in and securely locked up before the others were marched back to their cells. Nothing seemed settled for long. Within a week three of our group were moved again and, we learned later, had been sent off to an internment camp called Frongoch in North Wales. The five of us who were left were: Seán Milroy who had been with me all through, Dr Ned Dundon[33] who had been arrested a few hours after his marriage on Easter Monday, Pierce McCan[34] who was afterwards to die in Gloucester Jail where he had been held after his arrest in the 'round up' which followed the faked German Plot, Frank Healy[35] a barrister from Cobh, and myself. After the others had gone, the five of us continued our daily 'grind' and then for no apparent reason the strict regime was relaxed. We were still held in until the others were all out at exercise and were locked up safely before they returned, but we were allowed to mix together, to talk freely and to entertain ourselves as we liked while in the exercise yard. It was a small yard and not particularly inspiring. At one side there was the execution chamber and along the opposite wall were the graves of those unfortunates who had paid the supreme penalty.

It is, I think, worth noting that, as I remember these graves, each one was marked by a small stone or it could have been a small cement block

33. Dr Edward Dundon: born Carlow, arrested in Listowel on his honeymoon and interned in Frongoch 1916.

34. Pierce McCan (1882-1919): born Prospect Lodge, New Ross, County Wexford, farmed at Dualla, Cashel, County Tipperary, president of Tipperary Sinn Féin Executive 1906, member of Gaelic League 1909, member of Irish Volunteers, 1914, interned after Easter Rising 1916, imprisoned in Gloucester jail after 'German Plot', May 1918-March 1919, returned as Sinn Féin M.P. for East Tipperary, December 1918, victim of flu epidemic 1919, his fiancé, Josephine Aherne, was later Mrs James MacNeill.

35. Francis T. Healy: born Cóbh, Sinn Féin member of Cork County Council, delegate to Sinn Féin Convention 1914.

and on this were inscribed the initials and a date clearly indicating that each grave was separate and could be easily identified as the resting place of the person executed and the date of his execution. I mention this specially because, amongst many reasons which have been quoted for refusing to hand over the remains of our old friend Roger Casement, one was that it was impossible to locate his grave in Pentonville. It seems unlikely that, despite their intense hatred of Roger, the British authorities changed their regulations and that he was not even allowed the simple initials and date that have been granted to those who are buried in the quiet corner of Knutsford prison.[36] It may be that his executioners too well remember the words spoken by Padraic Pearse in his oration at Rossa's funeral: 'The fools . . . they have left us our Fenian dead'.

We managed to get a handball, and the gable-end of the execution chamber served to provide us with many a strenuous game. Our guards were reduced to two, one of whom was hard-boiled but really kindly old war-horse called Badland. How or why he or anyone else should have retained such a name often intrigued me, but such trifles did not worry him. Badland was loquacious and had a limited but picturesque vocabulary, most of it unprintable. Everyone whom he did not like was a 'bloddy prognosticator', though why I never found out. The other permanent guard was an elderly Cockney with the name of Sheehan. He was a hand-loom silk-weaver and his home, he told me, was in Spitalfields. I tried to trace him back to Weaver's Square in Dublin, but Sheehan had no knowledge of any roots outside of Spitalfields. Their duties were light. They unlocked the cell doors, let us out, brought us back in and locked the cells again.

After the first week or so we were allowed visitors and here let me pay tribute to the kindness and generosity of the Irish girls in Manchester who travelled down to Knutsford several times a week. They provided us with the only cheerful interludes in a rather dreary existence. They were stimulating in the news they brought of events at home and were full of cheerful good nature. They brought us all and more than all we needed in the way of cigarettes, fruit and other delicacies. I would have to live to be a very old man indeed before I could forget to bless them and particularly the two sisters Maura and Teresa McGeehin from County Donegal and Rose Killian from County Down who were particularly attentive to us.

Time dragged heavily indeed, for we spent at least twenty-one hours out of the twenty-four locked in our cells, but I realised that we had much to

36. In 1965 the British Labour government under Harold Wilson gave permission for the return of Casement's remains to Ireland and he was re-interred in Glasnevin cemetery, Dublin.

be thankful for, in comparison to the men who had been sentenced. We had our supplies from our friends at home and from the great girls who came down from Manchester. We had cigarettes and reading matter and could get through the long evenings. Smoking was prohibited, but after things showed signs of being relaxed in regard to the guards we took our chance, started to smoke and were not stopped from doing so.

Knutsford is the village made famous by Mrs Gaskell in her early Victorian classic published as *Cranford*. It was our fate to be brought back to our cells early on Sunday afternoons. Our after-dinner exercise was curtailed and we were locked in about half-past three, immediately after which our mug of tea was served. The weather was fine and at times oppressively warm and it was a long stretch to look forward to the interval between half-past three in the afternoon and the warder's knock on Monday morning. Just then the bells would start ringing. There were dull sombre tolls, there were gay trills and runs on joybells, and there were various in-between contributions. In the old days in Belfast I liked the sound of the bells. They seemed to add a charm and to emphasise the contrasting peace and quiet of a pleasant Sunday morning, but in Knutsford they became an intolerable irritation.

The spending of Sunday afternoon became for me a study in the art of time killing. With a book and my mug of tea and with some of the delicacies brought in by our good friends from Manchester, I was able to make the meal at the little table last for the most of an hour. A cigarette and then an hour's exercise pacing the cell. Then Rosary and night prayers and then another cigarette and I would continue reading until the light failed. This latter did not take place until about ten o'clock for it was the month of June.

Despite all, we were a reasonably happy family. Dundon was full of youthful vitality, but, like the rest of us, had his bad periods of depression when he swung to the other extreme.

Milroy had a great sense of quiet humour, somewhat sardonic perhaps, but quick and apt in his dry commentaries on the trifling events that made our day.

Pierce McCan was intensely religious and kept us all up to the mark in regard to our prayers and devotions. I do not mean that he was a 'craw-thumper' or Puritan, but he had a sound, sane Catholic outlook. He would take part in such games, arguments and fun as we tried for ourselves, but back of it all was the sound moral courage that made McCan what he was, a great spiritual influence wherever he went.

Pierce received quite a lot of letters from Ireland and many of these were from friends who were priests and nuns in various convents and retreat houses. Inevitably they contained a certain number of religious leaflets. Pierce occasionally passed an odd one or two of them over to us to comfort our hours of loneliness in our cells.

Coming out of our cells one morning I was amazed to see Dundon going straight over to Pierce and shaking his fist at him, he almost shouted: 'Well blast you McCan, you and your tracts'. I stepped up and said: 'What's the matter Doc?' 'Matter', said he, 'That so and so eejit . . . He gave me one of his leaflets just as I was going in to my cell for the whole night and look at the first thing I read: "I will take thy wife from thee and give her to thine enemy".' Poor Pierce was distressed, although the rest of us made a joke of it. It certainly was not the perfect message of spiritual comfort to the doctor who, as I have said, was whipped off to jail some two hours after he had been married.

Our other colleague Frank Healy of Cóbh, or as it was then called, Queenstown, was somewhat older than the rest of us. He was a barrister, but I do not think he bothered to practise much. He was comfortably off and prison life weighed heavily on him. He was kindly and a good companion, but brooded a great deal despite all our efforts to shake him out of his moods. I do not know in how far he was actively concerned with the Volunteers, but I know he was a great friend of Arthur Griffith and that he had intimate family ties with some of our most influential friends in the United States. It was to this latter fact, I think, that he owed his arrest and his later segregation with our small group. Before we were transferred from Knutsford, Frank Healy was released.

During the weeks we were detained in Knutsford groups were being transferred almost daily to the Camp at Frongoch until eventually all the prisoners save the four of us, Milroy, McCan, Dundon and myself, were all that remained. We got word of these movements from our guards, but they had no information as to what was intended regarding ourselves. We were not forgotten, for the faithful lady visitors continued to come and keep us supplied with all that we needed and often more than we could use.

The weather was hot and the life enervating physically and mentally. We all had letters from home, but as the censorship was strict our friends there could not give us much other than family news. My wife's letters were always bright and cheerful and full of encouragement, but I realised that, whatever the situation was, her letters would be like that.

One afternoon, when locking us up in our cells, Badland whispered to us that he thought we were likely to be sent off the next day. He did not know our destination, but he believed the move out was planned. The uncertainty was disquieting, at least I found it so. If we were being released that would be splendid, but if it meant going to camp or to another prison then I felt I would prefer to put in the remainder of my time where I was. We had got into a routine and had adjusted ourselves to conditions and to one another, and, unless we were being freed to go home, the thought of readjustment and getting used to new conditions did not appeal to me.

Our wishes and views were not asked, of course, but Badland was a good 'prognosticator' for the following day we were told to pack up and get ready for the road.

We were marched off to the station and must have presented a weird picture to the quiet respectable citizens of Knutsford. We had not had an opportunity to shave since we left Richmond and must have looked like a quartet of pirates as we stood on the platform encircled by our armed guards. Soon we were aboard the train bound for an unknown destination. When the train stopped at Reading we were told to get out and were then escorted to the prison and handed over to the deputy governor. I immediately thought of Oscar Wilde[37] and his 'Ballad of Reading Gaol' wherein he tells us:

> We tore the tarry ropes to shreds / With blunt and bleeding nails, / We rubbed the doors and scrubbed the floors / And cleaned the shining rails. / And, rank by rank, / We soaped the plank and clattered with the pails.

So this was Reading Goal and our new 'home'.

The deputy governor was an elderly quiet person, who told the four of us that the governor was an extremely reasonable man and if we played fair with him we would find him equally fair with us. This gave me an immediate inspiration, and I promptly told the deputy that there were a few things which, if permitted, would go a long way to make things run smoothly. I suggested that we should have our cell doors open all day and be allowed to associate together during the day and that we should be permitted to eat together at a table in the corridor. To my surprise he told us that he would put the proposals to the governor. He then showed us our cells. He explained that we were in what had been normally the female wing of the prison and showed us two double cells which were, he said 'maternity wards'. I suggested that he should allot the two 'wards' to the

37. Oscar Fingal O'Flahertie Wills Wilde (1854-1900): born Dublin, poet and playwright, tried on charges of sodomy, convicted and imprisoned 1895-97, his 'Ballad of Reading Gaol' appeared anonymously 1898.

four of us. He smiled as he informed us that such could not be permitted, but that, if we chose, three of us could have one of the cells and the other 'gentleman' could have the other one and share it with a couple of later arrivals. He then told us that others were expected and we agreed to this course. At the time, I was at a loss to understand the deputy's decision 'Three or one—but not two'! It dawned on me later!

Soon after the governor himself came long. He was a fine handsome fellow, a retired doctor who had taken up duty as his contribution to the war service. He was a Welshman and a genial one at that. We were, it would seem, the first bunch of 'rebels' that he had encountered. He looked the four of us over critically and with a rather quizzical smile on his face. 'Well, you look a fairly decent bunch, not what I expected', he said and then, whipping round to Seán Milroy, added: 'Except you, now you look the real thing'. Poor Seán at the time certainly looked anything but a Beau Brummel. We all had four or five weeks' growth of beard and we all needed haircuts, but Dundon was bald and McCan and I were dark and our hair and beards were somewhat smoothed out. Seán, on the other hand, was becoming very thin on top and was prematurely grey. His beard was a mass of grey bristles framing his highly complexioned face and looked as stiff as the stubble in a well cropped field. Later Milroy gurgled to me as we went to our cells: 'So he knew me as the real thing!'

The governor discussed our proposals with us and readily agreed to the cell doors being left open from breakfast time until bed time and to the provision of tables and forms so that we could eat together in the hallway which divided the tiers of cells. Later he provided a gas ring in the hall so that we could boil a kettle to make supper for ourselves.

We had barely completed these arrangements when a new batch of prisoners arrived and from then until late in the evening these arrivals continued. They came in twos and threes and fours with a quite sizeable bunch that was transferred from Frongoch. I do not know that I can entirely remember all those who eventually made up the Reading group but amongst them in addition to the four of us were: Terence MacSwiney[38]

38. Terence MacSwiney (1879-1920): born Cork, a teacher, co-founded Cork Irish Volunteers 1913, returned to First Dáil for West Cork 1919, lord mayor of Cork, March 1920, after his arrest in August commenced a hunger-strike and died seventy-four days later after capturing international attention for his cause.

1. Postcard sent by Seán Milroy from Reading jail to Joseph Connolly in September 1916, a few months after Connolly's release. Block L5 referred to the room in Richmond barracks where, with others, they had been lodged for three weeks. The message on the postcard read: 'Will you no come back again?'

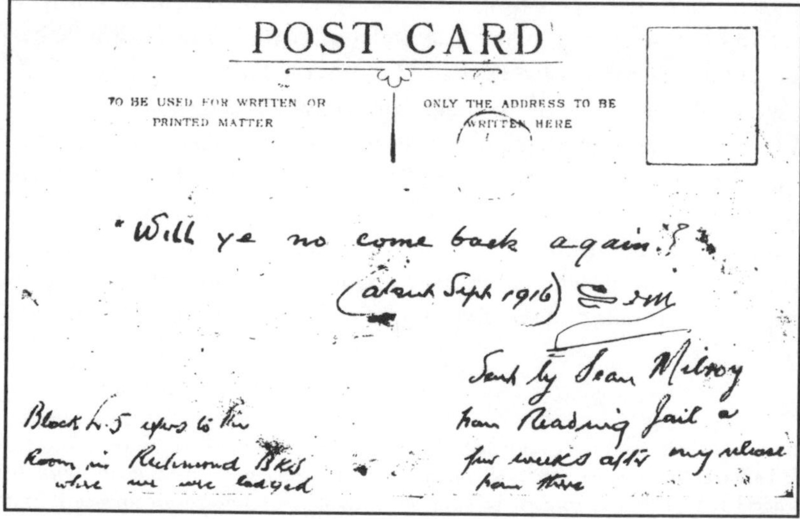

POST CARD

TO BE USED FOR WRITTEN OR PRINTED MATTER

ONLY THE ADDRESS TO BE WRITTEN HERE

"Will ye no come back again"?
(about Sept 1916) SM

Sent by Sean Milroy
from Reading Jail a
few weeks after my release
from there

Block L.5 refers to the
Room in Richmond BKS
where we were lodged

and Thomas MacCurtain[39] from Cork; Arthur Griffith, Seán T. O'Kelly,[40] Darrel Figgis,[41] Michael Brennan,[42] Eamon O'Dwyer, Conor Deere, Joe MacBride,[43] Francis de Búrca, P. T. Daly,[44] William O'Brien,[45] Cathal O'Shannon, Ernest Blythe,[46] Peadar de Loughrey, Peadar

39. Thomas MacCurtain (1884-1920): born Ballyknockane, County Cork, Gaelic League teacher in Limerick, Tipperary and East Cork, member of I.R.B. 1907, member of Cork Executive Committee of Sinn Féin 1909-11, brigade commandant of Irish Volunteers 1913, O.C. Cork brigade, I.R.A. 1919-20, lord mayor of Cork 30 January 1920, assassinated in his home by members of R.I.C. 20 March 1920.

40. Séan T. O'Kelly (1883-1966): born Dublin, founder member of Sinn Féin and Irish Volunteers, returned in 1919 for First Dáil, where he became Ceann Comhairle, opposed the treaty, founder member of Fianna Fáil, minister for local government and public health 1932-9, minister for finance 1939-45, president of Ireland, 1945-59.

41. Darrell Figgis (1892-1925): born Dublin, secretary of Sinn Féin 1917, returned for First Dáil for County Dublin 1919, Secretary of Commission of Inquiry into the Resources and Industries of Ireland 1920-21, acting-chairman of committee which drafted 1922 Constitution, committed suicide.

42. Michael Brennan: born Meelick, County Clare, member of I.R.B. and Irish Volunteers 1913, interned in Frongoch and Reading jail following Easter Rising 1916, commandant East Clare brigade, I.R.A. 1919-21, general in Free State army 1922-23, chief of staff, National army.

43. Joseph MacBride: born Westport, County Mayo, brother of Major John MacBride, member of Irish Volunteers 1913, interned in Frongoch after Easter Rising 1916, T.D. for Mayo.

44. P. T. Daly (1870-1943): born Dublin, member of Sinn Féin 1906, member of I.R.B. from which he was expelled in 1910 when secretary of its supreme council for alleged misappropriation of funds, secretary, Irish Trade Union Congress 1910-18, member of Irish Citizen Army 1914, interned after Easter Rising 1916, involved in life-long feud with William O'Brien as they vied for elective offices in Irish Transport and General Workers Union and later the Dublin Trades Council, allied himself to the Larkins in the feud that split the Irish labour movement.

45. William O'Brien (1881-1968): born Ballygurteen, Clonakilty, County Cork, member of Irish Socialist Republican Party 1898, a tailor by trade, chairman of the Amalgamated Society of Tailors 1904, co-founder of Irish Transport and General Workers Union 1909, secretary of Lock-Out committee 1913, through his involvement with James Connolly and the Irish Citizen Army interned 1916, general secretary of Labour Party 1919, supported I.R.A. in Anglo-Irish war and interned 1920, Labour T.D. for Dublin South 1922-3, Tipperary 1927 and 1932-8, general secretary of Irish Transport and General Workers Union 1923-46, financial secretary to Labour Party, 1931-9, chairman of its Administrative Council 1939-41, president of Irish Trade Union Congress 1914, 1918, 1925, 1941.

46. Ernest Blythe (1889-1975): born Lisburn, County Antrim, clerk in department of agriculture, joined Gaelic League, Irish Volunteers and I.R.B., member of Sinn Féin executive 1917, returned for County Monaghan in First Dáil, minister for trade and commerce 1919-22, minister for local government in Provisional government of Irish Free State 1922, minister for local government and public health 1922-3, minister for finance 1923-32, vice-president of Executive Council of Irish Free State 1927-32, senator 1933-6, founder of *An Gúm*, director of Abbey Theatre 1939-67.

O'Hourihan, an O'Kelly from London and a Brennan from Roscommon.[47]

Eventually there were some thirty of us gathered together, and we soon settled down to something of a community life. We soon discovered that in other wings of the prison there was quite a crowd of internees. Many of these were Germans who were probably working in Britain when war broke out, but there was at least one Belgian. One day a couple of men came to do some repairs to the plumbing in our wing. We took little notice of them until suddenly one of them emerged from one of the toilets shouting and swearing in broken English and French. I happened to be talking to Griffith as he came along and we inquired the cause of his excitement. His explanation was convincing: 'Someone he pulled the chain, damn fool'. Griffith asked him how he came to be locked up. He was still somewhat excited and cross and gesticulating wildly with his hands explained: 'What me . . . I Belgian, I marry a German . . . I did not know the war was going to be big war'. We did not learn any more from him for the warder who had charge of him came along.

The German internees had a large and pleasant exercise ground bordered with shrubs and flowers. They also had a canteen in which they could purchase various comforts and supplies. We were allowed to visit the canteen for half an hour on two days a week to make purchases. During these short visits the other internees were, of course, rightly excluded.

We did all our own 'fatigues'. Each person was responsible for his own cell but the general clearing up, serving of meals and so on were by a group of four 'orderlies' appointed for the day. Each of us took our turn as one of the four, so that we each had a day in the week on service duty. On the whole we were an agreeable group, but we had a couple of men who were suffering severe depression and who caused us some anxiety. Reading jail adjoins Huntly and Palmers biscuit factory; the weather in July was hot and when to this was added the heat from the biscuit factory and the sweetish smell and taste that seemed to permeate every breath of air our general apathy can be easily understood. We had a big 'blow-up' when, with improvised drums and flags, we had our Twelfth of July demonstration and toasted the memory of the prince of Orange. Speeches were made and ballads were sung, but I doubt if all of these would have had the approval of some of our loyal Orange friends in Belfast.

We had one major diversion to interrupt our spell in Reading and that was when we were all brought up to London and conveyed to Wormwood

47. Brennan from Roscommon, Francis de Búrca, Peadar de Loughrey, Conor Deere and Eamon O'Dwyer from South Tipperary and O'Kelly from London were transferred to Reading jail at the beginning of August 1916 from Frongoch and elsewhere.

Scrubs convict prison. Here we were brought in one by one before the Sankey[48] Commission. It was the Board of Appeal against internment, but all and sundry were brought before it whether they had appealed or not. I was brought into the room in my turn. A genial looking gentleman sat in the centre of a small group at a long table and was, I presume, Justice Sankey. His questions were few and my answers brief. I was Joseph Connolly and I resided at 38 Divis Drive, Belfast. Where was I in Easter Week? At home in Belfast. Yes, I had been in Dublin to see friends. I returned home on Easter Sunday. No questions about Drogheda or whom I had seen in Dublin. This surprised me, as I expected to be questioned on both matters and that I would have to decline to answer. I concluded afterwards that the Commission had abandoned any attempt to get informative replies to any questions and that the interview was the barest formality. In any case this constituted my examination and in a very few minutes I was ushered out to make way for the next examinee. We from Reading were fortunate as we were through in time to be brought back to our 'home goal' that evening and had not to spend the night in the 'Scrubs'. The lawn in front of Wormwood Scrubs was like a picture garden, but this to me only accentuated the depressing and gloomy atmosphere of the interior halls, in which I saw a few weird and sinister looking convicts moving around at work under their warders. We did not of course see much of Wormwood Scrubs, but the little we did see was not in harmony with the front garden and I for one was glad that we were brought back to Reading.

We had been in Reading for about four weeks when one day seven of us were called in to the governor's office and told to be ready to leave without delay. We were given travel vouchers to our home towns and we were so rushed and hustled by the warders that we had barely time to gather our few belongings and say goodbye to our colleagues whom we were leaving behind us. This was doubtless deliberate policy so that we would have no opportunity of carrying out special messages or concocting any mischief. However that may be, our farewells were hurriedly rushed and we were out of the building almost before we realised it. It was wonderful to get again that sense of freedom, but quite frankly much of the joy was lost when one realised that we were leaving behind more than twenty of our comrades. Almost immediately after we reached the platform the train steamed in, the warders at a respectful distance saw that we were all

48. John Sankey, Viscount Sankey (1866-1948): born Moreton-in-Marsh, barrister 1892, judge 1914, chairman of commission of inquiry into coal industry 1919, lord chancellor 1929, viscount 1932, described as 'the kindliest of men and very interested in matters religious and ecclesiastical'.

aboard and off to Holyhead and Ireland. The journey was without incident. Pim and I were the only two going North and having said goodbye to our fellow-travellers we were just in time to catch the Belfast train at Amiens Street. At Belfast Róisín and a few of my friends met me and we taxied home to Divis Drive. I was free and I was home. I leave it at that for there is all the meaning in the world in the two facts. There was only the constant sting in the thought not only of those I had left behind in Reading but the big crowd that still remained in Frongoch and, above all, the penal servitude men who had received sentences running from three years to life imprisonment. There could be little joy or peace of mind while any of them remained behind the bars or the barbed wire. Despite all, however, I was home and that meant that I was with Róisín and my family and friends. The house looked good, the garden was small but lovely, the Falls Park which bordered our home was at its best and towering behind it was my beloved black mountain stretching out to the far slopes of the real Divis behind it. Yes, life was good on that August morning!

For the first few days after my return from Reading, I felt somewhat bewildered and distrait but I quickly adjusted myself. There was no alternative, for I realised the urgency of getting down to the problems that awaited me in the business on which I depended for my home and living, and the responsibilities I had to my creditors and my handful of workers.

I might spare the reader any reference to this phase of my experiences, but there were several incidents which shed a reflection on conditions and outlook in the Belfast of that time.

I have already explained that I had started business on my own account in April 1915 and trade had been satisfactory and much more successful than I could have dared to hope. It was at the end of 1915 that my bank manager, who was controlling one of the most important central branches of the Belfast bank, asked me to come in to see him. When I did so, he expressed his satisfaction at the way business seemed to be going with me and told me that I could go ahead with confidence and that the bank would stand behind me. He assumed that we were on a rising market, a fact which I confirmed, and that I was perfectly safe in buying liberally. I explained to him that I was satisfied to go on building up a sound business out of its own strength rather than as a speculator, but that I was negotiating for the two floors above my present premises and that, if I succeeded in getting them, I would have the extension that I desired and of course would about double the amount of stock that I was at present able to carry. He assured me that I could go right ahead and that whatever credit facilities I required in the way of an overdraft were there for me. A week or so later I secured the upper floors on very favourable terms and proceeded to get ready for the much desired expansion. I also placed substantial orders for all the necessary stocks of finished goods and raw materials. From the beginning of 1916 these goods had been pouring in and we were just getting going in our upper floors before Easter. While in prison I was worried because I realised that the accounts for all these extra supplies in addition to the normal ones would be mounting up, but I tried to still my uneasiness with the assurance that the bank manager had voluntarily given me without any request from me.

The first job then that faced me on resuming was to have an early stocktaking and an examination of the stack of statements of accounts due. The review of the position was not pleasant, but it could have been worse. Business had been bad while I was away. That was only to be expected in the city of Belfast. Sinn Féin was not exactly loved by the Belfast loyalists and indeed it was at that time but a small minority of the so-called nationalists that would have a word to say in its defence.

I found on a close examination that I was considerably more than solvent, but that I was carrying heavy stocks and that a substantial overdraft would be needed to meet my due, and in some cases overdue, accounts. With these particulars I sought and had an interview with my bank manager and gave him the facts, reminding him of my last conference with him and his assurance of the necessary financial facilities.

I suppose I was somewhat shocked when he told me that in the altered circumstances and in view of what had happened the arrangement could no longer stand. He then gave me the benefit of his advice in these terms: 'Now look, Connolly, you have been away in prison. All your creditors know that. What you should do is call a meeting of your creditors, offer them ten shillings in the pound, they will be glad to get it and that will leave you all right'. I looked hard at him, not surprised so much that he should contemplate such a scheme, as that he should be so indiscreet as to state it so bluntly.

'But I am more than solvent', I protested.

'Yes, you may be', he replied, 'but you need cash to meet your pressing commitments'.

I asked him then if he was satisfied that he was adequately secured for the few hundreds that his bank had already advanced on overdraft and he told me he was. I told him that when he was giving me anything he could give me advice, but as he was not giving me anything he could reserve his advice for others. I told him that his suggestion did not fit in either with Catholic principles or Sinn Féin principles, that I believed in paying twenty shillings in the pound and, if it were necessary to sell out, not only what was in my warehouse and store, but what was in my home itself, I would do so rather than be listed in 'Stubbs' or let down my creditors. I added, as a final punch, that I thought it rather extraordinary advice for a bank-manager, occupying a position such as his, to give to any young business-man. Without any conventional leave-taking, I walked out of his office.

Emerging from the bank and walking back to my own place, I felt somewhat be-numbed and it was quite an hour or two before things levelled in my mind. I then sat down in the office to think out what was the best course to follow. I knew, of course, that I could call on friends like Simeon O'Leary and get more than all the cash I needed to settle the more pressing or overdue accounts, but I rejected the idea and for this reason. I did not know what the prospects were. I was in Belfast and, following recent events, trade might 'dry up' altogether. I had no intention of defaulting to my creditors or to the bank, but, if things were to go smash, I did not intend that any friend should lose a penny of loaned money.

Eventually, I decided that there was only one course to adopt and I there and then drafted a letter which I sent to all my creditors. In this I explained quite frankly what had happened and the position in which I now found myself. I was more than solvent though immediately short of cash and all I required was the necessary breathing space, while I got things under control. I pointed out that a forced realisation of stocks would be disastrous for me and might not work out satisfactorily even for my creditors. I recall, not with smugness but with genuine satisfaction, that with two exceptions all my firms wrote at once and the main theme and tone of their replies was: 'Go ahead, we are content to wait and meantime you can have what supplies you need'. With most of the concerns I had been doing business for quite a number of years before I started on my own account, but even so I was stimulated by their trust and confidence. Of the two excepted firms, one demanded immediate settlement and the other, a London agent for an American concern, slapped a writ on me by return, the only writ, thank God, that I had ever passed on me.

The experience had interesting repercussions later. During the period around 1918-1920 goods were in extremely short supply and almost impossible to obtain. For all that time all these firms, whom I had to ask to exercise patience, gave me all and everything I required. I was frequently able to supply even my biggest local competitors with their needs. Most of these competitors were anything but friendly. They had, I know, 'blackballed' me when, entirely unknown to me, my name had been put forward for membership of the trade association. Well, perhaps I got a little of my own back when they sought and got occasional urgently needed supplies, at a price.

Life is made up of compensations. A few days after my bank-manager had given me his shock treatment and before I had yet got replies from my creditors, I had a visit from a man from County Tyrone. I had never met him before, but he knew certain friends of mine he told me. He was due to be married in a couple of months, had got his house and figured that he would need to spend anything up to a thousand pounds on furnishing it. He wanted me to do the job and he was satisfied that I would give him a square deal. He and his 'intended' would be along in a couple of weeks to select their goods and in the meantime he thought maybe a cheque on account would be useful. He wrote out a cheque for seven hundred pounds. I do not need to explain to any businessman what such a gesture and action under the then circumstances meant to me.

It restored one's faith in humanity and in oneself. I think I can claim that his faith and trust were justified for he remained a good friend and customer for my remaining years in business.

Perhaps I have unduly laboured the business side of my affairs in this digression but, apart from their importance to me at the period, I was interested in the contrasting experiences I had with the bank-manager who favoured default and compounding with my creditors and the friend with the imagination for timing his friendly help. Before six months had passed I was in a comparatively easy position and within the year the business was running smoothly on an even keel. From that time forward I was able to settle all accounts promptly and secure full settlement discounts from my suppliers. This happy condition continued until, in the autumn of 1921, I was sent to the United States to represent the Republic as consul-general.

I have gone ahead of my narrative to complete the record of my experience with the banker. The first and almost immediate shock that awaited me on my return home was the news of Roger Casement's execution.

7

Casement hanged – A mixed reception – Herbert Moore Pim – Arthur Griffith restarts his weekly paper

It must be remembered that we, while in prison, received no papers and no news save such hints or remarks as might be surreptitiously dropped by a warder and that until I was back home I did not know how things stood with Roger Casement.

I had met Roger for the first time in 1913 when he, Denis McCullough and I had lunch together in the Olde Castle Restaurant in Belfast. I seldom base my estimate of people on first impressions, but I was more than impressed by Roger on that first meeting. So much has been written about his appearance, his courtly manner, his intensity and his wonderful personality that it is merely adding my testimony to the almost universal verdict of all those who knew him. To me he seemed to have an internal shrine within his soul and before it the flame of his devotion burned always. The shrine was Ireland, but it was a defined Ireland, if I may use the expression. The Ireland that Roger saw and wanted was an Ireland that would reflect all the finest qualities of his own soul and mind. It was an Ireland that would be gracious and chivalrous, that would be clean and straight and above board and that would preserve its honour and integrity.

I did not conceive my idea of Roger at that first meeting, but we met often in the months that followed and when he was a frequent guest, as a number of us were, in Frank Bigger's hospitable home in Ardrí. It was in these meetings that I sensed all that charm of character and all that burning devotion to his ideal that personified Roger Casement to me. I think it is not an exaggeration to say that Casement's interest in life, almost to the exclusion of all else, was concentrated on Ireland and her course of action in the events which, he foresaw so clearly, were impending. He had outlined in his pamphlet *Ireland, Germany and the next war* the course of events he had anticipated, and his whole life and future were dedicated to the seizure of that opportunity to gain Irish freedom.

He loved the simple things of Irish life, the plain honest-to-God people such as he loved to meet at a hurling match in Cushendun or that might gather together in the hospitable McCarry home at Murlough. Such meetings and gatherings were typical of the Irish way of life that he longed to see perfected in Ireland, and to him the whole scheme of things was corrupted by the shadow and the reality of the thing called the British empire. Till that evil was removed, Ireland could not breathe healthily. Her pores were clogged with the foul injection of distorted loyalties and poisoned bigotries deliberately applied in the interests of all who worshipped imperialism.

Roger's hatred of oppression and his fearless defence of those who suffered under it had long since been proved by his work in the Belgian Congo and in Putamayo and had earned for him the respect of all those who loved justice. It was the best type of Irishman that struggled successfully to end the rape, murder and plunder of these peoples. It was the same who devoted the remainder of his life to end the enslavement of his own people to an empire built on occupation and exploitation of subject peoples.

And now it was ended and we were saddened to know that never again would we meet with that gallant gentleman, that chivalrous soul who dared to stand against king and empire to proclaim that human freedom and human rights took precedence in justice over the money-changers and the empire builders. Yes, in justice sure but not in power. The pseudo-Orangeman, F. E. Smith, would outrage all the decencies by acting as leading prosecuting counsel at Roger's trial. As attorney general in the war cabinet he controlled the legal machinery of the government and elected to act as chief prosecutor himself. Doubtless he wanted to make sure of his victim, but the effrontery of the former Carsonite preacher of treason and the vindictiveness with which he conducted the crown case gave him a special niche in legal history. But Smith was not to be satisfied with having Roger convicted and sent to the gallows. He and his satellites planned and carried through their blackguardly campaign of calumny against Roger's personal character. The forged and faked infamous diaries[1] were prepared and shown to any and all of those who might be likely to enter a plea for mercy for Roger and urge a reprieve from the death sentence. Smith and his government feared pressure on Casement's behalf from many fair-minded Englishmen, but they feared still more pressure from the United States whom they were assiduously wooing to come in as their allies in the

1. Papers made available in the Public Record Office in London in mid-October 1995 seem to indicate that Casement's 'black diaries' were authentic. Sir Ernley Blackwell, assistant under-secretary at the Home Office, informed the British cabinet in a confidential document on 15 July 1916 that the diaries showed that Casement had 'for years been addicted to the grossest sodomitical practices'. In a memorandum of the same date, he suggested that there was no reason why the diaries should not be made known once Casement's execution had taken place. He continued: 'I see not the slightest objection to hanging Casement and afterwards giving as much publicity to the contents of his diary as decency permits so that at any rate the public may know what sort of man they are inclined to make a martyr of' (For more, see *Guardian Weekly* 29 October 1995).

great war. And so they succeeded and Carson's 'Galloper' could sit back and relax when eventually in August 1916 Roger met his death with exemplary courage on the scaffold at Pentonville. Smith would go on and prosper and achieve his life's ambition by becoming lord high chancellor and the keeper of the king's conscience. There was a wealth of irony in Galloper Smith becoming the keeper of anyone's conscience, but there it was! His leader, Carson, having reverted to his original loyalties and shed his pledged fealty to Kaiser Wilhelm of Germany, would find his reward by a seat in the war cabinet. Smith and Carson would appear again on the Irish scene as henchmen of the Welsh wizard, Lloyd George, to co-operate with him in his deceitful and double-crossing activities in the Irish treaty of 1921. Thus is British history in Ireland made. They are all gone now, Smith, Carson, and Lloyd George as well as Roger Casement. It is no exaggeration, I think, to claim that the one man among them who will stand out in history symbolising nobility of character, sincerity and honesty of purpose and heroic chivalry will be the maligned and despised victim, whom they buried in the felon's grave in Pentonville.

Just after resuming business I had an experience which I think was interesting and worthy of record. For a long time before the Rising, I had lunched every day at the Shaftesbury restaurant. There were six or seven of us who met each day and shared a table at the extreme end of the room. It was always a happy and welcome break for there were several of the group who were excellent company and interesting in various ways. Big Bob Rowan, a Presbyterian, was a liberal but without party affiliations. Bob had no time or use for politicians of any shade, but he hated oppression or wrong whether it came from a bad employer or the British empire. He was widely read but his two great favourites were Dickens[2] and Conrad.[3] He had always some new story or incident to record and his telling and his power of mimicry were a joy to me. It was Bob who first told the story of the Presbyterian minister who, deputising for a brother cleric, scarified the congregation by a vivid and lurid sermon on Hell. 'Brethren', said he, 'you will be there burning in the fire, your tongues will be hanging out and you will cry out for a drop of water but you will get no drop. And yis'll cry out: "but God we did not know, we did not know". But the Lord God, out of His Infinite Majesty and Mercy, will shout out to you, "Well yez know now".'

A collection of his stories and experiences would have made a valuable addition to the folklore of Belfast, Antrim and Down. They were all clean

2. Charles John Huffam Dickens (1812-70): born Portsea, novelist.
3. Joseph Conrad (1857-1924): born Mohilow, Poland, novelist.

and all tinged with that slightly satirical flavour that is the spice of Northern humour.

We had Hans Iten, a big genial and bearded Swiss who had come to Belfast as chief damask designer to one of the biggest linen manufacturers and had established himself as one of the best artists in the North. Hans for a long time had specialised in 'still life', but later his landscapes and seascapes were amongst the very best contributions of Irish artists of his period. He was a dear, big, simple soul who loathed everything that savoured of hypocrisy or pretension.

Then there was little Tommy, a manufacturer who had started work at ten years of age as a message boy, was a bundle of nervous energy, sparkling wit and one of the most honest men I have ever met. There were a couple of others, decent enough in their way but without any particular characteristics. An occasional visitor was Jimmy B–. Jimmy most nearly corresponded to what is traditionally accepted as the 'dour Ulster Protestant'. He was one of the 'brass hats' on the administrative side of the Orange Order. He was blunt and honest and made no secret and no apology for his views on politics, Home Rule or anything else. On resuming business, I was faced with the problem of the resumption of my accustomed place at the lunch-table. To those who do not know Belfast, it may sound absurd to suggest that any problem was involved, but our prejudices run deep in the Northern capital, and we were sufficiently provincial or parochial to know each other's form and history. Moreover, to go to our table meant walking down a long room to our corner and passing upwards of a hundred and fifty diners, to all of whom I was known. I decided that the ice had to be broken and accordingly ran the gauntlet of the stares that varied from mere surprise to ill-concealed hostility. As I approached the table, Big Bob stood up to welcome me back and to shake hands and all the others except one followed his example. The exception was our Jimmy. He grunted as though he were in pain, stood up, and glowered and said: 'A'm damned sure a'm not goin' to sit at the table with any Sinn Féin rebel', and off he shuffled to another table. There was an awkward pause for a second, until big Bob laughed and said: 'Sit down Joe and don't heed the eejit, we're all damned glad to see you back with us'. We had quite a happy re-union and our group continued to meet practically every day from then until my departure for America in 1921. The interesting thing was that big Bob and Jimmy were the closest of friends and continued to be so despite their differences of opinion. However, it was one thing to tolerate a misguided Presbyterian Home Ruler, but, when it came to rebel jailbirds!, well one had to draw the line somewhere.

As I recall the autumn and early winter of 1916, it was a period of concentrated effort in my business and as the weeks went by I had the satisfaction of feeling that 'things' were being quickly nursed back to order and security. In the movement itself there was a gradual awakening springing first of all from the National Aid Association and widening into other and more significant activities. The contrast between the hostility which we met immediately after the Rising and the friendly attitude which we experienced on our return was remarkable. This was of course less discernible in Belfast than in the rest of the country, but even in Belfast many of the supporters of the Parliamentary party and Mr Devlin had been doing some heart-searching and, while most of them were still hostile to Sinn Féin, there was a subdued note in their approach.

Belfast and the North-eastern counties were paying a heavy price at that time for their loyalty to the empire. The Ulster Division which was mainly built up from the Carsonite Volunteers, and the Irish regiments which had been largely recruited by Redmond and his associates had both suffered very heavily in the fighting on the Western front during the year. There was sorrow and bereavement in thousands of homes, there was anxiety about the course of the war, but there was unheard of prosperity and fantastic earnings in all the boom industries of the war.

Some short time after our release from Reading jail, Herbert Moore Pim, who had been released with us, arranged to publish his weekly paper *The Irishman*. Pim was to me the outstanding enigma of the whole movement. He has long since gone to his reward, God rest him. Even now, forty or more years since he was associated with us, I find it difficult to explain or even to understand his evolution. Extremely handsome in a rather soft purring way, he had abandoned his congenital Quakerism and been received into the Catholic Church. Soon after he became an active Home Ruler and by 'active' I mean he quickly became one of the most consistent propagandists for the Irish party. He wrote articles and delivered lectures; he wrote satirical quips and verses and was soon recognised as one of the brightest stars of the United Irish League intelligentsia. It was during this phase that I first met him. Pádraig Gregory,[4] our Ulster folk-poet, had occasional small parties in his home and there I met Pim for the first time. As it happened, he was due to deliver a lecture to one of the 'High-Hat' branches of the United Irish League and he regaled us with a rehearsal of the lecture. As a literary production it was excellent, but, as it was basically contrary to the whole doctrine which we held in Sinn Féin, I proceeded to challenge his whole thesis. Pim then either invited me or challenged me to

4. Pádraig Gregory (1886-1962): born Belfast, architect, balladeer, dramatist, folklorist, poet.

attend the lecture and make my arguments there. I did not particularly relish the suggestion, for the simple reason that I knew that most of those who would be present would be the hard-shelled devotees of Mr Devlin who were impervious to any criticism. However, I consented to go along and in due course Denis McCullough and I took our seats in the hall. It was an interesting evening and the first experience I had of hearing Pim proclaiming his dogmas. He spoke clearly and smoothly in a rather languid manner and without any spark of intensity or feeling. His material was clever and in spots witty, but it was essentially superficial and served only to reassure his hearers in their smug self-righteousness. The chairman called on various speakers, but did not follow the usual procedure of asking if any one else wished to speak and it was only as he was about to close the proceedings that I sought the privilege of having my say. I did and Denny McCullough followed up. We were subjected to interruptions, but we got a hearing with, however, a frigidly cold reception. I saw Pim at intervals during the next year or two, sometimes in the Ulster Arts Club or at Gregory's, but our contacts were few and in no sense intimate.

It was when the split in the Irish Volunteers was impending that I got a real shock when Pim called on me at my business place and announced that he had completely thrown over the Irish Party, that he was convinced that we in Sinn Féin were right and that henceforth he was with us all the way. I was surprised, I might almost say stunned by his avowal and, to be quite frank, I was by no means happy in having been a party to his conversion. It was not that I questioned his sincerity, but I had the conviction that he was a temperamental egotist, slightly neurotic, and with an artistic flair for exhibitionism rather than a solid conviction with regard to the principles which he espoused. From that day when he decided to support Sinn Féin he became the most active and the most prominent of our associates. He had the dark eyes and the pallor one associated with Parnell and what was more fitting than that he should proceed to grow a magnificent beard to complete the resemblance. Soon he was in close contact with the leaders in Dublin and intimate with most of them but, although he was never cold-shouldered in the slightest degree, he was never taken very seriously. He had been arrested with the rest of us in Belfast after the Rising and, as I have said, was released with myself and some others. Shortly after his return he launched his weekly paper. It was on the whole a very creditable production and, although it had to run the gauntlet of the strict censorship then operating, Pim managed to express the Irish Ireland and Sinn Féin viewpoints with reasonable success. *The Irishman* was his own concern in that he managed, directed and edited it without, so far as I know, any financial subsidy or support from any organisation. Some of us who knew Pim were at times anxious about the lines of policy he would pursue and I was not altogether surprised, but very much worried when, in one of the early issues, he indicated that while we were in Reading we had held conferences and decided on plans for the future. Now at this time there were still about thirty of our colleagues in Reading jail and they were still 'enjoying' the concession of constant association during the day and having their meals together in the main hall. My reaction on reading Pim's article was to groan and curse his stupidity, for I quite expected that all concessions would be immediately withdrawn and the governor, who was really a decent, reasonable man, would be moved to make way for a real 'jackboot'. I made contact with Denny McCullough who shared my anxiety when I drew his attention to the article, and we immediately summoned Pim for a conference. For a time he tried to defend his action and it was only under the threat of having him repudiated by headquarters in Dublin that he undertook to watch his step in the future. There were several other occasions when his indiscretions caused us worry and, what was more important, caused grave worry to the men in Reading. A few weeks later P. T. Daly, who was out on parole from Reading, brought us a memorandum protesting against several editorials and articles which had appeared in the paper. I sent for Pim and showed him the document without comment. He did not say much, but it registered. Following this repudiation and protest, Pim gave us little more trouble, but I have often wondered if this was the primary step in his ultimate withdrawal and his reversion to Ulster Unionism and recantation of his national faith.

At Christmas 1916, following a rash of rumours, the British decided to release all those who were interned, that is to say, the large number who were still confined in the Frongoch camp in North Wales as well as the thirty or so who were in Reading. Our happiness at their return was tainted with sorrow for the large number of sentenced prisoners who were still enduring penal servitude. Early in 1917 Arthur Griffith came to stay with us for a brief holiday and Róisín and I enjoyed his company, and I think he was happy with us and with our circle of friends. He and I sat late those nights discussing all that had happened and the possibilities of the future.

I urged him to get busy and launch his paper and then he disclosed that he had a proposal from Pim that he, Griffith, should join forces with him on *The Irishman.* I was somewhat shocked at the suggestion and pointed out to Griffith that the idea was preposterous and that he must have his own journal which he would edit, direct and control as he had done in the past with *The United Irishman* and *Sinn Féin.* He said that would of course be the desirable thing, but that the question of financing it raised a problem and he had thought that perhaps the Pim suggestion might serve in the meantime. I told him it was quite unthinkable, that he was not going to play second string to Pim and that with Pim, as the controlling owner or publisher, he might not have that freedom which was an absolute necessity for him. I suggested that I thought I could interest enough friends in Belfast and that between us we could find enough to get his paper going. The next evening we went along to my old friend Simeon O'Leary and I introduced Arthur to him. Simeon had kept aloof from politics since the Parnell split, but he was a sound Irishman, and, as I knew from experience, had a generous heart. Early in our talk and before I had time to suggest anything about the paper Simeon himself suggested that Griffith must get going quickly with a weekly journal and pledged himself to put up the necessary funds to start it. It was Arthur's first meeting with Simeon and to say that he was deeply touched and grateful is to put it mildly indeed.

It may seem strange to present-day readers that there should have been any difficulty facing such a brilliant journalist and leader of national thought as Griffith in starting a paper for which there was a crying-out need at the time, but there were reasons. For one thing Griffith had not been 'out' in the Rising, a fact which was in no way due to Griffith's outlook. He was not in the inner council of those who planned the insurrection and indeed was not regarded favourably by the I.R.B. or the extremists who made up the advanced guard of the Volunteers. Furthermore, the confusion of the weekend prior to the Rising, the calling off of the 'marches' on Holy Saturday and Easter Sunday by MacNeill and the general upset left him, as it left many of us, completely at sea as to what would happen.

These factors, added to the fact that Arthur was a singularly sensitive and independent type in regard to his personal needs, would prevent him making any approach for help. However, there were others than Simeon O'Leary who recognised his worth and the country's need of his pen, for a week after his return to Dublin he wrote me to say that a certain friend had stopped him in the street and insisted on putting up the necessary funds to launch the paper.[5] He sent his grateful thanks to Simeon and was glad that he was free to go ahead. For my own part I was delighted and relieved to know that Arthur would soon be in harness again, and that the Pim suggestion had been disposed of.

5. The 'certain friend' was James O'Mara. He gave £300 to Griffith to start *Nationality*. Nan Ryan (later Mrs Seán Nunan) subsequently recalled getting the cash from the safe in the office of O'Mara's bacon factory in Cork Street, Dublin, for James O'Mara who then handed it over to Griffith.

Perhaps I have pursued the Pim saga to an unreasonable length but to those of us who were involved at the period he was almost unique. To me he epitomised the type, and it is by no means uncommon, to whom a cause is great not because of its principles and qualities, but because of their personal participation in it. I have often said that Herbert Moore Pim might conceivably have been executed and, if such had been his fate, I am satisfied that his exit would have been dramatic and even heroic. However, such was not to be. He drifted from Sinn Féin and then startled us all in Ireland by disavowing all his nationalistic doctrines and proclaiming himself a re-convert, or pervert if you would have it so, to the doctrine of Ulster Unionism, the British empire and Sir Edward Carson. Letters from him appeared in the *Belfast Evening Telegraph* proclaiming his new allegiance, but no one seemed to take much notice.

I referred earlier to one, Jimmy B-, the dour Orangeman who left the dining table in the restaurant when I showed up after my release from Reading. Jimmy confided to my friend Bob Rowan that as secretary of the Lodge he had received a letter from Pim offering to go on the platform with Carson. Jimmy's decision and views as expressed to Bob were typical of the man: 'Not damned likely! He was a Quaker, he gives that up and becomes a papist; he joins the United Irish League and the Ancient Order of Hibernians; he gives them up and becomes a Sinn Féiner; now he gives them up and wants to speak with Carson at an Orange demonstration. No, be me sowl, he won't if I know it!'

Poor Pim, he was at once the most fantastic, the most irritating and, at the same time, the saddest case of mis-directed ability that I ever encountered in a long life-time. I last heard of him when he wrote me from Paris. It was in 1932 and he sent me his congratulations on being made a minister in de Valera's government and asked me to convey similar greetings to Séan McEntee.[6] I did so, but decided that it was wiser not to answer his letter. To do so might have meant recriminations about past events or an expression of interest which I did not feel. He died a few years later in Paris and it was consoling to know that, despite all the vagaries of his political career, he continued to be a practising Catholic until his death. May he rest in peace!

6. Seán MacEntee (1889-1980): born Belfast, an engineer, member of Irish Volunteers and fought in Easter Rising 1916, returned as Sinn Féin M.P. for South Monaghan 1918, opposed the treaty, national treasurer of Sinn Féin 1924, founder member of Fianna Fáil 1926, its national vice-president 1955-65, minister for finance 1932-9, minister for industry and commerce 1939-41, minister for local government and health 1941-8, minister for finance 1951-4, minister for health 1957-65, member of Council of State 1948-65, Tánaiste 1959-65.

8

Michael Collins and the National Aid Association – Ginnell leaves the House of Commons – Sinn Féin wins by-elections – The abortive Irish Convention – Release of the sentenced prisoners – Conscription – The 'German Plot' – Death of Tom Ashe – End of World War I

At the beginning of 1917 there were still over 120 men in Portland and Dartmoor, and Countess Markievicz[1] was still serving her sentence in Aylesbury. There were disturbing rumours and reports of serious trouble in various prisons and ultimately we learned that they had all been gathered together in Lewes. There could be no real contentment or sense of ease, while these prisoners were in the hands of their jailers.

At this time there was a growing awakening of national spirit and activity in Belfast and the surrounding areas. As in Dublin and the rest of the country, the National Aid Association served as a focal point of Sinn Féin and national activity. The National Aid Association was responsible for the administration of the funds raised to provide for prisoners' dependents and other victims of the Rising. It was the one organisation which could meet openly and carry on its work at the time and, whilst it kept strictly to its own functions, it did provide opportunities for contacts for all those who were connected with the movement.

It was early in 1917 that the Association appointed as its secretary a man of dynamic energy who was destined to be the most outstanding force in the national struggle in the years immediately ahead. Michael Collins[2] had already made his influence felt amongst the London-Irish in the insurrec-

1. Constance Markievicz, *née* Gore-Booth (1868-1927): born Lisadell House, County Sligo, married Count Casimir Markievicz 1900, member of Sinn Féin, founded Fianna Éireann 1909, member of Inghinidhe na hÉireann 1909, during Lock-Out of 1913 organised soup-kitchens and became an officer in the Irish Citizen Army, fought in Easter Rising 1916, president of Cumann na mBan 1917, returned as Sinn Féin M.P. for St Patrick's division, Dublin 1918, minister for labour 1919-21, 1921-2, opposed the treaty, Sinn Féin T.D. for Dublin City South 1923-7.

2. Michael Collins (1890-1922): born Woodfield, Clonakilty, County Cork, a post-office clerk in London, where he became an active member of Gaelic Athletic Association, member of I.R.B. 1915, fought in Easter Rising 1916, secretary of Irish National Aid and Irish Volunteer Dependants' Fund 1917, adjutant-general of Irish Volunteers, organiser and head of I.R.A. intelligence system, returned to First Dáil, minister of home affairs 1919, minister of finance 1919-22, organiser of national loan, president of supreme council of I.R.B. 1921, chairman of Provisional government 1921, commander-in-chief of the national army (Free State forces) during civil war, killed in ambush at Béal na mBláth, County Cork.

tion itself and, still more so, in the prison camps in Frongoch. His ability and qualities were recognised by his fellow-prisoners and by those who carried on the work after the internees had returned home, but few outside had any knowledge of him. As secretary of the National Aid Association, he gave a foretaste of his qualities as a brilliant administrator and executive.

Arthur Griffith had relaunched his weekly newspaper under the name of *Nationality* and all over the country there was a rapidly spreading turnover to Sinn Féin. We in the North East moved but slowly, and for obvious reasons. We were surrounded by a hostile population who were working feverishly on a war basis at a time when the war situation was particularly gloomy for the British and their allies. That element might have been ignored, but it has also to be remembered that the majority of the so-called nationalist population were equally or more hostile to Sinn Féin. This was due almost entirely to the extraordinary personal influence of Mr Joseph Devlin and his control of the Ancient Order of Hibernians. While all Ireland was shedding rapidly the illusions and spells with which they had been misled for years by Redmond's Home Rule party, Belfast and the North-East Hibernians clung tenaciously to Devlin. Idols are not quickly demolished and it is always difficult to admit that one was wrong. Devlin was little less than an idol to his Belfast supporters. It would be evident in some of the events of 1917 and particularly in the series of elections which took place that year and early in 1918.

A vacancy for the parliamentary seat of North Roscommon occurred early in the year and Count Plunkett went forward as a candidate. The count was the father of Joseph Plunkett[3] who had been executed immediately after the Rising and his other two sons, George and John,[4] were serving penal-servitude sentences. A short time before the Royal Dublin Society[5] had irrevocably stained its records by calling a special

3. Joseph Mary Plunkett (1889-1916): born Dublin, son of George Noble Count Plunkett, editor of *Irish Review* 1913-14, member of I.R.B. and Irish Volunteers, of which he became director of operations 1913, co-founder of Irish Theatre 1914, with Sir Roger Casement in Germany to secure aid for the Rising 1915, member of supreme council, I.R.B., Provisional Government 1916, and signatory to Proclamation of Independence 1916, married Grace Gifford on eve of his execution.

4. George Plunkett: member of Irish Volunteers 1913, interned after Easter Rising 1916, organiser of Sinn Féin 1917, member of I.R.A. 1919-21, opposed the treaty 1922, member of G.H.Q., I.R.A. 1922-40.

John Plunkett: member of Irish Volunteers 1913, interned after Easter Rising 1916, member of I.R.A. 1919-40.

5. Royal Dublin Society was established for 'improving husbandry, manufactures and other useful arts and sciences' on 25 June 1731. It has been responsible for the establishment of the National Library, National Museum, National Gallery, Botanic Gardens and the

meeting of the society and by a vote of 236 to 58 had expelled the count from membership.

There was a certain amount of discussion as to whether or not the election would be contested. The count had not committed himself to any particular policy, but it was decided that all the resurgent national strength should be given to him. The result of the election was the first defeat of the Irish Parliamentary party, Plunkett receiving over three thousand votes against the party's nominee, a Mr Devine, seventeen hundred. It was a staggering blow to the party to be followed by others and by the final débâcle that would come later.

In May a vacancy arose in Longford and Joseph McGuinness,[6] one of the prisoners still serving his sentence in Lewes, was nominated and carried the seat against a popular Longford man, Mr McKenna, by the narrow margin of thirty-seven votes. This was the second successive defeat for the party and the first election of a convicted rebel still serving his sentence. The tide was turning or had already turned. Mr de Valera would later win East Clare with a vote of over five thousand against Mr Lynch, the party's nominee who polled a bare two thousand, and Mr W. T. Cosgrave[7] would add another victory in Kilkenny.

About this time Laurence Ginnell announced his decision to withdraw entirely from the House of Commons and return to serve his people at home. Ginnell was not a member of the Irish Party. He was one of a small group of Independents and had been a consistent critic and opponent of the party machine. After the Rising he was the only outstanding defender of the Irish people in the House of Commons and was fearless in his condemnation of British policy and the savagery shown after the fight. It was

---

National College of Art. It maintains an interest in scientific matters, making grants available for research, the acquisition of scientific collections and the purchase of scientific equipment, and has published statistical surveys of the Irish counties. Besides housing a valuable library, its headquarters at Ballsbridge in Dublin is the centre for many exhibitions, displays and shows, including the Dublin Horse Show which was first held in 1868.

6. Joseph McGuinness: M.P. for Longford South 1917-18, Longford 1918-22, T.D. for Longford-Westmeath 1921-22.

7. William T. Cosgrave (1880-1965): born Dublin, member of Irish Volunteers 1913, fought in Easter Rising 1916, treasurer of Sinn Féin, Sinn Féin M.P. for Kilkenny 1917-18, minister for local government in First Dáil, president of Second Dáil and chairman of provisional government 1922, minister for finance 1922-3, president of executive council of Irish Free State 1922-32, founder of Cumann nGaedheal 1923, of which he was leader until 1933, president of Fine Gael 1935-44.

little wonder that Larry Ginnell[8] was accorded the title of 'The Member for Ireland'. Ginnell was a highly-strung, sensitive type, a man of outstanding courage and integrity, and his withdrawal from Westminster and his return home to work for his people was both symptomatic of the period and of great value to the movement.

It was in June 1917 that Bonar Law,[9] one-time leader of the Carsonite forces and like some of his fellow conspirators with the German high command now a minister in the Lloyd George government, made an announcement in the British House of Commons. He said: 'The Government, after long consideration of the position of the Irish political prisoners, feel that the governing consideration in the matter is the approaching session of the convention in which Irishmen themselves will meet to settle the difficult problems of the future administration of their country. We have decided therefore on the release, without reservation, of all the prisoners now in confinement in connection with the rebellion'.

I should explain perhaps that some time prior to this announcement the British government had announced the setting up of an Irish Convention.[10] No doubt some of the hand-picked nominees took the Convention seriously, but the country as a whole and, most of all, those who were now flocking to the Sinn Féin standard believed that the Convention was merely window-dressing.

At the time the wily Lloyd George, who had ousted his former chief, Mr. Asquith, out of the premiership and had taken to his bosom the Carsons and Smiths and Bonar Laws, was desperately trying to bring America into the war and to that fact we attributed both the setting up of the Convention and the release of the sentenced prisoners. Sinn Féin, which

8. Lawrence Ginnell (1854-1923): born County Westmeath, M.P. for County Westmeath 1906-18, after Easter Rising joined Sinn Féin, of which he became treasurer, returned to First Dáil, its director of publicity 1919-21, opposed the treaty, died campaigning against it in the U.S.A.

9. Andrew Bonar Law (1858-1923): born Kingstown, New Brunswick, Canada, first elected as an M.P. for a Glasgow seat 1900, leader of Conservatives 1911, gave unconditional pledge of British Unionist support for Ulster resistance to Home Rule 1912, supported formation of the Ulster Volunteer Force 1913, chancellor of the exchequer 1915, supported Government of Ireland Act 1920, resigned as leader of House of Commons and severed his relationship with Ulster Unionists 1921, prime minister 1922-3.

10. Irish Convention (1917-18) was an attempt by Lloyd George to secure a final settlement of the demand for Home Rule. Members, who met under the chairmanship of Sir Horace Plunkett, included representatives of the Ulster Unionist Party, the southern Unionists, the Irish Parliamentary Party and Independents. The Convention failed to reconcile the Nationalist demand for self-government with the Unionist demand that Ireland remain within the United Kingdom.

obviously was rapidly gaining the support throughout Ireland save in the four north-eastern counties, refused to take any part in the deliberations and the Convention was of little interest to the Irish people.

However, there was great joy and relief at the release of the prisoners and the enthusiastic receptions which they received on their homecoming were ample confirmation that the people had definitely repudiated the Parliamentary party and were on the march with Sinn Féin.

To those of us who were in Belfast and the surrounding counties there was an inevitable sense of frustration and disappointment. We naturally rejoiced at the re-birth of national faith and the vindication of the separatist doctrine that had spread over most of the country, but we realised that we were still surrounded by the forces of Ulster Unionism and a die-hard antagonism from the supporters of Devlin and Redmond. This found expression only in 1918 when a parliamentary vacancy arose in South Armagh. This was a 'Nationalist' constituency which, although it contained quite a big number of unionist voters, was always a safe seat for the Irish Party. Dr Pat McCartan,[11] who at this time was representing Republican Ireland in the United States, was chosen as the Sinn Féin candidate, but the forces of the Party, the Ancient Order of Hibernians and the unionist voters combined to defeat him. That was in February 1918 and two months later Seán Milroy, a 1916 man and one who had been a cheerful companion of mine in Knutsford and Reading jails, was defeated for the East Tyrone seat by over five hundred votes. These were discouraging results for us in the North, but despite them there was hard work and earnest effort going on all the time. Sinn Féin branches were being organised in Belfast and throughout the adjoining counties and, although the membership was not big, they were already proving a desirable leaven in the mind and conscience of the people.

My contacts with Dublin at this time were frequent, although they were mostly made up by the visits of some of my old friends who had 'business' up North and whom we were glad to welcome at our home.

As well as Griffith, some of my old associates in Reading would arrive from time to time, Seán Milroy, Darrell Figgis, Walter Cole,[12] Ginger

11. Dr Patrick McCartan (1878-1966): born Carrickmore, County Tyrone, member of Clan na Gael, Philadelphia 1905, editor, *Irish Freedom* 1910, M.P. for King's County 1918, T.D. 1919-23, representative of Sinn Féin in U.S.A. 1918-21, senator 1948-51.

12. Walter Leonard Cole (1866-1948): born Liverpool, member of Gaelic League 1894, member of Celtic Literary Society 1899, member of Dublin Corporation 1904, member of Sinn Féin 1905, its joint-secretary 1908, pacifist and not involved in Easter Rising 1916, interned in Frongoch and Reading jail after the Rising, T.D. for Cavan 1922-23, in 1920-21 he sheltered Sinn Féin leaders, including Collins and de Valera, and hosted sessions of Dáil

O'Connell,[13] and a few others. On these occasions the attendance of the ubiquitous G man, the special detectives of the political branch of the R.I.C., was constant. Their job was to 'shadow' these visitors all the time and to report their movements and contacts.

On one occasion Jeremiah O'Connell, later a colonel in the Free State Army and known to all in the movement as 'Ginger', was spending a few days with us. Our house was the last but one in a *cul-de-sac* which ended at a side gate to the Falls Park. With a few friends we were sitting around the fire and when some of the visitors were leaving we saw that the snow was falling heavily. We also noticed that the two G men were taking what poor shelter the bare trees at the Park entrance afforded. 'Ginger' was nothing if not original and when we had resumed our seats cosily at the fire he suggested that we should leave the lights still burning after we had retired to bed. He contended that the G men would be bound to stand out and keep watch, while the lights burned. Maybe he was right! He had his way, although I must confess that I had a sense of meaness as I went up to bed. It snowed heavily that night.

It was only occasionally I could pay a visit to Dublin and because of the pressure of work at home my stay would be short. Invariably I met Griffith and lunched with him, after which we would adjourn for a quiet chat and discussion on the latest developments.

The release of the prisoners and the setting up of the Irish Convention proved quite futile in the British government's shifting policy of dealing with the country. It is hard to believe that any motive other than to try to satisfy Irish-American opinion inspired their action, for in a few short months we find the Dublin Castle minions of the government again turned loose on the people. Of course in that short interval there was ample evidence that Sinn Féin was no longer a party but a people's movement. The results and the refusal to have anything to do with the so-called 'Irish convention' were significant enough, but there were other important developments.

Éireann, through his friendship with Michael Noyek he sheltered Jewish refugees from Germany on their way to the U.S.A. in the 1930s.

13. Lt-General Jeremiah J. O'Connell (1887-1944): born County Mayo, served in U.S. army 1912-14, returned to Ireland and joined Irish Volunteers 1914, assistant to Richard Mulcahy, chief of staff of I.R.A., 1919-21, after the treaty which he supported he became deputy chief of staff of Free State army, his kidnapping precipitated the outbreak of the civil war, assistant to General Eoin O'Duffy and General Mulcahy during civil war, chief lecturer to army school of instruction 1924-9, director of intelligence 1929-32, quartermaster general 1932-4, director of military archives 1934-44.

Meetings were being held all over the country and at the election meetings order was being maintained not by the uniformed R.I.C. but by young Volunteers. It is true that their only arms were their hurleys and sticks, but order was preserved. In August 1917 three of the leading men in the movement who had been released from Lewes were arrested for making speeches 'calculated to cause disaffection'. Austin Stack was sentenced to two years, Fionán Lynch[14] to eighteen months, and Tom Ashe[15] to twelve months. In Mountjoy they found themselves, with a number of others who had been sentenced for drilling and various other Sinn Féin activities, as prisoners who were to be treated as ordinary criminals. Stack, Lynch and Ashe had faced that problem before and had, during their time as 'convicts', successfully contested the decree and on their arrival in Mountjoy renewed the fight.

The result was a hunger strike. In the course of this the prison authorities adopted the foul practice of forcible feeding, and Tom Ashe after five days was removed in a dying condition to the Mater Hospital where he died within a few hours.

Ashe was a splendid character in every way. A fine looking man, he had distinguished himself in Easter Week at Ashbourne where, with Dick Mulcahy as his next in command, his small force of Volunteers had scored one of the most notable victories of the Rising. A schoolmaster of very wide culture and an outstanding Irish scholar, he was, as his writings prove, a deeply religious man.

Ashe's death and the revelations at the subsequent inquest shocked the whole country. Several of the leading specialists gave evidence at the inquest and it was conclusively proved that Ashe died as the result of being left on a cold floor for fifty hours and then subjected to forcible feeding, while in his weak condition after the hunger strike. The prisoners won their battle for recognition as political prisoners and Tom Ashe had received the answer to his poem-prayer 'Let me carry Your Cross for Ireland, Lord'!

14. Fionán Lynch (1889-1966): born Cahirciveen, County Kerry, national teacher 1912, member of Gaelic League 1912, member of I.R.B. and Irish Volunteers 1913, active in Easter Rising 1916, T.D. for South Kerry 1918-44, brigadier in Free State army 1922-3, minister for fisheries 1923-27, barrister 1931, judge 1944.

15. Thomas Ashe (1885-1917): born Kinard, County Kerry, principal of Corduff national school, Lusk, County Dublin, 1908-16, member of Gaelic League and Irish Volunteers 1913, led the Volunteers in successful engagement at Ashbourne, County Meath, Easter 1916, leading Republican propagandist and organiser of Sinn Féin and Irish Volunteers 1917, led a hunger-strike for political status among Sinn Féin prisoners at Mountjoy Jail and died while being force-fed.

In April 1918 Mr Lloyd George brought in a bill to the British parliament applying conscription to Ireland. It was passed in the Commons by 301 votes to 103, the minority being mainly made up of members of the Irish Parliamentary Party. John Redmond had died and John Dillon[16] had succeeded him as leader of the Parliamentary Party. After the passing of the Conscription Act, Dillon and his Party withdrew from the parliament and returned home to Ireland to join the rest of the country in an organised resistance to the new threat. They had unanimously 'decided to abandon attendance at Westminster and assist the people at home in their fight against conscription'. Perhaps they would have denied that their new departure was an acceptance of Sinn Féin, but to us it looked very like it.

The reaction in Ireland to the conscription threat was immediate. A conference of the leaders of all the parties, Sinn Féin, Parliamentary Party and Labour was held and declared for joint action in resistance to any attempt to enforce the decree.

The Catholic hierarchy in a session in Maynooth issued their pronouncement against conscription and on the following Sunday a pledge of resistance was available for signatures outside every Catholic church and chapel in the country. The Irish Labour Party called a one-day national strike to register their unanimity with all other bodies in the fight against the threat.

It will always be a question as to whether Lloyd George and his ministers really intended conscription as a means to fill the gaps in the ranks of the army or as an excuse to crush ruthlessly the rapidly growing Sinn Féin and Republican movement in Ireland. Most of us who tried to analyse the various shifting moves of the wily Welshman believed that the latter motive was the real one. This view would seem to be confirmed by what happened shortly afterwards. In May there was a 'round up' of some eighty leading Sinn Féiners throughout the country. Their homes were raided about midnight and those who were wanted and who were at home were arrested and deported to various English prisons.

The British government solemnly announced that the arrests were in no way connected with the anti-conscription movement, but because the arrested men were engaged in a plot with the Germans.

16. John Dillon (1851-1927): born Blackrock, County Dublin, M.P. for County Tipperary 1880-85, Mayo East 1885-1918, supported the Plan of Campaign 1886, opposed Parnell 1891, succeeded Justin MacCarthy as anti-Parnellite leader 1896, supported the United Irish League and John Redmond as leader of re-united Irish Parliamentary Party 1900, its leader 1918 and led it from House of Commons upon passing of military service bill 1918, defeated by de Valera at East Mayo, December 1918 and withdrew from public life.

The story of the 'German Plot' deceived nobody in Ireland and it is doubtful if it could have deceived any normally intelligent person anywhere else. The idea that a 'plot' in which nearly a hundred men scattered far and wide over the country could have been immediately concerned was ludicrous. There was also the fact that, with the military garrison, the R.I.C. and the G division of detectives, to say nothing of the forces at every port in the country, such contact with Germany as a plot would demand was impossible. It is noteworthy that Lord Wimborne,[17] then lord lieutenant and who had later to make way for Lord French, stated publicly that he had no knowledge of any evidence of the alleged plot with Germany. The 'German Plot' was a pure fabrication. It was crude and clumsy in conception and execution and deceived nobody. Lloyd George knew it but what matter! It would, he thought, serve his purpose; by removing up to a hundred of the trusted leaders of the people he could smash Sinn Féin and perhaps more easily have the young men of Ireland rounded up for the army. It was in keeping with so much else that was traditional in the British occupation of Ireland and in the treatment of those who resisted that occupation. It was in harmony too with the infamous forged 'diaries' that they circulated to ensure Casement's execution and to besmirch his reputation after they had hanged him.

Amongst the prisoners rounded up in the fake German plot arrests was one dear friend of mine. Pierce McCan was a fellow prisoner in Knutsford in 1916. Like myself he had been put into solitary confinement there. Later we were granted the privilege of associating together, but by ourselves and kept strictly apart from the main body of internees. The concession meant that we four 'solitaries' had our brief periods of exercise outside our cells together. Seán Milroy, Dr Ned Dundon, Pierce McCan and myself made up the four and it is good to remember the good-natured friendship and comradeship during that spell.

Following his arrest in 1918, Pierce was shipped over to Gloucester jail. There he contracted the bad influenza that was prevalent at the time and there he died. He was another of the many victims that British rule claimed from Young Ireland. Pierce McCan was one of the many fine characters I met in the various prisons. Widely read and cultured, he was yet an unspoiled simple soul. He was what we used to call in Ireland a 'gentleman-farmer' and in his case it was a literally true description. He had two all absorbing elements in life: his deeply religious fervour and his devotion to the cause of Irish freedom. We prayed and pray that his soul may rest in

17. Ivor Churchill-Guest: 1st Viscount Wimbourne (1873-1939): M.P. for Plymouth 1900-6, Cardiff 1906-10, paymaster-general 1910-12, lord lieutenant, Ireland 1915-18.

peace. To me after my intimate contact with him in jail, and nowhere else does one learn to know a colleague so well, it seemed that Pierce would go to his reward immediately. His whole life and his tragic death were but a fitting preparation for it.

The 'German Plot' stunt was, as I have said, ridiculed in Ireland and, although it had deprived the country of some of our best leaders, it hardened the will of the people to resist conscription and helped recruitment to the Volunteers. The English cabinet seemed to be uncertain as to what line of policy it would pursue. Having passed their Conscription Act, they decided to try out a new recruiting campaign in which the young men of Ireland were invited to join up, with the added threat that if they did not they would be taken. If there was ever bad psychology applied to an Irish appeal, surely this was it.

Looking back on the period it is difficult to trace any consistent line in the policy of the British government of the time. Consider that we had the abortive Irish Convention, the release of the prisoners, the arrests a few months later and the hunger-strike which resulted in the death of Tom Ashe. The big bombshell of conscription was followed by the 'German Plot' arrests and then a recruiting appeal for men to join the forces. This was followed by a proclamation demanding fifty thousand Irishmen for their army with an additional two thousand a month to maintain the Irish quota. A month later came the proclamation suppressing Sinn Féin, Sinn Féin clubs, Cumann na mBan[18] and the Gaelic League, and prohibiting all meetings, assemblies and processions except those for which written permits had been obtained. There is no record of any meeting having been held with the necessary permit, but on 15 August meetings were held over the country and without immediate interference. Later, however, many of the speakers at these meetings were arrested and sentenced to varying terms of imprisonment.

It may have been that, in its later phases, the game was being played to create uncertainty, a sort of war of nerves on the people or, as seems more likely, that the uncertainty regarding policy and tactics was within the British government itself. However that may have been, the fact seems to be well established that the government did intend to move actively to impose conscription in October. It has been generally accepted that it was the German approach for peace that caused the governments to cancel the

18. Cumann na mBan: Women's organisation founded in Dublin in November 1913 at the same time as the Irish Volunteers of which it became the women's division, led by Countess Markievicz and Mrs Kathleen Clarke, active in Easter Rising 1916 and during war of independence 1919-21, majority of its members opposed the treaty.

arrangements that had been perfected for the wholesale arrests of national and local leaders and the enforcement of conscription all over Ireland.

Although there was a certain amount of recruitment to the Volunteers during the conscription scare and support for Sinn Féin increased, Belfast and the border areas of Armagh and Down were slow to move. In the more westerly counties of Ulster definite progress was being made. In East Cavan, for instance, Arthur Griffith defeated the party candidate by a majority of twelve hundred votes, but I do not think that we could have won a single so-called Nationalist constituency in Antrim, Down, Armagh or Tyrone. Dublin was of course the pivotal centre of all that was moving at the time, but Sinn Féin and the Volunteer movements were spreading rapidly all over the country outside of our own little North-East corner. We had gained a certain amount of ground and many new recruits but, in comparison to the rest of the country, our progress was relatively slow. As I have explained, we in Belfast were almost swamped in an environment of war fever and Carsonite antagonism. The withdrawal of the Irish Parliamentary party from Westminster on the conscription issue did not mean that its supporters in our area came pouring in to Sinn Féin and the Volunteers. As I remember it, the Belfast and district supporters of the party adopted a sort of sullen neutralism and their loyalty was definitely a personal one to their own idol, 'Wee Joe' as they lovingly called Mr Devlin.

Such was the position when the war ended. The armistice was declared for eleven o'clock on the morning of the eleventh of November 1918. Germany had surrendered and the war was over. There was great excitement and jubilation in Belfast, but much less disturbance than we had anticipated. It brought a great sense of relief to many homes, but to many thousands of families it must have renewed the sorrow for those who would not return. Belfast and the Ulster division had suffered heavy losses during the four years carnage and Catholic Belfast had given more than a fair share of its young manhood in response to the recruiting campaigns of the politicians.

9

General election of 1918 – Sinn Féin's sweeping victory – The end of the Irish Parliamentary Party – Dáil Éireann established – The Peace Conference at Versailles – President Wilson's fourteen points – Irish-American delegation – Wilson's betrayal – De Valera goes to America – Rev Dr Irwin, his work, arrest and release

The war having ended, the British government announced a dissolution of parliament and a general election. The election was fixed for December and Sinn Féin decided that every seat would be contested and that a Sinn Féin candidate would be nominated even in the constituencies that were overwhelmingly Unionist and Orange. It was a bold and wise decision. Sinn Féin, for the first time, was able to put its programme and policy before the people of all Ireland. The policy was clear-cut and free from all ambiguity. The elected representatives of the people would meet and form a national assembly in Dublin. This assembly would claim its right to function as the government of Ireland and refuse to recognise the British parliament or government.

There were some of the supporters of the Irish Parliamentary Party who saw the folly of opposing Sinn Féin and urged the leaders of that party to stand aside and leave the way clear for Sinn Féin. Mr John Dillon, who had succeeded Mr Redmond as leader, quickly disposed of any such suggestions and announced the determination to fight Sinn Féin with all the resources that he and the party could command.

For us in the North the election promised to be a tough campaign indeed and fully lived up to its promise. There were constituencies in the Orange districts of Belfast, and that meant all of them except the Falls Road area of West Belfast, in which a Sinn Féiner dare not appear. There were others wherein a small minority of Nationalists lived and where, at considerable risk, canvassing and even open-air meetings were carried through.

It should have been a dispiriting experience but actually, due to the grand spirit that seemed to infect all our workers, there was a splendid enthusiasm and vitality that carried us through the campaign. One of the chief driving forces was our director of elections, Eamon Donnelly.[1]

1. Eamon Donnelly (1885-1945): born Middletown, County Armagh, clerk in Armagh prison, member of Irish Volunteers 1913, Sinn Féin director of elections in 1918 and 1921, opposed the treaty, director of elections for 'Sinn Féin Re-organised' 1923, Republican M.P. for Armagh 1925-9, Fianna Fáil T.D. for Laois-Offaly 1933-7, Republican M.P. for Belfast Falls 1942-5.

Eamon was an Armagh man, an excellent organiser with tireless energy and gifted with an irresistible sense of humour and caustic northern wit. He was director of elections for the whole north-east corner of Ulster with local and district directors working under him. I saw much of him at the time and worked closely with him and was amazed at his capacity. Arrangements for meetings, conventions for selection of candidates, detailed plans for the election itself and all the thousand and one things involved in elections were his responsibility. He saw to them all and with a gay laugh or a sardonic grin he had all of us going at top speed to carry out his directions.

At the outset of the campaign Donnelly arranged the opening meeting on behalf of de Valera in West Belfast. Here Dev had been nominated to oppose Mr Devlin. It was of course a forlorn hope but, in accordance with the policy of contesting every seat, a Sinn Féiner had to be nominated and de Valera was a candidate. To fight Devlin in his own home area was almost heretical at the time. The pope himself would not have won West Belfast against 'wee Joe'. Eamon arranged that Mick Carolan and I would open Dev's campaign. The meeting was announced to be held at the foot of Clonard Street and to start just as the two thousand or more members of the confraternity attached to Clonard were leaving the church after their devotions.

Carolan started off after he had been introduced by the chairman and it soon was clear that there would be little hope of a hearing from the vast crowd assembled. It was not the confraternity men nor indeed any other men that created the noise, but there was literally a multitude of young women, mostly the millworkers of the Falls Road, who created the din. Mick tried to shout them down and soon his voice gave out and I took up where he left off. It was tough going and I struggled through for about twenty minutes after which the chairman, as gracefully as the circumstances permitted, closed the meeting.

I have reasons to recall this meeting and to remember it. Apart from the fact that it was the first public meeting in Belfast for Dev as Sinn Féin candidate, it was earlier in that afternoon of 23 November that our first boy[2] was born. He is now, as I write, a Passionist missioner in Bechuanaland, but I sometimes remind him that he was born on the anniversary of the execution of the Manchester Martyrs and on the day that Dev's campaign against 'wee Joe' was launched.

The meeting over, we drove back to our election rooms in the horse-drawn 'brake' which, in those days, always served as platform and accom-

2. Fr Donal Connolly, C.P. (1918-1985): born Belfast, ordained 1943, missionary in Bechuanaland.

modation for the speakers. The brake was somewhat crowded and I was one of several who were standing upright to receive the boos, jeers and occasional cheers of the accompanying mob. Then something seemed to hit me. It was as though I had run headlong into a lamp standard or a telephone pole. I felt a bit queer, but only that. Then I realised that the blood was trickling down. However, after a temporary dressing in headquarters, I slipped across to the Mater hospital. I knew that my close friend, Harry Macauley, then recently qualified, was one of the house surgeons and he soon fixed me up. Harry and his wife, May, were amongst the best friends we and the movement had in Belfast. Later he would come to Dublin where, in the Mater hospital and in the Orthopaedic hospital at Cappagh, he would establish himself as one of the most highly-regarded surgeons in the country. His brother Charlie, who was a fellow-student of mine in St Malachy's College, was also a well-known surgeon and Harry and he were always available. Both of them were in constant service under fire during the civil war.

After Harry had dressed my wound I was faced with the problem of how I was to visit Róisín and the new boy before retiring. To go in with my head bandaged would be worse than not to call at all. The nurse attending solved it by removing the bandage temporarily, leaving only a night-light during my visit and restoring the bandage before I retired. From the opening of the campaign it was a constant rush of conferences and meetings. I was selected and nominated to contest Mid-Antrim against the Honourable Hugh O'Neill.[3] It was, of course, one of the safest of Unionist strongholds, but it included the major portion of the Glens of Antrim, where I was reasonably well known. My friends Tadhg Smyth and John Clarke,[4] the latter well known as 'Benmore', the Glenarm versifier, were my fellow-speakers at most of our meetings and our election expenses were negligible. Our chief objective in such constituencies was not only to get every nationalist and anti-partitionist vote recorded, but to secure sufficient votes to save the deposit of £150 which the British government had imposed as a corollary of nomination. There were a number of areas in the constituency where we just did not put in an appearance nor even provide and agent to look after our interest on polling day, but in most of the towns and villages we held meetings and got away unharmed. I received nearly

3. Sir Robert William Hugh O'Neill (1883-1960): born Belfast, barrister 1909, captain in British army 1914-18, M.P. for mid-Antrim 1915-22, for County Antrim 1922-55, M.P. in Northern Ireland Parliament for County Antrim 1921-29, 1st speaker in Northern Ireland Parliament 1921, under-secretary of state for India and Burma 1939-40.

4. John Clarke: born Glenarm, County Antrim, rhymer.

three thousand votes to the eleven thousand recorded by my opponent and in the circumstances the result was considered satisfactory. The fact that we had saved the election deposit of £150 was also gratifying. Somewhat similar results were recorded in North Antrim and North Derry. In North Antrim Pat McCarry[5] was our candidate. He was one of a grand Irish-Ireland family who had a beautiful farm and hospitable home at Murlough, County Antrim. Here we often had happy weekends and odd holidays in the early days of the Gaelic League and G.A.A. It was a favourite spot of Roger Casement's and Roger was often a welcome guest in the home. Poor Pat was killed by British forces in Ballycastle in 1920. There is a memorial cross erected to his memory in the headland beyond the house, and on it is also the inscription commemorating the death of Roger.

Casement had expressed the hope before his execution that his remains would not be allowed to rest in the prison grave of Pentonville and that his friends would have his body brought home to be buried in Murlough. Up to the present all succeeding British governments have refused to heed appeals for the handing over of the remains for removal to the grave that awaits them in Murlough.

Patrick McGilligan[6] contested the constituency of North Derry and like McCarry and myself saved his deposit and had similarly a vote of about three thousand. In West Belfast Devlin scored an easy victory over de Valera, but as I have said this was a foregone conclusion. His victory and that of Captain Redmond[7] in Waterford city were the only two which the Parliamentary Party secured in straight fights with Sinn Féin over the entire country. They had four other seats, but these they had secured by agreement with Sinn Féin in marginal constituencies in north-east Ulster. Sinn Féin had won seventy-three seats; the Unionists had held their twenty-six seats, all but one in the North-East, and the Irish party held six seats, the four agreed ones already mentioned, the West Belfast seat won by Devlin and the Waterford city seat held by Captain Redmond.

5. Patrick McCarry (1885-1920): born Murlough, County Antrim, member of Gaelic League, Irish Volunteers 1914, I.R.A. 1919-20.

6. Patrick McGilligan, S.C. (1889-1979): born Coleraine, County Derry, member of Sinn Féin 1910, secretary to Kevin O'Higgins in First Dáil, supported the treaty, professor in law faculty, U.C.D. 1934-57, T.D. for National University of Ireland 1923-37, Dublin North West 1937-48, Dublin Central 1948-57, minister for industry and commerce 1924-32, minister for external affairs 1927-32, minister for finance 1948-51, attorney-general 1954-7.

7. Captain William Archer Redmond (1886-1932): born Waterford, eldest son of John Redmond, M.P. for Tyrone 1910-18, Waterford 1918-22, T.D. for Waterford 1922-32, co-founder of Irish National League 1926.

We had heard much about 'Self determination' and President Wilson[8] had been very definite in his speeches and in his famous 'Fourteen Points'. Sinn Féin had answered with great certainty and surely if the voting power of an electorate was to have any meaning in a democratic state, then the will of the people had been adequately expressed.

Whatever the future might hold, the Irish people had elected its own government for the legislative control and administration of its affairs. That government would function in Ireland and without any obligation, responsibility or loyalty to any foreign government, British or otherwise.

That was the position resulting from the election of 1918. It established beyond question the moral right for every action that the new Sinn Féin government might deem it wise to take either in the defence of the people's rights or in advancing the material and cultural progress of the people. Sinn Féin had won 73 seats, but four of these were won by candidates who had been returned for two constituencies thus giving the party 69 representatives. Of these no less than 36 were in prison. The 1918 election terminated finally the attendance of an Irish Party in the British parliament.

In due course, all those who had been elected were summoned to the first meeting of Dáil Éireann which was held in the Dublin's Mansion House on 21 January 1919. All the Unionist members and the six who made up the remnant of the Irish Parliamentary Party received their invitations like the rest, but none of these attended.

Cathal Brugha[9] presided and Father Michael O'Flanagan[10] opened the session with a prayer.

The Dáil proceeded to elect a cabinet which included a minister each for finance, home affairs, defence and foreign affairs. It was in no sense a 'window dressing' or propaganda gesture, but a serious first step to give

8. Thomas Woodrow Wilson (1856-1924): born Staunton, Virginia, 28th president of U.S.A. 1913-20.

9. Cathal Brugha (1874-1922): born Dublin, co-founded candle-manufacturing business, member of Gaelic League 1899, member of Irish Volunteers 1913, a leader in Easter Rising 1916, I.R.A. chief of staff 1917-19, returned to First Dáil 1919, minister for defence 1919-22, a leader of the anti-treatyites, killed in civil war.

10. Fr Michael O'Flanagan (1876-1942): born Castlerea, County Roscommon, teacher at Summerhill College, Sligo 1907-12, involved in 'land agitation' demanding 'land for the people', vice-president, Sinn Féin 1917, suspended from his ministry because of his involvement in political activities 1918, Sinn Féin propagandist in U.S.A. against the treaty 1921-6, resigned from Sinn Féin 1927, supported I.R.A. members who fought against general Franco 1936-9, campaigned in Canada and U.S.A. on behalf of the Friends of the Irish Republic and the North American Commission to aid Spanish Democracy 1937, convent chaplain in archdiocese of Dublin 1940-2.

effect to the will of the people declared in a democratic way at the recent election. That there were difficulties and obstacles to be overcome were obvious even to the least discerning, but the country had unbounded confidence in their newly elected representatives and there was universal enthusiasm for the new development.

The major objectives to which An Dáil devoted its immediate attention were to try and secure a hearing at the Peace Conference which was already sitting in Paris and to launch a national loan to provide the funds necessary to carry on its administrative work. Three delegates, de Valera, Griffith, and Count Plunkett, were appointed to state Ireland's case to the Conference and an address was issued to the free nations of the world declaring our independence and calling on their support and recognition of our rights at the Peace Conference.

In view of President Wilson's declarations and particularly his historic 'fourteen points', we had the hope that our case for a hearing and recognition would be admitted. Alas, Wilson proved a broken reed and was no match for the wily Lloyd George and the serpentine Clemenceau.[11]

Seán T. O'Kelly in Paris as the accredited envoy of the Republic and Dr MacCartan in the United States worked tirelessly to have our case presented, but without success.

A delegation of prominent Americans representing the 'Friends of Irish Freedom'[12] came to Paris to try and obtain a hearing for the Irish delegates at the Peace Conference. Messrs. Frank P. Walsh,[13] Ex-Governor

11. Georges Clemenceau (1841-1929): born Mouilleron-en-Pareds, Vendée, French statesman, dominated the negotiations leading to the Peace of Versailles 1918-19.

12. Friends of Irish Freedom: A republican organisation founded in New York in March 1916 and dominated by Clan na Gael, supported Easter Rising 1916, organised a fund to help dependants of internees 1916, Diarmuid Lynch acted as its secretary 1918-32, promoted the sale in the U.S.A. of bond certificates to fund the newly declared Irish Republic 1920-1, because of a rift with its leaders, Judge Daniel Cohalan and John Devoy, de Valera founded the American Association for the Recognition of the Irish Republic to replace it 1921, following litigation it was wound up 1932.

13. Francis Patrick Walsh (1864-1939): born St Louis, Missouri, a Western Union messenger 1874, court reporter 1882, lawyer 1889, outstanding trial lawyer and holder of minor public office 1892-94, hated poverty and its causes and compaigned against corrupt business influence on the Democratic Party machine, member of Kansas City Tenement Commission 1906-8, president of Board of Civil Service 1911-13, chairman of Commission on Industrial Relations 1913-18, co-chairman of National War Labour Board 1918, chairman of American Association for Recognition of Irish Republic, lobbied for Irish Independence Paris Peace Conference 1919, handled a large number of high-profile civil liberties cases, for example those of Tom Mooney, a West Coast labour leader, William Z. Foster, the communist leader, and attempted to have a stay on execution of Nicola Sacco and Bartolomeo Vanzetti, was regarded as one of the leading labour lawyers in the U.S.A.,

Dunne[14] of Illinois and Michael J. Ryan[15] were the emissaries. All of them were high in the councils of the Democratic Party and the Wilson administration. They visited Ireland early in May and spent one day with us in Belfast. During their stay they had ample evidence of the repressive activities of the British forces and the concluding paragraph of their report to the Peace Conference summarises their findings:

> We sincerely urge if the Peace Conference refuses a hearing to the people of Ireland, in these circumstances, the guilt for the commission of these monstrous crimes and atrocities as well as for the bloody revolution which may follow must, from this time forward, be shared with Great Britain by the members of the Peace Conference, if not by the people which they represent.

It was not left to the American delegation alone nor to the Irish people themselves to express their views to President Wilson. The United States Congress had already passed a resolution calling on Wilson to secure a hearing of Ireland's case and later, in June 1919, the United States senate by an almost unanimous vote confirmed it in the following resolution:

> That the senate of the United States earnestly requests the American Peace Commission at Versailles to endeavour to secure for Eamon de Valera, Arthur Griffith and George Noble Count Plunkett a hearing before the Peace Conference in order that they may present the case of Ireland. And, further, the senate of the United States expresses its sympathy with the aspirations of the Irish people for a government of their own choice.

---

supported Alfred E. Smith in 1924 and 1928, organised National Progressive League to support Roosevelt 1932, member of Commission to Re-codify Public Service Law 1929, chairman of State Power Authority 1931, president, National Lawyers Guild 1936.

14. Edward Fitzsimons Dunne (1853-1937): born Waterville, Connecticut, admitted to bar 1877, judge, circuit court, Cook County, Illinois 1892-1905, mayor of Chicago 1905-07, in law practice 1907-13, governor of Illinois 1913-17, presidential elector 1900, president of League of American Municipalities 1906-07, member of delegation from Irish societies in U.S.A. to present claims of Ireland for self-determination at Paris Peace Conference 1919, chairman of National Unity Council, author.

15. Michael J. Ryan (1862-1943): born Philadelphia, Pennsylvania, in law practice 1884-1911, city solicitor, Philadelphia 1911-16, public service commissioner of Pennsylvania 1916-19, president, Girard Avenue Title and Trust Co. 1907-31, member of delegation from Friends of Ireland in U.S.A. to Paris Peace Conference 1919, member of American Bar Association, trustee of Temple University and Samaritan Hospital 1908-28.

These developments naturally raised high hopes in Ireland. The great Wilson, he of the fourteen points, he who, in his academic days in Princeton, had expounded his principles of freedom had now the entire support of his own congress and senate to put into practice the doctrines which he had preached. It did not seem possible that he could ignore the demand of his own people, but he did just that.

Ireland has had more than her fair share of outside 'friends' who failed her at her moment of crisis, but the evasive dishonesty and supine surrender of Woodrow Wilson to the crafty Lloyd George and Clemenceau will be long remembered as one of the worst examples of such failure and the least defensible.

Wilson would return to America to reap the reward of his vacillations and desertion of his own high principles. America would revert to its political isolationism and Clemenceau and the Welsh wizard would sow the seeds of another war in the Treaty of Versailles.

While the Irish-American delegation were being turned down by President Wilson, President de Valera was on his way to the United States. He had been elected president of the Republic and it was as our president that he appeared on the American scene in June 1919 to launch and consolidate the greatest and most successful American-Irish political movement of all time. Dr MacCartan, Harry Boland, Liam Mellows[16] and Diarmuid Lynch[17] were already in America and a very considerable amount of dollars had already been subscribed by the Friends of Irish Freedom. There were differences of opinion as to the ways and means of using these funds. Joseph McGarrity[18] held the view that all funds should be placed at the disposal

16. Liam Mellows (1892-1922): born Ashton-under-Lyne, Lancashire, clerk in Dublin 1905, member of Fianna Éireann 1909, member of I.R.B. 1912, member of Irish Volunteers 1913, active in Easter Rising 1916, in U.S.A. assisted John Devoy in editing *Gaelic American* 1917-20, assisted with de Valera's tour of U.S.A. 1920, I.R.A. director of purchases 1920, Sinn Féin T.D. for Galway 1921-2, opposed the treaty, edited *Poblacht na hÉireann* 1922, executed by Provisional government 8 December 1922.

17. Diarmuid Lynch (1878-1960): born Tracton, County Cork, clerk in British civil service, member of Gaelic League in New York 1896, on return to Ireland member of I.R.B. 1907, member of its supreme council 1911-16, active in Easter Rising 1916, back in U.S.A. secretary of Friends of Irish Freedom 1918-32, returned to First Dáil but resigned seat in 1920, opposed the treaty, returned from U.S.A. to Tracton 1939.

18. Joseph McGarrity (1874-1940): born Carrickmore, County Tyrone, settled in Philadelphia 1892, leading member of Clan na Gael 1893-1940, president of the American Volunteers' Aid Association 1914, supported I.R.A. and Sinn Féin during war of independence, founded and ran *Irish Press* to support the republican cause 1918-22, managed de Valera's tour of U.S.A. 1919-20, supported de Valera against Judge Cohalan and John Devoy in split in Friends of Irish Freedom, on behalf of de Valera headed up American Association for the Recognition of the Irish Republic, opposed Fianna Fáil's entry into Dáil

of Dáil Éireann and that de Valera should have all their support in the flotation of a loan. Despite the opposition of Judge Cohalan,[19] John Devoy[20] and some of the leaders of the Friends of Irish Freedom, a bond drive for ten million dollars was launched.

De Valera's tour of the United States was a phenomenal success. As president of the Republic he was received not only with mass meetings, but by city and State authorities from coast to coast. All the meetings were 'mass' meetings with overflow audiences, and it is no exaggeration to describe his nation-wide canvass of the United States as one long triumphal tour. In every city and town a branch of the organisation was formed to work for the cause of Irish independence, for the recognition of the Irish Republic and for the sale of the bonds.

Although these bonds were issued to bear interest at five per cent seven months 'after the territory of the Republic of Ireland is freed from the military control of England', I think it is fair to say that few, if any of those who bought, concerned themselves with the bonds as an investment. Our people in America, and many people who were not of our race, realised that we were in a deadly struggle with England and they responded with extraordinary generosity to help in our need.

It is an anticipatory digression perhaps, but here I may record that it fell to my lot as a minister of de Valera's government to make arrangements, in 1933 in New York, for the redemption of all these bonds with an ex-gratia bonus of twenty-five per cent. This redemption was made operative

---

Éireann 1927, supported demand of Seán Russell, chief-of-staff of I.R.A., for a war against Britain 1939, at a meeting in Hamburg unsuccessfully pleaded with Herman Goering for aid for the I.R.A. 1939.

19. Judge Daniel Cohalan (1865-1946): born Middletown, New York, important figure in Democratic Party, judge of supreme court of New York 1912, involved in preparations for Easter Rising 1916, chairman of Irish Convention in Philadelphia 1919, a leading figure in Friends of Irish Freedom 1916-32.

20. John Devoy (1842-1928): born Johnstown, County Kildare, joined Fenians and later enlisted in French Foreign Legion to gain military experience to assist in the fight for an Irish Republic 1860, organiser for Irish Republican Brotherhood 1862, with others recruited 15,000 Irish soldiers, serving in British army, into the I.R.B., successfully planned escape of James Stephens, head of I.R.B., from Richmond prison 1865, arrested 1866, released 1871, organised the escape of Fenian prisoners from Freemantle prison in Australia 1876, journalist in Chicago and New York and joined Clan na Gael 1871, supported the 'New Departure' and later the 'Plan of Campaign' in the struggle for a satisfactory conclusion to the 'Land Question', through his newspapers *The Irish Nation* and *The Gaelic American* he gave the British ample reason to consider him 'one of the empire's most dangerous enemies', he supported the treaty 1921, regarding it as the first step in securing the ultimate aim of the Republican movement.

at the time when Britain had defaulted on her war-debt payments to the United States. President Franklin D. Roosevelt[21] publicly commented on the fact 'that of all the debtor countries, the two small countries of Ireland and Finland were the only states who met their liabilities'.

The history of President de Valera's campaign in the United States has, I think, been adequately reported by those who so ably assisted him in the campaign. I had, however, one interesting experience in connection with it which merits recording.

On one of my visits to Dublin and while having lunch with him, Griffith asked me if I knew a Presbyterian minister named Dr Irwin. I had never met the reverend doctor and told him so. He then gave me his address and asked me to get in touch with him when I returned home. Dr Irwin had written to him and offered to go to the U.S.A. and speak there on behalf of the Republic, believing that it was desirable and perhaps essential to make it clear to America that there were others than the Catholic people of Ireland who believed in an Independent Republic. The importance of this was obvious as the whole fabric of the Carsonite movement had been mainly built around the frame-work of Orange bigotry.

On my return I invited Dr Irwin to meet me. He was a mild, gentle and kindly man with a fine mind and clear understanding of the past and present history of the country. His ministry was in the parish of Killead, a few miles from the town of Antrim and in the immediate vicinity of Aldergrove which at that time was the chief aerodrome in Ireland for the British forces.

I told him of my talk with Griffith and he in turn explained in detail what he had in mind. While I was completely satisfied about Dr Irwin's ability and his integrity, I was worried about the serious responsibility that he proposed to undertake. I pointed out to him that he had his parish and his parishioners, his home and farm and family. I wondered if he had fully realised the inevitable harvest of trouble that he must reap if he went to America and publicly advocated the cause of the Irish Republic there. I emphasised what seemed to me the minimum penalties which he must suffer. He would most probably be deprived of his church and congregation; he would be boycotted by his friends and church associates; he would almost certainly be 'on the run' like the rest of us. These, I said, were the very least of the punishments that would be inflicted and I rather feared that imprisonment or worse was possible. His quiet answer was typical of the man whom I came to know so well later and to esteem as one of my

21. Franklin Delano Roosevelt (1882-1945): born Hyde Park, New York, 32nd president, U.S.A. 1933-45.

best friends. 'Men have made sacrifices and are making sacrifices for the principles in which they believe, and I see no reason why I should not do the same.' There seemed little or no answer to that, and yet I was still uneasy. I asked him about Mrs Irwin and how she might view the situation and he told me that he knew she would agree with his proposal. Eventually I asked him to go back and consult Mrs Irwin, charging him to make clear to her all my fears of what would follow and to come back to me in a few days with her views and decision. He returned a few days later to assure me that he had given her my pessimistic picture of future possibilities and that she was wholeheartedly with him in his determination to do what he could to help the country in its struggle.

At this time I was visiting Dublin every fortnight for meetings of the Industrial Commission, and saw Griffith and some of the others at lunch or afterwards. I reported to Griffith the substance of my talks with the reverend doctor and both of us being satisfied that he fully appreciated all that was involved and of the great value his help would be to the American campaign, Griffith said he would make the necessary arrangements.

It is right to make it clear that Dr Irwin did not receive a cent for his services nor any allowance for the deputy minister who officiated during his absence and for whose services he was doubtless responsible.

Within the week of my talk with Griffith, one of Mick Collins' lieutenants—I think on this occasion it was Frank Thornton[22]—arrived up at home and handed me £200 which was to cover transportation and other incidental costs of the Irwins' journey to New York at which point they would be met and taken care of by our group there. Incidentally, on his return Dr Irwin handed me back some £58 out of the £200, explaining that the only expense incurred was the purchase of two second-class tickets to New York for himself and Mrs Irwin. All his hotel and travelling expenses had been paid by the American organisation.

Dr Irwin's campaign was of inestimable value to the organisation in the U.S. and of still greater value when the organisers had the wisdom to send him on a Canadian tour.[23] At his Canadian meetings and in areas in the

22. Frank Thornton: born Dublin, member of Irish Volunteers 1913, interned following Easter Rising 1916, member of I.R.A. and of Michael Collins' 'squad' 1919-21, supported the treaty, founder member of New Ireland Assurance Company.

23. The *Irish News* of 2 April 1920 reported the beginning of Dr Irwin's campaign as follows: 'The Rev J. A. H. Irwin, Presbyterian minister from a large congregation near Belfast, has come to the United States to present the case of the Irish Protestants in favour of self-determination of the Irish nation, says American Exchange.

In a statement which he issued from his hotel, Dr Irwin attacked the Carson delegation recently in the U.S.A. on the grounds that they had made a deliberate attempt to raise a

Southern States his very presence went far to dispel any suggestion that the fight for Irish independence was a sectarian struggle. Here was a nonconformist minister who lived in the heart of Orangeism and within a few miles of Belfast who stood for the Republic and freedom and had travelled over to convince his co-religionists and all non-Catholics that Ireland's fight was for freedom, for all Ireland irrespective of creed or class. Dr Irwin was a cool, calm and genial personality. His speeches were those of a sincere, thoughtful man and carried conviction. His contribution to the work in the United States and Canada was unique because he was what he was and he left a lasting impression wherever he went, as will be made clear by what happened after he returned home.

Some four or five months after I had said farewell to the Irwins on their departure for the States, I was sitting at my desk in the office when the door opened. To say that I was surprised would be an understatement for, with his genial smile, Irwin was standing before my desk. 'How, when, I mean how did you get here?', I spluttered. My surprise was not unreasonable for 'things' generally were pretty tough at the period, and, while most of us were able to go about our work during the day, not many of us were

---

religious issue which does not exist in Ireland. He said that Sir Edward Carson had tried to raise the religious issue only when every other effort on his part had failed.

'It is absolutely untrue', said Dr Irwin, 'that all Catholics in Ireland belong to the Nationalist Party, just as it is most untrue that all Protestants are Unionists'. Dr Irwin said that the so-called Ulsterites would not be afraid to attempt to protect their own rights in an Irish parliament.

'Do you mean to say that we could not hold our own in a Dublin parliament, even if we were in a three-to-one minority', asked Dr Irwin. 'You bet we could, and more. Further, it is stupid to think that a Dublin parliament would legislate to the detriment of any part of Ireland.' He said that, at present, Irish Episcopalians hold over 80 per cent of the positions of honour and emolument in Ireland, despite the fact that they form only 10 per cent of the population.

Dr Irwin, besides being minister of Killead, a large congregation in County Antrim, is manager of four national schools and is interested in the vital social problems of Ireland today.

Dr Irwin said: 'So far from expecting ill-treatment, we as a Church have from our unbroken experience of our Roman Catholic fellow-countrymen for generations good reasons to expect the contrary treatment. We have small bodies of Presbyterians in every part of the south and west of Ireland and these people and their ministers have experienced nothing but kindness at the hands of their Catholic neighbours, and very often they have got substantial help for their church funds from Roman Catholics.

No Protestant in any part of Ireland today is living in fear and trembling lest he may be murdered or attacked, as he is sometimes represented: and, in fact, he is in no way intimidated on account of his religion. There can be no difficulty in this respect as there is a common standard of morality held by all Irishmen'.

spending the nights at home. 'We just got off the boat and went home to Killead' was his reply. He then went on to tell me that he had just gone out and given the services on the previous Sunday, as if he had not been away at all. No, there had been no fuss or show of hostility, but of course he knew that there were deep and ominous rumblings. What interested him most and, in a sense amused him, was the fact that a number of the hard-shelled Orangemen in his congregation came over after the service, welcomed him back and assured him of their constant attachment. It all sounded reassuring, but I still had my doubts and fears. I could not conceive that his return would be allowed to pass unheeded either by his congregation or, by what I dreaded much more, the varied assortment of armed forces that were on the rampage at the time. Frankly I felt deep anxiety for his safety and thought a midnight raid and an unknown gunman the most likely development. However, Irwin continued to live at home and resumed his ministerial and parish duties, as if nothing untoward had happened. He visited me frequently at the office and one day announced that he proposed trying an experiment to test out the real atmosphere in his parish. He had decided to hold a garden party at which a fee for admission would be charged to raise funds for some church or parish requirements. Everything was planned accordingly, but I had a visit from him a few days before the event when he told me he had learned that a gang or group had been formed which would cause chaos or worse at the party. It was not in the good doctor's character to surrender quietly to threats of that nature and yet he dreaded the possible consequences which, from his information, might be very serious indeed. We talked the matter over and it was clear that what Dr Irwin wanted was a few of the right sort of boys who could mix with the crowd and yet be ready at a moment's notice to handle the situation. I saw Joe McKelvey[24] that evening and he, with a few of his company, took charge of the situation and everything passed off quite pleasantly. Irwin was satisfied that their presence did not pass unnoticed and accounted for the peaceful afternoon.

Eventually he had the inevitable raid. A group of the usual mixture of Auxiliaries and R.I.C. arrived at night and searched the house with their customary destructive efficiency. They had apparently found nothing incriminating, but the officer seeing an old blunderbuss, a relic of the United Irishmen, hanging in the hall decided to arrest the doctor for being in possession of firearms. He was taken to the Victoria barracks and duly

24. Joseph McKelvey (1885-1922): born Belfast, member of Irish Volunteers 1914 and later I.R.A. 1919-22, opposed the treaty 1921, acted as adjutant to Four Courts' forces, captured after its surrender and executed in Mountjoy jail 1922.

charged before a military court. Here they took the unusual course of releasing him on his undertaking to appear before them on a fixed date. We had tea together the evening before his trial when he told me that he had practically decided to hand in his resignation to the elders of his congregation at Killead. He expected to be sentenced and this did not seem to depress him. What was worrying him a great deal, however, was that the retention of his ministry was not helpful to the religious and spiritual guidance of his parishioners. I pointed out that as he was not responsible for his own arrest by resigning his ministry he was simply playing into his enemies' hands. As I put it to him: 'If you resign, they win: if they dismiss you or demand your resignation, you win'. I succeeded in dissuading him from resigning. He went before the military court the following day and was sentenced to six months imprisonment.

About two weeks later he walked into my office in his usual quiet way. I was surprised but delighted and asked him what had happened. 'I haven't a notion', he said, 'The warder opened the cell door and told me to take my things and go'. Later he learned the reason. It transpired that the Presbyterians in Toronto, most of them Orangemen, on learning of his arrest and sentence had 'raised Cain' and had caused a demand or request for his immediate release to be sent through officials in Canada. His address on behalf of Ireland to the people of Toronto had not been forgotten.

Dr Irwin quietly resumed his parochial work, but he was unhappy about the damage that might result from the religious point of view by his continuing as minister, and sometime later transferred as an assistant minister to a congregation in Edinburgh. His bank had withdrawn normal overdraft facilities which had been accorded to him for running his extensive farm and he was forced to dispose of his fine house and holding at a heavy sacrifice. He 'won back to Ireland' a few years later to serve the Presbyterian congregation at Lucan, just outside Dublin, and here he continued as minister until his death. He resumed his association with those of us who knew him in the dark and troubled days. His services, advice and help were always available to the Republican cause until the end. May his soul rest in peace!

It may seem perhaps that I have devoted an inordinate amount of attention to the Irwin story, but I think it merits it and for this reason. Some of us know that there were a number of Presbyterian ministers in Belfast and throughout Ulster who believed, as Irwin believed, in Ireland's right to independence, and who cherished the memory of their forbears in the '98 struggle and in the 'Tenant Right' movement. They were in a minority, and they were hemmed in by the intolerant and bigoted mass pressure that reached its peak with the Carsonite movement. Irwin deserves his historical niche for the simple reason that he was the sole North of Ireland minister of that church who, in our generation, dared to come out openly and declare his allegiance to his own people and to the cause of Irish independence and the Irish Republic.

10

Dáil Éireann functions – Local council elections – Proportional Representation introduced – The new terror launched – Tomás MacCurtain murdered – Terence MacSwiney on hunger strike – Revolt in the R.I.C. – The Partition Bill passed

The year 1919 saw the initial efforts of Dáil Éireann to take over, in so far as it was possible, the machinery of government and the immediate counter attacks by the British to kill all such efforts. Raids, arrests, long sentences to imprisonment were the order of the day. Lord French[1] was in command and Winston Churchill, in answer to a question in the House of Commons on 18 December 1919, said that the number of troops in Ireland was 43,000 and the monthly cost was £860,000. During the earlier months of the year there was comparatively little 'hitting back' by the Republican forces, but it was soon evident that the authorities in the Castle were determined to provoke trouble all over the country.

Sinn Féin and the Dáil departments were concentrating on the constructive side of their programme and, despite all suppression and interference, were succeeding to a remarkable degree. The canvassing for and collection for the Dáil Loan was carried on, meetings of the Dáil were held and the various departments were, step by step, working their way into the life of the country.

I had the privilege of being appointed a member of the Commission of Inquiry into the Resources and Industries of Ireland which had been set up by An Dáil. We held our opening session in September 1919 and for some time continued our work openly without being disturbed by the British. It was heavy but interesting work and for me it involved travelling to Dublin for the various Commission sessions every fortnight and in the intervals, studying and analysing the various technical and experts' reports. Darrell Figgis was our secretary and a most competent executive he proved himself. My fortnightly visits to Dublin gave me the opportunity to keep in contact with most of what was going on there and throughout the country, and it soon became clear that we were rapidly advancing to a period of struggle.

I found it difficult to deal with all my engagements and work. Business was flourishing and, although I had an excellent though small group of

1. John Denton French: Lord French of Ypres (1852-1925): born Kent, joined British army 1874, commander-in-chief British Expeditionary Force to France 1914, commander-in-chief of the Home Guard 1915-18, lord lieutenant in Ireland 1919-21, survived a dozen attempts on his life by the I.R.A.

employees, mine was very much a one-man business and required constant personal attention. It was, however, symptomatic of the times that one's own personal business did to a degree become of secondary importance to the urgent demands of the movement.

In Belfast itself there were occasional incidents, but on the whole things were superficially quiet. Sinn Féin was spreading in a somewhat slow growth and the Volunteers were quietly building up their organisation.

Belfast as a whole was continuing to enjoy its boom of good trade, big wages and much spending. Ironically enough, the wholesale merchants, some of whom I met at lunch, were jubilant at the big orders they were receiving from all over the South and West of Ireland. At that time and for many years before the wholesale distributors in Belfast had enjoyed the support and trade of the retail shops all over Ireland. It applied to every branch of the dry goods trade, drapery, linen, cotton and wollens, and equally to imported food stuffs. Now that the war was over, stocks were being replenished and the real problem, as one of the wholesalers explained to me, was to get enough supplies to meet the demands.

If things were relatively quiet in Belfast and the surrounding area, it was very different in Dublin and in other parts of the country. Each day saw an intensification of the struggle. Sinn Féin and the work of the Dáil departments must not be allowed to go on. Arrests, raids and savage sentences were increasing, and it seemed clear that Dublin Castle and the authorities were determined to provoke the whole country into open insurrection.

From this time forward it is but fair to say that the biggest share of directing the constructive work of Dáil Éireann and the work of national defence fell on the shoulders of Michael Collins.

I am, by nature, little disposed to anything in the way of hero worship, but I have always been convinced that during the fateful years from 1919 to 1921 the one man who, more than any other, carried the Herculean load of Ireland's fight was Collins. It would scarcely be necessary to say so, but for the events that followed the treaty and which to many obscured the real qualities and genius that made Collins what he was.

I met him only a few times, but he paid me the compliment of his confidence by entrusting to my care a number of special commissions and jobs that had to be carried out. What first surprised me was that, where particulars and instructions had to be communicated in writing, the letters were typed on official paper with the necessary references and finish that one would expect from an institution such as the Bank of Ireland. I soon learned that this was normal procedure. How any man, pursued as he was by day and night, with offices here and there over Dublin that had to be moved and switched as raid followed raid, was able to carry out his work so efficiently will always be a mystery to me.

One of the great achievements of Collins, and one which made all else possible, was the building up of his intelligence service and his complete destruction of the spy system in Dublin Castle. For those who are interested I would recommend them to read accounts of the life of Michael Collins written by his close associate, Piaras Béaslaí, To me these are fair, dispassionate records of Collins' life during those years. I leave aside all the controversial issues that marked the aftermath of the treaty and the tragedy of the split that followed but, with that reservation, I think Piaras Béaslaí's volumes[2] are an essential study for those who wish to know and understand Michael Collins and his work.

The elections to municipal and local boards were due to be held in January 1920 and the British government decided to introduce the system of election by proportional representation. It should be noted particularly that it was to be applied to Ireland only and, of course, the reason behind it was obvious. Under proportional representation it was anticipated that the pro-British vote would secure at least some representation in the local bodies.

Although the new system of voting was aimed solely at the reduction of Republican influence and power, it was willingly accepted by the country as a fair and democratic means of giving expression to minority opinion. The ultimate results showed that the country all over with the exception of the North-East corner was solidly behind Sinn Féin. Even in the city of Belfast we managed to secure upwards of a dozen seats in the city council. The counties of Fermanagh and Tyrone and the city of Derry, which were soon to be cut off from their fellow countrymen and forcibly engaged in the partitioned six counties, had Republican majorities, and Derry had elected a Catholic Nationalist as its lord mayor.

All over Ireland outside the North-East corner councils had Republican majorities who were in control of local government. They broke off administrative connections with the Local Government Board which was administered from Dublin Castle and recognised Dáil Éireann as the sole authority over them.

Such were a few of the immediate results of the proportional representation elections of 1920. The war on the people all over the country was being intensified and raids, arrests, shootings and murders were of daily or,

2. Piaras Béaslaí, *Michael Collins and the making of a new Ireland*, I-II (Dublin 1926) and *Michael Collins, soldier and statesman* (Dublin 1937).

perhaps it might more correctly be said, of nightly occurrence. As Dr Daniel Cohalan,[3] one of the bishops, said at the time: 'The policy of the British government seems to be to make use of every means and every opportunity to exasperate the people and drive them to acts of desperation.'

It was quite evident that there was a policy. It was a war on the people, a war of frightfulness without regard to age or sex. The Volunteers fought back and, thanks to the intelligence service which Collins had perfected, did it effectively.

I was in Cork early in 1920 to attend special sessions of the Industrial Commission that had been arranged to take evidence from people in the area. The meetings were to be held in the city hall and we had just assembled when the military arrived and ordered us out. The members of the Commission were staying at the Imperial Hotel and, after a brief consultation, we decided to return to the hotel, get one of the large reception rooms and proceed with our work there. We had started our work but a short time when the room was invaded by another detachment of military and again we were driven out.

This was the first occasion on which the authorities in Dublin Castle had openly interfered with our operations, but we were not surprised. It was in harmony with all else that was happening. The Reverend Dr O'Rahilly,[4] who was then Professor O'Rahilly of Cork University, a member of the Commission, made his own house available and there we examined all the witnesses and completed the work we had come to do. That was in January 1920 and many terrible things were to happen before my next visit to Cork. Tomás MacCurtain, the lord mayor, who had been one of our fellow-prisoners in Reading in 1916, was on the night of 19 March shot dead in his own home, and his successor, Terence MacSwiney, who had also been with us in Reading, would die after seventy-four days on hunger strike. The city hall and many of the finest buildings in Cork would be burned to the ground by the army of released criminals that we would come to know as the 'Black and Tans'.[5]

3. Daniel Cohalan (1859-1952): born Kilmichael, County Cork, professor, St Finbarr's seminary, Cork 1883-86, professor, St Patrick's College, Maynooth, 1886-1914, co-adjutor bishop of Cork 1914-16, bishop 1916-52, outspoken critic of both sides in Anglo-Irish war.

4. Alfred O'Rahilly (1884-1969): born Listowel, County Kerry, member of Society of Jesus, but left before ordination 1901-14, professor of mathematical physics, U.C.C. 1917-43, Sinn Féin member of Cork Corporation 1920-21, president U.C.C. 1943-54, following death of his wife in 1953 ordained for archdiocese of Nairobi 1955, monsignor 1960.

5. Black and Tans: During the war of independence the British government recruited this new force in England from demobilised soldiers and ex-convicts to supplement the R.I.C.

I would pause for a space in my narrative to pay my humble tribute to these two great men, MacSwiney and MacCurtain. They were close friends and associates in all their work together in Cork and in their work for Irish freedom.

MacCurtain was always a cheerful and kindly companion in jail and one of the most transparently honest men I ever met. He gave me the impression of being somewhat impulsive and was vehement and tenacious in argument when questions of national policy arose. A man of great courage and character and withal a simple soul who saw things straight. A thing was either right or wrong, and there could be no compromise on matters of principle.

I came somewhat closer to Terence MacSwiney than I did to MacCurtain or indeed to most of my other fellow-prisoners. Terence was gentle, quiet and thoughtful. His were the mind and soul of a poet and patriot. He was interested in literature and drama, but they were secondary to his interest in Ireland. The Ireland he worked for and eventually died for was the same Ireland that would be clean and pure and cultured, and freed from the sordid soul-killing elements of materialism. Prosperity was desirable, but it was to be a reasonable prosperity, widespread over all our people and free from the exploitation of any individual or groups. Terence was deeply religious, but without any unnecessary display of it was quietly tolerant of all our foibles. He had only one hate. It was not against English people or English things, but concentrated entirely on the British occupation of our country and their ruling over us as a subject people. He personified resurgent Ireland and all the finest ideals that the Ireland of his day sought to establish. I was to see him later when he was a prisoner in Belfast jail and to welcome his lovely wife and little baby at our home when she came to visit him. She took apartments near us and with her baby availed of every opportunity that the regulations permitted to visit Terence in the prison. It was my last contact with him, God rest his soul!

Lloyd George brought in his 'Better Government of Ireland' Bill in March. This was the Partition Bill passed by the Commons without an Irish

---

There was a shortage of R.I.C. uniforms and they were issued with khaki trousers (military) and dark green tunics (police). This combination reminded people of the County Limerick hunt known as the Scarteen Black and Tans. The Black and Tans were responsible for many outrages, including the murders of Lord Mayor Tomás MacCurtain, Lord Mayor George Clancy and former Lord Mayor Michael O'Callaghan, the killings in Croke Park on Bloody Sunday, 21 November 1920, as well as the burning of Balbriggan, County Dublin, Ballylongford, County Kerry, Bruff and Kilmallock, County Limerick, Cork City and Midleton, County Cork, Ennistymon, Lahinch, Miltown-Malbay, County Clare, Trim, County Meath, and Tubbercurry, County Sligo.

vote and the curse of which still hangs over us. It cut off not Ulster, be it noted, but the six North-Eastern counties, two of which, Tyrone and Fermanagh, had nationalist majorities as had the city of Derry and the area of South Down. Geographical Ulster, which included Donegal, Monaghan and Cavan, would have given a majority vote for the Republic and that could not be tolerated, while on the other hand to leave out Fermanagh and Tyrone would have reduced the British-occupied territory to the four counties of Antrim, Down, Armagh and Derry.

Carson was quite frank when he replied to his critics who demanded to know why all Ulster was not being partitioned from the rest of Ireland: 'You would bring in from these three counties an additional two hundred and sixty thousand Roman Catholics . . . There is no use in our undertaking a government which we know would be a failure.'

The super democrat who had earned hate and attack for his defence of the Boers in the South African war, the little Welsh lawyer Lloyd George, proceed to smash all the democratic canons and to carve out a pocket of occupation for the empire. As Carson said: 'You will have it as a jumping-off place from which you can carry on all the necessary operations.'

Carson had no compunction about throwing overboard the seventy or eighty thousand Protestants who live in the three counties Donegal, Monaghan and Cavan and equally little regard for the minority groups that were in the southern counties of the country. It may be that, being a Dubin man who had spent his academic life in Trinity College and had lived in Catholic Ireland, he knew perfectly well that bigotry did not prevail there, and that non-Catholics throughout the country enjoyed more than tolerance from their Catholic neighbours.

While Lloyd George and his associates were 'wangling' their legislative measures through parliament, they were at the same time intensifying their ruthless warfare all over the country. General Sir Neville Macready[6] was made commander-in-chief of the forces in Ireland and was working in close association with Sir Henry Wilson who was chief of the imperial staff.

6. General Sir Cecil Frederick Nevil Macready (1862-1946): born Aberdeen, lieutenant-colonel in Boer war 1900, became a general 1918, commissioner of London Metropolitan Police 1918-20, officer commanding British forces in Ireland 1920-3, disapproved of reprisals carried out by the indisciplined Auxiliaries and Black and Tans, informed Lloyd George that I.R.A. would not negotiate if laying down arms was a preliminary, arranged truce 1921, advised British government during treaty negotiations 1921, supervised withdrawal of British forces from Southern Ireland 1922.

That prince of liars, Sir Hamar Greenwood,[7] was made chief secretary and a general was appointed as police adviser. All over Ireland the combined forces of military, police, Black and Tans and Auxiliaries[8] carried on incessantly, and murders, raids and outrages were of daily occurrence. The Republican forces hit back and their guerrilla warfare, carried on by comparatively small active columns, was gradually pushing the British forces out of the scattered police barracks throughout the country to seek their safety by concentrating in the larger and heavily protected centres.

On the Saturday of Holy Week, 1920, one of the most effective blows against the British administration in Ireland was delivered successfully. On that night the Volunteers raided the income tax offices, not only in Dublin and Cork, but in practically every town in Ireland, destroyed all the records and books and set fires to the offices. The Belfast active-service group succeeded in their raid on the Belfast Custom House. The raids all over the country were in nearly every case successful and practically the whole machinery of income tax collection was put out of action. Apart from Belfast and the Six Counties, the collection of income tax by the British was permanently finished.

One of the interesting features in regard to the major coup was that during the Holy Week preceding it, the British authorities had been more active than ever. Apparently the rumour had got around that another insurrection would take place on Easter Sunday. Barricades and military detachments were placed on the main roads and passengers on the trains were questioned and searched. Soldiers were out on patrols and naval forces were around the coast, while the Volunteers were quietly carrying out their work.

A significant development emerged in 1920 when some members of the R.I.C., disgusted with the work which their superiors demanded, revolted and threw off their uniforms. The Royal Irish Constabulary from its

7. Sir Hamar Greenwood (1870-1948): born Whitby, Toronto, M.P. for York 1906, parliamentary private secretary to Winston Churchill 1906-10, M.P. for Sunderland 1910, under-secretary for home affairs 1919, chief secretary for Ireland 1920-2, a lawyer himself, at a time when coroners' inquests had returned over twenty charges against the crown forces he admitted to knowledge of only one, his stonewalling statements in parliament were even in British circles not unfairly caricatured as 'there is no such thing as reprisals, but they have done a great deal of good'.

8. The Auxiliaries were recruited from among demobilised officers of the British army in July 1920 to augment the Royal Irish Constabulary. They numbered 1,500 'cadets' and were divided into fifteen companies of 100 men. Their pay of £1 per day plus expenses made them the highest paid uniformed force of their time. They became notorious for the ferocity of their reprisals.

foundation had been noted for its loyalty to its controlling authority in Dublin Castle. It had always been much more than a police force. It was the eyes and ears of the British government in Ireland, and nothing happened, even in the smallest town or village in Ireland, that escaped notice. In its G division in Dublin Castle was operated the almost perfect organisation of political intelligence and espionage that could account for the movements and activities of practically every person who was deemed to be hostile to the British occupation of the country.

But strange things were happening. Michael Collins had succeeded in establishing within the G division itself his counter-espionage organisation, and from that time forward, thanks to the daring of a few men, it served Collins and the country. That was one phase and the most important one of the new developments, but the spontaneous spirit of mutiny in the ranks of the R.I.C. that would arise in various districts of the country could only be attributed to the policy of savage and ruthless warfare on the people which the new military and police chiefs laid down for the men under them.

What happened in Listowel in 1920 was symptomatic of the changing outlook in the ranks of the R.I.C. General Tudor,[9] the head of the police force, and Colonel Smyth,[10] the Divisional Police Commissioner for Munster, visited the barracks and Colonel Smyth assembled the men in the dayroom and addressed them. This was a real 'pep-talk'. Here is a report of his speech which one of the men concerned gave to Arthur Griffith:

> Well men, I have something of interest to tell you; something that I am sure you would not wish your wives to hear. I am going to lay all my cards on the table; I may reserve one card to myself. Now men, Sinn Féin has had all the sport up to the present and we are going to have the sport now. The police are not in sufficient strength to do anything but hold their barracks. This is not enough for, as long as we remain on the defensive, so long will Sinn Féin have the whip

9. Major-General Sir Hugh H. Tudor (1871-1965): born Exeter, served with distinction in Boer war and World War I, chief of police, Ireland 1920-1, air vice-marshall and officer commanding forces in Palestine 1922.

10. Lt-Colonel Gerald Smyth (1885-1920): born Dalhousie, India, distinguished service as a captain in British Expeditionary Force 1914, divisional commander of Royal Irish Constabulary in Munster 1920, at Listowel R.I.C. barracks on 19 June 1920 he told the police that in dealing with the I.R.A. and Sinn Féin the more people they would shoot the better he would. like it, a subsequent police mutiny prompted by this was led by Constable Jeremiah Mee. Smyth was assassinated soon afterwards in the Cork County Club by the I.R.A.

hand. We must take the offensive and beat Sinn Féin with its own tactics. Martial law, applying to all Ireland, is to come into operation immediately; as a matter of fact we are to have our scheme of amalgamation complete on 21 June. I am promised as many troops from England as I require: thousands are coming daily. I am getting seven thousand police from England. Now men, what I wish to explain to you is that you are to strengthen your comrades in the out-stations.

The military must be quartered in the large towns for the following reasons: (1) They must be convenient to railway stations to enable them to move rapidly from place to place as occasion demands and (2), unlike police, soldiers cannot act individually and independently but only in large numbers under a good officer; he must be a good officer, otherwise I shall break him for inefficiency.

If a police barracks is burned or if the barracks already occupied is not suitable, then the best house in the locality is to be commandeered, the occupants thrown out in the gutter. Let them die there, the more the merrier. Police and military will patrol the country at least five nights a week. They are not to confine themselves to the main roads, but make across the country, lie in ambush and when civilians are seen approaching shout 'Hands up!' Should the order be not immediately obeyed, shoot and shoot with effect. If the persons approaching carry their hands in their pockets or are in any way suspicious looking, shoot them down.

You may make mistakes occasionally and innocent people may be shot but they cannot be helped and you are bound to get the right parties sometime. The more you shoot, the better I will like you and, I assure you, no policeman will get into trouble for shooting any man. Hunger strikers will be allowed to die in jail, the more the merrier. Some of them have died already and a damn bad job they were not all allowed to die. As a matter of fact some of them have already been dealt with in a manner their friends will never hear about.

An emigrant ship left an Irish port for a foreign port lately with lots of Sinn Féiners on board. I assure you men, it will never land.

That is nearly all I have to say to you. We want your assistance in carrying out this scheme and wiping out Sinn Féin. Any man who is not prepared to do so is a hindrance rather than a help to us and he had better leave the job at once.

At the close of this speech Colonel Smyth addressed the first man of the ranks of the assembled constables saying: 'Are you prepared to co-operate?'

The man curtly referred him to the spokesman whom the members of the Listowel force had chosen. This constable stood forward and replied: 'By your account I take it you are an Englishman and in your ignorance forget that you are addressing Irishmen.' The constable then took off his cap, belt and bayonet and laid them on the table saying, 'These too are English, take them as a present from me and to hell with you, you are a murderer.'

Colonel Smyth immediately ordered the arrest of the spokesman; the other constables swore that if a hand was laid on him the room would 'run red with blood'. Colonel Smyth and his companions then retired.

A month later this Colonel Smyth was shot dead in the Cork County Club by a member of the I.R.A.

While a number of incidents similar to that in Listowel occurred, it has to be admitted that in most places the R.I.C. did co-operate with the Tudor forces and many attacks and much destruction could be credited to them up to the time of the truce. At the same time the old confidence and trust that Dublin Castle had in them was badly shaken. Between five and six hundred constables had resigned and recruitment to the force had ceased by August 1920.

11

Swanzy shot in Lisburn – Belfast pogrom – Murders and burnings – Craigavon gives his approval to the campaign – Kevin Barry tortured and killed – Republican courts operating – Dr Mannix arrested – Terence MacSwiney dies – The boycott of Belfast traders

The Macready-Tudor-Greenwood forces grew stronger throughout the country. British soldiers, Black and Tans and Auxiliaries, as well as the R.I.C. and the detective force of G men, were in constant action. In the summer of 1920 they seemed to be everywhere and for the most part were completely out of hand and indisciplined. It was evident that the doctrines enunciated by Colonel Smyth to the constables in Listowel were the permanent 'orders of the day' for all the operating forces.

In Belfast and the North-East we had our own share of the campaign, but in our area the British and anti-National authorities had always available their experienced and well-tried forces of the Orange and anti-Catholic organisations. There was ample evidence that the necessary influences and direction were under way early in 1920. As always, the first rumblings of trouble were apparent in the shipyards and an appropriate lead was given by Sir Edward Carson in his Twelfth of July speech. In this he called for action, and within ten days he had got a whole-hearted response, and the expulsion of the Catholics from the shipyards had commenced.

I had always been convinced that the intermittent but quite frequent outbursts of riots, pogroms and the savage attacks by the Orange mobs on the Catholic minority had their commercial and economic facets, apart altogether from their use by the anti-Home Rule politicians. The years 1920 and 1921 seemed to confirm that conviction. I remember a number of us discussing the position informally when the first shadow of trouble in the shipyards began to appear. With us was one of our friends who had achieved an outstanding status as one of the most brilliant engineers of our time. Frank MacArdle had been making his reputation as the outstanding man in the firm of Musgraves, the celebrated firm of engineers, and already had many patents to his credit. At the end of World War I, Lord Pirrie had sent for him and induced him to join Harland and Wolff. He had commissioned him to take charge of a huge development scheme for the building of new slips required by his firm for the construction of new liners and cargo vessels.

When the dangers and possibilities of an outbreak of the traditional type were being discussed, Frank expressed the view that Pirrie would stamp it out as he had done in 1910. He was referring of course to what had happened in that year. Then the first sign of trouble began to show up after the Twelfth of July. The Home Rule Bill seemed to be looming up as a threat. The Liberals, with the aid and support of the Irish Party, held office and Pirrie was an outspoken supporter of the Liberal Party and Home Rule. At the very outset of the threatened trouble, Pirrie issued a warning and stated clearly that, if anything in the nature of religious or other disturbance occurred, the Queen's Island would be closed down and all their works would be transferred to the company's other shipyards. As Harland and Wolff had extensive shipbuilding branches in Southampton as well as on the Clyde and elsewhere, it was no empty threat and the Belfast loyalists realised that. There was no pogrom and no interference with the Catholic workers in the yards. But that was in 1910, and we were now in 1920.

I pointed this out to Frank and emphasised the changes that had taken place during the war, arguing that Pirrie and his co-directors might see certain advantages in having the workers at one and another's throats and the solid front of the labour unions disrupted. I gave him my reasons and they were these:

In 1910 the tradesmen employed by the 'yards' were earning eight pence to eight pence half-penny an hour. That rate applied to joiners, ships-carpenters, upholsterers, polishers. I knew these rates because in my own business the rates of our tradesmen were based on the rate operating on the 'Island'. The rates of wages for the many other trades varied. Platers, rivetters and others worked in 'squads' as they were called and in most cases were operating on 'piece work' rates and earned very high wages.

During the war and up to the time of our discussion, in 1920, the rates had been steadily increased until in the trades mentioned they reached 2/2d to 2/4d per hour. It was an all time 'high', and whilst it might be justified during the feverish rush of war-time production, the war was now over and Pirrie and the firm of Harland and Wolff would have to adjust themselves to a competitive market. Frank did not see it that way. That may not have been a factor in Pirrie's reasoning or policy. Other forces or personal developments may have operated. I was not and am not in a position to know. What I do know and what we all soon knew to our bitter reflection in Belfast was that Lord Pirrie issued no warning and no threat of removal of plant to his other yards, and that the pogrom was launched and that, with beatings and murderous assaults, the Catholics were driven from their employment. Frank MacArdle himself had to be kept in close cover to protect him from the mob until late evening and then smuggled out of the premises. It was, I think, his final departure from the shipyards.

It may have been due to other causes that the rate of wages had been reduced to something around one and six pence per hour within a couple of years, but trade unions that are split wide open by bitter sectarian antagonisms are not in the best condition for upholding their claims or defending their rights.

Carson had called for action instead of words, and Craig had openly given his approval to the answer given by the 'Islandmen'. No Catholic dare show his face in any of the shipyards. To do so would, at that time, have been signing his death warrant.

The pogrom initiated by the 'Islandmen' spread at once all over the city and a veritable reign of terror had begun.

I had lived through and seen at close quarters many outbreaks of rioting in Belfast. In 1898 and 1899 the outbreaks were fairly prolonged but the areas involved were, on the whole, restricted and could be 'contained'. Moreover, most of the districts which housed what would be described as the 'respectable' and middle-classes and wherein quite a number of Catholics lived would be entirely free from disturbance. Not so in 1920! The Orange mob, armed and equipped with bombs and petrol, invaded many of these areas, ordered Catholic residents out at the point of the gun, seized the furniture and effects which they piled up on the street and, having sprayed them with petrol, set them alight.

I am not quoting from reports, but merely stating what we all saw happening before our eyes during the orgy of organised bigotry and fanaticism. The 'forces of the crown' provided no protection and the most the small groups of Volunteers could do was to try and defend the purely Catholic areas against the raids that were attempted.

The strangest irony to the Belfastman who has not entirely discarded his right and power to serious thought is the consistent and traditional miscalling of the Belfast outbreaks as 'religious riots'. I do not think any decent Belfast citizen would dispute the fact that scarcely one out of every hundred that make up the Belfast Orange mob takes the slightest interest in religion. Their creed is a purely negative one based on an inflamed hate which has been and can be fanned into flames as and when the political overlords deem it useful for their own ends.

In August District Inspector Swanzy[1] was shot in Lisburn. Swanzy was one of the R.I.C., charged by the coroner's jury in Cork for the murder of Lord Mayor MacCurtain in the previous March. The British authorities

1. District Inspector Oswald Ross Swanzy (1881-1920): born County Monaghan, member of R.I.C. 1899, district inspector 3rd class in Rathkeale 1905, district inspector 2nd class in Cork 1907, district inspector 1st class in Carlow 1917, Cork 1918, Lisburn 1920.

took no action against those who had been concerned in that crime, but had transferred Swanzy for his greater safety to Lisburn, a town about eight miles from Belfast. Following the shooting of Swanzy, fierce attacks were launched on the Catholic quarters in Lisburn, and upwards of a thousand Catholics had to evacuate the town. Their homes and furniture were burned. From our home in the Glen Road, seven or eight miles from Lisburn, we saw the inferno raging over the town. Similar warfare was waged on the Catholics of Banbridge and with similar results, while 'pockets' of Catholics in areas such as the Newtownards and Crumlin Roads of Belfast were driven out at the point of the gun and their homes looted and burned.

The London *Daily News* correspondent, Mr Hugh Martin, who must rank as one of the most fearless of the London reporters who were covering the Irish scene at the time, said in one of his reports: 'Refugees were pouring into Belfast by road and rail, though the city had its own problems to face. Since the early days of the German invasion of Belgium, when I witnessed the civil evacuation of Alost and the flight from Ostend, I had seen nothing more pathetic than the Irish migration. Over one hundred and fifty families, numbering seven hundred and fifty people in all, were dealt with in a single day at one of the Catholic receiving centres, St Mary's Hall, and it was to the credit of the afflicted Catholic population of the city that every family found a refuge before nightfall'.

It was in the light of such conditions that Sir James Craig, who would soon be Lord Craigavon, deemed it wise and politic to say to the Orangemen as he unfurled the union jack at a shipyard in Belfast: 'Do I approve of the action you boys have taken in the past? . . . I say yes!' Not one Catholic employee was then working in the yards and the plan of driving all Catholics out of their jobs was being carried out where possible in other large undertakings. Several employers, to their credit be it noted, refused to be bullied by the mob or by the pogrom directors, but many yielded. It seemed to me at the time that the situation might be summed up thus: 'We cannot exterminate the Catholics in Belfast but we will force them to evacuate, bag and baggage, from amongst us'.

It is important to record that the conditions prevailing in Belfast and many of the surrounding towns in the summer of 1920 continued with a few, but very few, intermittent lulls until 1922. The truce came in July 1921, but there was no truce on the part of the Orange leaders or mobs and some of the worst anti-Catholic crimes were carried out during the winter of 1921-22.

In a number of districts where relatively small pockets of Catholics resided an almost heroic resistance was made to the attacking forces. In these the Catholics refused to leave and fought back to preserve their homes and their family life, although surrounded on all sides by the Orange mobs. In Thompson Street in Ballymacarett, and in the Oldpark Road area of Marrowbone, the resistance was maintained for weeks, but the unfortunate people paid a heavy price for their courageous defence. In the Falls Road area, which housed an almost entirely Catholic population, a constant defence had to be maintained every night and the attacks here were not confined to the Orange mob, but were mainly carried out by the police and the auxiliary forces of the crown. While we were enduring the savage Orange attacks in Belfast, the war was raging all over Ireland and events and incidents of historical importance were of daily occurrence.

Dáil Éireann had set up its own Republican courts[2] and these were operating successfully. Where they functioned, and they were functioning in all but five of the thirty-two counties, the British courts were deserted. Litigants, solicitors and counsel carried on their business in the new courts which quickly won the support and respect of all creeds and classes both for the strictness of their justice and efficient administration. These courts had been operating publicly but, with the collapse of the British courts, the inevitable clash took place and the crown forces set out to smash them. Arrests, charges and imprisonment followed but the courts, though driven underground, continued to function. Their sessions were held in secret but counsel, solicitors and litigants appeared and the decrees of the courts were enforced by the Republican police.

One of the outstanding events of 1920 was the arrest of the archbishop of Melbourne, the Most Reverend Dr Mannix[3] who was on his way to Ireland to visit his mother. His Grace of Melbourne had been more than a thorn in the side of the Australian imperialists. He had joined issue with Mr Hughes,[4]

2. Republican/Dáil Éireann Courts: These courts were established during the Anglo-Irish war to replace the British courts. In June 1920 they came under the authority of the minister for home affairs, Austin Stack. The courts' decrees were executed by police provided by the Dáil. There were four types of court in operation: parish courts, district courts, circuit courts and a supreme court. These courts were forced underground but after the truce operated openly. They were replaced in 1924.

3. Archbishop Daniel Mannix (1864-1963): born Charleville, County Cork, professor of philosophy at Maynooth 1891, professor of theology 1894, president 1903-12, co-adjutor bishop of Melbourne 1912-17, archbishop 1917-63, outspoken nationalist and virulent critic of the excesses of the Auxiliaries and the Black and Tans.

4. William Morris Hughes (1862-1952): born London, teacher 1882-84, migrated to Queensland, Australia 1884, Labour member for constituency in Sydney 1894-1901, Commonwealth House of Representatives member for West Sydney 1901, prime minister 1915-23, member of United Australia Party 1931, represented Australia at League of Nations 1932, held a number of ministries 1934-41.

the prime minister, on the conscription question and routed him in the fight. Fearless and brilliantly clever, he had consistently advocated Ireland's cause and did not mince his words when he attacked British policy in Ireland. When the liner on which he was a passenger was a few miles off Cóbh (then Queenstown), a British destroyer came alongside and the archbishop was arrested, transferred to the destroyer and conveyed to England. The country, his Australian friends and parishioners and the Irish in America were shocked by what they regarded as an outrage. To some of us it was the greatest tribute that the British government could have paid to the archbishop, and was indicative of the blind frenzy that underlay their whole campaign in Ireland.

That was in August 1920. Today, as I write in August 1958, His Grace the archbishop is still in Melbourne and by no means inactive. For many decades his has been the voice and mind that guided not only his own archdiocese but most of Australia. He has survived the petty tyrannies of British governments and most of the gangsters and their directors who prevented him seeing his mother in 1920.

It was in August 1920 also that Terence MacSwiney was arrested in the city hall in Cork. He had been elected unanimously to take the place of Lord Mayor MacCurtain who had been murdered by the crown forces in his own home. He was a poet, dramatist and Gaelic scholar. He was also commandant of the 1st Cork brigade of the I.R.A. In a couple of paragraphs of his speech after his election as lord mayor he synthesised I think, the most perfect doctrine for Irish republicans and indeed for lovers of freedom everywhere. This is, in part, what he said:

> It is not those who can inflict the most but those who can suffer the most who will conquer, though we do not abrogate our function to demand that murderers and evil-doers be punished for their crimes. It is conceivable that the army of occupation could stop our functioning for a time. Then it becomes simply a question of endurance. Those whose faith is strong will endure to the end in triumph. It is not we who take innocent blood but we offer it, sustained by the example of our immortal dead and that divine example which inspires us all for the redemption of our country. Facing our enemy we must declare our attitude simply. We see in their regime a thing of evil incarnate. With it there can be no parley any more than there can be truce with the powers of hell. We ask no mercy and we will accept no compromise.

They tried him, sentenced him and brought him to Brixton jail and there, after seventy-four days of hunger strike, Terence MacSwiney died. His faith was strong and he endured to the end in triumph. His long hunger-strike and his death aroused attention in every corner of the world and focused attention on Ireland and on British atrocities in Ireland as nothing else that had happened had done.

Next to the death of Terence MacSwiney, the country and the friends of Ireland all over the world were most stirred by the torture and ultimate hanging of young Kevin Barry.[5] Kevin Barry was a bright, promising, young student in University College, Dublin. He was but eighteen years of age and immensely popular with all his fellow-students and friends. Like many of his contemporary students, he was active in the columns and was captured and made prisoner. While in their hands, his captors proceeded to torture him in a vain attempt to get him to disclose the names and addresses of his companions.

James H. Thomas,[6] of whom we will have something to say later when he became minister in Ramsay MacDonald's[7] coalition government, was at the time one of the Labour leaders in the British House of Commons. He made an impassioned protest there against the execution. In doing so he read an affidavit which the boy had made while awaiting execution and which described in some detail the torture to which he had been subjected. Thomas stated: 'They put him face down on the floor, the sergeant knelt on the small of his back while two other soldiers placed one foot each on his back and shoulder. His arms were twisted from the elbow joints'. Kevin Barry spoke no names and gave no information and on 1 November, All Saint's Day, they hanged him in Mountjoy jail. His name and memory became the symbols to Irish youth of all that was fine, noble and heroic

5. Kevin Barry (1902-20): born Dublin, a medical student at U.C.D. and member of I.R.A., captured after an attack on a British army detail in Dublin, court-martialled and hanged.

6. James H. Thomas (1874-1949): born Newport, Wales, began his working-life at nine years of age, eventually worked in the railway, chairman of Swindon borough council 1904-5, general secretary, National Union of Railwaymen 1919-31, M.P. for Derby 1910, colonial secretary 1924, played an important role in winding-up general strike 1926, lord privy seal 1929, dominions office 1930, dismissed from National Union of Railwaymen for his support for the Ramsay MacDonald coalition government 1931, colonial secretary 1935, developed a proneness to intemperance, dismissed from office for leaking budget secrets 1936.

7. James Ramsay MacDonald (1866-1937): born Lossiemouth, Scotland, of a humble background and had to endure considerable hardship in his early life, member of Independent Labour Party 1894, M.P. for Leicester 1906-18, M.P. for Aberavon 1922-37, prime minister 1924-35, lord president of the council 1935-7.

and will continue to be so. In Ireland we did not have to wait on Dachau or Buchenwald to learn how prisoners of war may sometimes be treated!

There were many other deaths in Ireland in the summer and autumn of 1920 and there would be many more before the truce in July 1921.

The Republican columns by guerrilla warfare and supported by a whole people were making government by the British entirely impossible. The British forces hit back by the burning and sacking of towns, factories, and the creameries and stores of the co-operative movement, while at the same time their raids, shootings and murders were of daily occurrence.

In Belfast and the surrounding towns the pogrom continued. Here the designation of Catholic was synonymous with Sinn Féin. It seemed such a short time since the war posters of 1914 shrieked for volunteers to defend Catholic Belgium, and the parliamentary leaders appealed from countless platforms for recruits to form the Irish brigade for Flanders. The bitter irony of it was that so many thousands of young Catholics had, like so many thousands of non-Catholics, been seduced into the army on these hypocritical war-cries. Many of them had paid the full price and did not return, but thousands of those who did return were now hunted from their employment and many from their homes. They were living under a rule of terror, denied employment and facing poverty and want. They were not entirely forgotten. The American Committee for Relief in Ireland[8] was busy and shiploads of food and clothing began to arrive. The American organisation later merged into what was known as the Irish White Cross and contributed most of the funds which enabled that society to relieve the want and distress which the British forces throughout Ireland and their allies of Belfast Orangeism had spread over the whole country.

In actual results the American contribution was over a million and a quarter pounds, nine-tenths of the total amount subscribed. There was intense feeling amongst the Catholics in Belfast about one aspect of the situation. I have already referred to the specially favoured conditions of trade throughout the whole country which the Belfast manufacturers and wholesale distributors enjoyed. It is a difficult position to explain and one

8. American Committee for Relief in Ireland was also known as the Irish White Cross. This was a Sinn Féin organisation founded on 21 February 1921 to assist in the distribution of the American-based White Cross Fund. The purpose of the fund was to assist republicans and their families who were suffering hardship through involvement in the Anglo-Irish war. The funds were also applied to aid expelled Catholic workers from Northern Ireland. Arthur Griffith was active in its organisation and Cardinal Logue was one of its patrons. Its accounts published on 31 August 1921 revealed that it had collected £1,374,795, £1,250,000 of this came from American sources. Count John McCormack contributed £35,000, Pope Benedict XV £5,000.

that had often intrigued me when I observed it in normal peaceful times. There seemed no obvious reason why the retail draper, furnisher or grocer in, say, Ballina, Ballinasloe or Ballyvourney should place his orders with Mr X of Belfast in preference to Mr Y in Dublin or Galway, but in fact in many cases he did. I spent thirty-six years of my life in Belfast and of these I spent eighteen in the manufacturing and distributing business. We had customers from one end of the country to the other. We despatched our goods to Dungarvan as often as we did to Cahirciveen and our travellers visited every sizeable town in the country at least four times a year.

I do not think Belfast enjoyed any more favourable terms from their suppliers than their competitors in Dublin and elsewhere, nor do I believe that the bankers afforded them special consideration in rates of interest or extensions of credit. I came to the conclusion that there could only be two possible reasons for the position as it then was. The first was that the Belfast trader was keener and more attentive to his customers' needs, prompter and more reliable in his deliveries and, where necessary, prepared to cut his prices more finely. All these factors were, I think, due to his whole psychological 'make up', for the Belfast business man as a rule, although there were exceptions, lived, ate, slept and got his major enjoyment out of his success in business. It was a combination of Samuel Smiles[9] and Calvin[10] and, however lacking it may have been as a soul-satisfying existence, it showed results in the ledger accounts and in the ultimate balance sheets.

The second reason is one that I am almost afraid to put forward, but it is based on a wide experience and close observation. It is my conviction that, up to the period with which we are now dealing, there was a definite tendency for the Catholic traders and the people generally throughout the country to favour the non-Catholic merchants in preference to those of their own faith. It may have been that the non-Catholic was, for the reasons already stated above, a more satisfactory merchant, or it may have been an exaggerated tolerance amounting to an inferiority complex on the part of the Catholic population. Whatever the cause, I think it will be admitted by those of my generation, who have survived, that in almost every town in Ireland, even where the Catholics constituted ninety per

9. Samuel Smiles (1812-1904): born Haddington, Scotland, an enthusiast for self-reliance and self-education, medical doctor, journalist, in 1859 there appeared his most successful book, *Self-Help*, which was translated into 17 languages.

10. John Calvin (1509-64): born Noyon, Picardy, France, Swiss divine and reformer, his insistence that the chief end of man was 'to know and do the will of God' made for a strict moral code.

cent and more of the population, the non-Catholics invariably had the lion's share of the distributing trade.

It is perhaps something of a digression to analyse these factors, but they bear directly on the next and very important phase of the Belfast and North-East Ulster situation.

The plight of the Catholic in Belfast grew worse. Dismissals from employment were general and some employers were seeking declarations of loyalty to the British government. It was in such circumstances that a boycott against all goods from Belfast was launched.[11] It is interesting to note that the Dáil only grudgingly gave its official approval to the boycott. Later in the year they issued a decree prohibiting any religious test as a condition of employment. The boycott was, nevertheless, enforced by the I.R.A. and spread rapidly all over the country with disastrous effects to the wholesale merchants and many manufacturers.

We had a small headquarters organisation in Belfast with an excellent intelligence service which kept us fully advised of all attempts to beat the prohibition. In a number of instances where goods were despatched they were suitably dealt with at the point of delivery. After a few experiences of that type the Northern traders ceased their attempts to get their goods through. I had the rather ironical experience myself of having to refuse business from customers in the prohibited area.

We discussed this aspect of the problem and it was suggested that a system of permits should be introduced whereby Catholic and nationalist manufacturers and distributors would be enabled to carry on their business throughout the country. I resisted this suggestion strenuously and convinced the other members that any such loophole would result in the collapse of the whole plan. The argument I made which convinced them was this:

I am doing a certain amount of trade down south and out west. Several of my competitors are similarly engaged. One of them, the biggest in the city, is doing a wholesale trade in these areas which must run to two or three thousand pounds a month. It would be a simple matter for me to arrange to supply them with my labels for the despatch of their goods, book them with my forwarding notes and collect ten per cent on the turnover.

11. Belfast Boycott (1920-22): The boycott of goods produced and distributed from Belfast was a reaction to the anti-Catholic pogrom and rioting in Belfast during the summer of 1920. It started in August on unofficial lines when shopkeepers in Galway city refused to stock goods originating in Belfast. Dáil Éireann appointed as director of the Belfast Boycott Joseph McDonagh from August 1921 to January 1922 and Michael Staines from January to February 1922. It ended officially, as a result of the Craig-Collins agreement.

It would be easy money for me, it would keep their organisation going and would defeat our whole purpose. I might refuse to act in this way, but I feared that the temptation might prove too much for some of our people. The only safe course was a complete 'shut down' of everything from Belfast. My colleagues saw it that way too and the boycott was made water-tight. There was no doubt as to its effectiveness. I lived in Belfast, heard the wails and groans of the traders and knew that Belfast was being hit where it counted.

The boycott continued until early in 1922 when Michael Collins made his fantastic agreement with Sir James Craig to cancel the boycott, provided Craig would 'facilitate the return of Catholic workers to the shipyards'. I was in New York when I read the announcement of this agreement and frankly I squirmed with vexation. It showed a complete lack of apprecia-tion on Collins' part of the realities in Belfast. I did not need to be told later of the dismay that his agreement caused to my colleagues and friends in Belfast and the North-East. They realised that Craig had as much power to have the Catholics admitted to work in the shipyards as he had to give them visas to take them past St Peter into heaven. It was 'a tongue in the cheek' promise on Craig's part!

While the campaign by the combined forces of military, Black and Tans, Auxiliaries and police raged all over the country including Belfast and the rural areas of Ulster, our situation in Belfast was aggravated by the fact that we were trying to live in the midst of a bigoted and bitterly-hostile com-munity. The Falls Road and the adjoining areas in West Belfast were almost exclusively Catholic and, following the pogrom and house-burnings and the reception of the countless refugees from other areas, it looked like developing into a Catholic ghetto. As might be expected, the forces of the crown, aided by Orange gangs, concentrated their nightly attacks in the district. Raids, shootings, arrests and murders would continue long after the truce. The people as a whole, apart altogether from the I.R.A., fought back as well as they could, but they were unarmed and practically defenceless against the attacking forces who were well supplied with arms.

One interesting development is worth recording. There had been instances of midnight and early morning house raiding where unfortunate people, men and women, had been shot in cold blood by the raiders. It seemed to be entirely indiscriminate as in many cases the victims had no connections with political or I.R.A. activities. The raiders invariably travelled in Crossley tenders and other motor vehicles and it became the universal practice of the women in the side streets off the Falls and Grosvenor Roads and those in the Clonard area to sound the alarm and gather together as soon as a military vehicle was heard approaching their street. The tocsin was sounded by banging the lids of their refuse bins and this was the signal for all neighbours to be on the alert, to gather together and to ensure that at least there would be witnesses to what was happening. 'Rattle your bin' became a Falls Road slogan at the time.

The I.R.A. had its columns, not only in Belfast but in many districts throughout Antrim and Down, and their active service units carried out many successful engagements and exploits during the whole campaign. When it is remembered that these small units were operating in an entirely hostile area, in contrast to other districts throughout the country where every house had an open door and welcome protection, it will be realised what courage and determination every 'operation' required. I do not feel free nor do I think it is opportune to mention the names of those who led their units successfully. That history is being recorded elsewhere.[12] It may be but a small fraction in the whole history of the national struggle, but when it is viewed in the light of the conditions under which these units operated and which I have attempted to describe their names ought not to be forgotten.

During all the period it was out of the question for most of us to live at home. We were and had been 'on the run' practically all the time from the autumn of 1919.

Being 'on the run' was a somewhat peculiar business. In effect it meant that you did not spend the evening or night in your own home. We went to our business each day openly, had meals in restaurants and then late at night discreetly made our way to whatever friend's house was sheltering us.

For the most part raids on our homes were made between midnight and three o'clock in the morning and it was up to us not to be there when they occurred. Occasionally the house would be raided in daylight, but such raids were rare and were usually made when some major action had just been carried out by the I.R.A. At such times it became necessary to lie low for a period. It also happened that friendly houses where some of the boys were being sheltered would be 'spotted' and raided during the night. Several of our best men were caught in them but, on the whole, the widespread net yielded few catches.

12. The Bureau of Military History 1913-21 was set up in 1947 to assemble and co-ordinate material to form the basis for the compilation of the history of the movement for Independence from the formation of the Irish Volunteers on 25 November 1913 to 11 July 1921. Michael McDunphy was its director, Colonel Dan Bryan, John McCoy, Major Florence O'Donoghue and Séamus Robinson were its members and it had an advisory committee, consisting of a number of distinguished historians.

The raids varied in their nature from the comparatively mild search party to the ruffianly destructive blackguards, whose object was to strike terror and create chaos. Much depended on the type of officer in charge and on the local police sergeant or head constable who accompanied them. There were other types of raids when the murder gangs went out. They did not concern themselves with inquiries or searches; they sought victims and got them. On one Saturday night they carried off five men and the next morning their mutilated bodies were found on the adjacent mountainside.

Needless to say I was not present when the various raids were made in our own home, and I had a few narrow escapes when raids were made on houses where I had been sheltered.

There were about twenty-five nocturnal raids on our house during 1920. At the time the family consisted of my wife and three children and our Aran Island maid, I myself being 'away from home'. My wife always considered that she was fortunate in the fact that most of the raiding parties were accompanied by the local R.I.C. sergeant. Sergeant L- was a non-Catholic and seemed to be a quiet person who did not want to make trouble. Apparently he always did his utmost to restrain his companions, to prevent them from doing any damage and generally to carry through his job with the minimum of disturbance. There were a few raids made without his company and several where his restraining influence was not effective, but on the whole we fared much better than some of our friends.

It may have been that Sergeant L- was not altogether forgetful of his own future well-being, but my wife insists that the simple fact was that he was a decent man who loathed having any part in the dirty work involved. There were a number of that type, but they were a minority of the R.I.C. as I knew them.

There were afternoons and evenings when it was advisable to keep away from home altogether and even to avoid the whole area of the Upper Falls and Glen Road. On such occasions I made my way to a quiet corner of the restaurant for my evening meal to pass the time until I could discreetly make my way to my billet for the night. My old Presbyterian friend, Bob Rowan, invariably joined me. Bob's normal schedule was to catch the five-thirty train to Bangor where he lived, but, if he learned at lunchtime that I was 'staying in town', he too stayed over and was there in our corner to keep me company. Occasionally we would be joined by Willie M-, a sound Methodist with an Irish heart in the right place.

I have referred earlier to my friend, Rowan, and his qualities of mind and heart and his fund of humour. Willie M- was another of the same type, but much less robust in his humour than Bob. Quiet and subtle, with a fine gentle ironical vein of wit illuminating his stories and talk, his company was a delight at all times.

I owed much to these two friends and not least of which was the many hours they helped me to spend pleasantly during a very difficult period. They have both gone to their rewards. I bless their memories and pray peace to their souls.

12

The terrorist policy continues – Protests from leading English authors, poets, artists and journalists – Most Rev Dr Clune as emissary – Father O'Flanagan's intervention – Canon Magner shot by Black and Tans – 'Guilty but Insane' – General Gough on British forces in Ireland – King George V opens parliament in Belfast – The truce

As 1920 drew to its close there was a number of significant developments. Lloyd George professed his belief that his mixed forces of military, police and gangster columns of Black and Tans were winning the war for him. There was, however, a growing revulsion of feeling spreading over England. More and more, the ordinary decent English people were feeling shame for activities of the forces that were carrying out their blackguardly campaign of murder and arson in Ireland.

The British Labour Party had demanded an inquiry into the conduct of the British forces in Ireland and this had been refused. They then decided to set up their own Commission of Inquiry[1] with Arthur Henderson, M.P.,[2] as chairman. Their ultimate report was a damning indictment of the reign of terror and destruction which the government had let loose on the Irish people.

The Society of Friends made their own inquiries and collected money for the relief of the suffering people and the most notable of the English publicists, authors, poets, playwrights and journalists were vehement in

1. British Labour Party Commission on Ireland was set up in October 1920. It consisted of the leader of the Labour Party, Arthur Henderson, M.P., William Adamson, M.P., John J. Lawson, M.P., William Lunn, M.P., John Bromley, of the Associated Society of Locomotive Engineers and Firemen, Alexander G. Cameron, of the Woodworkers, F. W. Jowett, of the Independent Labour Party, with Captain C. W. Kendall as legal adviser, Brigadier-General C. B. Thomson, as military adviser, W. W. Henderson, as press secretary, and Arthur Greenwood as secretary of the commission. The commission arrived in Dublin on 30 November and were taken on a fact-finding tour of the country by Tom Johnson, leader of the Irish Labour Party. The commission reported to a special conference of the British Labour Party on 29 December. The report of the commission's fact-finding tour was published as *Report of the Labour Party Commission on Ireland* (London 1921).

2. Arthur Henderson (1863-1935): born Glasgow, trade-unionist 1881, member of Newcastle City Council 1892, close associate of Keir Hardie and co-founder of Labour Party 1906, secretary of Labour Party 1911-34, president of Board of Education 1915, paymaster-general 1916, secretary of state for foreign affairs 1929, presided over world conference on disarmament 1932-35, winner of Nobel Peace Prize 1934.

their denunciations. Lloyd George and Sir Henry Wilson with their attendant satellites carried on.

Towards the end of the year various rumours began to circulate that efforts to establish peace were being made and tangible evidence emerged when it was learned that the archbishop of Perth, Dr Clune,[3] had interviewed Lloyd George and found him willing to consider the possibility of a truce. Dr Clune then came to Ireland and saw Arthur Griffith, then a prisoner in Mountjoy jail, and Michael Collins and crossed over to resume his talks with Lloyd George and discuss the terms of truce which he had secured from Griffith and Collins.

Lloyd George was apparently in a very different mood when Dr Clune again visited him. There were reasons for the change. Father Michael O'Flanagan, who was one of the vice-presidents of Sinn Féin, had gone to London with some others who were making 'behind the scenes' efforts to secure peace. I think most of us were startled when we read in the papers that Father O'Flanagan had sent a telegram to Lloyd George which was quoted thus: 'You state you are willing to make peace at once without waiting till Christmas. Ireland is also willing to make peace. What first step do you propose?' My own reaction to the announcement was one of shocked anxiety. Father O'Flanagan was one of the most active Sinn Féin priests in the country. He was a noted orator who could move vast audiences by his emotional and patriotic appeals. I knew too that he was inclined to be impulsive and I noted that his telegram did not presume to speak for Sinn Féin.

At this time Galway County Council passed a resolution which, whilst declaring its adherence to Dáil Éireann, called on 'that body to appoint three delegates to negotiate a truce' and on the British government to do likewise and thus 'arrange preliminary terms of peace, honourable to both countries'. At the time Galway County Council passed their resolution most of the Republican members of the council were in prison or 'on the run'.

It was soon made clear that Father O'Flanagan's telegram had no sanction from the cabinet of the Dáil nor from the Sinn Féin organisation; that it was, in fact, simply a personal intervention on his own part.

Lloyd George's reaction to these two approaches was what might have been expected. He quoted both incidents in the House of Commons and

3. Archbishop Patrick Joseph Clune (1864-1935): born Ruan, County Clare, ordained in All Hallows College, Dublin, for diocese of Goulburn, Australia, 1886, St Patrick's College, Goulburn, 1886-93, administrator in cathedral 1893, entered novitiate of Redemptorists 1893, conductor of missions and retreats 1894-1911, bishop of Perth 1911, archbishop 1913-35, chaplain-general to Australian forces 1916-18, negotiator between British cabinet and Irish leaders, December 1920.

said he was satisfied that the majority in Ireland was anxious for peace; that he was prepared to discuss peace with those who desired it, but that they were not prepared to consider any proposal which involved secession by any part of Ireland from the United Kingdom and that the Six Counties, which represented North-East Ulster, must be given separate treatment. It was obvious that Lloyd George believed that at least he had an Ireland ready for surrender and he was backed up by General Macready and Sir Henry Wilson who objected to any discussion until the Republicans had surrendered.

Thus ended the attempt made by Dr Clune to bring peace to Ireland. It is not for me to judge how far his efforts were nullified by the unwise and untimely intervention of the well-meaning priest and the weakened county council, but the feeling throughout the country was one of vexation with both.

It is reasonable to assume that the British government was satisfied that Ireland was at breaking point, and that their proper course was to intensify still further their campaign of death and destruction.

Within thirty-six hours of Lloyd George's speech the city of Cork was ablaze. All the principal shops in Patrick Street, the principal street and shopping centre of the city, were burned down. The city hall and the free library adjoining it, a quarter of a mile from Patrick Street and divided from it by the river, were completely gutted and members of the fire brigade were shot and wounded, while endeavouring to quell the flames.

The British Labour Commission which at the time was investigating conditions in Ireland had no hesitation in expressing its verdict.

> We would point out that the fires occurred after the crown forces had driven the people indoors and that, during the greater part of the time that outbreaks of fire took place, the curfew regulations were in force. We are of opinion that the incendiarism in Cork was not a reprisal for the ambush which took place on the same date at Dillon's Cross. The fires appear to have been an organised attempt to destroy the most valuable premises in the city and we do not think that arrangements could have been carried out if they had been hastily made after the unfortunate occurrence at Dillon's Cross.

The burning of Cork meant throwing thousands of workers out of employment and a bill of damages reckoned at three million pounds.

The burning of Cork seemed to be the essential sequel to Lloyd George's disclosures of the peace overtures in the House of Commons.

The Henry Wilsons, Macreadys and their associates in this campaign of horror and destruction supplied it. Miss Dorothy Macardle in her book *The Irish Republic* records that:

> The number of Republicans killed in action in this period (December 1 to 20) is not known. It is known, however, that, besides those who fell in action, thirty-three Irishmen and boys had during these twenty days been killed by the forces of the crown. Two of the number were brothers, Patrick and Henry Loughnane of Gort, whose bodies, showing traces of barbarous cruelty, were found in a pond on 6 December. Canon Magner,[4] parish priest of Dunmanway, County Cork, was over seventy-three years of age. The canon had received a letter on 10 November threatening him with penalties unless he tolled the bell of his chapel on armistice day. It was signed 'Black and Tans'. He took no notice of the order. On 15 December he was talking with a young man, Timothy Crowley, and a motorist on the roadway near Bandon when Auxiliary cadets from Macroom Castle drove up in a lorry, stopped, dismounted and began to speak abusively to Crowley and the priest. Suddenly an Auxiliary Officer shot Crowley dead. The priest rebuked him; they demanded his name; he gave it and was immediately shot dead by the same man. None of the other Auxiliaries intervened; some of them emptied the pockets of the victims and dragged the bodies behind the fence.
>
> The motorist who escaped was a resident magistrate under the British government. He insisted upon an inquiry and the cadet, named Harte, who had done the shooting was pronounced 'Guilty but Insane.

'Guilty but Insane!', it is and has been a useful British formula in Ireland. It saved Bowen Colthurst when he murdered Frank Sheehy-Skeffington[5] in 1916. It has served everywhere from Amritsar to Cyprus no less in Ireland. I have quoted Miss Macardle's record of the brief period merely as an example of the campaign and the nature of the warfare carried on by

4. Canon Thomas J. Magner (1847-1920): parish priest, Dunmanway, County Cork 1907-20.

5. Francis Sheehy-Skeffington (1878-1916): born Bailieborough, County Cavan, registrar, U.C.D., 1902-4, journalist on *The Nationalist* 1906, *The National Democrat* 1908 and *The Irish Citizen* 1912-16, staunch supporter of Irish Women's Suffrage Movement, disapproved of Easter Rising and while attempting to prevent the looting it occasioned was arrested by Captain J. C. Bowen-Colthurst who had him executed after a drumhead courtmartial.

the authorised Black and Tans and Auxiliaries which the Lloyd George government turned loose on our people.

Miss Macardle also records that 'the number of unarmed people killed by crown forces in Ireland during the twelve months of 1920 was two hundred and three; this included six women and twelve children under seventeen years of age'.

The close of 1920 was a period of gloom and tragedy only relieved by the fighting-back of the I.R.A. columns. With us in Belfast the dark curtain of Partition was already descending, for two days before Christmas the Government of Ireland Act became law. The crown forces and the Orange hooligans continued their raids and attacks. The British Labour Commission made its report which was a denunciation of the British forces of Black and Tans, their accomplices the Auxiliaries and their campaign of murder, arson, destruction and outrage. It was a fully documented report, but none of us had any illusions that it would in any way affect the Welsh premier or his chief associates, Sir Henry Wilson, General Macready or Hamar Greenwood.

We learned shortly after Christmas that President de Valera had eluded the British authorities and got safely back from America.

During this period it was quite impossible to go near my home and, indeed for most of the time, it was necessary to lie low during the day as well. Communication with both home and business was by messenger and my wife and I decided to try and have Christmas together with the children at her parents' home in Glenarm. Accordingly, she, with the youngsters and our always dependable maid, found their way there a couple of days before Christmas and I managed to join them on Christmas Eve. By no stretch of imagination could we call it a happy Christmas, but at least we were all together in what was our second home. There was always the danger and indeed likelihood of a raid and there was always the daily quota of Black and Tan crimes reported in the press. A few days after Christmas the family returned to our home in Belfast to find that the house had been forcibly entered during their absence. A thorough search had obviously been made and, although a certain amount of damage had been done, it was much less than might have been expected. From this my wife surmised that the local Sergeant L- must have accompanied the raiders.

The year 1920 ended and the year 1921 began with a continuation of the reign of terror which the British forces had established. Internment camps had been opened and were rapidly filling up and executions by shooting and hanging were taking place constantly, not only in the martial law areas but in Dublin and elsewhere. The murder campaign was intensified and prominent Republicans were marked down for execution by the murder gang. George Clancy,[6] the mayor of Limerick, Michael O'Callaghan, a former lord mayor, and Joseph O'Donoghue were murdered in Limerick on the same night in March 1921.

During April thirty persons were murdered and it must be emphasised that these were murders, not casualties in the fighting. Even the British army voiced its contempt for the methods employed by the British government. General Gough, who could hardly be described as a sympathiser with Sinn Féin or Republicans, wrote at the time:

> Law and Order have given place to a bloody and brutal anarchy in which the armed agents of the crown violate every law in aimless and vindictive and insolent savagery. England has departed further from her own standards, and further from the standards even of any nation in the world, not excepting the Turk and Zulu, than has ever been known in history before.

The Volunteer columns were hitting back and with considerable success all over the twenty-six counties, but particularly in the Dublin area and in Munster and Connacht. Many of their exploits have already been published and in due course the whole story will no doubt be made available by the organisation set up by the government to collect the entire history of the period from 1916 onwards. One of the most daring operations carried out by the I.R.A. was the burning of the Custom House in Dublin by the Dublin brigade. Next to Dublin Castle itself, the Custom House was the most important centre of British administration in Ireland. Here were housed the various sections of local government administration and the taxing departments and in them were the books and records covering the whole country. To put the 'machine' out of action it was necessary to destroy all these books, records and files, and the only effective means to do so was to burn the building. Over a hundred Volunteers took part in the operation and fires were started simultaneously all over the building with the result that the next morning the bare walls were all that remained of Gandon's masterpiece. The burning of the Custom House, one of Dublin's most beautiful buildings, was universally regretted, but there was

6. George Clancy (1879-1921): born Grange, County Limerick, teacher in Clongowes Wood college and later in Limerick, superintendent in Irish National Assurance Company 1918-21, Sinn Féin mayor of Limerick 1921 and shot in his own home by Black and Tans on 7 March, when two of the city's other leading citizens, Michael O'Callaghan, a former lord mayor, and Joseph O'Donoghue, met the same fate.

no alternative. As the *Irish Bulletin* declared: '. . . the destruction was an unavoidable military necessity'. The Custom House has long since been fully restored by the Irish government.

Looking back over the period as we lived through it in Belfast, the memory of it is one of a day-to-day strain, of constant tension, of incidents, raids and arrests. The local and district columns were active but, as has been said, their opportunities and activities were necessarily limited by their surroundings and the fact that they were operating in an almost entirely hostile area.

The 'Partition Election' was fixed for May. With us in the six counties it was fixed for 24 May while for the twenty-six counties the date was 19 May. The elections were under the Proportional Representation system, but in the twenty-six counties no elections were necessary. There were one hundred and twenty-four seats to which all the members were returned unopposed and all were pledged to the support of the Republic and its government. Trinity College, to which four seats had been allocated, supplied the only nominal or potential opposition to the Republican government of Dáil Éireann. Those of us who went through the six-county election campaign are not likely to forget it. Here the combination of police, Orange mobs and the whole personnel of the election machinery was set in motion to make it difficult, if not impossible, for Sinn Féiners or Nationalists to record their votes. In whole areas, where the Catholic population was a small minority, a non-Unionist voter ran the risk of his life if he or she attempted to go to the polling booth.

There were 52 seats in the six-county parliament and of these the Nationalists and Republicans secured twelve, the other forty going to the Unionists. The dishonesty of the whole six-county position was exposed by the fact that Fermanagh and Tyrone, two of the six counties, polled a majority of 7,831 votes in favour of the anti-partition candidates. Thus democracy and self-determination, as operated by the British in Ireland, worked in 1921. To those of us in Belfast and the six counties, who believed in Ireland, an undivided and free Ireland, the Partition election was a bitter dose to swallow. We no longer 'belonged' in our own country. We were less than an English shire and subject to a controlling regime, whose whole history was one of hostility and bigotry to everything that was dear to us. We had not long to wait to sample its temper.

The Unionists had the Northern Parliament to themselves as the twelve anti-partitionist members abstained from attendance. Some of the more virulent members immediately renewed their campaign of incitement to violence and declared their intention of 'driving Sinn Féin out of the six counties'. Now, while it is true that there had been a very definite swing to Sinn Féin all over the six counties, it is equally true that a very considerable number of Catholics were still loyal to Devlin and his Hibernian organisation,. To the Orangeman, however, every Catholic in the area was the enemy and his political leaders knew this and when they declared war on Sinn Féin by name they meant and intended the expulsion or extermination of Catholics.

Within a few days after the first meeting of the Northern Parliament we had a renewal of the pogrom. There were a number of murders including the seizure of five men who were taken from their homes at night and whose mutilated bodies were found the following morning. In addition there were eleven people killed in rioting, and hundreds of homes were wrecked. There would be even worse to follow, but in the meantime King George V[7] would formally open the parliament of Northern Ireland on 22 June.

It is understood, and can be reliably accepted, that the speech prepared for delivery by King George at the opening ceremony did not meet with his approval. He discussed it with General Smuts[8] and revised it to such an extent that the Lloyd George—Henry Wilson policy of ruthless war became well-nigh impossible. We in the North read with mixed and somewhat grim emotions that portion of his statement in which he said:

> I speak from a full heart when I pray that my coming to Ireland today may prove to be the first step towards the end of strife among her people whatever their race or creed.

No doubt King George was sincere in the expression of his hopeful prayer, but his memory was at fault in forgetting that Ulster Unionism, backed up by all that stood for reaction and bitterness in Conservative circles in Britain, owed but a qualified loyalty to the throne and had even

7. George V (1865-1936): born London, king of Great Britain and emperor of India 1911-36.

8. Jan Christian Smuts (1870-1950): born Riebeck West, Cape Colony, South Africa, barrister 1895, active in Boer war 1899-1902, facilitated its conclusion 1902, active in successful campaign against German forces in South West Africa 1915, chief sponsor of British Commonwealth of Nations and League of Nations 1918, prime minister of South Africa 1919-24, facilitated negotiations leading to Anglo-Irish treaty 1921, Britain left the gold standard and Smuts unsuccessfully advocated that South Africa do likewise 1931, as a consequence the fall of South Africa's export prices was acutely felt and South Africa forced off the gold standard 1932, active in World War II and became a British army field-marshal 1941, helped to create United Nations 1946.

been prepared to accept a continental monarch rather than a constitutional decision by the democracy of Britain. In another portion of his statement he declared:

> The future lies in the hands of my Irish people themselves. May this historic gathering be a prelude of the day in which the Irish people, North and South, under one Parliament or two, as these Parliaments themselves may decide, shall work together in common love for Ireland upon the sure foundation of mutual justice and respect.

This latter statement, in the light of after events, will seem an oversimplification of the position. Certainly it did not leave to one of the two parliaments how it might decide to work for Ireland. That decision had already been taken by the people of the twenty-six counties and it was practically an unanimous decision to be countered by King George's ministers by the threat of 'immediate and terrible war'. All that would emerge later, but, in the light of his speech, it seemed likely that a change of tactics, if not of heart, might be anticipated. It came quickly. Two days after the king had opened the Belfast parliament, Lloyd George addressed his historic letter to President de Valera. There was an exchange of correspondence and ultimately the terms of a truce were agreed.

General Macready, Colonel J. Braid[9] and A. W. Cope,[10] assistant under secretary, represented the British. Commandant Robert Barton, T.D.,[11] and Commandant E. J. Duggan, T.D.,[12] represented the Irish Republican Army. The truce came into effect on 11 July 1921.

9. Colonel J. Brind: member of general staff at HQ of British forces in Ireland, with Emmet Dalton, who acted in the interests of the I.R.A., he dealt with complaints about violations of the truce, signed in July 1921, subsequently he supervised the evacuation of British forces from most of the territory of Ireland.

10. Sir Alfred W. Cope (1880-1954): born London, civil servant and businessman, second secretary, ministry of pensions, 1919-20, assistant under-secretary in Ireland 1920-2, played important role in securing the truce of July 1921, later supervised the withdrawal of British forces from Ireland.

11. Robert Childers Barton (1881-1975): born Glendalough, County Wicklow, captain in British army during World War I, Sinn Féin T.D. for Wicklow 1919, minister for agriculture 1919-21, one of signatories to Anglo-Irish treaty 1921, later took anti-treaty side on civil war, at end of which he retired from politics to manage his extensive estate.

12. Eamon John Duggan (1874-1936): born Longwood, County Meath, qualified as solicitor 1914, member of Irish Volunteers 1913, director of intelligence Irish Volunteers 1918, T.D. for Louth-Meath 1919, one of signatories to the Anglo-Irish treaty 1921, T.D. for County Meath 1922-23, minister for home affairs in Provisional government, minister for defence 1927-32, senator 1933-6.

13

Belfast in 1920-21 – The big slump – Request to go to U.S.A. as consul general – Conference with Griffith and de Valera – I consent to go

Before continuing my record of experiences following the truce, I will pause to try and recall something of the general course of affairs that operated in Belfast during the eighteen months preceding it.

During 1919 and for most of 1920 trade was good. The shipyards and factories were busy and agents, representing British and foreign concerns, were making easy money in a 'buyer's market'. At the luncheon table the general complaint of these agents was not the difficulty of getting orders, but of getting deliveries. This was particularly the case in the spring of 1920. One of my friends, who represented a big Manchester concern in cotton yarns, described to me his visit to the Manchester headquarters. According to his reports, Manchester was simply alive with all sorts of foreigners seeking supplies of every type of merchandise that Manchester and Lancashire produced. He himself had gone over to press for speedier deliveries of yarns which were required by the Belfast mills for the production of 'unions' which were the fabrics of linen and cotton mixtures. Somewhat similar conditions prevailed in the linen trade and in most of the other manufacturing industries. There was in fact something of a minor boom in trade generally and Belfast was enjoying its share of it. In my own case business was good without being spectacular. I had always inclined to a steady programme of building up the business without undue speculation and was content to follow that course. The circumstances under which I was living were not exactly conducive to the undivided attention that most business demands. Home life did not exist for most of us and there were periods when business had to be directed by letter or messenger. Despite this and thanks to the loyalty and efforts of my relatively small but competent staff, we did manage to carry on with reasonable success.

It was sometime about the middle of 1920 that I had a caller to my office. It was early in the morning and I was dealing with the post when Miss Rogan showed him in. He explained who he was and said his father had asked him to call and give me a message. His father, I may explain, had drifted in one day attracted by a fine mahogany reproduction dining-room set which was shown in our window display. He examined it and wrote a cheque for the complete set which was to be delivered to his son, then about to be married. He was one of the principals in one of our large linen houses and a very pleasant person indeed. The business transaction was satisfactory to both of us. He gave me his father's message which was, briefly, that he had information about Dunlop's shares which were then standing at fifty shillings and advised me to buy and to hold them until they reached ten pounds, but to sell as soon as they touched that figure. He said that his father was laid up ill, but he had asked him specially to call and see me and give me the tip as, for some reason or another, he wanted to do me the good turn. I expressed my thanks and charged him to convey my gratitude to his father for his kindness in thinking of me, but I explained that I never touched the stock market and found an outlet for any surplus in the building up of my comparatively young business. I told him I would think it over and have a chat with my accountant, but that I doubted if I would break my rule to avoid the stock market. I thought over the matter after he had gone and had a brief run through the books. Now it so happened that a very important dignitary, who was a customer, had just been furnished with his account amounting to over five hundred pounds. I had done business with him on many occasions and his usual procedure was to call in a day or two after he received his account, have a chat and a cigarette and write a cheque for the amount due.

I had a word with my accountant, Bob Hillock, who was not only my accountant but also my trusted and reliable friend. I asked him to look over the books and confirm or otherwise what I thought they would show. This was that I could, without embarrassment to myself or the business, take the five hundred and have a 'flutter' on the 'Dunlops'. Bob did as I asked and, while he agreed that I could give the five hundred a 'run' on the Dunlop shares, he protested vigorously against chancing any speculations. 'Let well enough alone, your business is doing well and you are a damn fool if you start to get mixed up with stocks and shares' was his ultimate advice. Despite that, I decided that I would, as soon as the five hundred pound cheque was paid, buy two hundred 'Dunlops'. It so happened that within that week there was a strike of electricians and other corporation workers and things in the city were much upset. My friend did not come into town for more than a week and, when he did arrive and had his chat and cigarette and given me his cheque, 'Dunlops' had gone up to five pounds a share. I decided that I had 'missed my luck', felt a bit sore about it and left them alone.

In the meantime, however, I had told our little group at the luncheon table of the information that I had received, emphasising that they were to sell once the shares touched ten pounds. Most of them had been doing reasonably well in business and most of them bought. In due course the price mounted and when the shares reached ten pounds I implored them to rest satisfied, take their profits and quit but would they? No, they had not touched summit, they would go up and up and the tragedy was that they did go up and up. Then came the options to buy bonus shares, bank over-drafts to enable them to do so and so it went on until Dunlops were listed at fourteen pounds ten. A somewhat similar position was running parallel with regard to Mexican Eagles and the ultimate result was more or less the same.

The markets eased, began to sag and then to slump and, in a brief period, Dunlops fell from fourteen pounds ten to six pounds. At this point, so far as I can recall, the six pound share was quartered, that is to say, every shareholder got four shares for his one and the price dropped to thirty shillings. In the autumn of 1921 the Dunlop shares could have been bought for less than five shillings.

I have referred to this experience because it was a significant episode in the commercial life of Belfast at that time. Normally your Belfast business man is anything but a speculator or gambler. His early background, prior to the first world war, was ultra conservative and somewhat Calvinistic and, although the business magnates did their steady quota of investing, it was investing and not speculating or 'playing the market'.

Whether it was due to the big profits made during and after the war or a psychological revolt against their inherited traditions of caution and anti-gambling I cannot say, but the fact was that Belfast and the surrounding areas went crazy on Dunlops and, to a lesser degree, on Mexican Eagles and many business men were bankrupt when the orgy was over.

There were many tragedies as a result and we heard varied accounts of broken homes, ruined businesses and even suicides that followed the 'boom and bust' phase of the Dunlop shares. It was estimated that, all told, the losses of the Belfast shareholders amounted to over eight millions of pounds. How true or otherwise these stories and reports were, I was in no position to judge but I had enough personal contact with some of the sufferers to believe that they were not exaggerated.

Inevitably it was our friend Bob Rowan who told the best story about the Dunlop saga:

'He lives in a fine house down near our place in Bangor', said Bob.

> He's a grumpy sort of divil that would hardly bid you the time of day when you met him in the train. He travelled up and down like the rest of us and then for a whean o' days we missed him. Some of the boys heard he was ill and later it was serious. Then after a couple of

> weeks he was back as usual. Later I got the whole story from a friend of the family. It appears he got more grumpy than ever, was moody and sullen and was not sleeping and no food would tempt him. His wife was worried and insisted on calling in the local doctor who examined him, but could find nothing wrong with him. He was not improving, was still eating practically nothing and lying awake most of the night. The local doctor brought down a Belfast specialist for a consultation; the specialist told the patient's wife to arrange to have the family lawyer down the next day at three o'clock and that he, the specialist, would meet him there. The wife was alarmed and asked if he was 'as bad as that'. The specialist reassured her and told her not to worry and that he would have her man all right in a few days. The next day the lawyer attended and, under the direct orders of the specialist, 'Mr Grumpy' gave instructions to him to dispose of every share he possessed and sign the necessary authority. His Dunlops were sold at fourteen pounds and the others at equally satisfactory prices. He finished up with nearly two hundred thousand pounds to credit in his current account.

Bob shook his head and almost glowered at us. 'That's the other side of the Dunlop story', he said, 'and I wouldn't mind a damn but the big eejit is going around Bangor with his chest out as the one man in Bangor who knew when to sell'.

The stock market collapse synchronised with a general slump in business and the cry for supplies so common a few weeks earlier gave way to a hunt for orders and a wail about the condition of trade generally. Prices were being slashed and heavy stocks, most of which were held at inflated prices, had to be written down with disastrous effect on the ultimate balance sheets. To add to the general commercial discomfort, the boycott of Belfast traders and their goods was practically watertight and wholesale distributors in every line of business as well as the manufacturers were facing a bleak future. Wages had been greatly increased during the war years and conditions of labour had altered considerably. The six o'clock in the morning start in the shipyards, factories and mills had gone and very few workers started work until eight or half past eight in the morning. Many businesses would close down in the early nineteen-twenties and of these, the linen trade would be the most affected with resultant unemployment for the poorest element in the community, the spinners and weavers in the mills and the wareroom girls in the 'making up trade'.

I was fortunate in as much as my business was quietly but steadily growing and, despite the fact that I was shut out from trading with a number of customers owing to the boycott, was well content with my six years progress. I had been contemplating opening a moderately-sized factory in Dublin and had discussed my plans with my old friend and associate, Robert Burns. Mr Burns had been our principal traveller in the South and West of Ireland in Maguire and Edwards. He was a man of the highest character and integrity and commanded the support and respect of all his customers. Our plan was that we would, at the beginning, confine our manufacturing to bedding and wire mattresses, and 'wholesale' our other lines. It would be nominally a branch of the Belfast business, but run as a separate company on a fifty-fifty basis of partnership. I was able to make the necessary arrangements for capital allowing Mr Burns to pay off the purchase price of his shares out of earnings and dividends. We had not advanced very far in our plans when it happened! 'It' was a letter requesting me to get ready to go to America as consul-general for the Irish Republic in Ireland. It was signed by Ernest Blythe, who was minister for industry and commerce in Dáil Éireann, and his private secretary brought it to me by hand and was to bring back my decision.

The letter not only took me by surprise, but bewildered me by the conflicting emotions it caused. I confess I felt somewhat flattered by the request but, against that, I realised what the acceptance of the appointment involved. I was happily married with three grand youngsters and a very comfortable home. I had built up a successful if modest business and was ready to expand it. My income was more than adequate. I was, at the time, able to 'plough back' about two-thirds of the profits into the business and live comfortably on the other third. Over and above all, now that the truce had come, I was able to return home and hoped to resume a normal life with my wife and children. To face a complete disruption of all this was anything but pleasant.

At the time my wife was holidaying in the glens of Antrim with the children, and of course before I could decide anything it was necessary to discuss the whole problem with her. I was due to attend a meeting in Dublin the following week and I told Blythe's secretary that I would go up for this meeting and that I would see Mr Griffith and talk the matter over with him. Griffith was minister for foreign affairs at the time and I assumed that, in the ultimate development, I would be working for him. In view of our long and intimate association, that assumption had its attractions, but hardly sufficient to offset the opposing factors that I have mentioned. I had asked the secretary one question and that was if she knew whether the letter was a 'request' or an 'order' from the ministry. Her reply was that she thought that they would like me to treat it as a 'request'.

That weekend I joined the family in the glens, and my wife and I discussed the proposal from all angles and decided that, in all the circumstances, it was simply my duty to go. It is, perhaps, no harm to mention that there was no question raised regarding terms of salary, allowances or the like nor was there any reference to such in the letter. In those days consideration of such things was of minor importance.

I met Griffith on the Wednesday following. I pointed out to him what acceptance of the position would mean to me and stressed what I thought was the most cogent argument against my appointment and it was roughly in these terms: 'There surely must be many of our friends who would be suitable and who would jump at the opportunity. It does not seem to be wise to take a man who is reasonably well established, running a business and settled with his wife and family, when there must be many others available'. Arthur was his imperturbable self. He never argues vehemently in private talks, and he quietly summed it all up when he said: 'I want you to go Joe'. That decided it finally.

Now, I have never been what would be called a 'follow my leader' type. Far from it! I have had a life-long conviction that Ireland has invariably suffered when 'loyalty to a leader' overrode 'loyalty to principles'. It was so in the past and I think it is even more so today as I write. I had great regard and respect for Arthur Griffith. I had more than that, for Arthur was a generous, kindly soul and personality who won your affection and trust, and I knew I enjoyed his complete confidence. It was not, however, solely as a personal matter between Griffith and myself that I consented. The circumstances of the time must be remembered. There was a truce, but an uneasy truce and no one could forecast what lay ahead of us.

We knew, or thought we knew, what we were up against and we knew enough of our history to fear the British at the council table of negotiation. The Dáil and the country were up against innumerable difficulties and required every available contribution of help that could be given. We counted much on the influence and support of the United States and the Irish there. We had needed both up to the present, and our people there had given generously. We needed their help now, and might need it much more if negotiations broke down. These were the all-important considerations, apart from the persuasive powers of Griffith, that influenced me.

And so the die was cast and I had to proceed with my plans and arrangements to take up office at the consulate headquarters in New York. My major problem was what to do about my business. It was not a big business, but I had followed a definite and conservative plan of building it up on sound lines of quality goods and service. I aimed at creating a reputation which would ultimately reflect credit on the firm and pay dividends in the future. In no business is there more deceit or 'fake' production than in the furniture trade.

It was, in a way, tempting during the war years, when there was an overflow of money in the hands of discriminating purchasers, to bring in loads of cheap, shoddy Chesterfield suites, shoddy show cabinets and carpets and all the rest. There were ready sales and big money in it. The policy I pursued was the direct opposite of this. No upholstered goods were ever sold save those that were made in our workshops. 'You can put anything at all under a cover' and I knew that the only safe way was to have the goods made by our own workmen. It is almost tempting to go into some details on the relative merits, ways and means of the honest-to-goodness furniture and carpet firm, and compare them with the tricks and devices of the flashy, showy and almost entirely shoddy techniques of the multiple stores of today. However, that is outside my present objective. It is sufficient for my purpose if I can convey the nature and type of the business, the disposal of which was a major problem for me before I could leave Belfast for America.

It seemed a pity that a healthy and successful business which had already earned something of a reputation and was growing steadily should 'fold up' and disappear. I could have sold out as a 'going concern' to a certain group, but this would have involved giving over my name for all time and, frankly, I just could not accept that. There was a splendid man in the business with one of the highest-class houses in the trade. He was one of the few Catholics in the trade. I mention this not in a spirit of partisanship, but it was important for I had at that time a very big number of convents, colleges and institutions, all of which were under the control of religious communities and all were consistent and valuable customers.

I sent for him and discussed my proposal with him. My proposal was that he would take over control on a fifty-fifty basis of the profits with a first charge of £400 a year to him for salary. He would not be required to find any capital, though he could, if he so wished, buy into the concern later on a par basis. Now £400 a year was a big salary at that time and the equivalent today, 1958, would be about £1,200 to £1,300. Moreover, his salary at the time was about £4 per week.

As I have said he was a splendid young man. He knew his job in all its branches and was an inadequately rewarded treasure to the firm that employed him. He lacked one essential and that was the courage to make a change. He was quite candid about it. He feared responsibility and I was satisfied that it was as much his responsibility to me as his own future that deterred him. I have seen so many similar types in Belfast. They dread the possibility of being out of a job and will carry on for a lifetime at a poor wage rather than venture out of what seems a safe shelter.

When my man had turned down my offer and determined as I was that I was not selling my name and goodwill, there remained the only alternative and that was to dispose of my stock and close down the concern. It was, for me, a big break in my life. I had opened the business six and a half years before with that mixture of hope, fear and anxiety that are the inevitable accompaniments of a new business venture. I had survived the many difficulties of the time and had reached what I regarded as the quiet stream of steady progress and now it was to end! Across the street, and almost opposite my own door, was the shop and factory of Maguire and Edwards where, for over twelve years, I had been employed under happy conditions and comfort. Eighteen and a half years is a fair slice out of one's life and leaving Upper Arthur Street after that period of time and breaking with all its associations had its share of regrets. That, however, was a minor affair compared to the ordeal of leaving my wife and children at home. Our semi-detached house was in Divis Drive, a *cul de sac* ending on the upper area of the Falls Park, with the Black Mountain and Divis immediately behind it. We were on the fringe of the city and had the Park and a variety of lovely walks all around us. Our house, modest enough in its way, was comfortable and furnished just as we liked it. It was a home in every sense and I had been looking forward to the resumption of our quiet, happy home life now that the truce had been made.

There was no purpose in indulging in vain sentimental regrets. There was much to do to clear up all my affairs and I was being urged to hasten my departure and get across to New York to take up my duties with the utmost speed.

I spent some days in Dublin making my final arrangements, discussing my future work with Blythe and Griffith and the others. I had a brief conference with President de Valera. I had met him on two occasions only and neither was of any significance. My first was in the home of his father-in-law in, I think, 1912. My friend Hugh MacCartan was a great friend of Miss Bee Flanagan who was Mrs de Valera's sister and she kindly invited him to bring me along for tea. My recollection of it is of Mr and Mrs de Valera and several youngsters gathered around the table with the other members of the Flanagan family: de Valera, the tall, sallow, foreign-looking man, pleasant, quiet and unobtrusive; Mrs de Valera, bright and genial with that aura of spiritual kindliness that I always associate with her. My second meeting was a mere passing word in the Dundalk hotel during the South

Armagh election. My talk with him prior to my departure was comparatively brief. Griffith was along with me and the general sense of our meeting was that I was Arthur's charge and responsibility and would get all the direction I needed from him.

I hastened to wind up my business affairs. It was an unfavourable period for disposing of stock for, as I have said, there was a general slump in 1921. It could only be an estimate, but I figured that the winding-up process meant a loss to me of from £1,300 to £1,500. Griffith asked me to send in my statement, as he felt that it was a liability of the Dáil. I told him that I would leave it in abeyance until we knew how circumstances would be after the negotiations. Later, when I resigned from the position of consul-general, the minister for finance repudiated any liability. Arthur Griffith was then dead and so the matter ended.

I put aside for the present any reference to the trying ordeal of parting from my wife and children, my relatives and friends and the breaking up, for me, of that happy circle that made up our lives.

Being sent to America was, in its way, a minor 'judgement' on me. I had always proclaimed that under no circumstances could I be tempted to leave Ireland and that no prospect of making big money or success could compensate me for being an exile from Ireland and all that it held for me. One should go easy on vows and resolutions for it was my fate to make sixteen Atlantic crossings to and from the United States before I was finished.

14

In America 1921-1922 – British propaganda in the U.S.A. – Joseph McGarrity and Dr W. J. Maloney – Washington and some of its leading politicians

I sailed from Cóbh on 15 October 1921 on the *S.S. America*, one of the United States' liners. She was an excellent ship which, even in very bad weather, behaved splendidly. She had been I learned, the *Amerika* at one time, the flagship of the Hamburg-America Line, and had been built in Belfast by Harland & Wolff, and served as the model on which the later German liners were designed.

The trip across was uneventful. I had as my table companions two Capuchin fathers who were on their way to do a series of missions in California. One of them, Father Sylvester Mulligan, O.F.M.Cap., was afterwards to become archbishop of Simla. There were many Americans on board and of these, many were German-Americans and Irish-Americans who were returning home after 'doing' Europe. The German Americans, most of whom had been visiting relatives in Germany, were very depressed by what they had experienced in Germany and what they anticipated for the future. France had won the war and France would crush them. The terms of the Versailles treaty and the Clemenceau policy of revenge gave the German people little hope of re-establishing anything like a normal orderly life. They were not bitter, but they were infinitely saddened. They had to return to their own homes and affairs in America, but the remembrance of what they had seen and the conditions under which they left their relatives in Germany would haunt them. Such, in brief, was the story I had from most of them.

We had a fair sprinkling of Irish-Americans aboard, including Father Phil O'Donnell of Boston and a few priests and laymen who were of his party. Father Phil was a friend of Judge Cohalan and John Devoy and was one of the big men of the 'Friends of Irish Freedom', the organisation which had fallen foul of de Valera and his supporters during Dev's American campaign for the Republic.

Father Phil and his friends and I had many long talks and they gave their side of the argument in the controversy. I did not agree with them, but I realised quickly the inevitable developments that must arise when the Irish-American politician has to decide between his loyalties to his American party politics and his activities on behalf of the people of Ireland. I was to learn much more about such conflict of interest before I was long in America. Let me say that, despite our arguments and disagreements, Father Phil and his party were almost embarrassingly kind and good to me on the trip over and we parted good friends when the ship landed at New York.

The chief engineer on board the *S.S. America* was a fine strapping Irishman named Paddy Brennan. Paddy stood about six feet two or three inches and was built in proportion. He was a picture of physical fitness and his strong face and firm chin bore evidence of the strong character behind them. He was a rigid teetotaller who did not smoke and controlled his team of over two hundred and fifty engineers, fitters, electricians, firemen and the rest by a firm discipline. I was to see much of Paddy for I made five trips in the *S.S. America* within the next few years.

Paddy was a County Louth man and had trained in the Inchicore works of the Great Southern Railway. He had hurled in the Phoenix Park and, as he said himself, often followed the 'Inchicore Sheet Metal Band' to big meetings and parades. He had gone to America sometime around 1903 when the *S.S. Baltic*, another Belfast-built liner of the White Star Fleet, was carrying 3,000 steerage passengers to New York at twenty-five shillings a head and making a profit.

Paddy was in 'the movement'. He was a naturalised American citizen, but that did not prevent him remembering that he was Irish and that Ireland had a call on his services. As he crossed the Atlantic once a month and the ship was joined by the tender at Cóbh on the East bound trip from New York and the West bound trip from Bremen, Paddy could give useful service to the men at home. He did and I think he would not like me to say more than that.

I had so often read the recorded impressions of new arrivals at the port of New York that I was, to some extent, prepared for the impressive skyline, the skyscrapers, the Statue of Liberty and all the rest. The films have made it as well known to everyone as to those who have landed at the port. Dan McGrath,[1] the Irish consul, who would be my deputy and chief assistant in the consulate and with whom I was destined to have close associations for many years afterwards, met me at the pier. There were others there too, including two of the Ward girls from Belfast who were old friends of ours for many years and excellent workers in Irish circles.

I had the inevitable sense of bewilderment that marks the newcomer's arrival in a strange city but, under Dan McGrath's guidance, soon settled down to know my way about and get into work.

1. Daniel John McGrath (1884-1942): born Kilkenny, solicitor with a practice in Dublin, consul for the Irish Republic in New York 1920-22, businessman in New York 1922-32, consul for Irish Free State in Chicago 1933-42.

2. Joseph Connolly, consul-general of the Irish Republic to the U.S.A., October 1921 to November 1922

The work in the consulate was very varied and interesting. We had at that time no official recognition from the United States government. We did not issue passports nor grant visas and the British consul general, a Mr Armstrong, tended to ridicule our pretensions to be a consulate at all. Despite non-recognition by the government, the position was fully appreciated not only by Irish-Americans but by most Americans who were not Anglophiles.

My predecessor, Mr Diarmuid Fawsitt,[2] who was the first Irish consul general to the U.S.A., had already established many connections with shipping concerns, importers and exporters and agents and our people at home were slowly but gradually beginning to realise that the consulate was in a position to further and protect their interests. This was and continued to be the more or less routine work of the office. It was work in which I felt quite at home from the beginning, for it was second nature to me to pursue business contacts and negotiate deals and arguments. We had a constant stream of callers with various problems. Some of them would be concerned with family disputes over land or other settlements, others with regard to wills and intestacies. They afforded ample evidence of how little disposed many of our emigrants are to maintain correspondence with the folk at home. There is of course a reason for this. The early years are often difficult and involve movement and change of address often with little time or the facilities for letter writing. Time passes quickly, new interests are developed and the letter home is 'put on the long finger'. There are many such procrastinators but most of our emigrants, and particularly our women emigrants, are loyal in their attachment and a help to the parents at home. The American letters and remittances are evidence of that.

There was one evil which we set out to kill, and that was the slick operations of some American lawyers in the handling of the assets of our emigrants who had died intestate.

The technique of such American lawyers who specialised in this racket is probably well known now, but in 1921 it was not and, even after all the publicity and warnings we issued, it continued for many years and even now may be in operation.

2. Diarmuid Fawsitt (1884-1967): born Bandon, County Cork, secretary of Irish Industrial Development Association 1902-19, member of Gaelic League and founder-member of Ring College, County Waterford, member of Sinn Féin and Irish Volunteers 1913, Irish Republic consul-general in New York 1919-21, secretary, department of finance in Provisional Government 1922, confidant of Michael Collins who sent him to establish contact with Unionists 1922, assistant secretary, department of industry and commerce, Irish Free State, 1923-5, proprietor of tobacco shop, Dame Street, Dublin, barrister 1928, broadcaster, Irish correspondent for *Financial Times*, circuit court judge 1938-54.

The estates of the emigrants who die intestate are in the care of the Surrogate's Court and are listed in the Surrogate's Offices.

The wise gentlemen of the law who had access to this office were able to secure the lists and particulars of those emigrants who had died intestate. They got their home addresses in Ireland and had, as their agents, solicitors in nearly every district in Ireland. Through these Irish solicitors they got the next of kin to sign a power of attorney giving them authority to collect the total amount of the estate and at the same time agreeing to pay half the amount of same for the services and costs involved. What the Irish solicitors collected as their 'cut' of the costs I do not know, but the system was, if not universal, very widespread in 1921.

There was an even worse evil that we discovered, and that was the lawyer who, not content with staking his claim for fifty per cent, which he could do quite legally by the terms of his agreement, held on to the full amount and depended on getting away with it because there was no one to take action against him. It is but right to say that there were not many such, but there were a few that came to our notice. In a couple of cases they paid up, but we sent two of them to spend nine months in the penitentiary.

Dan McGrath, who was a native of Kilkenny and had been a practising solicitor in Dublin, had a commendable passion for looking after the interests of our people at home and was ruthless in tracking down the 'shyster' lawyers who were out to rob them. He was a man of ability, highly cultured and efficient, and his knowledge of America and American ways was invaluable to me and to the administration at home.

The development of trade formed a major section of our work and we handled many inquiries from Ireland and were able to secure valuable contacts for quite a number of our exporters.

We suffered many irritations in handling the affairs of some of our traders and professional men in Ireland. One of these was the difficulty in getting them to deal with correspondence or to give adequate and precise details in replies to the queries raised by potential clients or customers. Solicitors were particularly negligent in this respect. I have known cases where lawyers delayed for months to sign and return documents to close estates even when, apart from other considerations, there would be a substantial amount for their own fees coming to them. Another major difficulty was to get shippers to give adequate attention to the proper preparation, packing and despatch of their goods to the American buyer, as well as to the necessary documents, bills of lading, etc., that are essential for quick and orderly delivery of the goods. It was nearly impossible to get most of the shippers at home to realise that the American importers were exacting, that they were used to getting their goods in proper condition and according to their directions, and that the authorities at the Port just did not release the goods unless the necessary documents were available. Detailed instructions covering every essential requirement were issued from the consulate and then, when some call came through from the Customs or the Shipping Company, McGrath would explode: 'Why don't the so and so dumb-bells read the letters we send them . . . I bet they, the letters, are lying on their desks unopened'. However, despite these irritations and annoyances and the fact that we were not officially recognised, we were steadily gaining ground and influence. Much of this was due to the friendly co-operation and goodwill we received, not only from our Irish-Americans but from many Americans who had no kinship whatever with Ireland.

The 'feeling' for Ireland in the United States during the autumn of 1921 was widespread. As the Americans would say our 'stock' was high indeed. All America knew something of the fight that had been put up against the Irish people. Added to that was a general revulsion of feeling against the English which was, I guessed, a purely after-the-war reaction. One heard constantly sneering and contemptuous comments on the 'Limies', the fact that 'Uncle Sam had won the war', that he had paid for it too and that now they 'could whistle for the money they had lent the British'. Most of it was ill-informed perhaps and all of it was typical American emotionalism, but it had its effect in breaking Wilson and putting Harding[3] into the White House.

Back of it all, however, and where it counted most, English influence was in evidence. I was not long in America until I realised just how much it did operate. In trade and shipping it was everywhere in evidence. One learned or heard of the universal 'tie-up' in financial circles and in the better class stores goods were specially marked 'Imported from England' to make special appeal to the more wealthy buyers. Later I would see some evidence of its backstage power and influence in official governmental circles.

At this period the British were pursuing a definite and well organised plan of astute propaganda throughout the United States. One by one the English lecturers arrived to start off on a nationwide lecture tour. Novelists, poets, playwrights, artists, politicians and professors followed one another in quick and orderly succession. I noticed with considerable interest that, at intervals of a week or two weeks, there would be one or two new arrivals. There would be press interviews on arrival, a reception and a

3. Warren Gamaliel Harding (1865-1923): 29th president of U.S.A. 1921-3.

lecture, and the star of the moment would be launched on his 'coast to coast' tour.

One could not find fault with the British for their methods. Personally I thought they showed great sense and intelligence in the way they did their job. Their propaganda was subtle and insidious and sprang from the cultural reflexes conveyed to the Americans rather than from any particular message that the lecturer put over to his audience. Moreover, these tours were, I imagine, profitable to the lecturers and did not involve any expense to the directing council. American communities, particularly in the major cities and towns, have an insatiable appetite for talks and lectures. Women's organisations are widespread and are always eager to welcome the bearer of any messages of interest, whether it be historical, sociological or cultural. Schools and colleges are equally receptive and, if much of the appetite for lectures and culture generally is superficial, it would be foolish not to appreciate the fact that there is a core of earnest, intelligent people eager to hear and learn from the foreign visitor.

I was not long in New York until I had many demands for talks, lectures and meetings as well as numerous invitations to private dinners, suppers and the like. It was necessary to fit in as many engagements as possible, although I sometimes felt that the main purpose of some of these invitations was to 'vet' me or, as the New Yorker would say at that time, to give me the 'once over'.

The meetings and discussions were interesting. Sitting on the platform waiting my turn to speak, I found myself trying 'to place' the many and varied types that made up the audience and the speakers. There were the well-groomed and prosperous, the quiet and serious as well as the jovial and sporting, but what impressed me most was the middle-aged and elderly women who sat quietly listening with rapt attention to every word. Many of them were simply and quietly dressed by American standards. They were not demonstrative, but one could sense that, however many years they might have spent in Brooklyn or the Bronx, they had never in their hearts and souls left their own little corner of Ireland. It was the same in Boston and Philadelphia or wherever else one went. Rightly or wrongly, I found myself speaking to them rather than to the others. They, I knew, would grasp the whole spiritual, cultural and civilised nature of our conflict with the alien forces that had held us in subjection.

It would be quite impossible to mention all the men and women, Irish and Irish-American, whom I met in the first few weeks in New York. There were luncheons and dinners squeezed into a schedule which included conferences, talks and business appointments. Harry Boland, Seán

Nunan,[4] Gilbert Ward[5] and Liam Pedlar[6] were busy with a good staff at the headquarters of the American Association for the Recognition of the Irish Republic,[7] and dealing with the bond drive. Stephen O'Mara[8] had replaced his elder brother James[9] as fiscal agent and was looking after the funds.

Joseph McGarrity of Philadelphia was one of my earliest callers and was soon one of my best friends and helpers. McGarrity hailed from County Tyrone and had 'made good' in Philadelphia. He was the big man in the Clan-na-Gael movement and had been one of the chief driving forces that helped to make de Valera's mission and the bond drive the successes that they were. He was a complex mixture of tough ruggedness and boundless good nature. He did not indulge in much finesse, but was mostly blunt and at times aggressive and dogmatic. The driving impulse of his life was his love for Ireland and his hatred of British rule over it. For this he made every sacrifice in time and money and the outpouring of his tireless energy.

It was McGarrity who introduced me to Dr W. J. Maloney, a medical specialist in New York. He was an American citizen, although a graduate of Edinburgh University, who had been seriously wounded while serving as an officer with the British forces in World War I.

4. Seán Nunan (1890-1981): born London, member of G.P.O. garrison, Easter Rising 1916, interned in Frongoch and later served prison sentences for refusal to join British army, clerk of First Dáil Éireann 1919, toured U.S.A. promoting Dáil Éireann External Loan, of which he was registrar 1919-21, acted as secretary to de Valera in U.S.A. 1919-21, consul general, New York 1932-38, First Secretary, London 1938-41, counsellor, Washington 1941-46, consul general, New York 1946-47, minister, Washington 1947-50, assistant secretary, department of external affairs 1950, secretary 1950-55.

5. Gilbert Ward: born Dublin, member of Irish Volunteers 1913, interned in Frongoch following Easter Rising 1916.

6. Liam Pedlar: born Dublin, member of Irish Volunteers 1913, active in Easter Rising 1916, interned in Frongoch 1916.

7. American Association for the Recognition of the Irish Republic: was founded on 16 November 1920 by Eamon de Valera to bring Irish American support into a single effective movement. His action followed a split between him and Clan na Gael which dominated the Friends of Irish Freedom. The Association raised money for the I.R.A. during the Anglo-Irish war. The split in the I.R.A. over the treaty signalled the beginning of the end of the Association and by 1926 it had ceased to exist.

8. Stephen M. O'Mara (1885-1926): born in Limerick, entered family business, member of Irish Volunteers and Sinn Féin 1913, mayor of Limerick 1921, succeeded his brother as trustee of Dáil Éireann funds and fund-raiser in U.S.A. 1921.

9. James O'Mara (1873-1948): born in Limerick, entered family business, member of Irish Parliamentary Party until 1907, member of Irish Volunteers and Sinn Féin 1913, in which was active after Easter Rising 1916, T.D. for Limerick 1919, fund-raising in U.S.A. and acting as a trustee for Dáil Éireann funds, after a disagreement with de Valera in May 1921 resigned from Dáil Éireann and resumed his business interests.

Maloney was one of the cleverest and most subtle minds I encountered amongst the friends of Ireland in New York. He was the direct antithesis of McGarrity and they were very close friends. It became a frequent practice for the three of us to have lunch together in the Commodore Hotel and very soon Billy Maloney and I were intimate friends. He had a risible wit and a puckish sense of clothing the ordinary with a shroud of mystery and colour. Back of it all there was a cool, calm mind that was Maloney and the generous helping hand for anyone who needed help. He was linked up professionally and socially with many of those who were in the top flight of the American social register.

Maloney did not appear on platforms very often and I never heard him address a meeting, but he could, at short notice, get things going, bring the useful people together and get the job done. It was Maloney who, with de Valera's approval, got the Commission established for the purpose of investigating the conditions in Ireland in 1920.[10] The whole organisation and planning of that organisation bore the Maloney stamp. Years later he would write and have published his book, *The Forged Casement Diaries* (Talbot Press, Dublin, 1936). It is a book of 275 pages of which fifty pages are notes and references. Not a very long book by any standards but, with intimate knowledge, I can vouch for the work and expense that were involved in the writing of it. When back in New York in 1933, I looked through two four-drawer filing cabinets containing all the records, reports, particulars and details which Maloney had gathered for the making of the book. He was patiently meticulous in his pursuit of the facts and no effort was spared to check all the material so that his ultimate presentation would be accurate. The book is a brilliant example of compression and to my mind a convincing refutation of all the vile slanders that the Smiths and the Basil Thomsons[11] spread about Roger Casement. If for no other reason but

10. American Commission of Inquiry into conditions in Ireland was launched in August 1920 by Dr W. T. Maloney and Frank P. Walsh to check alleged excesses of British troops and police in Ireland. The committee of 150 eminent Americans included Cardinal Gibbons, one Catholic archbishop, four Catholic bishops, seven Episcopalian bishops, four Methodist leading churchmen, the governors of five U.S. States, eleven senators, academics, editors and leaders of labour and industry representing, in all, thirty-six States. The Commission heard evidence from witnesses from Ireland. Its interim report, issued early in 1921, focused world attention on the misconduct of British forces in Ireland and brought pressure to bear on the British government to bring about a cessation of hostilities.

11. Sir Basil Home Thomson (1861-1939): born York, colonial service in Fiji, Tonga and New Guinea, barrister and deputy-governor of Liverpool prison 1896, later governor of a number of other prisons, secretary to Prisons Commission 1908, assistant commissioner of metropolitan police 1913, responsibility for dealing with enemy espionage 1914-18, director of intelligence, Scotland Yard 1919, resigned 1921, prolific writer.

the compilation, writing and publication of the book, Ireland and those of us who knew and worked with Casement are under a deep debt of gratitude to Dr Billy Maloney.

It was one of the sorrows of McGarrity's life that de Valera and Maloney never really 'hit it off' as he would say. There never was any 'break' but, as Joe explained it to me, there never was any real trust or confidence between them. I never discussed either one of them with the other, but I could, I think, understand the clash of temperament and technique that would explain it.

I had many helpers in my work and they were from all grades of society, from leaders in the law and press to foremen in the trades and transport services of the city.

I could always count on Charlie Redmond[12] finding temporary jobs for a dozen new arrivals or men temporarily 'laid off'. Major Eugene Kinkead,[13] who was recently and deservedly awarded an honorary degree by the National University, never failed me once in finding an opening for a newly arrived graduate or clerical worker. Tom Mulholland, the kindly and efficient port officer for the National Catholic Welfare Council, had a special care for the Irish emigrants arriving at Ellis Island and his co-operation with the consulate was one of the most valuable supports we had. Liam Gleeson, an officer in the federal customs, looked after any and all our problems arising over passports and solved most of them.

I mention these because I called on their help so frequently, but it would be a long list indeed if I tried to record the names of the many who, at all times, were ready to give their voluntary help to the non-recognised consulate of Ireland. Most of them were Irish or first generation Irish, but not all of them by any means. We had many American friends. Real 'one hundred per cent Americans', as they would be called, who were for one reason or another interested in our work and in Ireland generally. Many of these were interested in Irish literature and drama, others in the sociology of AE, George Russell,[14] while others were insistently inquisitive on political issues.

12. Charlie Redmond: an Irish-American who had influential contacts in the New York Transit Authority.

13. Major Eugene Kinkead (1876-1960): born Buttevant, County Cork, brought to U.S.A. as an infant, businessmen, chairman of Colonial Bank and Trust Company of New York, Congress 1907-10, major in military intelligence at Washington 1914-18, co-founder of Friends of Irish Freedom 1916, vice-president of American Association for Recognition of Irish Republic 1920, director of American Irish Historical Society.

14. George William Russell ('A.E.') (1867-1935): poet, journalist, mystic, economist and artist: born Lurgan, County Armagh, assistant secretary of Irish Agricultural Organisation Society and editor of its journal *The Irish Homestead*, generous in his encouragement of

Inevitably, we had to deal with all sorts of 'chancers' from share pushers for new and bogus Irish shipping companies to new inventions for bog drainage. In some cases these caused us considerable trouble, but a word to the district attorney was usually sufficient to end their activities.

I cannot close these references without mentioning one quiet little woman who called at the consulate occasionally. Miss O'Reilly was a hard-working lady employed in one of the big stores. She had a little group of Irish women like herself who collected and subscribed to their own organisation and who were ready and indeed always on the 'look out' to find where and how they could best help. My first experience of them was when a ne'er-do-well lad from home had foolishly brought his wife and three children out to the United States, but who was off on a drunken spree when they were dumped in Ellis Island. Miss O'Reilly and her group stepped in, looked after them and booked them back home in much better condition materially than they were when they landed. She was outstanding, but at the same time typical of that quiet, selfless and unobtrusive charity that existed, and I am sure still exists amongst the ordinary Irish in America. There were others, of course, many of them, and they were something of a trial at times. They 'talked big' and sentimentally of Ireland, of their work and interest in the 'old country' and of their anxiety to help out, but one soon learned to distinguish between the genuine and the opportunist.

The most heart-warming experience I had was when a little, middle-aged man called and asked to see me. He asked me about Egans in Cork. He knew that their jewellery store and factory had been burnt down, when Cork had been sacked by the Black and Tans. Did I know anything about them or how they were making out? I told him I knew Mr Barry Egan[15] slightly, but that I did not know exactly how the firm had progressed since the destruction. He then produced his Bank Savings book which showed a credit balance of a few thousand dollars. He asked me if I would write to Mr Egan and tell him that he would like to send him his savings to help them out. I promised to do so, but told him that I thought the firm was quite sound and had already got going. He went on to tell me his story.

He had been in an orphanage and Barry Egan's father had taken him out of it as a boy, gave him a job and got him decent lodgings. 'He was good

literary talent, invited to U.S.A. by Franklin D. Roosevelt in 1935 to lecture on his idea of employing young people on public works for two years, died soon after returning home.

15. Barry Egan (1879-1954): born Cork, a gold and silver smith, chairman of firm of William Egan & Co, member of Sinn Féin, member of Cork Corporation, T.D. for Cork 1927-32, founder member of Irish Tourist Association.

to me always', he said, 'but when I grew up I decided I had better get to America. You see . . . well I did not quite know who I was . . . no parents, no relations . . . I thought it would be easier out here'. And so he had come to New York more than thirty years earlier. He had got a job in a wholesale warehouse shortly after landing and he was still there as storekeeper. I asked him if he had never thought of trying his luck in any other city or in another job but, no, he was quite content. He had his room near his work. He got Mass in the mornings in Barclay Street, had his breakfast and went on to his work. In the evenings he went for a stroll down by the Battery, called into the church and went home to his room. He had been up Fifth Avenue to see St Patrick's cathedral, but had never been in Central Park. When I expressed surprise at this he merely nodded his head: 'Yes, I agree it sounds queer but I am content. I shall put in my time'. I did not probe further but just sat and wondered. He was quite self-possessed and intelligent and seemingly content, yet for over thirty years he had spent his life within about a square mile at the end of Manhattan. Timidity! Fear of the crowds! An inferiority complex! I did not know. All I did know was that he remembered his Cork benefactor and was there to offer every dollar of his savings to help out in what he feared was an irreparable disaster to the firm and the family.

I wrote to the firm in Cork and in due course had their reply for him when he called a couple of weeks later. He was relieved to know that all was well and pleased with the terms of their appreciation and thanks. He thanked me for the trouble that I had taken and left, to return about ten minutes later and bring me a small box of cigars which he begged me to accept. It is, of course, a rule that officials must not accept anything in the way of gifts from those whom they serve. This was one occasion when I broke the rule!

Soon after I had settled down and got a grip on the work in New York I made my first visit to Washington. I was booked to give an address in the Catholic University there and afterwards to make contact with a number of the top flight statesmen and politicians, as well as some of our most prominent and active supporters in the city. The journey was interesting all the way. Passing through Philadelphia, Newark, Elizabeth, Wilmington and the other cities and towns gave but a brief glimpse of the big factories and warehouses and the layout of the residential areas, but it did convey something of the impulsive drive that charged American life. The countryside in between the towns and cities was disappointing. Frequently one could observe farm houses and buildings which were disorderly, unkempt and badly in need of paint. They may not have had a 'midden' in front of the house, but quite a number of them had dumps of old implements, broken machinery and the remnants and junk of old model T. Fords and most of them needed paint. Billboards on the borders of the permanent way shrieked two proclamations at me most of the way, one was for 'Carter's Little Liver Pills' and the other was 'Eventually, why not Now!', which I think referred to somebody's flour.

Washington impressed me as it must impress every first-time visitor. It has grace, beauty and dignity and an air of sheltered restfulness in its tree-lined residential avenues.

At the Catholic University we dined with the faculty and later proceeded to our meeting when Father Michael O'Flanagan and I delivered our talks. Later we adjourned to the home of Frank P. Walsh where we had an hour or two of entertainment and talk and where we sat around one of the very few open fires that I saw while in America.

For several days I was busy making my first contacts with the men who thought 'they counted' and the men who were content to go on with their work without caring whether they counted or not. It would be tedious to go into detail, but I was most impressed by Senator Borah[16] who was at that time chairman of the Foreign Relations Committee of the senate, Senator La Folette[17] and Senator Norris.[18] There were many others and one and all were kind and sympathetic to Ireland and, despite the fact that we had no official recognition, were at all times helpful.

After Washington there were meetings to be addressed in Boston, Philadelphia and some of the other eastern cities. In New York, Brooklyn and the Bronx the demand for one's presence was constant and it became something of a problem to get the quiet free nights that I felt were necessary for both my sanity and my digestion.

Our work in the office proceeded smoothly and satisfactorily. We had a small staff of seven. They were competent and earnestly interested and

16. William Edgar Borah (1865-1940): born Fairfield, Illinois, lawyer 1887, in practice at Boise, Idaho 1890, senate 1907, urged social reforms, opposed League of Nations, chairman of Senate Foreign Relations Committee 1924.

17. Robert Marion La Folette (1860-1925): born Madison, Wisconsin, governor of Wisconsin 1901-06, senate 1906-25, a leader of the Progressive Movement and one of the nation's most prominent and controversial politicians, his son, of the same name, who succeeded to his seat in the senate (1925-46), had acted as his political secretary and adviser 1919-25, both La Folettes were champions of organised labour.

18. George William Norris (1861-1944): born Sandasky County, Ohio, worked on family farm, lawyer 1883, teacher 1883-5, Beaver City, Nebraska, law practice 1885, local politics, Congress 1902, senate 1913-43, associated with the success of Tennessee Valley Authority and other such enterprises.

we could feel satisfied that, despite the limitations due to our lack of recognised status, we were getting results.

One of the projects that I determined to carry through was the establishment of an Irish Arts and Cultural Organisation. It was my plan to get this going, first of all in New York and then, if all went well, to have similar groups linked up in Chicago, Boston, Philadelphia and the other large centres. I thought then and I still think that such a body is the most essential Irish organisation that is needed in America.

At that time we had quite a fair sprinkling of Irish folk in New York who were well known in the literary, dramatic and art circles of the city. I had discussed the project with a few like Padraic and Mary Colum, John Campbell[19] and John Smiley[20] the artists and a few others and we were all agreed that with little effort we could muster a respectable force of Irish born and second generation Irish whose names were familiar to the literary and theatrical circles of the United States. It would be the purpose of the organisation to emphasise the cultural side of Ireland as distinct and separate from politics and to bring notice to a wider public of the achievements of our poets, dramatists and artists. The scheme, like a few others that were in the embryonic state, was arrested by the crash that was on its way and which would disrupt our efforts at home and abroad. It was not the only frustrating disappointment.

Early in my brief career in America I had correspondence with the Very Reverend Dr Yorke[21] of San Francisco. Dr Yorke was outstanding when in Ireland both as a churchman and as an Irish Irelander, and he enhanced his reputation in America. He was as brilliant as he was fearless in his defence of his Faith and his country and was unequalled in a verbal or published controversy. I had gladly accepted his invitation to do a brief lecturing tour in his area, but the signing of the treaty in London changed my plans and the tour was postponed indefinitely. I was selfishly sorry that it

19. John Campbell (Seán Mac Cathmhaoill): illustrator of Celtic legends, illustrated *Celtic Romances*; *Irish songs*; *the Táin*; *Four Irish Songs* 1909-12, continued to be prolific until 1919.

20. John McA. Smiley: born Belfast, spent time in India, probably with the British army, prolific painter 1913-21.

21. Peter Christopher Yorke (1864-1925): born County Galway, St Parick's College, Maynooth 1882-86, emigrated to U.SA. 1886, St Mary's Seminary, Baltimore 1886-87, ordained priest for archdiocese of San Francisco, December 1887, secretary to Archbishop Patrick William Riordan, chancellor, editor of archdiocesan weekly *The Monitor* and eventually parish priest 1888-1925, president of Gaelic League in California 1899, founder and editor of *The Leader* 1902, regent University of California 1903-12, successfully challenged the influence in San Francisco of the anti-Catholic American Protective Association, doughty champion of Catholic education, Irish emigrants, Sinn Féin, trade-unionists and workers, author.

had to be so for it meant that I never had the dual pleasure of meeting Dr Yorke and of visiting California.

Official correspondence with Dublin dealt mainly with commercial matters and such cases as called for special attention, but there was little reference to the big political issues or the vital discussions that were going on between our plenipotentiaries and the British.

The letters which I received from my wife in Belfast were disquieting. There was little evidence of truce or peace there. The army might be standing at ease, but the Orange 'lambs' and their Special Constabulary, a force recruited and paid to do the work which they would have done voluntarily, were still waging an incessant war on the Catholic minority.

It was a period of strain and worry and even the constant activities in the office and the distractions of meetings, lectures and journeys here and there did little to reduce them.

15

The treaty of 1921 – Repercussions in America –
McGarrity crosses to Ireland – The Collins-de Valera Election Pact –
Collins sees Churchill in London – Collins' speech in Cork –
The Pact is broken – Darrell Figgis and the 1922 election –
Rival delegations arrive in New York from Ireland –
We get Jim Larkin released –
Cigarettes or liquor the American women's viewpoint in 1921 –
Relaxations – Canada – Return to Ireland – The civil war

I would be glad to draw a curtain of forgetfulness over the months that followed the announcement of the signing of the treaty. Even now I shudder when I recall them to memory.

When the news first came through we were swamped out with inquiries by telephone and the invasion of pressmen. I had learned from experience that it was utterly foolish to say anything to an American newshawk. A plain statement of simple fact was liable to be distorted into something almost directly the opposite of what you had said. All American reporters were not like that, but most of them were and they had a persistent tendency to colour the story to their own shade rather than to report accurately. Accordingly the response in the consulate was that there was no comment, but that a statement might be issued later. We had of course no advice or guidance from Dublin nor did I expect any. I realised that they would be having such a time at headquarters in Dublin that our very existence might be temporarily forgotten. All the while the pressure from the American press for information, for our views and for all sorts of relevant and irrelevant details was kept on.

It was in these circumstances that I issued a brief statement to the press and to our people and friends in America. It was simple and to the point. Articles for a treaty had been signed by our representatives in London. The terms and conditions would in due course be submitted to Dáil Éireann, the only authority in Ireland with the right to decide on their acceptance or rejection. It was not within the rights or functions of any outside body here or elsewhere to judge what was right or wrong. That duty rested on the people of Ireland. Our people in America had been more than generous in helping us and we were more than grateful for that help. We might need it again and we would always need their goodwill and loyalty, but at this critical point in our history I urged a quiet waiting until all the issues were clear and above all that the ultimate decision rested with the people at home.

These were, approximately, the lines of my statement. Frank P. Walsh, our consulting lawyer, rang me a day or two later to compliment me on it and to say that it was the necessary steadying-message that our friends in the United States needed. It may have been with many of them, but I knew that the vast majority of our people there had a sense of dread and fear of what was impending. Distrust of the English was in their blood and marrow and how justified it was!

We were far from being a happy group that gathered together on Christmas Day 1921. It was arranged that those of us who were not already booked to spend the festival with friends would gather together for lunch and dinner.

I will always remember that Christmas morning. It gave me a minor shock to realise that, having gone to early Mass, I had to make my way to a restaurant and eat breakfast alone. My apartments were comfortable and well cared, but no meals were served. I had breakfast alone every morning in one or other of my favourite haunts but . . . well, Christmas morning!, that seemed altogether different! It was my first Christmas away from home and inevitably I recalled other Christmases and pictured the little family at home with all the excitement that youngsters enjoy on the morning of the great feast. However, I had tried to set my mind against futile regrets and to conquer the sense of loneliness that at times became almost unbearable.

After breakfast I made my way to the house of the Carmelites in Twenty-Eighth Street, where we were to meet, and here all sense of loneliness was dissipated by the atmosphere of friendliness and Irish hospitality that was always to be found in that house. Harry Boland, Stephen O'Mara, Liam Pedlar and a few others were already there and we were joined by Father O'Connor and those of the community who were free. Despite the wish to retain the spirit of Christmas, the discussion came back to the situation at home, the terms of the treaty and the possibilities of the future.

We dined together that evening at the Pennsylvania Hotel and here we were joined by Mrs Stephen O'Mara and her sister, Miss Kate O'Brien,[1] who would, in the near future, make her name as a writer and playwright. On me, and I think on all of us, there hung the shadow of the coming conflict at home. Enough had already been said and reported to indicate that there was more than a threat of a split in our ranks. We knew enough of our history, even if our Irish instinct did not warn us, to realise that, if the English succeeded in dividing us, then our hopes of achieving our aims would be dim indeed. 'Divide and Conquer' has been the trade mark of

1. Kate O'Brien (1897-1974): born Limerick, journalist, playwright, novelist.

the English, and it is the 'Divide' as much as the 'Conquer' that has bred that fierce hate that animates all the peoples who have had the misfortune to come under their insatiable maw. We in Ireland know it more than others. India and the Far East as well as Africa have had their share and today, as I write, the changeless policy is being applied to the unfortunate Cypriots and Pontius Pilate continues to wash his hands. 'If only we could get them to agree amongst themselves', they cry to the world, ignoring the fact that Arthur Balfour[2] committed himself to hand over Israel to two groups and that Lloyd George succeeded in bluffing the Irish with a Boundary Commission after guaranteeing the Six Counties to Sir James Craig. It will be a wise policy for young Ireland to resume the study of John Mitchel's writings!

It is not pleasant to recall the conditions under which we carried on in the United States in the early months of 1922. The routine work of the office continued, but even these activities were tainted and influenced by the growing uncertainty and anxiety about what was happening at home. The treaty debates were very fully reported in the American dailies. At three thousand miles distance and in a foreign country they made depressing reading from every point of view.

Most of the group that directed and ran the political and bond drive headquarters had been summoned home. Harry Boland, Seán Nunan, Liam Pedlar and Gilbert Ward[3] left together at the end of 1921 and I felt very much alone after their departure.

I had endless conferences and discussions with the leading men in the American Association. Some of our best and most unselfish workers from outside New York were constantly arriving and it was a delicate job to get them to understand that, as things were in Dublin, little or no attention was being given to Irish-American thought or opinion. Little or no news came to me officially regarding the crisis nor did I expect any. I could envisage all too clearly from the reports in both the Irish and American papers how the situation was developing. Everything was in the melting pot and boiling over at that.

The American groups had felt themselves to be such an important force in the movement that they could not readily accept the fact that their views

2. Arthur James Balfour, first earl of Balfour (1848-1930): philosopher and statesman, in November 1917 during his tenure of the foreign office he issued the so-called Balfour Declaration in favour of the Jewish national home in Palestine, as a result of which under a British mandate from the League of Nations the Jews were established in the Holy Land on equal terms with the existing inhabitants.

3. Gilbert Ward did not return to Ireland with Harry Boland, Seán Nunan and Liam Pedlar. He returned to New York to finish work on the Bond drive.

should not weigh heavily with the Dáil and the people at home. It was an extremely difficult and complex situation to deal with. I understood their point of view which had a certain justification by reason of the work and sacrifices they had made, but I knew equally that they had neither the right nor the power to influence the ultimate decisions of the Dáil.

I had an illuminating side-light on the American and Irish-American outlook during this period. It disclosed two things, the naiveté of some of our friends there and of their firm belief in the power of the dollar. It emerged at one of our many conferences. Joe McGarrity, Dr Maloney, John Hearne[4] of Springfield, Frank P. Walshe and myself were considering the latest developments and reports of what was going on at home. The election was in the offing and we could glean from the reports of the debates that the rift was getting wider and deeper. I am not certain which of them made the proposal, but I think it was Joe McGarrity. The suggestion was that we should go along at once to 'old man Doheny', as Joe called him, get him to throw a big lunch in the bankers and lawyers club, rope in the right people and raise a half-million dollars, send each of the parties an equal half of the fund to run the election and then let the Dáil get together and decide their future policy.

Edward L. Doheny[5] was a multi-millionaire Irish-American who had been one of the most prominent and certainly the wealthiest patrons and supporters of Dev's campaign and the bond issue drive. He had the connections and the power to influence many of the American magnates and I knew the raising of the money would be no difficulty for the oil king. The suggestion to me was not only fantastic, but quite ridiculous and I told them so. I argued that money had no bearing whatever on the issue and could have no effect on the minds and outlook of the members of the Dáil. McGarrity would not agree and argued that it would make clear to the 'men at home' their interest and support. He had his way and I was overborne and straight away we motored up to the Plaza Hotel, where Doheny always maintained a private suite as his home and headquarters when in New York. I felt worse than sore. I felt utterly foolish and, when it came

4. John P. Hearne: born Springfield, Massachussets, proprietor of a dry-goods business, a leading member of American Association for Recognition of Irish Republic.

5. Edward L. Doheny (1856-1935): born Fond du Lac, Wisconsin, mule-driver for government geological survey, New Mexico 1872, gold-prospector in western mountains 1874-92, oil producer Los Angeles 1892, Tampico, Mexico 1900, Hawaii and California 1921-2, senatorial investigation and later a trial into charges of bribery against him 1923-30, acquitted but lost government oil leases, erected a library on campus of U.C.L.A. to the memory of his only son, murdered by one of the household servants.

to the point of entering the elevator to ascend to Doheny's suite, I almost spontaneously pulled back. 'You boys go along and have your talk, I just can't go up, because I think the whole idea is utterly foolish and will get us nowhere. However, you think otherwise. I'll wait for you in the lobby'. In half an hour or so they returned. They reported: 'Everything was O.K., the old man would throw the luncheon and see that the right people were present'. That was as I had expected it to be, but it still left me bewildered to try and think how they could imagine that dollars had or could have the slightest influence on the position at home. However, we returned to the office to continue our vehement arguments and fray our minds and nerves still further with our anxieties.

McGarrity always returned home to Philadelphia at the weekends and indeed often did the two hours journey each way several times a week. I went down with him on the Friday afternoon and after dinner on the Sunday evening I suggested to him that the most practical thing he could do would be to pack a grip and jump over on the next available liner and see the principals at home. I had some difficulty at first in persuading him, but eventually he agreed.

I was not very optimistic, but I had a faint hope that his status and his influence might have a salutary effect. He was intimate with some of them and particularly close to de Valera, Boland and McCartan, while one and all of them knew that he had given almost a lifetime's service to the Irish cause in America. There was another aspect that I had in mind. McGarrity was the head and mainspring of the American Association. As such it was desirable, if not essential, that he should get a 'close up' of the realities and of all the facets of the crisis. The main purpose, however, was that he should try and bring the differing personnel together and try and bridge the gulf that threatened to swamp us.

Whether it was my persistent opposition to the Doheny half-million dollar scheme or the departure of McGarrity for Ireland that caused it, I heard no more of the luncheon nor did anyone else. I asked no questions, but was content to know that the proposal was dropped.

McGarrity was back in four weeks having spent a couple of weeks in Dublin. He was cheerful and inclined to optimism, because a pact had been made by de Valera and Collins which seemed to hold the promise of unity. There was a universal sense of relief in Ireland which had its corresponding echo in America.

It is not suggested that Joe McGarrity had a major hand in bringing about the agreement. There were others who were more intimately concerned and who were the real effective operators in the achievement, but that his presence and his influence did something to ease the strained relationships and make contacts less embarrassing may be credited to him.

Our hopes for the united efforts at home were short lived. The Collins-de Valera 'pact' was made on 20 May and the election was fixed for 16 June. Collins crossed to London and had an interview with Churchill on 13 June and delivered a speech in Cork the day after. In that speech it was clearly indicated that the pact and the agreement made on the voting at the election were abandoned.

He said:

> You are facing an election here on Friday and I am not hampered now by being on a platform where there are coalitionists. I can make a straight appeal to you, to the citizens of Cork to vote for the candidates you think best of, whom the electors of Cork think will carry on best in the future the work they want carried on. When I spoke in Dublin, I put it as gravely as I could that the country was facing a very serious situation. If the situation is to be met as it should be met, the country must have the representatives it wants. You understand fully what you have to do and I depend on you to do it.

I quote this from Miss Macardle's *The Irish Republic* and in the same volume is recorded the fact that on 25 May Darrell Figgis addressed a meeting of the executive council of the Farmers' Union and representatives of business interests and urged them to put forward pro-treaty candidates in the constituencies where a Republican might otherwise head the poll.

Now Darrell Figgis was a member of the standing committee of Sinn Féin and it was ominous that he, in his position, should make such a pronouncement and it could only have one purpose, the wrecking of the pact and the defeat at the polls of anti-treaty republican candidates

Darrell Figgis was to me something of an enigma in the movement. He had been one of the principal operators in the Howth gun-running and had been one of our companions when we were in Reading jail. He was clever as a writer and speaker and I had formed a high opinion of his administrative and executive competence when he was secretary and director of the Industrial Commission on which I had served. Despite all these contacts and the fact that our relationship with one another was always harmonious, I could never get that sense of trust and comfort that I enjoyed with most of my other colleagues. I was not alone in that for, to be quite frank, Figgis was regarded generally by those who counted as something of an interloper, a careerist or an opportunist. There was one notable exception and that was Griffith. Ever since our time in Reading I had noticed the close intimacy that had developed between them. On my frequent visits to Dublin and my meetings with Griffith, Figgis would generally turn up before we parted. Arthur would make many references to him and his work when we were alone.

This interested me for one reason only. I knew Griffith always appreciated men of keen intelligence and whose literary and journalistic contributions were of value to the national work, but Figgis had so many characteristics that were normally anathema to Griffith that I just wondered. Figgis had a double dose of vanity and egotism and seemed eager to dominate and hold the centre in whatever company he was. Most of us treated these characteristics with a good-natured tolerance and dismissed them as just the foibles of a clever but vain man. Normally I had always found that Griffith had little patience with anything that savoured of pretentiousness or vanity. Figgis was an intriguing study. I would not have devoted any attention to him here, but for his action in addressing the meeting of 25 May which would seem to have been a major step in breaking the pact and the election agreement. My reason for doing so and for stating the relationship between him and Griffith is simply this: that I cannot conceive that Figgis did what he did without the full consent and approval of Griffith. It is not to me a pleasant recollection of Griffith, but what seems to be the clear facts of that move must be recorded.

The pact and the election agreement were gone and the ultimate results showed that the Figgis appeal and the Collins direction had been effective. The Labour Party won 17 seats, the Farmers' Party 7, Trinity College had its 4 and 6 Independents were returned. Ninety-four candidates, who had been nominated under the panel as arranged by the pact, were elected and fifty-eight of these were pro-treaty and thirty-six were anti-treaty republicans.

It has been argued that 94 panel members were pledged to the pact and that the Labour candidates had also been pledged to the pact. The pact had stipulated for a national coalition 'on the ground that the national position requires the entrusting of the government of the country into the joint hands of those who have been the strength of the national situation during the last few years, without prejudice to their present respective positions'.

The argument was sound and, had the terms of the pact been observed, it is reasonable to think that the internal difficulties could have been surmounted and the subsequent tragedy of the civil war avoided. The British, however, determined otherwise. They maintained their pressure, and definite threats by Churchill and Sir Henry Wilson clearly indicated their decision to prevent any agreement between the Irish or their representatives. Churchill replying to Sir Henry Wilson said:

> The troops in Dublin are remaining in the position they hold and which I am assured are militarily completely secure . . .
>
> In the event of a setting up of a Republic it would be the intention of the government to hold Dublin as one of the preliminary and essential steps for the military operations.

Carson's 'Galloper' Smith, now Lord Birkenhead, would rattle his sabre again and assure the House that 'the resources of our civilisation are by no means exhausted'. It was the phrase that Oom Paul Kruger used prior to the Boer War and caught my boyish imagination at the time he used it. The civilised 'resources' of the British in the shape of guns, bayonets and everything down to 'Black and Tanism' have never been exhausted up to the present!

The breaking of the pact and the final result of the elections must have been an utterly depressing blow to the best of our people in Ireland, but to follow the events and to read the daily reports in the American press gave me a sense of despair. I felt isolated, three thousand miles away from the centre of all that went on and with little or no attention or advice from official headquarters. I had many good and worthy friends around me, all as deeply concerned as I was with the developments at home in Ireland, but they were not familiar with the cross currents, as I envisaged them, and inevitably they saw everything through Irish-American rather than Irish eyes.

Two delegations from home arrived together in New York, one representing the pro-treaty party, led by James O'Mara who was accompanied by Piaras Beaslaí[6] and Seán Mac Caoilte.[7] My friend Austin Stack along

6. Piaras Béaslaí (1881-1965): born Liverpool, member of Gaelic League in Dublin 1904, member of Irish Volunteers 1913, editor of Gaelic League's journal *An Fáinne* 1917-22 and Irish Volunteers' journal *An t-Oglach* 1918-22, close associate of Michael Collins during Anglo-Irish war, T.D. for East Kerry 1919, supported the treaty and major-general in the National army which upheld it, resigned from politics in 1923 and from the army in 1924 to devote his time to the Irish language movement, was a prolific author in Irish and English.

7. Seán Mac Caoilte: member of Gaelic League, member of Sinn Féin, Dublin City Council 1919-21.

with J. J. O'Kelly ('Sceilig')[8] came to represent the anti-treaty Republicans. When the news of their impending arrival reached us, I had a conference with a few of our selected friends, including McGarrity and Maloney. We were concerned with one major purpose and that was to try, if possible, to prevent the 'Split' spreading to the whole American organisation. We thought that whatever might happen in Ireland it was of the utmost importance to keep our people united solidly in the United States.

We decided to go out to the liner and interview both parties, and ask them to refuse to make any statements to the press pending a joint conference which we proposed to hold after we had landed at New York. We got the necessary permission to accompany the immigration officers on the tender and on boarding it found more than the usual complement of the American newshawks.

It was arranged that I would talk to Stack and that McGarrity would put our proposal to James O'Mara. Austin readily agreed to my appeal and McGarrity reported that O'Mara had also assented. However, before we had docked at the pier, a journalist friend, who was representing the *New York World* and a sincere worker for the cause in New York, came and told me that the press had received statements from the pro-treaty side. I immediately told Stack that, in view of this development, he was released from his promise and free to make or issue any statement to the press that he desired.

Both delegations went their ways and our proposed conference did not take place.

Later Professor Timothy Smiddy[9] arrived as the minister and accredited representative to Washington, and Denis McCullough came on a temporary mission which apparently was meant to consolidate the Devoy-Cohalan forces in support of the treaty. They kept somewhat aloof from the consulate, no doubt on the basis of an imaginary protocol which drew an equally imaginary line between the *Corps Diplomatique* and the consular

8. John J. O'Kelly (Sceilig) (1872-1957): born Valentia Island, County Kerry, president of Gaelic League 1919-23, T.D. for Louth-Meath and Leas Ceann Comhairle and minister for Irish 1919-21, minister for education 1921-22, opposed treaty 1921, president of Sinn Féin 1926, editor of *Banba, The Catholic Bulletin* and *An Camán*, prolific author under the penname 'Scéilg'.

9. Timothy A. Smiddy (1875-1962): born Cork, professor of economics, U.C.C. 1909-24, adviser to the plenipotentiaries during treaty negotiations 1921, envoy of Free State to U.S.A. 1922-24, minister plenipotentiary in Washington 1924-29, high-commissioner in London 1929-30, chairman of Free State Tariff Commission 1931-33, director of the Central Bank 1943-55, chairman of the commission of inquiry into post-emergency agricultural policy 1947.

service. As we had no official recognition from the United States government, the differentiation when pointed out to me amused me somewhat.

It was about the time of Smiddy's arrival that Dan McGrath called my attention to the decision that had been handed down in the courts in favour of Foster,[10] the socialist labour leader. Foster's counsel had raised the issue of his imprisonment on some technical grounds and had succeeded in securing his release. Jim Larkin, like Foster, had been under lock-and-key for what passed as sedition or provocation to public disorder in the United States and McGrath believed that a similar move on Larkin's behalf must likewise result in Larkin being freed. With my approval he prepared a brief for counsel who took the matter to court and, as McGrath had anticipated, secured Larkin's release.

I met Larkin a short time later and had a long talk with him. We discussed the position at home and all the personnel involved therein. The question came up as to how and with whom he would 'link up' on his return to Ireland. I went over the whole litany of them from de Valera to William O'Brien and from George Russell ('AE') to Tom Johnson, but was unable to find one with whom he would be prepared to work. One by one he analysed them critically, but with somewhat sweeping generalisations. He gave them credit for this or that good quality or ability, but . . . there was always that 'but'. Eventually I could not resist asking him the question: 'Now look, Jim, I have gone down nearly the whole list of them. There doesn't seem to be anyone with whom you feel you could work in Ireland. What do you propose doing when you return home? Are you going to try and carry the whole country on your shoulders like Atlas?' He did not tell me.

I quote from this talk with Jim Larkin not in any spirit of antagonism, but simply because it was so symptomatic of his personality and character. I have already stated my appreciation of what he did both in Belfast and Dublin. He had by his personality and forceful tactics put a badly needed spinal column into the workers of both cities and raised them from a degraded serfdom to an upright manhood, be that he was a 'Lone Ranger'. Not for him was the accurately compiled minute book and the audited

10. William Z. Foster (1881-1961): born Taunton, Massachussets, began his working life 1891, member of Socialist Party 1901, Wage-earners Party, Industrial Workers of the World 1909, founded Syndicalist League of North America 1912, founded Independent Trade Union Educational League 1915, organised steel-workers 1915-19, led unsuccessful steel strike 1919, visited Moscow, member of American Communist Party 1921, chairman of American Communist Party 1932-56, died in hospital in Moscow and given a State funeral.

accounts, but the unfurled flag and the barricade were his elements and the word of Larkin was an order.

Despite all the stress of anxiety, I had to attend various functions and to move around socially. There were lectures, occasional dinners and even county organisation balls at which attendance was practically imperative. Despite the shadow cast by events at home, some of these were entertaining and all were, in one way or another, informative of the American and Irish-American mentality.

Prohibition was the law of the land, but I quickly realised that the hallmark of the successful hostess was not so much the culinary achievements of her head cook but the quantity and quality of the liquors that were drawn from her cellars. The situation could be embarrassing for a teetotaller guest like myself. I remember a very special private dinner-party which was given to honour my arrival in New York and at which that Grand Old Man from Ireland, Judge Goff,[11] was the toast master. It provided me with my first and only embarrassment arising from the liquor conventions. Opposite me was a somewhat corpulent and rather greasy-looking gentleman who, it transpired later, was a very prominent and successful corporation lawyer. Observing that my various glasses remained unsoiled, he, who had already disposed of several replenishments, observed audibly: 'Well, all I can say is that if the consul general doesn't drink he won't get very far in America'. I was slightly stunned for a second or two by his bad manners, but ever so gently spoke across to him: 'When the consul general finds that he is not getting very far in America he will return home'. However, it was a lesson to me. After that night I always allowed the waiter to pour a share of wine into the glass and leave it there.

At another private party the two ladies that sat on either side of me raised the question of women smoking and wanted to know did the girls and women in Ireland smoke. I told them that some of them did. Did my wife smoke? I explained that, while she was not what I would call a smoker, she occasionally had a cigarette or two after an evening meal. They expressed their mild horror at women smoking at all and I was rather

11. John William Goff (1848-1924): born County Wexford, emigrated to U.S.A. 1853, his youth was spent in New York amid poverty and he had to forego attending school owing to the necessity of working for a living, in 1865 he entered the office of Samuel G. Courtney, U.S. district attorney and after serving as a junior clerk and attending night classes was admitted to the New York bar, prominent member of the Fenian organisation, with others he organised the escape of Fenian prisoners from Western Australia 1869, assistant district attorney, New York 1888, recorder of city and county of New York 1894, justice of supreme court of New York 1906-18, presided over some of the more celebrated criminal trials of the period.

surprised and somewhat amused to note that at the end of the evening they were both somewhat 'fuzzy' and incoherent. This was of course in 1921. Apparently it was an essential protest against the Volstead Act and Prohibition for all to break the law and acquire a taste for anything from imported Scotch to bathtub gin. It seemed to me that American women learned to drink in the Prohibition days and from then on taught many of their sisters all over the world to follow their example.

Such recreation as I managed to get was found in the theatres, in the Metropolitan Opera House and in the intimate family circles of a few good friends. I consider that I was fortunate that my first period of exile coincided with the early years of Gigli in the Metropolitan, the visits of the Moscow Art Theatre and Pavlova, to say nothing of the early production of Eugene O'Neill's plays and many other noteworthy dramatic performances. On one memorable night, I heard and saw Kreisler making his initial return visit after the war in Carnegie Hall. For two and a half hours he bewitched myself and a packed house with his exquisite playing and for nearly a week afterwards I felt exalted to a new plane of existence. I got a somewhat similar thrill from one particular performance of Anna Pavlova. I had seen her in my native city of Belfast some years earlier and was thrilled, but on the vast stage of the New York Hippodrome it was all so different. With her full company on the vast stage and the wonderful orchestra it was spell-binding. She performed one ballet called 'Autumn Leaves' in which she danced as the last chrysanthemum. I will not attempt to describe it. It was the quintessence of poetry and beauty and to this day, some thirty-six years afterwards and myself a decaying old man, the memory of that night still thrills me.

There were a few family homes, where I was welcome to drop in as and when I so inclined, and these were havens of refuge indeed. Here I could relax and talk freely, discuss plays and books or lapse into all sorts of discussions and arguments. In the homes of Peter Golden, Bill Gleeson, and the Wards, and with the Colums, John Campbell and a number of others I was always sure of a pleasant interlude and the sense of being back home in Ireland. The early months of 1922 passed. It was a curious mixture of routine work with fits and starts of activity on the part of different branches of the Irish organisation to cast their influence on affairs at home. All my main efforts were directed to preserve an unbroken line of unity in the American ranks of our movement and, despite minor incidents and the definitely hostile attitude of a certain section of the press, this unity was maintained.

The news I was receiving from my home in Belfast was worse than disquieting. Week by week my wife's letters brought me news of murders, riots, shootings and the reign of terror under which the Catholics of Belfast were struggling to exist. It was a nightmare of torture to think of it all and it added to my vexation of spirit to realise that the wrangling and disruption in Dublin was heading for chaos at the same time.

In May I made my first visit to Canada to carry through a lecture programme that had been arranged early in the year and to explore certain trading and commercial prospects that seemed promising. To be quite honest, I had little enthusiasm for my mission. The shadow of uncertainty that hung over the situation at home was more than sufficient to dampen one's fervour and made discussion on political matters extremely difficult. Despite this, I had a reasonably successful trip during which I established a number of valuable contacts both in governmental and commercial circles. I visited Montreal, Quebec and Halifax before concentrating on my various engagements in Ottawa.

Mr MacKenzie King[12] was prime minister at the time and was a kind and entertaining host during my stay. He was a Canadian Liberal with progressive ideas and a warm admirer of 'A.E.', with whose co-operative ideas he had great sympathy. My initial meeting with him caused a parliamentary flutter. He had arranged to give me an appointment at his office in Parliament House and his private secretary had told me that he would give me fifteen or twenty minutes. We were not long talking when he rang the bell, ordered his car round to the front and swept me off to his 'Country Club', where we enjoyed a light meal and much talk. I do not know just how long we stayed there, but it must have been several hours before we got into the car to return. We got back to the Parliament House to find a very anxious private secretary awaiting us with the information that Mr So and So was keeping the debate going until the prime minister would appear in the House and make the closing speech of the debate. It sounded like a near crisis and the prime minister had to make a hurried farewell and rush off to do his stuff. I was relieved to know that MacKenzie Kings's government had not suffered a defeat in the division lobby, owing to my intrusion.

My visit to Canada was a short one of about ten days and, with meetings and conferences, I had little opportunity of seeing much of either the cities or the countryside. The one place that attracted me above all others was Quebec. The whole layout of the city, its quaint old-world atmosphere and the pleasant and cheerful people that I met gave me a warm feeling of

12. William Lyon MacKenzie King (1874-1950): born Kitchener, Ontario, Canada, leader of Liberal Party, champion of Canada's independence of action, exceeded Walpole's record for length of service as prime minister in a parliament under the British system.

comfort and homeliness that I experienced nowhere else in my short visit to Canada. My last few days were made miserable by a sudden attack of illness, during which I carried out my engagements almost literally on my nerves. I had, perhaps, an exaggerated conception of the importance of keeping engagements, but it was only on my return home and when a further attack made the removal of my appendix essential that I realised how narrowly I had, by the Grace of God, escaped peritonitis. I got back from Halifax more dead than alive, but in a few days the attack passed. I was due to return home on leave a couple of weeks later and made all the necessary arrangements. It was quite impossible to return to Belfast for I had been advised that I was high up on the 'Black List' there. My wife arranged to take a house for two months in Glenageary, County Dublin. She and the four children would go there and I would join them on my arrival.

I had looked forward to my return with eagerness, and the prospect of being back with my wife and children added a new impulse to life, but everything was overshadowed by the situation at home. The elections were over and the situation had worsened to an alarming degree. All the reports indicated tension and strain between the pro-treaty and anti-treaty parties which threatened explosion.

Having left everything in order and under the safe care of Dan McGrath, I sailed on the *S.S. America* to Southampton and from there travelled on to Dún Laoghaire. I had expected that my wife and some of the family would be on the pier to meet me and was both surprised and disappointed to come off the mail boat and not find even one person that I knew. The explanation came later that morning, when I learned that my whole family had travelled up from Belfast on the previous day, had to leave the train somewhere between Dundalk and Drogheda and make their way by various circuitous routes and a variety of vehicles through County Meath into Dublin city. They had spent the night on the stairs and landing of a small hotel kept wide awake by the shooting that went on during the night. The civil war had been going on for several days before we landed!

16

Griffith's death – Brugha and Boland killed – Collins killed in ambush in County Cork – The 'Split' and the civil war a British achievement – I return to New York – I resign and return home – Childers executed – The 'Reprisals' executions of 8 December – Correspondence with de Valera in December 1922 – Conference with Austin Stack

I have 'come into port' many times and returned home after both short and prolonged visits abroad, but my first home-coming from America remains in my memory as one of my bitterest and most heart-breaking experiences. I had the joy of re-union with my family and of meeting for the first time my second little daughter who was five months old when I arrived, but not even these events could screen off the horror of the fight that was going on. It was nerve-wracking to read the treaty debates at a distance of three thousand miles and feel the humiliation of the press reports and commentaries on them, but it was devastating to realise on arrival that the very worst had happened, that our ranks were irrecoverably split and that the British had achieved their purpose by having former comrades waging war, one on the other, to the death.

I was not long home when I had a major distraction in the shape of a recurrence of the violent attack which I had experienced in Canada. A consultation with my friend, Surgeon Harry Macauley, led to a hurried admission to a nursing home, an operation for the removal of my appendix and a brief period of convalescence. It was on 12 August and while I was laid up that I heard the news of Griffith's death, and I had ample time to brood in melancholy recollection of all my long association with him and to think bitterly that he should be taken, while his former comrades and associates were locked in the bitter conflict of civil war.

Ten days later came the news that Michael Collins had been shot at Bealnablath, near Macroom in County Cork, while on a tour of inspection. Cathal Brugha had been killed in what I regarded as an act of frenzied despair in O'Connell Street, Harry Boland had been shot in Skerries and died shortly afterwards in St Vincent's Hospital, and so it went on. It was a summer of tragedy and gloom that filled me with a sense of futility and despair and was destined to leave a heritage of bitter discord for many a year ahead.

During this period, it was practically impossible to meet anyone officially or otherwise. I held open office for several weeks to interview commercial and other people who had interests and problems in the United States. I had a number of such callers and received their advice and gave mine, but it all seemed unreal and even callous in the atmosphere of chaos and disruption that prevailed.

During that time I had perforce to set about the securing of a new home for the family and the removal of our furniture from Belfast. The fact that I could not, without the certainty of arrest, return to Belfast added to the fact that I was still convalescing after my illness meant that the whole brunt of those arrangements fell on my wife's shoulders. It is, as I now write, thirty-six years since we bought and took occupation of our home, and here we have remained, facing the ups and downs of life as they come but content and happy with it as our home. This is the most eloquent tribute that I can pay to her judgement.

We had barely settled into our new home, when I had to hasten my preparations for my return to New York and my consular duties.

I try now to recall my outlook and my feelings at the time and how I viewed the situation as it existed.

It may have been that my enforced detachment from the centre of all the conflict and controversy that raged during the spring and summer of 1922 left me less fully informed than those who were at the very centre of the dispute, but against that it did, I think, enable me to review the situation more dispassionately.

Rightly or wrongly, it was my view at the time that the civil war need not and should not have happened. I do not propose at this stage to try and apportion blame. There were grave blunders on both sides and what seemed to be personal antagonisms rapidly developed to a crescendo of near hate. The treaty debates, the breaking of the pact in the 1922 election and the withdrawal of the anti-treaty opposition from the Dáil led up to the disaster. Back of it all, of course, was the Machiavellian policy of the Lloyd George government which ensured that every opening was widened to a major break until the unbridgeable gulf was perfected. The one outstanding fact that seemed to be receiving little or no attention from the principal contestants in the conflict was that it was British policy to divide our people. On the one hand the pro-treaty party were pursuing a policy that was dictated by the British under the dire threats of a renewal of war, while the anti-treaty leaders were inflaming their followers to opposition which must inevitably lead to physical conflict, not against the British but against their former comrades, and to a civil war.

The move that was introduced into the 'Pact' election by Figgis and the repudiation of the Pact by Collins which destroyed the agreement were perhaps the preliminary steps that led to the miserable debâcle that followed. These were, as we have seen, dictated not by Collins or the pro-treaty party, but by Churchill and Lloyd George backed up by Sir Henry Wilson, F. E. Smith and the whole British cabinet.

On the other hand, de Valera had declared that there was 'a constitutional way of settling their differences', but such a course was not followed. My own view, but this was formed some years later, is that, actually, control of things passed out of de Valera's hands at that time, that things were done and events precipitated that he would not have initiated or approved, but which he could not, in the circumstances then prevailing, have easily repudiated or condemned.

It was my view then, and I have had little reason ever since to alter it, that, when the vote for the treaty was carried, the wise course for de Valera and the anti-treaty party to pursue was to remain in the Dáil as a real Republican opposition, and to contest any and every move or motion that tended to sever us from our Republican policy.

That this is not *post factum* reasoning will, I think, be clear from what I have to record of my correspondence and contact with de Valera a few months later.

It will be understood that it was with a mind and heart loaded down with distress and worry that I returned to resume my work. Not only was most of my enthusiasm and incentive to constructive work destroyed, but I realised that I was returning to meet a bitterly disillusioned Irish-American public which had loyally supported us in our struggle. It was not a pleasant prospect, and only the faint hope of trying to steer the more important leaders of the Irish Association to keep their organisation intact in the United States justified my return. I think I can claim that, at the time, I did enjoy the complete confidence of all those who counted in the American Association for the Recognition of the Irish Republic. Frank P. Walsh, Joe McGarrity, Major Kinkead, Dr Maloney, Judge Campbell and John P. Hearne, and a host of others, scattered all over the country from Maine to California, were my constant friends and co-operative supporters. Almost every one of them, distressed though they were at the turn of events at home, were, at the same time, concerned to maintain the Irish-American supporting arm at its highest strength and efficiency.

It was to meet these and to try with them to safeguard the future that I returned. I brought no news or information for their consolation or comfort and it soon became clear that our stock in the United States had plummeted from an all-high rating to a near zero.

It is simply a matter of recording the true position when I say that the overwhelming majority of our people in America were opposed to the treaty and in favour of de Valera and his opposition to it. The Devoy-Cohalan element proclaimed themselves as supporters of the treaty but, bearing in mind what had developed during de Valera's campaign in the States, this was simply regarded as a continuation of their antagonism to de Valera and I think that view was justified. This group was, relative to the entire mass of Irish opinion in the States, comparatively negligible. De Valera had, in his intensive campaign over all the States, won for himself and for the cause of Ireland a respect and loyalty that was unique in the records of Irish-American activity.

The Irish in America remembered all the phases of the struggle. The Rising of 1916; the executions that followed; the murders and arrests and hunger strikes; the slow torturing death of MacSwiney and all the outrages of the Black and Tans. They remembered too the stories and histories of their forebears, the evictions and the emigrant ships and, for them, de Valera had personified the uprising and resistance to the England that had crushed them.

Back at my desk in New York I resumed my work. There was a sufficiency of the normal routine activity to keep me occupied, but it went on in an atmosphere of uninspiring sterility. It lacked all the driving stimulus of enthusiasm or the sense that I could, under existing conditions, do the worthwhile thing that I had envisaged for our prestige or progress in America. The reports of events in Ireland in the American papers became more and more depressing and I became convinced that events there had reached a stage which made it impossible for me to continue to hold office. Apart from the fact that I realised that all chances of doing worthwhile work for Ireland was just not possible, I was distressed at the ruthless nature of the campaign and the unnatural alliances with the friends of imperialist Britain that were in evidence.

I cabled my resignation to the head of the Free State government and prepared to return home without delay.

I believe my resignation caused something of a flurry at the time and I heard various opinions and reasons quoted as the cause of my decision. One of these was that I had yielded to the pressure of my friends in America who urged me to resign.

The late Joseph McGarrity was head of the Clan na Gael movement. He was the dominating chief of that organisation which itself was the most powerful driving influence behind the Irish Republican organisation in the United States. McGarrity was my closest associate during my whole period in America and one of my best friends, and Joe's wish was that I should continue to do all possible to go on with my plans and hold together all the friends I had made there to work for Ireland. So far from influencing me in my decision, it was reluctantly that he eventually conceded the admission that it was somewhat futile for me to try to carry on.

Another reason that was advanced was that my wife and friends at home had exercised their pleas and pressure to quit. There was no truth whatever in this story. I was naturally receiving a steady run of letters from my wife many of which gave particulars and news of events at home, but in none of these, nor, indeed, at any other time, did she seek to influence me in my political decisions.

The matter is of little or no historical importance and consuls-general of today are merely officials of the department of external affairs, but in 1922 and prior to that date the situation was somewhat different.

In consenting to go abroad to represent the Republican government of Ireland before the treaty, one did so to further the fight for independence and the recognition of the Irish Republic by every means in his power. It was one's main purpose by talks, lectures and publicity of every legitimate nature to advance the political and cultural prestige of the country, and to ensure that hostile and damaging attacks in the press were suitably dealt with. This does not imply that the material interests of the country in trade, shipping, finance and general commerce were to be neglected. Every available prospect that showed any promise of development in these spheres was pursued and all rights and claims by our citizens at home were fully protected, but in the period I write of, namely, 1921-1922, the national political situation was by far the outstanding objective in our work.

I sailed for home on the *S.S. Celtic* on her November sailing. She was one of the first big liners built in Belfast for the White Star Line about a quarter of a century earlier, but had many times been overshadowed by newer, bigger and more luxurious trans-Atlantic ships. In 1922 she was regarded as a second or third rater, but she was a steady, comfortable ship and we had a smooth, uneventful passage all the way over. It is not quite relevant perhaps, but it was of passing interest to me that the same *S.S. Celtic* on an East bound November sailing, went on the rocks at Roche's Point, Cóbh, County Cork, and became a total wreck there.

Our ship did not call at Cóbh and it was Sunday afternoon when we landed at Liverpool and I caught the connection for Holyhead a few hours later. My wife met me at Dún Laoghaire and we motored home. There was bad news, news that made one feel cold with horror and yet made one's blood boil with indignation. Erskine Childers had been shot at dawn on Friday, 24 November, two days before I had landed.

It was the circumstances accompanying the execution of Childers that shocked me. He had been arrested in a raid on the house of Robert Barton, his cousin and one of the signatories of the treaty, and had carried a small automatic pistol which, ironically enough, was a souvenir gift from Collins.

The day after his arrest and while the case was still *sub judice*, that fair-minded warrior, Winston Churchill, saw fit, against all the decencies of either law or honour, to launch a denunciation of Childers in a speech at Dundee which could prejudice not only his audience, which was a matter of no account, but which was of vital importance, the military court appointed to try him. Churchill referred to him as a 'mischief-making murderous renegade' and told his audience that 'no man has done more harm or shown more genuine malice or endeavoured to bring a greater curse upon the common people of Ireland than this strange being, actuated by a deadly and malignant hate of the land of his birth'.

It was a vicious indictment, gratuitously uttered by the great Churchill before the subject of his venom and hate had been brought to trial and, even to the dispassionate observer, outraged all the canons of decency.

Childers' trial took place *in camera* before the military court. The charge was 'being in unlawful possession of a Colt automatic pistol'. He was found guilty. Notice of appeal was served, but Childers was shot at Beggar's Bush barracks a few days before the appeal came up for hearing which caused Mr Justice Ronan to exclaim: 'Are we to understand that the prisoner has been executed pending an appeal to this court?' I am not a lawyer but many eminent lawyers held the view that the execution of Erskine Childers was a judicial murder.

George Gavan Duffy,[1] an eminent lawyer and judge, a signatory to the treaty and for a brief spell a minister of the government, gave his opinion in a speech in the Dáil in the course of which he said:

> I think Erskine Childers was executed upon a charge which does not sustain in the public conscience the capital punishment or else

1. George Gavan Duffy (1882-1951): born south of France, solicitor, Irish bar 1917, prepared Sir Roger Casement's defence 1916, Sinn Féin T.D. for South Dublin 1918, helped draft declaration of Independence 1919, Sinn Féin representative at Paris Peace Conference 1919, its envoy in Rome 1920, signatory to Anglo-Irish treaty 1921, resigned from ministry of foreign affairs 1922 after only a month upon the abolition of the republican courts, resigned from the Dáil upon its refusal to treat captured anti-treatyites as POWs 1923, judge of high court 1936, its president 1946.

> he was tried on that charge but other matters were allowed to influence those who confirmed his execution.
>
> If that were the case, the authorities have done something contrary to natural justice as understood in every part of the world.

Eoin MacNeill, a minister in the cabinet with somewhat egregious frankness which must have earned him the reproofs of his colleagues, really gave the show away when, in the course of the debate, he stated that: 'No man has been executed simply for having a revolver either in his own house or elsewhere'.

There was what to me was an even more ominous and shocking event that took place prior to the execution of Childers.

Four Republican prisoners, Volunteers of the rank and file who were quite unknown to the general public, were executed. The charge against them was 'Possession of revolvers without proper authority'. These executions caused a shock and members of the Labour Party raised the matter in the Dáil. Mulcahy[2] gave 'military necessity' as the reason for the executions, but Kevin O'Higgins[3] gave the real explanation when he said:

> If they took, as their first case, some man who was outstandingly active and outstandingly wicked in his activities, the unfortunate dupes throughout the country might say that he was killed because he was a leader, because he was an Englishman or because he combined with others to commit raids.

How is one to interpret that statement? Does it make clear that they had to execute the 'Englishman Childers' and, to justify that execution, must they shoot four ordinary Irish Volunteer republicans to show their impartiality? Does it mean that Childers must not be the 'first case' and, for that

2. General Richard Mulcahy (1886-1971): born Waterford, post office clerk, member of Gaelic League, Irish Volunteers 1913, second in command to Thomas Ashe at Ashbourne during Easter Rising 1916, Sinn Féin T.D. for Clontarf 1918, minister for defence 1919, I.R.A. chief of staff during Anglo-Irish war 1919-21, T.D. for Dublin constituencies 1922-43, Tipperary 1944-61, G.O.C. Free State army 1922-23, minister for defence 1923-4, chairman of Gaeltacht Commission 1925-6, senator 1943-4, leader of Fine Gael 1944-59, minister of education 1948-51, 1954-7.

3. Kevin O'Higgins (1892-1927): born Stradbally, County Laois, solicitor, barrister 1923, member of Irish Volunteers 1913, T.D. for Laois-Offaly 1918, assistant minister for local government 1919, advocate of treaty 1921, T.D. for South Dublin and minister for economic affairs 1922, minister for justice and vice-president of Executive Council 1922-7, assassinated by I.R.A.

reason, four ordinary rank and file Volunteers, 'in possession of revolvers without proper authority', must be the primary victims? And how did MacNeill reconcile the fact of these four executions with his statement that: 'no man was executed simply for having a revolver'. Look at it how one will it is difficult to resist the conviction that these four men, P. Cassidy, John Gaffney, James Fisher and R. Twohig, were the preliminary sacrifices which were considered essential to justify the execution of Erskine Childers. How far the outspoken condemnation by Churchill contributed is a question on which one can only speculate!

I have referred to the Childers execution at some length because it was and is, to most of us, one of the indelible blots on our national record. There were others and one of the worst, if not the worst, occurred within a couple of weeks after my return. This was the shooting of the four men as reprisals in Mountjoy prison yard. After the execution of Childers and the other four men, the I.R.A. had issued a warning to every member of the Provisional parliament who had voted for the resolution authorising executions that drastic measures would be taken unless the Free State forces observed the rules of war. On the basis of this warning, two deputies, Seán Hales[4] and Padraic O'Malley,[5] were shot in Dublin. Hales was shot dead and O'Malley was wounded. Late that night four leading Republicans were roused from their sleep in their prison cells and informed that they would be executed the following morning. All four of them had been prisoners for five months in Mountjoy from the time that they had surrendered in the Four Courts. They were Rory O'Connor,[6] Liam Mellowes, Joseph McKelvey and Richard Barrett,[7] and on the following morning, 8

4. Seán Hales (1890-1922): born near Bandon, County Cork, member of Irish Volunteers later I.R.A. 1913-22, O.C. Bandon battalion, West Cork Brigade 1919-22, T.D. for West Cork 1919-22, assassinated by anti-treatyite I.R.A. 1922.

5. Pádraig Ó Máile: born Kilternan, County Galway, farmer, member of Gaelic League and Sinn Féin, member of Irish Volunteers later I.R.A. 1914-21, T.D. for West Galway and leas-cheann comhairle 1922-27, wounded by anti-treatyites 1922, broke with Cumann na nGaedheal and joined National Group of T.Ds after army mutiny 1924, attempted to persuade anti-treatyites to enter Dáil Éireann 1925, senator 1932-36, 1938-45.

6. Rory O'Connor (1883-1922): born Dublin, railway engineer in Canada 1911-15, active in Easter Rising 1916, I.R.A. director of engineering 1919-21, opposed the treaty 1921, led I.R.A. military council which repudiated the authority of the Dáil 1922, a leader of anti-treatyite garrison in Four Courts, April 1922, executed 8 December 1922.

7. Richard Barrett: born near Crossbarry, County Cork, teacher at Gurranes National School, member of Irish Volunteers and later I.R.A. 1913-22, quarter-master West Cork Brigade 1920, interned at Spike Island 1921, leading figure in anti-treatyite I.R.A., quarter-master of Four Court's forces and executed in Mountjoy jail 1922.

December, while Catholic Dublin and all Ireland was honouring the feast of Our Lady, these four young men were taken out to the prison yard and shot.

The Childers execution and the execution of the four men that preceded it had shocked the country, but the killing of four prisoners who were in custody for five months and completely powerless in the hands of their jailers filled the minds of all decent people with horror.

I knew two of the executed men. Liam Mellowes was loved by all who had associated with him in Ireland and was equally regarded by the thousands of friends to whom he had endeared himself in America. Joe McKelvey was one of our good friends in Belfast. He was a splendid type of courageous soldier and yet a gentle, quiet soul without any ambition but to serve Ireland and work for her freedom. I had never met Rory O'Connor or Dick Barrett, but both were well known for their courage and integrity. It was doubtless their work and their qualities of mind and heart and character that singled them out for what the *New York Nation* described as 'Murder foul and despicable'.

It was a period of tragedy and bleak outlook with little or no gleam of hope to illumine the future.

My wife's mother, Annie MacGavock was on a short visit to us at the time from her home in Glenarm, County Antrim. She was distressed beyond measure at the succession of events and had gone to see her brother, Eoin MacNeill who was in the cabinet, to use her influence with him and to plead for peace and an end to the executions. I remember vividly coming into the sitting room on the evening after her interview with him. She was in a state of high tension and could scarcely sit at rest for a few minutes, but would rise and walk up and down the room. I was definitely worried about her for she was not in good health at the time and had been through a serious operation a year earlier. She said little about her interview with MacNeill, but it was clear that it had not relieved her anxiety nor given her any cause for hope. Soon afterwards she returned home, and then it happened.

The Royal Ulster Constabulary raided her home in Glenarm just after the morning post had been delivered. One of her younger daughters had, during the Black-and-Tan period, been active in 'Intelligence' and had continued her work with the North Antrim group after the treaty. There was a postal packet for her in the mail and no sooner had the postman delivered the letters than the police arrived at his heels. Mrs MacGavock had the letters in her hand when they arrived and without a moment's hesitation she pushed past them and put the whole mail into the kitchen fire. A short time afterwards she collapsed and had to be assisted to bed. The shock and excitement of the raid following on all the tension and anxiety that she had experienced in Dublin proved too much for her. The doctor was summoned and the priest administered the Last Sacraments. She died that night at the age of fifty-nine and with all of us, who loved and respected her, the conviction remains that her death was precipitated by the events which I have recorded. She had found that peace herself that she so eagerly sought for her country and for all of us.

I travelled North for the funeral. Surgeon Harry Macauley and his wife Mary and I motored up to Glenarm arriving there late on the night before the funeral to avoid notice or recognition. It was a sad and mournful group that gathered round the grave in Carnlough churchyard, for we were paying our last tribute to one of our most respected and most loved of the County Antrim Gaels.[8]

We were just finishing the Rosary after the grave had been closed when my father-in-law whispered to me that I was not to return to the house, but that it was urgent that I should get into the car and clear out. The Macauleys and I slipped off quietly and returned to Dublin. Within an hour after the funeral, the home, the house of mourning, was raided. It was one of the leading Orangemen who had 'tipped off' my father-in-law that I had better clear out as they would go up to the house to arrest me after the funeral. It was one of a number of experiences that I have had which showed that decent Orangemen could be and generally are decent Irish neighbours in the rural districts of Northern Ireland.

Shortly after I returned from America I wrote to de Valera. He was 'on the run' at the time and for many months afterwards, but I was able to have my letter conveyed to him through a mutual friend. In my letter to him I analysed the situation as it then appeared to me and was quite frank in my review. While I explained that, due to my absence in the United States, I could not speak with any authority on all the causes and events that led to the civil war, I condemned and deplored it and laid stress on his failure to find the 'constitutional ways of settling their differences' which he had proclaimed as being possible. I then went on to argue that the so-called Free State government was a *fait accompli* and that a prolongation of the civil war was a futile and tragic waste of life and energy, and that, in my opinion, the only sane course for him and his party was to end it and adopt the alternative policy of political opposition.

8. Alice Milligan recalled the occasion in a poem which she presented to Connolly. For this, see Appendix 2.

It is regrettable that I have no copy of my letter, but it has to be borne in mind that the practice of keeping no unnecessary documents, which we had following during the earlier days of British raids, still persisted during the civil war.

It was on 17 December 1922 that I wrote to de Valera and I received his reply by messenger some ten days later. I have still the letter in my files and it reads as follows:

Dáil Éireann
(Government of the Republic of Ireland),
Baile Átha Cliath,
26 December 1922.

Oifig an Uachtaráin
Confidential

A Chara,

I received your letter of the 17th and accompanying memo, every line of which I read with sympathetic understanding, but the difficulties remain.

Republicans will not regard the Free State government as an established government, either *de jure* or *de facto*.

The legitimate sovereign authority of the nation at this moment is the Second Dáil, which the Executive had no authority to suppress. If that Dáil is allowed to meet, it has power to make provision for the government of the country pending the next election; if it is not allowed to meet, I do not know what alternative there is.

Republicans cannot permit the Free State government and parliament to go on establishing itself and functioning as a *de facto* government, whilst the Republican government is suppressed. The people have already had enough 'accomplished facts' presented to them.

When the Articles of Agreement were brought over here, I felt as if a plague were being introduced into the country and every effort I have since made to save the people from its effects has been met on the other side by bad faith and the miserable short-sighted tactics of party politics. Frankly I have no hope that our opponents would even now keep any contract they might enter into with us.

Heaven knows there ought to be sufficient incentive! With a little commonsense we could now apply the Sinn Féin policy of ruling ourselves without any reference to the foreigner in a way that could not have been applied before, but blindness and partisanship deprives us of the power to seize the opportunity. It is heartbreaking.

I hope you are keeping well.

Le meas mór,

Mise,

Eamon de Valera

I think this letter is of considerable historical interest as reflecting, though in a guarded way, de Valera's outlook in December 1922, when the civil war went on. To me he seemed to refrain from expressing his own personal attitude to the civil war and his *cri-de-coeur* seemed to be in the final paragraph and to reinforce the argument and appeal that I had made to him. With the letter it was conveyed to me that de Valera thought it might be advisable if I would go along and have a talk with Austin Stack. Austin was an old friend and between us there was something just a shade deeper than ordinary friendship, perhaps bordering on affectionate regard and interest. He, like de Valera and most of the Republican leaders, was 'lying low', but a few evenings later I was brought to the house where he was sheltered. I had not seen him since our meeting in New York early in the year and we were both happy in the re-union.

We discussed the situation, the arguments that I had put up to de Valera and the latter's reply. Stack was unyielding. His was a 'no surrender' attitude. I tried to point out that, apart from every other consideration, the Republican forces were beaten militarily, that he and de Valera and most of the other leaders were on the run or, as he was himself, condemned to hiding and that, in these circumstances, it was worse than folly to continue the futile struggle. Austin would not agree that they were a beaten force, though to me his own very position at the time was evidence of the fact. He gave me no indication of where or how the power of the Republican resistance was to be restored, but held tenaciously to his refusal to give in. Our talk was long and, despite our disagreement, entirely friendly. It was in the small hours of the morning that I left and, as I was leaving, he asked me to continue my efforts in the direction in which I was working. I told him good naturedly 'to go and have sense'. 'Don't you realise, Austin, that its just nonsense to suggest that I go on trying to bring about an end to the fighting when you and, I assume, many of your friends are completely opposed to the idea?' 'No Austin, I'm through, from now on I am standing clear of both sides. I had hoped that maybe I could help to end the deadlock but, well among you be it!' And it was on this note we parted and my efforts and intervention ended there or so it seemed at the time.

17

I start banking – The organisation of Sinn Féin – Dismissed from the bank by order of the minister for finance – The 'Cease Fire' – The election of 1923 – The Ennis meeting – De Valera arrested by Free State troops

Sometime in February, when I was experiencing a restless idleness, Lionel Smith-Gordon[1] approached me with a proposal that I should join the National Land Bank, of which he was managing director. They planned to extend their activities and to go more heavily into the foreign import and export business. He thought my experience in the United States coupled with my consistent interest in Irish banking and economic problems would be of value to the bank. The fact that I had spent some seventeen years in the tough school of Belfast business was an additional factor in their interest.

The terms he offered were not extravagant but, in all the circumstances, were not ungenerous. I gave the matter a good deal of thought and eventually agreed to try out the experiment. There were a number of sound reasons that decided me.

At the time my income, since I resigned from my position of consul general, was exactly nil. I had 'burned my boats' when I had disposed of my comfortable business in Belfast to serve the Republic and now, well I was eating steadily into my limited resources.

The additional reason was that I thought it would be instructive to see the 'machinery' of banking in operation. I had in my study of Irish trade, commerce and finance contributed articles on various aspects of our position including the operations of the Joint Stock Banks. Such articles were all written from the Sinn Féin and national points of view with particular emphasis on the consistent drain of our national wealth through our banks to British and Bank of England securities. I had the pleasantest associations with my colleagues in the bank, but my period of banking education was to be terminated abruptly.

I had only been there a couple of months when, to my surprise, I received a brief note from de Valera asking me if I would be agreeable to meet him that night. If so, I could inform the messenger and a car would call at my home and collect me at 11 p.m. I was brought to a house in Mount Street Crescent, where he was waiting to see me.

1. Lionel Eldred Pottinger Smith-Gordon (1889-1971): 4th baronet 1933, Ullmann & Co., merchant bankers, London, 1911, managing-director, National Land Bank 1921.

We had a long conference without disturbance or interruption, during which we reviewed the whole position and he informed me that he had referred back to my memorandum of the previous December and that he now wanted me to act on the lines which I had suggested in it.

I pointed out that I was comparatively unknown in Dublin, that my contacts and friends were almost entirely in the North and that any effort on my part would be viewed with suspicion and looked upon as political opportunism. I could not imagine that I could expect to find any worthwhile support or supporters to enable me to do what he wanted. He assured me that he would find the supporters for me, that I could count on having a loyal committee who would back me up, but he wanted me to consent to act as chairman of the group and to guide the movement on the lines that I had broadly outlined in my memorandum. With certain misgivings I consented to do my best. We then got down to the bare outlines of the plan.

The movement would be 'Sinn Féin Reorganised' and the committee would be set up for the purpose of reorganisation. At an early date there would be a 'cease fire' and the Republican forces would be harnessed to Sinn Féin as a political organisation.

In the course of our discussion and when I had consented to act I made certain stipulations to which I later tenaciously held, despite de Valera's pleas to waive them.

The first condition I laid down was that, irrespective of what time and energy I put into the work, I was not to receive a penny of salary. It was instinctive with me to insist on that, but I also had the foresense to realise that, if I were to preserve my independence, I could only do so by refusing any remuneration whatever.

The second condition was that in any election, and there was every likelihood of an early election for the Dáil, I should not be asked to go forward as a candidate. There were several reasons for my negative attitude to this. I had no desire to become a politician and I had the hope of ultimately launching out in my own business again without being hampered by political responsibilities. There was the additional and all-important reason that by refusing to go forward as a candidate I would dispel any notion in the minds of the committee that I was a career-seeking politician. This, I knew, would be a desirable and even essential qualification to enable me to have and to hold the trust and loyal support of those with whom I would have to work.

The third and last condition that I made was that, as and when the organisation was successfully launched and the election completed, I would be released from my position as chairman and left free to start in to build up my own life and business.

De Valera demurred at some or all of these conditions, but I think he appreciated fully just how I felt and thought about them and he ultimately agreed.

In due course we met to form our committee. We met in the private house of Mr Malachy Muldoon,[2] a barrister then living in Herbert Place. I doubt if I could name all those who assembled there and from whom the committee was elected, but I can recall Eoin O'Keeffe,[3] Michael Comyn, S.C.,[4] Michael Foley,[5] George Daly,[6] Dr Kathleen Lynn,[7] Mrs Sheehy-Skeffington,[8]

2. J. Malachy Muldoon: solicitor, at his residence, 9 Herbert Place, two informal meetings were held in late May and early June, after which the organisation 'Sinn Féin Re-organised', was formally established at a meeting in the Mansion House on 14 June.

3. Eoin P. O'Keeffe (1891-1979): born Wexford, member of Sinn Féin and Irish Volunteers 1913, secretary of the Dublin Sinn Féin peace committee which attempted to get peace talks started between the pro- and anti-treatyites 1922-23, secretary of the Sinn Féin Re-organised Committee 1923, proprietor of Duffy's booksellers and newspaper distributors, 1950-79.

4. Michael Comyn (1871-1950): born Ballyvaughan, County Clare, barrister 1898, senator 1928-36, circuit court judge 1936-43.

5. Michael J. Foley: a chemist, he conducted his business at 136 Parnell Street, Dublin.

6. George Daly: he subsequently acted as secretary to the organising committee, later he was joint honorary secretary of Sinn Féin and as such attended a meeting of the anti-treatyite T.Ds on 7 August 1924.

7. Dr Kathleen Lynn (1874-1955): born Mullafarry, Killala, County Mayo, medical doctor 1899, fellow of Royal College of Surgeons of Ireland 1909, active with Irish Citizen Army in helping the destitute during Dublin lock-out 1913, member of Women's Social and Political Union and leading suffragette 1914, with Irish Citizen Army in Liberty Hall, Easter 1916, member of executive of Sinn Féin, vice-president, Irish Women Workers' Union 1917, co-founder with Madeleine ffrench-Mullen of St Ultan's hospital 1919, rendered medical assistance to I.R.A. 1919-21, member of Rathmines Urban District Council 1920, opposed the treaty 1922, Sinn Féin T.D. for County Dublin 1923-7, member of Save German Children Committee 1945.

8. Mrs Hanna Sheehy-Skeffington (1877-1946): born Loughmore, County Tipperary, founder of Women Graduates' Association 1901, co-founder with her husband, Francis Sheehy Skeffington, of Irish Women's Franchise League 1908, active in Easter Rising 1916, member of executive committee of Sinn Féin and a judge in the Dáil Éireann courts 1918-21, opposed the treaty 1921, member of executive of Fianna Fáil 1926, assistant-editor of *An Phoblacht* 1932, founder of the Women's Social and Progressive League 1938.

Robert E. Whelan,[9] Dr Conn Murphy[10] and Philip Ryan.[11] I was elected chairman, Eoin O'Keefe was appointed secretary and a committee was voted into office. Later Father Burbage[12] and several others were added to the committee.

It was decided to launch the organisation by a public meeting in the Mansion House. The holding of such a meeting at the time was a risky venture for the civil war had not ended, feeling was still tense and the Free State government were still making raids and arrests. There were conflicting opinions as to the wisest course of action, but to me there was only one that seemed worthwhile and that was to come out in the open, declare our policy and seek to win the people back to their early allegiance. The big question that faced us was whether or not we would be able to carry through the meeting successfully. The government might proclaim the meeting or launch a raid, while the meeting was in progress, and create disorder or worse. Whatever was to happen, I was convinced that we had no alternative, but to test the public reaction to the movement and in how far the government would refrain from interfering with it.

It was essential, too, that the speakers should be carefully chosen so as to avoid flamboyant and useless rhetoric and to ensure that the enunciation of our policy would be clear.

The Round Room in the Mansion House was packed to capacity. We had an orderly and enthusiastic meeting; our programme and policy were

9. Robert E. Whelan: proprietor of a clothing business, he followed de Valera into Fianna Fáil 1926, subsequently he resided at 'Garnavilla', Kilmacud Road, Stillorgan, County Dublin.

10. Dr Conn Murphy: he was well qualified academically, having an M.A. and Ph.D., during the civil war he was a leading propagandist for the anti-treatyites and later for Sinn Féin, in 1921 he was chairman of the Civil Service Alliance and had access to those involved in the treaty negotiations and, it seems, initially enthusiastically supported it. After it was announced that the treaty had been signed his colleague, Michael J. Gallagher, recalled: 'No one was more pleased than our chairman, who, whatever he may have thought of it later on, was then much in favour. The morning the news of the signing of the treaty broke I remember him throwing up his work and going out. We were then located at 45 Merrion Square. A little crowd had assembled at the offices of the National University, a few doors away. Nothing would do our chairman but to round them up and address them on the significance of the news, and what it meant for the country and all of us.' Dr Murphy was a Sinn Féin candidate for County Dublin in the general election of 1923.

11. Philip Ryan: a Dublin publican, he was a Sinn Féin candidate for County Dublin in the general election of 1923, in August 1924 with Austin Stack he attempted to buy the ailing *Freeman's Journal* and convert it into an anti-treatyite and Republican daily.

12. Father Thomas Burbage (1880-1965): curate in Geashill, County Offaly in 1920s, parish priest, Tinryland, Carlow 1935-44, parish priest, Mountmellick, County Laois 1944-65.

clearly stated and the movement for the re-organisation of Sinn Féin was launched.

Having successfully negotiated what seemed to be the first and major obstacle, I believed that the next and most urgent job was to come still more into the open, in other words, to hold a big open air meeting. I put this view to the committee and suggested that we should hold our next meeting in Cork, that it should be in the open air and that, if all went well there, it would be followed by a widespread series of Sunday and weekend meetings all over the country and the organisation of branches in every area. The committee agreed unanimously on the proposals and we went ahead.

The Cork meeting was more than a meeting. It was a huge demonstration. Daniel Corkery, that outstandingly cultured Gael, presided and set the right tone to the proceedings. The meeting was enthusiastic, orderly and in every way satisfactory. There is no purpose in recording all the activities that followed beyond saying that meetings were held all over the country, branches and committees were formed and that within a few weeks the Republican views were being openly preached in every district.

It was at the end of May 1923 that the order to 'cease fire' was issued. I interrupt the narrative to mention a personal experience arising out of my activities at this time.

As I have already recorded, I had taken up work in the National Land Bank and was so engaged when I was active in the re-launching of Sinn Féin. On the morning after the initial meeting in the Mansion House Smith-Gordon, the managing director of the bank, asked me down to his office. I was not altogether surprised when he told me that the minister for finance had been on the telephone 'raising Cain' about one of his staff presiding at an anti-government and Republican meeting in the Mansion House and demanding to know what he was going to do about it.

The Land Bank had been set up by the Republican government and was chiefly financed by the proceeds of the Republican Bond money. It was entirely controlled by the State with the minister for finance as the responsible authority. I had already anticipated all that would follow, but this did not prevent me exchanging good-humoured banter with Smith-Gordon. I pointed out that I had given no pledge, nor had the bank sought any pledge from me, that I would refrain from political activity. I pointed out that several of the directors, like Mr James Douglas[13] and Mr James

13. James Douglas (1887-1954): born Dublin, treasurer and trustee of the White Cross 1919-21, vice-chairman of senate 1922-25, member of Constitution Committee 1922, senator 1922-36, 1938-43, 1944-54.

MacNeill, who incidentally was my wife's uncle, were not inactive in the political sphere and that, if the minister ordered these gentlemen to stand aloof from politics, I would agree to do likewise. I went on further to emphasise that the money that kept the bank floating was the people's money, given for the Republic, and that it was somewhat ironical that a member of its staff was being 'carpeted' for his Republican affiliations.

I knew that my arguments were, in existing circumstances, somewhat specious and that in any event my days as a banker were numbered, but I could not resist the temptation to give them to Smith-Gordon to be passed over to the minister. Poor Smith-Gordon, who was really a good friend of mine before and since, was perplexed and worried and not less so when I said to him: 'Now look S.G. you're going to have to sack me and that's all there is to it'. 'Oh, for Heaven's sake, Connolly, don't put it that way', he replied. 'Well, there's no other way to put it for I am not resigning. I am on the staff of bank until I'm 'fired''.

Smith-Gordon on 1 June 1923 wrote me an official letter on behalf of the bank which I give below:

National Land Bank, Ltd.,
College Green,
1 June 1923.

Dear Mr Connolly,

I am now officially informed that the keeping of the registers, etc., for a large part at any rate of the government securities will be entrusted to this bank. The officer in charge of this branch of the bank's business will have a very responsible task and I would like to see the work in your hands if you care to undertake it, subject to the existing probationary period and terms.

Of course this development means that officials of the bank become for all practical purposes civil servants and it will involve definitely giving up for the time being any political activities or ambitions.

I would like you to consider whether you are prepared to do this and to let me know as soon as possible. For your own sake I would suggest that if you prefer to keep your independence of action in political ways it would probably be better to put an end to the probationary period as soon as possible.

I hope, however, that you will prefer to remain with us.

Yours sincerely,

Lionel Smith-Gordon

I did not stop to consider whether the offer was tempting or not. I knew that Smith-Gordon knew that my mind was already made up and that his letter was a graceful and kindly effort to soften the impact of my dismissal. And so ended my brief career as a banker. 'The Old Lady' in Merrion Street said 'No', not for the first nor the last time. The view at the time was that there was no place in Ireland for non-conformists, provided of course their non-conformity was in the political sphere.

Having been relieved of my work in the bank, I concentrated all my energies on the building up of Sinn Féin and the preparations for the coming election which was due to be held on 27 August.

Our old friend, Eamon Donnelly, was director of elections and, just as he did in 1918, he put all his energy and his genius for organisation into the work. It was even more difficult to carry out our election campaign than it was in 1918. Many of our most prominent men were in prison, others were still 'on the run' or lying low and, although the cease fire had been ordered at the end of May, raids and arrests were continued. The *Freeman's Journal* quoted official figures which estimated that on 1 July 1923 there were 11,316 military prisoners in the custody of the government. Apart from the enforced absence of most of the leaders, every sort of obstruction to our election campaign was experienced. Donnelly himself was arrested a week before election day.

During all this period I had conferences and meetings with de Valera all of which were held around the midnight hour and at the house in Mount Street Crescent. Paddy Ruttledge[14] sat in with us on a few occasions and it was then I first got to know him and to esteem him for the gentle, quiet man of real ability who, from that time, became one of my best and lifelong friends. At one of these conferences de Valera had declared his intention to be present and address his constituents at the election meeting which was 'billed' to take place in Ennis on 15 August. I tried to dissuade him but he was adamant. Frankly I feared that his attempt to get to Ennis would be a failure and that, if he did reach there, anything might happen, not excluding assassination. We discussed the arrangements and his final directions which were carried out were as follows:

14. Patrick J. Ruttledge (1892-1952): born Ballina, County Mayo, solicitor, member of Irish Volunteers and Sinn Féin 1913, member of I.R.A. 1919-23, opposed the treaty 1921, T.D. for County Mayo 1921, active in civil war on anti-treaty side 1922-3, acted as president of the 'Republic' while de Valera was in prison 1923-4, minister for lands 1932-3, minister for justice 1933-39, minister for local government and public health 1939-41.

Joe Delaney would provide a car and collect Miss Kathleen O'Connell[15] and myself on 14 August, the day before the meeting. We would report at Ennis and spend the night there. T. V. Honan[16] would preside and I would make the opening speech outlining our plans and policy after which de Valera himself would address the meeting. I did not ask him nor did he tell me how he proposed to get from Mount Street Crescent to Ennis.

Our programme worked out more or less as we had planned. Miss O'Connell and I were 'collected' by Joe Delaney and, except for two occasions when we were given a very superficial examination by military patrols, had an uneventful journey to Ennis. Early in the evening we were advised that the house in which we were to be guests would be raided that night and that it would be wise to find other accommodation. Our small party slipped off in the car and booked rooms in the hotel at Lahinch. The house was raided and searched, but no visitors were there.

We were early afoot the next morning. It was the fifteenth of August, the feast of Our Lady's Assumption and a Church holiday. We got early Mass, had a leisurely breakfast and put in the time until we were due to leave on our return journey to Ennis. When we arrived, the town was already crowded and people were still pouring in on all the adjoining roads. There was an air of tension, perhaps it was only in myself that I experienced it, but I hoped and prayed that the day would pass without tragedy. Soon the advertised time of the meeting came round and we ascended the platform. Just as we were doing so a motor appeared and from it emerged the long, gaunt figure of de Valera. There was great cheering and enthusiasm as he stepped up on to the platform and the meeting began. The chairman opened the meeting with a brief introductory speech. I followed as arranged and, as briefly as possible, outlined our policy and the importance of the impending election. As I concluded and de Valera came forward to address the vast crowd that filled the square, a detachment of soldiers marched in and surrounded the platform. There was a tense silence for a few moments as the officer shouted out his commands. The soldiers faced the platform, rifles were brought to the ready and the order given to fire. I watched the whole scene in a sort of fascinated detachment. The volley had been fired at an angle which would ensure that the discharge would go

15. Kathleen O'Connell (1888-1956): born Caherdaniel, County Kerry, emigrated to U.S.A. 1904, secretary, Gaelic League, New York 1912, member of Cumann na mBan, New York, and Friends of Irish Freedom 1916, de Valera's personal secretary and closest friend and confidante 1919-56.

16. Thomas V. Honan (1878-1954): born Kildysart, County Clare, general merchant, member of Sinn Féin 1912, Irish Volunteers 1913, chairman, Ennis Urban District Council 1917-45, senator 1934-6, 1938-54.

over our heads but just that. After the volley I saw the troops ascending the platform and at that moment I was, with the minimum of ceremony, pulled down from the back of the platform and found myself on the rough ground on which the platform had been erected. I quickly discovered that my bodily seizure was carried out by friendly hands, who hustled me down the street and into the shelter of a friendly house. Apparently they assumed that I would be arrested by the troops and took steps to ensure that I would not. It was quite some time before we got definite and accurate news and learned that de Valera had been taken off as a prisoner, but unharmed. It was bad enough to know that he was now a prisoner but, to be quite frank, I was relieved and thankful that the day had passed and that he was still alive.

I have often wondered about that meeting and the military tactics adopted by the Free State forces. The march in to the platform front by the soldiers and the firing of the volley by some twelve or more of their number, admittedly over the heads of the crowds though it was, was somewhat more than provocative. And this was Ennis, the capital of Clare, and Claremen were not often prone to take things 'lying down'. What was the plan for that day? I do not know and I never will know, but one thing seemed certain to me. Had a shot been fired by anyone of the thousands that were assembled around us that day, Ennis would have been a shambles. I leave it at that!

Late that night our little party was got together and we made our way back to Dublin arriving some time in the early hours of the morning.

The Ennis meeting was over, de Valera was still alive, though a prisoner, and the remaining days preparatory to the election were fully occupied with all the final, frenzied activity that only ends on polling day.

The result of the election exceeded my most optimistic hopes, despite the majority secured by the government party. The latter secured a total first preference vote of 415,000 and returned 65 members to the new Dáil, while the Republican first preference totalled 286,000 and elected 44 members. The majority would seem to be substantial in normal circumstances, but the circumstances were anything but normal in those days. For one thing, all the power, money and influence were available to the government. Nearly all Republicans of prominence, including the candidates themselves, were in prison, and it is putting it mildly to say that every possible coercive measure was applied during the election campaign. Apart from all these factors, I think I had some justification for feeling satisfied that in the few months, re-organised Sinn Féin had taken the Republican movement out of the catacombs, had bridged a gap with a restored platform and, above all, had ended the futility of a continuing civil war. Not everyone will agree with that analysis but to those who feel as I do, that of all evils there is none greater than civil conflict, the result of the 1923 campaign marked an important milestone in the history of our time.[17]

However that may be, I felt that my obligations had been fulfilled and that, with the election over and Sinn Féin firmly re-established, I could, without any breach of trust, seek my release from active participation on the political stage. It was becoming a pressing necessity to do so. It was now August and, save for the few months in the bank, I had been without income since the previous November. With a home, a wife and a young family to maintain, I had to face up to my responsibilities. It was, from the economic point of view, probably the most anxious and worrying period of my whole life and even now I do not relish the need to recall it.

17. Few would disagree with Connolly's assessment of the importance of 'Sinn Féin Re-organised'. It's importance and his major role in its establishment and early success was acknowledged in the following report in *Sinn Féin* in October 1923:

> 'Sinn Re-organised' was established at a meeting presided over by Dr Lynn, vice-president of Sinn Féin, held on 11 June 1923 at which the following resolution was passed: 'That it is the opinion of this meeting of present and former members of the Sinn Féin organisation, the declared object of which is to secure the recognition of Ireland as an independent Irish Republic, that the re-organisation of Sinn Féin as the national organisation is a national necessity, and, as the officer board and standing committee have not taken public action, that this meeting nominate a standing committee forthwith to undertake the task'.
>
> In accordance with that resolution the following were appointed on the committee: Dr Kathleen Lynn, Mrs Brugha, Mrs Ceannt, Seán Ó hUadhaigh, Mícheál Ó Foghlughdha, Joseph O'Connor, R. Emmet Whelan, Joseph Connolly, W. M. Cahill and Eoin P. Ó Caoimh. Joseph Connolly was appointed chairman, Mrs Brugha, hon. trerasurer and Eoin Ó Caoimh, hon. secretary. The following were subseqeuntly co-opted at various times: M. Comyn, K.C., Geo Daly, Fr Burbage, Dr Conn Murphy, Phil Ryan, Miss Maloney, Harry O'Hanrahan and Miss MacSwiney, T.D.
>
> Since their appointment the committee have secured the affiliation of 680 Cumainn and the return of 44 Teachtaí Dála . . . The sum of £2,040 for affiliation fees was duly lodged in a bank and remains intact except for the grant, on 5 October, of £300 to the Prisoners' Release Committee.
>
> The committee much regretted to lose the services of Seán Ó hUadhaigh, who resigned, and of the chairman, Joseph Connolly, whose resignation was consequent upon his going to America. To his initiative and ability much of the success which attended our efforts was due.

18

I return to New York and commercial life – Selling goods in New York – Senator Douglas, Alesburys and the bank – Fianna Fáil established – General election of 1927 – Shooting of Kevin O'Higgins – Fianna Fáil deputies take their seats in the Dáil – I revisit America – Cardinal Mundelin and Ireland – Al Smith for president – Some reflections on the U.S.A.

Immediately the election was over I took a ten days holiday. It was a welcome relief to get away from all the strain of election meetings, conferences and committee work even for a brief interlude.

On my return, I took stock of my personal position and decided to make arrangements to open showrooms and to resume activity in my own line of business of furniture and carpets. It is worth noting the trifling things that sometimes arise and have far-reaching effects on one's whole career.

For my business one of the main essentials was to have adequate showroom accommodation. I believed I had secured what would suit me just a few doors from Grafton Street, where a good ground floor and a spacious basement were available. I had practically decided to take up the tenancy, but on measuring the basement I found that the height from floor to ceiling was exactly six feet. That was, I reckoned, just a few inches too 'tight' and, as the basement was essential to provide enough showroom space, I decided against it. Three or four inches more and I would have signed the lease.

Later I had practically completed arrangements to lease premises from an old gentleman who was retiring from business but, on the day we were to complete the agreement, he decided that he was fit for another year or two on the job and so that prospect ended.

Just at that time my former consul and close associate and friend in New York, Dan McGrath, wrote to me about a business proposition in New York and after negotiations I purchased the business, packed my traps and sailed for New York. McGrath joined the concern as chief assistant and to act as manager in my absence. I had left him in charge of the consulate at the time of my resignation but the execution of Childers and the four men who were shot on 8 December caused him to send in his resignation. The re-union with Dan McGrath was an entirely happy one. He was the soul of honesty and reliability and had so many qualities of mind and heart that our friendship, begun in the consulate, was firmly cemented in our many years of close association that followed.

I have no intention of recounting in detail all the ups and downs of our business activities in the United States. They are scarcely relevant to the main purpose of these notes, however interesting or vital they may have been to me at that time. There are, however, one or two aspects of that period that, because of their nature, may be worthy of record. One of these affected me personally in a peculiar way.

In pushing our goods on the market I had decided that the wise course was for me to go out myself and seek to open the desirable accounts, then, having done so, to put the traveller on the road. In other words, I did not wish to have a representative or salesman in a position to claim that they were his accounts or that he had put us on the map. It was uphill work, particularly as in most buying offices the restricted hours meant being out on the job from eight-thirty a.m. to noon. I presented my card at Altmans which was one of the leading Fifth Avenue stores. The buying office was a big room with a counter at one end behind which a few clerks directed operations. One of these took my card and gave me a brass check, which immediately recalled Jack London's awful story of that title, and pointing to a long bench just said 'wait over there'. The check had a number. I was that number. My personality and individuality were gone. I was number 73. I took it, went over and sat down on the bench and after about half an hour I heard a voice from the counter shout out: 'No. 73 go to no. 6'. No. 73 went to no. 6 which was a cubicle somewhat bigger than a confessional box and there I interviewed the buyer.

It was all perfectly normal and good business, but I must confess that my first experience of the system gave me a jolt. Just more than a year earlier in New York and in other big cities in America, I was embarrassed and even irritated at being introduced as 'The Honorable, etc.'. Now I was a number on a brass check. The experience was salutary and was the most useful lesson on humility and a proper sense of values that I had up to that time received.

Our opening months were extremely difficult. There was a minor slump and it was nearly impossible to interest buyers in a new concern or a new line of goods. The expenses were heavy and the case of samples was not light. I tramped round the buying offices for nearly four months almost without results and then, in something less than a fortnight, I had opened practically all the accounts that we wanted in the city of New York. What had happened? It was just that there was a sudden note of optimism creeping into the market and that the buyers were less restricted in their purchasing by their directors. The way was now clear for me to 'put a man on the road'. Soon afterwards we appointed another traveller who, starting in

Chicago, worked his way to the coast and still another to cover all the Eastern States.

One of our main heart-breaks was to get our Irish exporters to give that care and attention to the finish, the packing and the accuracy of their goods that the American market demands and must have. Our imports were mainly suitings, serges, tweeds and other woollens. Hand-knit sports goods from Donegal in the shape of sweaters, pullovers, golf-hose and the like made up a big proportion of our imports. The woollen manufacturers were accurate and business-like in their despatch arrangements and in the preparation of documents, etc., but it was a near nightmare to try and educate the others. The actual monetary loss caused by rejected and returned merchandise was very heavy and what was almost as bad was the sense of humiliation that one experienced in trying to placate a disappointed buyer. No doubt the Irish exporters have learned much since those days and are now perfect in their attention to detail but, rightly or wrongly, I feel that the early education of some of the Donegal exporters was achieved at our expense.

I have noted these experiences for the guidance of those who may come after me and who may be tempted to launch out to sell goods on the American market. The Americans, including the Irish-Americans, are the most generous and hospitable people I have ever met, but the American buyers and the department stores they represent are not only exacting but quite ruthless in dealing with importers. Let the trend of trade or fashions show the slightest symptoms of change, they will not hesitate to cancel orders or contracts and leave the importer to 'get out' as best he may.

I continued for six years until 1929 with varying fortune in the American market, crossing over to New York at least once a year until 1926 and dividing my time almost equally between my home and my American activities. I still continued to keep contact with my Irish-American friends and was frequently called on to help out in the various activities of the organisation. Despite the inevitable recession in interest in Irish affairs that followed the treaty and the civil war, the American Association for the Recognition of the Irish Republic maintained its organisation and its support for the Republican movement at home. Joe McGarrity, Dr Maloney and most of my other intimates were always in touch and we had frequent and pleasant evenings together. McGarrity continued his *Irish Press* for quite a long time. The Ford papers, *The Irish World* and *The Monitor*, came out as usual. Devoy's paper, *The Gaelic American*, continued its course and, while it was fundamentally Irish in its tone and appeal, it was unalterably hostile to de Valera and his supporters and consistent in its support of the treatyites at home.

Dr Billy Maloney was steadily building up his dossiers and files on the Casement case which he would ultimately give to the public in 1936 as *The Forged Casement Diaries*, a book that I regard as concentrated essence from a mountain of material that Maloney had patiently collected.

In 1926 I was approached by Senator James Douglas and asked so take over control of the Alesbury factories in Edenderry and Navan. Douglas was chairman of the firm. Alesburys were furniture manufacturers and coach-builders and, at Douglas's request, I inspected the two factories, made such examination of the affairs of the company as was necessary and reported back to Douglas and the bankers concerned. The report was entirely unfavourable. The factory in Edenderry had grown up from small beginnings in the most haphazard fashion and, to me, was a collection of ill-planned and badly constructed annexes, while, for the most part, the plant was makeshift and out of date. The Navan factory was somewhat better and even there many alterations and improvements were needed.

I should make it clear that Senator Douglas's interest in the firm and his position as chairman of the company were due to the fact that, following the grant of an industrial trade loan of 28,500 by the government, he was put at the head of the board to protect the loan investment.

The government of the day had the natural and commendable purpose in trying to keep the Alesbury concern going. In Edenderry it was the only industrial concern and provided employment for upwards of two hundred and fifty workers. Had the money provided by the loan been used to reconstruct the factory and provide new plant all might have been reasonably hopeful, but the fact was that it had been used to pay off the trading liabilities of the concern and wipe out the bank overdraft. At my point of entry I found that not only had the entire money of the loan been disposed of but a new overdraft had grown up in the ledgers of the National Land Bank.

The proposition was not encouraging, but my friend Tim Caffrey, who was manager and later managing director of the National Land Bank, persuaded me to consent. I did so but firmly on the basis that I saw little or no hope of saving the concern and that the only justification for carrying on was to provide employment in the area. From 1926 until 1932 we struggled to do so. Our wage bill fluctuated from four to five hundred pounds per week. The overdraft and the interest were crippling handicaps and there was little to spare for improvements or the supply of new plant. We had some excellent craftsmen and workers in the factory, but they were in the minority, and, for the most part, the general run of the labour force was extremely poor in quality.

In 1931, owing to general trade depression and a worsening in the financial position, it became necessary to shut down one of the factories and consolidate our activities in the other. Navan was, by a considerable margin, the better of the two and accordingly arrangements were made to close down Edenderry and transfer such lines of production as were profitable to Navan. The decision caused consternation and something of an upheaval in Edenderry and I came in for more than a fair share of the abuse that followed. However, there was no alternative. Had the original company been liquidated and a new company formed with the government loan as the main support for modernising the buildings and plant instead of paying off old debts, the future of Alesburys could have been assured.

My appointment as a minister in de Valera's cabinet in 1932 involved my resignation from the firm, as no minister was permitted to act in outside businesses or occupy a seat on the directorate of any company. De Valera and I discussed the matter. He was himself chairman of the *Irish Press*, the new Republican daily that had been established a year earlier. I was also a director of the paper and several others of the proposed ministry held directorships in other companies. Following the announcement of the personnel of his cabinet, de Valera stated that all the ministers would relinquish their directorships in the concerns with which they had been connected.

During the years between 1923 and 1926 I had taken little active part in politics in Ireland. This was not due to any lack of interest but to the fact that, for more than half of each year, I was absent in America on my own business. When in Ireland I was in constant touch with de Valera and my other friends in the movement and was fully aware of the various developments as they occurred.

The new party, Fianna Fáil, was set up by de Valera and most of his active supporters, including practically all the elected Republican representatives. A general election was held in June 1927 and resulted in the return of 44 Fianna Fáil deputies to the Dáil. The government party, Cumann na nGaedheal, had only two more, having secured 46 seats, but they could count on the support of 11 deputies representing the Farmers' party, 8 from the National League and most of the 14 members who had been returned as Independents. The Labour Party had returned 22 representatives and was the official opposition. In addition there were five deputies returned as representing Sinn Féin and two Independent Republicans.

On Sunday, 10 July 1927, Kevin O'Higgins was shot dead at Booterstown Avenue and the tragic occurrence caused something of an upheaval in political groups in the country. The whole situation was fraught with danger and the threat of a renewal of civil war, reprisals and general disturbance. It was in these circumstances that de Valera and the Fianna Fáil party decided to enter the Dáil and take their seats as elected deputies. Their decision to enter provoked considerable controversy in the Republican ranks because, under Article 17 of the Constitution, it was laid down that all members must take an oath of allegiance before being permitted to take their seats.

The oath had been a real stumbling block that had kept the Republican deputies from taking any part in parliamentary work since the treaty. In the debate on the Constitution in September and October 1922 George Gavan Duffy and Thomas Johnson[1] had strenuously opposed the inclusion of the oath and argued that the Dáil had the right to grant exemption from the taking of the oath. Johnson had accurately summed up the position when he said that he believed that insistence on Clause 17 in the Constitution 'will inevitably have the effect of depriving this country of the services of quite a number of very estimable and very capable men and women'.

The oath prescribed to be taken by members of parliament of the Irish Free State was as follows:

> I, . . ., do solemnly swear true faith and allegiance to the Constitution of the Irish Free State as by law established and that I will be faithful to H.M. King George V, his heirs and successors by law, in virtue of the common citizenship of Ireland with Great Britain and her adherence to and membership of the group of nations forming the British Commonwealth of Nations.

Reading the debates and the controversy that took place over the Constitution in 1922 there would seem to be reasonable grounds for believing that, had the pro-treaty government of that time been so inclined, the barrier of the oath need not have been created. However about that, it had the effect of keeping the Cumann na nGaedheal party in power and

1. Thomas Johnson (1872-1963): born Liverpool, commercial traveller, Belfast 1901, served on Jim Larkin's Belfast strike committee 1907, co-founder of Irish Labour Party 1912, vice-chairmen of its executive 1912-23, vice-president of Irish Trade Union Congress 1913 and president 1915, secretary to Mansion House Conference to oppose conscription 1918, attended the Socialist International in Berne 1919, co-author of Democratic Programme 1919, secretary to Irish Trade Union Congress 1920-28, T.D. for County Dublin and leader of Parliamentary Labour Party 1922-7, senator 1928-36, founder member of Labour Court 1946-56.

preventing some fifty elected representatives from fulfilling their parliamentary duties.

De Valera and the Fianna Fáil party decided that the time had come when the policy of abstention must be abandoned, and they might ultimately, and as soon as possible, secure victory at the elections and become the government. Meantime there was the undesirable snag of the oath. De Valera announced the decision of the Fianna Fáil party. In the circumstances he would treat the oath as an 'empty formula', each deputy of the party would present himself to the clerk, whose duty it was to 'swear in' the newly elected deputies. He would kiss no bible, but would instead read a short statement to the clerk stating that he was merely signing the roll as the only means which would enable him to take his seat as an elected representative.

There was much argument about the ethics of this procedure, many holding the view that, by signing the form, one was morally bound by the oath; others contending that by the declaration and by declining to swear on the bible no oath or moral obligation had been incurred.

It was on the 12 August 1927 that the forty-four members of the Fianna Fáil party took their seats in the Dáil and on 16 August the leader of the Labour Party, Mr Tom Johnson, moved a motion of no confidence in the government. The division resulted in a tie of 71 votes for and against the motion was lost on the casting vote of the Ceann Comhairle (Speaker).

Nine days later, on 25 August, the Dáil was dissolved and an election, the second within three months, was fixed for 15 September. In this Fianna Fáil improved its position considerably. With 57 seats the party was but four behind the government party (61), but the Independents (12), the Farmers (6), and the National League (2) could be reckoned as certain supporters of the government. Labour was reduced to 13 with one Independent Labour member so that, even assuming the unanimous support of Labour to Fianna Fáil, the government could still count on a safe majority of eight to ten votes.

At the beginning of 1928 I made a short visit to America. I had not been across for nearly two years and there were matters which required urgent personal attention. I had kept close contact with affairs in the United States by correspondence, by trade and financial reports and the various journals that I received weekly. I knew that there was something of a trade and financial boom, that hire purchase had reached an all time high peak and that everything was, as the Americans described it, 'on the up and up'. I found on my arrival that the boom was even more hectic than I had imagined. Everyone, from the negro operating the elevator to the managing director in his revolving chair, was 'playing the market' which was the Americans' apt expression for buying stocks and shares.

I confess to a definite antipathy to the whole hire-purchase system. Perhaps my hatred of it stems from my early training when we were taught that 'to be out of debt was to be out of danger' and that if one wanted anything the wise course was to save up for it and pay cash.

There was always a big volume of trade on the hire-purchase basis in the United States. 'We bought it on time' would be the frank avowal of the lady who showed you her new Victrola or drawingroom suite, while her husband was equally frank when he pointed out the qualities of his new Chrysler car. I know all the arguments in favour of hire purchase, but I am still convinced that, by mortgaging an uncertain future, it is, in the ultimate, a danger to the social stability of the State and the people in it.

Now it was, in effect, in full swing in the stockbrokers' offices. Anyone and everyone was buying shares and prices rocketed. With five hundred or a thousand dollars of hard-earned savings the speculator might be holding, or rather his stockbroker would be holding for him, share script worth many times that amount. He would scan the market report on prices and would reckon his gains. Tips and 'inside dope' were the common jargon of the whole community and everyone seemed on a fair way if not to become a millionaire at least to look forward to an early retirement to Florida in the near future. Such was the atmosphere of New York when I returned in January 1928. I did not like it and I somehow remembered the Dunlop and Mexican Eagle boom in Belfast in 1921, but even some of the shrewd business men, to whom I mentioned my fears, laughed at my pessimism. I was told: 'No, you've got it all wrong. America is facing a period of wide expansion and development. Capital is needed which will multiply itself immeasurably as America grows and develops'. Even Herbert Hoover,[2] the president, proclaimed the same philosophy and the doctrine, not of every family having a car, but that of two cars in every garage. In 1928 all this cheerful optimism seemed to be justified. The rise in stock-market values continued and more and more of the ordinary people were infected by the 'get rich in the easy way' bug. The impact of this 'mass opinion' made one wonder if one's reasoning was all wrong, if one was unenterprising or lacked that American characteristic of 'taking a chance'. Despite it all, I still had my doubts and my fears.

2. Herbert Clark Hoover (1874-1957): born West Branch, Idaho, distinguished mining engineer, president, U.S.A. 1928-32.

In the course of my business I paid a short visit to Chicago and there I renewed acquaintance with my old friend, Monsignor Cahill. The monsignor was a Limerick-born priest closely associated with the Irish movement and was an intimate friend of de Valera and all who had been linked up with the strenuous work of the earlier years. The monsignor brought me along to meet His Eminence, Cardinal Mandelein,[3] who, though a German without any trace of Irish blood, had been such a staunch friend and supporter of the Irish cause. In the course of a very pleasant talk I asked him how it happened that he became so active and so interested in our struggle. His explanation would gratify any Irishman and it is solely to record it that I mention my visit to him.

He explained that as a young boy he had served Mass in the church in Hoboken, New Jersey, where he had grown up, a member of one of the German families that had settled there. The parish priest was an Irishman, a grand priest who was much loved by his parishioners. At that time the German parishioners were advised that a German priest was to come to Hoboken on a visitation and to see how the German Catholics were making out. His father and some other Germans approached the pastor and made the request that, during the German priest's visit, they might be allowed to have a special Sunday Mass for the Germans of the congregation and a sermon in German from their visitor. The pastor's response was that he would place the basement church at the disposal of the visiting cleric so that they could have two Masses each Sunday for the Germans and a sermon in German at each. I should perhaps explain that in the bigger American cities the basement church is not an unusual feature. It is really a duplicate of the church overhead and is, in many of the densely populated areas, essential to accommodate the large congregations attending Mass.

'In due time', His Eminence continued, 'our German population grew and we set about building our own church. I need hardly say that the support and the funds contributed by our Irish neighbours and friends made that possible. I have many good reasons for being interested in Ireland and the Irish people, but that is the primary one'. I was impressed by his explanation and I was equally impressed by the gentle, quiet dignity and kindliness of the cardinal and the sense of humility and spiritual grace that he conveyed.

My visit to Chicago was a brief one, but long enough to allow Monsignor Cahill to bring together a number of Irish people for a céilidh under

3. Cardinal George William Mundelein (1872-1939): born New York, auxiliary bishop of Brooklyn 1909, archbishop of Chicago 1915, cardinal 1924.

his hospitable roof. We had songs and stories and good talk and it was one of the happiest evenings that I ever spent in America.

During the evening the subject of the coming election for president cropped up. There was at the time a special and unusual interest for American Catholics in the election of 1928. Mr Alfred E. Smith,[4] popularly known as Al Smith, was almost certain to be the Democratic candidate and all Catholic America was stirred at the prospect of seeing a Catholic installed in the White House. It caused something of a stir at the party when I suggested that Catholic America should be on its knees praying that Al would not be elected. To most of those present it was rank heresy and defeatism of the worst possible type, but I quietly held to my viewpoint and gave my reasons. America was on a wild orgy of spending and speculation. Despite all evidence to the contrary, I believed that it could not go on indefinitely and that inevitably there would be a bad slump. It may happen any time but, if it happens when Al Smith is in the White House, every bigot in the United States will blame it on him and attribute it to Rome and the Catholic Church. They will look for a scapegoat and you will provide them with several: Al himself, of course, but the main indictment will be launched against the Catholic Church and the Vatican. You have your share of 'know nothing' bigots in the United States, as bad or worse than those in my home town in Belfast. Al Smith was defeated in the election and I must confess to a sense of relief when I learned that Herbert Hoover was returned.

It was part of my programme on this visit to discuss with my associates in business a proposition, whereby they would buy out my interest and take over the ownership and control of the import and export concern. My desire to do so was not prompted by any financial pressure, but was due simply to the fact that I was no longer free to cross over to New York frequently and to have the entire financial responsibility at three thousand miles distance was something of a burden. Moreover, my other activities in Ireland were more than sufficient to keep me fully occupied.

My chief anxiety was for my friend Dan McGrath who was managing the concern and our two principal travellers. All three had been with me since we opened back in 1923 and had given loyal and worthwhile service. They had done reasonably well and were happy and content in their jobs and I felt it incumbent on me to safeguard their future. However, they did not find the necessary cash or credit to enable them to take over and so

4. Alfred E. Smith (1873-1944): born New York, New York State Assembly 1903, governor of New York 1918-20, 1922-28, unsuccessful Democratic presidential candidate 1928.

the matter rested. Had I followed my own instinct and wishes, I would have disposed of the concern and terminated my interest in it, but to do so would have meant terminating the employment of all three or leaving them insecure in the employment of the purchaser and new owner. I just was not sufficiently 'hard-boiled', as the Americans would say, to do so. I returned home having been away just under five weeks, the shortest visit I ever made to the United States. It would be five years later when I would pay my next and final visit to America. There would be many changes there and at home before I would pass the Statue of Liberty again, but they will emerge in their proper sequence.

I am tempted at this stage to make a brief digression and to record a few of my impressions of a number of aspects of the American scene built up during my seven visits from 1921 to 1928. These visits averaged a period of six months and, apart from New York, included visits to some of the principal cities in the Eastern and mid-Western States. My visits to Washington, Boston and Philadelphia were frequent and those to Chicago, Detroit and St Paul and some of the less important centres only occasional.

Like most early arrivals in New York, I felt bewildered and to some extent irritated by what seemed brash and nerve-wracking. The crowds of people all seemed to be moulded in the one pattern and to have the same standards of speech, outlook and mentality that reflected the 'Main Street' so ably described by Sinclair Lewis.[5]

I realised later that my first impressions were wrong and that there were innumerable Americans, so many, in fact, that there was scarcely any limit to the number of groups and types that went to build up the American people.

There were the moronic types which H. L. Mencken[6] as well as Sinclair Lewis has made familiar to most of us. They were articulate, they were superficial and lived on a diet of slogans and clichés and one found them in every walk of life from Damon Runyan's[7] Broadway to the House of Representatives in Washington. Then there were the millions of strict conformists and by that I mean those who adhered strictly to the established conventions for their conduct in public, irrespective of their private activities. Many of these conventions were admirable in their way, but they

5. Sinclair Lewis (1888-1951): born Sauk Centre, Minnesota, U.S.A., newspaper reporter, author, his novel *Main Street* published 1920, Nobel prize for literature 1930.

6. Henry Louis Mencken (1880-1956): born Baltimore, U.S.A., journalist and author, contributing editor to *The Nation* 1921-32, editor *American Mercury* magazine 1924-33.

7. Alfred Damon Runyon (1884-1946): born Manhattan, Kansas, sportswriter for *New York American* 1911, known especially for stories about New York nightlife, collected in *Guys and Dolls* (1931).

did tend to bore one with their constant uniformity. At dinners, lectures, political meetings and at many social gatherings this uniformity prevailed and there was frequently the added trial of listening to the typical fulsome, grandiloquent and rehearsed speeches.

Such may not be everyone's first impressions of America, but they were mine and, to be quite honest, I found it all somewhat wearing and disappointing. Very soon I realised how wrong I was. As I came to know America and Americans more intimately, I found all sorts of people, men and women alike, who were steadily and seriously pursuing their work with an enthusiasm and application that provoked one's envy and admiration. They arrived at the highest standards of perfection and seldom spared themselves in their efforts to achieve them. They were to be found in every branch of activity and in every department of scientific and cultural development. The passing visitor may not have met them and may have formed his opinion of America and Americans by his superficial contacts on his way through the States, but they are there, myriads of them. They are in the lecture halls and research laboratories; they are in the hospitals and clinics and in the law libraries; they are in the schools of painting, music and drama. In short, they are in every branch of American life and devoting every ounce of energy, physical and mental, to achieve their objective and that objective is to do it better than it has been done before. They are doubtless the elite of American life and development and on them rests the credit for that amazing growth that has enabled America to impose her influence, for good or ill, on the rest of the world.

There is one phase of American social life on which I would wish to comment, but I do so with a certain hesitancy and the fear that my experience was too limited to express a just and fair estimate of the real situation. In recent years there has been in America a vigorous campaign against communism and anything bearing the slightest tinge of the Red stain. As an Irish Catholic, I am entirely and unalterably opposed to anything and everything that tends in that direction or towards any totalitarian regime. It was the world's greatest tragedy that the late President Roosevelt made it possible for the ruthless power of one totalitarian State to be substituted for another at the end of the last war.

At the same time, when I read the various reports of the 'witch hunting' that has swept over all America in recent years, I could not but recall my impressions of the early twenties in New York. As I remember them, there was amongst most reasonable and intelligent people a growing sense of disquiet at the conditions prevailing between capital and labour on the industrial front of America. There was wide publicity for the grievances of the cotton pickers, for the copper miners in Butte, Montana, and the coal miners of Pennsylvania and for many of the other industrial groups throughout the United States. Villard[8] in *The Nation* and the columns of *The New Republic* and *The Freeman* carried the stories week by week. They were not pleasant reports and they did indict the owners and the managements of many of the biggest industries in the United States. The reports of strikes, the employment of 'Pinkerton men',[9] the use of the gunmen to deal with the strikers; all these created a sense of revolt amongst many of America's leading intellectuals as well a a sense of outraged injustice in the minds of ordinary decent citizens. No doubt the propagandists of the extreme left-wing organisations made the utmost use of the incidents as they occurred, but the incidents did occur and, at the time I write of, the drift to a left-wing political outlook was considerable. It was inevitable that many of those who were emotionally aroused drifted into the Red camp without any real realisation of whither they were going.

The disclosure of some of those who have recanted their communistic faith give ample evidence of this.

Let it be recalled too that Franklin D. Roosevelt was elected president of the United States and on what mandate?: 'The Forgotten Man'; the curbing of the big interests; the control of big industry to ensure a fair deal for the workers. These constituted the more appealing pleas that he expounded on his platform, they were the principal planks in it and it was on these that he tried to mould his 'New Deal' for the American people.

I am not writing a memoir of Franklin D. Roosevelt here. I am convinced that he was a great, inspiring leader in 1933, filled with a burning zeal to raise the status and conditions of living for every worker in the United States. That his zeal and his interest were not merely a matter of political tactics, but were due to a genuine human urge to provide fair play to the underdog is my conviction. His weaknesses and his failures would emerge later. Politics, and such unique political power as he was fated to achieve, diverted him from his early idealism, but all I wish to skim from this brief analysis is that it was the revolt from the gross overlordship of the industrialists and the vested interests that made him president, and that Reds, near Reds and parlour Pinks, as well as the ordinary plain man,

8. Henry Villard (1835-1900): born Speyer, Bavaria, emigrated to U.S.A. 1853, newspaper reporter, purchased *The Nation* and New York *Evening Post* 1881, president of Northern Pacific railway 1881-93, president of Edison General Electric Company 1890-93.

9. Pinkerton men: members of organisation of detectives established by Allan Pinkerton (1819-84) in 1843. Pinkerton was born in Glasgow but emigrated to Chicago in 1842. One of his detectives secured evidence which led to the break up of the Molly Maguires.

forgotten or not, were responsible for the bloodless revolution that he led to victory.

And why all this bother and worry to recall what is now history? Merely that I would venture to express the opinion that many, who were associated with Roosevelt and continued in various offices after his death, were potential rebels against the state of social affairs that existed prior to 1932, but were not supporters of the Russian or any other form of communism.

I need mention no names, but a number of the most ardent and aggressive pro-Russians and avowed communists, who left America to live in the 'New Haven of the Russian Soviet', returned disillusioned and were honest enough to tell all America why they did so. There has been ample evidence of the widespread and internal espionage and corrupting intrigue that has been carried on by Soviet agents in the United States as elsewhere, and it was and is the obvious responsibility of the government there to uproot and destroy it. At the same time it would seem to be wise not to misinterpret what I might call Rooseveltian radicalism as communism or to quote in the late 1950s what Mr X or Y said in the early 1930s. Much has happened in the years between and there is the danger of forgetting the collapse of the early 1930s, the causes that led up to it and the revolutionary nature of the New Deal that averted a worse type of revolution. I was in New York when Roosevelt shut down every bank in the United States, when the bread lines were forming and panhandlers were everywhere. My thought at the time was that in any other city in the world the barricades would have been erected. America survived that and all the radicalism and communistic emotions that it provoked. Roosevelt and his New Deal rode the cyclone and in the humble opinion of at least one observer a new concept of the obligations between capital and labour emerged in America. It has, I think, persisted and is likely to do so, provided that the machinery of re-adjustment, conciliation and co-operation are maintained.

19

Elected to senate in 1928 – Public Safety Act of 1931 – The Irish Press *(de Valera's party daily newspaper) is published – The senate and some of its members – The turn of the tide – Fianna Fáil elected as government – The Eucharistic Congress of 1932 – Abolition of the oath – The land annuities and the economic 'War' – The Ottawa Conference 1932*

It was in the latter end of 1928 that de Valera invited me to go forward as a candidate on the Fianna Fáil panel for election to the senate and I agreed to do so. There were nineteen vacancies to be filled and it was the first opportunity that the Fianna Fáil party had since they entered the Dáil of nominating or voting for candidates in the senate.

We secured six of the nineteen vacancies. Mrs Kathleen Clarke,[1] the widow of Tom Clarke who had been executed in 1916, Joseph O'Doherty,[2] a former deputy in the First Dáil, Séamus Robinson[3] and myself were elected for the full nine-year term. Michael Comyn, Senior Counsel, and Seán McEllin,[4] a leading County Mayo merchant and farmer, were elected for the shorter terms.

Following the election, the six of us presented ourselves to the clerk of the senate, read our brief statement that we were signing the forms as the only means of enabling us to take our seats and ignored the bible which was on the clerk's table. It is only right to say that the clerk, Mr Donal

1. Mrs Kathleen Clarke, *née* Daly (1879-1972): born Limerick, married Thomas J. Clarke 1901, supported her husband in his I.R.B. activities, supported I.R.A. as a member of Cumann na mBan in Anglo-Irish war 1919-21, opposed the treaty 1921, T.D. for Dublin 1921-22, again in 1927, senator 1928-36, 1938-54.

2. Joseph O'Doherty (1880-1960): born Derry, teacher, barrister, member of Irish Volunteer later I.R.A. executive 1917-21, T.D. for Donegal 1918-27, member of Republican mission to U.S.A. 1922-24 and 1925-6, county manager, Carlow and Kildare 1929-33, senator 1929-33, T.D. for Donegal 1933-38.

3. Séamus Robinson (1890-1961): born Belfast, member of Irish Volunteers 1913, active in Easter Rising 1916 and later interned in Frongoch, commandant, South Tipperary brigade, I.R.A., 1917-22, opposed the treaty, T.D. for East Tipperary and Waterford 1921-2, senator 1928-35.

4. Seán E. McEllin: born Balla, County Mayo, merchant and farmer, member of Sinn Féin and Irish Volunteers 1914, I.R.A. 1919-23, opposed the treaty, member of Fianna Fáil 1926, senator 1928-36, 1938-51.

O'Sullivan,[5] raised no question and did not attempt or suggest the administration of an oath.

I was appointed chairman and leader in the senate of our small group of six. Soon after we had taken our seats we had the consistent support of Senator Dowdall[6] and Colonel Maurice Moore[7] and later the frequent support of Mrs Wyse-Power.

We were but a small group, but we were active and applied ourselves diligently to the work that came before us. At that time the senate had considerable powers which were later withdrawn from it, leaving it little more than a debating and advisory body. With the exception of matters of finance, the senate of 1928 could, by voting against the government proposals, reject any bill and, failing later agreement with the Dáil, hold up legislation for a period of eighteen months.

The senate was made up of sixty members, and, at our point of entry in December 1928, had still a residue of those originally selected at the formation of the senate in 1922. The senate chamber was ideally suited for its purpose. It is, I think, the most beautiful room in Leinster House and is the most comfortable and satisfactory debating room that I know. The whole layout, the semi-circular plan of seating, the raised dais in the circular bay for the presiding chairman and the clerks and the relatively small size of the chamber created an atmosphere of congenial intimacy in which one would expect reasoned argument and debate. That was the impression I formed on taking my seat for the first time and, despite the many hours and days I spent there and the many strenuous and sometimes bitter fights I waged there, that impression still persists.

There were some excellent speakers and debaters in the House, and there were some who, for the most part, put in a dignified appearance and contented themselves with a move to the division call of the whips. The outstanding example in this latter category is the brilliant professional man who has been a senator since 1922 and is still in 1958 an impressive figure

5. Donal O'Sullivan (1893-1973): born Liverpool, well-known internationalist and supporter of League of Nations, clerk of Irish Free State senate 1922-36, folk-musicologist, member of Royal Irish Academy 1929, author.

6. James C. Dowdall (1873-1939): born Cork, founder member and president of Cork Industrial Development Association, butter and margarine manufacturer, director of Lucania Cycle Co., Hibernian Insurance Co, Cork Gas Co, member of Governing Body, U.C.C., senator 1922-36.

7. Colonel Maurice George Moore (1854-1939): born Moore Hall, County Mayo, officer in Connaught Rangers 1875 and service in Kaffir and Zulu wars and in Natal 1877-79, service in Boer war 1899-1902, instructor with Irish Volunteers 1913, campaigner for withholding Land Annuities 1920s and 1930s, a founder member of Fianna Fáil 1926, senator 1922-36, author.

in the chamber.[8] In my eight and a half years in the senate I never heard him speak, and I think that golden silence preceded my entry and continues up to date. Small wonder that some of his professional colleagues have given him the title of 'Elected Silence' without apology to the author of that interesting book.

I do not propose to give a critical analysis of all those who were members of the senate in my time, but a few references to some of the more important and most active may be permitted. Two of the most effective members of the 'House' were, I think, James Douglas and Tom Johnson.

Johnson had of course been leader of the Labour Party in the Dáil from 1922 and his record there was consistent with all I had experienced from him, since I first knew him in Belfast. He was not what I might call a congenital Irish Republican, but he was always a courageous defender of what was right and just for the people and particularly for the under-privileged. In the worst years of the struggle he had shown an unswerving courage and had continued to do so as leader of the Opposition in the Provisional government and a Dáil depleted by the abstentionist policy of the Republicans.

There was nothing of the demagogue in his make up. He avoided rhetoric but made a thoughtful, intelligent analysis of every measure and motion that came before us. He spoke well always and with little emotion in a voice that tended to be somewhat soporific, if the speech was prolonged. To me he seemed to be an advanced Liberal rather than the traditional Labour leader, but over a long period of years I learned to respect his ability and his judgement as well as his integrity. He was the ideal senator or member of any second chamber, whose functions were of an amending or revisionary nature.

James Douglas was one of the 'elders' of the house having been one of the first selection made in 1922 and was for a period its Leas-Chathaoirleach or vice-chairman. He was a clever parliamentarian, a skilled debater and one of the most industrious students of the various legislative measures that came before us. To me his chief characteristic was his tendency to seem to vacillate on the issue before him, particularly if the issue was one of acute difference between the Free State government and the Republican opposition. I say 'seem' to vacillate because time and again I came up against that obscuring screen of sympathetic understanding which invariably had to yield to an over-riding necessity of voting against

8. Henry L. Barniville (1887-1960): born Belfast, surgeon, Mater Hospital, Dublin, professor of surgery, U.C.D. 1915, consultant to National Army 1922-25, senator 1922-36, 1938-57.

us. It is not easy to convey the somewhat elusive yet unconvincing technique that he pursued. Perhaps I nearly explained it in one charge I made against him in the course of a debate when I said that he invariably agreed with the opposition until he found his ultimate qualification and that qualification always nullified his agreement. Douglas was an interesting study and would, I always thought, have found a suitable arena for his undoubted talents in resolving political deadlocks in the lobbies of the United States congress. He did desire to stand well with all his contemporaries in the senate and it was a difficult thing to achieve when feeling was high and differences were fundamental.

We had a fair sprinkling of the old guard of the British ascendancy days in our midst. Some of these like Sir Andrew Jamieson[9] showed a reasonable acceptance of the new order of things, while a few others gave momentary flashes of their inherited traditions. Sir John Keane[10] was perhaps the outstanding independent member of the house. He was a reasonably good speaker, blunt and direct and completely devoid of any spark of humour or resilience in his talk, but he was sincere and honest and spoke his mind on every issue without regard to any party view.

One well-known member of the house was Dr Oliver Gogarty,[11] whose literary work and associations have made his name familiar in literary circles far beyond the boundaries of Leinster House and Ireland itself. I abstain from attempting any literary appraisal of Gogarty. His works speak for him and what is lacking therein is perhaps adequately made good by James Joyce,[12] W. B. Yeats and a host of his contemporaries in their references to him.

9. Rt Hon Andrew Jameson (1855-1940): born Alloa, Scotland, chairman, John Jameson & Son Ltd., director and governor, Bank of Ireland 1896-8, high-sheriff of County Dublin 1902, chairman, Irish Lights Commissioners, president, Dublin Chamber of Commerce 1921, senator 1922-36.

10. Sir John Keane (1873-1956): born Cappoquin, County Waterford, Lt.-colonel in British army, service in Boer war 1899-1902, World War I 1914-18, secretary to governor of Ceylon, A.D.C. to Lord Lieutenant of Ireland, barrister, senator 1922-34, 1938-48, a director of Bank of Ireland, Irish correspondent for *The Times*, Councillor of State of Republic of Ireland.

11. Oliver St John Gogarty (1878-1957): born Dublin, surgeon, *littérateur*, his wide range of literary friends included James Joyce, George Moore, George Russell and W. B. Yeats, senator 1922-36.

12. James Augustine Aloysius Joyce (1882-1941): born Dublin, poet, dramatist and renowned novelist, from 1904 onwards except for the period October 1911 to January 1912 he spent his life outside Ireland at Trieste, Paris and finally Zurich. For most of his life he was supported by his brother, Stanislaus, his publisher, Sylvia Beech, and an American benefactor, Harriet Weaver.

I would merely venture to express my assessment of him as a senator and as one whom I met in the senate and the smoking-room annexe of it. It was always absurd to treat Gogarty seriously as a senator and for one very good reason and that was that he never treated the senate seriously. He floated in and out and sometimes intervened in the debates. Mostly his contributions were spasmodic outbursts, irrelevant to the subject under discussion, but perhaps an opportunity to air his undying contempt for certain of his opponents and for de Valera in particular. I never attributed the worthlessness of his interventions to his lack of ability, but solely to his lack of real interest and the fact that he paid little attention to agendas, reports, bills or anything else that provided the groundwork for the debates.

I had the privilege of earning his contempt and hatred, but his ineffectiveness in the house made this a matter of no significance. One aspect of his senate activities intrigued me and that was the futility of his efforts to exhibit that wit or gift of 'wise cracking' for which he had something of a reputation. In over eight years in the house I cannot recall one reasonably witty spontaneous contribution by the learned doctor. It was this that caused me in the course of a rather acrimonious debate to remark that: 'Senator Gogarty's wit bore evidence of the midnight oil'. I think he never quite forgave me for that single remark.

Poor Gogarty, God rest him, was a senatorial misfit. Maybe he was not the only one but he was, I always think, one of the greatest sufferers by being a member. It diverted him perhaps from his professional work for which he had great ability and scope and it did not provide him with a circle or group wherein his literary talents or his gift of talk might flourish.

We had a number of able Labour senators and of these Tom Foran,[13] Tom Farren[14] and Michael Duffy,[15] along with Tom Johnson, were most closely allied with our small party in national outlook and action.

13. Thomas Foran: born Dublin, member later president, Irish Transport and General Workers' Union 1909, member of executive of Irish Labour Party and Trade Union Congress 1912, senator 1923-36, 1938-48.

14. Thomas Farren (1879-1955): born Dublin, a stonemason, secretary, building-workers section, Irish Transport and General Workers' Union 1909, president, Dublin Trade Council 1915-16, member of executive, Irish Labour Party and Trade Union Congress 1916-27, president 1919-21, member of Dublin City Council 1912-13, 1920-23, member of executive, Irish National Aid Association 1916, secretary, Dublin Workers' Council 1921-39, senator 1922-36.

15. Michael Duffy: born Kilskeer, County Meath, agricultural worker, roads foreman, Meath County Council 1911-23, member of executive, I.T.G.W.U. 1920-32, member of commission on agriculture 1922, member of committee on the relief of unemployment 1927, senator 1922-36.

Foran did not speak very often but his contributions were always stamped with wisdom and clear thinking and a sound national outlook. Farren was a more constant debater and his views reflected the outlook of a sound Catholic conservative trade unionist. Representing Labour also was Senator J. T. O'Farrell,[16] a first class speaker and debater, but who seemed to me to have little or nothing in common with the other members of the Labour group. His views were, for the most part, such as one would expect from a member of the British Labour Party. He made no pretence of having any sympathy with nationalistic or separatist views and, at times, gave the impression that he was contemptuous of all such tendencies.

Our own small group of six was kept busy. Although we were only six, we did represent the major opposition in the Dáil, where our Party at the time held fifty-seven seats and the official government Party totalled sixty-one. It accordingly rested with us to continue the opposition that had been raised by our colleagues in the Dáil and by amendments, motions and divisions to deal with every legislative measure that had been finally passed there.

Our opposition achieved only one purpose and that was to make public, for those who took the trouble to read the press reports of the proceedings, our views and the Fianna Fáil party's attitude on the legislative proposals that came before us. The records of the many divisions show that in most of these we had the support of the Labour group, but even this meant that we were invariably a minority of from fifteen to twenty in a house of sixty senators. There was little or no evidence of dissent from any of the so-called Independents to any measure or motion put forward by the Cosgrave government of the time. With one or two exceptions, their response to the government whips was one of consistent support.

It would be unpardonably wearisome to make reference to the debates that occupied the time of the senate. For the most part they were a *réchauffé* of the arguments that had already been offered in the Dáil and, as such, exploded the theory that the senate was a desirable and necessary revisionary institution. However it may be in theory, experience has shown that we have never yet had a senate that was sufficiently free from party control to give an independent verdict on any measure brought before it. While the power of election rests in the Dáil and in the nominations made by the Taoiseach, the senate must continue to be a superfluous reflection

16. John T. O'Farrell (1888-1960): born Ballinlough, County Roscommon, secretary, Irish branch, Railway Clerks' Association 1918-48, member of executive of Irish Labour Party and Trade Union Congress 1918-30, president 1926, member of First Administrative Council of Labour Party 1931, treasurer of executive, Irish Trade Union Congress 1945-51, senator 1922-36, 1948-51.

of the Dáil with no honour or credit to its members and no influence on legislation. Prior to its abolition in 1936, the senate had the power to withhold its approval of bills passed by the Dáil, to pass amendments or to reject entirely any bill brought before it after its final passage in the Dáil. Such rejection originally involved the delay or suspension of the operation of the measure for a period of eighteen months and a further delaying period of two months. By any standards the period of delay was absurdly long yet, when in 1933 a Constitutional Amendment Bill which had been passed by the Dáil and which proposed the reduction of the period of eighteen months to three, the entire senate with the exception of the Fianna Fáil and Labour representatives rejected the proposal. That was perhaps the most vital decision that the senate made in as much as it clearly exposed the menace of its restrictive delaying power. It finally stamped it not as a revisionary body, but as an obstructive assembly that was prepared to block any decision of the parliament which had been elected by popular vote, and of which they did not approve.

It is of interest to record the contrasting attitude of the senate on another Constitutional Amendment Bill which the Cosgrave government rushed through both houses of the Oireachtas in 1931. This was the amendment no. 17 to the Constitution which gave the Executive power to set up tribunals without reference to parliament and gave such tribunals the power to carry out their trials, to impose their sentences and to execute in secret. It was a Public Safety Act proclaimed as necessary to safeguard the government and the country from the alleged conspiracy of certain groups that were prepared to make government impossible by armed force, attacks on persons and intimidation.

It will be readily conceded that in certain circumstances all governments may find it necessary, for the protection of the State and its democratic institutions, to seek and acquire emergency powers so that they can deal with such conspiracy and those actively concerned with it, but such powers must have the full sanction of law and above all it must be exercised in the full light of publicity and convincing evidence of fair trial and justice.

Amendment no. 17 gave none of these assurances. On the contrary, everything from the first step by the Executive Council to the trial and possible execution of the person on trial could be carried out in secret. Was it to be 1922 over again? Were we to have a repetition of four rank-and-file members being executed to justify the execution of an important leader? Were we to have another group brought out and shot as reprisals as were the four men who were shot on the 8 December 1922?

I have never known in how far the action of the government in October 1931 was due to a real fear of disruptive forces within the State, a state of panic resulting from several isolated instances or a political move to reconsolidate their position with the electorate. Their argument was made to convey the impression that a widespread communistic organisation was operating in the country, that it was financed by a foreign power and that, if it were let go unchecked, there would be an end to democratic and orderly government. I am quite prepared to believe that there may have been a communist group within the State, but I am equally convinced that, in numbers and influence, it was a negligible quantity.

But it is to record the methods adopted in the senate with this bill that I recall our experience with it. The bill had been bulldozed through the Dáil with indecent haste and, even before it had received its final reading in the Dáil, we of the senate were summoned on a Friday afternoon, 16 October 1931. When we met we were faced with a motion which gave us the schedule of time to be allocated to the discussion of the bill. The second reading would be taken at 4.15 p.m. and the closure would be applied at 6.45 p.m. after which the senate would adjourn until 8 p.m. From 8 p.m. until 9.15 p.m. the committee stage would be taken and the house would again adjourn until the next morning at 11 a.m. For one hour, that is to say until 12 noon, the report and final stages of the bill would be taken.

It will be seen that a period of four and three quarter hours was the limit of time granted to sixty senators to discuss this piece of legislation which had such far-reaching powers of life and death, arrests, trials and executions, and that this time limit was fixed by the senators themselves voting forty-one against fourteen. It was little wonder that Tom Johnson said: 'Personally I think that any claim for respect as a legislative chamber that the Seanad had made hitherto has been forfeited by its conduct on this bill'.

The final stage of the bill was, as I have said, fixed for the Saturday morning and one hour was granted for the final debate. We, who were in opposition to the bill, had in the earlier stages and within the limited time allowed us endeavoured to expose the tyrannous power that was being vested not only in the Executive Council but in its agents, military, police and administration. Our efforts were of course futile in respect to the senate itself, but they did at least ensure that the people would know and understand something of what was being enacted in their name.

The normal procedure in the senate was for the minister in charge of a bill to attend, present his measure and, having listened to the debate, to reply to the various observations on it. The method adopted with the amendment bill was entirely different. No less than six of the cabinet ministers took part in the debate. As they had no reason to fear a close division, their presence and their speeches had only one purpose and that was to monopolise as much of the four and three quarter hours allocated to the debate and reduce to a minimum the criticism of the opposition.

I was cynically amused to note that even in the bare hour that was granted for the final stage of the bill it was thought necessary to bring in two of the most eloquent of the ministers to crush our opposition. As leader of the opposition I was entitled to be called and I was called exactly seven minutes before the 'dead line' of 12 noon.

There were fifteen votes recorded against the bill. Six were from Labour, eight from Fianna Fáil and one, Mrs Wyse Power's, from an Independent. Forty-one members, the solid block of government supporters plus the miscalled Independents, voted for the bill which was now the law. It was chastening to realise how, even in a democratic State, the machinery of government could be so manipulated in the course of a few days as to supplant the ordinary processes of law by Star Chamber tribunals and secret trials. The senate was not of course a democratically elected body. It still contained many of those who were originally hand-picked by the treaty party in 1922, and even we ourselves, who represented Fianna Fáil, were but the selection of the deputies of our party in the Dáil.

From the time that Fianna Fáil entered the Dáil in 1927 a more intensive campaign was carried on throughout the country and the organisation grew rapidly. There was evidence of this in the several bye-elections which took place from 1927 to 1931.

There were three bye-elections in 1927 and in all of them the Fianna Fáil candidates were defeated and by substantial majorities. Early in 1928 the only bye-election of that year took place with a similar result, Mrs Tom Clarke, the widow of the executed leader, being defeated by over eight thousand votes by the government nominee, Mr Vincent Rice,[17] a leading lawyer. The year 1929 saw an impressive swing away from the government and Oscar Traynor[18] representing Fianna Fáil was defeated by Dr

17. Vincent Rice (1880-1955): born Dublin, barrister 1904, T.D. for Dublin City South for National League and later as an Independent, June-September 1927, Cumann na nGaedheal T.D. for Dublin City North 1928-32, 1933-37.

18. Oscar Traynor (1886-1963): born Dublin, member of Irish Volunteers 1913, active in Easter Rising 1916, O.C., Dublin brigade, I.R.A. during Anglo-Irish war 1919-21, opposed the treaty 1921, a founder member of Fianna Fáil 1926, minister for posts and telegraphs 1936-39, minister for defence 1939-48, minister for justice 1957-61.

O'Higgins[19] by only 151 votes, the figures being O'Higgins 28,445, Traynor 28,294. That was in the month of March. In June General Seán MacEoin[20] defeated Eamon Donnelly by nearly four thousand votes. MacEoin was of course the famous 'Blacksmith of Ballinalee' and one of the most popular figures in the country. For Donnelly, representing Fianna Fáil, to receive 24,621 against MacEoin in his home territory read like the writing on the wall and this was confirmed when, a week later, the Fianna Fáil candidate, Mr James Geoghegan,[21] had over five thousand of a majority against a strong local candidate in Longford-Westmeath. I give these figures and results merely to indicate the impressive swing that was taking place all over the country and the rapid increase in the support for the Fianna Fáil programme and policy,.

It was on 5 September 1931 that the first issue of the *Irish Press* appeared. It was an event that had been eagerly awaited, not only by Republicans but by many who welcomed a new outlook and direction from our daily newspapers.

The *Irish Times* was, as it still is, regarded as the organ of the non-Catholic and what had been the old Unionist and Ascendancy elements in the country. It was an excellent newspaper, as a newspaper, but its whole trend and tone were pro-British. It is true that in many ways it showed a growing appreciation of things Irish and an acceptance of the new Ireland. This was particularly evident in the literary side of the paper where Irish writers, poets, essayists and critics found a ready welcome, but fundamentally it still represented the mind of the Southern Ireland Unionist.

The *Irish Independent* was the only Dublin daily that might be said to represent the Catholic views of the country. It had a nation-wide circulation and was in fact the daily newspaper of the vast majority of Catholics all over the country. It would be difficult to define what policy, if any, it

19. Thomas F. O'Higgins (1890-1963): born Stradbally, County Laois, brother of Kevin, minister for justice, medical doctor 1915, member of Sinn Féin and Irish Volunteers, medical corps, Free State army 1922-3, T.D. for North Dublin 1929-32, Laois-Offaly 1932-48, leader of Army Comrades Association 1933-35, vice-chairman of United Ireland Party 1935, T.D. for Cork city 1948-51, minister for justice 1948-49, minister for industry and commerce 1949-51.

20. General Seán MacEoin (1894-1973): born Bunlahy, County Longford, member of Irish Volunteers 1913, as a commandant of I.R.A., played a leading role in Anglo-Irish war 1919-21, during civil war was G.O.C. Western Command of the Free State army 1922-23, chief of staff 1923, T.D. for Sligo and Longford 1929-65, minister for justice 1948-51, minister for defence 1954-57.

21. James Geoghegan (1886-1950): barrister 1915, T.D. for Longford-Westmeath 1930-36, minister for justice 1932-33, attorney-general 1936, judge of supreme court 1936-50.

pursued beyond that of being basically Catholic in its outlook. It could be and was, at times, severely critical of many aspects of the Cosgrave administration, but it was consistently hostile to any of the movements favouring republicanism.

It was an excellent newspaper, less ponderous than the *Irish Times* and more up-to-date in its features, but its past record was remembered. Very few of its readers forgot the bitter strike of 1913 which its proprietor at the time waged against the grossly underpaid workers, and the attitude of the paper in 1916 and the infamous leading article which preceded the executions of Seán MacDermott and James Connolly.

It was in this promising field that the *Irish Press* first appeared as the third Dublin morning paper and the only one that was completely allied with Fianna Fáil and de Valera's policy.

It had been a hard uphill struggle to launch the paper and the biggest share of credit for its appearance must surely go to Robert Brennan,[22] who for quite a long period had worked day and night to bring in the capital necessary.

Bob Brennan, as he was affectionately known to all of us, was a Wexfordman, a journalist who had given a lifetime's service to the Sinn Féin and republican movements. He was gentle, quiet and gifted with a fine sense of humour, but he was firm and resolute in his convictions and outstanding in his ability and integrity. He would later on go to Washington as our ambassador to the United States government and defend our neutrality and safeguard the country during the dangerous years of World War II. His work there and the skilful diplomacy with which he overcame all difficulties were not the least of the defences that preserved us from being involved in the war.

Bob took over the management of the company and the paper. He had a nerve-wrecking time during the erection of the building and the installation of the plant. Sometime in 1930 I joined the board of directors at the invitation of de Valera and I continued as a director until the creation of the new ministry in 1932 made it necessary for both de Valera and myself to withdraw from the board. We were fortunate in having Frank

22. Robert Brennan (1881-1964): born Wexford, member of Gaelic League, Sinn Féin and I.R.B., member of Irish Volunteers 1913, Sinn Féin director of elections 1918, Sinn Féin propagandist during Anglo-Irish war 1919-21, organised Irish Race Convention in Paris 1922, propagandist for anti-treatyites during civil war 1922-23, general manager of *Irish Press* 1931-34, attached in various capacities to Irish legation in Washington 1934-47, director of broadcasting, Radio Éireann 1947-48.

Gallagher[23] as our first editor. Frank was a Corkman who had, when barely out of his teens, already made a niche for himself as an outstanding journalist. He had been chief lieutenant to Erskine Childers on the publicity work during the troubled years of the Black and Tans and continued his work on behalf of the Republicans. Under the *nom-de-plume* of 'David Hogan' he has contributed some of the best written and most interesting historical records of our time that have been published. Frank had and still has an almost worshipful admiration for Childers as he has for Abraham Lincoln and his appreciation of both has found frequent expression.

When the initial difficulties, which apparently are the inevitable birth pains of a new daily paper, had been overcome, the *Irish Press* settled down to be the one Irish daily that was distinctly pro-Irish. Under Frank Gallagher's editorship the paper established itself as a trustworthy and reliable journal, bright without being cheap, cultured without being ponderous, and, above all, Irish through and through in the things that mattered. It was to me a tragedy not only for the paper but for the country when Gallagher ceased to be editor. From that time the whole tone of the paper gradually deteriorated. A new and undesirable streak crept into its columns and has continued to grow until the present time, 1958. It may be that modern journalism and the fierce competition that prevails in the newspaper world demands these radical changes, but one looks back with nostalgia to the days when Frank Gallagher, M. J. McManus[24] and Aodh de Blacam[25] gave the people the right lead and direction on all that really mattered in Catholic Ireland.

For de Valera the launching of the *Irish Press* was the fulfilment of a long cherished hope. Like all his associates and colleagues, both before and after 1916, he fully appreciated the importance of a newspaper in the fostering and developing of the Irish mind. He had lived through the sterilising period of the Irish Parliamentary Party and had seen the effects of the

23. Frank Gallagher (1893-1962): born Cork, member of Irish Volunteers 1913, editor of the *Irish Bulletin* mouth-piece of the I.R.A., 1920-22, editor of *Irish Press* 1931-40, director of government information bureau 1940-54, member of staff of National Library of Ireland 1954-8, author.

24. Michael Joseph MacManus (1888-1951): born County Leitrim, teacher in Lancashire 1907-10, freelance journalist in London 1910-16 and in Dublin 1916-31, literary editor of *Irish Press* 1931-51, president of Bibliographical Society of Ireland and of the Book Association of Ireland, author.

25. Aodh de Blacam (1891-1951): born London, member of Gaelic League, convert to Catholicism 1914, journalist with *Enniscorthy Echo* and active in Sinn Féin 1915, member of Fianna Fáil 1926-47, member of Clann na Poblachta 1947-51, member of Commission on Emigration 1948-51, prolific author in Irish and English, best-known for his column in *Irish Press* 1931-48 over the by-line 'Roddy the Rover'.

Freeman's Journal in bolstering up that Party's control of the country. He, more than most, had suffered from misrepresentation and misinterpretation and, what was of greater importance to him, he had realised the power of the press to mould and guide the people for good or ill.

That early morning of the 5 September 1931, when the first copies of the *Irish Press* began to come off the machines, was a memorable one for de Valera, probably the most notable date in his diary next to Easter Monday 1916.

The new paper gave an added impetus to the already considerable growth of Fianna Fáil all over the country. While it adhered firmly to its motto of 'Truth in the News', it was nevertheless frankly a party paper and, as such, was zealous in spreading the gospel of Fianna Fáil in its daily issues. It was the necessary coping stone to all the speeches, lectures and propaganda of the movement. Gallagher's leading articles dealt with every aspect of the national situation and were, I think, the best contributions to national journalism since Arthur Griffith had written in the earlier years.

The result of the combined efforts of the Party and the daily *Irish Press* was soon to be seen.

On 29 January 1932 the Dáil was dissolved and an election was announced for 16 February. At the dissolution Fianna Fail held 56 seats, while the government Party, Cumann na nGaedheal, had 66; Labour 10, Independent Labour 2, Independents 13 and Farmers 6 made up the other representation in the House.

The election was keenly contested by all parties but with great intensity by the two major parties. Let me add that, despite the intensity of the conflict, it was on the whole an orderly and well-disciplined people that recorded their votes.

I had several interesting experiences during the campaign. They speak for themselves and I refrain from drawing any moral from them.

Elections are costly and funds are a primary essential for a successful campaign. I realised this but I have ever been the world's worst collector. Frankly I just had not what the Americans call 'the crust' to hold people up for subscriptions. Quite a few of my friends and acquaintances passed on their contributions to me and I was duly grateful. One of these, a very old friend but one whom I knew to be a strong supporter of the Cosgrave Government, handed me a cheque for £50. I was somewhat surprised and immediately asked him: 'How much are you giving to Cumann na nGaedheal?' His reply was prompt and unashamed: 'the same amount', he said. I thanked him, smiled and merely added: 'Backing it each way?' Certainly', he said, and we let it go at that!

Coming in to our committee room in Leinster House a few evenings later, I found a number of our party members handing in their collected subscriptions to the treasurers. I happened to lift up one of the cheques out of idle curiosity. It was a fairly substantial amount and was from a leading member of the senior bar and was being handed in by one of our members who was also a senior counsel. 'I had some doubt as to our prospects in the election', I said, 'but I have none now'. My lawyer friend looked at me and said: 'I always thought you were a charitable man, Joe'. I replied: 'That doesn't prevent me being a realist'. These are but two of the many incidents that indicated the somewhat indecent scramble that takes place to mount the 'Bandwagon', while there is yet time. The ultimate result of the 1932 election showed Fianna Fáil as the largest single party with seventy-two seats against fifty-seven held by Cumann na nGaedheal, a majority of fifteen. There were, however, 11 Independents, two Independent Labour members and four Farmers' representatives, all of whom could be safely reckoned as opposed to Fianna Fáil. Official Labour had lost three of their ten seats, but with their seven elected members could still hold the balance of power between the two major parties. However, Labour was supporting us, although there was no specific working agreement between us, and so the way was clear for de Valera to assume control and form his government.

Shortly after the election results were known de Valera sent for me and invited me to become minister for education. I confess that I was flattered by the proposal, but I quickly realised the snags and objections to my acceptance of the ministry. I pointed out to him that a minister for education required two qualifications which unfortunately I did not have. The first was that he should be a fluent Irish speaker and the second was that he should, if possible, have a university degree. He argued against both my objections and stressed his urgent wish to get someone with drive that would re-organise and galvanise the department into live action. He rather pooh-poohed the idea of the need for a university degree and I understood his arguments on that issue. We parted without having come to any decision and on my promise to consider it carefully and give him my decision on the following day.

I turned the problem over and over again in my mind, but decided against acceptance. The question of being without a B.A. or a B.Comm. degree was not a barrier worth consideration, but I think, and still think, that a minister for education not fully competent to transact all his business through Irish would be, in view of the policy of the Party, an anomaly. That was in 1932 when we were perhaps more sensitive to what constituted the responsibilities of a minister than we came to be later. However that may be, I finally declined the post of minister for education and entered the cabinet as minister for posts and telegraphs, the least important ministry of the cabinet. I say 'least important' for, while it has many and varied activities and an enormous staff of public servants, it is, for the most part, a big, highly-organised business which runs on routine and well-set lines.

As minister I had my place in the cabinet and had equal voice and responsibility for all decisions on policy and administration that came before us at cabinet level. There was a further advantage in the position and that was that it afforded a reasonable amount of free time which could be devoted to other and more important activities of the government. It was thus possible for me to take an active interest in external affairs, to go to Geneva as delegate to the League of Nations, and generally to work in close collaboration with de Valera on the many problems with which he had to deal.

Our association with one another during my years in the cabinet was continuous and intimate, and I take this opportunity of paying tribute to his unfailing consideration and kindness at all times. The 'going' was heavy and it was, thanks to the indefensible opposition that confronted us on national issues, an incessant grind of long hours and constant anxiety and work. De Valera, working from early morning until the early hours of each succeeding day, never let up. Save for the few hours of sleep he snatched, it was a continuous round of work. From a meeting of the cabinet over to the Dáil and from there back to his office desk. We all felt the strain, but by far the greatest burden rested on him and only an iron constitution could have carried it.

The cabinet was formed and took office in March and no time was lost in introducing the bill for the abolition of the oath. This was done on 29 April 1932.

The debates of the various stages of the abolition of the oath bill are available in the official reports of Dáil Éireann.

The speeches of the opposition members constitute, in my opinion, one of the really black spots in our parliamentary history. Every argument that one might expect from the most reactionary British Tory was made and enhanced by abuse, threats and warnings. There was no evidence of any wish on the part of the treatyites to forward 'the onward march of the nation' to greater freedom, and one sought in vain to find any evidence that the 'stepping stone' policy was being pursued. The discreditable and humiliating exhibition continued for a month and it was on 19 May 1932 that the bill received its final reading and was passed on to the senate.

It came before us in the senate for its first reading on 25 May and here the humiliating round of abusive opposition was repeated at all stages of the debate and on 28 June the bill was returned to the Dáil truncated with amendments which the government would reject. The senate would show its policy of obstruction, exercise its power of delay and incidentally take a major step towards its own abolition.

There is a temptation to quote from some of the more virulent and dangerous of the speeches that were delivered in both houses, but it must be resisted. They can, as I say, be read in the official record of the debates and the student of the history of the period will find them both illuminating and humiliating. The oath had been removed, the period of delay inflicted by the senate would run its due course and the chief barrier to a fully representative parliament for the twenty-six counties had been removed. It was a momentous step forward and there would be others to follow.

In June 1932 Ireland had the great honour and privilege of holding the Eucharistic Congress.[26] I say Ireland because, although Dublin was the selected centre for the Congress, all Ireland, from Murlough Bay to the Cóbh of Cork, was united in the greatest manifestation of religious joy and devotion that has ever been known in the country. The preparations for the great event had gone on for months. It was as if the homes in the country had been subjected to a vast spring cleaning and redecoration, and this applied to the poorest slum areas in Belfast and Dublin, as well as to the suburban villas, the mansions and the remote farm houses. There were of course the vast imposing schemes of decoration and illumination that had been planned and carried out by the organising committees, but even more impressive were the small shrines and the blaze of colour and light that expressed the spirit of Catholic devotion in every side street in every town in Ireland.

The late G.K. Chesterton, who was a welcome guest for that week, aptly described this feature of the Dublin scene when he wrote: 'Instead of the main stream of colour flowing down the main streets of commerce and overflowing into the crooked and neglected slums, it was exactly the other way; it was the slums that were the springs. These were the furnaces of colour; these were the fountains of light'. What Chesterton wrote about

26. Eucharistic Congress: The thirty-first international Eucharistic Congress was held in Dublin on 22-26 June 1932. It was sponsored by Edward Byrne, archbishop of Dublin, organised by Frank O'Reilly, secretary of the Catholic Truth Society of Ireland, and formally opened by Cardinal Lorenzo Lauri, the papal legate.

Dublin could be said about every city and town and village in Ireland—in all Ireland, including the partitioned six counties. In the Catholic quarters of Belfast, Derry and every other town in the area the manifestation of fervent unity and devotion was made. We are credited with a flair for big demonstrations in Ireland and, as one cynic remarked to me, 'we dearly love big funerals as much as we love big public meetings'. There is more than a grain of truth in this and it applies equally in the North as anyone who has ever seen the Orangeman parade in a Twelfth of July procession will admit.

June 1932 was different from all this. Evening after evening, as the different groups made their way to the Phoenix Park, men one night, women another, and children having their own special occasion, there was the quiet atmosphere that accompanies prayerful devotion. Ireland was on its knees not as former rulers would have wished to have it to a foreign monarch but in prayerful devotion to the only king that it would ever acknowledge.

So the week progressed in perfect June weather until the culminating event on the closing Sunday morning when it was estimated that upwards of a million people assembled in the 'Fifteen Acres' section of the Phoenix Park for the High Mass. It was an unforgettable scene. The magnificent high altar, the gorgeous vestments of the cardinals and prelates of the Church, the sea of white surplices and the vast assembly of a whole population kneeling in quite devotion as Count John McCormack's[27] beautiful voice floated over their heads in the *Panis Angelicus*.

By the accident of circumstances I was privileged to make an important contribution to the great occasion.

A few of us were having a cup of coffee together in the Winter Gardens. One of the group, Mr James Digby, who was in the radio business, expressed the hope that the broadcasting branch of the post office would complete the work at the Athlone headquarters so that a direct broadcast could be made by the pope from the Vatican radio station to the congress. He knew, he said, that the necessary plant had been bought and was actually in store unpacked and that the job could be completed in time. That was about a week before de Valera announced his cabinet.

I said nothing but I made a mental note of the suggestion. On the day that I was installed as minister for posts and telegraphs I called in the chief engineer, Mr Monahan, and several of those responsible for the radio

27. Count John McCormack (1884-1945): born Athlone, famous tenor and opera singer, became an American citizen 1917, papal chamberlain and a commander of the Order of St Gregory 1928, star-role in films 1930s.

administration and, with the co-operation of the Board of Works under Hugo Flinn,[28] the work was put in hand and, under extreme pressure, was just completed in time. Perhaps I was entitled to experience an extra thrill as the voice of His Holiness, Pope Pius XI,[29] sounded over the park to impart the papal blessing to the vast audience. Even more so were Chief Engineer Monahan and my friend, James Digby.

There was a repetition of the wonderful scene in the afternoon when the people assembled for Solemn Benediction of the Blessed Sacrament. For this a beautiful altar had been erected on O'Connell Bridge which, as most people know, spans the Liffey and divides the city right at its centre. The selection of the bridge for the ceremony was a stroke of imaginative genius. The four long quays, as well as the other main approaches to the bridge, afforded accommodation for the hundreds of thousands of devout worshippers. These formed a compact mass all radiating out in every direction from the pivotal centre which was the altar. Those responsible for the marshalling and stewarding of the vast multitude did a wonderful job and the discipline and co-operation of the people secured perfect order. It was, of course above all else, the sacred ceremonies that ensured this. Dublin for that day had become a vast open-air cathedral, where all Ireland was meeting in prayer and devotion and where dignitaries of the Catholic Church from all ends of the Christian world had come to join them.

It was the final act of the congress completing, what must have been for all those privileged to participate, the most memorable week that Dublin and Ireland had ever known.

My congress activities were not completed until after midnight. His Eminence, Cardinal O'Connell[30] of Boston, had made special arrangements for a link up on the American side to broadcast a talk to his people and had timed the American reception for about 6 p.m. This meant that he would speak from the Dublin station at midnight. I was there to see that all was in order and to receive the cardinal. His broadcast went over satisfactorily and Boston reported back that the reception there was

28. Hugo Flinn (1880-1943): born Kinsale, County Cork, electrical engineer 1901, chief engineer of Liverpool Electricity Supply Board, radio business Cork, T.D. for Cork city 1927-43, parliamentary secretary to minister for finance 1932-39, parliamentary secretary to minister for local government 1939-43, advocate of establishment of Bord na Móna.

29. Pope Pius XI (1857-1939): born Desio, near Milan, palaeographer, papal nuncio 1918, cardinal 1921, pope 1922-39, concluded Lateran treaty with Mussolini 1929.

30. Cardinal William Henry O'Connell (1859-1944): born Lowell, Massachusetts, rector, American College, Rome 1895, bishop of Portland, Maine 1901, archbishop of Constance and coadjutor in Boston 1906, archbishop of Boston 1907, cardinal 1911.

excellent. His address was, in the circumstances, less colourful than I had hoped it would be. It conveyed too little of the atmosphere and colour of the momentous day and tended to be slightly ponderous and of a mission sermon type. However, that was my personal reaction and His Eminence knew his people. I would meet him again in Boston a year later under different circumstances but always with the grateful remembrance that he was the first of the great Church dignitaries of America who came forward at the time we most needed help in the United States.

The week of the congress was a somewhat colourful and exciting interlude in the work of the ministry, but it was a very strenuous and exacting time. Apart from the religious services, there were many receptions and social functions which we were bound to attend officially. They were interesting and pleasant, but they did impose a rather breathless rush with little opportunity to relax.

In the immediate background lay the menacing shadow of all that conflict with the British government not only in regard to the oath but on the issue of our refusal to pay the land annuities and other monies which we contended were neither legally nor morally due. The chief factor constituting that shadow was the unpardonable opposition that we were facing in our own Oireachtas.

It is highly unpleasant to have a fight with your next door neighbour, but it is heart-breaking when some of the members of your household align themselves with the enemy. That was the situation we were facing and we knew it. The opposition to the oath bill indicated the lines that would be followed. It would scarcely be necessary for the MacDonald ministry to defend their policy in the British House of Commons. All that would be done for them by the former ministers and deputies that constituted the opposition in the Dáil and senate. It was not an attractive prospect and it was not an inspiring performance. The re-reading, a quarter of a century later, of all that is recorded in the debates of that period is a depressing experience. They are available in the Dáil Reports of 1932-1933 and might serve as an example for budding politicians of the future of how an opposition ought not to behave.

Mr James H. Thomas, the British minister for the dominions, and Lord Hailsham[31] visited Dublin. Mr de Valera conferred with them and made our position clear. In regard to the oath, he said that our position was

31. Douglas McGarel Hogg, first Viscount Hailsham (1872-1950): born London, barrister 1902, attorney-general 1922-3, lord chancellor 1928, advanced to viscountcy 1929, secretary of state for war 1931, represented U.K. at world economic conference 1933, lord chancellor 1935, lord president of the council 1938.

unchanged and 'that we intended to proceed to put that measure into execution as soon as we were able to do so', that is, when the period of delay caused by the senate had expired. He made it clear that, while we were prepared to accept the principle of arbitration, we were not prepared to agree to the restriction of the personnel of the tribunal solely to citizens of the States of the British Commonwealth.

There the matter rested for the time. Thomas and Hailsham returned to London and we were soon afterwards faced with the British punitive tariffs designed to paralyse our export trade and force us by economic pressure to yield to their demands. The 'Economic War', as it came to be known, was on. It was a ruthless effort on the part of the British to cause such hardship to the whole community in Ireland as would force the government either to yield or to be put out of office, and be replaced by the more supine government led by Mr Cosgrave.

It was another depressing feature of the time to find that, as in the case of the abolition of the oath, the entire opposition stood firmly behind the British government in the Economic War. There was, however, a bright side to it also for, despite all the efforts of the British and the very real hardships which the whole agricultural community suffered, the country held firm and de Valera's government enjoyed increased support even in the districts which were most adversely affected. The opposition campaigned vigorously to spread discontent amongst the people and to emphasise that by returning Fianna Fáil to power they had cut themselves off from the British market and were paying a heavy price for their folly. It was to me a despicable policy. In the struggle to assert the country's rights one would have expected that all parties would have joined together, closed ranks and presented a united front. However, that did not happen and the opposition continued their campaign on behalf of the British demands to the end.

It proved to be a bad policy and poor psychological analysis of our people by the party opposed to us. The reaction in Ireland was quite different to what the opposition had hoped for. To the ordinary people it was a new form of British bullying and there was only one answer to that. They gave it when some six months later, in the general election of January 1933, Fianna Fáil was returned with a greatly increased majority.

It was in July 1932 that a conference of the British Commonwealth of Nations was held in Ottawa. It was decided to send representatives, and three ministers were delegated to attend. Seán T. O'Kelly, Seán Lemass[32]

32. Seán F. Lemass (1900-71): born Dublin, active during Easter Rising 1916 and Anglo-Irish war 1919-21, opposed the treaty and active in civil war 1922-23, T.D. for Dublin city 1925-69, founder member and organiser of Fianna Fáil 1926, minister for industry and

and Dr Ryan[33] accompanied by Mr Dulanty,[34] our high commissioner in London, were our principal delegates and they had the assistance of several of the departmental chiefs.

I confess that I had no wish to see our representatives taking part in any conference restricted, as it was, to the so-called 'Dominions'. Our presence there seemed to me to be a condonation of something very much akin to the imperial conferences of the past, despite all the implications and interpretations of the Statute of Westminster. My chief antagonists in Leinster House would no doubt argue that I had an inferiority complex on this and on other things. It was a favourite comment by those pseudo-Freudians when one wanted to see things straight and face them squarely.

However, it was argued in our own circle that contact with the representatives of Canada, Australia, South Africa and the others was desirable and even necessary, and that it was particularly desirable that the situation that existed then between ourselves and Britain should be made clear to them. There may have been much in that argument. The conference was held and the delegates returned having brought nothing back and without giving anything away.

The Dáil continued its wearisome debates, in all of which the opposition continued to bring in the issues involved in the Economic War and the dispute between Britain and ourselves. It was early in August that the session ended and the House adjourned until October. I had been ill for a couple of months before the adjournment and an operation was necessary. I kept going on with my work until the Dáil rose and then went into a nursing home, where my friend, Surgeon Harry MacAuley, did the necessary job.

While I was convalescing in the nursing home, de Valera visited me regularly and on one of his visits he told me that he wanted me to accompany him to Geneva for the meetings of the League of Nations. The 'assembly', the big annual meeting of all member States, opened in September and he hoped that I would be well enough to travel with him.

---

commerce 1932-39, 1941-8, minister of supplies 1939-45, Tánaiste 1945-8, minister for industry and commerce 1951-54, 1957-59, Taoiseach 1959-66.

33. Dr James Ryan (1891-1970): born Tomcoole, County Wexford, doctor 1917, active in Easter Rising 1916, Sinn Féin vice-chairman of Wexford County Council 1919-22, T.D. for County Wexford 1921-65, opposed the treaty 1922, founder member of Fianna Fáil 1926, minister for agriculture 1932-47, minister for health and social welfare 1947-48, minister for finance 1951-54, 1957-65, senator 1965-69.

34. John W. Dulanty (1881-1955): born Newton Heath, Lancaster, U.K., secretary, faculty of technology in University of Manchester, examiner, Board of Education, Whitehall 1912-15, chief establishment officer, ministry of munitions 1916-18, principal assistant secretary, ministry of munitions 1918-20, deputy chairman and managing director of Peter Jones Ltd, London 1920-26, trade commissioner for Irish Free State in Great Britain 1926-30, high commissioner in London 1930-50, special consultant to Irish embassy in London 1950-55.

20

The League of Nations – Ireland's presidency of the council – De Valera's inaugural speech creates a sensation – World statesmen and politicians at Geneva – The Manchurian conflict between China and Japan – The question of 'Sanctions' – The beginning of the end of the League

At the assembly the year's work of the League was reviewed and various committees were appointed to examine all branches of the League's activities. The session usually lasted about a month during which the committees were in almost constant session and prepared their recommendations which in turn came before the assembly for confirmation at the end of the session. The September 1932 assembly had a special interest for us. It was Ireland's turn to preside at the council of the League. The procedure at that time in the League was that a member State had the privilege of acting for a term of three months as president of the council and it was purely fortuitous that our period synchronised with the meeting of the annual assembly. It was also part of the procedure that the representative of the State presiding at the council should open the assembly and make the inaugural address.

The session promised to be one of exceptional importance and interest for it was clear that it would be a veritable testing period for the League. The economic and financial collapse which had taken place all over the world had left the statesmen and governments bewildered and stunned. Trade was in a semi-paralysed state; the world was glutted with surplus commodities for which no markets could be found. It mattered little whether the experts called it 'over-production' or 'under-consumption' or whether it was due to financial and exchange collapse, the simple fact was that international trade and international finances were in a state bordering on chaos.

There were other problems before the League, some of which held the immediate threat of armed conflict, and the repercussions of which might have far reaching effects not only on the future of the League but on world peace itself. The outstanding cause of anxiety in regard to world peace was what was euphemistically called the 'Dispute' between China and Japan, but which really meant the seizure and occupation of Manchuria by the armed forces of Japan. The other, but less immediately acute, problem was the trouble between Poland and Germany over Danzig and the Polish corridor. The agenda included many items dealing with social, health and financial problems, and these would be dealt with by the various sectional committees which would work on them during the session, prepare their reports and recommendations which the different *rapporteurs* would present to the final meetings of the assembly. Consultations with the department of external affairs and particularly with Mr Frank Cremins,[1] who at that time was in charge of the League of Nations section of the department, gave me a reasonable understanding of the work before us and, under his guidance, I made myself as familiar as time permitted with the matters set out on the agenda.

With a comparatively small team of advisers, Mr de Valera and I arrived in Geneva and here we had the guidance of Mr Seán Lester[2] who was our permanent representative at the League. Lester was an old associate in Belfast in Sinn Féin and Freedom Club days. He had been a journalist in some of the provincial papers, had passed on to the staff of one of the Dublin dailies and thence to the charge of the Government Publicity Bureau. From this he had been appointed to succeed Michael MacWhite[3] as our permanent delegate at the League.

I was much impressed by my first view of Geneva and particularly by its orderliness and spotless cleanliness, but it had, despite these attractive qualities, somewhat the same atmospheric impact on me as I experience when I revisit Bangor, County Down. Bangor, like Geneva, is beautifully laid out and almost spotlessly clean, but it too has the cold, slightly

1. Francis Thomas Cremins (1885-1975): born Carrick-on-Suir, County Tipperary, department of posts and telegraphs 1903-22, publicity section, department of external affairs 1922-25, head of the League of Nations section and member of delegation to the League 1929-34, permanent delegate to the League of Nations 1934-40, *charge d'affaires* at Irish Legation, Berne 1940-49.

2. Seán Lester (1888-1959): born Carrickfergus, County Antrim, journalist in nationalist and republican newspapers, news editor of *Freeman's Journal* 1923, staff member of department of external affairs 1923-29, permanent delegate to League of Nations 1929-34, high-commissioner in Danzig 1934-37, deputy secretary-general of the League 1937-40, acting secretary-general 1940-46. In a submission to the Bureau of Military History, dated 9 April 1948, Connolly stated: 'I was not at any time a member of the I.R.B. Sometime, I think in 1911 or 1912, I was sounded by Seán Lester, later deputy secretary-general to the League of Nations. I explained my position quite frankly to him as follows: (1) I had personal conscientious objections to becoming a member bound by oath to commit myself to unknown obligations. (2) I believed that my word was my bond and that my promise as a man was sufficient warrant for trust. If not then there was nothing I was prepared to do about it'.

3. Michael MacWhite (1883-1958): born Clondara, County Cork, served in British army 1914-18, secretary to Dáil Éireann delegation to Paris Peace Conference 1920-21, permanent delegate to League of Nations 1923-29, vice-president of the International Labour Conference at Geneva 1928, envoy extraordinary and minister plenipotentiary to U.S.A. 1929-38, to Italy 1938-50.

inhuman, Calvinistic current of air permeating everywhere. It is probably due to my early associations with Bangor, but I never walk along its well kept streets without expecting to run into an evangelist who will threaten me with damnation or demand to know where I expect to spend eternity. I had the same sense of expectancy in Geneva.

The first and most pressing matter after our arrival in Geneva was the preparation of the president's speech and to this Mr de Valera applied himself. Lester brought to him a draft speech which was prepared by the secretariat of the League, but this was rejected and word was conveyed to them that the president proposed to make his own speech. This course was apparently unusual, the general convention being that the League secretariat prepared the speech which would embody a review of the previous twelve months and an assessment of the work confronting the assembly. Mr de Valera had, very rightly, other ideas which we all shared and he accordingly reviewed the position as he himself saw it and outlined the responsibilities and duties that devolved on all of them. There is no need to go into detail about the speech. It caused something of a sensation at the time and received great publicity all over the world. It was something of a mystery to me why it created such a stir. Granted that it was an excellent speech, it contained nothing save what any honest, intelligent observer of world affairs would have been found to express at the time. It was in simple clear-cut terms, but it did set out realistically the dangers that were threatening world peace and the definite responsibilities that rested on the statesmen and governments of the nations. It was the simple, blunt truth that made the speech something of a sensation. Geneva and the League were not accustomed to that type of speech. The statesmen and pseudo-statesmen who hovered around Geneva in 1932 preferred for the most part to express pious platitudes rather than face up to the harsh realities of the world situation. There were exceptions of course, but most of them, including some of the great powers, seemed to prefer to bury their heads in the sand and to cover their ineptitude and complete lack of policy with declarations of ambiguous insincerity. De Valera spoke of the threat of conflicts and pointed out that, after conflict and war, the contestants must eventually get together to hammer out terms of peace and agreement. Why not seek agreement now and avoid all the horrors of war and the destruction accompanying it? The assembly was slightly stunned when he sat down. There was a momentary pause of silence and then a loud outburst of applause, but the temporary pause enabled some of the less scrupulous of the British journalists to report that the speech was received in silence.

The assembly brought together many of the world's leading statesmen and ministers of State and I was interested to watch and see them in action, and in due course to meet most of them during the session. M. Herriot[4] the French premier was there, a big, broad man physically, with, I would say, a mind to match. With him were M. Paul Boncoeur[5] and M. Bonnet,[6] who were members of his cabinet, and a strong supporting team of officials.

We had little contact with the French and, with the exception of Herriot, they gave me the impression of being sharp politicians rather than statesmen to whom big decisions affecting the world should be entrusted. Sir John Simon,[7] the foreign secretary, led the British delegation and his chief colleague was his parliamentary secretary, a very handsome and extremely well-groomed young man, named Captain Anthony Eden.[8] Ramsay MacDonald was prime minister and made periodical 'swoops' on Geneva no doubt to ensure that everything was going on and on to better and brighter things.

Simon was suave and genial in his unconvincing way and was adroit in his handling of British interests at the council table and conferences. We were to meet fairly frequently at this and subsequent sessions, and I found it difficult to think that he was other than the brilliant lawyer handling his brief, rather than a minister intensely interested in the critical issues that faced the League. As a contrast, Eden gave one the impression that he was genuinely sincere in his efforts to make the League a real force for world peace and development. At meetings of committees Eden seemed to be

4. Edouard Herriot (1872-1957): born Troyes, Champagne, academic, scholar, mayor of Lyons 1905, 1945, leader of radical socialist party, served as premier and foreign minister on three occasions, liberated from German prison camp 1945, author.

5. Joseph Paul-Boncoeur (1873-1972): French lawyer and politician, deputy 1909-31, minister of labour 1911, Socialist Party 1919, formed Union Socialiste Republicaine and elected to senate 1931, minister of war 1932, premier 1932-33, foreign minister 1932-34, 1936, 1938, senator 1946-48, supporter of League of Nations, member of French Resistance in World War II, head of French delegation to U.N. Conference 1945, author.

6. Georges-Etienne Bonnet (1889-1973): French politician and diplomat, member of chamber of deputies 1924-40, held various cabinet posts from 1926 onwards, ambassador to U.S.A. 1936, minister of foreign affairs 1938-39 at the time of Munich conference, member of National Council 1941-42, deputy 1956-68.

7. John Allsebrook Simon, first Viscount Simon (1873-1954): born Manchester, barrister 1899, M.P. for Walthamstow 1906-18, Spen Valley 1922-40, solicitor-general 1910, attorney-general 1913, home office 1915-16, foreign secretary 1931-35, home office 1935, chancellor of exchequer 1937-40, lord chancellor 1940.

8. Sir Robert Anthony Eden, 1st earl of Avon (1897-1977): born Windlestone hall, County Durham, M.P. for Warwick and Leamington 1935, supporter of the League of Nations and United Nations, foreign secretary 1935-38, 1940-45, 1951-55, prime minister 1955-57.

3. President Eamon de Valera and Senator Joseph Connolly outside the League of Nations building in Geneva on 26 September 1932 after de Valera had, as chairman of the Council, delivered his speech declaring the Assembly open

somewhat slow in assimilating all the points at issue, but he spoke with reasonable fluency and with convincing sincerity.

There were a number of outstanding personalities whom I met for the first time. M. Beneš,[9] the foreign minister of Czechoslovakia, was perhaps the most active and dominant of them all. Beneš was involved in most of the back-stage management that was continuous at the time. He was constantly in consultation and negotiations on all sorts of problems, trying to straighten out difficulties, to reconcile differences and to find formulae that would meet conflicting viewpoints. The League meant much to Beneš and his country and no man could have worked so untiringly or so ably to sustain the League and all it proclaimed itself to stand for than Beneš. He impressed you by his simplicity and directness. His appearance always suggested that of a decent works-foreman or trade-union organiser, clean cut and unpretentious, yet I doubt if there were any amongst those assembled in Geneva who were his equal in real ability. He needed it all for he represented a state that was menaced on all sides. Poor Beneš! He lived long enough to see the complete destruction of all that he and his colleagues, the Masaryks,[10] had done so much to build up, to experience Munich and to see the chaos of World War II.

I met Litvinov[11] for the first time and we had several intimate talks. He was very unassuming and likable and knew something of Ireland, for he had been over there for a period before World War I. His sister was a Mrs Levison. She resided in Clones, County Monaghan, where her husband,

9. Eduard Beneš (1884-1948): born Kožlany, Czechoslovakia, academic, journalist, a leader of Czechoslovak nationalist movement, foreign minister 1918-21, prime minister 1921-22, president 1935-38, 1945-48.

10. Thomas Garrigue Masaryk (1850-1937): born Kopcany, Slovakia, academic, journalist, philosopher, M.P. 1891, M.P. and leader of Progressive Party 1900-14, president of Czechoslovakia 1918-35.

Jan Garrigue Masaryk (1886-1948): born Prague, secretary to Eduard Beneš 1921, ambassador in London 1925-38, foreign minister, Czech government in exile 1940-45, foreign minister in post-war government 1945-48, after communist *coup d'etat* it appeared he had thrown himself from his room in the foreign office.

11. Maxim Maximovich Litvinov (1876-1951): born Bielostok, member of Social Democratic Party 1895, member of bolshevik section of party 1903, after failed revolution of 1905 resided abroad and organised sending of weapons to revolutionaries, after Nov. 1917 revolution diplomatic agent of Soviet Union in U.K., people's commissar for foreign affairs 1930-39.

David Levison,[12] was a merchant with whom I had often done business. We discussed the possibilities of trade between Ireland and Russia, but when Litvinov explained that they expected to be paid cash for their exports and to be given credit for their imports I asked him if he was really serious and laughingly dismissed the matter.

I found Litvinov extremely interesting and well informed, and was satisfied then, as I am still satisfied, that he was entirely and wholeheartedly out for world peace not as a temporary expedient to suit the immediate needs of Russia but as a fundamental need for humanity.

It is not fair to try to assess his background or early history or the elements that contributed to his evolution, but in 1932 Max Litvinov seemed to be a loyal and hopeful supporter of the League, a man who hoped, if he did not pray, for world peace and who writhed at the futile 'dickerings' of the French and British ministers and the sterilisation of the disarmament conference. Bearing in mind that he represented Russia and that his early life was entirely devoted to the revolution and in association with Lenin,[13] Stalin[14] and company, I found him something of an enigma. Had he become softened with age or by his contacts with the realities of foreign diplomacy, or was he merely a clever, subtle diplomat who suited his terms to his audience? I asked myself these questions knowing that I could not hope to find the answer but tending all the time to believe that, for whatever reason I knew not, Litvinov had shed many of his illusions of 1917 and was more favourable to peaceful reconstruction than to world revolution. It was no surprise to me to learn that on the outbreak of the war of 1939 he was relieved of his post as foreign minister. The world heard little of him during the war and I feared that he had been quietly purged, and was surprised to read that after the war he had been sent to Washington.

12. David Levison: born Poland, a political refugee, he resided in Clones from 1899 to 1929, where he was known as 'Davy, the Jew', as a general merchant he conducted a large and successful business first in Analore Street and later in the Diamond at the premises now owned by Brendan Jenkins, butcher; well-known for his compassion for the less fortunate, in 1907 he hired a covered carriage to take a destitute patient from Newbliss to the County Workhouse, he participated in the civic life of the town and was a director of Clones Electric Light and Power Co. 1914, Levison's wife was a sister of Maxim Litvinov who, as a political refugee, visited her on a number of occasions in the mid-1900s.

13. V. I. Lenin (1870-1924): born Simbirsk on the Volga, life-long revolutionary, founder of bolshevik communism, chairman of the Soviet government 1917-24.

14. Joseph Stalin (1879-1953): born Gori, Georgia, expelled from Orthodox seminary 1899, revolutionary, adopted the Marxist Social Democratic programme, prison 1902-3, editor of *Pravda* 1912, secretary-general of Communist Party 1922, dictator of Soviet Union 1929-53.

I have since read what purport to be his notes for a contemplated memoir and these seem to confirm the impressions he conveyed in our 1932-33 talks. There is distress and even a sense of spiritual revolt at all the terrible things that went on in Russia. He escaped the liquidators and died in his bed but, and assuming that the published notes are genuine, it was a sadly disillusioned Litvinov that passed to the ultimate tribunal.

I have no intention of completing a *Who's Who* of all those who were assembled in Geneva for the assembly or the council, and it is a sobering and a salutary reflection to think that most of them have been forgotten, not only by their associates of the time, but even in the States they represented.

The work of the committees went on and we, with our relatively small staff, found it difficult to provide constant representation on them. However, the arrangements permitted substitute delegates and this enabled us to be represented at all the more important meetings but, added to the work of the council, it meant practically a morning to night constant job. De Valera had to return home after about ten days. As a government we were having a very tough time from the opposition. We had the 'Economic war' with Britain on our hands and we were determined to remove every vestige of British influence or even nominal control over the Oireachtas. The various legislative measures were being put through the Dáil and it is hard to realise the insensate and bitter opposition to which we were subjected at the time. I have already referred to that phase of our activities. Here I mention it to explain de Valera's departure and the responsibility that fell on me to preside at the council in his absence.

The meetings of the council demanded considerable patience rather than any special ability. Sir Eric Drummond[15] was then general secretary of the League and he had a highly competent staff so that everything was invariably in perfect order. The most interesting of the discussions to me was that between the representatives of China and Japan on the Manchurian issue. This was to be the subject of a special assembly of all the League delegates later in the year, but in the meantime there were many issues raised at the council dealing with incidents that were of almost daily occurrence.

Dr Wellington Koo,[16] whom I had met away back in 1922 in Washington, was leader and chief spokesman for China. He was the most

15. James Eric Drummond, sixteenth earl of Perth (1876-1951): born York, convert to Catholicism, British higher civil servant, secretary-general of League of Nations 1919-33, British ambassador in Rome 1933-39, House of Lords 1941-51.

16. Dr V. K. Wellington Koo: envoy extraordinary and minister plenipotentiary, Paris, Chinese representative on the Council of the League of Nations 1932.

effective and competent debater that I have ever heard. He spoke in English and his English was perfect in its phrasing, simplicity, and delivery, while his marshalling of argument was equally effective. Matsuoka,[17] who represented Japan, was the complete contrast to Koo. He was equally competent in his rebuttal of Koo's arguments and charges, but he was slow beyond belief. He would wait for what seemed an interminable delay before leisurely standing up to reply and then, gently and in a laboured hesitant manner, would proceed with his statement. During his speeches there would be long pauses when one felt inclined to cry out: 'Oh, get on with it', but Matsuoka was unperturbed. He just stopped, took his own time, looked around wearily and eventually continued his speech. His arguments and replies were clever, his English was good, if halting, and I could not resist the feeling that his technique was deliberately calculated. The contests between Koo and Matsuoka were mere preliminaries to what we experienced two months later when the whole Sino-Japanese dispute was the sole subject of a special assembly and of this we will have something more to say. An interesting personality associated with Dr Wellington Koo was Dr Yen[18] who was permanent Chinese delegate to the League. Yen was a rotund, sturdy figure, genial and benevolent and, while he had many of the Oriental characteristics in his appearance, might have passed for a pleasant, homely farmer. He was to me the genial philosopher deeply concerned with the fate of his country, and yet quietly confident and resigned to whatever came next. I was surprised when he joined me coming from Mass one morning and to find he was a devout Catholic. It may be that fact, superimposed on his national mentality, explained his good humour, his quiet tolerance and his philosophical summing up: 'There will always be a China. Two hundred years, five hundred years, what does it matter! There will always be a China'.

Amongst many issues that were brought to the council was that dealing with Danzig and the Polish corridor. Sir Eric Drummond came to me one

17. Yosuke Matsuoka (1889-1946): Japanese politician, member of Diet 1930-34, represented Japan at League of Nations 1932, pleaded for acceptance of Japanese policy in Manchuria, lost his case and led his delegation out of League 1933, president of South Manchurian railway 1935-39, minister of foreign affairs 1940-41, allied Japan with Axis powers, died while on trial as a war criminal.

18. Dr W. W. Yen (1877-1950), born Shanghai, academic, journalist, diplomat, minister of foreign affairs 1920, prime minister 1924-26, envoy extraordinary and minister plenipotentiary at Washington 1929-32, chief Chinese delegate at League of Nations 1933.

day and informed me that Baron von Neurath,[19] German foreign minister, wished me to have a special meeting of the council summoned for that afternoon and that, if I agreed, he proposed gathering the members for 5 p.m. It was then about four o'clock, but I did not feel that I could do otherwise than agree, although we had had a very heavy programme of activity all day.

We met at 5 p.m. as arranged and the Baron opened the session with a broadside attack on all the latest sins of the Poles. The Baron was a magnificently built man, tall and broad and well cared for, and seemed to meet exactly my concept of the Junker landlord. He was somewhat aloof and distant but, although always courteous, gave little evidence of geniality and less of humour. In dealing with Poland he would only address the council in German and, as the official languages of the League were English and French, this meant that he had to provide his own interpreter who translated his speech into English to be followed by the League's official translator who gave it to us in French. The Baron's speech took forty minutes and the two translations took about the same time so that it took two hours to cover the German's first barrage against Poland. The incident registered in my memory and for two reasons: the later fate of von Neurath who was sentenced as a war criminal after the World War II, and the fact that his interpreter-translator was a genial, pleasant person named Herr Schmidt,[20] who was afterwards interpreter for Hitler!

Baron von Neurath was given a life sentence when tried as a war criminal by that strange court whose code seemed to be that to be on the losing side stamped you as a criminal. Sometime in 1954 I saw a photograph of the Baron on his release from prison. He seemed an old, broken man and little wonder that he did. He spent years in prison and was in his eighty-first year. I have my own views on the question of war criminals, but these do not arise here except to say that there were a number hovering around Geneva in those days who had more responsibility for the creation of the war than von Neurath, but escaped the penalties that he suffered.

I had reason to remember that particular council meeting. It lasted over three hours and when I got back to the hotel Frank Cremins met me and asked me to come over and meet a visitor who was waiting on me. The

19. Baron Konstantin von Neurath (1873-1956): born Klein-Glattbach, Würtemberg, German foreign service 1903, ambassador in London 1930, foreign minister 1932-38, reich protector for Bohemia and Monrovia 1939-41, Spandau prison 1946-54.

20. Paul Schmidt: born Berlin, translation branch and later chief interpreter, department of foreign affairs 1923-45, employed by U.S. army in Germany 1945-9, author.

visitor was a gorgeously draped person who reclined in one of the lounge's easy chairs. He was young, big and handsome with a heavy, wavy crop of blond hair. He was dressed in a loose, black, silk robe with crimson facings and wore a fez-like headgear to match. He explained that he was the ruling head of the Assyrians who had, under the mandate of the British over Iraq, been transferred to the malarial swamps of Iraq. His people were mountainy folk and numbered some thirty thousand souls. Their transfer from their own mountainous area would simply mean their extinction. There was already ample evidence that their present living conditions were rendering them impotent and non-reproductive. I asked him how he thought I could help and then he explained that, within the next few days, Britain would apply to the council to be released from their mandate as they contended that their work and functions had been concluded. Britain, he claimed, had not completed their work and, until the Assyrians had been restored to their former territory or given suitable or equally good conditions elsewhere, Britain must not be allowed to relinquish its mandate or the responsibilities involved therein. There was much talk and explanation, but eventually I arranged that, when the motion to terminate the mandate was moved, I would ask for any objections and give him or his representative an opportunity of making their case to the council. In due course the matter came before us in the council. Sir John Simon moved for the termination of the mandate and seemed somewhat more than peeved when I asked if there were any objections. The Assyrian representative explained the position and the termination of the mandate was deferred and the question referred to a special committee. Ultimately this committee would get no satisfaction from the Iraqi government, but the problem was later solved by the government of Peru adopting the whole race and transplanting them to their country. If the other members of the race were anything like their handsome leader, then I would judge that Peru had made a splendid deal.

The incident was relatively a small one according to League standards and yet was indicative of much of the potential good work of the League. It was interesting too and made one curious to learn all the background and the details. I had no opportunity to do so, but I could conjecture that Britain was playing soft with Iraq. I could smell oil and see the shadow of T. E. Lawrence,[21] but that may be due to my suspicious imagination. I

21. Thomas Edward Lawrence (1888-1935): service against the Turks in Arabia 1914-18 when he earned the sobriquet 'Lawrence of Arabia', research fellow, All Souls college, Oxford 1919, colonial office 1921, his close friend Faisal, son of Husain, Grand Sharif of Mecca, appointed king of Iraq 1922, Royal Air Force 1922-35.

hope that my Assyrian visitor and his thirty thousand subjects are happily settled and raising many good Peruvian families. A few days before leaving Geneva I again saw the Assyrian leader. He was having an exercise tramp along the promenade and, with a companion, was going at a great pace. Gone was the silk robe with the red, silk facings. Instead one saw a big man with a tweed sport coat and a heavy tweed cap and both well worn at that. He might have passed for a Tipperary hurler making his way to Croke Park or an aspiring challenger for the world heavy-weight title doing his road work. Draped in silk or clad in his rough, well worn tweeds, I would say he was equally at ease and competent.

One of our most helpful and interesting friends in Geneva was Mr E. J. Phelan[22] who was assistant chief, and later chief, of the International Labour Office of the League. He was a native of Waterford and was one of the outstanding personalities in League circles. He was a tireless worker, gifted with a keen mind and accurate judgement and his constant interest and help were of inestimable value to the Irish delegation in our League activities.

Apart from the council meetings, the various committees were in constant session and it was by these committees that much of the practical and most useful work of the League was planned and decided and would later be made effective by the administrative staff. It was interesting and at times disturbing, however, to find that in many cases the resolutions which would ultimately be passed on the *rapporteur's* report would contain so many reservations by various states. I suppose it was inevitable, but it tended to make one cynical to note the efforts necessary to find suitable formulae that would reconcile the irreconcilable.

I was naturally keenly on the watch to see just how the British delegation, representing as it did the unnatural coalition of Conservative, Liberal and Labour parties, would operate. The prime minister, Mr Ramsay MacDonald, paid several brief visits during the period, but it was Sir John Simon, the foreign secretary, who led the British team. As one who had been reared on the traditional history of British astuteness, subtlety and clever diplomacy, I was watching closely to try and detect any evidence of these features in their technique. Perhaps it was due to my incompetence or that their adroitness or subtlety were so cunningly carried out that they

22. Edward J. Phelan (1893-1962): born Tramore, County Waterford, British civil service 1915, official in British delegation to Paris Peace Conference 1919, chief of diplomatic division, International Labour Office, Geneva 1920-33, assistant-director 1933-38, deputy director 1938-41, acting director-general 1941-48, chairman of UNESCO's Special Advisory Board on Personnel 1955.

escaped me, but my conclusion at the end of the month was that they did not then exist.

It seemed to me that the truth of the matter was that the British government at the time, September 1932, had no policy and were simply drifting on a day-to-day basis, leaving it to the various departments to administer.

Much has been written in criticism of Ramsay MacDonald and his period as prime minister. I met him at the time in Geneva and, to be quite frank, I was embarrassed by the experience. He had invited me to have dinner privately with him at his hotel, and our only companions were his daughter, Miss Isobel, and Sir John Simon. The daughter, a very charming and intelligent young lady, did all possible to make the evening interesting and pleasant but it was to no purpose. The prime minister talked jerkily on the merest trivialities. Sir John was a responsive 'Yes man' and one could scarcely resist the notion of a nurse attendant on a rather uncertain patient. After various futile efforts to divert the talk into some matter of real interest, I gave up. Then the prime minister called for his table bagatelle board, and we spent the remainder of the evening politely competing in this somewhat childish activity.

Eventually I escaped and breathed the refreshing air from the lake as I walked back to my hotel. I asked myself some questions on my way. I realised that in the strained relationship between us and the British which then existed the prime minister may have wished to avoid anything controversial, but there were a thousand and one things other than our problems on which intelligent people could exchange views. The League itself had enough under consideration to provide discussion for a regiment, to say nothing of the innumerable subjects from fashions to horse breeding that might pass the time. I am afraid I was worse than bored. I had the staggering realisation that this man who had just been entertaining me was the prime minister of Britain and that his attendant henchman was the foreign secretary. The former was either tired and exhausted or a completely spent force and his foreign secretary was a 'Yes man' politician keeping in step without marching. Was that the reality of the position or were they being politely rude to me by wasting an evening on piffle and bagatelle? I could not satisfy myself on the question, but later developments seemed to throw some light on it.

That was the British leadership as I saw it at the time. Poor Arthur Henderson, who was staying in our hotel, was devastating when he discussed the situation privately. He was doing his utmost to get things done at the disarmament conference and was getting nowhere. His comments on Ramsay and the 'set-up' in Downing Street were illuminating, but after events justified most of them.

At the time Japan and China were at each others throats, and the Manchurian problem would be the subject of a special assembly in a couple of months time when the all-important question of applying sanctions would be considered and the very existence of the League might be the ultimate issue. The Danzig corridor was at issue between Germany and Poland, and the world was in an economic collapse. It was terrifying to contemplate the future and to watch the manoeuvring of some of the world statesmen and pseudo-statesmen as they strutted on the world stage that autumn in Geneva. It is now a matter of hind-sight but, to be quite frank, I was depressed by the brief insight I had of the 'world parliament' in session. The French delegation, with the exception of Herriot, was an uninspiring group. I could find little to admire in the dandified Boncoeur or the hawklike Bonnet. Old William Hughes and the Honourable Mr Bruce[23] from Australia were only interesting as contrasting types; Hughes was a fussy, old man long past his age of usefulness and Bruce as a smoothly sleek, well-groomed apostle of empire. The Dutch Minister Colijn[24] looked what he was, a hard-headed, shrewd and cold realist, who spoke bluntly and to the point on all issues in which he was interested. Hymens[25] from Belgium and Hambro[26] from Norway were interesting, attractive and conveyed a sense of real sincerity combined with a genuine interest in international peace and progress.

The United States was not a member State and did not therefore take part in any of the official work of the League, but they had their observers who were by no means inactive in the corridors and anterooms of the main hall. America was of course vitally interested in the Sino-Japanese dispute

23. Stanley Melbourne Bruce, Viscount Bruce of Melbourne (1883-1967): Australian politician, M.P. 1918-29, 1931-33, prime minister 1923-29, representative at League of Nations 1933-36, high commissioner for Australia in London 1933-45, chairman, World Food Council 1947, viscount 1947.

24. Hendrick Colijn (1869-1944): born Haarlemmer Meer, Netherlands, member of parliament 1909, minister for war 1911-13, director of Royal Dutch Shell and other oil companies 1919-22, minister of finance 1923, prime minister 1925 and 1933, chairman of World Economic Conference 1933, imprisoned by the Germans 1940-4.

25. Paul Hymens (1865-1941): Belgian politician and diplomat, professor of history, Free University of Brussels, 1898-1914, member of chamber of deputies from 1900, leader of the Liberal Party, ambassador to Great Britain 1915-17, minister of economic affairs 1917, of foreign affairs 1918-20, first presiding officer at League of Nations 1920, minister of justice 1926-27, of foreign affairs 1927-35, member of council of ministers 1935-36.

26. Carl Joachim Hambro (1885-1964): Norwegian politician, member of Storting 1919-57, president of Storting from 1926, Norwegian delegate to the League of Nations and president of the League Assembly 1939-46, delegate to United Nations 1945-57.

and their influence was directed to try and ensure that the League would take a positive stand against the aggression of the Japanese.

I found it difficult to decide in my own mind whether the League could or would justify its existence. Undoubtedly a great amount of valuable work was being done, not only in the social service departments, but in resolving many difficult inter-state and internal national problems, but when the issues involved touched the big powers one had the sense that the League must fail. There was above all the feeling that one was living in an unreal world, a world that was screening itself from realities by euphemisms. The Manchurian issue was a series of 'incidents' which a generation earlier would have called 'war', but no one dare utter that dread word. The situation in Germany was deteriorating daily, but beyond the parleying over Danzig nothing was being done about it. A world glut of commodities for which no market could be found was causing an economic upheaval that had no historical parallel. These and many less notable situations left one somewhat bewildered and inclined to cry out for someone with power and authority to stand up and make an honest-to-God review of the whole situation.

However, we had to be content with less, but two major issues were on their way.

A special assembly to deal with the dispute between China and Japan was called for November, and plans were being prepared for the World Economic Conference to be held in London in 1933.

With these major events listed on the programme and after an exhausting but interesting month, we left Geneva for home. It was when we were pulling out of the railway station in Geneva that I realised that I had not had even one day's sail on the beautiful lake, and that, save for a one-day trip to Chamonix, I had been on a shuttle service between my hotel room and the headquarters of the League, a shuttle service that would be resumed a few weeks later.

It was in November 1932 that Mr de Valera and I returned to Geneva. The special assembly had been summoned to consider the Lytton report[27] on the invasion of Manchuria by the Japanese and the setting up of what the Chinese government described as the puppet government of the new State of Manchucko.

27. Lytton report: Victor Alexander George Robert Bulwer-Lytton, second earl of Lytham (1876-1947), was chairman of the League of Nations mission to Manchuria in 1932. The report, which condemned Japan's oppression against China, was widely praised but weakly ignored by the governments to which it was addressed.

The League had sent out a special commission to investigate the position. Headed by Lord Lytton, the commission had visited the area, collected evidence on the spot and furnished a comprehensive report. It seemed clear from this report that Japan, taking advantage of the internal conflicts within China itself, had created the necessary incidents and provoked the interference with their vested interests which, they claimed, justified their military and economic occupation. It was to me simply a repetition of imperial expansion and, as the Japanese representative, Mr Matsuoka, reminded the assembly, it ill became some of the States who presumed to sit in judgement of them to offer criticism on Japan for protecting what he claimed were their legitimate property rights.

I had studied the report carefully and the whole weight of evidence presented therein was a clear indictment of Japan, not only as the aggressor but as the crafty creator of all or most of the incidents which enabled them to achieve their purpose. It was a new modern version of the subordinate, satellite state. A local stooge was nominally in power, but he was a mere administrative agent for his Japanese masters.

It was realised of course that the big over-riding issue was whether or not the League would exercise its authority by the imposition of sanctions under the covenant against the offending power.

If sanctions were applied, then it meant the ostracism of Japan in international affairs. If they were not applied, then the prestige of the League would be reduced to nullity and the aggressor power could continue to pursue the old policy of grab, conquest and exploitation. It was obvious that everyone at the League, ministers, delegates and, above all, the officials of the League itself, fully realised that the very existence of the League was threatened.

Mr de Valera presided at the council meetings for a few days, but had to return home before the assembly opened. The assembly itself was attended by representatives of all member States and it fell to my lot to open the debate. This, I make haste to add, was not in any way a tribute to me personally. It was due simply to the fact that, as Ireland held the presidency of the council at the time, it was her privilege to lead in the assembly debate.

I do not propose to burden these notes with reports of speeches delivered or to bore my readers with unnecessary details. It will suffice to say that I made a brief analysis of the report which had convinced me of Japan's guilt in the seizure of Chinese territory by force and of the exploitation of people and property in the seized areas. The tactics were as old as history and some of us present had a keener understanding of them than others. The big issue for us at the moment was what was the League going to do about it. If the big powers, any of the big powers, could with impunity and without moral justification ride roughshod over weaker peoples, then I feared that the value of the League and the hopes that it had created for world peace and co-operation would be seriously diminished, if not destroyed. That is the bare substance of the line I took.[28]

Beneš spoke on similar lines and other delegates followed. Most of the speeches indicated that Japan was definitely in the dock and practically convicted and the general atmosphere suggested a determination to outlaw her. The question was still there, though, as to how far the assembly would go. Condemnation was one thing, but the imposition of sanctions was another.

Sir John Simon spoke on the second day of the session and it became clear that, whatever else anyone might propose, Sir John was not going to support any suggestion for the imposition of sanctions. He did not say so directly, but his suave, pussyfooting speech was a clever balancing by a legal juggler who was not prepared to come down on either side of the fence. Boncoeur followed in much the same strain, and there was much heartburning among the ardent supporters of the League and particularly among the chief administrative men of the League itself. It was quite clear that, while the assembly might pass its condemnation on Japan, there was no likelihood of imposing any punishment by way of economic sanctions or otherwise.

In short Japan had got Manchuria and would hold it and the League members would continue to trade with her as usual. There were several high spots during the sessions that clung to my memory. One was when Matsuoka in the course of his long speech defending the Japanese activities and policy paused for a moment and then said in his slow and rather halting deliberate way: 'Two thousand years ago Jesus of Nazareth was crucified. My friends, you will crucify every citizen in Japan before we yield to you on this issue'. It was a disquieting experience to hear him say this and there was a perceptible silence in the hall before he resumed. Moreover, one did not expect parallels from the New Testament to be given by an Oriental. Years later, and just before World War II, I read of Matsuoka's death in the United States and that he had been received into the Catholic Church some time prior to it.

On the day after his speech I happened to meet Sir John Simon as we collected our overcoats at the cloakroom. In the course of his speech he

28. Connolly's papers include a number of letters from Chinese officials and journalists expressing their appreciation of his criticism of Japan in his contribution to the debate on the Lytton report.

had made complimentary references to my contribution to the debate. Lester had suggested that I should mention this to him and thank him for his kindly references. I was so disgusted with Sir John's own speech that I rather abruptly told Lester that there was 'nothing doing'. Apparently it was part of the Geneva technique to acknowledge such compliments but, in this particular instance, I declined to observe the conventions. As I came to the cloakroom bench, Sir John referred to my speech and said he had spoken approvingly of it. I said that I had heard him, that it was kind of him to do so and that I appreciated the compliment. I then told him that I was somewhat surprised at thc line he took in his own speech and said I had been under the impression that Britain wanted the League, and wanted it to function successfully. He expressed surprise and protested that they certainly wanted the League and would do all they could for its success. 'Well', I replied, 'I don't suppose it matters much what a small country like Ireland thinks or does but, for what it is worth, my opinion is that the League is now dead and that your speech and that of the French delegate have about finished it'. He expressed shock and horror at such a suggestion and wanted to know why I thought so. I explained very briefly that Japan's action would be condemned and that they would go out but without any damage to their position in international affairs. The reaction of such a development on Russia and Germany would be interesting, to say nothing of its effect on the United States.[29]

I am not unaware of what must have been the very big issues that concerned both Britain and France at the time. Trade, investments and many enormous vested interests in the Far East were their concern, and there was the inherent danger that Japan, if crowded out by sanctions and reprisals, might have precipitated a war in which all the powers would become involved. If however that was the position, then there seemed little wisdom in exposing the complete futility of the League to the wide world and emphasising to Germany and Russia and every other State that 'Might' and not 'Right' was still the only factor that counted.

29. In retrospect Connolly's comments on Sir John Simon's speech were not unduly harsh. From 1931 to 1935 Simon was British foreign secretary and had to deal with Germany, Italy and Japan in general and disarmament in particular. He was severely criticised by contemporaries especially for his failure to take a stronger line over Japanese aggression in Manchuria. Nor was his view that 'we must keep out of trouble in Central Europe at all costs' calculated to deflect Hitler and Mussolini from their designs. By the time Simon left office these aggressors were well on their way to making World War II inevitable.

Japan left the League condemned but without even a 'suspended' sentence. Germany and Russia would follow them soon after, and in a few short months the pattern of things in Europe would begin to take a new shape. The picture of Briand[30] at the council of the League saluting 'Mon ami Stresemann'[31] would be but a faded memory, and the example of Japan would be followed by others nearer home.

There was a feeling of depression, a sense of futility and the shadow of other and even worse developments hanging over the halls and corridors of the League when we left for home. It was my second and last mission to the League.

During 1932 when I attended the meetings of the League of Nations I was minister for posts and telegraphs. I might perhaps explain that this is the one ministerial post that would permit the minister in charge to absent himself for periods of a month or longer to attend the conference without seriously affecting the work of his department. The department of posts and telegraphs is a large and important one, but it is for the most part a department of regular routine and does not present the day-to-day problems that emerge constantly in other State departments. In the years that followed, and when I had settled in as minister for lands and forestry, it was quite impossible for me to spare any time for the League or any other work outside my department.

In one sense I regretted this, as I had found the work and the contacts interesting, but, against that, my experience in Geneva tended to aggravate what I fear is an instinctive tendency to be somewhat cynical about the consistent integrity of the whole-time or professional politician.

I returned from Geneva in late December to resume my ministerial work and to find that the situation at home was becoming difficult, owing to political pressure or threats by the Labour Party in the Dáil. Following the election of February 1932, Fianna Fáil had secured seventy-two of the one hundred and fifty three seats and Labour had seven. The chief opposition, Cumann na nGaedheal, held fifty-seven seats. There were eleven Independents: two Independent Labour and four Farmers. Although there was no suggestion of coalition nor even any agreed understanding, we had had the support of seven Labour members during the many stormy sessions

30. Aristide Briand (1862-1932): born Nantes, a leader of French Socialist Party 1894, member of chamber of deputies 1902, holder of various ministries and 'premier more often than any other politician in France'.

31. Gustav Stresemann (1878-1929): born Berlin, entered Reichstag 1906, leader of National Liberal Party 1917, chancellor and foreign minister 1923, main promoter of Locarno pact 1925, Nobel Peace prize 1926.

of 1932. A withdrawal of the Labour Party support would mean our overthrow and precipitate a general election. The so-called Independents and the Farmers' representatives could be really counted as part of the opposition.

This was the position when the Dáil adjourned for the Christmas recess and it was not a comfortable one. To me it was an impossible one for, rightly or wrongly, I considered that as a party, we were, from every point of view, infinitely more progressive than the small Labour group. Moreover, for the biggest and most representative party in the country to be at the mercy or dictation of a small group of seven deputies was, to me, the antithesis of democratic government.

21

General election of 1933 – 'Paddy the Cope' and Donegal – Appointed minister for lands – I go to the U.S.A. – Roosevelt as president – Financial collapse and closing of the banks – Boston and John T. Hughes – Raymond Moley and 'The Brains Trust' – My conference with President Roosevelt – Redemption of Republican Bonds – Boston meetings and personalities – On a German liner with a Jewish professor – I prepare for the World Economic Conference in London

It was on New Year's day 1933 that we decided to dissolve the Dáil and have a general election. I had gone up North for a few days holiday after Christmas and when I returned home I learned that de Valera had telephoned several times inquiring for me. I went down to his office and found a cabinet meeting in progress. I anticipated his explanation by suggesting that they had decided to dissolve and expressed my agreement when I said: 'You've either got to be a government with power or in opposition'. It was, I think, the view of the whole cabinet and it was decided that we would announce the dissolution and the date of the general election. It was about 11 p.m. and we agreed that we would wait until after midnight before advising the press. The legal formalities were completed and several of the ministers went into conference to commence planning for the campaign.

During the course of the night de Valera told me privately that, if we were successful in the general election, he would want me to be ready to start off at once on a mission to the United States. He and I had, on several occasions, discussed the possibilities of using our support in America for the strengthening of our position at home and especially in respect to the economic war and the annuities dispute, but this was the first intimation that I was to be sent on the mission. He pointed out that we had already decided to pay off the Republican bonds which had been bought by our American friends, with a bonus of twenty-five per cent, in lieu of deferred interest, and that it was desirable that a minister should go out and complete the arrangements. He pointed out also that the president-elect would soon be taking over office and that we should make every effort to have him and his administration friendly to our cause and interests.

It was clear that he was very much 'set' on winning all possible support in America to our side and it was equally clear that he was more than happy at the prospect of being able to redeem the bonds to the American subscribers. Having been in America for the later stages of the bond drive, I shared his feeling of satisfaction. Meantime there was the election to be fought! That weekend I was deputed to go to Kerry and address a number of meetings[1] and to preside at the Kerry Convention at which the candidates for the election would be selected. I had just completed my work there when I received a telegram from headquarters saying that there was a demand for me in Donegal and asking me to get there as soon as possible.

As I was a senator and had no constituency, it was immaterial to me where I applied my efforts, but, as I knew Donegal well and liked the people there, I was more than happy to go along. My old friend Paddy Gallagher,[2] better known as 'Paddy the Cope', met me in Derry and we proceeded by car to his home and our headquarters in Dungloe. As time for electioneering was limited, we did several meetings on our way, opening the campaign at the little town of Doochary. Arriving in Dungloe, I found the election work and organisation well under way and in good working order. From my arrival until the eve of the poll the campaign was intense. Four or five meetings each evening was our average. Some of these were in halls, of which Donegal seemed to have an unusually good supply, but many were in the open air surrounded by lighted torches. The weather was dry but bitterly cold and the roads were icebound. My driver, Paddy Dempsey, had a difficult time covering the distance between towns and keeping to his time schedule, but he always did.

Election meetings are, I imagine, much the same the world over, but I have often regretted that I had no recordings of all the quaint incidents, the humour and the earnestness that emerged in that campaign in Donegal in 1933. I was in good form and, I think, reasonably effective, but 'the Cope', as Paddy Gallagher was affectionately known all over the country, was the star artist at all our meetings. He did not 'play to the gallery' nor indulge in cheap comedy, but there was a delightful blend of humour, satire and quaint analysis flavouring all the sound direction and advice that he gave out to the electors. He knew his local history and reminded his listeners of it with that natural, honest simplicity that they understood and loved.

I have always regarded the Donegal people as amongst the very best and most self-respecting people in our island. There was no evidence of any

1. Connolly addressed Fianna Fáil election meetings at Killarney, Listowel and Tralee and these were reported in considerable detail in the *Kerryman* of 14 January 1933.

2. Patrick ('Paddy the Cope') Gallagher (1873-1966): born in the Rosses, County Donegal, left school to augment the family budget 1882, with the help of George Russell started the pioneering Templecrone Co-Op Society 1906, published *My Story* 1939.

cringing, slave spirit there, no cap lifting and no servile playing up to the stranger. They were kindly, genial and good humoured, but they met you man to man on the basis of friendly equality. This had always been my experience with Donegal people and some years later I had interesting confirmation of their spirit. As minister for lands, I had responsibility for the Gaeltacht department and through this section was administered the grants for free meals in the Gaeltacht schools. County Donegal was entitled to some thousands of pounds a year as its share of the grant, but I was not surprised to find that not a penny of the grant was accepted by Donegal. The western seaboard of Donegal has more than its share of poor land and poor people, but they are workers and, above all, they have that fine spirit of independence and self-respect that makes the character of a grand people. It explains why they were able, under the leadership of Paddy the Cope, to establish the finest example of co-operative enterprise in Ireland in one of the poorest areas in the country.

The election campaign finished with a massed rally in Bundoran. It was held at the wide open approach to the sea front on a night of bitter frost. A large bonfire was lit to shed light and heat on the audience and speakers, and one faced the smoke and warmth of the fire, while the west wind of the Atlantic nearly froze one in the rear. It had been an exhausting campaign, perhaps no different to all the others that were being waged in every county of the twenty-six, yet for me it had certain features that made it memorable beyond any other election in which I had taken part. The kindliness of the people, the spirit of resistance to the bullying attitude of Britain in the economic war, which hit Donegal very severely, and the good humour that prevailed, even amongst those in opposing parties made an indelible impression on my mind. I returned from Donegal in time to record my own vote and then to relax and await the results.

It was an anxious period because I realised that, despite our efforts to 'cushion' the hardships of the economic war, the small farmers were suffering heavily under the punitive tariffs and restrictions which the MacDonald government in Britain had imposed. It was a testing time for our people and they did not fail. The final result of the election showed an increase of five seats for Fianna Fáil giving us seventy-seven seats. Cumann na nGaedheal was reduced to forty-eight, while Labour had eight and the Independents nine. A new party, named the Centre Party, had been formed under the leadership of Messrs. James Dillon[3] and Frank

3. James Dillon (1902-86): born Dublin, T.D. for Donegal 1932-7, co-founded National Centre Party 1932, vice-president of Fine Gael 1933, T.D. for County Monaghan 1937-68,

MacDermot[4] and captured eleven seats. It was largely made up of supporters of the old Irish Party and the Ancient Order of Hibernians. This group consistently supported the opposition to the government. I had a pardonable satisfaction in the fact that our campaign in West Donegal resulted in a net gain of two seats for the party in that constituency, and that we were within two hundred votes of defeating Mr Dillon for the last seat and gaining a third.

The 1933 election ranks with that of 1918 amongst the most vital elections that took place in Ireland, in as much as it was a defiance of British bullying. It had one feature that made it different from the 1918 fight and that was the internal opposition that argued the British case against their own people. That had not happened in 1918. Well, it was over, and we were confirmed as the government in power. I was now due for the United States and, almost certainly, for a change of ministry. De Valera soon informed me that he was appointing me as minister for lands and fisheries, later this was to be made the ministry of lands and would substitute forestry for fisheries, the latter section to be handled by agriculture.

The department of lands was one of the biggest and, at the time, one of the most important of the ministries and, while I did not shirk the work, I must confess to a feeling of dread of all that was involved. The ministry of posts and telegraphs was, by comparison, a mild stretching exercise which allowed me a great portion of my time to work with de Valera on questions of policy and to help out on external affairs, the League of Nations and various other activities. Lands would be an entirely different order of things. It was obvious to me from all the reports and the sidelights disclosed at the Executive Council that the department itself was in a semi-chaotic state. Land division had been held up. The annuities dispute and the campaign against payment of the instalments, which had been fostered by the opposition, added to the genuine difficulties of our small farmers, were partially responsible for this. There was, moreover, a vague sense that the administrative machine there was either not in proper gear or was not so helpful as the circumstances demanded. To add to my anxiety was the fact that I was setting off for an indefinite period to the United States while, nominally at least, having the responsibility for my new department. Frank

disowned by Fine Gael for attacking Irish neutrality 1941, minister for agriculture 1948-51, 1954-7, rejoined Fine Gael 1951 and its leader 1959-65.

4. Frank MacDermot (1886-1975): born Dublin, barrister, British army 1914-18, New York banker 1919-27, T.D. for Roscommon 1932-7, co-founded National Centre Party 1932, vice-president of United Ireland Party 1933, senator 1937-42, critic of Irish neutrality 1941, U.S. and later Paris correspondent for *The Sunday Times*.

4. Cabinet of Fianna Fáil administration after it was formed on 8 February 1933. *Seated, left to right:* Frank Aiken, minister for defence; Patrick J. Ruttledge, minister for justice; Eamon de Valera, president of executive council and minister for external affairs; James Ryan, minister for agriculture; Thomas Derrig, minister for education; James Geoghegan, S.C. *Standing, left to right:* Seán MacEntee, minister for finance; Seán T. O'Kelly, vice-president and minister for local government; Joseph Connolly, minister for lands and fisheries; Seán F. Lemass, minister for industry and commerce; Gerald Boland, minister for posts and telegraphs

Aiken,[5] who had been reappointed as minister for defence, agreed to act as my deputy and acting administrator during my absence and this lightened my anxiety. I knew that Frank would put energy and drive into the work, that his views and outlook were fundamentally sound and that real work would be pushed ahead in my absence.

I left Dún Laoghaire to catch the liner at Southampton on 8 February, the same evening as de Valera announced his selected cabinet in the Dáil. I was accompanied by my old colleague, Dan McGrath, who, having been reinstated to the civil service, was taking up his post as consul in Chicago.

The weather was bad as we boarded the liner and continued so for most of the voyage but I had more than enough work to keep me occupied.

Without delay I set about planning my activities, preparing statements on the issues which were involved in the economic dispute between ourselves and Britain and on the repayment of the Republican Bonds. In addition, I drafted quite a number of articles on our lines of policy and on such matters as would serve as useful propaganda when I arrived. I discussed with McGrath the possibilities of contact with Roosevelt and various keymen in his team. McGrath, who was intimate with the up-to-date position in America, was an invaluable help. He had lived many years in the United States and he was now returning after a brief visit home. Despite the almost continuous storm, we managed to have quite an appreciable amount of material prepared for my activities before we passed Nantucket.

We were only a couple of days out on the Atlantic when very ominous messages began to appear on the ship's bulletin board. The first of these announced 'runs' on the banks and the closing of certain banking institutions in Detroit, to be followed for the next couple of days by similar reports from other large cities and indicating an unprecedented financial collapse. It was a rather weird experience. The whole atmosphere of the liner was one of gloom for, with few exceptions, all the passengers were Americans. It was not that they whined or complained, but all, or nearly all of them, had a tense, strained look of anxiety as they paced around the promenade deck. Normally the tedium of the day on an ocean liner is dispelled by games or light entertainment of one sort or another, but it was not so on this trip, and it was a relief when we docked in New York and passed through the customs.

5. Frank Aiken (1898-1983): born County Armagh, member of Irish Volunteers 1913, Sinn Féin organiser in County Armagh 1917, I.R.A. commandant 1919-21, opposed the treaty 1922, and leading member of anti-treatyites 1923, T.D. for County Louth 1923-73, founder member of Fianna Fáil 1926, minister for defence 1932-45, minister for finance 1945-8, minister for external affairs 1951-4, 1957-68, minister for agriculture 1957, Tánaiste 1965-9.

I had sent word in advance to the consul general, Mr William Macauley,[6] that I would be glad if he would book my accommodation at the Commodore Hotel. It had been a favourite hotel of mine in the earlier years, was excellent in every way and provided every comfort that any reasonable person could wish. I was slightly irritated when Macauley informed me that I was 'booked' for the Waldorf. He had two reasons to give as his excuse. One was that it was desirable that as a minister I should be housed in the Waldorf from the point of view of prestige. I always hated that argument, for prestige could so often mean pretence. The other argument was that he had been approached by a number of the Irish-American employees of the Waldorf urging him to arrange for my stay there. This may have had some validity, but did not quite convince me. However, my rooms had been booked and I bowed to the decision.

The question of accommodation may seem a trivial digression, but I have always held definite views on the whole issue of prestige and the essentials for its maintenance. It goes far beyond the mere matter of my hotel address for a couple of months in America.

To me it has always seemed far more dignified and decent to avoid the ultrapretentious, either at home or abroad, and to accommodate ourselves, our guests and our visitors with a service and environment more akin to our circumstances. Let us live up to the highest traditions of Irish hospitality by all means, but let us not try to do so behind a facade that might suit the imperial power of Britain or the mighty Republic of the United States. Our 'window dressing' in this respect has, in my view, been excessive and has tended to be widespread both at home and abroad. It was to utter this homily that I digressed!

Mr Macauley and my old friend, Seán Nunan, met us at the pier. Seán was consul and next in charge to Macauley at the New York consulate. I was glad indeed when the latter told me that he had arranged that Seán would be at my disposal as private secretary during my visit. We had been closely associated in the old days and I knew no one who had the intimate knowledge of Irish-American connections that Seán had. Moreover, he was the most reliable of confidants and the pleasantest and most cheerful collaborator that one could wish to have.

It was early afternoon on a Friday when we landed and I had planned to spend a quiet weekend and get what the Americans call 'acclimated' before I started in to work, but after a meal I felt fit and well and decided that I might as well get busy. An appointment for the next day was made

6. William J. B. Macauley: consul general in New York 1932, envoy extraordinary and minister plenipotentiary to the Holy See 1939-44.

with Mr Martin Conboy,[7] who was the attorney representing the government in respect to the repayment of the bonds. I had met Martin Conboy in my earlier years in the consulate, but did not know him intimately. He was of course well known to all our people in New York as a brilliant lawyer, a man of the highest integrity and sincerely devoted to every movement, political and cultural, that could advance Irish interests and prestige. He had acted as Franklin D. Roosevelt's consul and legal adviser when the latter was governor of New York State, and particularly when the governor had to take action over the Jimmy Walker[8] crux, when Walker was forced to relinquish his position as mayor of New York City.

We had lunch with Conboy on the Saturday and a general 'run over' the work ahead of us. When we had arranged the preliminary plans for dealing with the repayment of the bonds and Conboy had explained the various legal formalities involved, I explained the other purposes of my visit and asked him what were the chances of making contact with the keymen in the State department and with Roosevelt himself. He pondered this for a moment and said he would let me know. Martin had a way of thinking things over that I noticed from the first of our many meetings and conferences. In his office he would swing a little to the side on his swivel chair and remain silent. It would be just for a moment, but it seemed almost as if he were saying a silent prayer for direction and then, quietly and deliberately, he gave you his opinion. Needless to add, perhaps, that this only occurred when he was deciding some knotty problem of law or procedure. In ordinary social conversation Martin was genial, interesting, well read, well informed and the pleasantest of company.

Late that evening, Martin telephoned me to the hotel to advise me that he had arranged an appointment with Roosevelt for the Tuesday morning at his private home in 65th Street and that he would call for me to bring me along to introduce me. That was a hopeful start. I had only arrived the day before and, thanks to Martin Conboy, I had already an appointment

7. Martin Conboy (1878-1944): born New York, lawyer 1903, director of selective service for New York 1914-18, president of Catholic club, New York 1922-7 and recipient of papal honour Order of St Gregory the Great 1926, supported Alfred E. Smith's presidential campaigns 1924 and 1928, chairman of Governor Roosevelt's advisory committee on narcotics 1929, his special adviser in investigation of Mayor Walker 1932, U.S. attorney for Southern District of New York 1933, senior partner in Conboy, Hewitt, O'Brien and Boardman 1929-44 and handled some of New York's most sensational cases, including acting as special prosecutor against Dutch Schultz and later acting as counsel for Charles (Lucky) Luciano and others.

8. James John Walker (1881-1946): born New York, mayor of New York 1926-32, involved in State legislative investigation of corruption in municipal government, summoned before governor Franklyn D. Roosevelt to answer charges and resigned.

with the president-elect. When it is remembered that we were within one week of inauguration day and that a few days earlier Roosevelt had narrowly escaped assassination at the hands of a crazy fanatic, the appointment seemed to indicate Martin's standing with the president.

During the weekend I made deliberate preparations for my talk with the president. I had given the matter considerable thought on the voyage over and had worked on the theory that, if I wanted to gain his interest not to speak of his confidence, it was essential that I should lead the talk round to the subjects that were of primary importance to America. If I could succeed in doing so, it might be possible to create the situation whereby Roosevelt might want to see me and to get my views on a variety of matters with which he and his incoming administration would be concerned.

By the accident of circumstances it had so happened that I was reasonably well briefed on the Sino-Japanese conflict and on the proposed World Economic Conference. I knew that the president of the United States must be vitally concerned with both and, as I had been in close grips with the problems in Geneva, I might succeed in arousing his interest. It worked out that way. I make no apology either for adopting such tactics or recording the fact. It is, to me, an elementary step in ordinary, social manners to express interest in what concerns the person you are meeting, whether as host or guest, and it is equally desirable and often rewarding to apply the same principle on the diplomatic level.

On the Tuesday morning Martin Conboy called for me at the hotel and we were at the house in 65th Street by ten a.m. We were immediately brought up to Roosevelt's bedroom and found him lying comfortably relaxed after his breakfast. He had apparently already read the morning papers for they were spread over the counterpane. We smoked Camels, while we got deeper and deeper into our talk on affairs generally. His contact with Ireland was apparently limited to a visit to Cóbh during World War I when he was assistant secretary to the navy in the Wilson administration. He remembered that visit, because they had nearly a riot in rounding up their men to get them aboard and away from the sirens of Cork and Cóbh. Very soon we were discussing the international situation and he was eager to hear all the latest developments at the League of Nations and particularly the details of the Japanese situation in Manchuria and the attitudes of Britain, France and the other European States. We were warmed up to our talk when Louis Howe[9] came in, rustled some papers and generally

9. Louis McHenry Howe (1871-1936): born Indianapolis, Indiana, assistant editor *Saratoga Sun* 1888, journalist with *New York Telegram* 1907, began a life-long friendship with Franklin D. Roosevelt 1911, Roosevelt's secretary and *alter ego* from 1913 until a few years before he died

fussed about for a moment or two, until Roosevelt said to him in the kindliest manner possible: 'All right Louis, leave us for a while'. I made a gesture of retiring, but was waved back to my chair and the talk continued. After another twenty minutes the attentive Louis reappeared and reminded Roosevelt of some appointment, but Roosevelt told him to cancel the car and gave him some directions.

I felt uncomfortable and looked to Conboy for guidance, but Martin gave me no help. I was uneasy because I certainly did not want to get in wrong with the great Louis Howe. I should explain that Howe had been the strong will and driving force that had been behind Roosevelt during the vital years when he overcame all his physical disabilities to achieve the summit of his career. Louis gave me a hard look as he left the room the second time, which I thought implied that I had sent his whole schedule for the day 'haywire'. However, the situation was not in my hands. It was the gentleman relaxed on the bed and who continued to smoke Camel cigarettes that was timekeeper. The talk continued and eventually after over an hour it was Martin and myself who, with profuse apologies for the long 'hold up', left the room with an indefinite agreement that we would have a further talk in Washington. Martin was on terms of friendship with Louis Howe and I left it to him to explain that, while we were sorry if the long session had cut across his programme, we were not really responsible.

This was my first meeting with Franklin D. Roosevelt and I was deeply impressed. I was not unconscious of the real charm of personality that he exercised and its great value to him as a politician, but there was more to it than that. However he would develop, he was, at that time, full of enthusiasm for the causes in which he believed. He dreaded totalitarianism in any shape or form. Democracy, protection of the underprivileged and the right of all countries to be self-governed made up his creed. The impression that I gave him of the situation in Europe as I saw it at the time obviously affected him, and he frequently gave expression to his views. It was hard to realise as he sat up in bed that this magnificently built man with a fine head and handsome face and a body with shoulders like an Olympic champion was crippled from the hips down, and that only dogged willpower and years of effort had rescued him from being a bedridden cripple for life. I felt privileged to have met him and more than glad that during our long talk we seemed to have found a common ground of sympathetic understanding and respect. His regard for Martin Conboy was evident all through, and various allusions indicated that Martin preferred to carry on his legal practice rather than become a top flight administrator in the 'machine' in Washington.

It was after eleven o'clock when we left the house in 65th Street. It was a public holiday and Martin had arranged that I would spend the day with his family at Riversdale, their pleasant home on the banks of the Hudson. We motored out there and on our way discussed the morning's experience. Martin was more than satisfied and that comforted me. At the same time, I began to ask myself in that introspective way, that I know is one of my defects, what it all amounted to for me? Would I get any results? What, in the last analysis, could I hope to achieve for the government at home or for the country?

For anyone, who takes his work seriously and applies his energy and such ability as he may have to his job, the work of a minister is an exacting responsibility. To be turned loose alone on a mission abroad without the benefits and comfort of conference with one's colleagues is much more nerve-straining. One must just go on making decisions where they must be made and planning one's activities to the best of one's ability. My one consolation was that, in giving me what was practically a free hand, de Valera knew America and knew most of the difficulties to be encountered there. However, sufficient for the day. . . . We had lunch with Mrs Conboy and the Conboy girls and the good humour and the genial family atmosphere quickly restored my spirits. After lunch Martin and I went for a long tramp through the woods and along the Hudson valley and returned to find a few of Martin's best friends assembled for dinner. We had an interesting and pleasant evening with good talk that ranged from high politics to the latest Broadway 'hits'. It was the first of many pleasant visits to that hospitable home, where I was always welcome for a day, an evening or a weekend.

The inauguration of the president was due to take place on the following week-end and Conboy was due to attend it. He suggested that I should accompany him, but later on agreed with me when I expressed the view that I should defer my assault on Washington until all the fuss and excitement of the ceremonies were over. Instead, I decided to visit John T. Hughes[10] in Boston and renew acquaintanceship with one of the best friends Ireland had in America.

John T. was an outstanding character, despite the fact that he shunned all publicity and public office and was always content to work quietly in the background and away from the political ferment that was constant with the Boston Irish. He was a lawyer by profession and a cultured student of

10. John T. Hughes: member of the committee of distinguished Americans who sponsored the American Commission of Inquiry into conditions in Ireland, launched in August 1920, and one of the most active supporters in the U.S. of Irish independence.

Irish history and literature by choice. He had a fine generous nature and a great fund of good humour. Although born in Boston and without ever having visited Ireland, he had learned Irish and had accumulated a fine Irish library which, after his death, would have a special Irish room in the library of one of the universities. I spent a long and happy week-end at the Hughes' home, and before leaving I had committed myself to a return visit which would include a couple of lectures and a press luncheon.

I returned to New York and was kept busy with the preliminary arrangements for the repayment of the bonds. The announcement of the redemption of the bonds by the Irish government caused quite a stir in the American press. The newspaper reporters and the special-feature men were eager to get all the particulars and, having already prepared a statement in anticipation of this, I had no difficulty in satisfying their demands. In this statement it was pointed out that, although few if any of those who had so generously subscribed to the bond drive had expected or sought repayment of their contributions, the Irish government recognised the bonds as a loan and felt in honour bound to discharge their liabilities. We had been accused of default by the British government because we refused to pay land annuities, but our answer to that was that there was neither a legal nor a moral right in the British claim. We were prepared to let the dispute go to arbitration, but the court of arbitration must be an international court and not one limited in its membership to the British Commonwealth. I give here but the bare substance of the press issue. It received nation-wide publcity, and was made the basis of many leading articles and special features in the press generally.

At the time America was very articulate on the question of the British debts and seething with indignation that Britain refused to make even a token payment on account. Simultaneously the British publicists were holding us up to the world as a defaulting nation and justifying the imposition of punitive restrictions on our export trade. The American press and people appreciated the ironical contrast, and I make no apology for having exploited the situation to the full.

On my return to New York, I found further evidence of the financial collapse and the economic blizzard that was hitting America. A number of the banks had closed and long queues could be seen at those that were open. There were bread lines and closed shops, and there were panhandlers seeking help. In the Waldorf two-thirds of the rooms were unoccupied, and new, skyscraper office blocks were empty. I called to renew my acquaintanceship with Mr Alfred E. Smith, known to all America as Al. He was managing director of the Empire State Building at the time. It was at that time the world's highest building, having over one hundred stories and the latest and best in service and equipment, but only a fraction of its accommodation had been rented.

Al Smith had been governor of New York State in my earlier years in America. He had risen from quite humble beginnings to be the most respected citizen of New York and then of the State, and ultimately the Democratic candidate for the presidency against Herbert Hoover who defeated him in 1928. He was outstanding not only in his integrity but in his administrative ability, and his best friends thought he should have the Democratic nomination in 1932 and that it was his religion that prevented him receiving it. Al was an exemplary Catholic who, in his domestic as well as his public life, reflected credit on his Faith and on his home city of New York. I found him considerably changed from the Al Smith I had known in the early 'Twenties'. The old buoyancy was gone and I felt that a sense of disappointment and frustration hung over him. Maybe the times that were in it explained it, maybe his responsibilities as manager of the world's biggest office building, most of it as yet unoccupied, was responsible, but I think the fact that a Democratic president other than Al himself would be in the White House for the next four years was a contributory factor. His grievance was, I think, in many ways justified, for few if any had done as much to bring respect and confidence to the Democratic Party. Some day perhaps a Catholic might be elected president, but the time was not yet and by then Al would be but an honoured memory.

A day or two before Roosevelt's inauguration, all the banks were closed by government order. It was a unique and startling experience to find oneself in the great city of New York with its ready-spending millions of people left high and dry without the cash to make even essential purchases, and to realise that the same situation existed in every city, town and village of the United States. What, I ask myself, would happen? Riots! Wrecking of stores! The barricades! No, none of these. Actually, so far as the visiting stranger could see, nothing unusual seemed to be happening. In the hotel no questions of credit or demands for payment were made and outside it there seemed to be a general extension of universal credit available. It spoke convincingly of the wonderful resilience of the people and of their sense of camaraderie that, before twenty-four hours, they were exchanging stories and wisecracks about the crisis.

After the inauguration Conboy and I went to Washington. The excitement of the installation of the president was over, but Washington was still buzzing with all the new activities, new executives and new planning. The Mayflower Hotel, wherein the consul-general, Billy Macauley, had booked me, was the big political hotel centre and from early morning until early morning following it was a hive of activity. Here one heard the strident tones of Huey Long or observed the more discreet *tete-à-tetes* of the political lobbyists and the architects of the New Deal. Fortunately one could occasionally escape to find an almost monastic peace in the shelter of one's private room. Martin was due to deliver an address at Georgetown University, the famous Jesuit Institution and one of America's oldest universities. Honorary degrees were conferred that evening, and amongst those being honoured was Paul Claudel,[11] the distinguished French Catholic poet, who at that time was ambassador for his country to the United States.

After the ceremonies we paid a visit to the home of one of Washington's leading lawyers who was that night entertaining some of the notable intellectual and political figures in the capital. H. L. Mencken and George Nathan[12] were the two who interested me, most probably because I had long enjoyed their brilliant commentaries on life, letters and the drama in the *American Mercury* of which they were joint editors. However, our real quarry was not either of these distinguished gentlemen but one Raymond Moley,[13] reputedly the chief of the Roosevelt Brains Trust. Martin's avowed object was to bring us together and then leave it to me to make my own way with him. He introduced me to Moley and we fixed an appointment for the following day. From that first meeting we became good friends and were to have many pleasant talks and conferences.

What appealed to me most in Moley was his quiet approach, free from any suggestion of arrogance of breeziness, characteristics which are not unknown in American political life. His thoughtful analysis of any matter under discussion and his almost gentle reasoning in argument were attractive and almost obscured the keen grasp that he had of the many problems with which he had to deal. I quickly realised that he was a man who wanted to do his job well and believed that the job to be done was more important than the fact that, by the Grace of God, it fell to his lot to do

11. Paul Claudel (1868-1955): born Villeneuve-sur-Fin, member of diplomatic service 1892, ambassador of Washington 1927-33, renowned poet and dramatist.

12. George Jean Nathan (1882-1958): born Fort Wayne, Indiana, drama critic, with H. L. Menken co-editor of *Smart Set* magazine 1914-23, with Menken founded and edited (1924-30) *The American Mercury*, founder and editor of *The American Spectator* 1932, author.

13. Raymond Charles Moley (1886-1975): born Berea, Ohio, professor of government 1923-8, professor of public law 1928-57 at Columbia University, assistant secretary of state and member of President Roosevelt's 'brain-trust' group of advisers 1933, editor of *Today* 1933-7, contributing editor to *Newsweek* 1937-68, author.

it. That by no means common characteristic impressed me and perhaps made our later association pleasant to both of us.

Moley, long before the election and when the structure known as the New Deal was being erected, had borne more than one man's share in its creation. During the campaign the grind continued and now, the election over, he was faced with a colossal amount of work if any degree of order was to be restored out of the existing chaos and confusion. There were other members of the Brains Trust, of course, all bearing their separate burdens and working like galley slaves but I think it is no exaggeration to say that Raymond Moley was to Roosevelt the lynchpin that joined the team together on the presidential policies.

On our second meeting Moley, who was almost a prisoner in his office, suggested that we should take an hour's run in the car so that he could get a much needed breath of fresh air. We had a pleasant run during which Moley gave me a share of his views on many things. Amongst others, he referred to the British debt to America and the coming world conference in London. I listened without saying much, but I was somewhat surprised to note that he had an almost awesome respect for the astuteness and craftiness of the British operators. I ventured to give him my own views and some of my recent experiences with them at close quarters in Geneva. I explained that we in Ireland had enjoyed the 'benefits' of their adroit management, but went on to point out that surely the United States were in a very different position. I said: 'It is Britain that is in debt to you people. One would think that you are the debtors from the way you talk'. From that time I deliberately set myself to remove what seemed to be a threat of a political inferiority complex. I think I had some measure of success and I had reason to hope that the views expressed penetrated through Moley to a still higher authority.

We had quite a number of meetings and conferences, all equally pleasant and valuable, and we would meet later in the year in London where Moley would come as Roosevelt's special liaison officer and be caught up in the most torturing conflicts that developed between the members of the American delegation themselves and the pressure of the British and French to secure stabilisation of the currencies. He told the whole story in his book, *After seven years* (New York 1939). It is the most interesting record of the early Roosevelt saga and gives an intimate picture of all that led up to the revolution in the social economy that was embodied in the New Deal. It is scrupulously fair and, considering the treatment that Moley received, more than charitable in its recital.

A few days afterwards I was officially received by the president and, accompanied by our minister, Mr Michael MacWhite, the formalities were fulfilled. At this, my second meeting with him, I found the same genial reception and the same atmosphere of good fellowship with a sprinkling of banter and wisecracking. Before I left he expressed the hope of seeing me later, that he had been talking things over with 'Ray' (Moley) and that there were a few things that we could talk about. I expressed the pleasure I would have in coming along when it would suit him.

A few days later Michael MacWhite gave a dinner in his apartment so that I might meet and get to know some of the more prominent members of the senate and congress as well as some of the leading pressmen.[14] The gathering reflected the esteem and popularity that MacWhite enjoyed amongst the 'Upper Ten' of political Washington. It was here that I had my first meeting with the vice-president, Henry Wallace.[15] Like his father before him who had controlled and edited the leading farmers' journal, he was interested in Ireland and more particularly in the co-operative movement and the gospel of George Russell ('AE'), as set out in the latter's book, *The National Being*. He was of the quiet, thoughtful type, a striking personality and, like most of the New Deal types, fervently opposed to the big monopolistic interests. We had an interesting talk in which I sensed a certain disappointment that we in Ireland had not advanced definitely on

14. Here Connolly seems to telescope two festive occasions. Among his papers are the following:

> (1) Supper for newspaper men to meet Senator Connolly on the 24th of March 1933: Michael McDermott, Chief of Division of Current Information, Department of State; Harold Horan, *Washington Post*; Russell Young, *Washington Star*; Charles P. Smith, Associated Press; George Abell, *Washington News*; Farmer Murphy, *Baltimore Sun*; Kingsborough Smith, International News; Bert Hulin, *New York Times*; Edward Roddan, United Press; William P. Flythe, United Press; Harry Slattery, former assistant secretary of interior (freelance); Guy McKinney, *Chicago Tribune*; Edward Folliard, *Washington Herald*; Robert Allen, Hearst newspapers; George Holmes, International News; William O'Donnell, *New York Daily News*; Thomas H. Healy, *New York Evening Post* and *Philadelphia Public Ledger*.
>
> (2) List of guests attending dinner on Tuesday the 28th of March 1933: Seantor Connolly, minister for lands and fisheries; Secretary of Agriculture Wallace; Senator Ashurst, Arizona; Senator Pittman, Nevada; Senator McNary, Oregon; Senator Couzens, Michigan; Senator Copeland, New York; Senator Walsh, Massachusetts; Senator Coolidge, Massachusetts; Senator Lewis, Illinois; Senator Lonergan, Connecticut; Senator McCarron, Nevada; Senator Murphy, Iowa; Senator Duffy, Wisconsin; Representative Britten, Illinois; Representative Peyser, New York; Henry Morgenthau, Jr., chairman, Farm Board (later secretary to the treasury).

15. Henry Agard Wallace (1888-1965): born Adair county, Iowa, editor *Wallace's Farmer* 1924, secretary of agriculture 1933-40, vice-president 1941-5, secretary of commerce 1945-6, founder and leader of Progressive Party 1948, author.

the lines of policy suggested by 'AE'. Senator Key Pittman[16] of Nevada was of the company. He was chairman of the Foreign Relations Committee of the senate and a close associate of Roosevelt and the administration. A keen politician, he was interested in the introduction of silver currency, as befitted a representative of the silver-producing State of Nevada. We would meet some months later at the London Economic Conference and meantime he was kind enough to give a lunch in the Capital to enable me to meet his colleagues of the Foreign Relations Committee. At this time, I was glad to renew acquaintanceship with Senators Borah and Norris, whom I had met some ten years earlier. Both had grown old since those days but, while Borah looked tired and listless, Senator Norris seemed as alert and keen as ever. Norris had spent the best years of his life fighting the big power-controlling interests and he was now within sight of seeing some of his most cherished hopes and plans realised. The Boulder dam and the Tennessee Valley projects would go ahead now and an amplitude of cheap power would soon be available for the consumers. We met afterwards in his senatorial chambers and had a long and interesting talk. I cannot claim to have learned all his views, but I would venture the opinion that, while he was in favour of the State protecting the citizens from exploitation and that there were certain responsibilities on the government in regard to housing, fuel and power and the general well being of the citizens, he was utterly opposed to anything of a totalitarian control whether from the Right or the Left. George Norris was one of the really big men who left their mark on American life and it was good to have known him.

The life went on in Washington. It was exacting and rather wearisome. There were frequent luncheons and occasional dinners. I continued to meet Moley occasionally and to discuss with him some of the problems that loomed ahead. It was during these that a further appointment was made for me at the White House. I attended at the time fixed, but one of the secretaries came out to ask me to defer it for an hour. He explained that the president wanted to be free from interruptions during our talk and this could probably be ensured by the delay. I, of course, agreed and returned at the time appointed.

It was an interesting evening and the president was in good form and spirits. He asked all sorts of questions about the European situation as

16. Key Pittman (1872-1940): born Vicksburg, Mississippi, lawyer in Seattle 1892, joined gold rush to Yukon territory and later Alaska 1897, joined gold rush to Nevada 1901, competent in mining law and became a notable political figure in the new State, and represented it in the U.S. senate 1913-40, chairman of Senate Foreign Relations Committee 1933.

experienced in my meetings with the 'brass hats' in Geneva. They included the position of the Disarmament Conference, the situation between Germany and Poland, the quality and calibre of the British government under MacDonald and the likely developments in Germany. I gave him frankly my views and impressions on all the matters raised with the qualification that they were only my views and that much 'back stage' stuff might be going on of which I had no knowledge. I told him that, unless there was an inconceivable subtlety going on under the surface, the MacDonald government was just drifting on without any definite policy. Arthur Henderson was fuming with vexation and frustration at the Disarmament Conference of which he was chairman, while at the same time the defence ministries were being curtailed in their defence programme. I told him in some detail of the pussyfoot tactics of both Simon and Boncoeur at the special assembly on the Manchurian question and of my talks with Simon afterwards. I expressed the opinion, which I had already given to Simon, that the League of Nations, as we knew it, was dead as an effective force for preserving peace. The failure to deal reasonably with Germany, when Stresemann and his colleagues were working for an understanding, had created Hitler[17] and the Nazi movement. For that I held France and Britain responsible and the results could not be foreseen, but the future was disquieting. At the mention of Hitler and the Nazi movement, Roosevelt winced and was vehement in his denunciation. He extended his hands, joined them at the finger tips and said: 'It's like that! Germany at the top of the globe, Russia at the opposite pole, both tyrannies, and democracy to be crushed between them.' I can recall the intensity of his talk and his denunciation of both. He talked of Ireland and of our dispute with Britain, and I gave him full details of the background of our problem. He was impressed by our redemption of the Irish Republican Bonds and reminded me that he had mentioned in one of his statements that the only two countries which were paying their debts to America were Ireland and Finland, two of the smallest countries in Europe.

He raised the question of the coming World Economic Conference which was already listed to be held in London the following June. He had not yet got around to a study of the agenda or all that was involved, but expressed some doubts as to the possibility of achieving worthwhile results. I gave him such information as I had garnered in Geneva about it and, basing my views on what I had experienced there, was not optimistic. There

17. Adolf Hitler (1889-1945): born Braunau-am-Inn, Austria, commercial artist 1910, founder of National Socialist German Workers' Party 1919, chancellor 1933, dictator and war-monger 1939-45.

could, I thought, be much talk about international credit, the cancellation of debts and the restoration of the gold standard, but, with a world glutted with commodities and with tariffs in most countries, I could see little hope of a realistic approach. He was obviously worried about the conference and, like Raymond Moley, was apprehensive of things being 'put over' on the American delegation. He was somewhat frank on this latter danger, and I suggested to him that he could take adequate safeguards by restricting the delegates' power to provisional agreement. That, he said, presented difficulties. The delegation would be made up of certain heads in the party, including senators and members of the Foreign Relations Committee, and led by the secretary of state, Mr Cordell Hull.[18] Despite that, I argued that his only safe course lay in limiting their authority and insisting that no agreement should be completed until it was examined in Washington, laid before him in the White House and finally signed by himself. 'This conference,' I said to him,

> is a job for friars in brown habits who are teetotallers. Your senators and representatives are hardly that. It is going to be a big social display where everything from the gold plate in Buckingham palace to the sixteenth-century castle of a royal duke will be on show. There will be wine, women, song and sport and some of your 'birds' may succumb. It would not impress you or me, perhaps, and for very different reasons. You, because you have been used to have all that you required to satisfy you, and as for me, because I have been reared to distrust John Bull particularly when, like the Greeks, he bears gifts.

He seemed to ponder that for a moment and then we went on to other matters, but not until he had asked me if I would sit in with Raymond Moley and others in conference with the secretary of state, Mr Cordell Hull. The suggestion rather shook me for my sense of what was fitting made me rather uneasy. I expressed something of this fear, but the president brushed it aside saying that it would be merely an informal chat, and that he felt that Secretary Hull and the others might benefit by it. He then went on to express the hope that, while I was in Washington, Rex Tugwell[19] and I might be

18. Cordell Hull (1871-1955): born Overton county, Tennessee, lawyer 1891, Congress 1907-21, senate 1931-3, secretary of State 1933-44, Nobel Peace prize for reorganising United Nations 1945.

19. Rexford Grey Tugwell (1891-1979): born Sinclairville, New York, taught economics at Columbia University 1920-37, adviser to Franklyn D. Roosevelt from 1933, under-secretary of agriculture 1934-7, chairman of New York City Planning Commission 1938-41, governor of Puerto Rico 1941-6, professor in Chicago University 1946-57, author.

able to work out something in the way of a trade agreement which would be mutually helpful. I expressed my readiness and willingness to get down to it with Mr Tugwell and said that nothing would please our government more, but I did mention that the 'most favoured nation' clause in most of their international agreements might prove to be an obstacle. His final gesture of friendship was to ask me to convey an invitation to President de Valera to come to Washington and be his guest at the White House.

It had been a long and, to me, an entirely excitingly interesting conference and I took a quiet hour to sort out my impressions and to take stock of it all. Like all his visitors, I was much impressed by the charm and personality of the prêsident and by the intensity of his desire to achieve his ideals for his people. Making all allowance for the fact that he was an 'ace high' politician, who knew all the notes on his instrument, I was convinced then and I still am so convinced that at that time Franklin D. Roosevelt felt himself to be the leader of a crusade for the plain people of America and for the well-being of a world at peace.

The informal conference suggested by the president was held a few days later. Moley picked me up and we went along to the secretary of state's room. It was my first meeting with Mr Cordell Hull. He seemed a benign, elderly gentleman, grave and quiet and rather reminded me of an elderly Belfast friend who was a leading elder in the Presbyterian Church there. There were six or seven others gathered together when Moley and I entered and these included a Mr Hiss[20] who was an economic adviser and, I think, a 'carry over' from the Hoover administration. I felt something of an interloper and said so. Mr Hull was gracious and explained that they were glad to have me. I did not do more than answer the many questions they asked me, but these did shed some light on events as I saw them. It will be borne in mind that all the members of Roosevelt's 'team' were new to the work ahead of them, and that it was due to this fact and not to any special qualifications of mine that my contribution was sought. Doubtless there was in the background all the wisdom and experience of the permanent staffs with a whole legion of experts in their foreign office, but against that it must also be remembered that America had stayed aloof from the

20. Alger Hiss (1904-86): American lawyer and public servant, private legal practice 1929-33, department of agriculture 1933, State department 1936, office of special political affairs 1944 preparing policy for United Nations affairs, attended the Yalta conference in 1945 as one of President Roosevelt's advisers, acting secretary-general for 1945 UN conference in San Francisco, president of Carnegie Endowment for International Peace 1946, denounced as a member of an underground communist network, he was jailed in 1950 but released in 1954 still maintaining his innocence, his trial led to an upsurge of anti-communist feeling and the rise to prominence of Senator Joseph McCarthy.

League of Nations and was not represented there. Moreover, a change in American government cuts deeply into the administration. However that may be, I found the conference with the secretary of state and his attending staff interesting enough without being in any way illuminating or exciting. The secretary himself seemed to be somewhat bewildered by all that faced him and anything but well informed on the issues involved. Moley and I returned to the Mayflower Hotel where he introduced me to the famous Huey Long,[21] the cyclonic senator from Louisiana. Huey Long had all the characteristics of the demagogue who ruled his state with an iron rod, or maybe it was another sort of 'rod', and the old system of sharing the spoils. There were endless stories about him and his methods of controlling his State, but it is not for an outsider to pass comment on them. Some of his political enemies passed the final comment when he was shot dead in his own headquarters.

About this time my good friends, the Jesuit Fathers in Georgetown University, paid me the great compliment of giving a reception in my honour at which four hundred guests attended. They included most of the leading social, political and cultural leaders in Washington. I might have been embarrassed if I had not recollected clearly that it was the minister from Ireland and not me personally that had brought them together. The reception in Georgetown had an interesting sequel. A week later I had a visit from a Father O'Connor at the hotel. I remembered having met him away back in 1921 when I was a guest speaker at the Catholic University. Father O'Connor called on behalf of the president and board of the university to invite me to dinner and to give an address to the students and friends of the university afterwards. It was an embarrassing invitation and for this reason. During one of the many acrimonious debates in the senate the previous year I had contrasted the attitude of Britain to us on the annuities issue with their own failure to pay off the huge debt which they legitimately and morally owed to the United States. I ventured the opinion that our friends in America would take cognisance of the fact and would doubtless call attention to the contrast.

At that time one of the leading professors of the Catholic University was a contributing editor to the well-known Catholic journal, *The Commonweal.* He wrote a vehement denunciation of my statement, resenting my daring to make any comment on what was purely a matter for

21. Huey Pierce Long (1893-1935): born Winnfield, Louisiana, lawyer 1915, senate 1930-5, demagogue, dictator in Louisiana, assassinated.

America.[22] I pointed this out to Father O'Connor and said I would hardly feel comfortable in the circumstances in accepting their hospitality. I went on to point out to him that I had had a long experience in America before I made my remark which incidentally was merely the expression of an opinion. His colleague, however, had had the temerity, after a brief visit of one week to Ireland, to write a pamphlet defending the Constitution which had been imposed by the British after the treaty. Father O'Connor then told me that the article had been the subject of bitter controversy in the journal, that it had done much harm to the university in as much as it had practically dried up their subscriptions to a building-fund which they had organised at the time. They were anxious that I should go along and I agreed to do so. On the night arranged we had a pleasant dinner which was attended by the leading lights of the university and a sprinkling of the top flight political figures in Washington. At a lecture afterwards I gave a brief summary of the events at home as well as a short survey of the economic crisis that was world-wide in its scope. It was published in the Bulletin issued by the National Catholic Welfare Conference and was thus ensured a nation-wide publicity.

It was announced that the British prime minister, Mr Ramsay Macdonald, would visit Washington. The press references were interesting in their surmises as to the reasons explaining it. These depended on the point of view of the controlling power of the paper and there were all sorts of views expressed. Some argued that he was seeking cancellation of the debt; others that the election of Hitler made a firm alliance between Britain and America essential, while others claimed that Ramsay was merely on a good-

22. Fr John A. Ryan, professor of moral theology in the Catholic University in Washington, published two articles under the heading 'The Irish Land Annuities' in *The Commonweal* of 28 September and 5 October 1932. The two articles in the highly-regarded Catholic weekly were extremely critical of the stand taken by the Irish government on the Annuities issue and were extensively quoted in the *Irish Independent.* Apart from these articles *The Commonweal* had been consistently unfriendly to the new Irish Fianna Fáil administration which came into office in early 1932. Alfred O'Rahilly wrote two letters to the editor of *The Commonweal* in which he rebutted the arguments and assertions in the articles in a characteristically able and robust manner. These he also published in *The Catholic Mind* of November 1932, under the heading 'A layman's thoughts No. 4: An American theologian on the warpath'. O'Rahilly's heading was not inappropriate. For instance, in his second article Ryan accused Connolly of 'a piece of crude impertinence, if not of impudence' when he compared Britain's pressing the Irish Free State for the Land Annuities and its own failure to pay the war debts it owed to the U.S.A. In fairness to Fr Ryan it should be noted that from the outset he had taken an active interest in Ireland's struggle for independence. Thus he was a member of the committee of one hundred and fifty distinguished Americans who sponsored the influential American Commission of Inquiry into conditions in Ireland which was launched in August 1920.

will mission to the new president. Shortly before his arrival I had a further session with Roosevelt and renewed our discussion about future events and particularly about the various issues that were to arise at the world conference. It was on this occasion that we went into some detail with regard to our economic dispute with Britain. I made it clear to him that we were fighting tenaciously for our rights; we desired nothing more ardently than to be at peace with all peoples, including Britain, but the facts of history were there and could not be avoided. Our country had been partitioned and he knew that Abe Lincoln[23] had fought a bitter civil war to preserve American unity. We had the Black-and-Tan savagery to be followed by a treaty imposed under the threat of 'immediate and terrible war' by the unscrupulous Lloyd George. Now we had an economic war aimed at the overthrow of the government and its replacement by a more docile one.

Roosevelt asked any questions and had a pretty clear picture of our whole position. He said he would raise the matter with MacDonald when he met him, but he foresaw difficulties in getting anything worthwhile as a result. He pointed out the delicacy of 'breaking in' on the affairs of another State, but at the same time he realised that a hostile Irish attitude to Britain in the United States was not going to help to any undersanding between Britain and the United States. Althought I was satisfied that Roosevelt was sincere and genuine in his interest and his wish to help, I had seen enough of Ramsay in Geneva to convince me that he was a mere figurehead in the coalition government and that, whatever about his past, he was now merely a time-serving politician whose only creed was his pride in his position. However, I kept these notions to myself having to rest content with the president's offer to raise the issue with MacDonald.

On a later and final conference with the president he had a good deal to say about MacDonald's visit but, in the circumstances, I will pass over all that save to say that he told me that he had discussed our issue with the prime minister, whose defence was that he could not carry his cabinet with him on the Irish issue. My comment on that may have been harsh, but I think not unjustified. MacDonald visited the various Commonwealth representatives in Washington and Michael MacWhite informed me that he had received word that he would be paying a courtesy call at the Irish legation. MacWhite was there to receive him.

While these events were occupying much of my time in Washington, there were many breaks in my time there. The arrangements for the repayment of the bonds were going ahead. Martin Conboy was completing the

23. Abraham Lincoln (1809-65): 16th president U.S.A., born Kentucky, lawyer, Congress 1847-9, senate 1858-60, president 1860-5.

various legal formalities and Garth Healy[24] had been appointed to take charge of the office administration. Healy had been one of the original 'team' that had looked after the registration and accountancy end of the business from the time that the bond drive had been launched. He was a most competent and reliable man and an excellent administrator. All the initial planning and arranging meant that I was dividing my time almost equally between Washington and New York with occasional interruptions when it was necessary to visit some of the other chief cities. One such interruption was when I revisited Boston to fulfil my promise to John T. Hughes to attend a press luncheon and address a meeting in the historic Faneuil Hall. It was an interesting weekend and for a number of reasons.

At that time James Curley[25] was mayor of the city and, to put it mildly, John T. had little in common with him. I was John T's guest and yet I felt that, as a matter of courtesy, I must call on the mayor. Feeling was somewhat tense apparently in Boston at the time. However, we solved the difficulty by making our call and leaving my card at a time when the mayor was engaged elsewhere. At the luncheon John T. had gathered together all the leading journalists, and the arrangement was that there would be no speeches but that I would answer questions. Fortunately I was in good form, the questions came one after the other with the inevitable supplementaries and anyone who has experienced the American newshawk in his inquiring mood will appreciate what that meant. However, the questions were not only relevant but penetrating and covered all sorts of issues. It was 'quick fire' stuff and I enjoyed it thoroughly but, after an hour and a half and when the party was breaking up, I discovered that I had not taken the first spoonful from my half grapefruit! John T. and I had a quiet cup of coffee together after the pressmen had gone.

The public meeting had been arranged for the Sunday night and on the Sunday forenoon, after Mass and breakfast, I went out to pay my respects to Cardinal O'Connell. His Eminence seemed much older than he had looked a year earlier at the Eucharistic Congress in Dublin, but he was still fit and vigorous and keenly interested in all that had been happening in Ireland. He was worried about conditions in the States and, I would say, was not very happy about things in Boston itself. We had a packed house

24. Matthew Garth Healy (1882-1954): acting-manager of the Dáil Éireann Loans Office 1919-38, secretary to the Irish Legation in Washington 1938-40, acting consul general in New York 1940-42, acting consul general in Chicago 1942-47, consul general in New York 1947.

25. James Michael Curley (1874-1958): born Boston, House of Representatives 1911-14, 1943-7, mayor of Boston 1914-18, 1922-6, 1930-4, 1946-50, governor of Massachusetts 1935-7, a typical urban 'political boss'.

at our meeting that evening and I renewed acquaintance with a number of old friends who had been active in the Irish movement in the earlier years. Afterwards there was a reception in one of the principal hotels and John T. and our other friends were happy that a representative of de Valera's government had paid tribute and his respects to the Boston Irish.

I had two other important engagements in Boston. The first was to be presented to the State assembly or parliament while in session. I was accommodated on a chair beside the speaker and took my seat, while one of the members was addressing the House. He was not making a good speech, but was vehemently repeating himself with considerable emphasis. When he had finished, I was called upon to address the House. Naturally my remarks were brief and mainly confined to friendly greetings from Ireland to the people of Boston and the State of Massachusetts and a sincere appreciation of all the generous help that they had given us in the past. A more exacting assignment awaited me at Harvard University, where I was invited to address a group, made up of graduates and post-graduates from the political and economic faculties, on the League of Nations and the world situation. It was pleasantly informal and without any sense of strain. Amongst others whom I met at Harvard were Felix Frankfurter[26] and a young Irish American, Judge O'Brien of the Massachusetts Supreme State Court. I had heard a great deal of Frankfurter and his close association with Roosevelt, the Brains Trust and the New Deal. My meeting with him was comapratively brief but long enough to impress me with the brilliance of mind that I had been led to expect. It was understood that he had refused many offers of judicial appointment on the basis that he was fulfilling a more useful service as head of the Harvard Law School by guiding and directing the talents of the law students under his care. Frankfurter was a Jew and, like many of his people whom I have met in America, was completely absorbed in his subject and in the social and cultural development of American life. It would be quite a few years later that Franklin D. Roosevelt would induce him to relinquish Harvard and fill a vacancy in the supreme court of the United States. Having fulfilled all my engagements in Boston, I spent a quiet, relaxed evening with John T. Hughes in his comfortable home and returned to New York.

The arrangements for the repayment of the bonds were practically completed. Such minor legal problems as were outstanding would be dealt with by Conboy, and Garth Healy was installed to deal with the administrative

26. Felix Frankfurter (1882-1965): born Vienna, Austria, to U.S.A. 1894, professor, Harvard Law School 1914-39, American Civil Liberties Union 1920, adviser to President Roosevelt, associate justice, U.S. Supreme Court 1939-62, author.

work in the office. I made a brief final visit to Washington to confer with Moley and a few others on the impending world conference in London and then completed my arrangements to return home. The last few days were fully occupied by farewell calls and hurried visits to my more intimate friends and then I was all clear to go aboard the *S.S. Hamburg* en route for home. There was quite a muster of friends on the liner to see me off and this, I may add, is always an acute embarrassment for me. I have always had the theory that it is by far the easier and more comfortable arrangement to be unaccompanied to a train or a steamer and slip off without having to go through a series of protracted farewells. However, in due course the warning for visitors to go ashore was given and, on the stroke of midnight, the liner was under way and soon afterwards the skyline, that is part of the wonder of Manhattan, was gone from view. I retired to my stateroom but not to sleep. Automatically I began trying to sort out all my impressions and to take stock of all that I had been through during my three months visit. I knew that everything that had to be arranged and fixed up in regard to the bonds had been satisfactorily completed, despite certain difficulties and obstructions that had to be overcome with a couple of Irish-American lawyers. All that was satisfactory but, I argued to myself, after all it was more or less routine work of a business-like nature. It involved conferences, discussions with the lawyers and putting things into order. There were delays and irritations of course, but on the whole these were eventually smoothed-out. It was in regard to my other activities that I was relentlessly cross-examining myself. Had I achieved anything to forward our interests? Had I succeeded in making clear to the American public the realities of our position *vis-à-vis* Britain? Had I succeeded in putting a spoke in the wheels of British propaganda, and in their efforts to have a docile America at the London conference? These and a host of other queries crossed my mind and kept me awake. Ultimately I had to content myself with the feeling that I had missed no opportunity that I could remember, that I had done everything I could do and leave the rest to the future.[27]

At breakfast the next morning I found myself at the captain's table and there for the voyage across I had my place. It was an interesting group that assembled there. There were nine of us and the captain, and of the nine five were Germans or German-Americans. Leopold Stokowski, the well-known conductor of the Philadelphia Orchestra, a Jewish professor of history and art in Hamburg University, an American businessman and I

27. Such self-questioning was typical of Connolly. His friend, Martin Conboy, had no doubts about the success of Connolly's mission to the U.S.A., as he made clear in a report to President de Valera. For this, see Appendix 3.

completed the group at our table. A couple of nights before we sailed there had been a monster demonstration in New York protesting against the pogrom that had been launched against the Jews in Germany by Hitler and the Nazis. From Brooklyn, the Bronx and Long Island, the Jews assembled to join with their co-religionsits of Manhattan in what must have been one of the greatest gatherings ever seen in New York. From many platforms poured fierce denunciations of the new tyranny that threatened the Jewish race with extermination in Western Europe. Leaflets showing ghastly pictures of savagery were distributed and the whole Jewish community was in a ferment of impotent rage and sorrow. It was distressing at that time and yet but a shadow of what the unfortunate race was yet to endure.

It was with some surprise that I found myself seated beside the Jewish professor at table. I thought that it was scarcely tactful to install him at the captain's table surrounded by five Germans and a German captain. However, we found many things to talk about apart from the general table talk and he proved to be an interesting and pleasant companion. It was on the second day out that a shade of atmosphere developed. Something had been posted up on the bulletin board which caused an unfavourable comment from one of the Germans about the Jews. The American at the table, in an obvious effort to ease the situation, made some reasonable comment on the pity of it all, the shortness of life and how we all ought to try to live together and make the best of it. The German in a quiet, smooth voice replied that everything would be all right if the Jews, who made the war and made the peace and grown rich out of both, were kept in their place. My Jewish friend remained silent and I was keeping my peace when one of the Germans spoke across to me and said: 'Now you're an Irishman, what's your opinion?' I was somewhat taken aback and felt that I was being 'put on the spot'. I explained that I did not know Germany and therefore was not competent to speak about what was going on there. I had of course read the papers, but like most people had a distrust of propaganda. I loved peace and longed for a time and a world when people could live and let live, but I hated tyranny in any form and I loathed pogroms. I would hate to be anti-Semitic or anti-anything else. I believed Germany got a 'raw deal' at Versailles and that they had not got a very good one since, but that the danger that I saw was that they were going to make thousands of innocent people suffer for other people's sins. It was a very obvious or even platitudinous sort of contribution, but it eased the table atmosphere and we had little reference to the German situation for the rest of the trip.

That night after dinner the Jewish professor and I tramped the promenade deck for a couple of hours. He was a gentle, quiet and cultured little man. He told me that he was returning after a two months lecture tour in the United States. He found it necessary to do such a tour each year to enable him to live in reasonable comfort in Hamburg. It was hard work, his lectures were mostly to women's colleges and societies in the smaller cities, but it provided him with a couple of thousand dollars to add to his salary and made all the difference in the standard of living for himself, his wife and three children. He was not particularly inteested in making money and so long as he could provide for the comfort and education of his children he was content. He loved his work and his subject, it was his life and he would be happy, if he was left free to pursue it. He was hurrying back home earlier than he had planned, as he had not heard from his wife for several weeks before he left America. He was torn with worry and anxiety and did not know what he was going home to, perhaps his family would be already gone to a concentration camp, perhaps he would be arrested on landing. He concluded: 'Perhaps but what's the good! God alone knows what's before us!'

I asked him if he thought that the allegations that the Jews had exploited the German people in trade and finance during the difficult years had any real substance or was in any way responsible for the Nazi attacks on them as a race. He replied: 'Too many of our people are out to exploit every chance of making money. They are quick to seize on the opportunities and often are ruthless in the use of them. We are not all like that. Many of us are genuinely interested in the various arts and sciences and money is a secondary matter, but it has to be admitted that many of our people in Germany did go after the money and, in the big cities, had many businesses in their hands. Many others, who were not Jews, did the same, but the Jews were noticed and their activities were noted, talked about and made into a gospel of hate.' We had several talks on the week's voyage home and seldom have I felt such pity for a distressed and anxious soul.[28]

It would be entirely wrong if I conveyed the impression that the trip home was one of morbid depression. On the contrary it was, for the most part, bright and interesting and the group at our table quickly settled in to enjoy our short spell together. There was a reasonable complement of

28. In a 'memo for minister' [for external affairs, de Valera?], dated 18 May 1933, Connolly described his meeting with 'Professor Panofsky, professor of art and history, Hamburg' and the latter's fear for his safety and that of his wife and children. Connolly recommended that a request should be made to '[Thomas P.] Bodkin [director of the National Gallery of Ireland], [Denis J.] Coffey [president of University College, Dublin], [A.] Mahr [D.Ph., M.R.I.A., Keeper, Irish Antiquities Division, National Museum of Science and Art] and Mrs [Josephine] MacNeill [wife of the former governor-general, James MacNeill]' to see if they could exercise any salutary influence on behalf of the professor and his family.

passengers and we had the usual evening entertainments with an excellent orchestra. Stokowski was excellent company and discussed nearly everything except music. The captain was a seasoned old sailor and, although he occasionally added an odd word or two which indicated his hope of a resurrected Germany, had a quaint sense of puckish wit. In the privacy of his own cabain he showed us proudly the autographed photograph that he had received the previous Christmas from his old friend Kaiser Wilhelm[29] sent to him from his exile in Doorn. Apparently in the good old days prior to 1914 the former ruler of Germany had been more than once his No. 1 passenger. For myself it was a week of complete rest and relaxation. I put aside all my notes and papers and just lazed. It was my sixteenth Atlantic crossing and would probably be my last and I gave myself up to the undisturbed rest that it afforded.

We touched Southampton in time to enable me to catch the night connection for Dublin and it was good to see most of the youngsters at the dockside when I landed. Gerry Boland,[30] who had replaced me as minister for posts and telegraphs, was there also to welcome me and to tell me that my stay at home would be a short one as I was listed to go to London to the economic conference a couple of weeks later. While I was not altogether surprised, the announcement made me feel tired. I felt that I had had my share of absence from home and I dreaded the worrying anxiety of meetings, conferences and all that would inevitably be involved in the London schemozzle. I had a long conference with de Valera the following day, supplementing the reports which I had constantly sent from New York and Washington. He confirmed the decision that I was to get ready for London but, with typical consideration, insisted on my going off for a week's holiday after which I could get down to work on the conference agenda. He explained that Frank Cremins, who was the principal officer dealing with League of Nations affairs, had been busy on the work for some weeks and was assembling the material and reports from the various departments. He would have these in order when I returned and would be acting as secretary and guide to the delegation. So it was arranged. Frank Cremins and I had a week together working out the details and completing our plans for London and then, with a small team of advisers, I was off again.

29. William II - Wilhelm von Hohenzollern (1859-1941): German emperor, following collapse of German resistance in 1918 he fled to Doorn in Holland, where he resided in complete retirement for the rest of his life.

30. Gerald Boland (1885-1973): born Manchester, member of Irish Volunteers 1913, active in Easter Rising 1916, I.R.A. 1919-21, opposed treaty 1922, founder member of Fianna Fáil 1926, minister for posts and telegraphs 1933-6, minister for lands 1936-9, minister for justice 1939-48, 1951-5.

22

World Economic Conference – King George V opens the proceedings – Prime Minister MacDonald's platitudes – Cordell Hull makes a 'Free Trade' speech – Confusion in the American camp – President Roosevelt's 'Bombshell' – Raymond Moley arrives and the confusion persists – Smuts calls MacDonald and Chamberlain to a 'showdown' on French currency proposals – Pork on Friday at 10 Downing Street for Litvinov and self – Invitations and entertainments – The Conference drags on to failure and collapse

Mr John W. Dulanty was our high commissioner in London at the time, 1933. Later he would be promoted to be our first ambassador to the Court of St James. I had met him several times on our journeys to and from Geneva but barely knew him. I was to see much of him during the succeeding three months when we were in almost daily contact, and I would like to pay tribute to his qualities both as Irish representative and as a kindly and entertaining colleague.

He was a colourful personality with a never-failing sense of good humour and a keen sense for the right approach to any situation that might arise. He was on intimate terms with most of those who 'counted', not only in political and governmental circles, but equally so with the literary, journalistic and commercial groups. He seemed to me to be not only a veritable *Who's Who* for all London but a *What's What* as well. He was, I think, at his best when, after a strenuous day, we would get a quiet hour or two to relax and swap stories and exchange views on all the passing show. Dulanty had booked our accommodation in the Piccadilly Hotel; there we settled in. It was a noisy corner, but it was almost beside the high commissioner's office, an obvious convenience for Dulanty and for us.

The World Economic Conference was held in the Geological Museum in Kensington and here, in addition to the huge auditorium, there were innumerable rooms for the use of the delegates. Committee rooms, lounges, press rooms and every other sort of room provided every comfort and convenience for the army of delegates, advisers, officials, pressmen and all the others that had been gathered together from every corner of the world.

His Majesty King George V opened the conference and made his speech welcoming all the delegates and expressing his hopes for fruitful results. I thought it an excellent speech, excellently delivered. It may have been prepared for him. I do not know but his shading and his variations of emphasis were to me convincing, and indicated an appreciation of his expressed views that was anything but superficial.

The prime minister, Mr Ramsay MacDonald, addressed us all. It must have been a great moment for Ramsay. Here he was, prime minister of Great Britain and Northern Ireland to say nothing of the Dominions and the Colonies, addressing the biggest gathering of representatives from all over the world that had yet been held. He made the type of speech that we had all come to expect from him. It was full of hope and optimism and the things that must be done so that we might 'go on and on' to 'better and still better' things. Later the American secretary of state, Mr Cordell Hull, made his contribution. It was to me, and I imagine to most of the delegates present, something of a shock. Mr Hull made a speech that would have done credit to the most ardent free-trader of the old British Liberal tradition. He did not seem to appreciate how ironical it was that the leading representative of the most highly protected nation in the world should be pleading earnestly for the breaking down of the tariff walls. It was a speech that might have been appropriate, if delivered in the United States senate or to a Democratic convention, but could only provoke a somewhat cynical amusement in those who listened to it.

In due course nearly all the principal delegates from the various countries addressed the conference stating, in broad general terms, their varying viewpoints and attitudes. On the third or fourth day my own turn came. I expressed my government's desire to co-operate and to work for world peace and security based on justice and with all due regard to the rights of others. I criticised the report of the agenda committee for seeming to suggest that a solution must be found within the conventional orthodox system. The real kernel of my statement was in the following extract:

> It may not be inopportune to ask ourselves at this stage if our whole basis of money, exchange, credit and distribution has not broken down, and if we allow that it is functioning is it not merely staggering along? Yet the position in which we are endeavouring to survive today has been built on the system of production, credit and finance that still seems to be acceptable as inevitable. Must we accept it as inevitable? Has it worked? Is it working? These are the questions that we may well ask ourselves when we are warned by the drafting committee that we must do nothing 'to diminish confidence in the banking system', that the 'machine is delicate' and so forth. My

> feeling is that the 'machine' is so 'delicate' that it has ceased to be effective and, as regards 'confidence', I ask where is that confidence to be found, to what extent does it exist today and if there is any indication of its early return?

Another section of my statement had its own implications:

> Reviewing broadly the present position, it is not easy to escape the feeling that the situation has been aggravated by the political and international conflicts of the past. These are not necessarily confined to wars, whether long past or recently experienced but include so-called treaties of peace imposed on weaker states, divisions of territories, border impositions and the like.
>
> I am not referring to the position of any particular country, neither my own nor others, but I think it cannot be disputed that, when might or power exercises its superior force in either the military or economic sphere, then the results are fear, bitterness and a spirit of antagonism that make impossible any co-operation or any approach to a fair and reasonable solution of the problems.

While it is true that I had our own position in mind, the Black-and-Tans, the treaty, the border shutting out the six counties, and the economic war, there was, at the time, the situation in Germany with Hitler as chancellor already sweeping ahead in the building up of a new European menace. That development could be traced back to the treaty of Versailles, but I also believed that the subsequent blundering obstinacy of both France and Britain had been a main contribution to the creation of Nazi Germany. The conference soon went into committee work, and sub-committees, as they were named, settled down to examine and discuss the many-sided problems.

From the outset, there seemed little likelihood of any worthwhile harmony or agreement being reached. In the Monetary Sub-commission many of the central and southern European nations wished to have the discussions confined to the problem of indebtedness. France, Germany, Italy, Spain, Poland and a number of others pressed for this course, but they were defeated on a vote. Efforts were made to secure temporary stabilisation of currencies, but this was turned down, the Americans arguing that any such move would cause a violent price recession. Their qualification of their refusal was to me somewhat bewildering. It read:

> The American delegation has already introduced a resolution designed for ultimate world-wide stabilisation of currencies and is devoting itself to the support of measures for the establishment of a co-ordinated monetary and fiscal policy to be pursued by the various nations in co-operation for the purpose of stimulating economic activity and improving prices.

The French representatives were keen to have currency stabilisation and regarded it as a necessary preliminary to restore price levels. There was a threat of deadlock in the Monetary Sub-commission and this probably accounted for the American promise of 'ultimate world wide stabilisation'. It can hardly have satisfied the French representatives, but with it they had to rest content.

I mention this 'break' because it was symptomatic of all that followed in regard to all the problems that arose in regard to monetary policy and stabilisation of currencies. The conflict of interests was too acute to yield to a solution and, as day followed day, the atmosphere became less and less hopeful. Strange rumours of acute discord within the American camp itself leaked out. I kept aloof from all the gossip of the lobbies and corridors, but I heard enough to indicate the difficulties with which the American delegates had to contend. It was difficult to see how the different viewpoints of the delegates themselves could be reconciled, and it was more than doubtful if they had crossed the Atlantic with any clear-cut programme or definite objectives. Moreover, it soon emerged that in actual fact they were not free to commit their government to any definite agreement or policy. That cardinal fact was the frustrating element that made every approach difficult. While all this confusion continued, various other activities were being pursued and in several of these circumstances forced me to figure somewhat prominently.

At the Economic Sub-commission on Commercial Policy which discussed the subject of tariffs and trade restrictions I intervened in the debate to bring to the notice of the conference the special punitive tariffs imposed by Great Britain by special emergency legislation because of our refusal to pay over monies which we argued were neither legally nor morally due. I drew a clear distinction between what were normal protective tariffs and the punitive tariffs which had been imposed on us. I gave a brief but complete summary of the position. Mr Walter Runciman,[1]

1. Walter Runciman, first Viscount Runciman (1870-1949): born South Shields, president of board of education 1908-11, president of board of agriculture and fisheries 1911-14, president of board of trade 1914-16, 1931-37, 'independent mediator' between Czechoslovak government and Sudeten German Party 1938, lord president of the council 1938.

who was at the time president of the board of trade in the British cabinet, was present. He sat through the speech and did not make any reply so the chairman, Herr Krogmann[2] of Germany, announced that the matters referred to would be put on the agenda for a future meeting. It was the first opportunity that had presented itself for bringing our case before an international assembly and I welcomed it. I had a further and somewhat more spectacular opportunity to raise the matter later when a resolution proposing a pact of 'economic non-aggression' was brought forward at the Economic Sub-commission. I discussed the resolution with some of my colleagues and decided that it afforded the best possible opportunity for a definite indictment of the British policy in the economic war, and I deliberately planned that if possible I would be ruled 'out of order' and that Frank Cremins would be ready with copies of my speech to hand out to all the pressmen present and those who were in or around the conference halls. I prepared my speech carefully, giving all the facts and background of the dispute and even indicating to Cremins the point at which I expected to be ruled 'out of order'. It worked out to the letter.

The chairman was Dr Colijn from the Netherlands, a shrewd Calvinistic looking old gentleman whom I had known well in Geneva. I was giving a brief historical review and instanced the Cromwellian plantations and how the land was given to the soldiers and adventurers when Colijn intervened and said I was getting away from the subject. I replied that I thought there was justification for giving in brief detail the historical background, but Colijn ruled that I must not go into historical details. I submitted that I could not speak intelligently on the subject unless I gave a minimal historical background and Colijn insisted on his ruling being obeyed. I then said that I bowed to his ruling, but reserved the right to circulate to the delegates what would have been my statement. With that I bowed to Colijn, left the rostrum and resumed my seat in the hall. There was an outburst of applause as I did so, but who was responsible for it was a mystery. Certainly none of our delegates or officials would dream of committing what would be a near sacrilege in the halls of the conference and we knew of no Irish people being present. However that may be, the chairman was angry and ruled out all demonstrations, which was right and proper.

2. Carl Vincent Krogmann: born Hamburg, mayor of Hamburg 1933, deputy head of German delegation to World Economic Conference 1933.

The immediate reaction was interesting and more than fulfilled my hopes. The journalists from all over the world eagerly sought copies of the statement and, for at least one occasion, the true story of the economic war was given world-wide publicity. The American press featured the incident and the reference that appealed to me most was that contained in the leading article of the *New York Sun* which, *inter alia* said:

> It must be clear now that the Irish government went the wrong way about repudiation. Perhaps it was not in a position to remove gold support from its financial obligations but surely it might have offered at least a token, say a peck of potatoes to the pound sterling, a reference to Britain's token offer. Or it might have adopted the French plan of declining to appropriate money wherewith to meet stipulated payments but without specifically denying responsibility for the debt. It might even have sent about one-fourteenth of the money over as Italy did.

Some few years later I read a sneering condemnation of my action as I have just recorded it.[3] It is true it was written and published by one who, having served in the British civil service, had been later assimilated into an important branch of one of our departments. To him the procedure adopted and the scene created was foolish, undignified and futile. I have no doubt that in conversation he would have said it was 'beastly bad form, old chappie'. Well that is his point of view, developed in his early training and in an environment to which he still belongs. My answer to it is that we have still the paper walls of England and, as Griffith often warned us, England writes on the one side what she wants us to accept and on the outside what she wants the world to believe. She was doing that in the economic war as she was doing it on all sorts of subjects; I fear she continues her practice to this day. However that may be,

3. Donal O'Sullivan who was not an admirer of Connolly or Fianna Fáil referred to this incident in his *The Irish Free State and its senate. A study in contemporary politics* (London 1940). After mentioning the economic war which began in March 1933 he continued that 'a *rapprochment* might perhaps have been effected through intermediaries at the world economic conference in July, but the will to negotiate was unhappily absent. Speaking on the pact of non-economic aggression, Senator Connolly, the Irish delegate, went back over the centuries to the Cromwellian plantations as an "historical background", and was ruled out of order by Dr Colijn, the prime minister of the Netherlands, who was in the chair. He thereupon left the chamber with his typewritten speech only half read. This inability to discuss present-day problems in terms of the present day is puzzling to foreigners and distressing to ourselves'.

our government at the time was being pressed by our traditional enemy for monies which we did not owe and being held up to the world as defaulters. To me there was offered a unique opportunity to state our case and give the facts as we saw and understood them, and it would have been a contemptible neglect to let that opportunity pass. I make no apology for not doing so!

The sub-commissions continued to meet and discuss various proposals and matters listed on the agenda, but an atmosphere of unreality and futility began to creep over the entire work of the conference. Rumours of disagreement gave way to bitter complaints openly expressed and mostly directed against the Americans. The debtor countries had no success in their efforts to get America to yield on their demands for payments of the instalments due. That should have been crystal clear to them following the discussions which had taken place in Washington before the conference assembled. Britain and Italy made token payments and France defaulted. But there were other and more pertinent causes for trouble. Secretary of State Hull had been having endless trouble and confusion with his own delegation. Secretary Hull had apparently set all hopes on his tariff reduction policy and this was by no means acceptable to certain members of his delegation. Moreover, President Roosevelt had specifically announced in Washington that he was not going to ask congress for tariff-bargaining powers. Overshadowing all this was the question of stabilising the dollar exchange. Several American experts in finance, representing the delegation, had been negotiating with the British and French representatives in regard to the dollar exchange rate and rumours spread that they had reached agreement, fixing the rate at $4.05 to the pound.

Apparently headquarters in Washington had not been kept informed of the progress of these negotiations, but some of the team must have sent a warning as Roosevelt sent the delegation a sharp reminder that any stabilisation proposal must be submitted to him and the secretary of the treasury, Mr Woodin.[4] Secretary Woodin immediately made a public statement on the issue and said:

> Various reports from London today concerning an agreement by the American delegates to stabilisation in some form have been

4. William Hartman Woodin (1868-1934): born Berwick, Pennsylvania, went to work in his father's iron foundry, director, American Car and Foundry Co. 1902, later director of other large companies, generous contributor to the Democratic Party, secretary to the treasury 1933, a talented musician and composer.

> brought to my attention. Such reports cannot be founded on fact. Any proposal concerning stabilisation would have to be submitted to the president and to the treasury. No suggestion of such a proposal has been received here. The discussion in regard to this subject must be exploratory only and any agreement on the subject will be reached in Washington, not elsewhere.

Poor Secretary Hull must have been ready to pack his grip and slip quietly back home. Surrounded with his own team of delegates who were in conflict with him and with one another, pressed by the British and the French to relieve the impasse and save the conference and subjected to the humiliations of criticism and abuse of the American team, his was the most torturing job imaginable. Little wonder that he would complain: 'Everything I do is misconstrued these days'.

It is outside the scope of my narrative to go into all the details that explain the confusion that developed as a result of the deadlock on the stabilisation of currency issue.

Raymond Moley in his book *After Seven Years* has told the whole story, but a few points may be mentioned.

Moley arrived in London about a fortnight after the conference had opened. Prior to his departure, he had discussed with President Roosevelt the whole question of temporary stabilisation and was satisfied that he knew the president's mind on the issue. Despite this fact, he had definitely limited himself in his functions to the position of messenger and liaison officer between the president and the American delegation and consistently acted on this basis while in London.

This did not, of course, prevent the press and indeed all concerned in the conference from rushing to the conclusion that Moley was the voice of the president and carried authority far exceeding that of the delegation or even of the secretary of state himself. Negotiations for temporary stabilisation proceeded after Moley's arrival and, having in mind the terms which he had discussed with Roosevelt, he agreed to the terms of a tentative proposal for agreement to be submitted to Roosevelt. In doing so he again emphasised that he was merely the agent-messenger for the president. The proposal was duly submitted to Roosevelt and after some delay his reply was received.

In it the president not only rejected the proposal but proceeded to administer a scorching dressing down of all those involved. His opening paragraph read:

> I would regard it as a catastrophe amounting to a world tragedy if the great conference of nations, called to bring about a more real and permanent financial stability and a greater prosperity to the masses of all nations, should, in advance of any serious effort to consider these broader problems, allow itself to be diverted by the proposal of a purely artificial and temporary experiment affecting the monetary exchange of a few nations only. Such action, such diversion, shows a singular lack of proportion and a failure to remember the larger purposes for which the economic conference originally was called together.

There was much more in the same strain and the whole statement read rather like a belligerent lecture from a very much annoyed headmaster to a class of disorderly pupils and finished with the final homily that: 'The conference was called to better and perhaps to cure fundamental economic ills. It must not be diverted from that effort'. To say that the message caused consternation would be inadequate. It aroused anger, bitterness and fierce denunciation of America and Roosevelt particularly. It was called the 'Bombshell' and bombshell it was for, although the conference would continue to stagger along for some more weeks, the possibility of achieving any worthwhile results was shattered. It was interesting to watch and to listen to all the movements, talk, discussion and abuse that swept through the halls and corridors of the conference. The Irish delegation was not involved nor indeed were most of the other delegations outside the big powers, and our position was willy-nilly one of interested observers. There was one interesting development however in which I was a silent participant.

The British prime minister's private secretary came to me one forenoon and asked me if I would please come along to a special conference in the prime minister's room an hour later. I told him I was due to attend a sub-commission meeting and that I would arrange for Mr Dulanty to attend. He told me that that would not do, as only ministers were to attend. Accordingly I arranged for Dulanty to take my place at the sub-commission, and at the appointed time went along to the prime minister's room. On going in I noticed that MacDonald and Neville Chamberlain,[5] the chancellor of the exchequer, were at the head of the table, while

5. Neville Chamberlain (1869-1940): born Edgbaston, Birmingham, businessman, lord mayor of Birmingham, minister of health 1924-29, chancellor of the exchequer 1931-37, prime minister 1937-40.

around it were Bennett[6] of Canada, Smuts and Havenga[7] of South Africa, Bruce of Australia and one or two others.

I had no inkling whatever as to the purpose of this hurriedly summoned gathering, but was soon made aware of it when Smuts explained that he had asked for this meeting because he had learned on the best authority that the prime minister and the chancellor were negotiating with the French and were on the verge of coming to an agreement with them for a restoration of the gold-standard by the British. Normally high in complexion, Smuts became turkey red as he denounced these secret parleys going on without the knowledge of the Commonwealth countries. It was a fierce attack finishing with the declaration that South Africa had gone off gold to accommodate Britain at a time when it did not suit South Africa to go off gold. Now Britain, at the urge and under pressure from the French, was prepared to go back on the gold basis. Well they could do so but South Africa would not and he wanted to make that clear and definite.

There was an awkward silence when he finished. MacDonald and Chamberlain sat and the impression I got was of two boys being found robbing an orchard. They had their heads together and the prime minister gave a rather stumbling and incoherent reassurance to Smuts after which we somewhat self-consciously slipped out of the room. I made no inquiries and, although I was meeting Smuts every day, there was no further reference to the matter. It was, I assumed, only one symptom of the confusion and chaos that was characteristic of the whole conference.

During the conference there were endless social functions and entertainments for the delegates and their chief assistants. I abstained from most of these, partly from lack of interest, but mainly because under the existing

6. Richard Bedford Bennett, Viscount Bennett (1870-1947): born Hopewell, New Brunswick, Canada, teacher, barrister 1905, member of Canadian House of Commons for Calgary 1911 and 1925, leader of Conservative Party 1927, prime minister 1930-35.

7. Nicolaas Christiaan Havenga (1882-1957): born Blesbok, near Fauresmith, Orange Free State, Boer war 1899-1902, attorney and partner in Olivier and Havenga 1906, member for Fauresmith in Free State Council and member of its Executive Committee 1910-11, M.P. for Fauresmith 1915-40, member of a delegation to Paris Peace Conference 1919, minister for finance 1924-39, co-founder of Afrikaner Party 1940, its leader 1942, helped to effect the political unity of the Afrikaner people which resulted in their winning the general eleciton of 1948, M.P. for Ladybrand and minister for finance 1948-55, farmer, director of *Die Vaderland*, director of Barclay's Bank 1955-57, in 1931-32 he strongly opposed the move to relinquish the gold standard but was forced by General Smuts and the parliamentary opposition to allow this at the end of 1932.

conditions between ourselves and Britain I had no particular desire to be pretending a friendship that I did not feel nor did I want to figure as the skeleton at the feast.

The first of the big functions was the government banquet for all the delegates. It was held in the Guildhall and carried through with all due pomp and ceremony. In the cloakroom I experienced an overwhelming odour of camphor moth balls indicating the presence of belted earls and worthy knights, wise enough to protect the ermine, the fur and the fabrics of their regalia. Marching down the passage of the banqueting hall to the cry of 'Oyez, Oyez, Oyez' was slightly embarrassing, but I was soon at my allotted table.

Here I had as two of my half dozen companions the two sons of the earl of Derby. The elder one, the Honourable Lord Stanley,[8] was an under secretary at the time. He looked a delicate man and much less robust than the younger brother who was a bright, genial and altogether cheerful companion at the table. Their father had won the Derby a few days before with *Hyperion* and the victory afforded a useful opening gambit in our talk. We had a pleasant and interesting group at our table and I enjoyed it thoroughly, despite the speeches that accompanied the various toasts.

It was the first and only occasion that I experienced the ceremony of passing around of the 'loving cup' and, to be quite frank, the ceremony somewhat disgusted me. When I looked around and took stock of the old boys and the not-so-old boys who drank out of the big silver vessel that passed as the loving cup I silently resolved that there was nothing doing so far as I was concerned. Of course I linked arms and put my lips to the cup, but they were closed lips, not just because I was a teetotaller but because I just could not bring myself to go nearer the trough.

Mr Thomas, the secretary of state for the dominions, also gave a big dinner for the delegates with lavish entertainment for all. The minister made what I thought was an extremely witty speech in which he gave imaginary conversations he had had with various ministerial delegates including

8. Edward George Villiers Stanley, seventeenth earl of Derby (1865-1948): born London, held numerous ministries, including secretary of state for war 1916-18, in an attempt to initiate negotiations between Sinn Féin and the British government he held a secret meeting with de Valera in Dublin, April 1921, won St Leger six times and the Derby twice, close friend of George V, his eldest son Edward, Lord Stanley, died in 1938 when secretary of state for the dominions, his younger son Oliver (1896-1950) had a distinguished military career and held a number of ministries including that of transport 1933-4, he enjoyed remarkable popularity.

myself. I was seated next to Mrs Thomas and commented on the brilliantly clever speech her husband had just made. I was somewhat stunned when she replied: 'Yes, it would be amusing if you had not heard it before'. I switched our talk to some other subject.

Perhaps the most interesting experience I had was when I was invited and went to a small semi-private lunch at 10 Downing Street where the prime minister was entertaining us. I was somewhat at a loss to understand the nature or purpose of this particular 'get-together' for the small company was an extraordinary mixture of personalities and interests. There were several Americans, a few British ministers and Max Litvinov and myself. I found myself seated between Litvinov and a lady who seemed to have a preoccupation about the Christian religion in Ireland. I did my best to enlighten her in the intervals between an exchange of views with the rotund Litvonov.

The day was Friday and to my intense amusement the *entree* served was roast pork. I side-glanced to Litvinov who was, racially at least, a Jew to see what his reaction would be but he was sphinxlike and then I ventured to whisper to him: 'It looks as if they are trying to get at both of us at the one stroke'. The course passed, both of us making our gestures without indulging. I have never been able to decide whether it was the MacDonald Scotch humour, Scotch mist, or purely accidental.

The various delegations had occasional social meetings and I had a few pleasant evenings, one with the Americans, another with the South Africans and a pleasant renewal of contact with Wellington Koo, the Chinese ambassador, and his charming wife.

Smuts was a lively and entertaining guest at one of our own small gatherings. At this he took me aside and asked me if I would go along informally with him to meet His Majesty George V. He went on to tell me that the king had been very much impressed by my speech and expressed the desire to Smuts that he would bring me along informally to meet him. It was an embarrassing proposal. For one thing, I did not accept for a moment that the king had taken the slightest interest in my statement to the conference and was convinced that it was only the wily old Dutch Afrikaner that supplied that bait. The chief thought in my mind was that de Valera had singled out Smuts as the one person at the conference that I should be wary of. He had broken faith with de Valera and had issued statements after his pre-truce interview with him in 1920, although it had been agreed between them that the terms of their discussion were not to be made public. I knew too that, despite all Smuts' assurances of privacy and informality, the fact of any such meeting having taken place would not be kept private, but would be widely circulated. I knew that Smuts was on the closest terms of intimacy with the king, and that he was one of the biggest influences for the consolidation of imperial interests.

I pointed out to Smuts that such a meeting was impracticable and could serve no useful purpose, but would only create mischief for our government at home. I assured him how pleased and interested I would have been to accede to his suggestion, but in the existing circumstances I was sure His Majesty would understand.

Any delegate placed as I was and who had a flair for a good time in the social whirligig of that summer in London might have had the time of his life. All doors were thrown wide open. The House of Commons, various clubs, seats at the Epsom Derby and all sorts of other diversions were available. Lady Astor invited the visiting ministers for a long weekend to share company with the Prince of Wales, afterwards Edward VIII[9] who abdicated. The prime minister had his garden party at Chequers and, to crown it all, I was invited to a special ring-side seat to watch the ubiquitous Jack Doyle[10] being disqualified for fouling a Mr Petersen in a fight for the British heavyweight championship. An invitation to have lunch with their majesties the king and queen gave me an elementary lesson in court etiquette. 'The Master of the Household', I learned, 'had received a command' to invite me to lunch at Buckingham Palace on Tuesday, 18 July 1933, at 1 o'clock. It was explained to me that I had 'to request that I might be excused from obeying the command'. In due course I was advised that their majesties graciously excused me. And so these wonderful opportunities for 'seeing life' passed me by. I have never seen the Derby, and this to my regret, nor the inside of Buckingham Palace nor of Chequers, while the wonders of Cliveden are still for me an unknown quantity. I have never even seen Mr Doyle in the square ring, in which he was, for a brief period, such an imposing presence. There were less glamorous but pleasant consolations in the occasional private little gatherings with intimate friends. Dulanty had a few attractive restaurants on his list and in these we would get together with a few kindred spirits to relax and try to shed some of the gloom and depression that hung over the conference.

9. Edward VIII (1894-1972): born London, king of Great Britain and emperor of India 1936, abdicated 1936.

10. Jack Doyle (1913-1978): born Cóbh, County Cork, joined Irish Guards in British army, successful amateur boxer, later a professional boxer and colourful personality, fought Jack Petersen in 1933 for British heavy-weight title but the bout was ended with his disqualification in second round, thereafter he was better known as a stage-Irishman and playboy than as a boxer, he had minor roles in a number of Hollywood movies.

I renewed acquaintanceship with Robert Lynd,[11] whom I had last seen when we travelled to Belfast by the narrow gauge railway and the long car to Cushendall, and with Herbert Hughes,[12] whose songs had been the delight of our earlier years. There were many other old friends who had settled in London, some who had made their mark in the journalistic and literary world, others who had slipped or fallen by the wayside, but all were interesting and meeting them at a social evening was more rewarding than the formal receptions.

The conference dragged on, though it was obvious to all concerned that it had failed and that for all practical purposes we might as well pack up and get back to our real work at home. There was a sense of unreality at the occasional meetings of the sub-commissions and desperate efforts to get agreement on minor issues to try to 'save face' for the conference, but no window dressing could obscure the fact that the World Economic Conference had been a miserable failure.

It would be presumptuous perhaps to try and analyse the causes of the failure, or to assess the degree of responsibility that rested on the different governments and their statesmen for the confusion and chaos that resulted. Inevitably the American president was the chief culprit in the eyes of the British, the French, and those other countries that were acutely concerned in the whole currency problem. They seem to have overlooked the fact that Roosevelt himself was desperately involved in a domestic struggle to get America on its feet after the most sensational financial and economic collapse that the United States had ever known. There were millions of unemployed in America and every effort was being made to restore industry and provide credit so that something like normal conditions could be restored there. That was Roosevelt's big and over-riding problem and, important though it might be to world peace and stability, what happened in other States had to be of secondary consideration. Having said that, it must be charged against Roosevelt that he did encourage the whole idea of the conference and with such interest and near enthusiasm as to create entirely justified hopes of what the conference might achieve. In the selection of his delegation his judgement seemed entirely at fault, for there was fundamental disagreement amongst them from the beginning. There was

11. Robert Lynd (1879-1949): born Belfast, worked as a journalist in Belfast, Manchester and London, member of Gaelic League 1905, member of Sinn Féin 1907, prolific author.

12. Herbert Hughes (*c.* 1885-1937): born Belfast, musician, collector of Irish folk-music and editor of *Irish country songs* I-IV, after a meeting with Bulmer Hobson in Belfast in 1906 he founded the London Dungannon Club in the following year, he was the Club secretary and among its members were George Gavan Duffy, Robert Lynd and P. S. O'Hegarty.

no defined line of policy apparent, and no evidence of set objectives with the result that not infrequently the delegates and their advisers had only the vaguest ideas on the technical problems with which they had to deal and were frank enough to admit it.

The delegation had no power to decide anything. That, it was argued, was one of the chief causes of their failure. I do not agree with this. Tentative agreements, suggestions, and alternatives could all have been discussed and submitted to the White House to be rejected, amended or confirmed, but the delegation never got within sighting distance of an agreed suggestion until Moley arrived in London. When he did arrive, he found some of their financial experts, outside of the delegation, ready to agree on a proposed submission to Roosevelt for a temporary stabilisation that would be entirely unfavourable to the United States and would certainly not have been approved in Washington. States have suffered through the delegation of powers to its representatives and misunderstandings have arisen on the instructions and directions of plenipotentiaries. We in Ireland know that!

It seemed to me that there emerged in the course of the negotiations between Roosevelt and his delegation, and even between Roosevelt and Moley, a characteristic of the president that would become more apparent as the years went on. This was his tendency to think and believe that if he insisted vehemently enough that a thing was to be done it was already accomplished. He believed implicitly in himself and that his vision of what was right was infallible. Another characteristic which I would condemn as a weakness, and one that caused confusion and annoyance amongst his loyal henchmen, was his tendency to put a new man 'on the job' without withdrawing the one originally appointed and in many cases without advising either of them of the true position. I had several examples of this when I was in Washington and Moley's book reflects the same tendency.

Apart altogether from the American delegation, it was difficult to discover any real worthwhile objective in the work of the big powers. Britain and France, disappointed on the debt issue and later distressed and demoralised at the lack of progress on the stabilisation issue, seemed to have no life left in them, and the same might be said to have applied to the other major States.

Meetings were held and various conferences on side-issues went on, but they all had the same sense of unreality and futility. It was with a sense of relief that we learned that the conference was 'recessed' on 27 July and we were free to pack up and return home to Ireland. 'Recession' was a euphemism for complete and abject failure, and complaints and recriminations on all sides took the place of the gospel of peace and co-operation with which the conference had opened.

23

The department of lands – I try to learn my job – The land commissioners – The 'team' gets busy and we get results – Official figures for land division – Forestry taken over by department – Our German director of forestry – The migration scheme – Mr Commissioner Shiels' review on migration results – The Gaeltacht problems

A few days after our return from the London conference I took up my new position as minister for lands and fisheries. The new responsibilities made me anxious and somewhat frightened, and not without reason.

I was not familiar with land problems and had had no experience of life on the land and even less of the fishing industry. Moreover, I knew in a general way that the land commission[1] organisation had been the subject of adverse criticism all over the country. It was condemned as slow and ineffective and without any urge to acquire the landlord's estates and divide them into economic holdings.

There was a nation-wide cry out for the acquisition and division of estates. Farmers with small agricultural holdings were asking for additions which would make their farms reasonably economic, and landless men, many of them employed on the estates at poor wages, were equally insistent with their claims.

My first job was to familiarise myself with the working of the 'machine', and to try to understand all the varied and complicated sections of the organisation and how they worked out from the first step of acquisition to the completion of the newly-settled farms.

I called the commissioners together and had a frank discussion with them. I explained that President de Valera and the government were not satisfied with the slow rate of progress that was operating in the work of land division, that I had been assured that I would be provided with what-

1. Land Commission: Established under the Land Act of 1881, its main purpose was to work out 'fair rents' under the Act. It was also given responsibility for overseeing the land purchase schemes introduced under later acts. Under the Free State Act of 1923 it took over the estates where landlord and tenant had a dual interest and arranged for the land to be passed to the tenant under the stipulated land annuities. In 1923 it absorbed the functions of the Congested Districts Board. In 1992 the Irish Land Commission Dissolution Act was passed but it has not yet been brought into operation and so the Land Commission continues to re-distribute land.

ever money and staff would be required to expedite the work and that with these assurances it was my job to see that the work was done.

I explained that, as a person who was city born and reared, I knew little about land problems, but I hoped that I could correct my ignorance by a close study of the Acts and the machinery of the commission and by constant conferences with them and with the various heads of the department. It was the first of many conferences for it became an established practice for us to meet once or twice a month to report progress and to keep under constant review the work that was going on all over the country.

I prepared an exhaustive questionnaire for my private secretary with directions that he was to gather together all the information that I required to make me intimate with every branch of the department, internal and external. In addition I had all the land acts to study and digest. The land commission at the time was made up of six commissioners. These were Mr Kevin O'Shiel,[2] S.C., who had been a land court judge in the Sinn Féin courts, Mr J. Heavey,[3] Mr M. Deegan,[4] who was also the secretary of the department, and Mr Sam Waddell who was also chief inspector;' Mr Dan Browne[5] and Mr Eamonn Mansfield[6] were recent appointees of the government as commissioners on the appeals tribunal, but also functioned as ordinary land commissioners. Mr Justice Wylie,[7] a former high court judge in the British time, had been judicial commissioner on appeals, but he is now joined by Browne and Mansfield, the three of them forming the appeals tribunal. Justice Wylie was outside the group of six which con-

2. Kevin R. O'Shiel (1891-1970): born Omagh, County Tyrone, barrister 1915, a leader of Sinn Féin in Ulster 1916, Republican/Sinn Féin Court judge 1919-22, land commissioner 1923-63.

3. M. J. Heavey (1885-1945): civil service 1902, assistant land commissioner 1923, land commissioner 1930, retired owing to ill-health 1934.

4. Michael Deegan (1883-1960): civil service 1901, secretary of land commission 1930-48, land commissioner 1930-51.

5. Daniel Browne (1895-1959): born Listowel, County Kerry, solicitor 1917, member of Irish Volunteers 1918, secretary, department of home affairs 1920-22, when he helped to organise the Republican courts and police, solicitor in Tralee 1922-33, secretary, department of justice 1933, land commissioner 1934-59, chairman of Drainage Commission 1938-40.

6. Eamonn Mansfield (1876-1954): national school teacher 1894, president (1910-11), vice-president (1913) and general secretary (1913-16) of Irish National Teachers' Organisation, principal of Cullen national school 1913, land commissioner 1934-50.

7. William Evelyn Wylie (1881-1964): born Dublin, barrister 1905, served with Trinity College officers training corps during Rising, Easter 1916, attended trial of Patrick Pearse 1916, high-court judge 1920, judicial commissioner in Land Commission 1920-36, chairman of Irish Racing Board 1920-36, chairman of Royal Dublin Society, steward of Irish Turf Club and judge at horse-shows at home and abroad.

stituted the land commission, his functions being purely judicial. The team of six was an interesting and highly competent body and, as soon as we had settled down with our lines of policy defined, gave of their best in hard and constant work and consistent co-operation.

Sam Waddell, well known to the world of the theatre as 'Rutherford Mayne', the playwright, was our chief inspector and was responsible for the big force of inspectors that we had spread over the country. We had been old associates together in the Ulster Theatre where Sam was one of our leading playwrights and actors and for which he had written *The Turn of the Road, The Drone, Red Turf* and other plays. His playwriting and theatre interests in no way militated against his ability and work as a land commissioner and chief inspector. His knowledge of the country was unique and I doubt if there was a single estate or a stretch of land in any part of the country with which he was not familiar.

Kevin O'Sheil, who was a senior counsel at the Irish bar, had been a judge in the land courts of Sinn Féin. His experience there, his legal training and his outstanding ability made him one of our most valued colleagues.

Dan Browne was a leading solicitor in Tralee who, at the request of the government, gave up a highly successful practice there to help us through the difficult period of the Blue Shirt agitation. As secretary of the department of justice, he had helped steer the government through all its problems of legal administration and it was good news to me when I learned that he had consented to join the land commission as a commissioner and a member of the appeals tribunal.

His colleague on the appeals tribunal was Eamonn Mansfield, a national school teacher and headmaster. It may have seemed strange to select a headmaster of a national school to serve as a commissioner, but Mansfield was a unique personality in Ireland. As a teacher and as president of the Irish National Teachers' Organisation, he had waged war against the bureaucratic control of the department of education not only in regard to the rights of the teachers but against everything that was opposed to the national outlook and development in the whole system. This of itself would hardly have qualified him as a land commissioner, but Mansfield was an outstanding authority on the land laws and especially on land commission finance. His heart and soul and mind were in the business of land settlement, and I can say from experience that every hour of his time was unselfishly devoted to that work from the day he joined the commission.

Michael Deegan was appointed secretary of the department and as such was made a commissioner. Transferred to the land commission from the department of justice, he was a good administrator and controller of staff and, if he had not the burning urge for acquisition and resettlement that stimulated his colleagues, he was an excellent department head and gave his full co-operation during my term as minister,

Mr Heavey, who had been a commissioner under the previous government, continued for a period, but retired for personal reasons and went abroad. During the short period of his service under my ministry I found him working whole-heartedly for our policy of acquisition and resettlement and it was with much regret that I learned of his retirement. These men constituted my headquarters staff and very soon we got down to the details of a working policy. At the time there was a total staff of nearly eight hundred, but this would be gradually increased until in 1935-36 we had a total staff of 1,019, of whom one hundred and thirty one were inspectors.

After various conferences and much study a plan of operation was completed. I decided to ask for a total division of 100,000 acres and this amount was to be made up by an allocation of a quota for each county. This I decided was essential in the interest of fair and equitable treatment for each area and it also prevented anything in the way of being misled by aggregate figures of acquisition. For example, it would not serve our purposes to have a mountain which might contain 10,000 to 15,000 acres acquired and reported in our returns which would give little or no land for distribution.

There was something approaching consternation when I made my demand but, backed up by several of the commissioners and emphasising the fact that I had been guaranteed the necessary funds and the power to recruit the necessary staff, I held out for my programme. As a preliminary to our 'big drive', I had all the inspectors from all over Ireland called together for a conference at headquarters. This I asked de Valera to attend. He came along and, after I had introduced him and explained the purpose of the conference and outlined our plan of campaign, he addressed them and made an effective appeal for their earnest work and co-operation. We then left them together to pool their ideas and experience and to hammer out the ways and means whereby our demands could be met. Needless to say, the mere holding of the conference and outlining our needs did not solve our problems. There was constant watching and checking of reports, there were bottlenecks to be broken, there were questions of staff movements to be decided and, above all, there was the rapid examination and approval of the schemes submitted. In a short time the land commission was geared to get on with its work. Inspectors knew that schemes had to be prepared within reasonable time and headquarters knew that the headquarters machinery had to be put in motion to keep pace with them.

Putting things 'on the long finger' for a week, a month or indefinitely had to cease. All this may sound somewhat self-laudatory and nothing is further from my wish or intention. All I would claim is that the land commission was merely doing its job and giving reasonable returns for the numbers employed and the amount of money expended on it.

That it had not been doing so prior to 1934 and that it has not been doing so since 1937 is my firm conviction and I am equally convinced that the responsibility for the position must rest on the ministers in charge.

Lest that may seem too sweeping an assertion, I quote the official figures for the work of the department for the years 1933-1942 with the numbers of staff engaged and the cost to the State for their services:

Year	Staff incl. legal staff	Estimated cost of staff £	Total vote £	Acres divided	C.D.B. Estates acres	Total acreage
1933/34	789	227,765	446,254	32,868	366	33,234
1934/35	860	257,795	1,196,574	97,033	21,477	118,510
1935/36	984	279,832	1,369,474	93,946	6,767	100,693
1936/37	1002	291,181	1,578,379	69,135	4,725	73,860
1937/38	1056	319,520	1,743,146	60,324	2,395	62,719
1938/39	1112	338,740	1,743,080	41,034	3,811	44,845
1939/40	1113	341,840	1,792,028	36,402	2,836	39,238
1940/41	1108	335,955	1,583,672	25,093	1,833	26,926
1941/42	1109	337,282	1,468,547	19,000	2,810	21,810
1942/43	1108	335,119	1,338,533			

It has been argued that the war seriously interrupted the work of the land commission and doubtless this was to an extent true, but the argument can hardly explain the drop of nearly 27,000 acres in the year 1936-37 and the further drop to 62,719 acres in 1937-38. Moreover, it will be noted that the staff of 860 in 1934-35 had grown to no less than 1,113 in 1939-40 and that the staff cost had grown from £257,795 in 1934-35 to £341,840 in 1939-40.

There is another explanation that is often given and that is that the area of land for acquisition is much less now than it was twenty years ago, and that accordingly the estates are fewer and smaller and that acquisition and division will not show equal results for the time and effort expended on the work. There is a certain element of justification in that argument, but not enough to offset the facts and figures which I have quoted and which have bewildered not only me but more important persons involved in the administration of State departments.

An interesting sidelight on the administration of the land commission emerged on the issue of the C.D.B. estates. These are the estates which were formerly under the administration of the Congested Districts Board.[8] They are amongst the most difficult problems that face the land commission and the most worthy of attention. They are all located in the poorest parts of the western seaboard and the aim of the land commission is to acquire additional land, re-arrange the holdings and abolish the 'rundale' system whereby three, four or more holders will have several furrows in the one field. New houses are erected and small compact farms are arranged and allotted. It is slow and difficult work, but from the social and humanitarian points of view it is, in its way, the most soul-satisfying job in the commission.

In 1933-34 the land commission dealt with only 366 acres, but following up our intensive work plan of 1934-35 we succeeded in allotting 21,477 acres. In the following year this figure dropped to 6,747 acres. When we were discussing the programme for 1936-37, the secretary called attention to the reduction in allotment in the C.D.B. estates and urged that increased attention should be given to them. I readily agreed and indicated that I would be satisfied to drop from 100,000 to 75,000 acres in our ordinary programme of division, provided I got a proportionate increase in the allocation of the C.D.B. estates. The ultimate returns, so far from showing an increase, reported a further drop of 2,000 acres. It was no longer, since June 1936, my privilege nor responsibility to seek an explanation. It was just another of the 'mysteries' that the land commission presented to the government after 1936. I say 'mysteries' and I mean that literally for, with the best will in the world, I cannot give an explanation. Only those who are actively engaged and responsible for the administration of the department could give the explanation.

8. Congested Districts Board: Established by Chief Secretary Arthur J. Balfour in 1891, it consisted of a body of commissioners whose duty was to dispense assistance to the 'congested districts' in Donegal, Sligo, Leitrim, Roscommon, Galway, Clare, Limerick, Kerry and Cork. It was part of the Conservative policy of 'killing Home Rule with kindness'. The Board consisted of two land commissioners, five experts appointed by the chief secretary with the chief secretary himself sitting in as an *ex officio* member. The territories under the Board's authority added up to around three and a half million acres with a population in 1901 of half a million. The grants at its disposal were spent on building harbours, encouraging the fishing industry, curing fish, cottage industries and modernising farming methods. Under the Wyndham Act of 1903 the C.D.B. was authorised to purchase extra land from large estates to enlarge small holdings. In 1909 it was granted compulsory powers of purchase. It re-distributed 1,000 estates totalling 2,000,000 acres. The Board was dissolved in 1923 by the Free State government and its functions handed over to the Land Commission.

On a number of occasions, after I had ceased to be minister, I was consulted and asked if I could explain the extraordinary shrinkage in 'output' of work. On several occasions I told the head of the government in reply to these queries that he had in the land commission at least three men who were not only outstandingly competent to direct the organisation but were enthusiastically interested to get ahead with the work. These three were Commissioners Browne, O'Shiel and Mansfield. I suggested that he should consult one or other or all three of them, be advised by them and see that the direction of the work was left in their hands and I thought all would be well. Consultations did take place on more than one occasion and views were frankly expressed but nothing happened and the land commission continued its steady downward course. The 'slump' will be fully appreciated by the comparative returns of the years 1934-35 and 1941-42 as set out in the official reports:

	Staff	Vote	Acres divided
1934-35	860	£1,196,574	118,510
1941-42	1,109	£1,468,547	21,810

Making all allowances for increased difficulties in the acquisition of the smaller blocks of land, there is such a wide discrepancy in the results achieved that I can only come to one conclusion and that is, to be quite frank, that in the years between 1936 and 1942 the land commission did not do its job.

With a steady increase in the staff and an increase in the annual vote, it continued to fall lower and lower in the 'output', that is, the division of land, which was its function and for which it was being maintained. It is not a pleasant survey that I have to make and it is no less unpleasant for some of those, including the three commissioners I have mentioned, who worked so whole-heartedly to complete the work of land resettlement in Ireland. All their efforts were of no avail. They were practically sterilised in their work. They did not always know why and the mystery has not, so far as I am aware, been solved.

The natural question arises as to when, if ever, the land commission will have completed its work?

There will of course be its collection branch which has the responsibility of collecting the reduced annuities every six months from our half a million annuitant debtors. This section must continue until the last payments of the terminable annuities have been paid. There is also the section which must complete the vesting of lands, and there will be the completion of the re-arrangement of the C.D.B. holdings. Outside of these operations, I had estimated in 1936 that, by keeping up our consistent efforts, we should have completed land division in a period of from eight to ten years. Writing now, twenty-two years afterwards, I hear no word of an approaching completion of the work. No doubt the 'machine' is still running, the inspectors and administrative staff are still 'on the job' and I cannot resist asking myself: 'What are they all doing?'

I look back on my period of minister for lands as the most interesting period of my life and for one reason. The reason is that I was given an opportunity to make a really worthwhile contribution to the welfare and comfort of thousands of my own people by establishing them in homes and farms where they could work and live and rear their families in reasonable comfort and full security.

I have written at considerable length of my experience as minister in charge of the department of lands. My only excuse for doing so is because of the vital element that the land contributed to our whole national life and history. Our centuries of struggle centred on the land. Territorial occupation by invaders; seizures of whole areas from the natives and grants to the soldiers, freebooters and camp followers of the conquerors; to be followed by the Cromwellian clearances, the rack-renters and the evictors. The land war, waged by the whole people during most of the nineteenth century, was fought almost inch by inch to regain what had been stolen from them. The ultimate in all that history is the land commission and with it rests the final responsibility for the final chapter.

It may be that the interest in 'The Land' has waned, that our people are turning their eyes outward and seeking a different life in the narrow streets of industrial cities at home and abroad. It may also be that our statesmen have similarly lost interest in the preservation of our people on the land of Ireland, that they are content to revert back to the position when the land should be made available for the investing rancher or the playground for the speculative businessman. I do not know in how far such and similar suppositions are justified. I do know that our policy in 1932 was to break up the big estates, to provide economic holdings and on these to build decent homes in which a family could be reared in decency and comfort. That was the concept we had of rural Irish life in 1932 and it was to that end the land commission was working and working successfully. Why did it slow up? Why did it almost stop? I do not know. I have asked and got no answer. When, in one of our many discussions on the land commission after I had left the department, I told de Valera that my only conclusion was that he had changed his policy, he denied it vigorously. I had no more to say!

With the department of lands went the relatively small but highly important department of fisheries. In other words, the same minister was responsible for both. Soon after my return from the London conference, while I was settling in to my new work, Dr Jim Ryan, who was minister for agriculture, brought forward the proposition that the section of his department which dealt with forestry should be transferred to the department of lands, and that fisheries could be taken over by agriculture.

I had no objection to the proposed swop and so it was arranged. There was much to be said for the change because in the course of their work of acquisition, the commission inspectors would be in the right position to decide on the lands that could be most suitably allocated for forestry purposes.

The amount of planting by the forestry section was at the time, 1933, miserably small. Dr Ryan reported that his chief forestry director would not plan for more than 4,000 acres of annual planting and contended that it would be unwise and impractical to increase that amount, if the work was to be done on an economic basis. Such was the position when forestry became part of the ministry at the end of 1933.

I had consultations with the director and found him somewhat obdurate in clinging to his policy of the restricted area of economic forestry. I pointed out to him that our concepts of what was 'economic' differed, and explained that, if we engaged another couple of hundred men who would otherwise be drawing unemployment insurance, the ultimate net cost to the State would be merely the difference between the two rates. The real reason that I sensed behind the 'Go Slow' policy was that our forestry was being directed by men who had grown up and were trained in 'Demesne Forestry'. Within that sphere they were doubtless excellent forest managers, but for our purposes and for large widespread development they were quite unsuited. It was fortunate that they were approaching the time of retirement and that it would be possible to introduce a new direction and a new point of view in our forestry programme. In the meantime I pressed hard for more activity and had the minor satisfaction of getting some 5,500 acres planted within the first year of action. It was by no means anything like a sufficient amount, but it had at least broken the traditional barrier of four thousand acres to which the forestry branch had been so long wedded.

Arrangements were made for the establishment of additional nurseries, and year by year these were increased. They were well spread all over the country and formed the pivotal centre of large schemes of development. By 1936 we had gradually worked up to a planting programme of 8,500 acres and, with our nursery schemes coming on, we would advance by reasonably rapid stages to my ultimate planting programme of 20,000 acres a year. This I regarded as a minimum for which we should plan, and I thought that we should speedily reach that amount.

There has been a great deal written about forestry in Ireland, all of it well intentioned but much of it not well informed. It has to be kept in mind that in many of the districts, where forestry would be desirable, the forester is faced with difficulties that are nearly insuperable. In the poorer districts of the western seaboard, land, that is in any sense arable, is of almost priceless value to the inhabitants. Those of us, who have seen the small patches levelled out among the rocks and stones and that serve to supply the potatoes and meagre grain crops for the small farmer, realise that, important though forestry may be, the first essential for the struggling holder is to use such land as is available for the production of food. Trees need land and reasonably good conditions, if they are to survive and flourish. The western Atlantic gales constitute another factor that has to be considered. Experiments were tried in various areas. Some were moderately successful, but many more were complete failures, due partially to the poverty and sourness of the land but mainly to the harshness of the winds.

This is not to argue that forestry is not a worthwhile and necessary development in Ireland. No development is so urgently required and no better long term investment so apparent, but it is wise, I think, to sound this mild note of warning to those who, with a sweep of the hand over a wide area in Connemara, exclaim: 'Why isn't all this planted?' In the latter end of 1935 the way was clear to seek a new forestry director and advertisements were published in the principal newspapers on the continent and the United States. Our hopes was that we would secure a really first-class man of established reputation and wide experience of State forestry development and to that end we offered what was, at that time, the tempting salary of £1,300 a year, incidentally, just £300 a year more than the remuneration of the ministers of the various departments.

We had some seventy applications for the position and eventually picked Herr Otto Reinhardt,[9] a German forestry expert who had experience in Austria, Hungary, France and South Africa. Reinhardt was engaged in State

9. Otto Reinhardt (1887-1946): German forestry master, German army reservist, director of Irish forestry Nov. 1935-June 1939, Wehrmacht 1939-45.

Michael Deegan, secretary of the land commission, was the member of the interview board who queried Reinhardt about the state of his health. Edward MacLysaght, the proprietor of a nursery, was another member of the board and complements Connolly's recollections in his *Changing times: Ireland since 1898* (Gerard's Cross 1978) 222-4.

forestry work in Germany when he applied. He came over for interview and we of the small selection board were more than favourably impressed. I was amused by a little incident at the interview. Reinhardt was a magnificent type physically. Standing well over six feet and built like a block of granite, he fitted my concept of the real Prussian guardsman. The chairman of the selection board was a thin and rather delicate-looking man, but that did not prevent him asking the Prussian Goliath if his health was sound. Reinhardt looked at him for a second and then with a mighty thump to his chest exclaimed: 'My healt! I dink I am all right!' He looked it! I had only a few months experience of his direction before I ceased to be minister, but I was somewhat disappointed when I read the progress reports for the two succeeding years. In June 1939 Reinhardt took his annual leave and with his wife and family returned to Germany for his vacation. I think that was the last we saw of him in Ireland and I could not but think that he had his place awaiting him in the ranks of Hitler's Nazis.

Forestry development was slow and during the period from 1935 to 1939 fell much below the scheduled plan. There were practical difficulties, however, which might explain some if not all of the failure. For one thing it became increasingly difficult to get adequate supplies of seed for the nurseries, and equal difficulty was met in procuring the wire netting which was essential for the protection of the young saplings from rabbits. Even allowing for these difficulties, I believe that the forestry section tended to relapse into the leisurely routine of early days. The relatively small areas of land planted, which is the real test, seemed to indicate little or no progress.

Forestry continues today, more than twenty years later, to receive the spasmodic publicity and the occasional attention of governments, and to serve as a gospel of pious aspiration in the speeches of the politicians, but it would be hard to convince me that the necessary drive to secure the real and potential results has, up to the present, been applied.

There was still another section of the department of lands that called for active attention. This was the department dealing with the Gaeltacht. In this section grants and loans were made available to the poorer residents for the rebuilding of their homes or their replacement by new houses. Free grants from 70% to 85% were given, and loans were made on special terms. A worthwhile feature of the scheme was that the department sought and got competitive tenders from the wholesale suppliers of builders' materials, arranged contracts for them and ordered the essential materials, and with neighbourly co-operation in the actual work and free architectural supervision, excellent results were achieved. This scheme, it is only right to state, was introduced by our predecessors in office, and I always regard it as one of the wisest and most socially valuable of the various efforts to help districts of the Gaeltacht.

In 1934 I had the satisfaction of carrying through the first experiment in the policy of migration. The planning and carrying through of a migration scheme presented many difficulties and required exceptional care at each step of the way.

Briefly stated the arrangement was that in some areas, where large blocks of land were being acquired, a certain area would be marked out for a migrants' colony. In our first scheme we decided to plan for twenty migrants' holdings in Athboy, County Meath. Certain preliminary precautions have to be taken before local district opinion is satisfied to show a spirit of agreement to the influx of newcomers. All reasonable claims for increases to existing holdings must be satisfied, and all landless men who are anxious for holdings and are deemed competent and trustworthy must be equally satisfied. Any failure to have the local farmers and labourers content with the plan would create an atmosphere of hostility and antagonism to the migrants and that would kill any hope of success.

Twenty allottees from one of the poorer districts of Connemara were selected. They were all married men with families and picked for their ability to work their new farms. Each farm consisted of about twenty-two acres of prime arable land, and on this we erected a well-built house with suitable out-offices. Provision for the primary stocking of the farm was made and the new migrants were comfortably installed. We had grave anxiety as to how the new migrants would make out, how they would adapt themselves to the new conditions on the rich lands of Meath away from the hills and the seas of the western seaboard and, above all, how they would succeed in establishing good neighbourly relationship with the local people. There were difficulties at the beginning, but time and patience surmounted them and soon our new migrants began to show their appreciation of their new conditions by excellent results.

Following the experiment in Athboy, new and additional schemes were planned and with equal or greater success. Mr Commissioner O'Shiel, S.C., summarised the results in a portion of an address on 'Land Settlement in Ireland', when he reported on one of the larger migration schemes. He stated:

> I can just refer briefly in passing to a large migration venture carried through successfully some years ago. Full details are given in the land commission report. The land commission acquired some 5,233 acres in County Meath from seven owners, only two of whom were

> living on their lands. Almost the whole area was in grass and over 1,000 acres were let constantly to graziers. An area of 2,300 acres went to compensate discharged employees and to provide for deserving local applicants.
>
> On the remaining 3,000 acres some 122 Irish-speaking families, comprising 772 individuals, were settled at a cost of £49,000 all of which, save for the State's liability for half the annuities, was recovered on re-sale. The total cost with regard to buildings and improvements was £104,612 which was about £37,000 more than it would have been had the land not been used for migration, but against this excess has to be put the 2,820 acres surrendered to the State in the West for relieving congestion and abolishing rundale there. The latest returns show that these new holdings carried a total of 1,375 cattle, 210 pigs, 177 horses, 90 sheep and, of course, poultry. Over 700 acres have been tilled, a further 240 acres have been taken by the migrants in conacre, as well as another 388 acres in grazing for which a total sum of over £5,000 a year was paid in rent. These people have acquired tractors and harvesting machinery and supply milk locally, a boon in County Meath, and as far away as Dublin. These colonists are a progressive and go-ahead type that have brought vitality and life into what had hitherto been a deserted and almost manless countryside.

Further on he says:

> In that area there are upwards of 700 human beings now, where there were fewer than one hundred before. Eighty of them have married locally and all of them are living mainly by and from the land, and all are making substantial contributions to the State's assets by their supply of food and animal stock every season and of human stock every generation, to say nothing of their continuous contributions to the State's increasing demands in direct and indirect taxation.

Before passing comment on Mr Commissioner O'Shiel's interesting analysis, I would refer to one factor that emerged when we were planning our second migration scheme. As has been mentioned, our first group of migrants were brought from Connemara, County Galway. Our second venture was more ambitious, as it proposed to settle sixty families. It was suggested that these families should be brought from Donegal, but it occurred to me that it might be wise to bring twenty from each of three different counties. The main reason that I had in mind was that in due course and as the families grew up and reached marriageable age they might find their life partners outside their own kinship. We have suffered to some extent from inbreeding in the remote and isolated areas of the country and with families from Donegal, Mayo, and West Kerry this would be less likely to happen. The commissioners readily accepted that view, and on that basis the new additional colonies were established.

Commissioner O'Shiel's survey of the migration experiment calls for little additional comment from me, but I would stress the important factor that he mentions of the '2,820 acres surrendered to the State'. It was part of the arrangement that the migrants who were allotted new holdings in the midlands had to give up their holdings in the West. These farms were small and much of the land was poor in quality, but with it the land commission was in a position to give additions to the neighbouring farmers and thus convert what were small, poor farms into reasonably economic holdings.

Land resettlement by migration is difficult and is superficially costly but, as will be admitted on a fair reading of Mr Commissioner O'Shiel's analysis, it is a sound national investment if we have not ceased to regard human beings working on the land of Ireland as our best national asset.

Let it not be argued that there is no land available for division in Ireland until an examination has been made of how a great deal of the land is being used by present holders. Drive through the country going north, south or west from Dublin, count the farms and farmsteads that show evidence of life, of tillage, of mixed farming, and there perhaps you will find the answer to the problem of the vanishing Irish.

I may be wrong, but it seems to me that we have reverted to the policy of ranching that our forbears cursed and fought, and that the speculator, with the connivance of the land commission and the government, has a free hand to carry on the traditions of the nineteenth-century landlord. That was not the policy that operated in 1932 and the succeeding years. Then we aimed at having a country of moderate-sized farms with people decently housed earning their living from the soil and stock that they cared and worked. Now, well we have the bullocks and where the bullocks flourish the people disappear!

The Gaeltacht section organised and managed various industries in the remote Gaeltacht areas. I would be glad to pass over without criticism or comment the condition in which I found this section of the work in 1933, but there have been many and varied opinions expressed and a certain amount of controversy on the changes that were effected in 1933-34.

The purpose of these industries was of course to provide employment for the people and the making of profits was not a consideration. At best, such industries could only provide a small ameliorative treatment in the economy of the people, but with intelligent and businesslike management they could be expanded and developed to worthwhile proportions. The chief activities were in hand-weaving of tweeds and the production of hosiery, sweaters, pullovers and sportswear and centres of production were established all down the western coast.

The only hope of establishing permanently successful results in these lines of goods was by having proper designs, perfect goods and service, and proper business attention. To be brutally frank, none of these conditions was being fulfilled and a complete 'clean up' and re-organisation was immediately necessary and was carried through. It was an unpleasant job and caused a certain amount of bad feeling, but there was no alternative. With a new designer and a textile expert, plus a re-organisation of our sales and office department, the Gaeltacht Industries section was transformed into a reasonably competent and efficient business. How it has progressed in recent years I know not, but I still see its products in good-class stores and I think it is no longer necessary to 'job out' the vilest looking patterns of tweeds at one shilling per yard. At that price I was glad to dispose of some 70,000 yards in 1934.

The Gaeltacht industries will not solve the employment problem in the Gaeltacht areas. They have been, are, and will be, but a minor 'sop', or even a cheap political gesture, to the poor inhabitants there. I may have more to say about that problem later.

I have written at considerable length on all that concerned me as minister for lands, and if I have dealt in some detail with what I consider of most importance it is simply in the hope that my experience may serve some purpose in guiding those who come after us. The chief lesson that I think I learned in my period of four-and-a-half years as a minister was that it was a primary essential for the successful administration of a department that the minister must know every section of his department and all the general lines of activity in each section.

That is a formidable undertaking but, as I see it, there is no escape from it. The greatest weakness in a minister will be found if he has not the moral courage to admit to his principal executives that 'he does not know'. He may not know and very few ministers taking over a department do know, but they can learn, they can demand the information, they can study their problems and make up their minds and give their directions according to the policy that they are to implement. To act otherwise is the sure road to becoming a mere figurehead and possibly a weak 'yesman', rather than the director of the administration which he is supposed to control.[10]

10. Ministers meet with mixed re-actions from senior civil servants on taking over their departments. For the recollections of one such civil servant, see Appendix 4.

24

The 'Blueshirt' movement – Government boards and ministers' responsibilities – 'Government by order' – Industrial development – Neglect of the most needy areas – Dublin grows and rural Ireland suffers – The senate is abolished

It need hardly be said that a minister in the cabinet has many duties and responsibilities outside those of the particular department to which he has been appointed. As a member of the cabinet he has equal responsibility with his colleagues for every line of policy that is carried out by the government in all departments. This collective responsibility is perhaps the most serious of the commitments that must be accepted by the minister. Ministers have their difficulties and their disagreements and, while it is the invariable aim to reach unanimous decisions on all issues that arise, the situation can arise whereby a minister, disagreeing on some fundamental proposal, may find himself compelled to quit his position and retire from the cabinet. Moreover, it is entirely desirable that he should do so rather than continue and condone something that he is convinced is wrong or unjustified.

That, I suggest, is the strongest argument against coalition governments. Any cabinet composed of the representatives of two, three or more political parties, all or most of whom are pledged to different and often conflicting policies, can only continue to function by constant compromise of the principles for which their respective parties stood at election. As I have said elsewhere, a cabinet should embody 'a state of mind', based on the detailed policy and programme which the party had put before the electorate and for which they received a mandate.

We were fortunate in 1932 and 1933 in that we had clearly defined our policy and programme of action and there was little room for disagreement within the cabinet on the fundamental issues such as the abolition of the oath and the retention of the land annuities and other monies which our predecessors had been handing over to Britain.

I have referred earlier to the consistent opposition that was maintained against us on the abolition of the oath legislation, and on the land annuities issue. Most of the time of Dáil Éireann and the senate during 1932 was devoted directly or indirectly to these issues. Every measure of legislation, every proposal or motion was diverted to the main opposition track of the conflict between ourselves and Britain. Day after day the dreary talk went on with the monotonous argument that the government was in the wrong and every opposition speech was a defence of the British claim. I was spared much of the distasteful performance. As a member of the senate it was not necessary for me to be in attendance in the Dáil except on such occasions as I had to deal with specific matters affecting my own departments. Against that, I had the somewhat unpleasant job of 'leading' in the senate, where the government was in a minority.

Here the opposition was equally consistent in its attacks on government measures and had the voting power to defeat them and thus defer their effective application. The abolition of the oath bill, for example, which had been finally passed by Dáil Éireann on 19 May 1932, did not become law until 3 May 1933. The senate had the power to delay, and it exercised it, despite the verdict of two general elections. It was the major step that would later lead to the abolition of the senate as originally formed and the creation of an alternative second chamber with greatly curtailed powers.

It was in 1933 that certain elements in the opposition, finding themselves frustrated by the increased strength of the Fianna Fáil government, adopted a new and somewhat sinister line of policy. This was the organisation of the Blue Shirts.[1] At that time Europe was experiencing the full development of the 'shirt' movements which Mussolini[2] had launched in Italy and Hitler had perfected in Germany. Black has been the chosen colour of Mussolini's fascists and Hitler had his Brown Shirts and so the neo-fascists of Dublin selected blue. It was an ominous development. We were still too near the period of civil war and the struggle against the British not to realise the potential dangers that threatened the democratically controlled government of the State. There was anxiety concerning certain departments of the State, such as the administration of the law, and the control of the armed forces. Certain precautionary steps were taken and changes were made,

1. Blueshirts was the popular name given to members of the Army Comrades Association which, under the leadership of Commandant Edmund Cronin, adopted blue shirts as a uniform in April 1933. General Eoin O'Duffy became their leader in July and renamed the movement the National Guard. The basic philosophy of the movement was that of the corporate state. In September 1933 Cumann na nGaedheal, the National Centre Party and the Blueshirts merged to form the United Ireland Party or Fine Gael, with the National Guard becoming a youth movement within Fine Gael. O'Duffy led a brigade of the Blueshirts to Spain in support of General Franco in 1936-37.

2. Benito Mussolini (1883-1945): born Dovia, Forli, Italy, teacher 1901, journalist 1908, prime minister 1922-28, dictator 1929-45.

including the replacement of the commissioner of the Gardaí, General Eoin O'Duffy,[3] by Colonel Broy.[4]

I cannot say what were the immediate grounds on which General O'Duffy was 'retired', as I was in America at the time and read the announcement in the New York papers. I confess that I was somewhat surprised as, from my slight experience with him, I had not considered him as a potential conspirator nor did I form any high opinion of his judgement or ability. However, it was following his enforced retirement that the Blue Shirt organisation was formed with O'Duffy at its head and many, but not all, of the frustrated politicians supporting him. It is only right to add that a number of the leading members of the opposition, including several former ministers, frowned on the new development without openly condemning it. That did not prevent most of the opposition deputies and their henchmen falling into rank and creating an awkward period of unrest and disturbance. It was only for a brief period, however, and at no time did the Blue Shirt movement achieve any worthwhile support from the people throughout the country. O'Duffy's final gesture as a military leader was to bring a contingent of his Blue Shirts to assist General Franco[5] in the Spanish civil war. I have no knowledge of how they fared there, but I do not think his force included any of the leading politicians who had 'goose stepped' with him in Ireland. I missed, or should I say I escaped, much of the turmoil that developed over O'Duffy's retirement and the early stages of the Blue Shirt movement. My mission in America followed by nearly three months in the World Economic Conference in London meant that I was out of the country and delayed for a period of six months in taking over control of the department of lands.

I have already outlined my experiences in that department and its subsidiaries and these covered my administration activities until, following the abolition of the senate in June 1936, I had perforce to relinquish my position as a minister of state.

3. General Eoin O'Duffy (1892-1944): born Castleblaney, County Monaghan, worked as an engineer, an architect and an auctioneer, member of HQ staff, I.R.A. 1919-21, T.D. for Monaghan 1921, assistant-chief of staff, Free State army 1922-23, chief of Garda Síochána 1922-33, dismissed by Fianna Fáil government and became leader of the Blueshirts 1933, his *Crusade in Spain* published in London 1938.

4. Colonel Eamon Broy (1887-1972): born Ballinure, County Kildare, civil servant in Dublin Castle, assisted Michael Collins in his intelligence activities during Anglo-Irish war 1919-21, opposed the treaty 1922, commissioner of Garda Síochána 1933-38, recruited anti-treatyite ex-I.R.A. members into an auxiliary force known as the 'Broy Harriers' to cope with the Blueshirts 1935.

5. General Francisco Franco Bahamonde (1892-1975): born El Ferrol, Galicia, career soldier 1907-39, leader of victorious side in civil war, dictator 1939-75.

As I have said a minister has his very important responsibilities, apart altogether from his specific administrative duties as minister in charge of a department. These included the examination of all major proposals which other ministers bring forward for the consideration and approval of the cabinet as a whole. They also include, or should include, a watchful or even critical observance of the way in which policies already adopted are working out in actual practice. The examination of new proposals involves a considerable amount of careful study, if one is to formulate and express opinions on them. That seems obvious perhaps, but in actual practice it does not always happen. There are reasons. In the first place a busy minister may be confronted with quite a number of such proposals each one covered by a long explanatory memorandum prepared by the department and the minister concerned. It will take time and concentrated attention to give the prepared memorandum that critical examination which it merits and the tendency on the part of the busy or less energetic minister is to leave it aside and depend entirely on the judgement and guidance of the minister concerned. That tendency is by no means uncommon. It is the line of least resistance. It avoids friction and discord perhaps, but it can also mean that a minister may get acceptance for certain proposals which, on a closer examination by his colleagues, would not have been approved.

The second problem which I have mentioned is liable to create an even greater difficulty. To criticise or condemn a line of policy which is being followed by a cabinet colleague within his own department is, to say the least of it, a delicate undertaking. It requires a certain degree of moral courage and an accurate knowledge of the results and effects of the policy as being administered departmentally. This latter is not always easy to acquire unless the minister concerned is fully co-operative and willing to put all his cards on the table. Not all ministers will be found to be so agreeable, and there will be those who will resent anything in the nature of critical enquiry, however honestly or impersonally it may be made. This attitude is, in a way, natural and easily understood. The minister has, presumably, gone fully into all aspects of the problem and, with his officials, has set up the machinery to give effect to a measure already approved. To have to meet criticism from his colleagues may not be to his liking and he is liable to overlook the all-important fact that each of these colleagues has an equal share of responsibility with him for all his administrative decisions and actions.

The argument that all cabinet decisions must eventually find their confirmation or rejection by legislation in the Oireachtas does not adequately meet the situation. In modern legislation, due to the complexity and urgency of the many problems that arise, 'Government by Order' has become a universal practice. Granted that, within certain limits, 'Statutory Orders' form an essential part of the machinery of government, the use and abuse of these orders by ministers has been and is a real danger.

No less has been the development whereby a minister bluntly disavows any departmental or government responsibility for any action that may be taken by any of the numerous boards that he may have created within his department.

These boards have been set up by government legislation, the government has selected the personnel of the boards, and has provided the necessary funds and credits enabling the boards to carry on their work. In many cases these boards have a complete monopoly of services which the public must use, and in all cases they are subordinate departments of the government. It is agreed that, in the day-to-day control and administration of the work entrusted to the board, all unnecessary interference should be avoided, but that should not excuse the minister or the government from its responsibility of seeing that the people's interests are protected.

On the whole the people have been well served by the boards created by the government, but there have been occasions when serious and justifiable grievances have been raised in the Dáil to be met by the peremptory reply that: 'The minister has no function or responsibility in the matter'. In my opinion he has, if the matter is of sufficient importance to the majority of the citizens who are dependent on a monopoly service as the only one available and who have provided the capital to create it.

I have emphasised these important factors of governmental administration because they have steadily grown in recent years and because they are a real danger to the basis of democratic government. The present lack of interest on the part of the ordinary people in what the government does or fails to do seems to me to have reached an 'all time low'. During my period in the ministry there was or seemed to be a live alertness that exists no longer and this tended to make both ministers and departments careful in their administration and conscious of the fact that they were the servants and not the masters of the people. If this apathy is not replaced by a reawakening of active interest in political and governmental affairs by the young people of Ireland, then the future is by no means bright.

It is a difficult and delicate business to refer to all or any of my experiences as a member of the cabinet as distinct from my personal and departmental activities. Apart from the legal or other restrictions defining the confidential nature of cabinet procedure, there is an instinctive reticence which forbids any abuse of the privileged position that one happened to occupy.

In these days we seem to be surfeited with disclosures, attacks and counter-attacks, as well as dissections of personal character, motives and all sorts of extraneous matter. Statesmen, politicians and army chiefs contribute their share of what satisfies the appetite of the readers of the Sunday newspapers. If their contributions fail to supply the spice of conflict, bitter criticism or a breath of scandal, then they are unlikely to make the headlines.

Let me, therefore, try to summarise briefly and dispassionately my recollections of the period from March 1932 to June 1936, during which I was a member of the 'Front Bench'. It was a period of intense activity, during which every effort was concentrated on giving effect to the main issues on which we had been elected to office. The major stumbling block to the full democratic representation of the twenty-six counties in the Dáil had been removed. The abolition of the oath from the Constitution was a slow process, made so by the unconscionable opposition that I have already described. The chief burden of work in planning and steering the various measures through the Oireachtas rested on de Valera who, apart from being president of the executive, was also minister for foreign affairs. In this, as in all the other vital issues affecting our relations with Great Britain, he had of course the ardent support of the entire cabinet. I think I can say with justification that no group, cabinet or otherwise, could have worked together with such harmony as did the government during the years I was associated with it. We had, of course, differences of opinion on many matters, but they were on minor issues and our concentration on the major problems, guided with infinite patience by de Valera, invariably resolved them.

Most of the ministers were more than fully occupied by the work of their respective departments and this, with the constant attendance to their parliamentary duties, left too little time for critical attention to the work of their colleagues. Apart from the legislation necessary to amend the Constitution and remove the oath, and the changes required to give authority for the retention of the monies hitherto transferred to Britain, we were committed to a speedy implementation of our industrial development policy and our programme of land division.

From the day on which we assumed office the planning of ways and means to protect our home manufacturers and to create new productive organisations was commenced. It was a staggering undertaking that had to be faced by the minister for industry and commerce and his department. It involved the imposition of tariffs, the operation of quota orders, and a spate of legislative measures, most of which provided the opposition with opportunities for long, obstructive debates. In the latter we had endless repetitions of the same arguments that were made on the oath bill, the economic war and on our relationship with Britain. The speeches are all on record and to be found in the official reports. They provide a rather depressing commentary on the attitude of the opposition party of those years.

The rush to protect our existing industries and the market for our new enterprises gave me a considerable amount of anxiety at that time. I realised that, while many of our manufacturers would not abuse the favourable position which the greatly increased protection would give them, our policy would open wide the doors for all sorts of 'get-rich-quick' exploiters. I had been sufficiently long in trade to know of the many devices that could be adopted to exploit the public and convert a protective tariff into a profiteering one. There was also the problem of the foreign manufacturer who found it profitable to open a branch factory in Ireland and retain and expand his existing trade here, taking full advance of the enhanced profit margin ensured by the tariff imposed. Efforts to circumvent this latter problem were made and a Control of Manufacturers Act was passed in the Oireachtas, but enough loopholes were found to evade the obstacles that the Act provided. As time went on my anxieties and fears were replaced by the conviction that we were in fact creating around us a circle of quick-thinking, money-making gentlemen who were not slow in exploiting the situation to its uttermost limits.

It was a worrying situation, one that I feared from the beginning, but there was not much that I could do about it. Speedy action was necessary and the situation created by the economic war increased the urgency. I discussed the position frequently with my colleagues and still more frequently with de Valera but, in the last analysis, the problems were those of the minister for industry and commerce who was worn to exhaustion trying to reach on all the load of work which was his. Apart from that, my own department and the big drive for land division and re-settlement was keeping me hard at work for a twelve-hour day.

It is not my intention to submit here an exhaustive analysis of our industrial development since 1932. It would be a job worth tackling and I would suggest it as a suitable subject for a thesis by one of our university students in economics. I have, however, one definite protest to record against the policy of the department and its minister. We had two planks included in the Fianna Fáil platform when we were appealing to the electorate. One was the decentralisation of industry, and the other was the preservation and development of the Gaeltacht areas. They were not precisely correlated, but it was definitely understood that, if the people of the Gaeltacht were to be saved from extinction by emigration and otherwise, work must be provided for them. A limited amount of decentralisation was effected in as much as factories were started in many of the larger provincial towns. It was limited, for after more than twenty years activity a survey is hardly needed to convince us that most of the manufacturing industries are centred in Dublin city with a sprinkling scattered over the more important east coast towns. Our vision of potential development prior to 1932 was not distorted, it was obliterated. What was that vision? It was that the country should become, in so far as our natural resources permitted, self-supporting and provide for our needs by the labour and energy of our own people: that the ranch-lands should be taken over and divided to provide economic farms by the land commission with suitable houses and out-offices: that factories and industrial plants would be placed where practicable in those areas where it was most essential to provide employment and halt the flow of emigration.

I have in an earlier publication *How does she stand* (Dublin 1953) ventured to examine the position and see how far we have drifted from the policy preached prior to 1932 and I feel justified in quoting it here:

> Perhaps the chief complaint should be made against the failure to decentralise the new industries and to spread them widely throughout the State. Many reasons will be given to show that it was not possible to do so, but these will not, in most cases, bear examination.
>
> It is true that there are industries which, by their very nature, must be located at or near a port. But it is also true that many industries that are located in the city of Dublin could, with relatively little inconvenience and with no economic disadvantage to the industry itself, have been spread over the most needy and poorest areas along the western seaboard.
>
> Of course the manufacturer objected to 'going west' or indeed to go anywhere outside Dublin, particularly if he was one of the many British industrialists who opened his Irish factory with its nominal fifty-one per cent of Irish capital. In most cases he got his way. Well, we have the result today and, mark you, it is a permanent result, for factories and workshops, once established, cannot easily be transported to new areas.
>
> The result is a grossly overgrown Dublin now holding within its boundaries practically one-fifth of the entire population of the State.

> I have said that in most cases the manufacturer objected to going west or anywhere outside Dublin. It is agreed that there was no power to compel him to go where he was sent any more than there was any power to bring him in at all or to get him to start at all. The State was, however, giving him protection and a tariff which in some cases amounted to a practical monopoly and there was every justification for the State and its department making the granting of the protective tariff conditional on the factory being located in one of a number of areas selected by the department.
>
> It was surely ironical to read within the past few months the statement of one of our ministers that: 'it was realised that it would be necessary to establish new industries in the poorer and remote areas of the West'.
>
> The fact was realised many years ago and long before the period, over twenty years ago, when the existing ministry first took office. At that time we had the illusion that, with protective tariffs and State guidance and direction, we might hope to see the western areas from Donegal to West Cork getting their due share of the production work necessary for our home market. Instead we have our Dublin, the pride of the country, the source of admiration to our tourists with its extravagantly expensive hotels and restaurants, its hundreds of thousands of picture 'queuers', its pre-1914 Viennese atmosphere, while rural Ireland and that Gaeltacht, which we were assured contains all that is best in the Irish nation, steadily shrinks in hope and population.

That was written in 1953 and now, 1959, I see no reason to alter the opinion expressed. If I were to do so, it would be to stress the further deterioration that the intervening years have brought and the continuous increase in the number of our departing emigrants.

My years in the ministry, 1932-36, were for the most part the primary years of development in the industrial sphere, but even then the symptoms and trends were obvious. I had many long and earnest discussions with de Valera on this aspect of our development. He expressed his anxiety and concern but, as I later experienced in regard to the 'slow down' policy of the land commission, nothing was done about it. This has always been one of the major mysteries of my whole career. I have tried honestly to find the answer and the reasons, but so far without success. I will have reason to refer later to the aftermath, but my concern with the mis-direction of our industrial policy was only secondary to my main job of administering the land commission and creating as many home farms for families as possible. These two interests constituted in the main my ministerial life, and to say that I am bitterly disappointed and disillusioned by what followed would be a gross understatement.

Perhaps my whole concept of Irish development is all wrong. Perhaps, when all is said and done, we do want Ireland as a prosperous ranch for the favoured few, and that we now agree with the landlord's scheme of plenty of bullocks and very few workers. It makes one think of the days of the land war, the evictions and clearances and all that accompanied the bitter struggle for the home and the little holding. Maybe that sounds like gross exaggeration but let us face the facts and what are they?

More and more are the big holders of land creeping into our life in Ireland, and less and less is the land commission exercising its functions and powers to settle the small man in a comfortable farm-home and unit of land. Our balance of trade depends more and more on the export of fat and store cattle. That means bullocks and it is my deep-set conviction that the more we encourage the production of bullocks the more we throw across the gangway for the emigrants. In the days immediately preceding our election as a government I had an experience which left an indelible imprint on my memory. I had a good friend down in the midlands. He was a grand type of good Irish manhood, handsome, intelligent and the pleasantest of company. He was bringing me out for tea to his home, and called for me with the family car. On our way out he called at one of the shops where he purchased a pound of butter, a couple of pounds of tomatoes and several heads of lettuce. We proceeded to his home which was not a mansion, but so nearly one as to make no difference. We had a delightful meal presided over by his mother, and in which we were joined by his father and two brothers. It was a very pleasant evening. Later I remembered the purchases, butter, tomatoes, lettuce, and wondered!

That family owned and 'ran' a holding of over six hundred acres as well as another 'out farm' of over two hundred, in all between eight and nine hundred acres. They employed three or four herds who were paid, in 1929, about a pound a week with a free cottage and half-an-acre. The young men journeyed to the fairs throughout the country, bought young stock and turned them on to their pastures. It was a good life for them. They were free at any time to go to the races and coursing meetings, while their profit margin was being earned by the silent beasts cared for by the herdsmen.

I am giving the bare facts without embellishment. The amount of land held may be greater than the average ranch of that time. I do not know, but from the little experience I had the situation of my friend and his family was more or less typical of those who lived and swore by the bullock. I leave it to the agricultural economist to figure out how many families could have been bred, reared and supported on that holding of over six hundred acres not to mention the 'out farm' of over two hundred.

I had another experience of a different nature but linked up with this all-important matter of the use of land for living people and the break up of the big ranches.

It was during the economic war and one of the Roscommon deputies asked me to accompany him and address a couple of open air meetings in his constituency. I agreed to do so all the more readily because, just at that time, we were proceeding in the land commission to acquire some three thousand acres of the fertile plains of Boyle and to establish upwards of a hundred families to take the place of grazing cattle.

I was somewhat shocked to read the glaring headlines in the following morning's opposition paper, quoting as a statement that I had made that 'I thanked God that the cattle trade was going'.[6] The words were accurate, but it was the old device of taking them out of their context and without the qualifications that I had included in my speech. The simple truth was that I had pointed out that our opponents were crying out about the destruction of the cattle trade due to our conflict with Britain and that, if the preservation of the cattle trade meant that we must surrender in the economic war and that if it meant that instead of people on the land they must make way for the bullock, then 'I thanked God that the cattle trade was going'. Inevitably the matter was raised in the Dáil where de Valera gave a clear explanation, but that did not and does not prevent a repetition of the unqualified quotation. It was a minor incident and typical of what anyone involved in politics must expect with grim resignation.

I need hardly add that I realise as fully as most that cattle we must have, and that the export of beef cattle must figure in our all-round economy just as we must have the dairying industry. Nevertheless, I still hold to my conviction that to direct our main energies to the production of bullocks and beef cattle for export can only result in less employment, fewer family farms and homes in rural Ireland, and more passengers with one-way tickets on the emigrant ships. Our industrial programme must depend on the primary essential of the purchasing power within the home market. With that as a foundation, we may find outlets for our surplus production in the export market, but with the persistent drain of our population by emigration we are steadily losing a big percentage of our potential consumers. The purchasing power of our cattlemen, horse dealers and the like, however

6. *Irish Independent* 9 June 1934. See also *Irish Independent* 19 June 1934.

wealthy they may be and however lavish in their expenditure, cannot offset the economic loss inflicted by the loss of the thousands who depart annually to seek a living outside the country. One could go on for many pages writing on the various aspects of this problem but for the present, and bearing in mind my immediate purpose, I restrain myself in an effort to preserve my sequence.

My work in the land commission was incessant but entirely satisfying. The team of outside inspectors was working at top pressure and effectively, while the clearance at headquarters by the commissioners and their indoor staffs exceeded my expectations.

Attendance at the meetings of the senate was essential and at times worse than irksome but, compared with the lot of my cabinet colleagues, was relatively light. All of the other ministers had to attend in the Dáil whether they had departmental business before the House or not. Their presence as voting units in the divisions was obligatory with the result that most of them had to carry out their departmental work in their 'cubby hole' offices in the back passage. As the Dáil generally sat for three days a week and from 3 p.m. to 10.30 p.m. their lot was not an enviable one. In the senate we seldom sat for more than a day or two each week and it was seldom that the sittings were not concluded by 7 p.m. Our debates prior to 1932 had been on the whole decorous, but the new legislation provoked the grave and dignified senators and the bitter and acrimonious cross fire of the Dáil had its repercussions with us in the senate.

I have already referred briefly to our days in the senate before we became the government in power. Following our election as the government, the position was entirely changed. We were in a minority and the senate had the power to outvote us, a power which they exercised on all the vital issues and thereby caused the delay on such measures as the abolition of the oath.

It would be somewhat dreary to recall all the long-drawn-out debates of those days. The lines of attack were set by the opposition in the Dáil and repeated with painful monotony. It is sufficient to record that their powers of obstruction and delay were exercised to the full and ultimately led to the abolition of the senate as then constituted. My own position was somewhat difficult. As leader of the government party I was leader of the House and also leader of the minority within the House. Save when ministers came in to the senate for the debates on their own parliamentary measures, it was generally my responsibility to put forward government proposals and make the necessary defensive replies.

The outstanding debates for which any historical value might be claimed were those which took place on the Constitutional Bill (Amendment No.

24). The bill came before the senate on 30 May 1934 having already been passed by the Dáil. The initial debate was made interesting by two departures from the customary conduct of business in the senate.

Immediately preceding the opening of the debate Senator Douglas referred to the standing orders and specifically to that one which forbade the reading of speeches within the House. The Cathaoirleach of the senate, Mr Westropp Bennett,[7] announced that there was of course a standing order which provided that 'No senator shall read his speech', but it had been the custom to allow ministers and senators introducing an important measure or making prepared statements on grave issues to read their speeches and in his opinion that was a desirable practice. Accordingly he ruled that 'on this occasion of special gravity' if anyone had thought fit to prepare a careful statement of his views and chose to read it he would not interfere.

I protested against his ruling. His arguments about ministers reading statements was a mere quibble. Ministers and senators read or quoted references and statistics, but these were incidental to and embodied in their speeches. However, he would not have his ruling questioned. The second departure was consequential on the first for Westropp Bennett vacated the chair, came into the members' benches and read a long and skilfully prepared statement dealing with Second Chambers generally and our own Second Chamber in particular. The reading of the statement occupied two hours. (It is recorded in Volume XVIII of the *Official Reports*, cols. 1218-1264.)

I had no doubt in my mind as to the authorship of the long and excellently compiled statement and I do not think that a single member of the senate credited its composition to Mr Westropp Bennett.

It was tempting to ask the Cathaoirleach when he resumed the chair if, in granting permission to members to read their speeches, he would ask for a guarantee that such speeches were their own productions. However, I refrained, but I did definitely charge that, apart from breaking an existing standing order, he had read a long thesis which had been prepared for him by others.

The debate was concluded on 1 June 1934 and the bill rejected by the senate by thirty-three votes to our fifteen. It went into 'cold storage' for

7. Thomas Westropp Bennett: born Kilmallock, County Limerick, land-owner and farmer, district councillor, county councillor 1906, member of governing body of University College, Cork, member of executive committee of Irish Agricultural Organisation Society, director of Irish Agricultural Wholesale Society, chairman of County Limerick Rate-payers Association, chairman of Limerick and Clare Farmers' Association, president, Kilmallock Agricultural and Industrial Society, senator 1922-36.

the long delaying period that the senate had then the power to impose. Two years later and when the delaying period had run its course, the senate, as originally established in 1922, would cease to exist.

It was on 11 December 1922 that the then governor-general of the Irish Free State, Mr T. M. Healy,[8] had summoned the selected nominees of the first senate and directed that the oath be administered to them. On the following day Lord Glenavy[9] was elected chairman. Mrs Wyse Power and Colonel Maurice Moore objected to the selection and issued their objections in brief statements, but there was no other nomination and he was elected. It was, to me, not without significance that he was proposed for the chairmanship by Senator John McLaughlin[10] who was an intimate friend of Healy's. Perhaps association in the law library counted more effectively in climbing the ladder of success than national or political endeavour. Perhaps it still does! The selection of Lord Glenavy must have come as a severe shock even to those who were whole-heartedly supporting the treaty government. As James H. Campbell, K.C., he had been one of the foremost members of the Unionist Party and had taken his full share in the Anti-Home-Rule campaign and the building up of the Carsonite campaign. Emerging out of this I had an interesting experience

During the 1923 election campaign and while I was chairman of reorganised Sinn Féin, I referred to the selection of Glenavy as chairman of the senate and condemned it as an outrageous insult to our people. I went on to charge Glenavy with his full share of responsibility for all that our people in Belfast and the North East had suffered at the hands of his associates there with their organised pogroms and murder campaigns. The sequel was interesting. Senator James Douglas, with whom I had occasional contacts, wrote to me saying that Lord Glenavy had spoken to him about my attack on him and was considering what action he would take about

8. Timothy Michael Healy (1855-1931): born Bantry, County Cork, M.P. for Wexford 1880-83, barrister 1884, M.P. for County Monaghan 1883-85, for South Derry 1885-86, North Longford 1887-92, after split in Irish Parliamentary Party was a leading anti-Parnellite, M.P. for North Louth 1892-1910, M.P. for North-East Cork 1910-18, governor-general of Irish Free State 1922-28.

9. James Henry Mussen Campbell, first Baron Glenavy (1851-1931): born Terenure, Dublin, barrister 1878, unionist M.P. for St Stephen's Green division, Dublin, 1898-1900, solicitor-general for Ireland 1901-05, M.P. for Trinity College, Dublin, 1903-16, attorney-general 1905, member of Edward Carson's Anti-Home Rule provisional government 1912, attorney-general 1916, lord chief justice of Ireland 1916, lord chancellor 1918-21, senator 1922-28.

10. John MacLaughlin (1871-1950): born Buncrana, County Donegal, shirt-manufacturer, proprietor of Ormonde Woollen Mills, Kilkenny, Justice of the Peace 1912-18, senator 1922-26, 1938-43.

it. Douglas said he had urged Glenavy to do nothing until he communicated with me. There was a scarcely veiled threat of legal action by Glenavy with the implication of Douglas acting as peacemaker to save me from calamity. My reply to Douglas was brief and to the point. In this I simply stated that I would welcome any opportunity afforded me by Lord Glenavy to bring forward adequate evidence in proof of my statement and, in view of his lordship's objection, I proposed to repeat my charge at every election meeting I addressed. A few days later Douglas wrote me to say that he had shown my letter to Glenavy and that the latter had said he supposed that, considering everything, he would have to 'accept it as fair political comment'.

The first senate nominated by the government included in its membership W. B. Yeats, Dr George Sigerson[11] and Mrs Alice Stopford Greene, but these three eminent figures in our literary and national 'renaissance' had, I regret to say, vanished from the floor of the senate before we of Fianna Fáil took our seats in December 1928. Altogether the senate had thirteen and a half years of existence when its career was terminated in June 1936. For seven and a half years I had been a member and, of these, approximately four and a half years were spent as a minister.

During the two years that intervened between the rejection of the senate abolition bill and its automatic enactment after the delaying period had expired, the policy of obstruction was maintained. The debates and speeches of the government opposition were a reflection of those that continued to be made in the Dáil. It was all rather wearisome and futile, but it was part of the essential machinery of government. To me, driving all out on our big programme of land acquisition and division, it was an unwelcome diversion from what I regarded as my real worthwhile work.

11. Dr George Sigerson (1836–1925): born holyhill, Strabane, County Tyrone, a fellow of the Royal University, he was professor of biology at University College, Dublin, senator 1922–25.

25

I leave the cabinet and become a reinstated civil servant – Chairman of the Commissioners of Public Works – Commission for a new senate – The Office of Public Works and some of my colleagues – Drainage Commission

As June 1936 came near and the end of the senate was in sight, the question of my future career had to be faced. I was the first and, until many years later, the only senator who had a seat in the cabinet. The abolition of the senate meant also the termination of my career as a minister. All ministers had to be selected from the members of the Dáil save that one only might be selected from the senate.

To continue as minister meant that I would have to find a seat as a deputy and, failing this, there was no alternative but to retire from the ministry. A deputy came to me and proposed to retire and so provide me with a safe seat, but I declined to avail myself of his kindly offer. At the time I do not think anything would have induced me to become a deputy in the Dáil, despite my interest in my soul-satisfying work in the department of lands. The thought of seven and a half hours attendance in Leinster House for three days a week, the dreariness of the debates and the load of correspondence directed to most deputies simply appalled me.

The fact that I had an alternative may have influenced me and all the more so because it would mean that I would be spared the limelight and publicity that, to a greater or less degree, surround ministerial activity. That alternative linked back to my brief career as consul-general to the United States in 1921-22. My appointment then by Dáil Éireann made me a civil servant of that body.

There were many contemporary servants of the Dáil who, like myself, felt constrained to relinquish their posts rather than carry on their work for the pro-treaty government. There were others who, for various political activities, were dismissed by the government.

It was very soon after we had been returned to power in 1932 that a bill was introduced and passed which provided for the reinstatement of all those who had resigned their offices on grounds of political principle or who had been dismissed from their positions for the same reasons.

It was under this legislative Act that I was reinstated, and at the time, which was long before the issue of the abolition of the senate had emerged, I had no notion of how, if at all, my nominal reinstatement would affect me. When in 1936 it was clear that I could not continue as a cabinet minister, the question arose as to what post in the civil service would be mutually satisfactory to me on my reinstatement and to the government. At that time there were two vacancies. One was the chairmanship of the Revenue Commissioners and the other the chairman of the Commissioners of Public Works.

I discussed the situation with de Valera and, while I believed the former would probably be the less arduous, we decided that the duties of the Office of Public Works or Board of Works would be more in line with my earlier commercial life and experience. There was an additional reason in de Valera's mind which he explained to me. Arterial drainage for the whole country was something on which he had set his heart and he expressed the hope and wish that, once I had taken up duties, I would launch a big drive to have drainage carried out. It was part of the work of the Commissioners of Public Works to carry out drainage schemes and a section of the organisation existed for that purpose. A considerable amount of work had been done but, with the possible exception of the Barrow Drainage Scheme, most schemes had been done on a piece-meal basis rather than on the comprehensive method which was subsequently adopted. I will have more to say about this later. I transferred to the Board of Works early in June, and at once settled in to get to grips with the innumerable functions and activities of that department.

At the time of the change over de Valera suggested to me that he would like me to keep in constant touch with him on the many issues and problems which the government was constantly facing. It was a suggestion that I instinctively felt might, if adopted, have awkward repercussions for both of us. I do not think I am exaggerating when I say that, at that time, I was as closely or more closely akin to de Valera in his cultural and economic outlook for the future Ireland than any of our cabinet colleagues. We did not always agree and I had perhaps an inclination to be somewhat blunt in expressing a difference of opinion, but we had pulled together in fundamental harmony from the time in 1923 when I had, at his request, led the re-organisation of Sinn Féin.

In pointed out to him that, as I was now a civil servant and no longer a member of his cabinet, I could not go along and raise matters of policy with him which were the sole responsibility of the cabinet. I told him frankly that, if I were still a minister, I would be inclined to resent any outside interference on issues that were solely for cabinet decision. As a civil servant I would be always available and, if he wanted to talk over anything, a call on the telephone would bring me to his office, but that in no circumstances would I take the initiative on questions of policy. It was on this agreed basis that I left the cabinet and ceased to join the other ministers even at the lunch table.

Leaving the ministry and taking over my duties was still another change added to the many that I had experienced since I had relinquished my own business in Belfast in 1921. It was in its way a big break. I was cut off, not only from my cabinet colleagues, but from my associates who were doing such splendid work in the department of lands. We had become an enthusiastic team, wholeheartedly co-operating on the re-settlement of our people on the land.

The whole organisatiaon, which numbered upwards of a thousand officials, was running smoothly and efficiently and seemed set fair for the completion of the work. It was the termination of my direction and association with this work that gave me the greatest wrench, but it had to be.

I was but a short time in the Board of Works when I was invited by de Valera to act on a commission which he was setting up to advise the government on the creation of a new senate or Second Chamber of the Oireachtas and the method of election thereto.

It was a commission made up of twenty-three members under the chairmanship of Chief Justice Hugh Kennedy.[1] We were asked to apply ourselves actively and without any delay, so that our report could be completed by the end of August or some five weeks after we were first brought together. To do this would mean intensive work and establish an all-time record for a government commission. It meant meeting each afternoon from 3 p.m., except on Saturdays and Sundays. The meetings lasted until 6.30 or 7 p.m. and our very competent secretary, Mr Seán Malone, posted to each of us a summary of the day's proceedings, the same evening. The Senate Commission only merits reference because of a unique development.

After a month or longer hammering out our views and proposals, we had reached the point when a report was in draft, ready for final passing over to the government. The report proposed a blend of vocational and political representation with provision for representation of the universities and various cultural and professional organisations. When we were practially at the end of our work, Professor O'Rahilly put in an appearance. He had been at the first meeting or two, but from this he had ceased to attend and

1. Hugh Boyle Kennedy (1879-1936): born Dublin, law officer to the Provisional government 1922, attorney general in Irish Free State 1922-24, chief justice of Irish Free State 1924-36.

had taken no part in our discussion. Despite this, on his reappearance he had no hesitation in condemning all our proposals. Our chairman, Chief Justice Kennedy, quietly pointed out to the learned doctor that the work had been proceeding for more than a month and that each evening progress reports were posted to eahc member. He wondered why Dr O'Rahilly had not thought it wise to set out his views before things had reached their present advanced stage.

Dr O'Rahilly rather brusquely explained that he had been away from home for the past month and that he had not had the reports forwarded to him. Our poor chairman was somewhat stunned and so were we all. There was a strained silence which I had the bad manners to break by saying that I did not know how the other members of the commission viewed Dr O'Rahilly's conduct, but to me it was a 'damned outrage'. The sequel was interesting. Dr O'Rahilly, with three [sic] of his colleagues, submitted a minority report, and it was this report that formed the basis of the form of the new senate.[2] Whatever its merits or defects, it would be radically changed after the first election, the chief charge against it being that under the system of voting it was not impossible for an aspirant for senatorial honours to secure his return by the judicious expenditure of a certain amount of cash.

I note that even today the government is still seeking a method of electing a senate and that a further commission has just reported its findings. The plain fact emerges that the government has never had a senate that could claim to have had the approval of the country. It has been made the haven or refuge for party candidates who have suffered defeat in the elections for the Dáil; it has been used to place party supporters who were unwilling or unsuitable to serve as deputies, and it has provided resting places for six representatives of our universities. In no sense has it ever had any claim to being a democratically elected representative body, and until it is such it is futile and provocative of derision to have a senate at all.

The Office of Public Works is responsible for practically all the essential services required by State departments. Accommodation, furnishing, heating and lighting and maintenance are the principal services demanded. In addition the provision of national schools, training colleges and all State institutions, except military barracks, is the responsibility of the department. Certain public parks such as the Phoenix Park, St Stephen's Green, Muckross estate in Killarney and the harbours of Dún Laoghaire, Howth

2. For more on this, see J. A. Gaughan, *Alfred O'Rahilly II: Public Figure* (Dublin 1989) 275-8.

and Dunmore East are also in their care. The authority for all arterial drainage is vested in the Board.

The department is governed by a Board of three commissioners, of whom one is chairman, and a secretary. It maintains a large architectural section, an engineering and drainage section, a schools section and various subdivisions dealing with accommodation, rentals, furniture, fuel and so on. In addition, a very large section is responsible for maintenance, repairs and renewals. Altogether it is a very varied and comprehensive organisation, covering everything from the provision of a waste paper basket to the erection of a new building costing a quarter of a million or more.

Mr Diarmuid O'Hegarty[3] and Mr Pierce Kent[4] were the two commissioners in office and Mr George Fagan,[5] who would subsequently become a commissioner and eventually chairman, was secretary when I joined the board as chairman. I soon settled down to work and had the fullest co-operation and help not only from my fellow commissioners but from all my associates.

I have no intention to weary my readers with a detailed account of all the many and varied activities that occupied our time and energies during the thirteen and a half years that I spent as head of the Board. An interesting book could be compiled on all the difficulties and problems that arose almost daily for solution and led to ulcers for many of our chief officers. Orders from ministers and departments, invariably declared to be urgent and demanding immediate attention, were constant, often ill-considered, and frequently made without regard to reasonable economy or foresight. However, as I once described our position, we were the 'skivvies' of the ministry and the civil service, and seldom were we allowed to 'reason why'. Ours was to do what we were told and accept the abuse or criticism that might follow! Naturally we always submitted our advices and reports. Sometimes the advice would be taken, at other times we would get our

3. Diarmuid Ó hÉigeartaigh (1892-1967): civil service 1910, a leading figure in I.R.B., director of organisation, I.R.A. 1919-21, clerk of 1st Dáil Éireann 1919-21, acting secretary to cabinet of 2nd Dáil Éireann 1921-22, major-general in Free State army 1922, secretary to Executive Council of Irish Free State 1923-32, commissioner of Office of Public Works 1932-49, chairman of Office of Public Works 1950-57.

4. Pierce Kent (1877-1950): born Dublin, civil service 1901, assistant secretary (1912-22) and acting secretary (1922-27), National Health Insurance Board, commissioner of Office of Public Works 1927-43.

5. George P. Fagan (1894-1970): born Dublin, civil service 1914, department of finance 1923-31, accountant in Office of Public Works 1931-37, secretary (1937-44), commissioner (1944-57) and chairman 1957-9) in Office of Public Works.

orders to go ahead, despite our disapproval of the proposal. There was the occasion, for instance, when we were asked to inspect and report on hotel premises which were picked on by a certain minister to satisfy his urgent need. We inspected and reported our opposition to the purchase. Pressed further we estimated the very outside value at £12,000. The property was to be sold at auction and we were ordered to attend the auction and buy it. I protested and asked that, if we must buy, our ultimate bid should have a price limit fixed, but no, we must buy. We did and paid £30,000 for it. It was robbery of course but, even at that, I wondered where we would have stopped if the seller had given his bogus bidders a longer rope or if he had known the directions we had received. That of course was exceptional, and usually our advice and recommendations were given due consideration, but frequently there were decisions and directions that made us squirm.

It was in 1938, when the shadow and threat of war hung over us, that some of us began to think of the possible effects that an outbreak of war would have on our supplies of essential stores. Our director of fuel supplies was Colonel O'Reilly,[6] known to us all as Joe O'Reilly. Joe had been 'right-hand man' to Michael Collins and a more trustworthy, honest and courteous gentlemen I have never met. He was deeply religious, neither smoked nor drank, yet, withal, was entirely devoid of either smugness or priggishness. I was in constant contact with him and had quickly reached the stage when respect merged into trust and affection. We discussed the fuel situation and came to the conclusion that, war or no war, we were very unlikely to place contracts for coal at more favourable prices than were then on offer. 'The situation seems to be, Joe', I said to him, 'that we can lose nothing by buying now. If there is no war we are at no loss; if war comes, well, we have our stocks in at reasonable rates'. Joe agreed and, having got Johnnie Hanna,[7] of the department of finance, to see it our way,

6. Joseph F. O'Reilly (1895-1943): born Limerick, post-office official, Bantry, County Cork 1910-11, London 1911-16, member of Irish Volunteers, London 1913, close associate of Michael Collins, fought in G.P.O., Easter Rising, interned at Frongoch 1916, assistant to Collins, then secretary of Irish National Aid Association 1916-19, member of 'Collins' Squad' 1919-21, aide de camp to Collins 1921-22 and Colonel in Free State army 1922-23, after reorganisation of National Army reduced to rank of major in 1924, aide de camp to President William T. Cosgrave 1924-27, aide de camp to governor general 1927-32, director of purchases, Office of Public Works, 1932-43.

7. John Ernest Hanna (1888-1960): born Dublin, civil service, department of agriculture and technical instruction 1907, British army 1914-19, department of finance, second secretary (1923), assistant principal officer (1932-9), principal officer (1939-45) and assistant secretary (1945-9).

we went ahead and stored up coal in every available space where it could be safely kept. Coal contracts were placed at prices averaging 38s 3d per ton. The war came and, helped out by supplementary supplies of turf, the end of the war found us with some 3,000 tons of our 1938 purchases, having during the war-period provided rationed but reasonable heating for all departments.

To a lesser extent we endeavoured to anticipate and provide for our other many and varied needs and to escape, to some extent, the sky-rocketing prices that followed the outbreak of hostilities. The situation reflected the difficulties that often arise in governmental purchasing due to the necessary 'finance sanction' which normally must be obtained before expenditure is incurred. On the whole, I was fortunate in getting reasonable and quick decisions when the opportunity for favourable purchase or completing a deal arose. The restrictive operations of the finance sanction and control are sometimes irksome and frustrating but, against that, one must realise how essential these are to preserve the discipline and integrity of the service and prevent obvious dangers and temptations.

The government decided to set up a commission to examine the whole problem of arterial drainage on a national scale and to report on the most efficient means for its execution. Mr Commissioner Dan Browne was appointed chairman and Mr Candy,[8] our chief engineer, and myself were appointed to represent the Board of Works. Drainage, like so many of our other national needs, had been neglected and such drainage as had been carried out was on a local or area basis. Most if not all of the schemes, with the notable exception of the Barrow which our predecessors in office had carried out, had been fundamentally unsound and for one reason. The reason was that in very few of the schemes did the 'run-off' find its ultimate outlet to the sea.

Joseph Candy was our chief engineer. He was born and reared in Derry and had graduated as a fully qualified engineer, M.Sc. and M.E. at Queen's University, Belfast. He had spent quite a number of years on big engineering schemes in Burma, Haifa and other centres abroad. His experience was wide and varied, and included drainage, irrigation, harbour construction, tidal embankments and indeed every type of work proper to his profession. I doubt if we had in the whole country his equal in judgement and knowledge and in his devotion to his work. He had, moreover, the character to stand over his advice and reports, and no pressure would force him to

8. Joseph P. Candy (1895-1960): born Derry, chief engineer in Office of Public Works 1934-60.

undertake work that his knowledge and judgement would condemn as unsound from the engineering point of view.

Guided by Candy, the Commissioners of Public Works and later the Drainage Commission itself laid it down as a *sine qua non* that every scheme of drainage must be a comprehensive one covering certain defined areas and must be planned so that the total water-ways may join in the ultimate run-off to the outfall at the sea. Any divergence from this policy would mean that drainage would simply be a removal of excess water from one area to find its level in another.

The special difficulties of drainage in Ireland are largely due to the saucerlike formation of the country and, with this in mind, the wisdom of Candy's resistance to any piecemeal drainage is obvious. This objection to piecemeal local or district drainage had not prevented a considerable amount of such work being done in the past. Local pressure and political expediency had played their part in having such schemes carried out and in most cases the ultimate results were far from satisfactory.

The Drainage Commission first assembled in September 1938 and, despite the incidence of the war emergency, continued its work and made its final report to the government in July 1940. There were tours of inspection covering every county within the State and an examination of the areas which presented the most complex and difficult problems from the drainage point of view. Sittings of the Commission were held in Dublin and in various centres throughout the country, and at these the county and local authorities gave evidence and advice through their engineers, senior officers and public representatives. Meantime the drainage survey staff in the Board of Works prepared the scheme in outline and the approximate estimates of cost.

Considering all that was involved and the immense amount of material that had to be studied and analysed, the fact that the Commission was able to furnish its final report to the government twenty-two months after its opening session was worth noting. Most of the credit for the achievement must go to Mr Commissioner Dan Browne, who, as our chairman, kept resolutely to the work and by his quiet competence and keen direction steered us to a concentration on what was relevant and essential. This was no more than I expected from Dan for I had experienced his great qualities and his tireless co-operation while minister for lands. Some little time ago Dan passed to his reward and Ireland lost one of its most able and most sincere patriotic workers. I make no apology for repeating what I have often said elsewhere: 'If we had a cabinet of a dozen Dan Brownes, this country would leap ahead not only in desirable material progress but in integrity and in the moral qualities that are or should be the primary essentials of Irish nationality'. That is not a sentimental tribute to a good friend and colleague, but a realistic appraisal based on practical and intimate experience of a man and his work. May God rest his grand soul!

Following the report of the Drainage Commission, the government passed the necessary legislation and since then real, comprehensive drainage work has proceeded. As I write, some of the major schemes have been completed, but there are years of work still ahead. Let us hope that those for whose benefit the work is being carried out will take full advantage of the results, for one has always the fear that the essential co-operation of the individual farmer and his responsibility for doing his share are not so fully realised in Ireland as they would need to be.

Friday, 1 September 1939, opened with as perfect a morning as one could desire. I was enjoying the early days of a brief holiday in Portstewart and a welcome relief from all official work. There was a background of anxiety that everyone was experiencing over the position in Europe and the threat of an upheaval, for day by day the pendulum seemed to swing between the hope of peace and the dread of another world war. Reading the papers that morning, the outlook and the prospect of peace being maintained seemed to me to be brighter than they had been for some days. It was with that feeling of hope that a few of us set off from the hotel to have our dip in the sea. Bright, warm sunshine with little or no wind, a calm sea and the long stretch of the beautiful strand made everything just right for a morning of luxurious relaxation. On arriving back to the hotel, the clerk in the office met us with the awesome news that had just come over the radio. Hitler had launched his attack on Poland. Momentarily stunned, I quickly realised the implications of the announcement and that my immediate job was to pack up and get back to headquarters without delay.

I had no provisional arrangements with de Valera or the government in regard to any emergency, but I realised that in any such development the Board of Works must inevitably be called on to provide all sorts of services. Within an hour I had packed up and was on the train to Belfast and later caught the evening train to Dublin, arriving home at about 10 p.m. There I learned that de Valera had been telephoning several times and left a message asking me to report to government buildings as soon as possible after I had arrived.

I went there and found the cabinet in full session. De Valera told me that they had decided to ask me to take on the job of the controller of censorship. This came as an unpleasant shock, for I had no inkling whatever that I was to be 'drafted' for the post and had definite qualms about all that would be involved and genuine fear of the responsibility.

It was explained to me that a 'shadow' organisation had been planned on paper for some time and that various 'keymen' and officers from other departments had been listed and would be made available. From these the organisation must be built up, but immediate action was the order of the day or rather of the night. Mr Coyne from the department of justice, who had been responsible for planning the 'shadow' organisation, would be my chief assistant, and deputy controller. The question of acceptance or refusal did not of course arise. It was simply a matter of being told to do a certain job and that was that! It was long after midnight when I left the cabinet still at work and made my way homewards. The streets were already 'blacked out', such few lamps as were lighted being heavily 'cowled'. The transition from the glorious sunshine of the forenoon on the Portstewart strand to the sepulchral gloom of the city was a depressing experience. Even more so was the contemplation of all the horrors that lay ahead. Those of us who had lived through the war years of 1914-18 needed no forecast of what the world and all humanity was facing, only this time it seemed to me it would be a thousand times worse. Scientific development in the implements of war and the colossal forces of military power that had built up on land and sea and in the air must inevitably mean a world-wide holocaust of millions of victims who had neither voice nor power to influence decisions.

I recalled to memory and with bitterness all the futility of the long debates at the League of Nations and the ostrich-like activities of the statesmen-politicians. I remembered also how, on a Sunday night early in 1938, de Valera had asked me to go out to his home to discuss some urgent matters of importance. He had just come back for the weekend from London, and was due to return a day or two later. He and certain members of his cabinet were negotiating with Neville Chamberlain, the British prime minister and other members of the British cabinet, a settlement of the differences that had arisen in 1932 over the oath, the land annuities and the other payments involved in the dispute. We had a long session in the course of which de Valera explained that they had practically achieved agreement on a lump sum settlement on the financial issues and, most important of all, they had secured the control of all our twenty-six counties ports at that time held by the British.

While I appreciated the tremendous importance of the evacuation of the British from our ports and the great step forward it represented in our path to complete freedom, I raised the question of Partition. I am afraid that I argued rather vehemently that, if the partition of the country was not solved then when the other matters were being settled, the prospects of having it raised and decided in the near future were not very bright. De Valera explained that Neville Chamberlain was sympathetic and had described the partitioning of the country as an 'anachronism', but that, despite all de Valera's pleas, he, Chamberlain, could not carry his cabinet with him on the six-counties issue. My reaction to de Valera's news may have been disappointing to him, but he was infinitely patient with me. He understood my intense interest in the almost abandoned position in which our people in the North-East were placed and my real fear that any settlement, which left them as they were, would be a further consolidation of the existing state. I returned home from that Sunday evening conference with very mixed feelings. It was good to know that the last round of the economic war was about to end and that our ports within the twenty-six counties would soon be in our own care and under own control, but it was galling to know that the six counties of Ulster and my own home area would continue to be dominated by the British army of occupation and their satellites in the North. However, that was or would soon be the position and it was outside my power or functions to do anything about it. I appreciated fully that it was an act of courtesy on de Valera's part to take me, no longer in the ministry, into his confidence and to discuss with me the whole situation frankly.

On my way home in the early hours of Saturday morning, 2 September 1939, I remembered vividly our talk and realised that, despite all else, de Valera had got back the ports, and that the chances of asserting and maintaining our neutrality were not only made possible but were reasonably hopeful. It is hardly necessary to say that, had the ports been in the control of the British admiralty, the country would most probably have been the cockpit of the conflicting forces

We were early astir on the Saturday morning planning our organisation and taking over occupation of premises for our operations. The Hospitals Trust Sweepstakes[9] building in Exchequer Street was taken over for the postal censorship. Here, under the direction and control of Mr Jack Purcell,[10] accommodation and equipment for a staff numbering nearly three hundred was quickly provided. In Dublin Castle we found space for

9. Irish Hospitals Sweepstake: this was established mainly by Joseph McGrath. The first 'Sweep' was held on the Manchester November Handicap of 1930. Over four hundred institutions which afforded free medical or surgical treatment were beneficiaries of the 'Sweep' which was wound up in 1985.

10. Jack Purcell: civil servant, department of local government and public health.

the entire press censorship and accommodation for my deputy controller, Mr Coyne,[11] and myself. Our chief assistant, Mr Daly,[12] who had been loaned to us by the department of local government and who proved to be a man of outstanding ability, shared our accommodation. The press censorship was under the direction of Mr Michael Knightly[13] who was editor-in-chief of the reporting staff of the Oireachtas and responsible for the official reports of the Dáil and senate.

On Sunday, 3 September, and just after the British prime minister, Mr Neville Chamberlain, had broadcast his message that Britain was now at war, Mr Coyne and I met the editors and press representatives in Government Buildings. I explained to them the arrangements that had been made for the censorship of all newspapers and journals, the vital importance of preserving our neutrality and their heavy responsibility in co-operating with the government to that end. It was, on the whole, a quietly subdued conference, most of us realising the serious crisis that we were facing and that one of the most important matters affecting our neutrality was probably the printed news-sheet. The late Mr R. M. Smyllie,[14] who was then editor of the *Irish Times*, the leading Unionist or pro-British paper in the State, made no secret of his objections to censorship in any form. He protested his right to express his views on the war and everything connected with it. It took Coyne and myself some time to convince him that, despite our belief in the freedom of the press in normal times, the preservation of our neutrality was the over-riding consideration of the present, and that nothing that might in any way jeopardise that neutrality could or would be tolerated. That night the press censorship was put into action.

11. T. J. Coyne (1901-80): born Dublin, graduated in legal and political science, U.C.D. 1920, barrister 1922, private secretary to Kevin O'Higgins, minister for home affairs 1923, seconded from department of justice to external affairs and secretary to the representative of the Irish Free State at the Vatican 1929-32, secretary to the permanent delegation at the League of Nations 1932-34, principal officer, department of justice 1934-39, deputy controller of censorship 1939-41, controller 1941-46, assistant secretary, department of justice 1946-49, secretary 1949-61.

12. Patrick J. Daly (1900-75): born Dublin, clerk in G.P.O., London 1916, clerical officer, London 1920, dept. of local govt., Dublin 1920-29, duty in New York 1929-32, dept. of local govt. 1932-39, office of controller of censorship 1939-41, dept. of supplies 1941, principal officer in roads section, local govt. 1941-48, assistant sec. 1948-65.

13. Michael T. Knightly (1888-1962): born Tralee, County Kerry, member of Irish Volunteers 1913, fought in G.P.O., Easter 1916 and afterwards interned at Frongoch, journalist and later member of editorial staff of *Irish Independent*, 1914-23, close friend of Thomas Ashe and Austin Stack, also close friend of Michael Collins and his main channel to the press 1919-21, editor of paraliamentary debates in Dáil Éireann 1923-55, keen follower of horse-racing.

14. Robert M. Smyllie (1894-1954): born Glasgow, journalist and eventually editor *Irish Times* 1919-54.

It was something of a nightmare experience for all of us. Knightly and his staff were amazingly competent and tireless in the care and energy they applied to their work. A rotation of duties was arranged so that press censorship was in constant operation from 9 a.m. to 3 a.m., when the last submissions for the morning papers were cleared. Inevitably we had incidents and occasional friction with editors and sub-editors but, looking back on it all, I think we can claim that the press censorship emerged from it with credit to all concerned. To Michael Knightly, the chief of the press censorship, must go the major credit. He was firm without being arrogant, he was steadily calm under stress, and his judgements and decisions were sound.

The postal censorship under Mr Purcell functioned efficiently from the commencement. It is true that at the beginning we were only able to do 'spot checking' and this meant on the average about ten to fifteen per cent of the letters passing through. With the acquisition of increased help this percentage was speedily increased and the staff quickly acquired an almost uncanny instinct for picking out the potential trouble makers. These latter formed an interesting, if somewhat irritating, factor in our work. Many of the letters that were opened displayed vivid imagination on the part of the writers. Some of the latter claimed that they had seen the German submarines being supplied with petrol on the south-west coast, while others were convinced that various agents of Hitler were active in their particular districts. Most of them, however, concentrated on vehement abuse of the government and protests against the various restrictions to which they were subjected. Several ladies of title were the most consistent, not only in their abuse of the government but in their fantastic reports to their friends in Britain and America of the German activities within the country. I can only describe these reports as figments of their imaginations, for in all cases that we investigated there was not the slightest justification or shadow of a reason for their stories. One of these titled dames became such a persistent menace that we decided to summon her to call and explain the numerous false reports, which she was attempting to send to her friends abroad. Colonel Liam Archer[15] was attached to us as military intelligence adviser and he was in attendance and in full uniform when her ladyship, attended by my lord her husband, arrived at our office. It was a quiet interview, during which the various penalties for such offences were explained with the intimation that the decision had not yet been made as to our ultimate action. If her ladyship was upset, it was mild indeed compared with the

15. Liam.Archer (1892-1969): born Dublin, civil servant in post-office 1908, officer in Free State army 1922, O.C., signals corps 1922-29, member of inspector-general's staff 1929-31, military intelligence 1932-41, assistant chief of staff 1941-49, chief of staff 1949-52.

reaction of his lordship. He stormed not at us but at his loving spouse, and growled about 'damned fools and people minding their own business'. He repeated his assurances that we would have no more trouble as far as his household was concerned, and marched off with a subdued and scared ladyship. I mention this incident merely as an example of some of our experiences on the postal side of censorship nor was it all a one-sided affair. A number of the dangerous correspondents were violently pro-German and provocative, while a few, a very few, persistently let off steam on behalf of Stalin and the U.S.S.R. There were other types of letters that emerged from time to time that one wanted to forget about. There were only a few of them, but they were a revelation of the depths to which the human mind can sink. Needless to add that only the letters that required special consideration reached the controller's desk. The others, and these represented practically the entire foreign mail, were checked, re-sealed and dispatched within twenty-four hours of arrival.

The censorship of telegrams was somewhat difficult and particularly so in dealing with newspaper correspondents. We were anxious to deal promptly with all telegrams and this meant immediate service between the telegraph headquarters and ourselves. Some of the journalists were reasonable, but many were ready to make trouble and create difficulties both for us and the government, and a continuous alert had to be maintained both on the telegraph and telephone services. Journalists are naturally resentful of restrictions. It is their job to get their stories 'hot' to their papers and to surmount every obstacle that would prevent them. One can understand and sympathise with their professional zeal, but in our circumstances of the time we just could not afford to allow them a free run on all the rumours, reports, stories and impressions that they wished to send to their papers. Most of the British and American journalists, who were covering the Irish situation on periodical visits, were deeply resentful of our neutrality, and a few of them were disposed to create incidents that might endanger it.

While censorship control was more than a whole-time job, I had stipulated with de Valera that I would continue in close contact with my colleagues in the Board of Works. I had the utmost confidence in my fellow commissioners, Messrs Pierce Kent and Diarmuid O'Hegarty and the department chiefs subordinate to them, but I was anxious to keep myself informed of all that went on. I realised that sooner or later I would be resuming my full responsibilities as chairman and accounting officer, and I did not wish to do so ignorant of all that had been carried through in my absence. Accordingly, I invariably spent an hour or two each afternoon at the Office of Public Works and dealt with the more important cases and problems in consultation with my colleagues. It added that much extra to the day's work and strain, but it left me more content to know all that was moving in my own department.

The minister responsible for the censorship was Mr Frank Aiken, who had been appointed minister for co-ordination of defence and who had, prior to that, been minister for defence. It was, in the last analysis, his function to take responsibility in the Dáil and senate for all our actions and accordingly it was also his job in difficult cases, which might be provocative of trouble, to give us the final word of direction. As the peak hours for the morning papers to pass in their reports for censorship were from 10 p.m. to 2 a.m. he had, like the rest of us, many disturbed nights. In the Dáil he had to face many difficult and mischievous questions and debates. Despite the fact that all parties in the Oireachtas were unanimous on the issue of neutrality, this did not prevent a few of the deputies from airing their views on the war and questioning the impartiality that was being exercised in the censorship. However, Frank was invariably able to dispose of these critics without much trouble and for the simple reason that cold impartiality was the ruling dogma of the whole censorship organisation. Frank had been one of my closest friends and co-operators, when I was a member of the cabinet, and it may not be out of place to place on record for all time one of his contributions to the welfare of the State and its contributory effect in enabling us to keep out of the war.

From the earliest days of de Valera's government in 1932, Aiken urged the immediate development of the bogs and the use of turf. We were all enthusiastic about our wheat and beet production policies, as well as the protection and development of our manufacturers, but I am afraid a few of our number were not convinced that turf afforded anything like a reasonable economic prospect. Transport from the bogs to the distant towns and cities would be costly, and coal at that time was relatively cheap. Some of the earlier experiments in producing and transporting turf to Dublin by rail and canal boat were disappointing, but that did not deter Frank. His middle name was 'Tenacity' for, despite all discouragement and disappointment, he held on persistently. Eventually he secured the services of Todd Andrews[16] as administrative head of the turf section of the depart-

16. Christopher S. Andrews (1901-85): born Dublin, member of Irish Volunteers 1917, member of I.R.A. 1919-24, opposed the treaty, member of Fianna Fáil 1926, executive in Irish Tourist Association 1926-30, E.S.B. 1930-46, Bord na Móna 1946-58, C.I.E. 1958-66, chairman of R.T.E. 1966-70. In his *Man of no property: an autobiography*, II, published in 1982, Andrews, in recalling the mid-1920s, wrote: 'I became very friendly with Joseph

ment of industry and commerce. At a later stage Andrews and his Board were freed from the shackles of department control, and Bord na Móna started to grow rapidly and to become the most spectacular success of the various enterprises, sponsored and financed by the State.

I am not proposing to analyse all the economic advantages that turf production and the development of our bogs have meant to our people. The production of fuel in the form of briquettes and machine-won turf, to say nothing of the power plants on the bogs to supplement our supply of electricity, has saved us millions in our balance of trade and provided employment for a big number of workers. My only reason for referring to it is to pay tribute to the one man who, in spite of all obstacles, held on grimly in his determination to make, in so far as it was possible, turf the national fuel for the country. That man was Frank Aiken.

He was fortunate that Andrews, who was director and manager from the beginning, was not only an optimist as to the future of turf but was a great organiser, gifted with courage and imagination and the capacity to get things done. A graduate of University College, Dublin, Andrews a few years ago received an honorary doctor's degree from his *alma mater*. I know of very few instances in which the honour was so well deserved.

My period as controller of censorship was inevitably a more or less constant strain, particularly with respect to the press and the visiting journalists. Eventually we settled down and, while at no period could it be claimed that a routine had been established, 'incidents' were less frequent and the exercise of our authority less subjected to criticism. At the same time we were constantly on the edge of an explosion. Any 'slip up' on the part of one of our press censors, whereby an item that had been passed for one of the papers and ruled out in another, could be made the medium of an attack in the Dáil. Fortunately they were few and far between, but such as did occur revealed the inevitable and continuous conflict that existed between ourselves and the editorial control of some of our leading newspapers.

It was while I was in control of censorship that I had my first contact with the then American ambassador, Mr David Gray.[17] He came to me

---

Connolly. He was a northern businessman, one of the few who continued actively to support Sinn Féin after the civil war. Of all my acquaintances in Republican circles he was the only one who showed any concern for economic policy. I actually heard him discussing the democratic programme of the First Dáil which had been long since forgotten by even the most radical among us. I found his company all the more interesting because of my late introduction to economics. He was, of course, much older than I, a very intense and humourless little man.'

17. David Gray (1870-1968): born New York, wealthy newspaper publisher, married an aunt of Eleanor Roosevelt, U.S. ambassador to Irish Free State 1940-7.

apparently about some deadlock that existed between himself and the department of finance. I had to explain that I had no function whatever in the matter and that the problem was one which he could only resolve with the minister for finance himself. I could not understand why he should have sought me out. Censorship did not of course attempt to interfere with foreign representatives, whose 'diplomatic bags' were exempt from all interference. Perhaps he wished to unburden his feelings. Our neutrality outraged all his sentiments and I think nothing would have pleased him more than to see us dragged into the conflict. I have met many members of the diplomatic service representing various countries when in Geneva, London and Washington and here at home, and the only one that seemed to me to be dangerously incompetent was the one who represented the United States government here during the war and mis-represented Ireland to the United States at that critical time.

The war had many repercussions which affected our whole life and economy. That was inevitable, but some of them were peculiar and unexpected. One of the latter was the sudden and at times overwhelming inrush of visitors and the crowding out of hotels and restaurants at all hours of the day and night. The explanation was simple. In Belfast and the six counties they were swamped with war work. Wages were high and overtime was constant, and there was 'money to burn'. At the same time the area was subjected to severe rationing. The meat supply was reduced to the minimum and the same applied to butter and most other essential commodities. Ration cards and a system of 'points allowances' operated with the result that, despite the high earnings, the ordinary citizen found himself with a superabundance of paper money and little on which he could spend it. In the twenty-six counties there was, in the early years of the war, practically a free market, and Dublin city and most of our border towns were invaded by hordes of visitors with plenty of money and insatiable appetites not only for food and drink but for every conceivable commodity that their home restrictions denied them.

Naturally all this had its effect on the normal economic standards of Dublin life. Traders reaped a rich harvest and this was particularly so with the drapers, butchers, spirit merchants and hotel and restaurant owners. The ordinary Dublin resident experienced certain drawbacks, as a result of these continuous invasions. Prices, which the war-time economy had increased, were raised still higher by the new boom demands of the Northern shoppers. Queues lined the streets at the pork-butchers, waiters became selective of the guests to whom they would give attention, and the man with a northern accent was a better prospect both as a customer and source of tips.

There was another aspect of the position at that time which had an immediate relevance, and that was the income-tax and super-tax demands that operated in the six counties as in Britain. Even deep-seated loyalty, such as we are told exists in the partitioned area of Ireland, does not always encourage the handing back of substantial sums of trading-profits to the tax collector. Bank accounts could be inspected, and those whose trading was for the most part in cash and who did not wish to part with the major portion of it in income-tax found themselves with the problem of the storage or disposal of paper currency. This in itself was a factor in the boom prosperity of the war in which Dublin and our border towns shared. There were many stories of the results of all this abnormal economic development, of men becoming mental wrecks worrying about the safe storage of their currency and the fear of disclosures. One of the most interesting explained the technique adopted by some of the gentlemen who were embarrassed by the load of concealed wealth which they had stowed away. They attended the various race meetings and placed heavy bets on a number of horses in each race. Their selections and bets were almost certain to include the winner. Instead of drawing their winnings in cash, the bookmaker was asked to send them a cheque. This they could lodge in their bank. They might, and no doubt invariably did, lose substantially on the day's operations, but they had their lodgement in the bank and gambling winnings apparently were not subject to income-tax.

As the war went on and after it had ended, the 'invasion' of Dublin spread to Britain and the war-workers flocked over in their thousands to enjoy their brief holidays and, what was unusual to them at the time, the luxury of good feeding. There was, at times, a certain bitter irony in all this for our own people. We too had rationing of essential foodstuffs. Butter, tea and for a brief period even bread itself were rationed but, while this was so, I never heard of any lack of supplies in the hotels and restaurants which catered for our visitors.

The population of Dublin continued to grow. Many from outside the State, who had 'done well out of the war', found it a congenial place in which to settle at least temporarily, while others drifted in from the rural areas to find employment. By far the biggest number from rural Ireland crossed to Britain to find employment in the war-industries and the building, mining, road-making and all the ancillary activities begotten of the war. That this had the approval of the government was evident from the fact that employment-recruiting-agents openly advertised their days of visitation to various centres to select and engage applicants for every type of employment. Young men and women were signed on in thousands and to a less extent this exodus continues. Perhaps it had to be so and will continue to be necessary, but I must confess to a spirit of resentment to the whole trend that our economy and social life has taken. Those of us who had, more than half a century ago, grown up with the hope and ideal of creating a new Ireland, who felt deep bitterness when we recalled the enforced emigration, the land clearances and evictions, can hardly escape the sense of bitter disillusion. From time to time I discussed most of these problems with de Valera at our occasional talks, but without any appreciable result. Our original lines of policy seemed to have been, if not forgotten, at least watered down to a point of near extinction.

After some two years as controller of censorship I had suggested to de Valera that I was anxious to be relieved of the position and to be free to devote all my time to the Board of Works. After a brief delay, I was released and Mr T. J. Coyne, my deputy, replaced me as controller. There were justifiable reasons for this. Censorship was running as smoothly as any such organisation could hope to function and the work of the Office of Public Works was becoming more difficult and complex. The demands for accommodation for the emergency staffs that had to be recruited for all sorts of services, such as rationing, passports, emigration and the like, were almost insatiable. The demands were mostly peremptory and often ill-considered by the departments concerned, so that we were frequently faced with the need to move and remove a section two, three or four times before it was finally housed. The supply position steadily deteriorated and, despite the anticipatory pre-war purchases of supplies that we had made, we found it necessary to dole out our reserves with miserly care and caution. This had its inevitable repercussions, some of which were amusing but others were provocative of trouble and friction.

It was relatively easy to explain to a newly promoted principal officer that until the war was over he would have to be content without the new Axminster carpet to which he might normally be entitled. It was somewhat more difficult but still possible to explain to the wife of a newly elected judge that the carpets for all the judges' rooms were comparatively new and that we just could not supply the special one of a 'French Empire' pattern that she had selected at one of the leading furnishers to adorn her beloved one's room. It was quite a different story when one of the ministers, transferred from one department to another, demanded a complete clearance of everything out of his ministerial room. The said office had been occupied by three or more predecessors. It was furnished in old mahogany, a fine large old desk, with 'spoonback' chairs in leather, and the usual accompaniment of old mahogany bookcases, tables and so on. I pointed out to finance the unnecessary waste and, above all, the great difficulty we would find in getting good quality furniture in the gaudy walnut veneering which the minister insisted he must have. We got our orders: the ministerial requirements must be supplied. They were. After chasing after a number of manufacturers without success we eventually got one to undertake the job. He was a Cork cabinet-maker and ultimately the minister had his bright glossy suite with its walnut veneers glistening in his pad, as he gave his ministerial approval or dissent to the submissions before him. His case was not unique, and I am afraid I was often tempted to growl under my breath: 'Beggar on horseback', or, alternatively, to chuckle inwardly at some of the absurd vanities which surround us.

However, these were very minor incidents in the day's work. In so far as it was possible, our building programme was maintained and our drainage engineers were busily engaged on all possible preparations for the big schemes that would follow the report and the anticipated legislation. A sizeable volume might easily be compiled covering any commissioner's experience in the administration of the Board of Works. I once described the officials of the Board, including the commissioners, as the 'skivvies' of the civil service and the government. Now I am not so sure that the designation was not a libel on that worthy body of general servants who were vulgarly described as 'skivvies' in my youth. They had at least certain defined functions, they knew their masters and mistresses and their orders were definite. That was not always our experience and conflicting interests were not always easy to reconcile. When it is remembered that we had the responsibility for replacing a pane of glass in an office equally with the erection of the Dublin airport, and of satisfying innumerable people of all sorts of taste and of no taste at all, our day-to-day job will, perhaps, be understood.

I do not propose to record a monotonous list of works and functions, of buildings and schools erected, of the parks, harbours and institutions that are maintained and managed by the Board. A few brief comments on some aspects of the administration of the very varied activities of the Board for the various departments may, however, be relevant. They are mentioned in the hope that they may be of some value in the guidance of those who come after us.

One of the problems that caused me disappointment and irritation was the neglect of the proper maintenance of national schools throughout the State. The maintenance of the schools is almost invariably the responsibility of the manager, and while most managers were prompt in their attention to necessary repairs quite a number neglected them. A few broken windows, a few slates blown off the roof and a couple of broken spouts or gutters will, if left without repairs, soon transform a reasonably comfortable school into a miserable shambles. Most of the very old schools are being replaced by good modern and well-equipped buildings, but it is surprising how rapidly even reasonably recent buildings have deteriorated for want of the 'stitch in time'.

There is one serious source of trouble that emerges occasionally for the commissioners and the technical administrative staffs of the Board, and that is the recruitment of overseers, tradesmen and general manual workers such as firemen, boiler-attendants, gardeners and so on. The professional and technical staffs such as architects, engineers and inspectors are, of course, like the administrative staff, all appointed by the Civil Service Commission and are fully established civil servants. In addition to these there are hundreds of skilled and unskilled workers engaged in every variety of work. These jobs are eagerly sought, and no doubt the chief attraction is that they are permanent and that the standard trades union conditions apply. When vacancies occur the commissioner and their officers would naturally seek to fill them with the best and most competent of the applicants, but in actual practice the decision does not rest with them. The final selection is made by the parliamentary secretary to the minister for finance who is, with certain limitations, the acting minister over the department. During my years as chairman the system worked reasonably well because most of our parliamentary secretaries were reasonable and sensible of the need to secure competent and reliable workers. There were occasions, however, when the dangers in the system emerged. As might be expected, when a vacancy occurred the parliamentary secretary would receive a bunch of recommendations and almost all from deputies and political associates of his party. The ultimate appointment might be satisfactory, but all such appointments should be on the basis of a period of trial, and the confirmation or termination of employment should be solely the function of the Board. To have any employee, whether he be tradesman or ordinary labourer, feel that he is safe and secure under the wing of his political nominator is a danger to discipline and the authority of his superiors. It may seem that I am laying undue stress on this matter of employment by public authorities, but some of my experiences convinced me that it is a problem that requires more attention than it receives from those who are concerned with it. To give one outstanding example of these experiences I will mention the case of a Mr X. Mr X was a tradesman, a mechanic employed in an important centre. He was active in party politics in his area and owed his original appointment to the recommendation of a minister. Directed by his overseer to proceed with a certain job, he flatly refused. The overseer suspended him and reported the facts to the architect for the district, who in due course submitted the case to the Board. There were some thirty-five employees, mostly skilled tradesmen, working in the centre and, when the file came before me and after a careful examination of the facts, I had no hesitation in ordering his dismissal. A short time afterwards we had a change of parliamentary secretary and a few weeks later the annual Ard Feis of the political party was held. I was somewhat shocked when, on the morning after the meeting of the Ard Fheis, the parliamentary secretary asked for the file on the case. I sensed interference from outside and quite bluntly told the parliamentary secretary that, while the file would of course be submitted to him, the case was closed and the man had been dismissed. The file was sent to the parliamentary secretary and to my amazement came back to me with a direction that Mr X was to be reinstated in his job. I realised, of course, that the direction, if followed, would mean an end to any discipline in that particular section, that the authority, not only of the overseer and architect but of the Board itself, could be treated with contempt. I prepared a minute to this effect and called in my two colleague commissioners for an emergency meeting of the Board. We all three signed the minute, but again the file came back to us with a simple repeat of the earlier direction to reinstate Mr X. My colleagues and I felt that we were being placed in a difficult, if not almost impossible, position, and there did not seem much that we could do about it. I later adverted to the fact that I was accounting officer and that I had to answer before the Public Accounts Committee for every penny of our total expenditure which, at the time, amounted to about one and a half million pounds a year. I also remembered that, in any case where critical questions arose, it was no defence for the accounting officer to cite the approval of a parliamentary secretary. The approval of a minister, in our case the minister for finance, was essential, if the accounting officer was to defend any particular expenditure that might be the subject of criticism at the Public Accounts Committee.

It might seem unlikely that any inquiry would emerge about a particular workman's work and wages considering the hundreds of men who were in our constant employment, but the fact was that it was expenditure of funds and I found it expedient to use that fact. It was my somewhat unpleasant job to submit a minute to the parliamentary secretary pointing out that, in the circumstances, his direction and authority were not sufficient, and that if he still insisted that Mr X must be reinstated then I, as accounting officer, must receive the specific sanction of the minister. The reply to my submission was prompt and to the point: 'Submit case to the minister'. I did so and merely cited the different pages of the file which covered the matter at issue. The commissioners heard no more about it. Whether there was any discussion of the case at a higher level or not, I do not know. The one thing we did know was that neither the file nor any direction ever reached us from the minister for finance and Mr X was not reinstated.

Does this seem to be making a fuss over a 'storm in a teacup'? I am convinced that it is of vital importance to our public life and administration that the whole question of nomination and recommendation for jobs in the public services should be examined. I would be inclined to go further and prohibit any minister, deputy, alderman or city councillor from making any recommendations for any job. The humblest employee, if he feels he is in any way under the protection of anyone in authority, is prone to play on that fact. His foreman or superior is made conscious of the position and, unless he is a very strong character, often fails to insist on that discipline and attention to work which are his primary functions. The menace spreads like a dry rot until real control and authority disappear. It will never be possible to ensure absolute integrity and fair play in this matter of public employment, but I would suggest that where responsibility and authority are entrusted to any body, whether it is a city or county manager, a board of directors or the Commissioners of Public Works, there should be no interference with that authority. If they fail in their administration they can be dealt with, but, if their authority is undermined by the subtle implication that subordinates have influence at a higher court, then a portion or even the whole organisation can be infected.

I hesitate to refer to a somewhat similar problem which arises in respect to the appointments that are made at the highest level, and I do so because I am conscious of the inherent difficulties that face the cabinet of the day in making their selection. It has been the accepted practice all over the world as we know it to appoint men to important positions within the State, who were, if not active party men, sympathetic supporters of the party in power. The judiciary and the various law-officers of the State, as well as many State representatives on various boards and companies, are invariably selected on this basis, though there have been a few commendable exceptions. The only comment I would venture on these appointments is that it is of primary importance that the presence of the highest standard, not only of competence but of integrity, should govern the selection and that anything in the shape of nepotism should be avoided as an evil.

It may be suggested that I myself owed my position as chairman of the Commissioners of Public Works to my political affiliations. While it is true that I was appointed by de Valera's government in 1936 of which I had been a member, the fact was that it was as a reinstated civil servant of the first Dáil Éireann that my appointment took place. As former consul general to the United States representing the Republic, I resigned my position following the treaty and the civil war because I would not conscientiously continue to represent the government at that time. It was the invariable practice to appoint reinstated civil servants in positions as nearly akin as possible to those from which they had resigned or from which they had been dismissed, and it was on this basis I passed from the cabinet to the Board of Works. I do not make a boast of it, but I may add that in all my career I have never sought preference, privilege or position for myself or for any member of my family or relatives.

Recently I had a long talk with an old friend on the evolution of national life and politics in our time. He is a priest and a very saintly one. We had been classmates over sixty years ago in St Malachy's College and he belonged to a family that had a well earned reputation for national service right back to the Fenians and the land war. Amongst other things, we discussed the old question of the priest in politics and recalled some of the difficulties and dangers that were created in the North when individual priests lined up on one side or the other of party differences. We were agreed that it was altogether regrettable and unwise for priests to take sides publicly as party advocates. While I agreed with my friend on that point, I did contend that there were many aspects of public life and conduct that merited more attention from the pulpit than they seemingly received. In other words, I suggested that the matter of ethics in public life should be subjected to close analysis and definition, and should be made the subject of sermons and direction more frequently than they are today. Perhaps I am treading on dangerous ground and that I am not competent to judge such matters, but I am sometimes afraid that there is amongst our public representatives a hazy notion that the ten commandments do not apply when the matter is one of politics. How often have we heard it said: 'Oh well, you know what politics are' or 'Oh but that's different, this was purely a matter of politics'. I do not see it that way, and I think the potential harm of the politician taking the wrong course in public affairs or on condonation of political jobbery far outweighs what he might or could do in his role of private citizen.

All this may sound smug or even pharisaical, but I am referring to these things because I still cling to the hope that in this small country of limited material resources but of immense reserves of national idealism we will attract the best of our young people to participation in the political and national guidance of our people. That is my apology for an old man's sermonising. I have digressed at some length from the consecutive run of my experiences in the Board of Works and my remote contact with affairs of State, but I leave off my preaching to mention a few of the events or works that were outside the boundary of our day-to-day routine.

It was early in 1943 that de Valera telephoned me to ask me if I remembered making a suggestion about the Chapel Royal in Dublin Castle when he, James Geoghegan, then minister for lands, and I were going over the Castle to see how we could best plan the use of it for the ceremonies and entertainments of the Eucharistic Congress in 1932. I remembered our inspection and that, when we visited the Chapel Royal, I suggested to de Valera that it should be converted and equipped as a Catholic chapel and that daily Mass should be offered there. De Valera agreed, but pressure of events and the acute political controversies of the intervening years accounted for the delay in dealing with the matter. He told me that the time had now come when the change was to be made and that His Grace, the Archbishop, the Most Reverend Dr McQuaid,[18] had deputed the Reverend Father Cathal MacCarthy,[19] dean of Clonliffe College, to act for him in making the necessary arrangements.

As the Board of Works would be responsible for the carrying out of the work, he directed me to contact Father McCarthy and go ahead with the necessary alterations and equipment. I did so and under Father McCarthy's direction one of our architects, Mr Basil Boyd-Barrett,[20] planned the alterations. The chief adaptation was of course in the sanctuary, and here a new altar and surrounds with communion rail, sanctuary lamp and candelabra were installed. The whole scheme was designed to fit in with the existing panelling and woodwork. The altar was in wood and the sanctuary lamp was in wood and bronze. The sacristy was equipped with a new vesting chest, and a complete set of vestments for all liturgical needs was

18. Archbishop John C. McQuaid, C.S.Sp (1895-1973): born Cootehill, County Cavan, dean of studies in Blackrock College 1928-31, president 1931-9, archbishop of Dublin 1940-72.

19. Fr Cathal McCarthy (1913-): born Dublin, professor of liturgy, Holy Cross College, Clonliffe 1939-64, dean 1940-55, president 1955-64, adviser to Radio Éireann on religious programmes 1940-62, member of Irish Liturgical Commission 1957, parish priest, Church of the Holy Name, Beechwood Avenue, Dublin 6, 1964-83, chairman of Catholic Television Interim Committee 1965, archdeacon of Glendalough 1977.

20. Basil Boyd-Barrett (1908-69): born Dublin, architect in Office of Public Works 1931-69, brother of distinguished architect, Rupert Boyd-Barrett.

supplied. Thanks to Father McCarthy's impeccable taste and Mr Boyd Barrett's sense of what was fitting and artistic, what was the Chapel Royal was now a very beautiful Catholic chapel and on the feast of Pentecost, 13 June 1943, his grace, the archbishop, said the first Mass and solemnly consecrated the chapel to the Most Holy Trinity with full ceremonial and in the presence of all the ministers of State, the judiciary and a distinguished congregation. It was a day to be remembered and I cherish it as one of the happiest in my official service. From that day Holy Mass is offered daily in the chapel and at least one little corner of Ireland has been reclaimed from the clutching grasp that had held it for centuries and restored to life in the heart of Catholic Dublin.

I have mentioned Father McCarthy as the guide and director of the conversion and rightly so, but I may add that it was the beginning of a friendship with him that has grown with the years. He is now a Very Reverend Canon of the diocesan chapter and president of Clonliffe College. I am indebted to him in many ways that are too personal to mention, but I value the opportunity that was afforded me of being associated with him in the establishment of the chapel of the Most Holy Trinity. As invariably happens in effecting any major changes in this country, some incident or other arises which marks the new development and the lines of demarcation between the old and the new. The Chapel Royal was not an exception.

It so happened that one of the Board's staff who was officially concerned with the building was a sound Protestant. When I informed him of what we proposed to do, I saw a look of horror creep across his face and spontaneously he said: 'But chairman, that is under the control of the cathedral chapter. You surely can't mean . . .' and then he stopped. Theoretically he was right. In the pre-treaty days the chapter of St Patrick's Cathedral was responsible for the Chapel Royal and a chaplain was appointed, but it would seem that from 1922 onwards no action had been taken to define the position. Gently I reminded him that the Castle and everything in it was State property and that it was surely within the competence of the government to decide how it should be used. I was tempted to add that both the cathedrals, Christ Church and St Patrick's were, by right, Catholic Church property and that the restoration of at least one of them would not be amiss. However, I resisted the impulse and felt that he had had shock enough for one day in his official life.

One of the most interesting events that occurred during my chairmanship was the munificent gift of Iveagh house and gardens to the State. The splendid entrance hall and the somewhat ornate reception rooms were preserved as they were and became the headquarters of the department of external affairs with access to the grounds. Some time afterwards the question of additional accommodation for University College was under consideration and Mr de Valera was discussing it with me. I suggested that the problem could be solved by the erection of buildings in a quadrangle around the grounds and, by taking in Harcourt Street and such houses as became available in St Stephen's Green, adequate accommodation could be provided. At that time, and I think the position is similar today, the only two premises in Harcourt Street that seemed to present any difficulties in regard to acquisition were the Children's Hospital and the Standard Hotel, and I thought these difficulties could be overcome. De Valera reminded me that there was a restrictive clause in the deed of gift that prohibited the erection of any buildings on the 'Grounds'. I suggested that, if the position was explained to Lord Iveagh, he might be willing to withdraw the restriction. I pointed out that by intelligent planning along Harcourt Street and Hatch Street a very reasonable portion of the grounds could be preserved as a campus or university gardens and still provide the building space necessary for the expansion. I also suggested that the department of external affairs could be accommodated elsewhere, preferably in Dublin Castle, and that Iveagh House should be made the official entrance to University College.

Mr de Valera seemed interested but non-committal, but the fact is that he informed me subsequently that he had approached Lord Iveagh[21] and that the latter had graciously consented to the withdrawal of the clause in the deed, prohibiting the erection of buildings on the grounds. In view of the conflict of opinion on the future development of University College, I think the facts as recorded have some significance and are not entirely irrelevant in the present controversy.

During the war and for quite a few years after it had ended, the work in the Board of Works provided us with a continuous series of problems. These were mainly due to the scarcity of supplies. We had our plans ready to get started on large comprehensive drainage schemes, but we found it nearly impossible to get deliveries of the heavy-plant necessary. It was only when we started to 'tap' the American market that we noticed an awakening on the part of the British-makers to show a live interest in our needs and give us reasonable deliveries. As our needs were extensive, we were able to buy from both as prices and dates of delivery suited us.

21. Guinness, Rupert Edward Cecil Lee, 2nd earl of Iveagh (1874-1967): born Dublin, served in Boer war 1900, M.P. for various English constituencies 1908-10, 1912-18, 1918-27, chancellor of Dublin University 1927.

It was not always easy to convince some of the departments of our difficulties. Some of those in the highest authority proved very difficult indeed. At times one was amused, but at other times the pressure and strain were acute. I always relish a minor experience that I had with one head of department. It was at the time of acute shortage when all fuel; coal, turf and firewood; was being doled out in meagre rations. In the month of August, when all heating was of course cut off, I got an official call from the department of finance that a coal fire and an adequate supply of coal was to be provided for this gentleman's private office. It was on medical authority and so there was no more to be said about it, and he got his coal fire and enough coal to keep him warm all day. We felt no grievance about that. He was elderly, on the brink of retirement and was understood to be delicate.

Early in October I sat down beside him in a bus homeward bound at about six o'clock in the evening. We exchanged the usual small talk of the day and I suggested that he would be glad to get into his slippers and relax at the fire. He stunned me when he said he was going out to Bohernabreena to have a swim before he went home to dinner. I thought of the coal fires in August and September, but said noting about them yet I wondered what new treatment had been evolved whereby you are cooked all day at 70% to prepare for a plunge into fresh water at twilight.

It would be dull and uninteresting to attempt any record of all the innumerable activities of the Board during the years, and I have already said enough to indicate their variety and nature and some of the interdepartmental and ministerial problems to which they gave rise. It will be sufficient if I sum it up by saying that from the start of the war in 1939 there was little of what had been established routine left undisturbed. My occasional talks and conferences with de Valera continued, but they were less frequent than they had been. I would stress the fact that on all occasions such talks only took place when I was invited over to his office. At no time did I feel that I was entitled to raise any issue on my own initiative. I was a civil servant and it was outside my province to offer criticism or opinions, unless my views were sought. While that was my definite line of action, I had no hesitation in being entirely frank if and when my views were sought. Our talks over the years have been many and covered most aspects of government activity and policy. I cannot flatter myself that either my talk or advice had any appreciable influence for, to be quite candid, there were quite a number of issues on which we seemed to agree that radical change was essential, but no change or action followed. Well, that was his job! Perhaps circumstances or political exigencies explained the position. I did not know, I did not inquire and I do not know today. What I did realise was that most of our economic and land policy of 1932 was rapidly disappearing and that the drift from internal self-reliance and development had become a steady stream.

In the course of these *tête-a-tête* conferences de Valera referred to a number of problems that were causing him concern, and adverted to the question of land division and the land commission. I smiled at this and asked him if he were serious. He seemed irritated and asked me what I meant, and said of course he was serious. I said it was difficult to realise that; that we had discussed the position frequently; that he had consulted Mr Commissioner Dan Browne, who with Commissioners Mansfield and O'Shiel were my chief support in the land ministry, at least twice and got his advice on what was needed to restore the land commission to its full functioning power, and that nothing had been done. I said I could only conclude that he had changed his policy. This remark sparked off a minor fireworks display. He denied that there was any change of policy and I retorted that, looking at the position, how was one to think otherwise? I pointed to some of the more obvious instances which seemed to bear out my charge, and this did not improve the atmosphere. To sum it up briefly, de Valera was more than annoyed, and I myself was in a raging bad temper. I turned at the door as I was leaving and my parting benediction was simply: 'All right, you do what you think is best, as far as I am concerned, I'm through'. It was my last private talk or conference with de Valera. It is and will be always the most bewildering problem of my political career to try to understand de Valera's change on this and a number of other major lines of policy which were, prior to 1932 and for some years afterwards, articles of faith to which he had pledged himself. There may have been very good sound reasons for the changes but, if so, they are not obvious and, what is more important, they have never been disclosed either to his supporters or the electorate. For my part I believe the changes were fundamentally bad for the ultimate future of the State and people.

One other comment and I will have finished with the unpleasant break in a close association that had lasted from 1923 to 1945, and it is this. In my later talks with de Valera I formed the opinion that he no longer welcomed discussion much less criticism, and that what he wanted beside him was a group of 'yes men' who agreed with everything and anything that the party, with himself as leader, approved. I think he achieved this! This has been by far the most difficult and certainly the most unpleasant section of these notes to put on record, and I would have been glad to have omitted them, but for the fact that they were a vital part of my experiences and seem to me to shed some light on the trend of things since war broke out in 1939 and a trend that has been alarmingly accelerated in recent years.

Save for my occasional conferences with de Valera, I was out of touch with politics and politicians since my retirement from the ministry. Apart from the fact that I had more than a full day's work every day, I enjoyed a sense of relief in being freed from meetings and debates and the environs of Leinster House. At times I would run into some of my old associates on the street or in a restaurant but, irrespective of the party to which they belonged, politics were seldom mentioned. Occasionally I had a tramp over the Dublin hills or a long chat over a cup of coffee with an old friend and associate, who was later to figure in a somewhat fantastic phase of political acrobatics.

I first met Noel Hartnett[22] at a meeting of the Historical Society of Trinity College at which I had been asked to preside. That was in 1932 and shortly after Fianna Fáil had been elected as the government, and Hartnett was the leading evangelist for Fianna Fáil and republicanism in the Elizabethan stronghold. I was much impressed by his personality and by his skill in debate which veered between extremes of vehemence and acidulous satire. Later we became more intimate and ultimately good friends. He had two qualities which appealed to me: one was his interest in the underprivileged, and the other was his ability to laugh at himself. He had an immense vehemence and flow of language to match, which were somewhat devastating when released. I have seen him here at home after one of these outbursts sit back immediately afterwards, run his hand through his hair, laugh boisterously and say: 'Amn't I the awful eejit to get worked up over such a darned trifle?' Another characteristic in those days was his indifference to his material advancement. He worked hard. He and our friend Harry Kennedy,[23] whose early death shocked and distressed his many friends, wrote and produced some of the best programmes then broadcast by Radio Éireann, while at the same time he produced and issued the Bulletin Service for home and foreign newspapers on the Partition

22. Noel Hartnett (1909-60): born Kenmare, County Kerry, teacher, press officer for Irish Tourist Association, barrister, broadcaster in Radio Éireann, member of National Executive of Fianna Fáil 1933-7, co-founder of Clann na Poblachta 1947, after the indecisive general election of 1951 he organised the Independent support which put Fianna Fáil and de Valera back in power, senate 1951-3, rejoined Fianna Fáil 1953, co-founder of National Progressive Democratic Party 1957.

23. Harry Kennedy: journalist, broadcaster, close associate of the leaders of Clann na Poblachta.

problem.[24] I was closely associated with him in the latter project and I can say with all sincerity that the work, and not the meagre monetary reward, was the driving impulse behind his efforts.

It can be assumed that my purpose in recording my knowledge and experience with Hartnett has a purpose other than a mere character study. It has, and simply because he was a pivotal power and influence at a vital stage in our political history. I had been meeting him only on rare occasions not because of any straining of our friendship but simply that our ways seemed to diverge and that, since the war, there was less inducement to go out to meet friends. On such occasions I found him more vehement than ever in his denunciation of those in power with a particular bias against certain ministers and their departments. I pointed out to him that he had developed a completely 'anti' and negative attitude, which was ill-balanced and of little value. I stressed this particularly when he told me that, on his initiative and that of Seán MacBride[25] and others, a new party was being formed to give a lead to the country and replace the existing government.

He mentioned some of those who were already linked up, and my immediate reaction was to advise him that, in my opinion, they were embarking on a foolish and forlorn hope. I pointed out that what they seemed to be attempting was to gather together all the 'old timers' who had, for one reason or another, been opposed to de Valera and Fianna Fáil; that many of the men he had mentioned, while very decent men, definitely bore the 'scars' of a political past, and were liabilities rather than assets to a new movement. I told him that the only hope I saw for the future was a new movement which would seek to bring the best of our young men and women together to work for the development of the country, and discard all of us who were tainted with the aftermath of the treaty and all that followed. It was the only talk I had with him about the new movement, and I cannot flatter myself that my arguments made any impression on him

24. The first issue of this service appeared in mid-April 1938, the last on 29 January 1945. Connolly, in fact, was in charge of the Northern Ireland Publicity Service on which he reported indirectly to de Valera. He also occasionally contributed articles to the Bulletin over a variety of pseudonyms.

25. Seán MacBride (1904-88): born Paris, I.R.A. 1921, active anti-treatyite 1922-3, leading member of Comhairle na Poblachta 1929, organiser of Saor Éire convention 1931, I.R.A. chief of staff 1936-8, barrister 1937, left I.R.A. in protest at its 1939 bombing campaign, leading barrister defending I.R.A. activists during 1940s, founder of Clann na Poblachta 1946, minister for external affairs 1948-51, secretary general of International Community of Jurists 1963-70, founder member and later chairman of Amnesty International, co-author of the United Nations Declaration of Human Rights, Nobel Peace Prize 1974, Lenin Peace Prize 1977.

or his associates, for a short time afterwards Clann na Poblachta was launched with MacBride at its head, and with many of those I looked upon as liabilities on the governing board. Well, it was their job and after all I myself was one of the older generation for whose relegation I had pleaded. In the circumstances and being absorbed day by day in my official work, I can perhaps be pardoned for having taken but the merest casual interest in the passing show of politics.

Even the election in February 1948 afforded little or no stimulus to my political instincts. I had no faith whatever in the new movement, despite the fact that I was told that many of the younger people were supporting it in the hope of breaking up the two principal parties. The result of this election was interesting. Fianna Fáil held 68 seats against a mere 31 seats won by Fine Gael; Labour had 14, National Labour 5, and Clann na Poblachta 10; Clann na Talmhan/the Farmers had 7, and there were 12 Independents. Fianna Fáil was the largest single party, but de Valera had definitely declared that under no circumstances would he or his party form a coalition. I share his views on coalitions for the simple reason that I cannot see how any definite policy can be pursued and maintained if ministers, representing various and invariably conflicting interests, have to be satisfied or placated before every piece of legislation and every government decision is made effective. The combined votes of the opposition to de Valera put him and his government out of office. It was the first defeat since Fianna Fáil had been given power sixteen years earlier in the election of 1932.

Mr John A. Costello[26] was elected Taoiseach, and his cabinet reflected the strength of the different parties which formed the coalition. Mr Seán MacBride was installed as minister for external affairs and his colleague, Dr Nöel Browne,[27] was made minister for health. The acceptance of office by MacBride and Browne sounded the death-knell of Clann na Poblachta and created a cynical reaction, particularly amongst the younger and more idealistic of the Clann's supporters. Memories were not so short in Ireland as to let people forget MacBride's own conflicts with his new associates in the pre-Fianna Fáil days. A wiser political course seemed to me simple

26. John A. Costello (1891-1976): born Dublin, barrister 1914, attorney-general 1926-32, T.D. for County Dublin 1933 and for other Dublin seats up to 1965, Taoiseach 1948-51, supported the Act which formally established the Republic of Ireland 1949, Taoiseach 1954-7.

27. Nöel C. Browne (1915-): born Waterford, medical doctor, Clann na Poblachta T.D. for Dublin South East 1948, minister for health 1948-51, Independent T.D. 1951-3, member of Fianna Fáil but failed to secure the Party's nomination 1953, Independent T.D. 1957, National Progressive Democratic Party T.D. 1958-63, Labour T.D. 1969-73, senator for Trinity College, Dublin 1973-7, Socialist Labour Party T.D. 1977-81.

enough. He had simply to lead his party in the Dáil as an independent group, alert and ready to deal with each and every matter according to their decision as to what was good for the nation.

In the then existing political situation MacBride and his party of ten had a wonderful opportunity of setting a new headline for young Ireland, in accordance with Clann na Poblachta's published programme. A very few years of such leadership might well have seen the Clann emerge as a strong young Ireland party and a new complexion stamped on our political life. Instead, the party as such practically disappeared from public life. In 1951 two Clann deputies were elected to the Dáil and in 1954 three were returned. MacBride himself was defeated in 1957 and today, 1959, there is but one single deputy of the party in the Dáil.[28]

It is not for an outsider like myself to assign blame or responsibility for the decision of the Clann to merge the party into the coalition. It was currently understood that my friend Hartnett was the main influence in that direction. However, surely the ultimate decision rested with Mr MacBride himself who was not only the principal minister concerned but was also the leader of the party. My chief interest in the position was the realisation that the party had injected a further dose of disillusionment into their younger supporters and, what was even more important, had made it still more difficult for a real worthwhile national lead to be given a hearing. This latter result was and still is the major damage that can be charged against Clann na Poblachta.

I have described, as briefly as possible, the evolution of Clann na Poblachta. It was a peculiar evolution but the aftermath was more than peculiar, it was almost Gilbertian. Something 'went wrong with the works' for in a relatively short time we find that Hartnett, Dr Browne and a new deputy, Dr ffrench-O'Carroll,[29] had broken away from the Clann and MacBride, and were now campaigning as vigorously against them as they had in 1947-8 been fighting Mr de Valera and Fianna Fáil. The two doctors were elected to the Dáil and my friend Hartnett was a senator. All of them were nominally 'Independent'. The situation was intriguing, if one could stand back and look at it dispassionately. Perhaps the simplest way of

28. This was John Tully of Cavan who held his seat in 1961 and 1965. The party was dissolved and in 1969 Tully was defeated when he ran as an Independent.

29. Michael William ffrench-O'Carroll (1919-): born Dublin, medical doctor 1944, member of Clann na Poblachta 1947, Independent T.D. for Dublin South West 1951-3, reverted to career in medicine 1958, post-graduate studies, University of Michigan 1968-73, worked in public health in U.K. 1973-74, joined Irish Public Health Authority 1974-75, medical officer of health and director of medical services for Cork 1975-80, director of Alcohol and Drug-Addiction Centre, Cork 1980-92.

explaining my reaction to it is to quote from the final chapter of my pamphlet, *How Does She Stand?*, which was published in 1953.[30] In this I say.

> A final word! It is to those who may protest that there is no just cause for pessimism and that, politics being what they are, expedience must play it part in the affairs of the government. There are two answers that come to mind. The first is that, when expediency involves a breach of principle or a departure from either truth or integrity, then expediency must go. The second is to point to our present government of October 1953 and examine its basis of power. To do so involves a short retrospective study.
>
> A few years ago a new party was formed. It combined within its ranks many divergent elements but all united on one purpose and that was the overthrow of the existing Fianna Fáil government.
>
> It had, of course, a proclaimed policy, but it was difficult from the very beginning to see how the constituent elements could merge or fuse together on a really national policy. It is an open secret that one of the main driving forces behind the movement was one whom we might designate as the 'Dynamo' for that exactly describes him. It is no libel or an injustice to him to say that he at least believed sincerely that Fianna Fáil must be ejected from office. He had his reasons and his experience! He and his party worked hard and, although not very successful as a party, he and they did succeed sufficiently to defeat the government party and form part of the coalition that succeeded it.
>
> It is history now how the second cleavage occurred and this cleavage was within the party, and then our dynamic friend found that the power that he had done so much to build and which had dethroned Fianna Fáil must itself be destroyed and that the only means whereby that could be achieved was by the restoration of Fianna Fáil and the government of the country. There is one other aspect of the situation which it would be wrong to evade, however distasteful it is to have to refer to it. It is on record, not once but several times, that the head of the government does not favour coalition governments in any shape or form. I have every sympathy with that point of view and believe with him that it is practically impossible for any cabinet to follow any clear-cut line of national policy successfully unless they are united on the basic principles of that policy.

30. Joseph Connolly, *How does she stand? An appeal to Young Ireland* (Michael F. Moynihan publishing company, Dublin, 1953).

> It amounts to a 'state of mind' which, for real progress, must operate harmoniously through all the departments of State and create a unity of purpose and action. Bearing this in mind, it is diffficult to reconcile the existence of the government of today with that expressed objection to any form of coalition.
>
> It is granted that the so-called 'Independents' do not occupy ministerial or other posts, but it must also be granted that the government holds office solely at the will and pleasure of these so-called 'Independents'.
>
> It can safely be assumed that Mr de Valera never discussed, negotiated with nor dealt with these representatives, but it is not unreasonable to assume that some of his subordinate leaders did. It is further reasonable to assume that he knows what voters, other than those of his own party, he has to depend on to give his government the strength to keep his party in power. There is a certain grim humour behind it all when it is remembered that the very power, dynamic and explosive as it was, that ousted him and his party from power is now the same power that keeps the party in office today. Is this another of the factors that make our young people cynical about politics and politicians? It could be!

As I have explained earlier, the pamphlet was ignored by the government's daily paper, but it was not without significance that within a period of a few weeks the supporting 'Independents' were assimilated into the Fianna Fáil party as full members. Doubtless it was purely 'coincidental', but a study of the statements of the new re-assimilated prodigals afford an interesting study when compared with their earlier arguments for the dethroning of de Valera and the Fianna Fáil government. The marriage of convenience was short-lived, and when the 1954 election took place the olive branch had withered and the new allegiance was ended.

I have gone ahead of my period and it may be thought have devoted too much attention to what was perhaps considered to be a passing phase on the political stage but, as I have said, I look back on the whole performance of Clann na Poblachta and its leaders as a most damaging factor to our young people's faith in our political future. Many will disagree with that analysis and it is not for an old man to be dogmatic, but I can only record the events as I saw them and my personal reactions to them.

I have moved rapidly from the mid-1940s and right into the fifties, but it was unavoidable if the Hartnett-MacBride and Clann na Poblachta saga was to be complete and in any sense coherent. Let me emphasise the fact that I was merely an outside observer of all that went on. I scarcely ever met any of the politicians of any of the parties and when we met we did not discuss politics. My work in the Board of Works was all-engrossing and I had practically ceased to have any faith in either the deputies or the parties they represented.

I had several disappointments in planning our Board of Works schemes. One was the provision of adequate, modern accommodation for government offices. My idea was that we could provide a major portion of what was needed by a progressive rebuilding programme of most of the old buildings of Dublin Castle. Certain unique and historical sections would be preserved and restored, but many of the old buildings which were being used as offices were in danger of collapse. The plan was to erect the first, new modern building then transfer into it the staffs from building number two, have this demolished and a new building erected to accommodate those from building number three. Proceeding in this way the old, crumbling buildings and rabbit warrens that constitute most of the accommodation of officials would have been replaced by modern offices. It was inevitably a long-term programme which would probably have been spread over a period of twelve to fifteen years. The advantages I saw in the scheme was that the State already owned the site and so could proceed without the expense of purchase or compulsory acquisition; that it would cause no disturbance to existing interests and that a very big section of government administration would be carried out in the heart of the city and within easy reach of the law courts, the main banking and commercial offices and with convenience to all concerned. Quite a number of government offices are scattered over different sections of the city and some are in old and unsuitable buildings that would scandalise any efficiency expert.

Another project was the erection of a short-wave radio station. During the war and after it, the lack of short-wave broadcasting was acutely felt and Mr de Valera had determined that, as quickly as possible, a short-wave transmission station should be erected. The radio experts reported that the most favourable location for such a station was in the Donnybrook area. As our function in the business included the provision of a suitable site and the erection of the necessary buildings, a site giving us ample space, including a fine residence, was purchased.

When, in February 1948, the first coalition government took over from Fianna Fáil both these projects were dropped and all development in connection with them was suspended. I thought both decisions were wrong. I was tempted to think that they may have been influenced by a desire, from the party point of view, to show the lack of wisdom on the part of their predecessors in office.

I understand that the site and house, which had been purchased for the short-wave station, have been transferred to University College. It may be so, but I have no authoritative information on all that is included in the big scheme of University College development as at present planned.

Apart from a few such decisions regarding change of plans, the change over from Fianna Fáil to the coalition government did not affect our normal work in the Board of Works. School building, arterial drainage and all the other major works were being pushed forward and, with a gradually improving position in respect of supplies, we were able to place more and more contracts and expedite the work.

The change of government brought us a new parliamentary secretary, Mr Michael Donnellan,[31] a deputy representing Galway and a leading member of the Clann na Talmhan/the Farmers' Party, which had returned seven deputies to the Dáil. Like most new political heads of departments, he found the work of the Board in all its many sections and ramifications somewhat bewildering, but he was a reasonable and agreeable 'head' and always willing to be guided. He had one characteristic, however, that was at times embarrassing: he just could not give no for an answer. He was liable to promise that a major drainage scheme, on which a survey had just begun and which could not possibly be commenced for a couple of years, would be opened up in a few months time. It was this consistent tendency which made me describe him, in his presence, as 'the most promising parliamentary secretary we had in my time'.

There was little, if anything, to give me any excitement during the few remaining years I spent in the Board of Works. The work was always heavy and was often made more so by lack of decision or conflict of opinion between departments. My colleague, the late Diarmuid O'Hegarty, often suffered torture when such occurred. He suffered all the more because he was one of those quiet, long-suffering souls who listened patiently, while groaning internally. Diarmuid was a man of outstanding ability, who, while thoughtful and disarmingly quiet in conference, never missed a point in an argument or brief. He had been secretary to the Executive Council in the Cosgrave government and had been made a commissioner of public works in 1932. He would succeed me as chairman in 1950. He died in March

31. Michael Donnellan (1900-64): born Dunmore, County Galway, Sinn Féin member of Glenamaddy District Council 1917, member of Galway County Council 1927-45, founder of Clann na Talmhan 1938, T.D. for Galway 1943-4, 1948-51, parliamentary secretary to minister for finance 1948-51.

1958, a few months after his retirement, and those of us who worked with him down the years lost a good friend and a brilliant colleague. God grant him eternal rest!

Despite the war and all the confusion and upsets that accompanied it, the years in the Board of Works passed rapidly and I woke up to the fact that I was within sight of my sixty-fifth birthday and my retirement. The realisation of this did not cause me much emotion one way or the other. I was in reasonably good health and felt quite competent to do a full day's work or participate in conferences, however difficult or diverse they may have been. Some months before I was due to retire the parliamentary secretary informed me that our minister, Mr McGilligan, had asked him if I wished to have a period of extended service continued after my retirement date. This was a concession that was occasionally granted to retiring officials and periods of retention were from six to twelve months. I asked the parliamentary secretary to express to the minister my appreciation of the offer, but told him that, as a matter of principle, I would prefer to relinquish my position on the due date and gave him my reasons. The regulations stipulated for retirement at sixty-five years and, unless there were very exceptional circumstances such as difficulty in finding a suitable successor, there should be no departure from this rule. No such difficulty arose in my case as Diarmuid O'Hegarty was there and fully ready to take over. By remaining on for an extended period, I would be barring him from well-earned promotion and consequential promotions would be similarly held up right down the line. From the personal economic point of view the extension would have been welcome, for two of my sons had not yet completed their academic studies, but I had always been opposed to the system of extended service for the reasons already stated and saw no justification for being an exception.

While on this subject of retirement, I may refer to what I consider is an even greater evil than the retention concession that seems to have crept into our administration in later years. This is the tendency to appoint retired officials to positions on various government or semi-government boards. The argument may be used that their experience in administration is valuable, but in most cases the argument is unconvincing. If there is any logic in the continuation of official service beyond the stipulated sixty-five years of age, then the obvious course is to extend the period of service and defer the age of retirement. I would not favour such a change, but mention the alternative to show the anomalies that exist. Despite the evidence we have of the elder statesmen who cling on to power and authority long after they have passed the sixty-fifth milestone, I am still satisfied that here in

Ireland we can afford to dispense with the 'ancient mariners' and let youth have its chance to bring a breath of fresh air into our political and national life.

There is one other comment that I would venture to make before I close finally on my experiences of government generally and as commissioner of public works in particular. I have always been critical of the consistent tendency towards extravagance, both at home and abroad, in the provision and furnishing of accommodation for our State representatives. Some of our legations abroad are, to put it mildly, on the grandiose scale and scarcely in keeping with the economy of a twenty-six county Republic of a partitioned Ireland with a population of less than three million people. At home we have somewhat similar tendencies, which I need not exemplify. I know that the argument urged in favour of all this is that of 'prestige and the dignity of the country', but may it not create the very opposite effect? After all, most of those who are likely to visit or frequent these establishments are fully aware of our true position, and do we run the danger of the sneer at our 'pretentiousness'? We are not the British empire or the United States government, but one is sometimes tempted to think that it is on their standards we try to impress the foreigner. I am entirely in favour of maintaining the prestige and dignity of the State at home and abroad, and that our hospitality and generous welcome to our guests should be maintained, but all this can be secured while still preserving a sense of proportion that would more accurately reflect the real position of the country. I am sure this commentary will be rejected as 'carping criticism' or the groaning of a 'tight-fisted Northerner', but let those who criticise look through the book of estimates and the appropriation accounts and they may find some food for reflection after a brief study of both. Some of the many sub-heads are not altogether in harmony with the shilling per week increase that has been awarded to our old-age pensioners. I leave it at that!

On 19 January 1950 I was sixty-five years of age and I spent it, my last official day as chairman of the Commissioners of Public Works, in handing over my 'keys of office' to Diarmuid O'Hegarty and bidding farewell to my colleagues. I had spent some thirteen and a half years in the department and it was difficult to accept the fact that my work had now ended, and that from the following day I was a free agent and had shed my official responsibilities.

It was a new experience and I paused to reflect that it was the first time since I was a youngster at the national school that it had happened to me. Retirement had no terrors for me and I knew that, if the Lord granted me my health and the use of my faculties, I had enough interests to preserve me from boredom and a sense of futility. I did not play golf, I was a teetotaller and my interest in outdoor sport had diminished almost to vanishing point. However, I still enjoyed a long tramp, I had a reasonable library of books and a circle of friends and my family circle. In these circumstances it was pleasant to relax and take a detached interest in all that went on around me.

While I continued to remain detached and nothing on earth would have provoked me to participate in any movement, political or otherwise, the inevitable discussions emerged frequently when some of my old associates and friends visited me for a social evening. One one such occasion, when some young friends of my own boys were spending the evening with us, the talk turned on existing conditions and the apathy of the younger generation to problems of national importance. I was probably somewhat vehement or scathing in my criticism of the situation and the lack of interest and activity on the part of our young men because one of them promptly said: 'Well, if that's how you feel about it why don't you say so in public or publish your views in the press?' Without much consideration or deliberation I said: 'I will, I'll do just that.'

That was what prompted me to sit down and prepare a series of twelve articles in which I tried to analyse the national position from the point of view of modern youth; to try and find the reasons for his almost cynical apathy, and to suggest the need for shedding it. The writing of these articles was made difficult, not from any lack of material, but simply because I believed that my criticisms must be confined to such matters as had been made public in the press, and that I had to steer entirely clear of much that I knew as a former minister and as a head of a department of State.

I submitted the articles in turn to the *Irish Independent*, and the *Irish Times*. Needless to say I did not send them to the *Irish Press*, as their very nature eliminated any possibility of them being considered suitable for loyal party readers. Both the other Dublin dailies rejected them and so I decided to publish them in pamphlet form under the title 'How Does She Stand?' and the sub-title 'An Appeal to Young Ireland'. I have already referred to its publication and even quoted from it so I shall not go beyond saying that it had, despite the *Irish Press*, and party 'freeze over' on it, a reasonably good circulation. I am satisfied that all of my charges are still valid and indeed could be augmented by still later developments. However, I leave the further criticism to some of the younger generation if and when they awake to the glaring facts that the country is being rapidly 'put in pawn' to the foreign combines; that our emigration continues; that our people are not being planted in farms and homes of their own by the land commission as was planned in our original policy; and that a mountain of debt bearing heavy interest rates has been built up to lay on the shoulders of future generations. 'What did future generations ever do for us?' was a common jest when I was a youth. They will have no doubt as to what we did to them in the years ahead. Today, as I write, I remembered an advertisement which appeared in yesterday's *Irish Independent*, of 18 May 1960. It reads thus: 'Farms wanted! Required for German clients, 4 farms of 200-250 acres each, preferably in coastal regions. Interested parties should communicate in writing giving full details to . . .' Maybe it is all wise and right and farseeing! Maybe my strictures are but the croakings of an old man who has become cranky in his old age. I am ready to be convinced that such is the case, but only when I am convinced that our people do not find it necessary to emigrate, and that we have not reverted to the policy of fostering the interests of the big rancher in all branches of agriculture at the expense of the family farm.

There is little of importance or excitement to disturb the twilight years of the average quiet man who has survived the turbulent years and has glided into retirement. I had, however, one experience which is, perhaps, worthy of being recorded. Some time after I had completed my articles I conceived the notion of attempting to write a play. I have had a life-long interest in the theatre from my earliest years, an interest which I maintained at home and abroad, despite all the pressure and strain of my other activities.[32] I have already mentioned my previous efforts to write for the stage and the relative success of what I considered a rather poor play in the Abbey.

That was away back in 1913 and, although the 'itch' to try and develop as a dramatist was always there, circumstances and my essential work made it impossible for me even to contemplate any such effort. My new freedom and relative idleness must have stirred some of the old hankering, for I found myself almost sub-consciously thinking of possible themes and envisaging stage settings. However that may be, I found myself settled in to work seriously on a modern play which I planned would be a satirical study of the evolution of one of our modern tycoons of the dominating type and his relationship with his workers, his associates and his family. I need not bore the reader with further details. It is sufficient to say that in due course the job was finished and the play submitted to the Abbey Theatre. My political relationship with the chief mogul of the Abbey had

32. This is evident in the splendid tribute to F. J. McCormick which Connolly provided in the *Capuchin Annual* of 1948.

been worse than strained since 1923 and, frankly, I had little hope of a sympathetic reading. However, I was assured that the play had been submitted to four different readers and the consensus of opinion was to reject it. That sounded fair enough and it was not for me to dispute their verdict.

The play was put on by a group of Dublin amateurs who gave a somewhat mixed but, on the whole, rather poor production of it. Despite that, the production gave me the sense that the play had certain qualities both in its dialogue, characterisation and ideas, and a short time later I wrote to Harold Goldblatt,[33] who was director and leading actor in the Belfast Group Theatre,[34] asking him if he would be interested in reading it. He replied at once, askng me to send it on to him, and after a few weeks wrote accepting it for production by his company.

There were the usual delays and difficulties that seem to attend everything in the world of the theatre. At times it seemed as if I would have to enforce the fulfilment of the contract. However, in April 1958 the play, *Master of the House*, was played to a packed house and had its three weeks run in the excellent intimate theatre which the Group Theatre has had provided for them in the Ulster Minor Hall. The production was by James Ellis who was doing his first show for the 'Group', and was entirely satisfying. Ellis had been producing in the Bristol Old Vic and later in Bangor, County Down. Those who saw his production of Sam Thompson's[35] *Over the Bridge* will need no tribute of approval from me of his qualities as a producer. Harold Goldblatt took the leading part and Margaret D'Arcy and Elizabeth Begley were the leading women. The cast was excellent and I was immensely satisfied with the whole show. I may be pardoned for mentioning that the packed house seemed to be equally satisfied. Goldblatt gave of his best in a very heavy part and Goldblatt's 'best' is very good indeed. I first saw him on the stage when he came as special guest artist to take the principal part in *The Dybuck*, a Jewish play which the Dublin Jewish Dramatic Society put on for a week in the Gaiety Theatre. I was therefore happy when he advised me that he was taking the leading part in 'The master' and I was even more so after seeing the performance.

Since then the Group Theatre in Belfast has been somewhat torn asunder with internal disruption and the final dispute over Mr Sam

33. Harold Goldblatt (1901-82): one of the many fine actors associated with the Ulster Group Theatre.

34. Ulster Group Theatre (1940-60): actors developed by it included, among others, J. D. Devlin (1908-87), Elizabeth Begley (1909-93) and Margaret D'Arcy.

35. Samuel Thompson (1916-65): born Belfast, painter, actor, his *Over the Bridge*, a play about religious bigotry in Belfast, was highly acclaimed, its rejection by directors of the Ulster Group Theatre caused the break-up of that body.

Thompson's excellent play *Over the Bridge*. Some of their leading players, including Goldblatt, Devlin and others, have cut their connection with it and they have lost their brilliant producer James Ellis. I look upon this as a tragedy not only for the Belfast theatre but for the whole Irish theatre. The 'Group' in Belfast was to Belfast what the 'Abbey' is to Dublin. It had built up a group of brilliant actors as competent as their Dublin contemporaries, and their productions were equally satisfying. The company is being continued, but it must be facing serious difficulties in trying to fill the gaps created by the many resignations.

I got a minor jolt at one of the intervals between the acts at the first performance when I suddenly remembered that the last occasion on which I was in the building was on 4 May 1916. It was not then the Group Theatre, but the Ulster Minor Hall, a rather unattractive annex to the big Hall, and I was there as one of the adjudicators in the play competitions for the Belfast Feis. I sat through the evening's performances and made my notes and was of course booked to do the same for the succeeding shows. I never knew what happened to my notes or how the competitions progressed for, on the following morning, the gentlemen of the G Division of the R.I.C., acting on behalf of His Majesty, George V, took me to Crumlin Road jail from which I proceeded to visit various 'theatres' where, although the houses were 'big', the audiences were cold and unsympathetic.

It was hard to realise that forty-two years had passed since then and that an old fellow of seventy-three had taken the place of the thirty-one year old in saying a few words of thanks and appreciation to his fellow-townsfolk.

One of the consolations of my retirement was that I re-discovered Cushendun, that nest of quiet peace on the Antrim coast. I had never really lost it, but circumstances had prevented me from visiting it. For some years after the treaty I was on the 'black list' in so far as the six counties were concerned. Then my activities, both political and administrative, tended to bring me more and more to Donegal, Kerry and Connemara.

I came back to Cushendun as one comes back home after a long absence and recaptured all the beauty and peace of the surrounding glens, the background of its hills and the sheltered bay. It has not the widespread grandeur of Kerry, nor the wild beauty of Connemara with its ravishing skies of ever-changing colours, but it has enough of each on a smaller scale to make it for me closer and more intimate and homely. Coming out from Mass on a summer morning, the vale of Glendun, stretching back to where it joins Glenann with the conical peak of Tievebulliagh towering behind and the gentle flow of the Dun river making its way to Cushendun and the sea, always gives me that sense of peace and restfulness that I have never found elsewhere. It was good to be there in June and return again for a 'round off' of the summer in early September before one finally settled in by the hearth for the winter months.

It is my sorrow and one of my very few grievances that I am no longer able to go there and the prospect of ever visiting the glens again is extremely dim. On Good Friday 1959 I had a severe heart attack and was prepared for the last journey and anointed for death. I really felt that I had finished my course and was content that it should be so, if it was God's will. I recall reflecting that Good Friday was a good day on which to die, that I had to be grateful to God for sparing me to see all my family happily-settled, that, although by no means encumbered with property or riches, I had no financial or other worries. In short, I reflected that my job was done and that I must trust in God to forgive me my sins and grant me His great Mercy.

However, thanks to the care of my wife and all at home and the medical attention of my son-in-law, Dr Ivo Drury, and my doctor daughter, Eithne, I pulled through and since then have led the quiet life of a chronic heart invalid. It is a restricted existence, but the garden, my easy chair, my books and the visits of friends and, above all, the constant care and attention from my family leave no possible excuse for complaint. So many more worthy people are suffering agonies of pain or are passing their remaining days in drab tenements that I can but offer up my prayer of thanks to God for all the blessings and comforts that are mine in the evening of my life.

The last chapters of these notes have been completed under difficulties, having been written since I was first laid low by the heart attack of 1959. It has been something of a struggle to complete them for, inevitably, I had many bad days when any effort to concentrate or write was just not possible. Against that I had a certain satisfaction in completing them and, if they reflect a certain weariness at times, let me claim for them and the chapters preceding them that they are sincere and honest and record the thoughts, impressions and views of the period and events as I then saw them.

It has been a good and interesting journey for me and, although my course of life was almost entirely diverted from what I had originally planned and expected, I do not think, looking back on it all, I would have wished it to be different. That is not to say that I can look back smugly on the past. Far from it! The blunders and mistakes and worst offences of a long life still arise like effigies from the past to haunt and humble me. But it is interesting and somewhat ironical to recall some of my early hopes and plans, and how differently circumstances and events combined to direct them.

In my youth and young manhood I had certain fixed ideas of what I wanted to do and was resolved that I would not do. I was determined that I would work to have an independent business, however small or big, of my own. I was equally resolved that I would not leave Ireland to go abroad, believing, as I still do, that Ireland had everything that made life worthwhile for me. Another resolution was that nothing would induce me to enter politics as a paid or dependent politician or to enter the civil service. Man proposes, and note what happened! I crossed the Atlantic sixteen times and had to stay in America for periods of from three to nine months at a time. My independent business, which was successful and expanding and made our position comfortable, had to be given up. I became an official of Dáil Éireann, later a minsiter of state at a thousand pounds a year, and finally finished up as a reinstated civil servant.

Maybe it was a 'judgement' on the dogmatic cocksuredness of my youthful plans. Maybe there is a moral in it somewhere! However that may be, it gave me a life of infinite variety and experience, some of it good and some of it the very opposite, but all of it worthwhile and at least providing me with a host of memories of light and shade to colour the closing days of life.

I have reached the end of my retrospective journey. I have deliberately restricted it to what I might describe as the 'bare bones' of my experiences. To have covered these with additional commentaries, criticisms or colourful incidents was not my purpose, however much they might have added to their interest. My sole purpose and intent in trying to respond to the pressure and urge of my reverend and revered friend, who is really responsible for it all, was to make a simple record of what I knew, saw and experienced during an eventful period of our history.

Old contemporaries will disagree with some or many of my views and that will not distress me. Young Ireland may learn at least a little of what, to many of them, is a somewhat confusing period of our history. If they can glean some few grains of inspiration from the best of those that I have mentioned and learn some few lessons of what to avoid, then my reward will be more than adequate.

Postscript

In compiling these notes I have, for the most part, abstained from introducing the personal, family and social associations that prevailed during the period.

It has been suggested that such omission may be misinterpreted. Actually it was deliberate policy in my plan and for a number of reasons. There is a distinct art, I think, whereby some writers can weave the combined threads of their subject's public life with those of his domestic and social environment. It seems to me a delicate art requiring a fine balance of the two phases to blend harmoniously and convey a worthy composite picture. If it is not well done, then the ultimate result is likely to be unbalanced, confusing and somewhat irritating to the reader. It was to avoid this latter result that I, realising my limitations, decided to confine my narrative to my actual personal experiences in so far as they covered the political and national activities in my career.

The fear that it might be misleading to let these notes go forth without any reference to my home and family life prompts me to add this postscript.

I have already mentioned that my wife, Róisín MacGavock of Glenarm, County Antrim, and I were married in January 1916. I cannot adequately convey all that she has meant and still means to me after our forty-four years of married life together. Her courage, good humour and widespread charity, combined with her unselfish devotion to our home and family, are unbounded.

We have eight children now grown up to be four men and four women. Three of the boys are ordained priests. The eldest is a Passionist father engaged in the missionary work of that Order in Bechuanaland and the other two are serving in the home archdiocese of Dublin.[1] The other son, Darach, is a solicitor carrying on his own practice in Dublin. In 1951 he married Joan MacKenny and, with their four children [later five], they make a very happy family. Two of our daughters are in religion. Sheila is a Little Sister of the Assumption and Eithne, a doctor, is a member of *Opus Dei*. Róisín is married to Dr Ivo Drury, a consultant physician in Dublin, and their family of three boys and two girls [later four], along with Darach's

1. Fr Brian Connolly (1926-94): born Dublin, ordained 1953, bursar and professor of sacred eloquence, Holy Cross College, Clonliffe 1954-69, curate, St Michael's, Dún Laoghaire 1969-82, parish priest of St Jude the Apostle, Willington, Dublin 1982-94.

Fr Diarmuid Connolly (1929-): born Dublin, ordained 1955, parish priest of Our Lady, Mother of the Church, Castleknock, County Dublin 1984-.

5. The Connolly family photographed after the ordination of Donal as a priest of the Passionist Order on 3 June 1944 at Mount Argus, Dublin. *Seated, left to right:* Sheila, Mrs Róisín Connolly, Fr Donal Connolly, C.P., Joseph Connolly, Ethna. *Standing, left to right:* Róisín, Brian, Darach, Diarmuid, Nuala

team of four, help to keep us aware and alert by their frequent and welcome invasions.

Our other daughter, Nuala, is engaged in business in Dublin and is now the only one of the eight to share our home. Still we have the great consolation that most of them are near at hand and that they are unsparing in their visits, kindness and attention.

This is the simple ordinary story of the family quietly going their separate ways without fuss or excitement, but a great comfort and consolation to an old man in his seventy-sixth year who can almost see the stage manager ready to give the signal to ring down the curtain on the last act. I pray that it may be a good 'curtain' and that I may have a favourable and merciful reception when it falls.

Appendix 1

ACCOUNT BY SENATOR JOSEPH CONNOLLY OF HIS FAMILY BACKGROUND

My father was born in Lissaria near Monaghan in the year of the Great Famine of 1847 the son of Charles Connolly. His mother was a McKenna and was according to all reports something of a stormy petrel being the only girl in a family with seven brothers.

The Connollys of which there were doubtless many branches were widespread in County Monaghan. Father Lorcan Ó Ciaráin, who was something of an expert in genealogy, told me once that having been overcome by other clans in Meath the Connollys took service under the MacMahons in Monaghan and gradually grew strong enough to assert themselves and contest leadership with the MacMahons themselves.

I often intended to discuss the family with my friend James Connolly who was executed as one of the leaders in 1916 but there were always other and more important things to talk about when we met. The intuition was due to this fact. We have a presentation oil painting of my father painted in 1881 and it bears many characteristic features of the executed patriot which suggests that they sprang from the same genealogical tree. The portrait was not presented by a devoted tenantry but by the trades union of operative bakers of which he was president for some years. Apparently, although foreman bakery manager of the well known and still successful firm of Bernard Hughes Limited, at that time the principal bakery firm in the North of Ireland, he was a staunch trades unionist and continued his membership all his life.

In the year 1851, when he was four years old, the family had left Monaghan and settled in Belfast which was then a steadily growing city in which the shipbuilding and linen industries were rapidly expanding.

I have recollections of all his reports and stories of the Belfast of his early years for he had an excellent memory and a gift of vivid descriptive powers which made everything live as he recounted them. However it is outside the scope of my present purposes to recall them, but his intimate knowledge of the events and personnel of his seventy years in the northern capital would have made interesting reading.

I have no recollection of my father's parents or of his brothers. I only knew one but he was a host in himself. He called himself 'Black Pete' when he had a few glasses taken or occasionally as the mood seized him, 'the dark captain'. Both were apt descriptions. He had a deep sallow complexion, penetrating brown eyes and a full black beard. The most typical memory I have of him was watching him being introduced to an attractive young ladyfriend of the family and his 'follow up' with the question to the surprised young lady of 'Well fair damsel how would you like to pace the quarter deck with the dark captain?' The fact that he had never been to sea in his life did not diminish the grandiloquence of his query nor the chivalrous sweep of his manner. He was an engineer and was, despite his rather frequent 'binges', all his life employed in the firm of Victor Coates, then owner of one of the most successful firms in engine building in the country.

Another brother who was in the flax business had to clear off to the continent during the Fenian round-up. He settled in Northern France and raised a family there. We had occasional correspondence with the family up to the outbreak of war in 1914 but since then the correspondence lapsed.

In 1876 my father and mother were married.

My mother's name was Margaret MacNeill. She was born and reared in the village of Cushendall, County Antrim, where her father had a posting business and public house. Her mother was Susan O'Drain from Cushlake, a fluent Irish speaker who had by some means acquired a knowledge of the Latin and Greek classics and had also studied navigation with her brothers.

I have a definite and clear cut recollection of this 'grandma' for she was something of a martinet to us youngsters. She was firm and strong in her discipline but punctilious in giving her reasons for such advice and guidance as she handed out to us. She survived to the early years of the Gaelic League and her home for the last few years of her life became a centre of social evenings with Gaelic speakers and enthusiasts like P. J. MacGinley (Cú Uladh) and many others.

There are many branches of the MacNeill clan throughout the Glens of Antrim and, to be quite frank, I have never been sufficiently interested in genealogical 'forestry' to try and trace our particular offshoot. I know that one of my sons, who has a flair for that sort of research, has, in conjunction with one of my cousins and, I think, one of Professor MacNeill's family, worked out the whole mysterious ladder down to the roots but my sense of values does not stimulate any interest.

Of my mother's family I knew only three. There was an uncle James who died at the age of 22 while an excise officer in Greenock. I remember him as a rather sombre student who played the piano very well but I was a very small boy when he died.

Uncle Patrick who survived to the age of 87 was one of the most brilliant men I have ever met and certainly one of the most widely read. As a young country student under the care of a Mr Ferris, the principal teacher in the Cushendall village school, he sat for the excise examination and secured first place in what was then known as the 'United Kingdom'. He was a good Irish scholar, had his share of the classics and was an excellent mathematician. It was, however, as a brilliant conversationalist and philosopher that I admired him. His logic and his art of analysis, tinged with a kindly but dry caustic Northern wit, were always a delight to me and they persisted with him practically up to the time of his death. He took no part in public affairs which, as I often told him, was to his discredit and the national loss.

Our Aunt Eileen MacNeill was a national teacher and, when I was old enough to recognise individuals, she was principal teacher in Dromiskin, County Louth. Later she transferred to the Ballyhackamore Girls School in Belfast. She was an ardent worker in the Gaelic League from its inception and for many years was a member of the Coiste Gnotha, the governing body of the League. She gave most, if not all, of her spare time to the language movement and her national school, which was in one of the best suburban residential areas in Belfast, was practically a bi-lingual institution. She was very kind and well disposed to all the numerous nephews and nieces but she had, to me, definite limitations. She was very much the elderly schoolmarm, not dogmatic but persistent, and, although tolerant and patient with all our kinds and foibles, inclined to be somewhat ponderous and pedantic. We of course looked upon her as a settled old maid but she gave us all the shock of our lives when, at sixty-one years of age, she retired on pension and married another retired teacher, a Mr Donnelly from County Mayo. She had a happy and contented married life until she went to her reward at the age of eighty-five or eighty-six.

I have it on my father's word that he commenced work at the early age of ten, continuing his studies by night classes in the Belfast Model School under a Mr Eardley who was later on a school inspector for the National Board. Two of Mr Eardley's sons became priests and were friends of mine. One was parish priest in Culfreightrin, Ballycastle, County Antrim, and was one of the intimate group that visited Murlough, the McCarry home, where Casement, Bigger and the rest of us enjoyed the McCarry hospitality. His brother I remember as parish priest in Rockcorry, County Monaghan, as one of the wittiest and best story tellers of my acquaintance.

It was in the firm of Bernard Hughes that my father started work and there he remained for twenty-five years when, as boss of the bakery, he broke with them to start his own modest venture as a master baker.

There were fourteen of us but five of the children died in infancy, of these five are alive as I write.

Appendix 2

POEM BY ALICE MILLIGAN AND PRESENTED BY HER TO JOSEPH CONNOLLY[1]

IF THE DEAD KNOW

(to Joseph Connolly in Clare)

If the dead can know,
Oh! there is one who died
Not long ago:
With rapture and with pride
Her soul would glow,
If in death she could know,
That when fell the trait'rous blow
You were there by his side.

When I saw you last,
And when last you spoke to me,
It was by her grave
In Antrim by the sea:
So great your grief
You had scarce a word to say:
Far you had fared
And were first to go away.

1. The poem was written following the arrest of de Valera at Ennis on 15 August 1923. It refers mainly to Connolly's attendance at the funeral of his mother-in-law, Annie MacGavock (*née* MacNeill), at Glenarm in February 1923. At that time Connolly was banned from entering the six counties. Nonetheless, he had motored up from Dublin on the previous evening for the funeral. At the funeral Connolly's father-in-law was 'tipped off' by the leading Orangeman and deputy lieutenant of the county, William Crawford, that he ought to get Connolly out of the district immediately after the funeral. Crawford warned that Connolly should not return to the MacGavock home after the funeral, as it had been decided to arrest him there. Connolly heeded the warning and returned directly to Dublin. When those attending the funeral returned to the MacGavock home the police searched the premises for Connolly.

You were first to haste
From amid the funeral band
When the last sod was placed,
Then the wreaths with loving hand:
And your bright Rose of the Glen,
I could not greet her then
In the view of many men,
She was so tearful faced.

Then you stole away
From the funeral train,
Lest an armed hand
Your going might restrain:
For though, for treaty signed
Stood her kit and kin
Peace is not granted us
Ulster within.

Now she would be glad,
Whose dust is in that grave,
To know, in trial's hour
You are true and brave,
Who held the place of son,
When died the only one,
Far far away
From Glenarm beside the wave.[2]

2. The last four lines refer to the only son of Annie MacGavock, Eoin, who, aged twenty-one, died in an explosion on a munitions ship off Halifax, Nova Scotia, Canada, during World War I.

Appendix 3

LETTER FROM MARTIN CONBOY TO EAMON DE VALERA (Dated 12 May 1933)

Dear Mr President,

While Senator Connolly will have made to you ere this a report on his activities while here, he is so modest about what he has done that you may be interested in having from me an appreciation of his worth, as a representative of your government, in circumstances such as made the presence of a member of your cabinet peculiarly important.

For myself it is enough to say that I have had genuine pleasure in every phase of my association with him. It has been for me the gratification of an old desire, since it has given me the opportunity to inform myself concerning the really significant features of the many problems you have to face. I might mistrust this feeling, thinking it to be governed by the friendship I have formed for him, were it not that I have found my admiration for his wide knowledge, calm confidence and modest demeanour shared by others who have not this prepossession.

The president of Georgetown University, for example, is continuously in touch with those who constitute the diplomatic and political life of Washington, and has, besides, both the capacity and the habit of discrimination in his estimation of those with whom he comes in contact. Nothing has pleased me more than to note how the respect and the admiration he formed for the senator gradually gave place to personal attachment. Mr Moley, the assistant secretary of state, had no hesitation in expressing to me his liking for the senator; and he certainly took advantage of what he saw to be the senator's knowledge and experience to clarify his own mind on some matters of immediate and pressing interest to the State Department.

Vastly more important is the fact, which I assure you does not admit of question, that he inspired President Roosevelt with the same sentiments as the rest of us have for him. You will be able to judge of how friendly was the attitude of the president to him by the willingness with which he acceded to one request made by the senator, which he will have mentioned to you, and which I am sure you will consider somewhat unusual.

Quite probably there is a reason other than personal for the friendly reception of one of your ministers. What information the senator was able to impart, especially, perhaps, on the basis of his experience in Geneva, came from one who so obviously was an observer friendly to the United States that his comments could be received and their purport weighed with that fact in mind by the president, Secretary of State Hull and Assistant Secretary Moley, all of whom have these matters much in mind. I was informed that what the senator had to say served to dissipate uncertainties that were in the minds of those who spoke with him, on subjects of immediate concern. In none of these conferences were there such reserves as would be inevitable if the parties to them had conflicting interests.

With that footing established, other seed that he sowed fell upon good ground. I doubt if there ever was a time when men high in office in this country were as willing as on this occasion to fully open their minds to the realities of Irish interests and difficulties as they did during these conversations. That there should be manifested a reciprocally friendly disposition has in fact been indicated to me, both in relation to London and to Geneva.

What especially impresses me about the senator's visit, as I look back upon it, is the amount he was able to do without getting himself into the limelight in doing it. It is the first time, in my experience, that a representative of Ireland could dispense with open appeals designed to bring influence to bear indirectly upon the government. Nevertheless, he was able to get a great deal of desirable publicity for the Irish outlook on Ireland's problems. He met the Washington correspondents, they liked him, listened to him, had quite informal discussions with him, and will not be easily led into disseminating what unfriendly suggestions may reach them from your side of the Atlantic in coming months. When he went to address a Harvard student body the article devoted to him in the *Boston Transcript* was so friendly that it must have been a novelty to readers of that paper beloved of the blue stockings of Massachusetts.

The senator's appearances in Washington were equally fortuitous. I have mentioned the good impression he made on Father Nevils at Georgetown, but that reference would be incomplete without mention that the reception and dinner tendered to him there meant to serve as a gesture of friendliness to Ireland. Coming at the time when representatives of several European countries were in Washington or expected there, it did not fail of that effect. Much the same might be said of his reception by the authorities of the Catholic University. I can bear witness that an excellent disposition towards Ireland, and towards its present government, was manifested by those present at a number of gatherings, and that I have been favoured by senators of my acquaintance with the most unreserved tributes of admiration of his ability and his knowledge of European and even American affairs. In short I think it not too much to say that the air of

Washington is charged with a much more friendly and more understanding spirit, as affecting Ireland and also yourself, than those who have not experienced its reflexes would be inclined to credit. The fact probably will be reported, in other quarters, with infinitely less satisfaction than I find in notifying it to you.

With renewed assurances of my regard, and all personal best wishes,

Sincerely yours,

Martin Conboy

Appendix 4

A CIVIL SERVANT'S RECOLLECTION OF SENATOR JOSEPH CONNOLLY[1]

There was a switch of government portfolios, as a result of which our minister, Mr Ruttledge, was transferred to the department of justice, and Senator Connolly was appointed minister for lands and fisheries. Reflecting on this I thought that our departmental affairs would receive more thoughtful consideration in the more serene atmosphere of the senate. Amateurish and hopeful wishful thinking! I did not get much time to indulge my speculations, for I was brought into touch at once with the new minister, who took up his official residence in our offices in Kildare Place, thus reversing the practice of his predecessor. It was obvious that he was going to devote the major portion of his time to us, and, although all of us should have been glad at this turn in our fortune, I noticed a strange air of doubt throughout the office, which I was at a loss to explain. Perhaps I had too little experience of the ways of political heads.

One day Senator Connolly sent for me and told me that he had decided to appoint me as his private secretary, and that he would be depending on me to keep him straight on fishery and Gaeltacht affairs. This took the wind out of my sails completely; I had no previous intimation of it, nor could I have guessed it, but my colleagues immediately connected it with my previous service in the Press Bureau, and I am sure that they felt that I was a bit of a mystery man. I could hardly blame them. Probably it did have something to do with it, but I should have been better pleased if I had known that the secretary had proposed me. Perhaps he did. I do not know.

I had never seen Senator Connolly until he sent for me, nor did I know anything about him. I thought my appointment, or indeed the appointment of any private secretary on that side of the department, was rather unusual, for there was already a private secretary on the Land Commission side. It was a pointer to the facts that the new minister did not know much about his new job; that he was determined to learn, and that there were, in all probability, some more changes in the offing.

Entering on my new duties it did not take me long to see that he was prepared to let the Land Commission run for a while on its own momentum.[2] While he was with us I can recall only one instance in which he did

1. Typescript containing 'Memoirs of Michael Joseph Gallagher (1895-1974), a civil servant from 1911 to 1964', 123-28.

2. See pp. 316-18.

anything noteworthy on the lands side, and that was the initiation of the migration scheme whereby migrants from the Gaeltacht were moved and settled in County Meath.[3] Possibly he handled that because of its bearing on our Gaeltacht problems. Much of my time was devoted to introducing the minister to the various sections of his department and its officials. I discovered that he had a commercial background, and from him I gathered that that was the prime reason for his appointment. The new government were taking the view that our section of the department was a business, and should be run as such. It was to be his task to introduce business methods. When I got to know him better I tried to get him to understand the disabilities under which we had to carry on or extend our industries, and the severe handicaps we suffered in competing with other entrepreneurs, who were better sited, had less carriage costs, and more homogeneous workers.

He was an early bird, and having gone through his mail each morning he would send for me, when I would induce him to refer all letters of purely departmental interest to me, letting him deal with those which had a personal touch. For those I would prepare replies, letting him put his own gloss on my drafts. I was only partially successful, for even in those cases which were strictly official, and could have been answered as if they had been addressed to the secretary, instead of to the minister, he wanted to see the replies before issue. Evidently he had little trust in us, but he soon tired of that and left me to deal with most of it, as indeed he should have done from the beginning. When he got to know the several sections of the department he got made for himself a set of rubber stamps imprinted 'For Secretary'; 'For Accountant'; 'For Private Secretary' and so forth, and took great pride in banging them down on letters as appropriate. I thought this rather puerile, but, as it might be business practice from the great big world outside our limited knowledge and, therefore, something of which I was palpably ignorant, I kept my mouth shut and said nothing.

Naturally and properly he had frequent consultations with the secretary and other high officers. When these would be in progress he would brook no interruption, often chasing me away when I would seek to break in with a message. This left me a bit scared about interrupting him during those sessions, but once when Mr de Valera wanted to speak to him on the telephone I had great satisfaction not only in interrupting him but in breaking up the session. I was occasionally put on the spot when he would consult me afterwards, and I felt that he was trying out on me what he had learned from my superior officers, but he never found anything incom-

3. See, however, pp. 358-65.

patible with what I told him and what he had learned from them. Once he was in a towering rage over the accounts of the Sea Fisheries Association, and he told me he was going to put in a commercial accountant, as he could not make head nor tail of the accounts. I strongly dissuaded him and pointed out that the comptroller and auditor general had at the department's request lent one of his experienced officers to take over the accounting work and bring it up to date. This officer was Jack Haughey, who subsequently had such a distinguished career in the service. I got him up to explain matters to the minister, and as a result the appointment of a commercial accountant was staved off. However, he was not to be deterred from putting in an outsider as chairman (part time) of the Association, and to that office he appointed Mr Eoin O'Keeffe. Now this gentleman, courteous and affable, painstaking and conscientious, was a bookseller, and I trembled for him taking over on a part-time basis such a difficult assignment. I need not have worried, for after a few months, I cannot now recall the exact duration, Mr O'Keeffe threw in the sponge. At that time I had quit the scene, so I must not anticipate.

Mr Connolly had a very poor opinion of the little industries we were running in the Gaeltacht, and he gave me to understand that the government took a poor view of them and of our efforts. Here also he wanted commercial managers put in. In vain I pointed out to him the uncompetitive conditions under which such industries must necessarily be carried on, and the need to harmonise development with the language so that it would not be injured. He did not set much store on the language,[4] and I once was so bold as to tell him that if he made a whopping success of the industries at the cost of the language the department would have failed in its *raison d'être*.

All the time the head of the department carried on under great difficulties, for it was plain to him and to me that his position was being undermined. He understood my position, too, and, while not giving me any of his confidence, he did not bother me much. On the sea fisheries side the minister never ceased to wonder at the negative attitude displayed by the inspectors, of whom the head was Charles Green. He was the inheritor of a long tradition of fisheries administration, particularly on the inland fisheries side, and his panacea for all ills appeared to the minister to be to make a by-law! I must say that I had great sympathy with the minister in this, which appeared to me to be a hang over from the old landlord days, when the lords of the soil also held sway over the waters of the country.

4. Connolly's papers indicate that he was a life-long enthusiast for the Irish language.

I did not think that the minister ever got as far as considering these things deeply enough to form an opinion on them.

Then there was a world economic conference held in the British Museum in London, and the government felt the situation called for some representation of Ireland at it. Anyway Senator Connolly was sent as our representative to it. It never produced anything of worth as far as I can remember, and the senator was the butt of many shafts of opposition wit on account of his participation in it, such as, 'the senator should have been left there as an exhibit'. While this was going on Mr Frank Aiken had been appointed to act for the minister, and when taking a land bill through the senate he accepted a proposal that a Commission of Inquiry should be set up to investigate the position of our inland fisheries and the question of their tenure. On his return Senator Connolly found himself faced with the problem of appointing, or at least nominating, such a Commission. I obtained a list of suggested nominees from the department, and he went through these with me, adding a name or two, and then finished the list by putting my name to it as secretary. I was aghast when I saw him do this and offered objection. I told him I knew nothing about fishing and rated myself poorly as a secretary. 'There is not much you will have to learn about fish when you are done with this' was his answer, 'and as for your ability as secretary, I have no fear'.

I asked what he was going to do about replacing me as private secretary and he told me it would not be necessary, as his plans had been perfected. He told me he had done a deal with Dr Ryan, the minister for agriculture, whereby he would take over forestry from the department of agriculture and give them fisheries instead. The Gaeltacht industries were to remain in the department of lands, as that department would henceforth be known. He was to get government approval for these changes, and then it would be merely a matter of administration as to the details.

Thus the department of lands and fisheries was to be dismantled. The change was carried through swiftly, and in the operation the head of the department was retired, and, as it affected me personally, I was transferred to the department of agriculture.

I had not known the senator long enough to become familiar with every aspect of his character. He told me his family originally came from Monaghan, but he did not appear to have any connections that he knew of there. He was most familiar with County Antrim and held a warm spot in his heart for the sturdy people of the glens. Stemming from his upbringing, he had in common with those good people a deep seated respect for authority, but he seldom displayed his own. He had an attentive ear for everyone, and was in the habit of pondering everything he would hear, weighing it against what he knew or seeking to verify or confute it by the opinion of others. It would then be dismissed from his mind but he would retain a vivid memory of what was found to be right or expedient. He had a consuming determination to get to the bottom of things and would keep worrying a problem like a terrier. Indeed his slight build and sad, lined features gave one the notion that he was continually worrying and depressed over something. Meeting a colleague one day from the department of industry and commerce, she asked me how I was getting along with Atlas. Momentarily perplexed, as I must have appeared, she explained that that was her mental description of the senator, who always seemed to her to be bearing the burdens of the world on his back. He seldom relaxed, as far as I know, and he was a deeply religious man. I often thought that if he played a round of golf or did something similar he would be the better of it, but an evening's run out to Dún Laoghaire and a walk along the pier was all he permitted himself.

It is true he was given a difficult and nasty assignment. The new government had no great opinion of the department or its chiefs. How much of this was the result of the reports of the special inspectors put in by Mr de Valera I do not know, but presumably it is permissible to assume that they had some part in forming that opinion. It was the senator's job to clear out the Augean stables and shape the department nearer to the government's desire. In the event, he disestablished it, and just as the governor general had been stripped of is functions, so the secretary of the department was to be stripped of his and cashiered. The nucleus of a department which was to have ameliorated the conditions of a section of our people was nipped in the bud, and its functions distributed among others, which had, perhaps, enough on their plates.

No sooner had we transferred to the department of agriculture than the assistant secretary, L. C. Moriarty, was invited to retire, which he was obliged to do under some pressure and to his great stupefaction. Instead of trying to perfect the machine, it was knocked down, and the sad remnants transferred to already overburdened administrations, where so far as I could see they were allowed to tick over, just keeping alive, unwanted children who were never to be allowed to grow up. In fact some of the work was abandoned and at a later date I was to deplore the virtual cessation of outdoor scientific work on the fisheries side which dated from this redistribution of functions.

One can see errors in retrospect. Twenty-five years later a new department was to be set up to deal with Gaeltacht problems specifically, whether it will succeed or not is a moot point. It came from an inter-departmental committee which was called into being in an effort to co-ordinate the work of the several departments whose functions extend to the Gaeltacht. Not a very happy body it staggered along somehow, like a poor relation who can only beg for what he needs, in other words to make recommendations to the departments that have the gift of spending moneys. But the new department has the power and the moneys, and is equipped with the usual hierarchy of minister, secretary, assistant secretary, accountant, Uncle Tom Cobley and all, just as had existed for a very much bigger outfit, wider in scope by far, thirty years ago. Thus has Senator Connolly's work been reversed.

In fact it has been further undone, for the very redistribution of functions which he carried out has been reversed. The fisheries branch of the department of agriculture, poor outcast that it was, has been returned after twenty five years to the department of lands; which in turn had disposed of the Gaeltacht industries to the new department of the Gaeltacht. It, in its turn, has got rid of those industries by setting up a State company to take them over, thus neatly, it may be, solving a problem by getting rid of it.

Nor is that the end. The most recent newsflash is that another interdepartmental committee has been set up to deal with the problems of the inhabited islands. Maybe it too contains the seeds of another ministry. Such proliferation would have been a dreadful worry to Senator Connolly, and his hopes of a business-like approach, but he has departed this mortal scene and it cannot now affect him. He had left the political scene to take up the chairmanship of the Office of Public Works, and I know he enjoyed his work there free from the trammels of office, even though his activities in parliament were confined to the senate and the even tenor of its ways.

I enjoyed my time with him, particularly when I had to attend him in the senate. This gave me an introduction to the backstairs and rabbit warren of ministers' rooms which encumber Leinster House, and which I was to get to know so well in the years ahead. There is no officials' gallery as such in the senate as there is in the Dáil. Private secretaries and officials in attendance have to wait in the visitors' gallery, or about the chamber until the business in which they are interested comes up. Then they enter the chamber and take their places just beside or behind the minister in charge. It is all very intimate and interesting, and an improvement on the railed off gallery in the Dáil.

But, I, too, had been disposed of and I would have to tidy up my papers and face my new department and my newest job, the Inland Fisheries Commission.

Sources

for footnotes

A

MANUSCRIPTS

Dublin, Darach Connolly, 6 Stonepark Abbey, Rathfarnham
Papers of Senator Joseph Connolly.

Wicklow, County, Father Colm Gallagher, Parochial House, Wicklow
Typescript containing 'Memoirs of Michael Joseph Gallagher (1895-1974), a civil servant from 1911 to 1961'.

B

PUBLISHED WORKS

Andrews, C. S., *Dublin made me: an autobiography* I (Dublin 1979).

——, *Man of no property: an autobiography* II (Dublin 1982).

Bell, J. Bowyer, *The secret army* (London 1970).

Bell, Sam Hanna, *The Theatre in Ulster* (Dublin 1972).

Beyers, C. J. (ed.), *Dictionary of South Africa* (South Africa 1981).

Blackrock College Annual 1908, 1967.

Breathnach, Diarmuid, agus Ní Mhurchú, Máire, *Beathaisnéis a ceathair: 1882-1982* (Baile Átha Cliath 1994).

Busher, J., *Consecrated thunderbolt: a life of Father C. Yorke of San Francisco* (Hawthorne, New Jersey, 1973).

Checklist of British artists in the Witt library (London 1991).

Clare Champion 24, 30 June; 7, 14, 21 July 1972.

Cleeve, B. T., *Dictionary of Irish writers* (Dublin 1971).

Connolly, Joseph, *How does she stand?: an appeal to Young Ireland* (Dublin 1953).

Cork Examiner 4 March 1954.

Deasy, Liam, *Towards Ireland Free: the West Cork brigade in the war of independence 1917–21* (Cork 1973).

Donegal Democrat 21 January 1933.

Dublin Magazine, The, XII, July-Sept 1937; XIII, April-June 1938.

Flynn, W. J. (ed.), *The Oireachtas companion and Saorstát guide* (Dublin 1930, 1932, 1939 and 1945).

Foster, R. F., *Modern Ireland 1600-1972* (London 1988).

Gaughan, J. A., *Austin Stack: portrait of a separatist* (Dublin 1977).
——, *Thomas Johnson (1872-1963): first leader of the Labour Party in Dáil Éireann* (Dublin 1980).
——, *Alfred O'Rahilly I: Academic* (Dublin 1986).
——, *Alfred O'Rahilly II: Public figure* (Dublin 1989).
——, *Alfred O'Rahilly III: Controversialist, Part I: Social reformer* (Dublin 1992).
——, *Alfred O'Rahilly III: Controversialist, Part 2: Catholic apologist* (Dublin 1993).
Guardian Weekly 29 October 1995.
Hickey, D. J., and Doherty, J. E., *A dictionary of Irish history since 1800* (Dublin 1980).
Hogan, Robert (ed.), *The MacMillan dictionary of Irish literature* (London 1980).
Houfe, Simon, *The dictionary of British book illustrations and caricaturists 1800-1914* (London 1978).
Irish Catholic Directory 1900-60.
Irish Independent 9, 19 June 1934; 17 January 1959.
Irish News 29 April, 26 June 1913; 14 February 1914; 2 April 1920; 13, 14 December 1962.
Irish Press 17 January 1959.
Irish Times 11 October 1960; 9 April 1994.
Johnson, Allan (ed.), *Dictionary of American biography I-X, with supplementary volumes* (New York 1964).
Johnson, J., and Greutzner, A., *The dictionary of British artists 1880-1940 . . .* (Woodbridge Antique Collectors' Club 1976).
Kerryman 14 January 1933.
Kotsonouris, Mary, *Retreat from revolution: the Dáil courts* (Dublin 1994).
MacLysaght, Edward, *Changing times in Ireland since 1898* (Gerards Cross 1978).
Maynooth College Calendar 1903-10.
Moody, T. W., Martin, F. X., Byrne, E. J. (eds.), *A new history of Ireland* VIII: *a chronology of Irish history to 1976: a companion to Irish history* Pt I (Oxford 1982).
Ó Broin, León, *W. E. Wyllie and the Irish revolution 1916-21* (Dublin 1989).
O'Connell, T. J., *History of the Irish National Teachers' Organisation 1868-1968* (Dublin 1969).
O'Mahony, Seán, *Frongoch: university of revolution* (Dublin 1987).

O'Sullivan, Donal, *The Irish Free State and its senate* (London 1940).

Phoenix, Eamon, *Northern nationalism: nationalist politics, partition and the Catholic minority in Northern Ireland 1890-1940* (Belfast 1994).

St Malachy's College, Sesquicentennial (Belfast 1988).

Senan, O.F.M.Cap., Fr (ed.), 'F. J. McCormick (Peter C. Judge): a symposium of tributes', *Capuchin Annual* 1948.

Sinn Féin 7 March, 9 May 1914; 20 October 1923.

Standard 21 July 1944.

Taub, Michael, *Jack Doyle* (Dublin 1990).

Thom Directory (Dublin 1923-57).

Walsh, James P., 'Father Peter Yorke of San Francisco', *Studies* LXII (1962).

Walsh, James P., and Foley, Timothy, 'Father Peter C. Yorke, Irish American leader', *Studia Hibernica* 14 (1974).

Who was who in America, vols 1 and 2 (Chicago 1943, 1950).

Williams, Sir Edgar (ed.), *The compact edition of the dictionary of national biography* I-II (Oxford 1975).

Yost, Walter (ed. in chief), *Encyclopaedia Britannica* I-XXIV, *with supplements* (London 1957).

C

PERSONS

Archer, Liam M., 67 Blackheath Park, Dublin 3.

Boyd Barrett, David, 'Brigadoon', Station Road, Glenageary, County Dubin.

Browne, C.S.Sp., Fr Kevin, Willow Park, Blackrock, County Dublin.

Byrnes, Michael, 33 Deramore Park, Belfast BJ9 5JU.

Collins, Lavinia, Department of Foreign Affairs, 80 St Stephen's Green, Dublin 2.

Collins, Margot, United States Embassy, 43 Elgin Road, Dublin 4.

Connolly, Darach, 6 Stonepark Abbey, Rathfarnham, Dublin 16.

——, Sister Gemma, Little Sisters of the Assumption, 3 Thorndale Avenue, Belfast BT14 6BJ.

Donnellan, John F., Cloonmore Park, Dunmore, County Galway.

Dowdall, Thomas F., Dunsland, Glanmire, County Cork.

Duffy, Sgt John P, Garda archives and museum, Phoenix Park, Dubin 8.

Dwyer, J. Ryle, 49 St Brendan's Park, Tralee, County Kerry.

Farragher, C.S.Sp., Fr Seán, Blackrock College, County Dublin.

Fawsitt, Carol, 12 Peter's Row, Aungier Street, Dublin 2.

Flinn, Hugo V., 4 Erskine Avenue, Greystones, County Wicklow.

Fullerton, Fr Robert, St Teresa's presbytery, Glen Road, Belfast BT11 8BL.

Killen, John, The Linen Hall Library, 17 Donegall Square North, Belfast BT1 5GD.

McCarthy, Archdeacon Cathal, 43 Upper Beechwood Avenue, Dublin 6.

Moore, Philip, Newtownbutler Road, Clones, County Monaghan.

Morrow, Rev Trevor W. J., 19 Chalet Gardens, Lucan, County Dublin.

Murray, Patrick, 'Windlea', Hodson Bay, Athlone, County Westmeath.

Myler, Thomas, *Evening Herald*, 90 Middle Abbey Street, Dublin 1.

Nolan, John, Registrar, National University of Ireland, 49 Merrion Square, Dublin 2.

O'Carroll, Thomas J., 25 Kincora Drive, Dublin 3.

Ó Ceallaigh, Cormac, 46 Killiney Road, Killiney, County Dublin.

O'Connell, Betty, 77 Barclay Court, Blackrock, County Dublin.

O'Shea, Anne, Office of Public Works, Department of Finance, Government Buildings, Merrion Street, Dublin 2.

Ruane, Maeve, 31 Royal Terrace, Dún Laoghaire, County Dublin.

Ruddy, Maura, Department of Agriculture, Food and Forestry, Kildare Street, Dublin 2.

Sagarra, Edith, 30 Garville Avenue, Dublin 6.

Schon, Karl-Georg, Embassy of the Federal Republic of Germany, 31 Trimleston Avenue, Booterstown, County Dublin.

Woods, Christopher J., Office of the 'Dictionary of Irish biography', Earlsfort Terrace, Dublin 2.

Young, Comdt Peter, Military archives, Cathal Brugha barracks, Dublin 6.

Index